HIDDEN SOUTHWEST

The Adventurer's Guide

Hidden Southwest
The Adventurer's Guide

Richard Harris   Madeleine Osberger

Carolyn Scarborough   Laura Daily

Steve Cohen   Mary Ann Reese   Ron Butler

Executive Editors
Ray Riegert   Leslie Henriques

Ulysses Press

Published by: Ulysses Press
          3286 Adeline Street   Suite 1
          Berkeley, CA 94703
          510/601-8301

Library of Congress Catalog Card Number 92-80233
ISBN 0-915233-60-6

Printed in the U.S.A. by the George Banta Company

10 9 8 7 6 5 4 3 2 1

Managing Editor: Claire Chun
Editorial Director: Roger Rapoport
Editor: Bob Drews

Maps: Wendy Ann Logsdon, Phil Gardner
Cover Designers: Bonnie Smetts, Leslie Henriques
Editorial Associates: Wendy Ann Logsdon, Laurie Greenleaf
Indexer: Sayre Van Young

Cover Photography: Front cover photo by GALA/Superstock;
  back cover photos by Leslie Henriques, Roger Rapoport

Distributed in the United States by Publishers Group West, in
Canada by Raincoast Books and in Great Britain and Europe by
World Leisure Marketing

Printed on recycled paper

Notes from the Publisher

Throughout the text, hidden locales, remote regions, little-known spots and special attractions are marked with a star (★).

* * *

An alert, adventurous reader is as important as a travel writer in keeping a guidebook up-to-date and accurate. So if you happen upon a great restaurant, discover a hidden locale, or (heaven forbid) find an error in the text, we'd appreciate hearing from you. Just write to:

Ulysses Press
3286 Adeline Street   Suite 1
Berkeley, CA 94703
510/601-8301

* * *

It is our desire as publishers to create guidebooks that are responsible as well as informative. The danger of exploring hidden locales is that they will no longer be secluded.

We hope that our guidebooks treat the people, country and land we visit with respect. We ask that our readers do the same. The hiker's motto, "Walk softly on the Earth," applies to travelers everywhere . . . in the forest, on the beach and in town.

Contents

SPECIAL FEATURES

MAPS

CHAPTER ONE

The Southwest

The Why, Where, When and How
of Traveling in the American Southwest

Why

The Southwest is a land unlike any other. It is sheer sandstone cliffs and slickrock mesas, secluded beaches on bright blue lakes, vast deserts alive with giant cactuses and unusual animals, high mountain peaks that guard some of the largest wilderness areas in America.

Strange landscapes conceal Indian ruins as old and haunting as Europe's medieval castles. And unlike in other parts of the United States, the people who lived in the Southwest when the first white men arrived still live here today. Although it was the first part of the United States where European colonists settled permanently, today it remains, on the whole, one of the least-populated parts of the country.

The Southwest attracts vacationers from around the world at all times of year. It is warm in the winter (some places), cool in the summer (other places) and sunnier than Florida. People come for the climate, the great outdoors, the unique cultural mix and the scenic beauty. Most of all, people come to explore, for the best places in the Southwest are not necessarily marked by big green-and-white signs or entrance gates. In this land of astonishing diversity, you'll find something new around every curve in the road.

Land of contrasts, proudly provincial, the Southwest lives up to its romantic reputation. Lost cities and hidden treasures await your discovery. If curiosity is in your nature, the Southwest is one of the best places on earth to unleash it.

Hidden Southwest is designed to help you explore Arizona, New Mexico, southern Utah and southwestern Colorado. It covers popular, "must-see" places, offering advice on how best to enjoy them. It also tells you about many off-the-beaten-path spots, the kind you would find by talking with folks at the local café or with someone who has lived in the area all his or her life. It describes the region's history, its natural areas and its residents, both human and animal. It suggests places to eat, to lodge, to play, to camp. Taking into account varying interests, budgets and tastes, it provides the information you need whether your vacation style involves backpacking, golf, museum browsing, shopping or all of the above.

This book covers the Southwest in three sections. Arizona, the most recently settled and fastest-growing part, claims among its virtues warm winter weather, famous sunsets and the largest Indian reservation in the country. New Mexico offers antiquity and a unique tricultural heritage that set it apart from anyplace else in America. The land north of the Grand Canyon and Navajo Reservation extending into Utah and Colorado, still largely unpopulated, is best known for its wild canyons and rugged mountains, portions of which are made accessible to the public in no less than six national parks.

The traveling part of the book begins in Chapter Two on the rim of the Grand Canyon. The same chapter also offers side trips from the national park to see other natural wonders in central Arizona. Chapter Three wanders through Indian Country in northeastern Arizona to help you experience the world of the Navajo and Hopi people. The greater Phoenix area, including nearby Scottsdale, Wickenburg and Payson, is revealed in Chapter Four. Chapter Five leads you to the best places in and around Tucson, then on to explore more remote areas along the Mexican border.

Chapter Six covers northern New Mexico, focusing on Santa Fe and Taos and suggesting additional expeditions to old Spanish villages as well as ancient cliff dwellings and modern Indian pueblos. Chapter Seven takes a good look at Albuquerque, from the top of a mountain as well as from the city's historic center, then investigates an array of central New Mexico side trips to lakes and volcanic badlands, ruins of abandoned pueblos and Spanish missions. Chapter Eight ranges across southern New Mexico from Carlsbad Caverns through Billy the Kid country to the remote canyons of the Gila Wilderness.

The terrain and culture of the Southwest do not stop at the arbitrarily squared-off state lines of Arizona and New Mexico but sprawl untidily over the Four Corners area into neighboring parts of Utah and Colorado. Chapter Nine takes you through the geological wonderland of southwestern Utah, including Bryce Canyon, Zion and Capitol Reef national parks. Chapter Ten continues into southeastern Utah with visits to Arches and Canyonlands national parks and all the information you need to rent a boat and cruise Lake Powell. Finally, Chapter Eleven is your guide to the southwestern corner

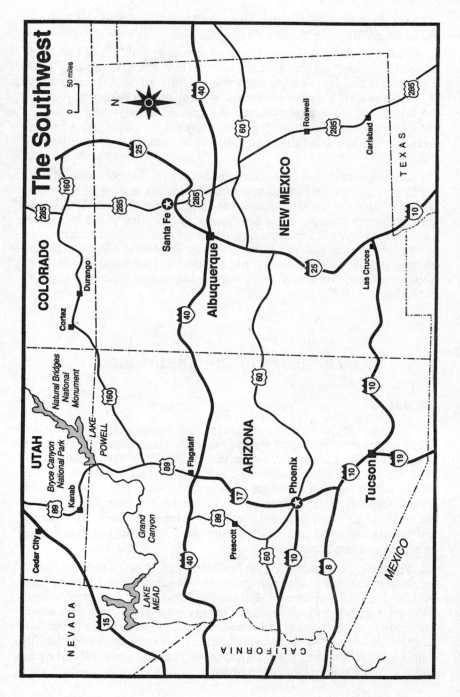

of Colorado, where the top attractions are Mesa Verde National Park and the Durango-Silverton Narrow Gauge Railroad.

What you choose to see and do is up to you. The old cliché that "there is something for everyone" pretty well rings true in the Southwest. In this book, you'll find free campgrounds with hiking trails and fantastic views as well as several playgrounds for the wealthy and well-known. And you can take some of the most spectacular scenic drives anywhere as well as hikes into wild areas that can't be reached by car. Or check into a bed and breakfast that has delightful little galleries and boutiques within walking distance.

There's so much to experience in the Southwest that even most lifelong residents can count on making new discoveries once in a while. First-time vacation visitors are hard pressed just to make brief stops at the best-known highlights of the region, while seasoned travelers often prefer to explore a more limited area in depth and then return on later trips to different spots, perhaps in different seasons. Either way, people generally come back, and often to stay. For the Southwest has so many unique ways—food, landscapes, customs, climate, art, architecture, languages—to create lingering memories.

The Story of the Southwest

GEOLOGY

The walls of the Grand Canyon reveal one billion years in stone. Over countless centuries, geological shifting raised the plateau up to slowly higher elevations as the Colorado River sliced it in half. The dark rocks at river level, which contain no fossils, are some of the oldest matter on the face of the earth. The different layers of color and texture in the layered cliffs attest to times when the area was sea floor, forest and swamp. Tiny fossilized sea creatures from the Paleozoic era, long before dinosaurs, trace the development of some of the first life on the planet up through strata of shale, limestone and sandstone.

The geological features of the Southwest are so varied and spectacular that it is certainly possible to appreciate the landscapes for their beauty without knowing how they formed. But travelers who take a little time to learn about the region's geology in natural history museums or park visitor centers along the way develop a different perspective. They come to see how the many different colors and kinds of surface rock connect in a wonderfully complex formation hundreds of miles across. They learn to explore the panorama in three dimensions, not just two.

For example, Kaibab limestone, the 250,000,000-year-old, 300-foot-thick, grayish-white layer along the top rim of the Grand Canyon, is also visible at Lee's Ferry, a half-day's drive to the east, and at Capitol Reef National Park, a similar distance to the north. The orange Wingate sandstone layer is seen in Capitol Reef as well as in Arches National Park, the Island in the Sky and Newspaper Rock units of Canyonlands National Park, and at Dead Horse Point State Park—all part of the same rock.

The delight of Southwestern geology lies not only in its grand overviews but also in its myriad unique details. Dinosaur tracks. Petrified wood. Pure white gypsum sand dunes. Huge underground caverns. Salt domes, arches, natural bridges, hoodoos and goblins fancifully shaped by water and weather. Huge volcanic boulders pushed great distances by glaciers.

Volcanoes created some of the most dramatic scenery in the Southwest. In some places, like New Mexico's Valley of Fires Recreation Area and El Malpais National Monument, lava has paved the desert floor for many miles into tortured, twisted, surfaces that cannot be crossed, laced with ice caves where water stays frozen even on the hottest summer days. Elsewhere, as in the volcano fields northeast of Flagstaff, Arizona, fields of pumice gravel prevent vegetation from growing but make hiking easy at the foot of picture-perfect volcanic cones.

The Jemez Mountains in northern New Mexico formed from the crumbled remnant of what many scientists believe may have been the world's tallest volcano nearly two million years ago. In the canyons of Bandelier National Monument on the slope of the Jemez stand tent rocks, strange spires left behind when steam vents hardened volcanic ash in the distant past. Farther north, near Taos, the massive lava flow from the Jemez volcano forms the walls of deep gorges along the Rio Grande. There are no active volcanoes in the Southwest today, but that could change at any time. Volcanoes have been erupting in the Southwest for millions of years, and the most recent ones exploded less than a thousand years ago. As geologists reckon time, a thousand years is just yesterday.

HISTORY

NATIVE PEOPLE

Spear points found near Clovis, New Mexico, prove that human beings lived in the Southwest at least 10,000 years ago. The Clovis points are some of the oldest Indian artifacts found anywhere, dating back to the last Ice Age. At that time, the region that is now the American Southwest was rich, green countryside where mastodons and giant bison grazed just beyond the reach of glaciers. The hunting and gathering tribes who followed the animals' tracks may have been some of the first people to walk on North American soil. They stayed. Across millenniums, their descendants walked softly through the Southwest leaving few traces—only small bone and obsidian tools and mysterious paintings of magical beings on the red walls of canyons in southern Utah.

Less than 2000 years ago, the people of the Southwest learned how to grow corn, beans and watermelons. This new technology allowed them to establish permanent homes. By about 1000 A.D., individual pit houses gave way to cliff dwellings like the ones at Mesa Verde in Colorado and large multifamily stone pueblos like the ones at Chaco Canyon in New Mexico. Besides agriculture and architecture, Pueblo people of the Anasazi, Mimbres and Sinagua civilizations were known for pottery making, cotton weaving and sophisticated astronomical observations and spiritual practices. They had extensive trade contacts including the Toltecs of central Mexico.

The saga of the pre-Columbian Southwest is one of migration and change. The great Anasazi pueblos of the Four Corners region, then the largest cities in what is now the United States, were occupied for a century or two and suddenly abandoned. Archaeologists disagree about the reasons. The Mesa Verde people may have moved to Acoma, the Mimbres of the Gila canyons to Zuni Pueblo or perhaps Casas Grandes in Old Mexico, the Chacoans to sites along the Rio Grande such as the pueblos at Bandelier National Monument. The Hopi people stayed on their remote desert mesa tops, where some structures standing today have been used by the same families for 900 years.

During the century just before Columbus's ships reached American shores, a new group of people arrived in the Southwest. They were Athabascans, nomads from the far north who had gradually wandered down the front range of the Rocky Mountains in small groups. They would become the Apache and Navajo nations—but only after another kind of stranger had come to change the character of the Southwest forever.

SPANISH CONQUEST

In the year 1540, a Spanish expedition under the command of *conquistador* Francisco Vasquez de Coronado set out from Mexico City and headed north across the parched, forbidding Chihuahuan Desert in search of the fabled Seven Cities of Cibola. Instead of the gold-paved cities of legend, he found pueblos such as Zuni, occupied by subsistence farmers who drew magical lines of cornmeal in unsuccessful attempts to fend off the Spaniards with their armor, horses and steel swords. Coronado and his followers were the first Europeans to visit the Hopi Mesas, the Rio Grande pueblos or the Grand Canyon. For two years they explored the Southwest, but finding no gold they returned to Mexico City with disappointing reports. After that, exploration of the territory Coronado had visited, which came to be called Nuevo Mexico, was left to Franciscan missionaries for the rest of the 16th century.

In 1598, a wealthy mine owner from Zacatecas, Mexico, named Don Juan de Oñate mounted an expedition at his own expense to colonize Nuevo

Mexico under a grant from the Spanish government. The group consisted of 400 soldiers and settlers, 83 wagons and 7000 head of livestock. Oñate founded the first permanent Spanish settlement near modern-day Española, New Mexico, but the cost of his expeditions bankrupted him and he resigned his position as governor. The new governor, Don Pedro de Peralta, moved the capital to Santa Fe in 1610.

The Spanish colonists grew in number and established villages, farms and ranches up and down the Rio Grande over several generations, but slavery practices and erratic religious policies toward the Indians inspired the Pueblo Revolt of 1680. The people of the Rio Grande pueblos, aided by fierce Athabascan nomads, attacked the Spanish towns and ranches, killing hundreds of settlers and driving the survivors downriver all the way to the site of present-day El Paso, Texas, where they camped for 11 years before soldiers arrived from Mexico City to help them regain Nuevo Mexico.

The Pueblo Revolt created the Navajo nation. To persuade their Athabascan neighbors to help chase away the Spanish, the Pueblo leaders agreed that the Athabascans could keep the livestock driven off from ranches they attacked. In that way, the tribe came to own sheep and horses, which would profoundly change their culture. When the Spanish colonists returned, many Pueblo people who had participated in the revolt fled to avoid retaliation and went to live with the nomads, bringing with them such advanced technologies as weaving cloth and growing corn. The Athabascan descendants who herded sheep and farmed became known as the Navajo people, while those who held to the old way of life came to be called Apaches.

After the Pueblo Revolt, Nuevo Mexico endured as an outpost of the Spanish empire for another 130 years. During all of that time, the conquerors and colonists were never able to settle the surrounding areas of the Southwest or even establish roads between Nuevo Mexico and other Spanish colonies in California and central Texas. The lands to the north and east were controlled by warrior horsemen of the Comanche tribe, whose raids forced abandonment of Spanish missions such as those at Pecos and Gran Quivira. To the south and west, the Apache and Navajo people used fear to keep Europeans out of the land that is now Arizona.

Nor did the Spanish settlers have any contact with English-speaking American colonists. Near the end of the colonial era, explorers from the United States, such as early U.S. Army explorer Captain Zebulon Pike, who accidentally strayed into Nuevo Mexico were arrested.

TERRITORIAL PERIOD

Beginning in 1821, distant events changed the lives of the Spanish inhabitants of the Southwest. Mexico won its independence from Spain, and government policies changed. The border was opened, and trade was established along the Santa Fe Trail, which linked Nuevo Mexico to United

States territory. At the same time, all Franciscan monks were exiled from Mexican territory, leaving Nuevo Mexico without spiritual leadership. They were replaced by a lay brotherhood of *penitentes* whose spiritual guidance did much to create a uniquely New Mexican culture and tradition that survives to this day in remote mountain villages around Santa Fe and Taos.

When the Texas republic won its independence from Mexico in 1836, many Texans contended that Nuevo Mexico should be part of their new nation—a sentiment that the people of Nuevo Mexico did not share. Texas troops occupied Nuevo Mexico in 1841, but their authority was not acknowledged. Five years later, when Texas had joined the United States and the Mexican War was underway, federal soldiers took possession of New Mexico. When the war ended in 1848, the peace treaty with Mexico ceded the territories of California and Nuevo Mexico (which included the modern-day states of New Mexico and Arizona) to the United States. To confuse the local people further, 13 years after they had become Americans, the Civil War broke out and Confederate troops from Texas fought numerous battles in New Mexico, briefly capturing Albuquerque, Santa Fe and Mesilla. Before the war ended, New Mexico and its people had been part of five different nations in about 40 years.

The first English-speaking settlers in the Southwest were Mormons, who chose to live free from persecution in the empty desert. Beginning in the 1840s, they established settlements throughout southern Utah and northern Arizona, often in places that are still remote today.

The United States government in the late 19th century was far less tolerant of Indians than the Spanish and Mexicans rulers had been. After the Civil War, the Army set out to make the lands ruled by the Comanches, Apaches, Navajos and Utes safe for homesteaders. The Comanches were annihilated. The Utes, who had roamed from the eastern slope of the Colorado Rockies to the canyonlands of southern Utah, were confined to a narrow reservation south of present-day Durango, Colorado. Kit Carson rounded up the entire Navajo tribe and marched them from their homeland to a reservation in eastern New Mexico, but after explorations revealed nothing of value on the Navajo land, and after thousands of Navajo people had died, he marched the survivors back home to the land where they live today. The longest and most violent army campaign against the Indians was the Apache Wars. Though never numerous, the Apaches were so fierce and elusive that the wars lasted for 19 bloody years, ending in 1884 with the surrender of the rebel leader Geronimo. Only then could settlers from the United States establish the first towns in Arizona.

Law enforcement was unreliable in the territorial era, giving rise to timeless legends of the Wild West. In New Mexico, Billy the Kid and his gang fought against an army of gunmen hired by a ruthless cattle baron in the Lincoln County War. In Utah, Butch Cassidy robbed trains and plundered banks and always eluded capture. In Arizona, Ike Clanton and his boys shot it out with lawman Wyatt Earp and gunman Doc Holliday at Tombstone's O.K. Corral. Out of all the turmoil and gunfire emerged a new multicultural society. In 1910, Arizona and New Mexico became the 47th and 48th states in the union—the last to be admitted until Alaska 50 years later.

MODERN TIMES

The traditional Spanish and Indian cultures of the Southwest remain strong even as waves of visitors and newcomers have swept across the land during the 20th century. Beginning shortly before World War I, artists and writers fleeing Paris's West Bank began to congregate around Taos, New Mexico. Since the 1940s, the Institute of American Indian Arts, the only federal Indian school dedicated to teaching traditional and contemporary art, has established Santa Fe, New Mexico, as the world's leading Indian art market. Exotic locations and reliable sunshine have drawn film production companies to the Southwest ever since 1898 and continue to do so. Today, visual and performing arts form one of the most important industries in many parts of the Southwest.

In World War II, the Southwest became America's center for nuclear research. The nation's best physicists were sent to a top secret base at Los Alamos, New Mexico, deep in a labyrinth of volcanic canyons, to develop the world's first atomic bomb. They tested it in 1945 in the desert near White Sands, New Mexico. After the war ended, nuclear weapons research continued at Los Alamos, as did development of peacetime uses for nuclear energy, bringing a stampede of prospectors and mining companies to the uranium-rich badlands of the Four Corners area. Today, Los Alamos National Laboratory and other federal laboratories in the region also study nuclear fusion, geothermal and solar energy research and genetic studies. The technologies developed at the laboratories have brought private high-tech companies to the major cities of the Southwest. Meanwhile, the nuclear industry has reached the top of the list of environmental controversies that stir heated debate in the region.

Although population growth since World War II has been phenomenal in the Phoenix, Tucson and Albuquerque areas, most of the Southwest remains sparsely inhabited. Water is the limiting factor. Although a series of huge manmade reservoirs—Lake Powell, Lake Mead, Lake Havasu and others—along the Colorado River runs through the heart of the desert Southwest, the water and electricity from them is used far away in southern California, while the land along the banks of the river remains almost entirely undeveloped.

Well over half of the land in the region covered by this book is owned by the public. Large expanses of grasslands and canyonlands are administered by the federal Bureau of Land Management and leased to ranchers for cattle grazing. Other stretches are military reservations. The region includes 15 national forests, 12 national wildlife refuges and 54 national parks, monuments and recreation areas—more than any other part of the United States.

Tourism is key among the forces that have shaped the modern Southwest. With a relatively small population, few manufacturing industries and limited agriculture, the economy relies heavily on travelers, who support hotels, restaurants and other service businesses. In general, Southwesterners display a friendly, positive attitude toward tourists. Beauty is one of the region's most important natural resources, and there is plenty to share. Besides, as locals like to point out, who would want to live in a place strangers didn't want to visit?

FLORA

Drivers crossing the Southwest at high speed on interstate highways can easily form the mistaken impression that this region is mostly open ranchland so arid that it takes 50 acres to graze a single cow. This is because main highways follow the flattest, most featureless routes. All one has to do is take a detour into the mountains and canyons where the main highways don't go in order to discover that the dry climate and extreme elevation changes create a surprising variety of ecosystems, each with its own unique beauty.

At low altitudes where winter temperatures rarely dip to freezing, cactuses and other succulents thrive. Ocatillo, century plants, yuccas and prickly pear, barrel and cholla cactuses, as well as mesquite and creosote bushes, are found throughout both the Chihuahuan Desert of southern New Mexico and the Sonoran Desert of southern Arizona. The Sonoran Desert is best known for its magnificent forests of giant saguaro and organ pipe cactuses. When spring rains come, which may be once in five years or more, the deserts burst forth for a few weeks in a fantastic display of wildflowers.

Miniature evergreen forests of piñon, juniper and cedar cover the desert hills at higher elevations where winter temperatures fall below freezing. Once every seven years in the fall, the piñon trees produce pine nuts, considered a delicacy in many parts of the Southwest. Cactus and yucca stay small in the high desert. The tallest of them, the cholla cactus, prefer areas that were once stripped of vegetation, such as old Indian ruins.

Mountain forests change with elevation, forming three distinct bands. On the lower slopes of the mountains, ponderosa pine stand 50 feet tall and more. At middle elevations, shimmering stands of aspen trees fill the mountainsides and paint them bright yellow in early October. Douglas fir dominates the higher reaches of the mountains. In some parts of the forest, accessible only by hiking trail and out of reach of timber cutters, fir trees 100 feet tall and bigger around than a man's reach stand spirelike in ancient forests dripping with moss and silence. The San Juan Mountains near Durango, Colorado, contain peaks reaching above timberline, where temperatures always fall below freezing at night and trees will not grow. There is only the alpine tundra, a world of grassy meadows rooted in permafrost where tiny flowers appear for brief moments in midsummer.

Of all the various ecosystems that characterize the Southwest, the real gems are the riparian woodlands. Since almost all of the Southwestern landscape is dry and can only support the hardiest of plants, plant life flourishes around even the least trickle of year-round running water. Creek and river banks support thick forests of cottonwood trees and tamarisks, along with isolated stands of hardwood trees such as maple and hickory.

FAUNA

The last grizzly bear sighted in the Southwest was in the San Juan Mountains near Silverton, Colorado, in the mid-1970s. Packs of Mexican wolves in Albuquerque's Rio Grande Zoo and the Desert Museum in Carlsbad, New Mexico, are the last of their species, preserved from extinction by a federal captive-breeding program.

But other animals of Western legend still roam free in the forests and canyons of the Southwestern back country. Mountain lions, rarely seen because they inhabit remote areas and hunt in the dark, sometimes flash past late-night drivers' headlight beams. Many black bears live deep in the mountains, and in drought summers when food is short they may stray into Albuquerque, Flagstaff or other towns to raid trash cans. Coyotes, the most commonly seen Southwestern predators, abound in all rural areas and frequently surround campgrounds with their high-pitched yipping and howling.

Open rangelands throughout the Southwest support sizable herds of pronghorn antelope alongside grazing cattle. Most visitors to national parks and other protected areas will spot mule deer, and in some parks such as Mesa Verde as well as in the remote canyonlands of southern Utah, wild horses still roam. The elk population in the Southwestern mountains is the largest it has been in this century. Because elk prefer high mountain meadows, only serious hikers are likely to spot one. Herds of mountain sheep live above timberline on the highest mountains of the San Juan and Sangre de Cristo ranges, while their solitary relatives, desert bighorn sheep, live in most desert areas.

One of the most distinctive regional birds is the magpie, an exotic-looking, long-tailed, iridescent, black-and-white cousin of Asian mynha birds. Another is the roadrunner, which is often seen hunting lizards alongside the highway. Large birds often seen by motorists or hikers include turkey vultures, ravens and many different kinds of hawk. Both golden and bald eagles live throughout the Southwest and are occasionally spotted soaring in the distance. Eagles and vultures are about the same size, and the easiest way to tell them apart is to remember that eagles glide with their wings horizontal, while vultures' wings sweep upward in a V-shape.

A thought that preoccupies many visitors to the Southwest is of living hazards like rattlesnakes, gila monsters, scorpions and tarantulas. Poisonous animals live in most parts of the region except for the high mountains. Yet even local residents who spend most weekends hiking say that they rarely encounter one. When outdoors in desert country, walk loudly and never put your hand or foot where you can't see it.

Where to Go

The Southwest is no more all of a piece than is Europe. Don't try to "see it all" in a single trip or you may find yourself focused so much on covering large distances that you sacrifice quiet opportunities to appreciate the natural beauty you came to see. Deciding what to see and where to go is a tough choice. The good news is, you'll just have to keep coming back and exploring at different times of year to get to know the "real" Southwest.

To help you with your decisions, we'll entice you with a brief description of each area covered in this book. To get the whole story, read the introduction to each chapter, then the more detailed material on the regions that appeal to you.

Begin exploring the **Northwestern Arizona** by heading for the largest single geological feature in the Southwest, which splits the region between north and south. The "village" on the South Rim of the Grand Canyon, just an hour's drive from interstate Route 40, is developed on a grand scale, complete with an airport. Hikers discover that only a tiny part of either rim of the Grand Canyon is accessible by vehicle, and that a moderate walk can provide total solitude. A visit to the South Rim fits in well with exploring other places in central Arizona such as the volcano fields and Indian ruins of the Flagstaff area, the canyon country around Sedona, and such offbeat sights as the real London Bridge at Lake Havasu and the ferry ride across the river from Bullhead City to the gambling casinos on the Nevada side. The North Rim, farther by road from major cities and main routes, is more relaxed and secluded, though still busy enough to make advance lodging or camping reservations essential. Closed during the winter months, the North Rim combines perfectly with visits to Lake Powell and the national parks of southwestern Utah, as well as Las Vegas, Nevada.

Northeastern Arizona, also known as Indian Country, includes the vast, sprawling Navajo Reservation, larger than some East Coast states, as well as the remote, ancient mesatop pueblos of the Hopi Reservation, fiercely traditional and independent although completely surrounded by Navajo land. The center of the Navajo world according to legend, Canyon de Chelly is still inhabited by people who herd sheep and live without electricity. Visitors can view their hogans and pastures from high above on the canyon rim but can only enter the labyrinth accompanied by a Navajo guide. Another national park service unit operated by the tribe, Navajo National Monument protects some of the best Anasazi ruins in the Four Corners area. The monument's biggest Indian ruin is only accessible on horseback. The third major park on the reservation is Monument Valley Tribal Park, a landscape so familiar from the many films, television shows and advertisements filmed here that visitors may feel like they're driving through a movie as they travel the backcountry road around the valley and visit the hogans of the people who live in this, one of the most remote places in the United States. A tour of Hubbell Trading Post National Historic Site and perhaps a stop at a still-operating trading post will round out your Indian Country experience.

It is amazing that a city of a million people could survive at all in this sunbaked desert valley, but a complex system of dams and aqueducts has made Phoenix, the state capital and focus of **Central Arizona**, the largest city in the Southwest and the ninth-largest in the nation. At first, this rectilinear sprawl of suburbs and shopping malls, giant retirement communities, towering office buildings, industrial parks and farmlands full of year-round citrus and cotton crops may seem to offer few charms for the vacationer. But those who take time to explore Phoenix and beyond will discover that this city where it is often better to spend daytime hours indoors has more than its share of the finest museums in the west. The winter months are the time for outdoor adventuring in the Phoenix area, and hiking, horseback riding, boating and fishing opportunities abound. Nearby Scottsdale blends the architecture of the Old West with exclusive shops, galleries, restaurants and night clubs, while other towns within easy day-trip distance of Phoenix, such as Payson and Wickenburg, recall grittier and more authentic memories of the rough-and-rowdy mining boom town era of turn-of-the-century Arizona.

Southern Arizona in the springtime, when the desert flowers bloom, is as close as most of us will find to paradise on earth. The secret is well-kept because during the summer tourist season, when most visitors come to the Southwest, Tucson is considerably hotter than paradise—or just about anyplace else. Those who visit at any time other than summer will discover the pleasure of wandering through the forests of giant saguaro cactus that cover the foothills at the edge of town, perhaps learning more at the wonderful Arizona-Sonora Desert Museum and seeing the 18th-century Spanish Mission San Xavier del Bac. For more desert beauty, drive west through the cactus forest of the Tohono O'Odham (Papago) Reservation to Organ Pipe Cactus National Monument on the Mexican border. Many people consider the monument to be the most beautiful part of the Southwestern desert. Another great side trip from the Tucson area is Cochise County to the east.

National monuments in the rugged, empty mountains preserve the strongholds of Apache warlords and the cavalrymen who fought to subdue them. Old Bisbee, until recently the headquarters for one of the nation's largest open-pit copper mining operations, has been reincarnated as a picturesque, far-from-everything tourist town. Tombstone, meanwhile, milks the tourist appeal of a famous gunfight that occurred more than a century ago to sustain one of the most authentically preserved historic towns of the Old West.

Visitors to **Northern New Mexico** find themselves in the land of the descendants of the Anasazi Indians who built the great pueblos at Mesa Verde, Chaco Canyon and other sites, as well as the descendants of the Spanish colonists who settled in the area 400 years ago, before the Pilgrims landed at Plymouth Rock. The unique population mix also includes the world's foremost nuclear scientists and major communities of visual artists, performers and writers. The center of activity in the area is Santa Fe, the state capital and oldest colonial city in the United States, where art openings and opera complement rodeos, horse races and wilderness adventures. Driving north from Santa Fe takes you to Indian pueblos, vast forests and mountain villages centuries old along the way to Taos, a legendary artists' community that adjoins one of the most traditional Indian pueblos. Visitors can venture into the maze of volcanic canyons in the Jemez Mountains at Bandelier National Monument to see some of the best examples of the ancient pueblos and cliff dwellings found throughout the area. Even more impressive Indian ruins await to the west in the lonely San Juan Basin, where the Anasazi pueblo city at Chaco Canyon once dominated the region, linked by an ambitious road system to satellite pueblos such as those at Aztec and Salmon Ruins national monuments.

New Mexico's urban crossroads is the hub for excursions around Albuquerque in **Central New Mexico**. The University of New Mexico provides a venue for cultural events. Places like the Indian Pueblo Cultural Center and the Spanish History Museum showcase the city's multicultural heritage. A fine museum of natural history is located within easy walking distance of Old Town Plaza, a historic district that preserves the architectural grace of Albuquerque's Spanish Colonial era. With a gnarled old forest of cottonwoods along its banks, the Rio Grande has great, secluded trails for urban hiking, jogging, bicycling and horseback riding. Sandia Crest, the massive mountain that flanks the city's Northeast Heights, offers skiing, wilderness hiking, a thrilling tramway ride, cool forests and a view of vast stretches of New Mexico. Albuquerque makes a good hub for exploring. To the west are the many outdoor attractions of the Grants/Gallup area, including El Morro and El Malpais national monuments and Acoma, the most remote and beautiful occupied Indian pueblo in New Mexico. Traveling east from Albuquerque takes you into the high plains, where the major tourist spots are all lakes. Driving south from Albuquerque can take you to Bosque del Apache, where huge flocks of cranes spend the winter months, or to Salinas

Missions, a group of national monument units preserving the ruins of Indian pueblos and old Spanish missions.

Travelers who continue into **Southern New Mexico** face a choice among three different areas, each with its own character. In the east, the premier attraction is Carlsbad Caverns National Park, which draws millions of visitors annually to this remote corner of the state. A visit to Carlsbad Caverns combines easily with a side trip to Ruidoso, a bustling mountain resort town that caters primarily to Texans with its Indian-owned ski slopes and some of the richest horse racing in the country. Nearby, the historic town of Lincoln still remembers the days of Billy the Kid, when it was one of the most lawless places in the Wild West. In south central New Mexico, a series of unique sightseeing highlights— lava fields, Indian petroglyphs, wilderness hiking trails and the vast dunes of White Sands National Monument—invites vacation travelers to leave the interstate and loop through the Tularosa Valley. The dominant feature in the southwestern sector of New Mexico is the Gila Wilderness, the largest roadless area in the 48 contiguous United States. Gila Cliff Dwellings National Monument is the starting point for hikers entering the wilderness, whether for an afternoon or a month. Visitors with plenty of time to explore the area can drive around the wilderness boundary to see the well-preserved ghost town of Mogollon or walk up a sheer-sided canyon on a series of narrow footbridges known as The Catwalk.

Few people actually live in the wild landscape of hoodoos and slickrock canyons that comprise **Southwestern Utah** and **Southeastern Utah**, but millions of visitors come each year to visit the remarkable string of five national parks, each within a few hours' drive of the next. Each of the five is strikingly different from the others. Arches, Bryce Canyon and Zion national parks all present distinctively shaped stone landscapes, erosion as an artform, en route to the North Rim of the Grand Canyon. Canyonlands, the most challenging to explore thoroughly, is reached by any of three dead-end roads into the park that start a hundred miles apart and do not connect. In Capitol Reef, the least known of Utah's national parks, the remains of an old pioneer community provide a hub for a network of dirt roads and trails through side canyons and among strange rock formations. Canyonlands and the Moab area are favored by backpackers, mountain bikers and river rafters. Besides the national parks, another major destination in southern Utah is Lake Powell, the largest reservoir on the Colorado River. Most of its shoreline is far from any road and only accessible by boat. You can rent anything from a speedboat to a houseboat at one of the marinas and cruise for days, exploring side canyons and isolated desert shorelines.

Southwestern Colorado's top visitor attraction is Mesa Verde National Park, the site of the largest, most impressive and mysterious cliff dwellings in North America. While crowd control to protect archeological sites means that backcountry hiking opportunities are limited at Mesa Verde, the park roads are ideal for bicycles. Those who prefer to visit Indian ruins in solitude can see less-known ruins at Hovenweep National Monument and sites around nearby Dolores, Colorado. Durango, the area's principal town, has a quaint Old West-Victorian ambience in the central historic district, which is the departure point for the Durango & Silverton Narrow Gauge Railroad. The popular passenger train follows an old rail route to an old mining town in the heart of the San Juan Mountain. Drivers, too, can explore the San Juans and find alpine hiking trails, old mining towns and great campgrounds along the San Juan Skyway, one of the most spectacular scenic routes anywhere.

When to Go

SEASONS

Many people imagine the Southwest to be a scorching hot place. Part of it—Tucson, Phoenix, southern and western Arizona—lives up to expectations with daytime high temperatures averaging well above the 100-degree mark through the summer months. Even in January, thermometers in this area generally reach the high 60s in the afternoon and rarely fall to freezing at night. The clement winter weather and practically perpetual sunshine have made the Arizona desert a haven for retired persons and migratory human "snowbirds."

Yet less than 200 miles away, the North Rim of the Grand Canyon is closed in the winter because heavy snows make the road impassable. Northern Arizona, northern New Mexico and southern Utah and Colorado experience cold, dry winters with temperatures usually rising above freezing during the day but often dropping close to zero at night. The high mountains remain snowcapped all winter and boast several popular ski areas. At lower elevations, lighter snowfalls and plenty of sunshine keep roads clear most of the time.

In the Southwest, where the high, rugged Rocky Mountains collide with the subtropical Chihuahuan and Sonoran deserts, small changes in elevation can mean big variations in climate. As a rule, climbing 1000 feet in elevation alters the temperature as much as going 300 miles north. For instance, the bottom of the Grand Canyon is always about 20 degrees warmer than the top rim. In Tucson during the winter, some people bask by swimming pools while others ski on the slopes of nearby Mount Lemmon.

Springtime in the Southwest is a mixed blessing. Flooding rivers, chilly winds and sandstorms sometimes await visitors in March and early April, but those who take a chance are more likely to experience mild weather and spectacular displays of desert wildflowers. Leaves do not appear on the trees until late April at moderate elevations, late May in the higher mountains.

Throughout the region, June is the hottest month. Even in cool areas such as northern New Mexico, the thermometer frequently hits the 100-degree mark. In July and August the thunderstorms of what locals refer to as the "monsoon season" usually cool things down quickly on hot afternoons. The majority of the moisture for the entire year falls during these two months, so try to plan outdoor activities in the morning hours. Although New Mexico and Arizona are pretty much safe from natural disasters like earthquakes, tornadoes and hurricanes, meteorologists have discovered from satellite data that the region has more lightning strikes than anywhere else in the United States.

Autumn is the nicest time of year throughout the Southwest. Locals used to keep this fact to themselves, and until recently tourists in October were about as rare as snowflakes in Phoenix. Nowadays the secret is out, and record numbers of people are visiting during the fall "shoulder season" to experience fall colors and bright Indian summer days.

CALENDAR OF EVENTS

Besides all-American-style annual community celebrations with parades, arts-and-crafts shows, concerts—and, in the Southwest, rodeos—the region has other, less familiar kinds of festivals. Most towns that trace their heritage back to Spanish colonialism observe annual fiestas, normally on the feast day of the town's patron saint. Fiestas tend to mix sacred and secular, with solemn religious processions and dancing in the streets. Indian pueblos mark their patron saints' feast days differently, with elaborately costumed ceremonial dances that include a pueblo's entire population, from toddlers to elders. Besides ceremonials, all Indian nations host annual powwows—gatherings of people from many tribes around the country who compete for money in colorful contest dances.

JANUARY

Northern New Mexico: **New Year's Day** is celebrated with dances at Picuris, Santa Clara and Taos pueblos. Most pueblos also celebrate **Three Kings Day** in early January. San Ildefonso Pueblo's **Fiesta de San Ildefonso** features all-day animal dances including an awe-inspiring dawn procession that descends from nearby Black Mesa.

Central New Mexico: **New Year's Day** is observed at Cochiti Pueblo with an all-day ceremonial including Comanche and animal dances. Dance ceremonies are also held at Laguna, San Felipe, Santa Ana and Santo Domingo pueblos. Most pueblos also celebrate **Three Kings Day** in early January.

FEBRUARY

Central Arizona: **Gold Rush Days** in Wickenburg features a parade, rodeo, arts-and-crafts show, melodrama, gold mucking and drilling competitions and a beard-growing contest. **Lost Dutchman Days** in Apache Junction near Phoenix is another community celebration full of traditional small-town events—like a Fourth of July in February. Casa Grande is the site of **O'Odham Tash—Casa Grande Indian Days**, including Indian rituals and arts and crafts.

Southern Arizona: The **Tucson Gem and Mineral Show** draws jewelers and collectors from around the world.

Northern New Mexico: **Candeleria** is observed with ceremonial dances at Picuris Pueblo.

Central New Mexico: At the **Mid-Winter Rendezvous** in Gallup, modern-day mountain men compete at black powder marksmanship, knife and tomahawk throwing and telling outrageous lies. **Candeleria** (Candlemas) is observed with ceremonial dances at Cochiti, Santo Domingo and San Felipe pueblos.

MARCH

Central Arizona: The **Scottsdale Arts Festival** features dance and music performances and crafts exhibitions.

Southern Arizona: The high point of **Tombstone Territorial Days** is a reenactment of the events leading up to the gunfight at the O.K. Corral. The **Tucson Festival of the Arts** presents a three-day program of orchestral, choral and ensemble music, modern and interpretive dance and theater performances in the city parks, along with one of the Southwest's largest arts-and-crafts shows.

Northern New Mexico: Each March 9, Columbus holds a military-style **Memorial Ceremony** to remember the victims of Mexican revolutionist Pancho Villa's 1916 raid.

Central New Mexico: Laguna Pueblo observes the **Fiesta de San Jose** with harvest and social dances. The **Four Corners Area Exposition** at Red Rock State Park near Gallup has arts and crafts, Indian fashion shows, a science fair and live entertainment.

APRIL

Southern Arizona: The **Tucson Festival**, which runs for three weekends, incorporates **Pioneer Days** and the **San Xavier Pageant and Fiesta**, both living-history re-enactments with Spanish priests, conquistadors, mountain men and the cavalry, as well as traditional Tohono O'Odham Indian dances. The Festival also includes the lively, Mexican-style **Fiesta de la Placita**.

Central New Mexico: At the **Gathering of Nations Powwow** in Albuquerque, more than 5000 costumed dancers from all over the country compete for prize money in one of the biggest Indian events anywhere.

Southwestern Utah: The **St. George Art Festival** fills Main Street and the art center with juried art exhibits and continuous musical performances.

MAY

Northwestern Arizona: **Bill Williams Rendezvous Days,** held on Memorial Day weekend in Williams, re-creates the days of the mountain men with barn dances, black-powder shoots, a pioneer costume contest and evening "whooplas."

Southern Arizona: Tombstone's **Wyatt Earp Days** celebration fills the Memorial Day weekend with Old West costumes, staged shootouts in the streets and arts and crafts.

Northern New Mexico: The **Northern New Mexico Arts and Crafts Fair** in Los Alamos displays work by over 100 artisans. The **Spring Festival at El Rancho de las Golondrinas** near Santa Fe presents Spanish colonial craft demonstrations and re-creates 17th-century hacienda life.

Central New Mexico: The **Fiesta de San Felipe** is observed at the San Felipe Pueblo with a large, spectacular corn dance involving more than 500 dancers.

Southern New Mexico: **Mayfair,** held on Memorial Day weekend, is the big community festival in Cloudcroft.

JUNE

Northwestern Arizona: The **Festival of Native American Arts** opens at the Museum of Northern Arizona in Flagstaff, with extensive exhibits and craft demonstrations continuing through early August.

Central Arizona: An **Oldtime Country Music and Bluegrass Festival** is held at the rodeo grounds in Payson.

Northern New Mexico: The **Taos Spring Arts Celebration,** continuing over several weekends, features artists' studio tours, performing arts and live entertainment. San Juan Pueblo observes the **Fiesta de San Juan** with buffalo and Comanche dances.

Central New Mexico: **Madrid Summer Festival** enlivens the old mining town on the Turquoise Trail between Santa Fe and Albuquerque with an old-fashioned country fair, live music and art studio tours. **Old Fort Days** in Fort Sumner feature a rodeo, staged bank robbery, melodrama and barbecue. The **New Mexico Arts and Crafts Fair,** held at Albuquerque's State Fairgrounds, is the state's largest.

Southwestern Colorado: The **Telluride Bluegrass Festival** packs this little mountain town to overflowing with musicians and fans.

JULY

Northwestern Arizona: The **Hopi Craftsman Exhibit** is presented at the Museum of Northern Arizona in Flagstaff in early July in connection with the Festival of Native American Arts. The **Navajo Craftsman Exhibition** opens there later in the month.

Central Arizona: The rodeo grounds in Payson are the setting for the **Loggers Sawdust Festival**, a weekend of cutting, chopping, pole climbing and log burling contests. The **Phoenix Parks Department Summer Show** is one of the Southwest's largest arts and crafts fairs.

Northern New Mexico: The **Taos School of Music Summer Chamber Music Festival** combines concerts by top classical musicians with educational seminars. Later in the month, the **Taos Fiesta** fills the streets with dancing. The **Rodeo de Santa Fe** comes to the state capital with a parade and pancake breakfast on the plaza. About a week later, the **Santa Fe Opera** season opens and the city's lodging accommodations fill to capacity through August. The **Eight Northern Pueblos Arts and Crafts Fair**, held each year at a different Indian pueblo north of Santa Fe, hosts hundreds of Indian exhibitors. The Jicarilla Apache tribe sponsors the **Little Beaver Roundup**, a three-day celebration in Dulce with dances, an Indian rodeo and an arts and crafts show. Santa Clara Pueblo holds its annual **Puye Cliffs Ceremonial** at their ancestral mesatop pueblo with dances and arts and crafts exhibits. In Española, the **Fiesta de Oñate**, commemorating the founding of the first Spanish settlement in New Mexico, includes a costumed procession and climaxes in a rowdy all-night street dance.

Central New Mexico: The **Piñata Festival**, Tucumcari's annual celebration, features sporting events, a beauty pageant, parade, rodeo and chili cook-off.

Southern New Mexico: The **Ruidoso Arts Festival** is a major juried arts and crafts fair with continuous live entertainment.

Southwestern Utah: The **Utah Shakespearean Festival**, from mid-July through August in Cedar City, features three plays performed on an outdoors stage along with related seminars and entertainment events.

Southwestern Colorado: The **Telluride Rock Festival** presents three days of top rock and pop bands. Durango's 11-day Navajo Trails Fiesta offers rodeo events, horse racing and square dancing.

AUGUST

Northern New Mexico: The **Santa Fe Indian Market**, the largest Indian arts show and sale anywhere, takes place on Santa Fe's main plaza and draws collectors from around the world.

Central New Mexico: Santo Domingo Pueblo's observance of the **Fiesta de Santo Domingo** with a huge corn dance in the streets and narrow plazas of this ancient village is one of the most spectacular Indian ceremonials in the Southwest. At the **Inter-Tribal Indian Ceremonial** held in Red Rock State Park near Gallup, Indians from more than 50 tribes participate in ritual and contest dances, an arts and crafts show, a rodeo and other events.

Southern New Mexico: **Old Lincoln Days** features costumed re-enactments of scenes from the Lincoln County War, including Billy the Kid's last jailbreak. The **Zuni Tribal Fair**, held in late August, includes an arts and crafts show, food booths and competition dancing. Deming hosts the **Great Deming Duck Race**, where waterfowl race for money and compete in such events as a Best-Dressed Duck Contest and a Duck Queen pageant.

Southeastern Utah: **Navajo Mountain Pioneer Days** in Blanding focuses on the area's Native American heritage with horse and foot races, Indian food booths and live entertainment.

Southwestern Colorado: Telluride hosts its annual five-day **Chamber Music Festival** featuring outstanding classical music performers. Later in the month, the **Telluride Jazz Festival** is one of the biggest in the country.

SEPTEMBER

Northwestern Arizona: The **Call of The Canyon Festival of the Arts**, held in Sedona, draws artisans from all over the West to participate in one of the region's major arts-and-crafts fairs.

Northeastern Arizona: The **Navajo Nation Fair** in Window Rock has carnival rides, a rodeo, horse races, dance competitions, a pretty-baby contest, the Miss Navajo pageant and a wonderful arts and crafts pavilion.

Central Arizona: Payson hosts the **Old-Time Fiddlers Contest and Festival** at the rodeo grounds.

Southern Arizona: **Wild West Days**, one of several practically identical town festivals held in Tombstone throughout the year, features a parade, rodeo, melodrama and quick-draw contest. Nogales joins its twin city across the border in celebrating **Mexican Independence Day** with food, live music and street dancing.

Northern New Mexico: The **Santa Fe Fiesta** starts with the ritual burning in effigy of a 70-foot-tall "Old Man Gloom" and continues through a weekend of parades, processions and wild celebration in the streets. The **Taos Arts Festival** presents art exhibits, lectures and an arts-and-crafts fair, coinciding with the **Fiesta de San Geronimo** ceremonial dances at the nearby pueblo. **Go-Chee-Ya**, the Jicarilla Apache tribe's annual celebration in Dulce, includes a rodeo and powwow.

Central New Mexico: In Albuquerque, the **New Mexico State Fair**, one of the nation's largest, has horse racing, top country-and-western performers, a rodeo and lots of livestock.

Southern New Mexico: The **Pan American Fiesta** in Mesilla celebrates harmony between the United States and Mexico with three days of folk dancing, mariachi music and food.

OCTOBER

Northwestern Arizona: In Lake Havasu City, **London Bridge Days** commemorates the relocation of the bridge to this improbable site with a parade, live entertainment, costume contests and lots of Olde English fun.

Central Arizona: The **Arizona State Fair,** held in Phoenix, runs until early November. Tombstone celebrates **Heldorado Days** with music, arts and crafts and gunfight re-enactments.

Southern Arizona: The **Bisbee Copper Queen Fling** celebrates the town's flamboyant boom days with tours of the now-defunct Copper Queen open-pit mine and revelry all over Old Bisbee.

Northern New Mexico: Costumed volunteers re-create the Spanish colonial era at **Harvest Festival** at the Rancho de las Golondrinas, a historic hacienda near Santa Fe that still operates as a working farm using pioneer methods. The artists of secluded Dixon, near Taos, open their homes and workplaces to the public in the **Dixon Studio Tour;** the even more off-the-beaten-path artists' community of El Rito also sponsors a studio tour this month.

Central New Mexico: The **Albuquerque Balloon Fiesta** lasts for a week and a half with races, mass ascensions and other events featuring hundreds of hot-air balloons—the world's largest such event.

Southern New Mexico: Ruidoso celebrates fall foliage with a boisterous **Oktoberfest,** coinciding with nearby Cloudcroft's **Aspencade.** In Alamogordo, the once-a-year **Trinity Site Tour** is your only chance to see where the first atomic bomb was tested. In Las Cruces, the **Whole Enchilada Festival** features a parade, live entertainment throughout the weekend, races (including a grocery cart race) and the "World's Largest Enchilada." **Columbus Day** is observed in Columbus with a parade, all-day live music and a street dance.

NOVEMBER

Central Arizona: The **Four Corner States Bluegrass Festival** in Wickenburg presents three days of music as bands compete for thousands of dollars in prize money.

Southern Arizona: The **Papago All-Indian Fair** at Sells, west of Tucson on the Indian reservation, features outstanding pottery, rug and jewelry exhibits as well as a rodeo.

Northern New Mexico: Tesuque Pueblo celebrates the **Fiesta de San Diego** with dances.

Central New Mexico: Jemez Pueblo observes the **Fiesta de San Diego** with dances and a trade fair. The **Southwest Arts and Crafts Festival,** an invitational show focusing on visual arts, presents the works of over 150 artists at the State Fairgrounds in Albuquerque. Thousands of Indian and non-Indian spectators brave the cold to see kachinas walk the night during **Shalako,** the annual house-blessing ceremony at Zuni Pueblo.

Southern New Mexico: Nearly 100 exhibitors participate in the **Holy Cross Renaissance Arts and Crafts Fair,** a juried art show in Las Cruces.

DECEMBER

Northern New Mexico: The **Fiesta of Our Lady of Guadalupe** is observed with dances and ceremonies at Nambe and Pojoaque pueblos. **Christmas** is celebrated with ceremonial dances at all Indian Pueblos. The Christmas holidays hold particular charm in Santa Fe and Taos, where instead of colored lights, building exteriors glow with thousands of small candles called farolitos.

Central New Mexico: **Luminarias** (altar candles) light up the skyline of Albuquerque's Old Town. The **Fiesta of Our Lady of Guadalupe** is celebrated with dances at Jemez Pueblo. Between Albuquerque and Santa Fe, the **Turquoise Trail Artisans' Open House** lets visitors see the studios of regional artists. Christmas is celebrated with ceremonial dances at all Indian Pueblos.

Southern New Mexico: The city of Las Cruces celebrates the fiesta with a **torchlight ascent** of a nearby mountain, musical concerts and other festivities.

How to Deal With . . .

VISITOR INFORMATION

For free visitor information packets including maps and current details on special events, accommodations and camping, contact the following offices: the **Arizona Office of Tourism** (1100 West Washington Street, Phoenix, AZ 85007; 602-542-3687); the **New Mexico Tourism and Travel Division** (Montoya Building, Room 106, 1100 St. Francis Drive, Santa Fe, NM 87503; 505-827-0291); the **Utah Travel Council** (Council Hall/Capitol Hill, Salt Lake City, UT 84114; 801-538-1030); and the **Colorado Tourism Board** (1313 Sherman Street, Denver, CO 80202; 800-433-2656). In addition, most towns have chambers of commerce or visitor information centers. Many of them are listed in *Hidden Southwest* under the appropriate regions. As a general rule, these tourist information centers are not open on weekends.

PACKING

The old adage that you should take along twice as much money and half as much stuff as you think you'll need is sound advice as far as it goes, but bear in mind that in many parts of the Southwest you are unlikely to find a store selling anything more substantial than curios and beef jerky.

(Text continued on page 26.)

People of the Southwest

The population of the Southwest is often called "tricultural"—Indian, Spanish and Anglo. Each of the three cultures has been an enemy to the others in centuries past, yet all live in harmony as neighbors today. Through centuries of life in close proximity, and despite persistent attempts by both Spanish and Anglos to assimilate the Indian people, each group proudly maintains its cultural identity while respecting the others. The resulting tricultural balance is truly unique to the region.

All three cultural groups share freely in each other's ways. For example, Southwestern cooking blends traditional Anasazi/Pueblo foods—blue corn, beans and squash—with green chili and cooking techniques imported by early Spanish colonists from the Aztecs of central Mexico, and the result is a staple in Anglo kitchens. The distinctive architecture of the desert uses adobe bricks, of Moorish origin and brought to the New World by the Spanish, while the architectural style derives from Anasazi pueblos and incorporates refinements Anglos brought west by railroad.

An Anglo, in local parlance, is anyone who comes from English-speaking America. Anglos first came to the Southwest less than 150 years ago, after the end of the Mexican War, and are still a minority group in many parts today. Newcomers are often surprised to learn that Americans of Jewish, Japanese and African ancestry, among others, are referred to as Anglos. Many Anglos in the more remote parts of the Southwest, from traditional Mormons in rural Utah to residents of old-fashioned hippie communes and artists' colonies in the mountains of New Mexico, hold to ways of life that are a far cry from modern mainstream America.

The Spanish residents of New Mexico trace their ancestry back to the pioneer era around the year 1600—the time of Don Quixote, of the Spanish Inquisition, of the conquest of the New World by the Spanish Armada. Today, the Spanish remain the dominant political and cultural force in many parts of New Mexico, and travelers can still find isolated mountain villages where many aspects of everyday life remain unchanged since the 17th century. Mexican immigration in the 20th century has created a separate Hispanic subculture in southern New Mexico and Arizona.

Visitors today have little opportunity to experience the uniqueness of such tribes as the Apache, Ute, Paiute and other nomadic tribes for whom confinement to reservations has meant adopting conventional ways of rural life. But among groups such as the Pueblo and Navajo people, who still occupy their traditional homelands, the old ways are still very much alive.

The Pueblo people who live along the Rio Grande in Isleta, Santo Domingo, Cochiti, Tesuque, San Ildefonso, Santa Clara, Taos and other Indian communities are descendants of the Anasazi, or "Ancient Ones," who built the impressive castlelike compounds at literally thousands of sites such as those we know as Chaco Canyon, Bandelier, Pecos and Salinas. Although they have lived in close contact with Spanish and Anglo neighbors for centuries, the Rio Grande Pueblo people have carefully guarded their own cultural identity. They often have Spanish names and attend services at mission churches, yet they observe Catholic feast days with sacred dances and kiva ceremonies that reach back to pre-Columbian antiquity. While most Pueblo Indians speak English, they converse among themselves in the dialect of their particular pueblo—Tewa, Tiwa, Towa or Keresan.

The more isolated pueblos of western New Mexico and northeastern Arizona retain their own distinctive cultures. The Acoma people, thought to be descendants of the Mesa Verde Anasazi, practice secret rites that are closed to outsiders. The people of Zuni, who speak a language unrelated to any other Indian group and may be the heirs of the Mimbres who lived in southern New Mexico, follow the ancient kachina religion, becoming embodiments of nature's forces in strange, colorful blessing ceremonies. The Hopi people, whose Sinagua ancestors once lived throughout central Arizona from the Grand Canyon to the Verde Valley, have banned non-Indian visitors from many of their religious ceremonies because of their objections to the publication of various books sensationalizing their snake and eagle dances and their ancient tradition of prophecies.

Nowhere is the blending of cultures more evident than among the Navajo, the largest Indian tribe in the United States. The roots of their religious traditions stretch far into the past, and their hogan dwellings originated in the frozen northlands from which they came. Since arriving in the Southwest in the 1400s, they have borrowed from their neighbors to create their own unique culture. They learned to grow corn and weave textiles from the Pueblo people, and to herd sheep and ride horses from the Spanish. Early Anglo traders helped them develop their "traditional" art forms, rugs and silver jewelry. Even the more modern aspects of Navajo life—pickup trucks, satellite dishes, blue jeans—are not so much signs of assimilation into the white man's world as of the continuing evolution of a uniquely Navajo way of life.

Southwesterners are casual in their dress and expect the same of visitors. Restaurants with dress codes are few and far between. Even if you attend a fancy $100-a-plate fundraiser or go out for a night at the opera, you'll find that a coat and tie or evening gown and heels instantly brand you as a tourist. Chic apparel in these parts is more likely to mean a western-cut suit, ostrich hide boots and a bolo tie with a flashy turquoise-and-silver slide, or for women, a fiesta dress with a concho belt, long-fringed moccasins and a squash blossom necklace—all fairly expensive items that you may never have an occasion to wear back home. Relax. Sporty, comfortable clothing will pass practically anywhere.

When packing clothes, plan to dress in layers. Temperatures can turn hot or cold in a flash at any time of year. During the course of a single vacation day, you can expect to start wearing a heavy jacket, a sweater or flannel shirt and a pair of slacks or jeans, peeling down to a T-shirt and shorts as the day warms up, then putting the extra layers back on soon after the sun goes down.

Other essentials to pack or buy along the way include a good sunscreen and high-quality sunglasses. If you are planning to camp in the mountains during the summer months, you'll be glad you brought mosquito repellant. Umbrellas are considered an oddity in the Southwest. When it rains, as it sometimes does though rarely for long, the approved means of keeping cold water from running down the back of your neck is a cowboy hat.

For outdoor activities, tough-soled hiking boots are more comfortable than running shoes on rocky terrain. Even RV travelers and those who prefer to spend most nights in motels may want to take along a backpacking tent and sleeping bag for irresistible urges to stay out under star-spangled southwestern skies. A canteen, first-aid kit, flashlight and other routine camping gear are also likely to come in handy. Cycling enthusiasts should bring their own bikes. Especially when it comes to mountain biking, there are a lot more great places to ride than there are towns where you can find bicycles for rent. The same goes for boating, golf and other activities that call for special equipment.

If you're the kind of person who likes to pick up souvenirs for free in the form of unusual stones, pine cones and the like, take along some plastic bags for hauling treasures. A camera, of course, is essential for capturing your travel experience; of equal importance is a good pair of binoculars, which let you explore distant landscapes from scenic overlooks. And don't, for heaven's sake, forget your copy of *Hidden Southwest*.

HOTELS

Lodgings in the Southwest run the gamut from tiny one-room mountain cabins to luxurious hotels that blend Indian pueblo architecture with contemporary elegance. Bed and breakfasts can be found not only in chic destinations like Santa Fe and Sedona but also in such unlikely locales as former ghost towns and the outskirts of Indian reservations. They come in all types, sizes and price ranges. Typical of the genre are lovingly restored old mansions comfortably furnished with period decor, usually with under a dozen rooms. Some bed and breakfasts, however, are guest cottages or rooms in nice suburban homes, while others are larger establishments, approaching hotel size, of the type sometimes referred to as country inns.

The abundance of motels in towns along all major highway routes presents a range of choices, from name-brand motor inns to traditional mom-and-pop establishments that have endured for half a century since motels were invented. Older motels along main truck routes, especially interstate Route 40, offer some of the lowest room rates to be found anywhere in the United States today.

At the other end of the price spectrum, the height of self-indulgent vacationing is to be found at upscale resorts in some destinations such as Tucson, Sedona, Ruidoso and Santa Fe. These resorts offer riding stables, golf courses, tennis courts, fine dining, live entertainment nightly and exclusive shops right on the premises so that guests can spend their entire holidays without leaving the grounds—a boon for celebrities seeking a few days' rest and relaxation away from the public eye, but a very expensive way to miss out on experiencing the real Southwest.

Other lodgings throughout the region offer a different kind of personality. Many towns—preserved historic districts like Tombstone and Lincoln as well as larger communities like Durango and Flagstaff—have historic hotels dating back before the turn of the century. Some of them have been lavishly restored to far surpass their original Victorian elegance. Others may lack the polished antique decor and sophisticated ambience but make up for it in their authentic feel. These places give visitors a chance to spice up their vacation experience by spending the night where lawman Wyatt Earp or novelist Zane Gray once slept and awakening to look out their window onto a Main Street that has changed surprisingly little since the days of the Old West.

Both rims of the Grand Canyon, as well as Bryce Canyon and Zion, have classic, rustic-elegant lodges built during the early years of the 20th century. Though considerably more expensive than budget motel rooms, the national park lodges are moderate in price and well worth it in terms of ambience and location. Reservations should be made far in advance.

Whatever your preference and budget, you can probably find something to suit your taste with the help of the regional chapters in this book. Remember, rooms can be scarce and prices may rise during the peak season, which is summer throughout most of the region and winter in low-lying desert communities such as Phoenix, Scottsdale and Tucson. Travelers planning to visit a place in peak season should either make advance reservations or arrive early in the day, before the "No Vacancy" signs start lighting up.

Those who plan to stay in Santa Fe, Sedona, Grand Canyon National Park or Mesa Verde National Park at any time of year are wise to make lodging reservations well ahead of time.

Accommodations in this book are organized by region and classified according to price. Rates referred to are high-season rates, so if you are looking for off-season bargains, it's good to inquire. *Budget* lodgings generally run less than $50 per night for two people and are satisfactory and clean but modest. *Moderate* hotels range from $50 to $90; what they have to offer in the way of luxury will depend on where they are located, but they generally offer larger rooms and more attractive surroundings. At a *deluxe* hotel or resort you can expect to spend between $90 and $130 for a double; you'll generally find spacious rooms, a fashionable lobby, a restaurant and often a group of shops. *Ultra-deluxe* facilities, priced above $130, are a region's finest, offering all the amenities of a deluxe hotel plus plenty of extras.

Room rates vary as much with locale as with quality. Some of the trendier destinations have no rooms at all in the budget price range. In other communities—especially those along interstate highways where rates are set with truck drivers in mind—every motel falls into the budget category, even though accommodations may range from $19.95 at run-down, spartan places to $45 or so at the classiest motor inn in town. The price categories listed in this book are relative, designed to show you where to get the most out of your travel budget, however large or small it may be.

RESTAURANTS

Restaurants seem to be one of the main industries in some parts of the Southwest. Santa Fe, New Mexico, for example, has approximately 200 restaurants in a city of just 50,000 people. While the specialty cuisine throughout most of the Southwest consists of variations on Mexican and Indian food, you'll find many restaurants catering to customers whose tastes don't include hot chili peppers. You'll also find a growing number of restaurants offering "New Southwestern" menus that feature offbeat dishes using local ingredients. Green-chili tempura? Snow-crab enchiladas? If a newly invented dish sounds tempting, by all means give it a try!

Within a particular chapter, restaurants are categorized by region, with each restaurant entry describing the establishment according to price. Dinner entrées at *budget* restaurants usually cost $8 or less. The ambience is informal, service usually speedy and the crowd often a local one. *Moderately* priced restaurants range between $8 and $16 at dinner; surroundings are casual but pleasant, the menu offers more variety and the pace is usually slower. *Deluxe* establishments tab their entrées from $16 to $24; cuisines may be simple or sophisticated, depending on the location, but the decor is plusher and the service more personalized. *Ultra-deluxe* dining rooms, where entrées begin at $24, are often the gourmet places; here cooking has become a fine art and the service should be impeccable.

Some restaurants change hands often and are occasionally closed in low seasons. Efforts have been made in this book to include places with established reputations for good eating. Breakfast and lunch menus vary less in price from restaurant to restaurant than evening dinners.

DRIVING THE SOUTHWEST

The mountains and deserts of the Southwest are clearly the major sightseeing attractions for many visitors. This is a rugged area and there are some important things to remember when driving on the side roads throughout the region. First and foremost, believe it if you see a sign indicating four-wheel drive only. These roads can be very dangerous in a car without high ground clearance and the extra traction afforded by four-wheel drive—and there may be no safe place to turn around if you get stuck. During rainy periods dirt roads may become impassable muck. And in winter, heavy snows necessitate the use of snow tires or chains on main roads, while side roads may or may not be maintained at all.

Some side roads will take you far from civilization so be sure to have a full radiator and tank of gas. Carry spare fuel, water and food. In winter, it is always wise to travel with a shovel and blankets in your car. Should you become stuck, local people are usually quite helpful about offering assistance to stranded vehicles, but in case no one else is around, for extended backcountry driving, a CB radio or a car phone would not be a bad idea.

TRAVELING WITH CHILDREN

Any place that has cowboys and Indians, rocks to climb and limitless room to run is bound to be a hit with youngsters. Plenty of family adventures are available in the Southwest, from manmade attractions to experiences in the wild. A few guidelines will help make travel with children a pleasure.

Book reservations in advance, making sure that the places you stay accept children. Many bed and breakfasts do not. If you need a crib or extra cot, arrange for it ahead of time. A travel agent can be of help here, as well as with most other travel plans.

If you are traveling by air, try to reserve bulkhead seats where there is plenty of room. Take along extras you may need, such as diapers, changes of clothing, snacks and toys or small games. When traveling by car, be sure to take along the extras, too. Make sure you have plenty of water and juices to drink; dehydration can be a subtle but serious problem. Most towns, as well as some national parks, have stores that carry diapers, baby food, snacks and other essentials, though they usually close early. Larger towns often have all-night grocery or convenience stores.

A first-aid kit is a must for any trip. Along with adhesive bandages, antiseptic cream and something to stop itching, include any medicines your pediatrician might recommend to treat allergies, colds, diarrhea or any chronic problems your child may have.

Southwestern sunshine is intense. Take extra care for the first few days. Children's skin is usually more tender than adult skin and severe sunburn can happen before you realize it. A hat is a good idea, along with a reliable sunblock.

Many national parks and monuments offer special activities designed just for children. Visitor center film presentations and rangers' campfire slide shows can help inform children about the natural history of the Southwest and head off some questions. However, kids tend to find a lot more things to wonder about than adults have answers for. To be as prepared as possible, seize every opportunity to learn more—particularly about Indians, a constant curiosity for young minds.

BEING AN OLDER TRAVELER

The Southwest is a hospitable place for older vacationers, many of whom turn into part-time or full-time residents thanks to the dry, pleasant climate and the friendly senior citizen communities that have developed in southern Arizona and, on a smaller scale, in other parts of the region. The large number of national parks and monuments in the Southwest means that persons age 62 and older can save considerable money with a Golden Age Passport, which allows free admission. Apply for one in person at any national park unit that charges an entrance fee. Many private sightseeing attractions also offer significant discounts for seniors.

The **American Association of Retired Persons** (AARP) (3200 East Carson Street, Lakewood, CA 90712; 213-496-2277) offers membership to anyone over 50. AARP's benefits include travel discounts with a number of firms. Escorted tours and cruises are available through AARP Travel Service (P.O. Box 5850, Norcross, GA 30091; 800-927-0111).

Elderhostel (75 Federal Street, Boston, MA 02110; 617-426-7788) offers educational courses that are all-inclusive packages at colleges and universities. In the Southwest, Elderhostel courses are available in numerous locations including: in Arizona—Flagstaff, Nogales, Phoenix, Prescott and Tucson; and in New Mexico—Albuquerque, Las Cruces, Santa Fe, Silver City and Taos. Courses are also offered in Durango, Colorado, and Cedar City, Utah.

Be extra careful about health matters. In the changeable climate of the Southwest, seniors are more at risk of suffering hypothermia. High altitudes may present a risk to persons with heart or respiratory conditions; ask your physician for advice when planning your trip. Many tourist destinations in the region are a long way from any hospital or other health care facility.

In addition to the medications you ordinarily use, it's a good idea to bring along the prescriptions for obtaining more. Consider carrying a medical record with you, including your history and current medical status as well as your doctor's name, phone number and address. Make sure that your insurance covers you while you are away from home.

BEING DISABLED

All of the Southwestern states are striving to make public areas fully accessible to disabled persons. Parking spaces and restroom facilities for the handicapped are provided according to both state law and national park regulations. National parks and monuments also post signs that tell which trails are wheelchair-accessible.

Information sources for disabled travelers include: the **Society for the Advancement of Travel for the Handicapped** (347 5th Avenue, Suite 610, New York, NY 10016; 212-447-7284); the **Travel Information Center** (Moss Rehabilitation Hospital, 12th Street and Tabor Road, Philadelphia, PA 19141; 215-329-5715); and **Mobility International USA** (P.O. Box 3551, Eugene, OR 97403; 503-343-1284). For general travel advice, contact **Travelin' Talk** (P.O. Box 3534, Clarksville, TN 37043; 615-552-6670), a networking organization.

BEING A FOREIGN TRAVELER

PASSPORTS AND VISAS   Most foreign visitors need a passport and tourist visa to enter the United States. Contact your nearest United States Embassy or Consulate well in advance to obtain a visa and to check on any other entry requirements.

CUSTOMS REQUIREMENTS   Foreign travelers are allowed to carry in the following: 200 cigarettes (or 100 cigars), $400 worth of duty-free gifts, including one liter of alcohol (you must be 21 years of age to bring in the alcohol). You may bring in any amount of currency but must fill out a form if you bring in over $10,000 (U.S.). Carry any prescription drugs in clearly marked containers. You may have to produce a written prescription or doctor's statement for the customs officer. Meat or meat products, seeds, plants, fruits and narcotics are not allowed to be brought into the United States. Contact the United States Custom Service (1301 Constitution Avenue Northwest, Washington, DC 20229; 202-566-8195) for further information.

DRIVING   If you plan to rent a car, an international driver's license should be obtained before arriving in the United States. Some car rental agencies require both a foreign license and an international driver's license. Many also require a lessee to be at least 25 years of age; all require a major credit card.

CURRENCY   United States money is based on the dollar. Bills generally come in denominations of $1, $5, $10, $20, $50 and $100. Every dollar is divided into 100 cents. Coins are the penny (1 cent), nickel (5 cents), dime (10 cents) and quarter (25 cents). Half-dollar and dollar coins are rarely used. You may not use foreign currency to purchase goods and services in the United States. Consider buying traveler's checks in dollar amounts. You may also use credit cards affiliated with an American company such as Interbank, Barclay Card and American Express.

ELECTRICITY   Electric outlets use currents of 110 volts, 60 cycles. For appliances made for other electrical systems, you need a transformer or other adapter.

WEIGHTS AND MEASURES   The United States uses the English system of weights and measures. American units and their metric equivalents are: 1 inch = 2.5 centimeters; 1 foot (12 inches) = 0.3 meter; 1 yard (3 feet) = 0.9 meter; 1 mile (5280 feet) = 1.6 kilometers; 1 ounce = 28 grams; 1 pound (16 ounces) = 0.45 kilogram; 1 quart (liquid) = 0.9 liter.

The Sporting Life

CAMPING

RV or tent camping is a great way to tour the Southwest. Besides saving substantial sums of money, campers enjoy the freedom to watch sunsets from beautiful places, spend nights under spectacularly starry skies and wake up to find themselves in lovely surroundings that few hotels can match.

Most towns have commercial RV parks of some sort, and long-term mobile-home parks often rent spaces to RVers by the night. But unless you absolutely need cable television, none of these places can compete with the wide array of public campgrounds available in national and state parks, monuments and forests. Federal campground sites are typically less developed and only the biggest ones have electrical hookups. National forest campgrounds do not have hookups, while state park campgrounds just about always do. The largest public campgrounds offer tent camping loops separate from RV loops and backcountry camping areas offer the option of spending the night in the primeval Southwest.

With the exception of both rims of the Grand Canyon, where campsite reservations are booked through **Ticketron** (Reservation Office, P.O. Box 617516, Chicago, IL 60661-7516; 800-452-1111—credit cards only), you won't find much in the way of sophisticated reservation systems in the Southwest. The general rule in public campgrounds is still first-come, first-served, even though they fill up practically every night in peak season. For campers, this means traveling in the morning and reaching your intended campground by early afternoon. In many areas, campers may find it more convenient to keep a single location for as much as a week and explore surrounding areas on day trips.

For listings of state parks with camping facilities and reservation information, contact **Arizona State Parks** (800 West Washington Street, Phoenix, AZ 85007; 602-542-4174); **New Mexico State Park and Recreation Division** (141 East De Vargas, Santa Fe, NM 87503; 505-827-7465); **Utah Division of Parks and Recreation** (1636 West North Temple, Salt Lake City, UT 84116; 801-538-7221); and **Colorado Parks and Outdoor Recreation** (1313 Sherman Street, Denver, CO 80216; 303-866-3437). Also see the "Parks" sections in each chapter of this book to discover where camping is available.

Information on camping in the national forests in New Mexico and Arizona is available from **National Forest Service—Southwestern Region** (Public Affairs Office, 517 Gold Avenue Southwest, Albuquerque, NM 87102; 505-842-3292); for those in Utah, **National Forest Service—Intermountain Region** (324 25th Street, Ogden, UT 84401; 801-625-5347); and for those in Colorado, **National Forest Service—Rocky Mountain Region** (11177 West 8th Avenue, Lakewood, CO 80225; 303-236-9431). Camping and reservation information for national parks and monuments is available from **National Park Service—Southwest Regional Office** (1100 Old Santa Fe Trail, Santa Fe, NM 87501; 505-988-6340) or from the individual parks and monuments listed in this book.

Many Indian lands have public campgrounds, which usually do not appear in campground directories. For information, contact the **Navajo Cultural Resources Department** (P.O. Box 308, Window Rock, AZ 86515; 602-871-4941); **Hopi Tribal Headquarters** (P.O. Box 123, Kykotsmovi, AZ 86039; 602-734-2415); **Havasupai Tourist Enterprise** (Supai, AZ 86435; 602-448-2121); the **White Mountain Apache Game and Fish Department** (P.O. Box 220, Whiteriver, AZ 85941; 602-338-4385); the **Mescalero Apache Tribe** (P.O. Box 176, Mescalero, NM 88340; 505-671-4427); and **Zuni Pueblo** (P.O. Box 309, Zuni, NM 87327; 505-782-4755).

WILDERNESS PERMITS

Tent camping is allowed in the back country of all national forests here except in a few areas where signs are posted prohibiting it. You no longer need a permit to hike or camp in national forest wilderness areas, but plan to stop at a ranger station anyway for trail maps and advice on current conditions and fire regulations. In dry seasons, emergency rules may prohibit campfires and sometimes ban cigarette smoking, with stiff enforcement penalties.

For backcountry hiking in national parks and monuments, you must first obtain a permit from the ranger at the front desk in the visitor center.

The permit procedure is simple and free. It helps park administrators measure the impact on sensitive ecosystems and distribute use evenly among major trails to prevent overcrowding.

BOATING

Most of the large desert lakes along the Colorado, Rio Grande and other major rivers are administered as National Recreation Areas and supervised by the U.S. Army Corps of Engineers. Federal boating safety regulations that apply to these lakes may vary slightly from state regulations. Indian reservations have separate rules for boating on tribal lakes. More significant than any differences between federal, state and tribal regulations are the local rules in force for any particular lake.

Ask for applicable boating regulations at a local marina or fishing supply store or use the addresses and phone numbers listed in "Parks" or other sections of each chapter in this book to contact the headquarters for lakes you plan to visit.

Boats, from small power boats to houseboats, can be rented for 24 hours or longer at marinas on several of the larger lakes. At most marinas, you can get a boat on short notice if you come on a weekday, since much of their business comes from local weekend recreation. The exception is Lake Powell, where houseboats and other craft are booked far in advance. Take a look at "Chapter Ten: Southeastern Utah" for details on how to arrange for a Lake Powell boat trip.

River rafting is a very popular sport in several parts of the Southwest, notably on the Chama River and Rio Grande in northern New Mexico, the Green River in southern Utah and the Animas River near Durango, Colorado. The ultimate whitewater rafting experience, of course, is a trip through the Grand Canyon. Independent rafters are welcome, but because of the bulky equipment and specialized knowledge of river hazards involved, most adventurous souls stick with group trips offered by any of the many rafting companies located in Page, Flagstaff, Taos, Santa Fe, Moab and Durango. Rafters, as well as people using canoes, kayaks, windsurfers or inner tubes, are required by state and federal regulations to wear life jackets.

FISH AND FISHING

In a land as arid as the Southwest, many residents have an irresistible fascination with water. During the warm months, lake shores and readily accessible portions of streams are often packed with anglers, especially on weekends. Vacationers can beat the crowds to some extent by planning their fishing days during the week.

Fish hatcheries in all four states keep busy stocking streams with trout, particularly rainbows, the most popular game fish throughout the West.

Catch-and-release fly fishing is the rule in some popular areas such as the upper Pecos River near Santa Fe, allowing more anglers a chance at bigger fish. Be sure to inquire locally about eating the fish you catch, since some seemingly remote streams and rivers have contamination problems from old mines and mills.

The larger reservoirs offer an assortment of sport fish, including crappie, carp, white bass, smallmouth bass, largemouth bass and walleye pike. Striped bass, an ocean import, can run as large as 40 pounds, while catfish in the depths of dammed desert canyons sometimes attain mammoth proportions.

For copies of state fishing regulations, inquire at a local fishing supply store or marina, or contact: the **Arizona Game and Fish Commission** (2222 West Washington Street, Suite 415, Phoenix, AZ 85007; 602-542-4174); the **New Mexico Department of Game and Fish** (Villagra Building, Santa Fe, NM 87503; 505-827-3292); the **Utah Division of Wildlife Resources** (1636 West North Temple, Salt Lake City, UT 84116; 801-596-8660); and the **Colorado Division of Wildlife** (6060 Broadway, Denver, CO 80216; 303-291-7533). State fishing licenses are required for fishing in national parks and national recreation areas, but not on Indian reservations, where daily permits are sold by the tribal governments. For more information about fishing on Indian lands, contact the tribal agencies listed in "Camping" above.

CHAPTER TWO

Northwestern Arizona

"The Grand Canyon—you've come too far not to see it," billboards declare along Route 40 all across Arizona. In fact, most vacation travelers who pass through this part of the state come mainly to see the world's most famous hole in the ground. With four million visitors a year, it is one of the most popular national parks in the United States. No matter how many spectacular landscapes you've seen in your lifetime, none can quite compare with the Grand Canyon. It is as long as any mountain range in the Rockies and as deep as the highest of the Rocky Mountains are tall. For centuries it posed the most formidable of all natural barriers to travel in the West, and to this day no road has ever penetrated the wilderness below the rim. No matter how many photographs you take, paintings you make or postcards you buy, the view from anywhere along the Grand Canyon rim can never be truly captured. Nor can the mind fully comprehend it; no matter how many times you have visited the Grand Canyon before, the view will always inspire the same awe and wonder as it did the first time.

The North Rim and the South Rim of the Grand Canyon are essentially separate destinations, more than 200 miles apart by road. This chapter covers the developed national park areas on both rims and, for the adventuresome, hiking possibilities in the canyon as well as two less-known areas of the Grand Canyon that are challenging to reach—Toroweap Point in the Arizona Strip and the scenic area below the Indian village of Supai.

When it comes to exploring Northwestern Arizona, the Grand Canyon is just the beginning. To the south and west, visitors discover a number of unusual communities, each surrounded by a distinctive landscape and each quite different from the others. These places vary dramatically in altitude:

37

9000 feet on the North Rim of the Grand Canyon, cool in the summer months and closed off by snow in the winter; 7000 feet in Flagstaff, shaded by ponderosa forests; 4500 feet in Sedona, with its well-balanced, moderate climate year-round; and 500 feet above sea level at Lake Havasu City where the winter months are summerlike and the summer temperatures soar well above 100 degrees.

Set in the midst of the world's largest ponderosa pine forest, at the edge of a huge volcano field, Flagstaff grew up as a railroad town. It was founded in 1881, less than a year before the first steam train clattered through town. It thrived first on timber and later on tourism. Today, both freight and passenger trains still pass through Flagstaff. The largest community between Albuquerque and the greater Los Angeles area on Route 40, one of the nation's busiest truck routes, its huge restaurant and lodging industry prospers year-round. In fact, casual visitors detouring from the interstate to fill up the gas tank and buy burgers and fries along the commercial strip that is Flagstaff's Route 40 business loop can easily form the misimpression that the town is one long row of motels and fast-food joints. A closer look will reveal it as a lively college town with considerable historic charm. A short drive outside of town will take you to fascinating ancient Indian ruins as well as Arizona's highest mountains and strange volcanic landscapes.

Less than an hour's drive south of Flagstaff via magnificent Oak Creek Canyon, Sedona is a strange blend of spectacular scenery, chic resorts, Western art in abundance and New Age notions. You can go jeeping or hiking in the incomparable Red Rock Country, play some of the country's most beautiful golf courses, shop for paintings until you run out of wall space or just sit by Oak Creek and feel the vibes. People either love Sedona or hate it. Often both.

Prescott is a quiet little town with a healthy regard for its own history. Long before Phoenix, Flagstaff or Sedona came into existence, Prescott was the capital of the Arizona Territory. Today it is a city of museums, stately 19th-century architecture and century-old saloons. Change seems to happen slowly and cautiously here. As you stroll the streets of town, you may feel that you've slipped back through time into the 1950s, into the sort of all-American community you don't often find any more.

In the forbidding, rocky hills of the Mohave Desert west and south of Kingman, real estate promoters used to sell lots in planned communities sight-unseen to gullible people in the East. Most of these towns never came close to reality, but two "cities" in the middle of nowhere along desolate stretches of the Colorado River have become the twin hubs of a genuine phenomenon, now often referred to as Arizona's West Coast.

Bullhead City, the fastest-growing town in Arizona with a population of about 25,000 people, is an isolated resort and retirement community. It has no visible reason for its existence except daily sunshine, warm weather year-round, boating and fishing access to the Colorado River—and a booming casino strip across the river in Laughlin, at the extreme southern tip of Nevada.

Even more improbable than Bullhead City is Lake Havasu City, which the *Los Angeles Times* has called "the most successful freestanding new town in the United States." Though it enjoys a great wintertime climate and a fine location on the shore of a 45-mile-long desert lake, there is really no logical explanation for Lake Havasu City—except that, in the 1960s, chainsaw tycoon Bob McCulloch and partner C. V. Wood Jr., planner and first general manager of Disneyland, decided to build it. Since their planned community had no economic base, they concluded that what it needed was

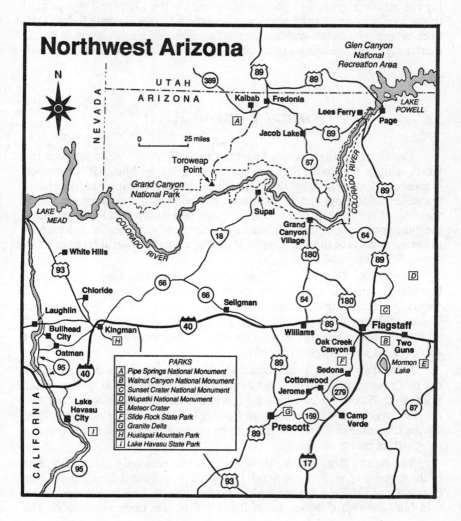

a tourist attraction. They came up with a doozie—the London Bridge. Yes, the real London Bridge, bought at auction and moved block by massive granite block across the Atlantic to be reassembled over a channel to an island in Lake Havasu. The audacious, seemingly absurd plan actually worked, and you can see the result for yourself today. The London Bridge is the second-biggest tourist attraction in Arizona, surpassed only by the Grand Canyon, and Lake Havasu City is a prosperous, attractive town of more than 25,000 people.

En route among these unusual Arizona communities, you'll also have the chance to visit some of the state's best-preserved ghost towns. Jerome, a booming copper town a century ago, was abandoned in the 1950s and repopulated in the 1960s by artists and hippies to become a tourist favorite today. Oatman, where wild burros outnumber the full-time residents, claims as its top tourist sight the wedding-night bed of Clark Gable and Carole Lombard.

Grand Canyon Area

The Grand Canyon comes as a surprise. Whether you approach the North Rim or the South Rim, the landscape gives no hint that the canyon is there until suddenly you find yourself on the rim looking into the chasm ten miles wide from rim to rim and a mile down to the Colorado River, winding silver through the canyon's inner depths. From anywhere along the rim, you can feel the vast, silent emptiness of the canyon and wonder at the sheer mass of the walls, striated into layer upon colorful layer of sandstone, limestone and shale.

The Grand Canyon is 277 miles long, extending from the western boundary of the Navajo Reservation to the vicinity of Lake Mead and Las Vegas, Nevada. Only the highest section of each rim of the Grand Canyon is accessible by motor vehicle. Most of Grand Canyon National Park, both above and below the rim, is a designated wilderness area that can only be explored on foot or by river raft.

More than five million years ago, the Colorado River began carving out this canyon that offers a panoramic look at the geologic history of the Southwest. Sweeping away sandstones and sediments, limestones and fossils, the river made its way through Paleozoic and Precambrian formations. By the time mankind arrived, the canyon extended nearly all the way down to schist, a basement formation.

The **North Rim** of the Grand Canyon receives only about one-tenth of the number of visitors the South Rim gets. Snowbound during the winter because it is 1200 feet higher in elevation, the North Rim is only open from mid-May through October, while the South Rim is open year-round. The

South Rim is much more convenient for more travelers since it is much closer to a major interstate highway route and to the large population centers of southern Arizona and California. But if your tour of the Southwest includes destinations such as the Navajo Reservation, Lake Powell, Bryce Canyon and Zion national parks—or even Las Vegas, then your route will take you closer to the North Rim, giving you an opportunity to explore the cooler, quieter side of the canyon.

The North Rim does not have the long, heavily traveled scenic drives that the South Rim has. The main road into the park dead-ends at the lodge and other tourist facilities at **Bright Angel Point.** The only other paved road is **Cape Royal Scenic Drive,** a 23-mile trip through stately ponderosa pine forest that takes you to several of the national park's most beautiful viewpoints—**Point Imperial, Vista Encantadora, Walhalla Overlook** and **Cape Royal.** Another road, unpaved and only passable in a high-clearance vehicle, runs 17 miles to **Point Sublime.** Other viewpoints on the North Rim are reached by foot trails. (Information on these can be found in the "Hiking" section at the end of the chapter.)

Extremely adventuresome motorists can visit a separate area along the North Rim of the Grand Canyon, Toroweap Point, by leaving Route 89A at Fredonia, about 75 miles north of the North Rim entrance. Don't forget to fill up the gas tank in Fredonia, because you won't see another gas station for nearly 200 miles. Next, proceed west for 15 miles on Route 389 to **Pipe Springs National Monument** (602-643-7105). Take time to see the monument. The remote, fortresslike old Mormon ranching outpost, which had the only telegraph station in the Arizona Territory north of the Grand Canyon, was home to the Winsor family and their employees, thus its historical nickname, Winsor Castle. The ranch buildings and equipment are well-preserved, and the duck pond provides a cool oasis. Volunteers costumed in period dress re-create the pioneer lifestyle during the summer months.

Backtracking, nine miles from the Fredonia turnoff and six miles before you reach Pipe Springs, an unpaved road turns off to the south. It goes 67 miles to the most remote point that can be reached by motor vehicle on the Grand Canyon rim. The road is wide and well-maintained, easily passible by passenger car, but very isolated. You will not find a telephone or any other sign of habitation anywhere along the way. You may not see another car all day. Several other dirt roads branch off along the way, but if you keep to the road that goes straight ahead and looks well-used, following the "Toroweap" and "Grand Canyon National Monument" signs whenever you see them, it's hard to get lost. Have fun experiencing this wide-open countryside as empty as all of Arizona used to be long ago.

There is a small, primitive campground at **Toroweap Point** (★) but no water. As likely as not, you may find that you have the place all to yourself. The elevation is 2000 feet lower than at the main North Rim visitor area, so instead of pine forest the vegetation around Toroweap Point is desert scrub. Being closer to the river, still some 3000 feet below, you can watch the parade of river rafts drifting past and even eavesdrop on passengers' conversations.

The **South Rim** of the Grand Canyon is the busy part of the park. From **Grand Canyon Village**, the large concession complex where the hotels, restaurants and stores are located on the rim near the south entrance, two paved rim drives run in opposite directions. The **East Rim Drive** goes 25 miles east to the national park's east entrance, which is the entrance you will use if you are driving in from the North Rim, Lake Powell or the Navajo Reservation. The first point of interest you come to after entering the park on East Rim Drive is the **Desert View Watchtower**, built in the 1930s as a replica of an ancient Hopi watchtower. It offers the first panoramic view of the Grand Canyon. As you proceed along East Rim Drive toward Grand Canyon Village, other overlooks—**Lipan Point, Zuni Point, Grandview Point, Yaki Point**—will beckon, each with a different perspective on the canyon's immensity.

There are two interesting museums along East Rim Drive to visit. The **Tusayan Museum** (602-638-2305), 23 miles east of Grand Canyon Village near the park's east entrance, has exhibits on the Hopi people and their Anasazi ancestors who used to live along the rim of the Grand Canyon. In the Hopi belief system, the canyon is said to be the *sipapu*, the hole through which the earth's first people climbed from the mountaintop of their previous world into our present one.

The **Yavapai Museum** (602-638-7890), about half a mile east of the visitor center, offers detailed information on the canyon's geology, showing the ages and compositions of the many colorful layers of rock that make up its walls. You'll also find explanations of how and why the Colorado River could have formed the canyon by slicing its way through the highest plateau in the area instead of simply meandering around it.

The **West Rim Drive**, which follows the canyon rim for eight miles west of Grand Canyon Village, is closed to private vehicles during the summer months. Visitors see it by free park shuttle bus or by bicycle. The drive runs past the Powell Memorial, honoring Major John Wesley Powell, the one-armed adventurer who first surveyed the Grand Canyon for the U.S. government in 1869—in a wooden boat. The road clings to the rim of the canyon as it takes you to a series of overlooks, each more spectacular than the last. **Pima Point**, in particular, offers what is probably the best of all Grand Canyon views. The drive ends at a place called **Hermit's Rest**, a former tourist camp where there are a snack bar and a hikers' trailhead.

The **Grand Canyon Visitor Center** (602-638-7888) is located about one mile east of Grand Canyon Village. We suggest leaving your car in the village and walking to the visitor center on the paved, magnificently scenic Rim Trail (or, if you're not spending the night at park lodgings, parking at the visitor center and walking to the village). The most interesting exhibit in the visitor center is the display in the outdoor central plaza of boats that have been used to explore the Grand Canyon by river. A burned fragment is all that remains of one of the original wooden boats used by Major Powell in 1869. Other wooden boats are of more recent vintage. There is also one of the original inflatable river rafts used by the woman who in 1955 invented whitewater rafting as we know it today.

You can take a romantic trip into yesteryear on the **Grand Canyon Railway** (Route 40, Williams; 800-843-8724). A turn-of-the-century steam train leaves Williams in the morning for a two-and-a-half-hour trip through Coconino National Forest, tracing the route that brought early tourists to the national park, arriving around noon at the historic 1908 Santa Fe Railroad depot in Grand Canyon Village. The return trip departs for Williams in the late afternoon. Trains run daily from June through September, with a more limited schedule the rest of the year.

Just outside the park's south entrance, the town of Tusayan has an **IMAX Theatre** (602-638-2203) that show films about the Grand Canyon on a seven-story, 82-foot-wide wraparound screen with six-track Dolby sound. The **Over the Edge Theatre** (602-526-4575) also features Grand Canyon films. Why one should wish to watch a movie when the real thing is just a few minutes away is not immediately apparent, but in fact the theaters add an extra dimension to the Grand Canyon experience by presenting river-rafting footage, aerial photography and close-up looks at places in the canyon that are hard to get to.

For the adventuresome, an intriguing Grand Canyon experience that is only accessible by foot is found far downriver near the west end of the canyon. The **Havasu Canyon Trail** (★) (16 miles), entirely within the Havasupai Indian Reservation, is reached by leaving the interstate at Seligman (westbound) or Kingman (eastbound) and driving to the Supai turnoff near Peach Springs. From there, the Supai Road goes for 62 miles before the pavement ends. In another 11 miles, the road dead-ends and a foot trail descends 2000 feet in eight miles to the Indian village of **Supai** where about 500 people live. All hikers must check in at tribal headquarters. From there, the main trail continues for about four more miles into Havasu Canyon, a side canyon from the Grand Canyon, which includes a series of three high waterfalls—75-foot Navajo Falls, 100-foot Havasu Falls and 200-foot Mooney Falls—with large pools that are ideal for swimming. There is a campground near Mooney Falls, and from there the trail continues down to the Colorado River in the bottom of the Grand Canyon, while another trail forks over to Beaver Canyon, where there is another waterfall. Whether you plan to stay in the campground or the modern lodge at Supai, advance reservations are essential. For camping, write Havasupai Tourist Enterprise, Supai, AZ 86435 or call 602-448-2121. For lodging, see "Grand Canyon Area Hotels" below.

GRAND CANYON AREA HOTELS

On the North Rim of the Grand Canyon, the only lodging within the park is the **Grand Canyon Lodge** (602-638-2611), which consists of a beautiful 1930s-vintage main lodge building overlooking the canyon and a number of cabins—some rustic, others modern, a few with canyon views. Clean and homelike, both rooms and cabins have an old-fashioned feel. About half the units have television sets, and a few have fireplaces. Rates vary from budget to moderate. North Rim accommodations are in very high demand, so reservations should be made far ahead. They are accepted up to 23 months in advance. Reservations are booked through TW Recreational Services Inc. (451 North Main Street, Cedar City, UT 84720; 801-586-7686), which also handles reservations for the lodges at Bryce Canyon and Zion national parks.

Aside from the national park lodge, the closest accommodations to the North Rim are 44 miles away at **Jacob Lake Lodge** (602-643-7232). This small, rustic resort complex surrounded by national forest offers both motel rooms and cabins, including some two-bedroom units, all priced in the budget range. Again, reservations should be made well in advance.

The South Rim offers many more lodging choices. The phone number for all South Rim accommodations is 602-638-2631. Reservations at any of them can be made up to 23 months in advance by writing **Grand Canyon National Park Lodges** (P.O. Box 699, Grand Canyon, AZ 86023; 602-638-2401).

Top of the line is the deluxe-priced **El Tovar Hotel**. Designed after European hunting lodges, El Tovar was built by the Fred Harvey Co., a subsidiary of the Santa Fe Railroad, in 1905 and some staff members still wear the traditional black-and-white uniforms of the famous "Harvey Girls" of that era. The lobby retains its original backwoods elegance, with a big fireplace, massive wood ceiling beams and dark-stained pine decor throughout. The rooms were renovated in the 1980s. All have full baths, color television and telephones.

More affordable historic lodging is available nearby at **Bright Angel Lodge**. The main log and stone lodge was built in 1935 on the site of Bright Angel Camp, the first tourist facility in the park. Its lobby features Indian motifs and a huge fireplace. Rooms are clean and modest and most have televisions and phones. Besides rooms in the main building, the lodge also rents several historic cabins on the canyon rim, some with fireplaces. Budget to moderate.

Also in Grand Canyon Village, on the rim between El Tovar and Bright Angel Lodge, are the modern twin stone lodges, **Thunderbird Lodge** and **Kachina Lodge**. Located on the rim trail, these caravansaries are within

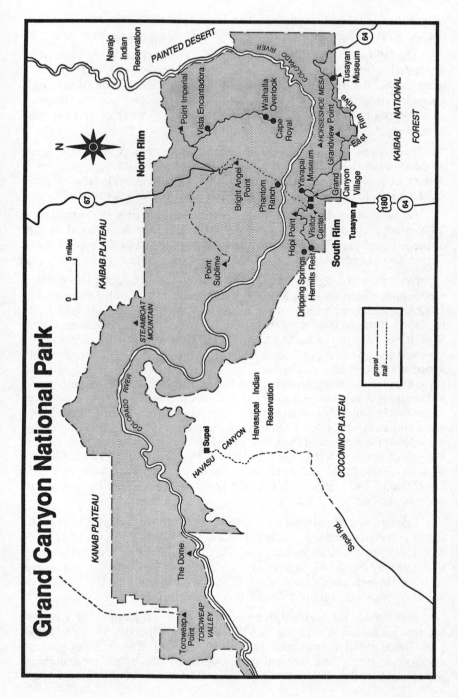

easy walking distance of the restaurants at the older lodges. Rooms are in the moderate price range. All have televisions and phones.

The largest lodging facility in the park, **Yavapai Lodge** is situated in a wooded setting about one-half mile from the canyon rim, near the park store, across the road from the visitor center and about a mile from Grand Canyon Village. Rates are moderate and the contemporary rooms are equivalent in quality to what you would expect for the same price at a national chain motor inn.

The newest option is **Maswik Lodge**, set away from the canyon rim at the southwest end of Grand Canyon Village. Maswik Lodge presents a variety of motel-style room choices as well as cabins, with rates ranging from budget to moderate. About half the rooms have televisions.

An elegant modern-rustic building with the look of a ski lodge and a lobby with multistory picture windows, **Moqui Lodge** is managed as part of the national park lodge system although it is located in Kaibab National Forest just outside the park entrance. Rates are moderate.

No survey of lodgings at the Grand Canyon would be complete without mentioning **Phantom Ranch** (★). Located at the bottom of the canyon, this 1922 lodge and cabins is at the lower end of the North Kaibab Trail from the North Rim and the Bright Angel and South Kaibab trails from the South Rim. It can only be reached by foot, mule or river raft. Cabins are normally reserved for guests on overnight mule trips, but hikers with plenty of advance notice can also arrange lodging. Prices, included in overnight mule trips, are in the moderate range. Bunk beds are available by reservation only in four budget-rate ten-person dormitories for hikers. There is no television at the ranch, and only one pay phone. There is outgoing mail service, however, and mail sent from Phantom Ranch bears the postmark, "Mailed by Mule from the Bottom of the Canyon." Meals are served in a central dining hall which becomes a beer hall after dinner. Do not arrive at Phantom Ranch without reservations! You can reserve space up to a year in advance by calling 602-638-2401 or writing Grand Canyon National Park Lodges at the address above.

Located in a remote red rock canyon on the Supai Indian Reservation, the 24 carpeted motel-style units at **Havasupai Lodge** (★) (Supai; 602-448-2111) is a truly hidden destination. There's a café next door, swimming in the nearby creek and a convenient barbecue pit. Just two miles away are Navajo, Havasu and Mooney falls. You can also enjoy Native American led horseback and hiking tours of this scenic region.

Just outside the South Rim entrance gate, the community of Tusayan has several motels and motor inns that are not affiliated with the national park. Rates are in the moderate range at all of them. If you cannot get reservations at one of the national park lodges, try one of the typical chain motels such as the **Red Feather Lodge** (602-638-2414); the **Grand Can-**

yon **Squire Inn** (602-638-2681); or the **Quality Inn Grand Canyon** (602-638-2673).

GRAND CANYON AREA RESTAURANTS

At the North Rim, the **Grand Canyon Lodge Dining Room** (602-638-2611) offers moderately priced breakfast, lunch and dinner selections. The food is good, conventional meat-and-potatoes fare and the atmosphere—a spacious, rustic log-beamed dining room with huge picture windows overlooking the canyon—is simply incomparable. Reservations are required for lunch and dinner. The lodge also operates a cafeteria serving budget-priced meals for breakfast, lunch and dinner in plain, simple surroundings.

The South Rim offers a wider variety of restaurant options. The most elegant is **El Tovar Dining Room** (602-638-6292). Entrées such as filet mignon with crab legs béarnaise are served on fine china by candlelight. Prices are in the deluxe range, the ambience is classy, but casual dress is perfectly acceptable.

More informal surroundings and moderate prices are to be found at the **Bright Angel Restaurant** in the Bright Angel Lodge. Menu selections include chicken piccata, grilled rainbow trout and fajitas. Cocktails and wine are available. Adjoining the Bright Angel Lodge, the **Arizona Steakhouse** specializes in steaks and seafood and has a good, large salad bar. The open kitchen lets you watch the chefs cook while you eat. Moderate. The phone number for these and all other South Rim Grand Canyon restaurants is 602-638-2631 and reservations are not required.

In the Yavapai Lodge, across the highway from the visitor center, the **Yavapai Grill** serves fast food—burgers and fries, hot dogs, chicken nuggets—while the **Yavapai Cafeteria** offers a changing selection of breakfast, lunch and dinner items. Both are in the budget range. Nearby in the general store, **Babbitt's Delicatessen** features sandwiches, salads and fried chicken box lunches to go or eat on the premises.

There are two other cafeterias in the park—the **Maswik Cafeteria** at Maswik Lodge, at the west end of Grand Canyon Village, and the **Desert View Trading Post Cafeteria**, 23 miles east of the village along the East Rim Drive. Both serve a changing selection of hot meals. Ice cream, hot dogs and soft drinks are available at the **Hermit's Rest Snack Bar** at the end of the West Rim Drive as well as at the **Bright Angel Fountain** near the trailhead for the Bright Angel Trail. All are budget.

Outside the park entrance, the town of Tusayan has nearly a dozen eating establishments ranging from McDonald's to the beautiful, moderately priced **Moqui Lodge Dining Room** (602-638-2424), which specializes in Mexican food. One of the best dining bets in the area is the **Moqui Lodge Cowboy Cookout** (same phone), where a chuckwagon-style barbecue beef dinner is followed by a Western music show nightly in the summer season.

GRAND CANYON AREA SHOPPING

Of several national park concession tourist stores on the South Rim of the Grand Canyon, the best are **Hopi House** (602-638-2631), the large Indian pueblo replica across from El Tovar Hotel, and the adjacent **Verkamp's Curios** (602-638-2242). Both have been in continuous operation for almost a century and specialize in authentic Indian handicrafts, with high standards of quality and some genuinely old pieces.

Other Grand Canyon shops, at least as interesting for their historic architecture as their wares, include the old **Kolb Studio**, originally a 1904 photographic studio and now a bookstore, and the **Lookout Studio**, which has rock specimens and conventional curios. Both are in Grand Canyon Village. Other souvenir shops are the **Hermit's Rest Gift Shop** (at the end of West Rim Drive) and the **Desert View Watchtower** (East Rim Drive).

GRAND CANYON AREA NIGHTLIFE

On the South Rim, there is dancing nightly at the **Yavapai Lounge,** and **El Tovar Lounge** has a piano bar. In general, though, Grand Canyon National Park does not have much in the way of hot nightlife. We suggest taking in one of the ranger-produced slide shows presented in the amphitheaters on both the North Rim and the South Rim or simply sitting in the dark along the canyon rim and listening to the vast, deep silence.

GRAND CANYON AREA PARKS

Kaibab National Forest—This 1,500,000-acre expanse of pine, fir, spruce and aspen forest includes both sides of the Grand Canyon outside the park boundaries. Most recreational facilities are near the North Rim, where they supplement the park's limited camping facilities. Wildlife in the forest includes mule deer, wild turkeys, and even a few bison.

Facilities: Picnic areas, restrooms, visitor center; information, 602-635-2681.

Camping: Demotte Campground has 22 sites ($7 per night) and Jacob Lake Campground has 53 sites ($10 per night); information, 602-643-7395. RV hookups are available at the privately owned Jacob Lake RV Park (602-643-7804); $15 to $17 a night per vehicle with two persons.

Getting there: The national forest visitor center is located at Jacob Lake, the intersection of Routes 89A and 67. Jacob Lake Campground is at the same location, while Demotte Campground is 24 miles south on Route 67, about 20 miles from the national park entrance.

Lee's Ferry, Glen Canyon National Recreation Area—Halfway along the most direct route between the North Rim and South Rim of the Grand Canyon, this beach area on the river below Glen Canyon Dam makes a good picnic or camping spot. It is situated at the confluence of the Colorado and Paria rivers, which often have distinctly different colors, giving the water a strange two-toned appearance. Historically, Lee's Ferry was the first crossing point on the Colorado River, established by John D. Lee in 1871. Lee, a Mormon, was a fugitive at the time, wanted by federal authorities for organizing the massacre of a non-Mormon wagon train from Arkansas. He lived here with one of his 17 wives for several years before federal marshals found and killed him. Today, Lee's Ferry is the departure point for raft trips into the Grand Canyon.

Facilities: Shaded picnic tables, restrooms; information, 602-645-2471. *Fishing:* Good.

Camping: There are four campgrounds; $7 per night.

Getting there: Located in Marble Canyon about two miles off Route 89A, 85 miles from the North Rim entrance to Grand Canyon National Park and 104 miles from the east entrance to the South Rim.

Flagstaff Area

Visitors who view Flagstaff from the mountain heights to the north will see this community's most striking characteristic: It is an island in an ocean of ponderosa pine forest stretching as far as the eye can see. At an elevation of 7000 feet, Flagstaff has the coolest climate of any city in Arizona. Because of its proximity to slopes in the San Francisco Peaks, Flagstaff is the state's leading ski resort town in the winter. It is also a lively college town, with students accounting for nearly 20 percent of the population.

A good place to start exploring the Flagstaff area is downtown, toward the west end of Santa Fe Avenue (the business loop of Route 40). The downtown commercial zone retains its turn-of-the-century frontier architecture. Neither run-down nor yuppified, this historic district specializes in shops that cater to students from Northern Arizona University, on the other side of the interstate and railroad tracks. A building-by-building historic downtown **walking tour brochure** is distributed by the Arizona Historical Society—Pioneer Museum (2340 North Fort Valley Road; 602-774-6272), the Main Street Foundation (114 North San Francisco Street; 602-774-1330) and the Flagstaff Visitor Center (101 West Santa Fe Avenue; 602-774-9541). Take time to stroll through the old residential area just north of the downtown business district. Attractive Victorian houses, many of them handmade from volcanic lava rock, give the neighborhood its unique character.

On a hilltop just a mile south of downtown is **Lowell Observatory** (1400 West Mars Hill; 602-774-3358; recorded schedule information, 602-774-2096; admission). The observatory was built by wealthy astronomer

Percival Lowell in 1894 to take advantage of the exceptional visibility created by Flagstaff's clean air and high altitude. His most famous achievement during the 22 years he spent here was the "discovery" of canals on the planet Mars, which he submitted to the scientific community as "proof" of extraterrestrial life. Building the observatory proved to be a great accomplishment in itself, though. The planet Pluto was discovered by astronomers at Lowell Observatory 14 years after Dr. Lowell's death, and the facility continues to be one of the most important centers for studying the solar system. Take a guided tour of the observatory and see Dr. Lowell's original Victorian-era telescope. On some summer evenings, astronomers hold star talks and help visitors stargaze through one of the center's smaller telescopes.

Overshadowed by Lowell Observatory, the **Northern Arizona University Campus Observatory** (★) (west side of San Francisco Street on campus; 602-523-7170) actually offers visitors a better chance to look through a larger telescope. Public viewing sessions are held every Thursday night when the sky is clear. The campus observatory specializes in studying eclipsing binary stars and pulsating stars.

Another sightseeing highlight in the university area is **Riordan Mansion State Historic Park** (1300 Riordan Ranch Road; 602-779-4395; admission), a block off Milton Road north of the intersection of Route 40 and Route 17. The biggest early-day mansion in Flagstaff, it was built in 1904 by two brothers who were the region's leading timber barons. Constructed duplex-style with 40 rooms and 13,000 square feet of living space, the mansion blends rustic log-slab and volcanic rock construction with turn-of-the-century opulence and plenty of creative imagination. Tour guides escort visitors through the mansion to see its original furnishings and family mementos.

Just north of town on Route 180, the **Museum of Northern Arizona** (301 North Fort Valley Road; 602-774-5211; admission) is known worldwide for its exhibits of Indian artifacts, geology, biology and Southwestern art. During the summer months, the museum hosts separate exhibitions of Navajo, Hopi and Zuni artists.

Nearby, the **Coconino Center for the Arts** (2300 North Fort Valley Road; 602-779-6921) provides space for fine-arts exhibits, musical performances, workshops and a folk-arts program. In summer, coinciding with the Museum of Northern Arizona's Indian artists exhibitions, the Center for the Arts presents a two-month Festival of Native American Arts.

In the same vicinity, the **Arizona Historical Society—Pioneer Museum** (2340 North Fort Valley Road; 602-774-6272; admission) exhibits memorabilia and oddities from Flagstaff's past, including a stuffed bear, Percival Lowell's 1912 mechanical computer and early-day photos of the Grand Canyon.

Not far beyond the Museum of Arizona on Route 180 is the turnoff for **Schultz Pass Road**. This unpaved scenic drive offers a close-up look at the spectacular San Francisco Peaks, which tower above Flagstaff. About 14 miles long, the road comes out on Route 89 a short distance north of the turnoff to **Sunset Crater National Monument** (602-527-7024). Sunset Crater, a bright-colored 1000-foot-tall volcanic cone in the San Francisco Volcano Field, is of recent origin. It first erupted in the winter of 1064–65 and kept spraying out molten rock and ash until 1250. A one-mile self-guided nature trail leads from the visitor center through cinder and lava fields. The ice cave along the trail has been closed because of unstable conditions since a 1984 cave-in. Hiking is no longer permitted on the slopes of Sunset Crater, either, since footprints create streaks visible from a great distance and mar the beauty of the perfect cone, but rangers guide trips up nearby O'Leary Crater, outside the monument boundary in the national forest. Several other volcanic craters in the national forest are also open to hikers and off-road vehicles.

Near Sunset Crater National Monument, **Wupatki National Monument** (602-527-7040) preserves numerous pueblo ruins on the fringes of the volcano field. They were inhabited in the 12th and 13th centuries, at the same time the volcanic activity was at its peak. Repeatedly, fiery eruptions would drive the Native Americans out of the area and volcanic ash would fertilize the land and lure them back. As a result, Wupatki's communities were small, architecturally dissimilar, often designed for defense as different groups competed for use of the rich farmland. A paved 36-mile loop road takes motorists through Sunset Crater and Wupatki national monuments, rejoining Route 89 about 15 miles from its starting point.

Sinagua Indians (the name is Spanish for "without water," referring to their farming methods) lived from the Grand Canyon southward throughout central Arizona and are thought to be the ancestors of the Hopi people. One of the most interesting Sinagua sites is at **Walnut Canyon National Monument** (602-526-3367). Take exit 204 from Route 40 just east of Flagstaff. Here, the Indians built more than 300 cliff dwellings in the walls of a 400-foot-deep gorge. A paved trail takes visitors around an "island in the sky" for a close-up look at the largest concentration of cliff dwellings, while a second trail follows the rim of this beautiful canyon.

Another fascinating bit of Northern Arizona's flamboyant geology is **Meteor Crater** (602-289-2362; admission), about 30 miles east of Flagstaff, five miles off interstate Route 40 at exit 233. A shooting star 80 feet in diameter and moving at an unimaginable speed struck the earth here 49,000 years ago and the impact blasted a crater 570 feet deep and a mile across. Geologist Daniel Barringer theorized a century ago that this was a meteor impact crater. Experts scoffed at the idea, especially since volcanic craters, so common east of Flagstaff, suggested a rational explanation for the phenomenon. He staked a mining claim to search for the huge, valuable mass of iron and nickel which, he was convinced, lay buried beneath the crater. An ambitious drilling operation did not strike a mother lode from outer space but did come up with fragments proving the theory and the geologist's family has been operating the claim as a tourist attraction ever since. The visit is worth the fairly steep admission fee if you take time to hike out along the rim on the spectacular three-mile trail that goes all the way around.

FLAGSTAFF AREA HOTELS

Flagstaff offers a good selection of bed-and-breakfast accommodations. Among the antique-furnished vintage lodgings available in the downtown area is **The Inn at Four Ten** (410 North Leroux Street; 602-774-0088), a beautifully restored 1907 home with three guest suites featuring period decor. Rates are moderately priced in the summer months, budget off-season. Other bed and breakfasts in the historic district include the homelike, moderately priced **Birch Tree Inn** (824 West Birch Street; 602-774-1042) and the budget-priced **Dierker House** (423 West Cherry Street; 602-774-3249), where the three guest rooms have king-sized beds with down comforters and share a common sitting room.

A large, rather elegant modern hotel in the moderate price range is the **Woodlands Plaza Hotel** (1175 West Route 66; 602-773-8888). Rooms are spacious and modern, with pastel color schemes and king-size beds. Facilities for guests' use include indoor and outdoor whirlpool spas, a steam room, sauna, fitness center and heated swimming pool. Room service, valet service and complimentary limousine service are also among the hotel's amenities.

The **Monte Vista Hotel** (100 North San Francisco Street; 602-779-6971), a 1927 hotel now listed on the National Register of Historic Places, has spacious rooms that feature oak furniture, king-size brass beds, velvet wall coverings and gold-tone bathroom fittings—a touch of old-time elegance priced in the budget range. Movie stars used to stay here in the hotel's glory days and some rooms bear plaques naming the most famous person who ever slept in them: Humphrey Bogart, Cornell Wilde and Walter Brennan, to name a few.

The other downtown historic hotel, the **Weatherford Hotel** (23 North Leroux Street; 602-774-2731) operates as a youth hostel and also offers a few very plain private rooms in the budget price range. Flagstaff has two other hostels as well—the **Downtowner Independent Youth Hostel** (19 South San Francisco Street; 602-774-8461) and the **Du Beau Motel International Hostel** (19 West Phoenix Avenue; 602-774-6731). Especially in the summer months, all three host backpack travelers of all ages from all parts of the world, and solitary travelers are sure to make instant friends here.

In the pines just five minutes out of town, the **Arizona Mountain Inn** (685 Lake Mary Road; 602-774-8959) offers bed-and-breakfast rooms in the main inn at the low end of the moderate price range and one- to five-bedroom cottages with fireplaces and cooking facilities at the high end. Amenities include baseball, volleyball, horseshoe and basketball areas as well as hiking and cross-country skiing trails.

FLAGSTAFF AREA RESTAURANTS

For fine dining in Flagstaff, one good bet is the small, homey-feeling **Cottage Place Restaurant** (126 West Cottage Avenue; 602-774-8431). Specialties include châteaubriand and roast duck à l'orange, as well as a vegetarian pasta con pesto. Moderate; reservations recommended.

Another good place for a romantic dinner is the **Woodlands Café** (1175 West Route 66; 602-773-9118). There's booth and table seating at this Southwestern dining room with atrium windows and forest views. Navajo white walls are decorated with Navajo rugs and baskets; the chandelier is crafted from deer racks. You can select from such entrées as Atlantic salmon with béarnaise sauce and chicken breast with smoked gouda cream sauce. Moderate. Reservations are recommended.

Yet another of Flagstaff's finest restaurants is **Chez Marc** (503 Humphreys Street; 602-774-1343), a small, intimate restaurant in a house listed on the National Register of Historic Places. A typical dinner might consist of duck pâté with pistachio hors d'oeuvre, salad niçoise and roast Arizona squab atop green cabbage and wild mushrooms. Prices start in the moderate range.

The **Main Street Bar and Grill** (4 South San Francisco Street; 602-774-1519) is a student favorite serving an array of budget-to-moderate-priced dishes such as fajitas, Philly cheesesteaks, quiche Lorraine and barbecued ribs. Other great little contemporary restaurants in the downtown area, featuring menu selections that emphasize healthy gourmet food, include **Charly's** (23 North Leroux Street; 602-779-1919) on the ground floor of the Weatherford Hotel youth hostel and **Café Espress** (16 North San Francisco Street; 602-774-0541), both in the budget-price range.

As a university town, Flagstaff has a plethora of budget-priced pizzerias—18 of them at last count. We recommend **NiMarco Pizza** (101 South Beaver Street; 602-779-2691). Besides the largest pizza-by-the-slice selection, NiMarco also has Italian-style baked stuffed sandwiches including exceptional stromboli.

For an unusual dining environment, head out of town to the **Mormon Lake Lodge Steak House & Saloon** (Mormon Lake Road; 602-354-2227), which has been in operation since 1924 and is reputed to be one of the West's finest steak houses. The restaurant also features ribs, chicken and trout, all cooked over a bed of mountain oak embers. The authentic brands from ranches all across Arizona which have been seared into the wood paneling of the restaurant's walls are said to be the result of one of the wildest branding parties ever. Moderate.

FLAGSTAFF AREA SHOPPING

The **Art Barn** (2320 North Fort Valley Road; 602-774-0822) next to Coconino Center for the Arts offers works of local and reservation artists for sale. A nonprofit, member-supported organization, the Art Barn provides artist facilities including classes, exhibition space and a bronze foundry.

Flagstaff also boasts quite a few regional arts-and-crafts galleries, most of them featuring traditional and contemporary Navajo and Hopi work. One of the largest is **Four Winds Traders** (118 West Santa Fe Avenue; 602-774-1067). Wander around the downtown area and you will find a number of others. East of downtown, **Jay's Indian Arts** (2227 East 7th Avenue; 602-526-2439) is a branch of Tucson's famous Native American arts-and-crafts "supermarket." In operation since 1953, Jay's keeps mobile units on the road throughout the Southwest buying rugs, jewelry, pottery, kachinas and the like direct from artists on the Navajo, Hopi, Papago, Apache and Pueblo reservations.

FLAGSTAFF AREA NIGHTLIFE

Because of the university, Flagstaff boasts both a busy cultural events calendar and a lively nightclub scene. On the cultural side, the performing arts roster includes the **Flagstaff Symphony Orchestra** (602-774-5107), **Coconino Chamber Ensemble** (602-523-3879), **Flagstaff Master Chorale** (602-523-2642), **Flagstaff Oratorio Chorus** (602-523-4760) and **NAU Opera Theatre** (602-523-3731). Most performances are held at the **Coconino Center for the Arts** (2300 North Fort Valley Road; 602-779-6921) or at the **Northern Arizona University School of Performing Arts** (602-523-3731).

The **Theatrikos Community Theatre Group** performs at the Flagstaff Playhouse (11 West Cherry Street; 602-774-1662). For current performance information, inquire at the Flagstaff Visitor Center (101 West Santa Fe Avenue; 602-774-9541) or tune to the university's National Public Radio station, KNAU, at 88.7 on your FM dial.

As for nightclubs, the most popular university hangout is **Fiddlestix** (702 South Milton Road; 602-774-6623), featuring live rock and Top-40 dance music. Another hot spot is **The Monsoons** (22 East Santa Fe Avenue; 602-773-9923), a rock-and-roll club attached to a barbecue restaurant. **Charly's** (23 North Leroux Street; 602-779-1919), on the ground floor of the Weatherford Hotel youth hostel, features jazz and blues.

For a more intimate atmosphere, check out **Granny's Closet** (218 South Sitgreaves Street; 602-774-8331) or the **Mad Italian** (101 South San Francisco Street; 602-779-1820), known locally as the "Mad I."

The sometimes rowdy **Museum Club** (3404 East Santa Fe Avenue; 602-526-9434), better known among the locals as the "Zoo Club," is one of the best examples in the West of an authentic cowboy club. The huge log-cabin-style building began as a trading post and taxidermy shop in 1918 and has operated as a nightclub since 1936. Decor includes an ornate 1880 mahogany back bar and an astonishing collection of big game trophies. Legendary country-and-western artists who have performed here include Willie Nelson, Bob Wills and the Texas Playboys, Commander Cody and the Lost Planet Airmen and many others.

FLAGSTAFF AREA PARKS

Lake Mary—Actually two long reservoirs, Upper and Lower Lake Mary provide the primary water supply for Flagstaff. They were created by damming Walnut Creek, which explains why there is no longer any water flowing through Walnut Canyon National Monument. The National Forest Service operates picnic areas on the wooded lakeshore and the small Lakeview Campground overlooks the upper lake. Both lakes are popular places to fish for northern pike, walleye pike and catfish. The upper lake is also used for power boating and waterskiing.

Facilities: Picnic areas, boat ramps; for information call, 602-556-7474. *Fishing:* Good.

Camping: Lakeview Campground has 25 sites at $6 per night. Pinegrove Campground has 45 sites at $7 per night. Showers are available at Pinegrove.

Getting there: Located eight miles south of Flagstaff on Lake Mary Road. From Route 40, take exit 195-B and follow the signs.

Mormon Lake—The largest natural lake in Arizona, covering over 2000 acres when full, is very shallow, averaging only ten feet in depth and can shrink to practically nothing during spells of dry weather. Because the shoreline keeps changing, there is no boat ramp and anglers must carry their boats to the water by hand. Still, it is a good place to catch pike and catfish. Several hiking trails run along the lakeshore and into the surrounding forest.

Facilities: Nature trail, lodge, restaurant, groceries, winter sports; information, 602-556-7474.

Camping: There are 30 sites at Dairy Springs and 15 sites at Double Springs; $6 per night.

Getting there: It's located 20 miles southeast of Flagstaff via Lake Mary Road.

Sedona/Prescott Area

Oak Creek Canyon is the most accessible of several magnificent canyons that plunge from the high forests of northern Arizona down toward the low deserts of southern Arizona. A major highway—Route 89A from Flagstaff—runs the length of Oak Creek Canyon, making for a wonderful, though often crowded, scenic drive. After a long, thrilling descent from Flagstaff to the bottom of the canyon, where the creek banks are lined with lush riparian vegetation, the highway passes a number of picnicking, camping and fishing areas. Midway down the canyon is one of Arizona's most popular state parks, **Slide Rock State Park** (see "Sedona/Prescott Area Parks" below). At the lower end of the canyon, travelers emerge into the spectacular Red Rock Country, the labyrinth of sandstone buttes and mesas and verdant side canyons surrounding Sedona. The elevation drop from Flagstaff to Sedona is 2500 feet, and the temperature is often 20 degrees higher in Sedona than in Flagstaff.

Sedona is a town for shopping, for sports, for luxuriating in spectacular surroundings. It is not the kind of place where you will find tourist attractions in the usual sense. Other than Oak Creek Canyon, Sedona's most popular tourist spots are spiritual in nature. The **Chapel of the Holy Cross**, south of town on Route 179, is a Catholic "sculpture church" built between two towering red sandstone rock formations. It is open to visitors daily. The **Shrine of the Red Rocks**, on Table Top Mesa two miles off Route 89A on Airport Road, features a large wooden cross and a great view of the Red Rock Country.

And then there are Sedona's **"Vortices."** The Vortex idea was "channeled" through members of the town's highly visible New Age community several years ago and keeps evolving. Believers expound at length on various theories underlying the Vortices' existence, from their being focal points in the earth's "natural energy grid" to their energy seeping out of fissures in the earth and explain them in terms of electrical and magnetic forces, yin/yang energy, ancient Indian beliefs and so on. It is commonly claimed that psychic powers, emotions and talents are stronger there and that UFOs frequently visit them. Before either accepting the Vortexes as real or discounting them as nonsense, why not go there yourself and see whether you can feel the power that is said to draw many thousands of people to Sedona every year. It is as good an excuse as any to explore deeper into the Red Rock Country.

While some local visionaries claim to have identified as many as 13 Vortices, only four are generally recognized. The **Airport Mesa Vortex** is a little more than a mile south of Route 89A on the way to the airport. The **Boynton Canyon Vortex**, one of the area's most popular hiking areas, is several miles north of West Sedona via Dry Creek Road and Boynton

Pass Road (for more information see "Hiking" at the end of the chapter). The **Cathedral Rock Vortex** is by a lovely picnic area alongside Oak Creek, reached from Route 89A in West Sedona via Red Rock Loop Road and Chavez Ranch Road; the rock itself is one of the most photographed places in the area. The **Bell Rock Vortex**, a popular spot for UFO watchers, is just off Route 179 south of Sedona near the Village of Oak Creek.

For Sedona visitors who wish to explore the surrounding Red Rock Country, the town has an extraordinary number of sightseeing tour services. **Pink Jeep Tours** (204 North Route 89A; 602-282-5000), **Sedona Adventures** (Uptown Mall; 602-282-3500), **Time Expeditions** (276 North Route 89A; 602-282-2137) and **Sedona Red Rock Jeep Tours** (270 North Route 89A; 602-282-6826) all offer four-wheel-drive backcountry trips ranging from one hour to all day and will pick you up at any Sedona lodging. While each of these tour companies offers trips to Sedona's highly touted "sacred places," two other companies promote explicitly New Age trips to the area's "Vortices" with guides who will share secrets of the Medicine Wheel, magic plants, crystal energy and such. They are **Sacred Earth Tours** (260 North Route 89A; 602-282-6826, with a second location at 251 Route 179; 602-282-2026) and **Earth Wisdom Tours** (293 North Route 89A; 602-282-4717).

A half-hour's drive south of Sedona via Route 179 and Route 17, **Montezuma Castle National Monument** (Camp Verde; 602-567-3322; admission) protects 800-year-old cliff dwellings built by the Sinagua people, ancestors of the Hopi. The ruins got their name from early explorers' mistaken belief that Aztecs fled here and built the structures after the Spanish conquest of Mexico. Though there is no truth to the old theory, archaeologists now know that several centuries before the Spanish arrived, Toltec traders used to visit the Southwest, bringing with them architectural methods from central Mexico. The main "castle" is a five-story residential structure set high on the cliff. Although visitors cannot climb up to the ruin, the view from the nature trail below will tingle the imagination. The visitor center displays artifacts of the Sinagua and Hohokam cultures.

Adjoining the national monument, the **Yavapai-Apache Visitor Activity Center** (602-567-5276) offers museum exhibits of the culture and crafts of Native Americans who have occupied the area during historic times. Eleven miles north of the main unit of the national monument is a second, smaller unit called Montezuma's Well, a pool of water in a limestone sinkhole surrounded by small pueblo ruins.

South of Montezuma's Castle via Route 17, in the small town of Camp Verde, portions of an old cavalry fort from the Apache Wars in the 1870s and early 1880s are preserved as **Fort Verde State Historic Park** (Lane Street; 602-567-3275; admission). Visitors can walk through the former hospital and officers' quarters, and there is a museum of Native American, pioneer and military artifacts. The fort formed the end of the General Crook

Trail, the major patrol and supply route during the Apache Wars, which followed the Mogollon Rim west for more than 100 miles from Fort Apache. The trail is driveable today, as a mostly unpaved road, from Camp Verde through Coconino and Apache-Sitgreaves national forests.

Near the little town of Cottonwood, on Route 89A en route from Sedona to Prescott a few miles below Jerome, is **Tuzigoot National Monument** (602-634-5564), an uncharacteristically large Sinagua Indian pueblo ruin. Once home to about 250 people, the limestone pueblo stood two stories high and had 92 rooms. Today its white walls still stand on the hilltop and command an expansive view of the valley. Although the vista is marred by slag fields from a refinery that used to process Jerome's copper ore, the museum at the national monument offers a good look at the prehistoric culture of the Sinagua people.

One of the most beautiful canyons in the area is **Sycamore Canyon,** which parallels Oak Creek Canyon. Turn off at Tuzigoot National Monument and follow the well-maintained dirt road past the golf course for about 12 miles to the trailhead at the end of the road. Sycamore Canyon is a designated wilderness area, meaning that no wheeled or motorized vehicles are allowed. The Parsons Trail takes you up the wild, lushly wooded canyon for most of its 21-mile length, passing numerous small cliff dwellings resting high above. Camping is not permitted in the lower part of Sycamore Canyon.

A historic railroad that carries sightseers through some of Arizona's most spectacular country is the **Verde River Canyon Excursion Train** (300 North Broadway Street, Clarkdale; 602-639-0010). Revived in November 1990, this train achieved instant popularity as a major tourist attraction. It takes passengers on a 40-mile round trip from Clarkdale, 26 miles west of Sedona and just below Jerome. The diesel-powered train winds along sheer cliffs of red limestone in curve after curve high above the Verde River, through a long, dark tunnel, over bridges, past gold mines and Indian Ruins, to the ghost town of Perkinsville and back.

Jerome is one of Arizona's most intriguing ghost towns. After having been completely abandoned in the 1950s, it was resettled by hippies in the late 1960s and now has a population of about 500 people—a mere shadow of the 15,000 population it had in the first decades of the 20th century, when it was a rich silver mining district and the fifth-largest city in Arizona. The history of Jerome's mining era is brought to life in three museums. The old Douglas Mansion in **Jerome State Historic Park** (602-634-5381; admission) at the lower end of town offers a glimpse into the lifestyle of a turn-of-the-century mining baron, from marble-paneled bathrooms and a large wine cellar to balconies from which you can see 100 miles. For a look at mining tools, old photos, and other exhibits about old-time copper mining enter the **Jerome Historical Society Mine Museum** (602-634-5477; admission) on Main Street. The **Gold King Mine Museum** (602-634-0053;

admission) at the upper end of town has a re-created assay office, a replica mine shaft and a petting zoo.

The real pleasure of Jerome lies in strolling the streets that switchback up Cleopatra Hill, browsing in the shops along the way and admiring the carefully preserved turn-of-the-century architecture. Many of the town's buildings were constructed of massive blocks of quarried stone to withstand the blasts that frequently shook the ground from the nearby mine. The entire town has been declared a National Historic District.

Over the top of the hill from Jerome, in the next valley, sits the city of **Prescott**, the original territorial capital of Arizona from 1864 to 1867. President Abraham Lincoln decided to declare it the capital because the only other community of any size in the Arizona Territory, Tucson, was full of Confederate sympathizers. Today, Prescott is a low-key, all-American city with a certain quiet charm and few concessions to tourism. Incidentally, Prescott is located at the exact geographic center of the state of Arizona.

The major sightseeing highlight in Prescott is the **Sharlot Hall Museum** (415 West Gurley Street; 602-445-3122), which contains a large collection of antiques from Arizona's territorial period, including several fully furnished houses and an excellent collection of stagecoaches and carriages. Sharlot Mabridth Hall was a well-known essayist, poet and traveler who explored the wild areas of the Arizona Territory around the turn of the century. In 1909, she became the territorial historian, a position she held until Arizona achieved statehood. Seeing that Arizona's historic and prehistoric artifacts were rapidly being taken from the state, Ms. Hall began a personal collection that grew quite large over the next three decades and became the nucleus of this large historical museum. The museum's collections are housed in several Territorial-era buildings brought from around the county, including two governors' mansions, in a large park in downtown Prescott.

Prescott also has some other noteworthy museums. The **Phippen Museum of Western Art** (Route 89; 602-778-1385), six miles north of town, honors cowboy artist George Phippen and presents changing exhibits of works by other cowboy artists. It is generally considered one of the best cowboy art museums in the country.

The **Smoki Museum** (100 North Arizona Street; 602-445-2000; admission) houses a large collection of Indian artifacts from throughout the Southwest, as well as some pseudo-Indian items. The Smoki "tribe" is a secret society of non-Indian Prescott residents that was formed in the 1920s and still performs spectacular ceremonials annually in August despite the objections of legitimate Native American tribes.

Probably the most unusual of Prescott's museums is the **Bead Museum** (140 South Montezuma Street; 602-445-2431), displaying a phenomenal collection of beads, jewelry and other adornments from around the world and explaining their uses as trade goods, currency, religious items and status symbols. Visitors to this one-of-a-kind nonprofit museum discover that there's more to beads than they ever suspected.

Thirty-four miles south of Prescott you'll find **Arcosanti** (Route 17, Exit 262 at Cordes Junction; 602-632-7135; admission), a planned community that will eventually be home to 5000 people. Arcosanti was designed by famed Italian designer Paolo Soleri as a synthesis of architecture and ecology. It is pedestrian-oriented, and its unusual buildings with domes, arches, portholes and protruding cubes, make maximum use of passive solar heat. Tours are offered daily. Continuing construction is financed in part by the sale of handmade souvenir items such as Cosanti wind bells.

SEDONA/PRESCOTT AREA HOTELS

As you drive down Oak Creek Canyon from Flagstaff to Sedona, you will notice several privately owned lodges and cabin complexes in the midst of this spectacular national forest area. You can reserve accommodations at these places and enjoy the canyon in the cool of the evening and early morning, avoiding the midday throngs and traffic of peak season and weekends. Several places are located just below Slide Rock State Park.

Top of the line, **Junipine Resort** (Oak Creek Canyon; 602-282-3375) offers modern suites and two-bedroom "creekhouses" with rates in the ultra-deluxe range. These individually decorated one- and two-story units are all crafted from wood and stone. Offering mountain and forest views, each 1300 to 1500 square foot unit comes with a kitchen and redwood deck overlooking the canyon.

Slide Rock Cabins (Oak Creek Canyon; 602-282-6900) offers one old-fashioned log cabin and three chalets with loft bedrooms, all in the deluxe-price range, within walking distance of swimming holes, fishing spots and hiking trails. In the same part of the canyon, at the more modest accommodations at **Don Hoel's Cabins** (Oak Creek Canyon; 602-282-3560), rates range from budget to moderate. Moderate-priced cabins, some with fireplaces, are available at **Forest Houses** (Oak Creek Canyon; 602-282-2999).

Farther downcanyon, **Oak Creek Terrace** (Oak Creek Canyon; 602-282-3562) offers resort accommodations ranging from moderate-priced motel-style rooms with king-sized beds, color television and fireplaces to ultra-deluxe two-bedroom suites with heart-shaped jacuzzis.

Sedona specializes in upscale resorts. Among the poshest accommodations in town is **Los Abrigados** (160 Portal Lane; 602-282-1777). Situated next to the atmospheric Tlaquepaque shopping area, Los Abrigados features fanciful Mexican-inspired modern architecture throughout and elegantly stylish suites with kitchens, fireplaces and patios or balconies. Guest facilities include tennis courts, swimming pool, weight room, golf parcourse and spa. Rates, of course, are ultra-deluxe.

Another top-of-the-line Sedona accommodation is **L'Auberge de Sedona** (301 L'Auberge Lane; 602-282-1661). Individually designed guest rooms and cottages are decorated with furnishings imported from Provence, France, to re-create the atmosphere of a French country inn on ten acres of creekside grounds within walking distance of uptown Sedona. Deluxe to ultra-deluxe.

Charming, more affordable lodging in Sedona can be found at the **Rose Tree Inn** (376 Cedar Street; 602-282-2065) which strives for an "English garden environment" and has patios and a jacuzzi. Rates are in the moderate range for units in this small bed-and-breakfast inn close to uptown.

A Touch of Sedona Bed and Breakfast (595 Jordan Road; 602-282-6462), uphill from uptown, offers four individually decorated theme rooms with corresponding motifs—the "Contemporary Eagle," "Hummingbird," "Kachina" and "Roadrunner"—all in the moderate to deluxe range.

Greyfire Farm (1240 Jacks Canyon Road; 602-284-2340) is one of the area's more unusual bed and breakfasts. Nestled among the pines in a rural valley between the Red Rock Country and Wild Horse Mesa, near hiking and horseback riding trails in the national forest, the "farm" can accommodate two guest horses. It provides bed and breakfast for human guests as well. Rooms are bright and contemporary; moderate.

For basic motel rooms in Sedona, the **White House Inn** (2986 West Highway 89A; 602-282-6680) in West Sedona at the Dry Creek Road turn-off provides lodging with phone and cable television in the budget-price range. Near uptown Sedona, the **Star Motel** (295 Jordan Road; 602-282-3641) also offers standard rooms in the budget to moderate range.

Visitors seeking to change their lives in Sedona might want to consider staying at the **Healing Center of Arizona** (25 Wilson Canyon Road; 602-282-7710). Rates for accommodations in this dome complex are in the moderate range and budget-priced gourmet vegetarian meals are served. Amenities, offered for reasonable fees, include a sauna, a spa and a flotation tank. Holistic therapies available to guests at the center include accupressure treatments, herbology, rebirthing, crystal healing, psychic channeling and more.

In Jerome, you can spend the night in Victorian style and comfort at a very affordable rate. The **Jerome Inn** (311 Main Street; 602-634-5094)— formerly the Miner's Roost, the oldest hotel in Jerome—offers comfortable, budget-priced rooms. In the same price range is the **Conner Hotel** (168 Main Street; 602-634-5792), which has the town's most popular saloon on the ground floor. It can be noisy.

Smaller and very homey is **Nancy Russel's Bed & Breakfast** (P.O. Box 791, Jerome, AZ 86331; 602-634-3270), in a turn-of-the-century miner's house with guest rooms decorated in the style of the period. Rates are moderate.

Prescott has several historic downtown hotels. The most elegant of them is the **Hassayampa Inn** (122 East Gurley Street; 602-778-9434), a 1927 hotel listed on the National Register. The lobby and other common areas have been restored to their earlier glory and furnished with antiques. The rooms have been beautifully renovated and all have private baths, telephones and color televisions. Rates are moderate, with some suites in the deluxe range.

A smaller hotel on a quiet side street is the **Hotel Vendome** (230 South Cortez Street, Prescott; 602-776-0900). Rooms in this 1917 hotel have been nicely restored and decorated in tones of blue. Some have modern bathrooms, while others have restored Victorian-style baths. Moderate.

More modest rooms, all with private baths, are available at budget prices at the **St. Michael Hotel** (104 South Montezuma Street; 602-776-1999). The location couldn't be better for those who wish to enjoy the Wild West nightlife of Prescott's Whiskey Row, on the same block.

A posh bed and breakfast in a 1902 main house with four guest houses is the **Prescott Pines Inn** (901 White Spar Road; 602-445-7270). It has 13 Victorian-style guest rooms beautifully decorated in subdued color schemes. Some have fireplaces and others have kitchens. Sumptuous full breakfasts are served on rose patterned china. Reservations are recommended as much as a year in advance for peak season. Moderate.

Prescott also has more than its share of low-priced, basic lodging from which to explore the wild canyons and forests surrounding the city. The prices can't be beat at the once charming, now somewhat run-down Mediterranean-style **American Motel** (1211 East Gurley Street; 602-778-0787), rooms have telephones and wonderful old murals on the walls.

SEDONA/PRESCOTT AREA RESTAURANTS

A favorite Sedona restaurant since 1958, the **Oak Creek Owl** (561 Route 179; 602-282-3532) serves Continental and New Southwest cuisine at deluxe prices. Specialties include Southwest shrimp (sautéed with chilis, cilantro, garlic, tomato and sherry), chicken Sedona (layered with prosciutto, spinach and parmesan cheese) and roasted quail stuffed with piñon nuts.

L'Auberge de Sedona (301 L'Auberge Lane; 602-282-1661) has an outstanding French restaurant with a view on Oak Creek and memorable prix fixe dinners. The six course menu, which changes nightly, typically features pâté, soup, a small baby green salad and entrées such as poached salmon, grilled lamb or chicken. Prices can reach into the ultra-deluxe range.

Another outstanding Continental restaurant in the deluxe price range is **Rene at Tlaquepaque** (Tlaquepaque; 602-282-9225), also specializing in French fare. The most elaborate neo-Spanish-colonial decor in the Southwest makes this restaurant extra special. Open-air patio dining is available.

A good moderately priced Mexican restaurant is **Oaxaca** (231 Route 89A; 602-282-4179), which has an outdoor deck for dining with a view of uptown Sedona.

Italian food at moderate prices is featured at the **Hideaway** (Country Square; 602-282-4204), with tables on a balcony over the creek, surrounded by a stand of sycamore trees. For health-conscious Thai food, made with all natural, organic ingredients, try **Thai Spices Natural** (2986 West Route 89A; 602-282-0590), a budget-to-moderate-priced restaurant in the White House Inn motel in West Sedona.

And for a synthesis of ethnic cuisines—European, Mediterranean and Oriental cooking techniques used to create highly original, healthy dishes such as red cabbage with goat cheese, hazelnuts and apples or Cajun fish with raspberry glazed cucumbers—head for the **Heartline Café** (1610 West Route 89A, Sedona; 602-282-0785). Moderate.

For just plain good, just-like-mom's food at budget to moderate prices in Sedona, the place to go is **Irene's Restaurant** (Castle Rock Plaza; 602-284-2240) at the corner of Route 179 and Verde Valley School Road. Irene's is famous for home-cooked desserts, including deep dish apple pie, peach cobbler and giant cinnamon rolls.

Another good budget place is **Phil and Eddie's Diner** (1655 West Route 89A; 602-282-6070), offering all-day breakfasts, burgers and fries, blue-plate specials and soda fountain suggestions in a 1950s nostalgia ambience.

In Jerome, the elegant place to dine, open for dinner on weekends only, is the **House of Joy** (Hull Street; 602-634-5339), a former house of ill repute whose past is recalled in the decor—red lights, red candles, red flowers, red placemats, red everything. The fairly limited menu features veal, lamb and poultry. Prices are moderate to deluxe.

The **Jerome Palace** (Clark Street; 602-634-5262) specializes in moderately priced barbecue, served in an upstairs dining room with a spectacular view of the Verde Valley. For breakfast or lunch, try **Macy's European Coffeehouse & Bakery** (Main Street at Hull Avenue; 602-634-2733), serving croissants, scones and pastries along with gourmet coffees and teas in historic surroundings. Budget.

Prescott's finer restaurants include the **Peacock Room** (122 East Gurley Street; 602-778-9434) in the Hassayampa Inn. Here you'll find a full menu of moderately priced Continental and American specialties in an elegant old-time atmosphere. An etched-glass peacock ornaments the front door of this art deco dining room. Choose between seating at tables or semicircular booths. Tiffany-style lamps add to the quaint atmosphere of this high-ceilinged establishment.

A century old general merchandise store that has been transformed into a popular restaurant, **Murphy's** (201 North Cortez Street; 602-445-4044) is a walk through history. A leaded-glass divider separates the bar and restaurant sections decorated with photos of Prescott's mining heyday. Mahogany bar booths and a burgundy carpet add to the charm of this establishment. You can also enjoy a drink in the lounge offering views of Thumb Butte. Specialties include mesquite-broiled seafood and prime rib of beef along with fresh home-baked bread.

With many plants and a creekside view, the **Prescott Mining Company** (155 Plaza Drive; 602-445-1991) is a large, modern restaurant with an entrance styled after a mine shaft. Its steak and seafood dishes are moderately priced.

For breakfast or lunch in Prescott, a very popular place in the downtown area is **Greens and Things** (106 West Gurley Street; 602-445-3234), which serves homemade Belgian waffles, build-your-own omelettes and homemade soups. Also good is the **Prescott Pantry** (1201 Iron Springs Road; 602-778-4280) in the Iron Springs Plaza shopping center. This bakery-deli-wine shop has restaurant seating and offers ever-changing daily specials, hearty sandwiches, espresso and cappuccino and fresh-baked pastries. Prices are in the budget range at both places.

Some of the best low-budget home-style cooking in Prescott is to be found at the **Dinner Bell Café** (321 West Gurley Street; 602-445-9888). It may not look like much from the outside, but give it a try and you'll find out why this is one of the most popular restaurants in central Arizona. For breakfast try the hubcap size pancakes or three egg omelettes. Lunch specials include pork chops, chicken fried steak and chili. Be sure to try the homemade salsa.

SEDONA/PRESCOTT AREA SHOPPING

Sedona's shopping district is one of the three or four best in Arizona. Many of the galleries, boutiques and specialty shops are labors of love, the personal creations of people who spent years past daydreaming about opening a cute little store in Sedona. The town has more than 60 art galleries, most of them specializing in traditional and contemporary Native American art, "cowboy" art and landscape paintings. Quality is relatively high in this very competitive art market. You can easily spend a whole day shopping your way up and down the main streets of town, leaving your feet sore and your credit cards limp.

Most galleries and boutiques, as well as tourist-oriented shops, are in "uptown" Sedona, on Route 89A above the "Y" (the junction where Route 89A curves right toward West Sedona while the road continuing straight becomes Route 179). Virtually all supermarkets, shopping malls and places where practical things can be purchased are in West Sedona.

Our favorite art gallery in Sedona is **Elaine Horowitz Galleries** (Schnebly Hill Road at Route 179; 602-282-6290). The late Ms. Horowitz endowed this and her other galleries in Scottsdale and Santa Fe with an eye for quality in contemporary art and a rare sense of humor.

The most relaxing and enjoyable place in Sedona to browse is **Tlaquepaque**, a large, eye-catching two-story complex of specialty shops and restaurants below the "Y" on Route 179. Built in Spanish colonial style with old-looking stone walls, courtyards, tile roofs and flowers in profusion, Tlaquepaque looks more like Old Mexico than the real thing. Representative of the range of stores here are several that deal in animal motifs: **Aguajito del Sol** (602-282-5258) exhibits animal sculptures; **Mother Nature's Trading Company** (602-282-5932) carries games, playthings and educational toys having to do with endangered species; the **Cuddly Coyote** (602-282-4480) presents a wide selection of stuffed toy animals; and **Geoffrey Roth Ltd.** (602-282-7756) has taxidermy and painted birds.

Across the highway, from Tlaquepaque, you'll find the **Crystal Castle** (313 Route 179; 602-282-5910), one of the larger New Age stores in this town which, according to many, is the New Age capital of the known cosmos. It carries unusual books, incense, runes, visionary art and, of course, crystals. In front of the store, a "networking" bulletin board lets you scan the array of alternative professional services in town—channelers, psychic surgeons, clairvoyants, kinesiologists, numerologists and many more. Other stores in the same vein include **Angels, Art & Crystals** (3006 West Route 89A; 602-282-7089), the **Golden Word Book Centre** (3150 Route 89A; 602-282-2688), **Crystal Magic** (2978 West Route 89A; 602-282-1622) and the **Crystal Pyramid** (6446 Route 179; 602-284-1737). Can't get enough? The **Center for the New Age** offers Vortex information, networking for New Age activities, psychic readings daily and a "Psychic Faire" every Saturday.

Shopping enthusiasts will also want to visit **Oak Creek Factory Stores**, a mall south of town on Route 179 in the village of Oak Creek. This is factory-direct outlet shopping with a difference. The factories represented include **Capezio** (602-284-1910), **Sarah Coventry** (602-284-1965), **Mikasa** (602-284-9505), **Izod/Gant** (602-284-9844) and **Anne Klein** (602-284-0407)—designer goods at discount prices.

Many of Jerome's residents are arts-and-crafts people, and a stroll up and down the town's switchback main street will take you past quite a few intriguing shops that offer pottery, jewelry, handmade clothing, stained glass and other such wares. A good place to hunt for a souvenir that recalls Jerome's mining origins is **The Copper Shop** (Main Street; 602-634-7754).

Because it is old as Arizona towns go, and perhaps because of Sharlot Hall's recognition that it was important to preserve the everyday objects of 19th-century Arizona, Prescott is a good place for antique shopping. As in most antique hunting areas, some items offered for sale do not come from the Prescott area but have been imported from other, less visited parts of the country. Most, however, are the real thing, and antique buffs will find lots of great shops within walking distance of one another in the downtown area, especially along the two-block strip of Cortez Street between Gurley and Sheldon streets.

Some of the best places to browse are the indoor mini-malls where select groups of dealers and collectors display, such as the **Merchandise Mart Mall** (205 North Cortez Street; 602-776-1728), **Prescott Antique & Craft Market** (115 North Cortez Street; 602-445-7156) and **Deja Vu Antique Mall** (134 North Cortez Street; 602-445-6732), which also features an old-fashioned soda fountain.

SEDONA/PRESCOTT AREA NIGHTLIFE

Sedona has surprisingly little nightlife. Besides the lounges in the major resort hotels, your best bet is to call the **Sedona Arts Center** (Route 89A at Art Barn Road; 602-282-3809) for their current schedule of theatrical and concert performances.

The Old West saloon tradition lives on in Jerome, where the town's most popular club is the **Spirit Room** (Main Street at Jerome Avenue; 602-634-5792) in the old Conner Hotel. There is live music on weekend afternoons and evenings and the atmosphere is as authentic as can be.

If old-time saloons appeal to you, don't miss Prescott's **Whiskey Row**, downtown on the block of Montezuma Street directly across from the Yavapai County Courthouse. Most of the bars that line Whiskey Row have been in operation since the late 19th century, when they served up their own home brew and this was one of the most notorious sin strips in the west. Today, the saloons remain authentically Old Western, and so do most of the customers.

The fanciest of the bunch is the **Palace** (120 South Montezuma Street, Prescott; 602-778-4227) in the center of the block. Others typical of the genre include the **Bird Cage Saloon** (148 South Montezuma Street, Prescott) and the **Western Bar** (144 South Montezuma Street, Prescott; 602-445-1244), which has live country-and-western music Thursday, Friday and Saturday.

For non-drinkers, there are the nonalcoholic hangouts **Hikkups** (116 South Montezuma Street, Prescott; 602-776-8715) and the San Francisco-style coffee house in the **St. Michael Hotel** (104 South Montezuma Street, Prescott; 602-776-1999) where, on weekend evenings, folk singers take you back into a different era.

SEDONA/PRESCOTT AREA PARKS

Slide Rock State Park—Very popular with students from the University of Northern Arizona, this swimming area midway between Flagstaff and Sedona in the heart of Oak Creek Canyon is almost always packed during the warm months. It is like a natural water park, with placid pools, fast-moving chutes and a wide, flat shoreline of red sandstone for sunbathing. The state park also includes apple orchards and abandoned homestead from the 1920s. Visitors are not allowed to pick the apples, but cider made from them is sold at a stand on the trail to the swim area.

Facilities: Picnic area, restrooms, volleyball court, nature trail, snack bar; information, 602-282-3034. *Swimming:* Excellent.

Getting there: Located seven miles north of Sedona via Route 89A in Oak Creek Canyon.

Watson Lake and Granite Dells—A labyrinth of granite rock formations along Route 89 just outside of Prescott surrounds pretty little Watson Lake, a manmade reservoir that is locally popular for boating and fishing. The area used to be a stronghold for Apache Indians. More recently, from the 1920s to the 1950s, there was a major resort at Granite Dells and some artifacts survive from that era.

Facilities: Picnic area, restrooms, showers, hiking, rock climbing; information, 602-778-4338. *Fishing:* Good.

Camping: There are 50 sites (25 with electrical hookups); $11 per night with electricity, $8 without.

Getting there: Located four miles northeast of Prescott on Route 89.

Colorado River Area

Downriver from the Grand Canyon, the Colorado River becomes a series of manmade desert lakes formed by the dams of the Colorado River Project, which provides electricity for Southern California and a steady supply of irrigation water for Imperial Valley agriculture. With Nevada and California on the other side, the river and lakes form the Arizona state line, often called "Arizona's West Coast."

In Kingman, the **Mohave Museum of History and Arts** (400 West Beale Street; 602-753-3195) offers a look at many of the unusual aspects of Northwestern Arizona. A mural and dioramas in the lobby depict the settlement of the region and show how camels used to be used as beasts of burden in these parts. Kingman is the source of much of the turquoise mined in the United States, and the museum has a fine collection of carved turquoise objects. Native American exhibits include portrayals of the traditional ways of the local Hualapai and Mohave people. Other rooms contain a collection of paintings of U.S. Presidents and their first ladies by local artist Lawrence Williams and memorabilia of the town's most famous one-time resident, the late actor Andy Devine.

(Text continued on page 70.)

Don't Be Spooked

Arizona has two types of ghost towns—those that have been completely and irrevocably abandoned to the ravages of time and those that have risen into new life thanks to tourism. Good examples of both types can be found along the beat-up old segment of Route 66 that climbs and winds over the mountains between Kingman and Topock near the state's western boundary.

Goldroad, a once-prosperous town whose residents dug $7 million worth of gold ore out of the desert hillsides between 1901 and 1931, is just about gone now. All that remains are mine shafts, a few crumbling adobe walls and stone foundations of the town's larger buildings.

Oatman, just nine miles away, was another gold-mining town of about the same size, founded at about the same time as Goldroad and abandoned around the same time. The old buildings still stand. Some are boarded up, but many others have become curio shops and snack bars. People today come from all over the state on weekends to wander through town.

Why the difference? The landowners of Goldroad destroyed their buildings on purpose to reduce their property-tax assessments. In Oatman, though, a small group of "never say die" citizens stayed on through the lean years, surviving by selling refreshments to passers-by on the old highway. Eventually, Hollywood discovered Oatman, spruced up the old storefronts and used it as a set for several Western movies, including *How the West Was Won*. People around Oatman realized early on that one day

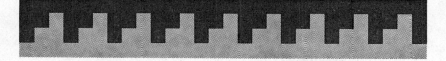

old buildings might be worth more than the gold ore that some say still lies in the ground beneath both Goldroad and Oatman.

In recent years, Oatman has been declared a National Historic District, as have other famous Arizona ghost towns like the copper-mining towns of **Jerome** and **Bisbee** and the silver boom town of **Tombstone.** Historic status virtually assures their continued survival and prosperity by offering special tax breaks to investors who restore the old buildings and by prohibiting anyone from tearing them down and erecting modern structures instead. Bed and breakfasts, espresso cafés and frozen-yogurt shops are beginning to spring up behind the old storefronts, and parking is becoming a problem.

And that's good. Without tourism as an economic base and incentive for preservation, we would never have the opportunity to wander the streets of a town from yesteryear. But for those travelers with vivid imaginations, a good local history book or two and an urge to explore away from the well-trodden tourist paths, the nearly vanished towns also have something special to offer. You can find history unadorned in the dusty remains of places like **White Hills** and **Mineral Park** north of Kingman, **Walker** and **McCabe** in the national forest near Prescott and **Stanton** and **Weaverville** north of Wickenburg, as well as dozens of sites in the southeast part of the state. The **Arizona Office of Tourism** (1100 West Washington Street, Phoenix, AZ 85007; 602-542-8687) publishes a free brochure telling how to find these and other ghost towns. Most often, getting there is the real adventure—and the trip itself is well worth it.

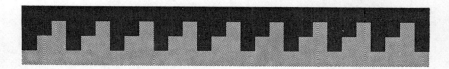

The largest of the reservoirs is 115-mile-long **Lake Mead**, which lies about 80 miles north of Kingman on Route 93, not far from Las Vegas. A scenic drive runs along the Nevada side of the lake, where there are marinas, a campground, a popular public beach and a few small resorts. The only access to Lake Mead from the isolated Arizona shore is at **Temple Bar Marina** (602-767-3211), reached by a well-marked, paved 28-mile road that turns off Route 93 about 55 miles north of Kingman. The marina has a motel and cabins in the moderate-price range, an RV park, a restaurant and fishing boat rentals. There is also a public campground.

Hoover Dam, which impounds Lake Mead, was a tourist attraction in the area even before the first casino was built on the Las Vegas Strip. This huge dam rises 726 feet above the river and generates four billion kilowatt-hours of electricity in a year. Containing over three million cubic yards of concrete, it was completed in 1935. Its Depression-era origins are evident in the art deco motifs that decorate the top of the dam, including two huge Winged Figure of the Republic statues and a terrazzo floor patterned with mystical cosmic symbols. Guided tours (702-293-8367; admission) take visitors down into the interior of the dam on an elevator.

Downriver from Hoover Dam is **Lake Mohave**, 67 miles long but only four miles across. It is held back by Davis Dam at Laughlin/Bullhead City. Lake Mohave is accessible at only two points in Arizona: Willow Beach, off Route 93 about 60 miles north of Kingman, and Katherine Landing, six miles north of Bullhead City and Laughlin. **Lake Mohave Resort** (Katherine Landing; 602-754-3245), six miles north of Bullhead City, rents houseboats and other craft for use on Lake Mohave, as does **Willow Beach Resort** (602-767-3311).

Bullhead City, Arizona's fastest-growing community, owes its prosperity to the recently established gambling town of Laughlin, Nevada, on the far side of the river. Laughlin has no residential areas, no shopping malls, nothing at all but casinos. Most of the thousands of people who work there live, shop and send their kids to school in Bullhead City. Others live in the smaller, lower-rent freeway towns of Kingman, Arizona, and Needles, California. The closest gambling zone to the greater Phoenix area, Laughlin is packed to overflowing every weekend. The rest of the week, the casinos, buffets, lounges and showrooms play host to motorhome nomads who appreciate the opportunity to avoid Las Vegas traffic and avail themselves of Laughlin's vast, free RV parking lots.

In the Laughlin/Bullhead City and Lake Havasu City areas, commercial boat cruises are a popular pastime. Before the bridge across the Colorado River was built a few years ago, visitors used to park on the Arizona side of the river and ride passenger ferries across to the casinos on the Nevada side. Now, on busy weekends when parking lots in Laughlin are full, the ferries still carry people across the river, making for a brief, fun free cruise. Several companies also offer longer riverboat sightseeing tours down the river from the casino docks. Among them are **Blue River Safaris** (702-298-0910), which operates the *Colorado River King* jet cruiser from the Riverside Casino dock, and **Laughlin River Tours** (702-298-1047), which runs the *Little Belle* paddlewheel steamer from the Edgewater Casino dock and even offers on-board weddings.

In the little town of **Topock** (★), midway between Bullhead City and Lake Havasu City at the junction of Route 40 and Route 95 South, **Jerkwater Canoe Co.** (602-768-7753) rents canoes to explore otherwise inaccessible areas of the **Havasu-Topock National Wildlife Refuge** and can provide directions to the beautiful Topock Gorge, ancient petroglyph sites and the Topock Maze, where Mohave Indians used to go to cleanse their spirits after long journeys.

Farther downstream, **Lake Havasu** may be the prettiest of the manmade lakes along the Colorado River. Cool and bright blue in the heart of the desert, this 46-mile-long lake has become a very popular recreation area. Its main claim to fame is **London Bridge** in Lake Havasu City. Except for the Grand Canyon, London Bridge is the most visited tourist attraction in Arizona. The audacity and monumental pointlessness of the city fathers' moving the bridge here when the city of London decided to replace it draws curiosity seekers in droves. To believe it, you have to see it. Originally built in 1825 to replace a still older London Bridge that had lasted 625 years, this bridge was sold at auction in 1968. Lake Havasu City's promoters bought it for $2,460,000. The 10,000 tons of granite facing were disassembled into blocks weighing from 1000 to 17,000 pounds each, shipped and trucked 10,000 miles to this site and reconstructed on the shore of Lake Havasu when the city was practically nonexistent. Then a canal was dug to let water flow under the bridge. It is 35 feet wide and 952 feet long, and you can drive or walk across it. Every year, millions do. Is it worth seeing? Absolutely! It's a giant object lesson in the fine line between madness and genius—and one of the strangest things in Arizona.

In Lake Havasu City, a number of boats offer sightseeing tours from London Bridge. They range from the first cruise boat on the lake, the cute little *Miss Havasupai* operated by **Lake Havasu Boat Tours** (602-855-7979), to the large Mississippi riverboat replica *Dixie Belle* (602-855-0888). **Bluewater Charters** (602-855-7171) runs daily jet boat excursions from London Bridge up to Topock Gorge and the Havasu-Topock National Wildlife Refuge.

The road through Oatman runs between Kingman and Topock, both on interstate Route 40. There is also a shortcut from Route 95 midway between Bullhead City and Topock. Back before the interstate was built, this narrow, deteriorating paved road winding steeply over the barren mountains used to be the most difficult stretch of Route 66 across the Southwest to California. Hard to believe. **Oatman** is one of Arizona's better-preserved ghost towns, thanks largely to the fact that it has been used several times as a movie set. As a gold mining boom town, Oatman flourished from 1906 to 1942, then nearly vanished. Today, a healthy tourist trade keeps the town going. Weekends are lively with country music and staged shootouts in the streets. Tourism also keeps dozens of wild burros, descendants of the work animals who hauled gold ore out of the mines, loitering in the streets. They've learned that panhandling snacks from sightseers beats scrounging around for food in the Mohave Desert any day.

COLORADO RIVER AREA HOTELS

On Sunday through Thursday nights, rooms cost significantly less in the casino hotels of Laughlin, Nevada, than they do in Bullhead City on the Arizona side of the Colorado River. In fact, on weeknights, you can rent a spacious, modern room with a king-size bed, remote control television, art prints and designer wallpaper in Laughlin for about the same rate as a plain, somewhat threadbare room in an aging mom-and-pop motel by the interstate in Kingman.

All hotel accommodations in Laughlin are in the budget range at all times, but they can be in short supply. Reservations are essential on weekends and a good idea at other times. Laughlin's strip consists of ten casino hotels.

Top of the line and the closest to the bridge across the river from Bullhead City, is **Don Laughlin's Riverside Resort** (702-298-2535). The resort's owner conceived the idea of promoting a casino strip here, founded the town that is named after him, and in 1977 converted the old Riverside Bait Shop on this site into Laughlin's first casino. With 661 rooms, the hotel remains the largest in town.

Some of the other hotels are famous-name spinoffs from well-known Las Vegas and Reno casinos, such as the **Flamingo Hilton** (702-298-2453), the **Golden Nugget** (702-298-4600) and **Harrah's Del Rio** (702-298-4600), a very nice hotel over a hill from the others at the south end of Casino Row. The **Colorado Belle** (702-298-2285) a showy casino hotel shaped like a giant riverboat midway down the strip, was created by the same company that owns Circus Circus and the Excalibur in Las Vegas, as was the high-rise, 450-unit **Edgewater Hotel** (702-298-2453).

For most visitors to the Laughlin/Bullhead City area, there is probably not much point to staying on the Arizona side of the river. Most of the motels in Bullhead City are clean and modern but unexceptional, and room rates tend to run higher than in the Laughlin casino hotels. They seem to thrive on weekend and peak-season overflows. It's hard to believe that many people with aversions to the gambling scene would go out of their way to stay in Bullhead City when they could as easily proceed south to the more family-oriented Lake Havasu City. But if they did, they'd find good noncasino lodgings in Bullhead City at places like the moderate-priced **Park Oasis Motel** (7th and Lee streets; 602-754-2829) and, in the same price range, the **Bullhead Riverlodge Motel** (455 Moser Street; 602-754-2250). Both are all-suite motels, ideal for families, and the Riverlodge has a boat and fishing dock available for guests' use at no charge.

Lake Havasu City boasts many fine resort hotels. The **Ramada London Bridge Resort** (1477 Queen's Bay Road; 602-855-0888), with its blend of Tudor and medieval castle-style architecture and beautiful contemporary guest rooms, has its own golf course, lovely green landscaped grounds and a waterfront location right next to London Bridge and the Olde English Village. Moderate to deluxe.

Across the bridge, on the island, the **Nautical Inn** (1000 McCulloch Boulevard; 602-855-2141) also has a golf course, as well as a private dock with waterskiing, sailing, boating, jetskiing and windsurfing equipment for guests. All the rooms are on the waterfront. Each carpeted unit comes with two double beds, a patio and direct access to the lawn and beach. The suites include refrigerators and kitchenettes. Deluxe.

Within a mile of the bridge, budget-priced standard motel rooms are available at the **Windsor Inn** (451 London Bridge Road; 602-855-4135) and the **Shakespeare Inn** (2190 McCulloch Boulevard; 602-855-4157).

Spacious one-bedroom suites are available at the **Sands Vacation Resort** (2040 Mesquite Avenue; 602-855-1388). Pictures of the Southwest decorate the pastel walls of these courtyard units. Each carpeted suite includes a living room, dining area and kitchenette. A two-night minimum stay is required. Budget to moderate.

In the ghost town of Oatman, the old **Oatman Hotel** (★) has reopened as a bed-and-breakfast establishment. You probably wouldn't want to call ahead for sight-unseen reservations here, even when they get a telephone installed, but the spirit of adventure might very well inspire you to take a room in this authentic two-story adobe with corrugated iron walls and ceilings on the spur of the moment—as Clark Gable and Carole Lombard did on their wedding night after a surprise ceremony in Kingman. Oatman was on the main highway to Hollywood back then and a peek into the honeymoon "suite," with its bare hanging light bulb and crumbling walls, will give you an idea of how eager Clark and Carole must have been. Today, rates are still in the budget range.

COLORADO RIVER AREA RESTAURANTS

In the Bullhead City/Laughlin area, hit the casinos for budget-priced feasts. Just about every hotel on Casino Row has an all-you-can-eat buffet featuring 40 or more items, in the budget range for dinner and almost absurdly affordable—no more than you'd spend at a franchise hamburger joint—for breakfast and lunch. To sweeten the deal even more, two-for-one buffet coupons are included in free "fun books" widely distributed in visitor centers and truck stops in Kingman and elsewhere along Route 40. The largest buffet in town is at the **Edgewater Hotel** (702-298-7111).

Each casino also has a full-service 24-hour coffee shop, most of them featuring breakfast specials priced between 99 cents and $1.99. Notable among the 24-hour casual places is **Lindy's** (702-298-2453), a classic New York-style deli, at the Flamingo Hilton.

Many, though not all, casinos also have moderately priced fine dining restaurants. **Harrah's Del Rio** (702-298-4600) offers an intimate atmosphere and a riverside view at William Fisk's Steakhouse or authentic Mexican fare at La Hacienda. In the **Colorado Belle** (702-298-4000), seafood is a specialty in the casually classy Orleans Room. And **Sam's Town Gold River** (702-298-2242) serves fine American and Continental selections in Sutter's Lodge, designed on hunting lodge theme with wood-beamed ceiling and big stone fireplace, all so convincing that you may completely forget that you're in a casino.

Lake Havasu City, oddly, has virtually no high-priced haute cuisine, but it does have a good selection of pleasant, affordable restaurants. A good place for salads, steaks and seafood in the moderate price range is **Shu-grue's** (1425 McCulloch Boulevard; 602-453-1400) in the Island Fashion Mall, which has an unbeatable view of London Bridge from the island side through tall wraparound windows. Fresh bakery goods are the specialty.

Also on the island, the **Captain's Table at the Nautical Inn** (1000 McCulloch Boulevard; 602-855-2141) serves a wide range of traditional American menu selections with a lakeside view overlooking the resort's private dock. Moderate.

Away from the water, a local favorite in the moderate range is **Krystal's** (460 El Camino Way; 602-453-2999), featuring seafood specialties such as Alaskan king crab legs, lobster tails and mahi mahi. Another long-time local favorite is **Nicolino's Italian Restaurant** (86 South Smoketree Avenue; 602-855-3484), serving 30 varieties of pasta with prices ranging from budget to moderate. In the English Village on the mainland side of the bridge, there's the budget-priced, usually busy **Mermaid Inn**, serving fish and chips.

COLORADO RIVER AREA SHOPPING

Arizona's "West Coast" holds a number of enticements for visitors, but shopping isn't one of them. The most interesting shopping district in the area is the **Olde English Village** on the mainland side of London Bridge in Lake Havasu, and the most remarkable thing about it, other than its vast expanse of bright-green lawn in the heart of one of America's most desolate deserts, is that the land on which it was built is owned by the city of London—making the bridge a symbolic link between London and Lake Havasu City. The cute Olde English buildings housing the shops and snack bars remind us that the city and the bridge were the brainchild of the retired general manager of Disneyland. The Olde English Village has about two dozen theme gift shops such as the London Bridge Gift Shoppe, the Copper Shoppe, the Gallerie of Glasse and the Curiosity Shoppe, as well as the London Bridge Candle Factory, which claims to be the world's largest candle shoppe.

At the other end of the bridge, the **Island Fashion Mall** houses about a dozen shops selling men's and women's fashions, sportswear and fine jewelry.

COLORADO RIVER AREA NIGHTLIFE

Nightlife on the river all happens in Laughlin where each of the casinos has at least one, often two, cocktail lounges that don't charge for watching musical acts that perform here while practicing for Las Vegas. Only one of the casinos has a showroom where name acts appear: the **Riverside** (702-298-2535) hosts such performers as the Gatlin Brothers, the Smothers Brothers, the Oakridge Boys, the McGuire Sisters and Willie Nelson. The Riverside also has the only movie theater in town, with three screens. Sam's Town Gold River (702-298-2242) has **Sandy Hackett's Comedy Club** where three stand-up comics appear in two shows a night Wednesday through Saturday.

COLORADO RIVER AREA PARKS

Hualapai Mountain Park—This island of forested slopes in the middle of the Mohave Desert is a locally popular picnicking, camping and hiking area. These mountains were once the ancestral home of the Hualapai Indians, who now live farther north on a reservation as the west end of the Grand Canyon. Managed by the Mohave County Parks Department, the park offers cool, protected habitat for wildlife including deer, elk, coyotes and occasional mountain lions.

Facilities: Picnic areas, restrooms, cabins, softball diamond, hiking trails, winter snow play area; information and cabin reservations, 602-757-0915.

Camping: There are 70 tent sites and 10 RV hookups; $6 per night for tent sites, $12 for hookups. Besides tent and RV campgrounds, there are 15 cabins built in the 1930s as part of a Civilian Conservation Corps camp that can be rented for the night at budget prices (reservations required).

Getting there: Located 14 miles southeast of Kingman on the paved Hualapai Mountain Park Road.

Lake Havasu State Park—This shoreline park area in and around Lake Havasu City encompasses most of the Arizona shore of this broad blue lake nestled among stark, rocky desert hills. The park has several campgrounds, boat launching ramps and rocky swimming beaches in four developed units— Windsor Beach and Crystal Beach, both north of the center of town, and Cattail Cove, about 15 miles south of town. Cattail Cove has a state-operated marina. Besides these four areas, the park encompasses the Aubrey Hills Natural Area, a wild shoreline that can't be reached by road.

Facilities: Picnic areas, restrooms, showers, boat ramps, marina, nature trails; restaurants, groceries and lodging nearby in Lake Havasu City; information, 602-855-2784. *Swimming:* Good. *Fishing:* Good.

Camping: There are 74 sites at Windsor Beach (602-855-2784) and 40 sites with full RV hookups at Cattail Cove (602-855-1223); $7 per night at Windsor, $12 per night at Cattail. Also available are 150 primitive boat-in sites along the shore in the Aubrey Hills Natural Area north of Lake Havasu City; vault toilets, picnic tables and shade structures; $7 per boat.

Getting there: The main automobile accessible areas are at Windsor Beach and Crystal Beach in Lake Havasu City and Pittsburg Point on the island across London Bridge from town, as well as Cattail Cove 15 miles south of Lake Havasu City on Route 95. Other areas of the park, which includes most of the east shore of Lake Havasu, are only accessible by boat.

The Sporting Life

HORSEBACK RIDING

At the Grand Canyon, the **Moqui Lodge stable** (602-638-2891) in Tusayan, near the park's south entrance, offers a selection of guided rides to remote points along the South Rim. Most popular is the four-hour East Rim ride, which winds through Long Jim Canyon to a viewpoint overlooking the Grand Canyon. One- and two-hour rides are also available. Horseback rides do not go below the canyon rim. For information on burro trips into the canyon, see "Tours" in the "Transportation" section at the end of this chapter.

Other areas offer interesting horseback outings including guided "Indian Sacred Ceremonial" rides in Sedona. Try **Hitchin Post Stables** (448 Lake Mary Road; 602-774-1719), **Fairfield Flagstaff Resort** (2380 North Oakmont Drive; 602-526-3232), **Ski Lift Lodge Stables** (Route 180 at Snow Bowl Road; 602-774-0729), **Perkins Wilderness Trail Rides** (Route 40 exit 171, Williams; 602-635-9349), **Kachina Stables** (Lower Red Rock Loop Road, Sedona; 602-282-7252), **High Country Stables** (200 Stable Lane, Prescott; 602-776-4192), **Black Mountain Trail Rides** (710 Lochiel Road; in Kingman, 602-656-2902 evenings only; from Bullhead City, 602-763-0883; from Laughlin, 702-298-1870) and **Havasu Horse Rental** (Lake Havasu City; 602-680-2939).

SKIING

Arizona's premier downhill ski area is the **Fairfield Snowbowl** (Snowbowl Road; 602-779-1951; snow report, 602-779-4577), 14 miles north of Flagstaff on the slopes of the San Francisco Peaks. The ski season runs from mid-December to mid-April. The small **Williams Ski Area** (602-635-9330) is located on Bill Williams Mountain, four miles south of the town of Williams.

For cross-country skiers, the **Flagstaff Nordic Center** (Route 180; 602-774-6216), 14 miles north of Flagstaff in Coconino National Forest, maintains an extensive system of trails from mid-October through mid-April. The center offers equipment rentals, guided tours and a ski school. Another great cross-country skiing facility is the **Mormon Lake Ski Touring Center** (Mormon Lake Village; 602-354-2240), 28 miles southeast of Flagstaff off Lake Mary Road.

BOATING AND WATERSKIING

The lower Colorado River and Lake Havasu are a mecca for watersport enthusiasts, and craft of all kinds are available for rent.

In Lake Havasu City, pontoon boats are available at **Island Boat Rentals** (1580 Dover Avenue; 602-453-3260) and **Rick's Pontoon Boat Rentals & Sales** (602-453-1922). Power boats for fishing and waterskiing are for rent at **Village Boat Rentals** (1600 West Acoma Street; 602-855-6668), **Rent A Boat** (London Bridge Resort; 602-453-9613), **Lake Havasu Marina** (1100 McCulloch Boulevard; 602-855-2159) and **Resort Boat Rentals** (English Village; 602-453-9613). Thirteen miles south of Lake Havasu City, **Sand Point Marina** (602-855-0549) rents fishing boats, pontoon boats and houseboats. Waterskiing lessons are offered by **Havasu Adventures Water Ski School** (1425 McCulloch Boulevard; 602-855-6274).

RIVER RAFTING

A Grand Canyon adventure that has become popular is river rafting. Raft trips operate from April through October. Most start at Lee's Ferry, northeast of the national park boundary near Page, Arizona, and just below Glen Canyon Dam. Rafting the full length of the canyon, 280 miles from Lee's Ferry to Lake Mead, takes eight days. Many rafting companies also offer shorter trips that involve being picked up or dropped off by helicopter part way through the canyon. Among the leading raft tour companies are **Grand Canyon Expeditions** (P.O. Box O, Kanab, UT 84741; 801-644-2691) and **Arizona River Runners** (P.O. Box 47788, Phoenix, AZ 85068; 602-867-4866). A complete list of river trip outfitters is available from the South Rim visitor center (602-638-7888).

BALLOONING

For the most spectacular guided tour in town, see the Red Rock Country from the sky with **Red Rock Balloon Adventure** (3230 Valley Vista Drive; 602-284-0040) or **Northern Light Balloon Expeditions** (P.O. Box 1695, Sedona, AZ 86336; 602-282-2274).

GOLF

This area of Arizona is a golf paradise. Tee off at **Fairfield Flagstaff Resort** (2380 North Oakmont Drive; 602-527-7997), **Sedona Golf Resort** (7256 Route 179; 602-284-9355), **Village of Oak Creek Country Club** (690 Bell Rock Boulevard, Sedona; 602-284-1660), **Canyon Mesa Country Club** (500 Jacks Canyon Road, Sedona; 284-2176), **Poco Diablo Resort** (1752 Route 179, Sedona; 602-282-7333) and **Antelope Hills Golf Course** (19 Club House Drive, Prescott; 602-445-0583).

Golf is an important pastime in the resort communities along the Colorado River. Try the **Riverview Golf Club** (2000 East Ramar Road, Bullhead City; 602-763-1818), **Chaparral Country Club** (1260 East Mohave Drive, Bullhead City; 602-758-3939), **Emerald Lake Golf Course** (1155 South Casino Drive, Laughlin; 602-298-0061), **Queen's Bay Golf Course** (1477 Queens Bay Road, Lake Havasu; 602-855-4777), **London Bridge Golf Club** (2400 Clubhouse Drive, Lake Havasu; 602-855-2719), **Valle Vista Country Club & Golf Course** (9686 Concho Drive, Kingman; 602-757-8744) and **Kingman Municipal Golf Course** (1001 East Gates Road, Kingman; 602-753-6593).

TENNIS

Public tennis courts in Flagstaff are located in **Thorpe Park** (Toltec Street) and **Bushmaster Park** (Lockett Road). Sedona has no public tennis courts. For a fee, courts are available to the public at the **Sedona Racquet Club** (West Route 89A; 602-282-4197) and **Poco Diablo Resort** (1752 Route 179; 602-282-7333). In Prescott, tennis courts are open to the public during the summer months at **Yavapai College** (1100 East Sheldon Street; 602-445-7300), **Prescott High School** (146 South Granite Street; 602-445-5400) and **Ken Lindley Field** (East Gurley Street at Arizona Street).

Tennis courts are available for a fee in Lake Havasu City at **London Bridge Racquet and Fitness Center** (1425 McCulloch Boulevard; 602-855-6274).

BICYCLING

At the South Rim of the **Grand Canyon**, the **West Rim Drive** is closed to private motor vehicles during the summer months but open to bicycles. This fairly level route, 16 miles round-trip, makes for a spectacular cycling tour.

Although trails within the national park are closed to bicycles, **Kaibab National Forest** surrounding the park on both the North and South Rims offers a wealth of mountain biking possibilities. The forest areas adjoining Grand Canyon National Park are laced with old logging roads and the relatively flat terrain makes for low-stress riding. One ride the National Forest Service recommends in the vicinity of the South Rim is the **Coconino Rim Trail**, which starts near Grandview Point and continues for more than ten miles north through ponderosa woods.

For other suggestions, stop in at the Tusayan Ranger Station just outside the South Rim entrance or the National Forest Information Booth at Jacob Lake or contact Kaibab National Forest Headquarter (800 South 6th Street, Williams, AZ 86046; 602-635-2681).

Toward the west end of the Grand Canyon on its North Rim, visitors to **Toroweap Point** will find endless mountain biking opportunities along the hundreds of miles of remote, unpaved roads in the Arizona Strip.

Flagstaff has about eight miles of paved trails in its **Urban Trail System and Bikeways System**, linking the Northern Arizona University campus, the downtown area and Lowell Observatory. Maps and information on the trail system are available upon request from the **City Planning Office** (211 West Aspen Street; 602-779-7632).

Outside the city, a popular route for all-day bike touring is the 36-mile paved loop road through Sunset Crater and Wupatki national monuments, starting at the turnoff from Route 89 about ten miles northeast of town.

For mountain bikers, several unpaved primitive roads lead deeper into the San Francisco Volcano Field in **Coconino National Forest**. Check out the forest road that leads to the base of Colton Crater and SP Crater. For complete information, contact the **Peaks Ranger Station** (5075 North Route 89; 602-526-0866).

The **Flagstaff Nordic Center** (Route 180; 602-774-6216), 14 miles north of Flagstaff in Coconino National Forest, opens its extensive trail system to mountain bikers from mid-May through September and offers mountain bike and helmet rentals.

The same network of unpaved back roads that makes the **Red Rock Country** around Sedona such a popular area for four-wheel-drive touring is also ideal for mountain biking. Get a map from one of the local bike shops and try the dirt roads leading from Soldier Pass Road to the Seven Sacred Pools or the Devil's Kitchen. Or follow the Broken Arrow Jeep Trail east from Route 179 to Submarine Rock. The Schnebly Hill Road climbs all the way north to Flagstaff, paralleling the Oak Creek Canyon Highway. The upper part of the road is steep, winding and very rough, but the lower part, through Bear Wallow Canyon, makes for a beautiful mountain biking excursion.

BIKE RENTALS   In Flagstaff, you can rent mountain bikes and get trail information at **Absolute Bikes** (18 North San Francisco Street; 602-779-5969), **Cosmic Cycles** (113 South San Francisco Street; 602-779-1092) or **Mountain Sports** (1800 South Milton Road; 602-779-5156). In Sedona, you'll find trail information and bike rentals at **Mountain Bike Heaven** (1449 West Route 89A; 602-282-1312) and **Canyon Country Mountain Bikes** (inside Sedona Sports at 245 North Route 89A; 602-282-6985).

HIKING

GRAND CANYON AREA TRAILS   The ultimate hiking experience in Grand Canyon National Park—and perhaps in the entire Southwest—is an expedition from either rim to the bottom of the canyon and back. With an elevation change of 4800 feet from the South Rim to the river, or 5800 feet from the North Rim, the hike is as ambitious as an ascent of a major Rocky Mountain peak, except that the greatest effort is required in the last miles of the climb out, when leg muscles may already be sore from the long downhill trek. Strenuous as it may be, hiking the Grand Canyon is an experience sure to stay vivid for a lifetime.

Though some people claim to have done it, hiking round-trip from the rim to river level and back in a single day is a monumental feat that takes from 16 to 18 hours. Most hikers who plan to go the whole way will want to plan at least two, preferably three, days for the trip. A wilderness permit, required for any overnight trip into the park back country, can be obtained free of charge at the visitor center on either rim.

The main trail into the canyon from the North Rim is the **North Kaibab Trail** (14.2 miles). The trail starts from the trailhead two miles north of Grand Canyon Lodge and descends abruptly down Roaring Springs Canyon for almost five miles to Bright Angel Creek. This is the steepest part of the trip. Where the trail reaches the creek, there are several swimming holes, a good destination for a one-day round trip. The trail then follows the creek all the way to Phantom Ranch at the bottom of the canyon. Park rangers recommend that hikers allow a full day to hike from the rim to the ranch and two days to climb back to the rim, stopping overnight at Cottonwood Camp, the midway point. Because of heavy snows on the rim, the trail is only open from mid-May through mid-October.

The **Bright Angel Trail** (7.8 miles to the river or 9.3 miles to Phantom Ranch), the most popular trail in the canyon, starts at Grand Canyon Village on the South Rim, near the mule corral. It has the most developed facilities, including resthouses with emergency telephones along the upper part of the trail and a ranger station, water and a campground midway down at Indian Garden where the Havasupai Indians used to grow crops. A one-day round-trip hike will take you along a ridgeline to Plateau Point, overlooking the Colorado River from 1300 feet above, just before the final steep descent. Allow about five hours to hike from the rim down to the river and about ten hours to climb back up. A lot of hikers use this trail, as do daily mule trails—not the route to take if you seek solitude.

Another major trail from the South Rim is the **South Kaibab Trail** (6.4 miles to Phantom Ranch), which starts from the trailhead on East Rim Drive, four-and-a-half miles from Grand Canyon Village. The shortest of the main trails into the canyon, it is also the steepest, and due to lack of water and shade along the route, it is not recommended during the summer months.

Several less-used trails also descend from the South Rim. All of them intersect the **Tonto Trail** (92 miles), which runs along the edge of the inner gorge about 1300 feet above river level for the length of the Grand Canyon. The **Grandview Trail** (3 miles), an old mine access route that starts at Grand-view Point on East Rim Drive, goes down to Horseshoe Mesa where it joins a loop of the Tonto Trail that circles the mesa, passing ruins of an old copper mine. There is a primitive campground on the mesa.

The **Hermit Trail** (8.5 miles) begins at Hermit's Rest at the end of West Rim Drive and descends to join the Tonto Trail. Branching off from the Dripping Springs Trail, which also starts at Hermit's Rest, the **Boucher Trail** (11 miles) also goes down to join the Tonto Trail and is considered one of the most difficult hiking trails in the park. Ask for details at the rangers' counter in the South Rim visitor center.

Without descending below the canyon rim, hikers can choose from a variety of trails ranging from short scenic walks to all-day hikes. On the North Rim, the easy, paved, handicapped-accessible **Transept Trail** (2 miles) runs between the campground and the lodge, then continues gradually downward to Bright Angel Point, which affords the best view of the Bright Angel Trail down into the canyon.

The **Uncle Jim Trail** (2.5 miles) starts at the same trailhead as the Roaring Springs Canyon fork of the Bright Angel Trail, two miles north of the lodge. It circles through the ponderosa woods to an overlook, Uncle Jim Point.

The **Ken Patrick Trail** (10 miles) forks off the Uncle Jim Trail, continuing straight as the shorter trail turns south, and eventually reaches a remote point on the rim where it descends to follow Bright Angel Creek and eventually joins the Bright Angel Trail. It is possible to make a strenuous, all-day 15-mile loop trip of the Ken Patrick Trail and the upper portion of the Bright Angel Trail.

Another quiet North Rim trail that leads through the forest to a remote canyon viewpoint is the **Widforss Trail** (5 miles), named after artist Gunnar Widforss, who painted landscapes in the national parks during the 1920s. The viewpoint overlooks a side canyon known as Haunted Canyon.

On the South Rim, the paved, handicapped-accessible **Rim Trail** (1.5 miles) goes between the Kolb Studio at the west side of Grand Canyon Village and the Yavapai Museum. A one-third-mile spur links the Rim Trail with the visitor center. At each end of the designated Rim Trail, the pavement ends but unofficial trails continue for several more miles, ending at Hopi Point near the Powell Memorial on West Rim Drive and at Yaki Point, the trailhead for the South Kaibab Trail, on East Rim Drive.

Visitors to remote Toroweap Point on the North Rim may wish to try the **Lava Falls Trail** (★) (2 miles), which begins as a jeep road midway between the old ranger station and the point. Although this trail is not long, it is rocky, edgy and very steep, descending 2500 feet to the Colorado River and the "falls"—actually a furious stretch of white water formed when lava spilled into the river. Allow all day for the round-trip hike and do not attempt it during the hot months.

FLAGSTAFF AREA TRAILS   Just north of Flagstaff rise the San Francisco Peaks, the highest in Arizona. Numerous trails start from Mount Elden and Schultz Pass roads, which branch off Route 180 to the right a short distance past the Museum of Northern Arizona. Other trailheads are located in Flagstaff at Buffalo Park on Cedar Avenue and near the Peaks Ranger Station on Route 89.

From the ranger station, the **Elden Lookout Trail** (1.5 miles) climbs by switchbacks up the east face of 9299-foot Mount Elden, with an elevation gain of 2400 feet and, waiting to reward you at the top, a spectacular view of the city and the volcano fields around Sunset Crater.

Fatman's Loop Trail (1 mile), branching off Elden Lookout Trail for a shorter hike with a 1600-foot elevation gain, also offers a good view of Flagstaff.

From the Buffalo Park trailhead, the **Oldham Trail** (3 miles) ascends the west face to the top of Mount Elden. The longest trail on the mountain, this is a gentler climb. The Oldham Trail intersects Mount Elden Road three times, making it possible to take a shorter hike on only the higher part of the trail. **Pipeline Trail** (1.5 miles) links the lower parts of the Oldham and Elden Lookout trails along the northern city limit of Flagstaff, allowing either a short hike on the edge of town or a long, all-day loop trip up one side of the mountain and down the other.

Perhaps the most unusual of many hiking options in the strange volcanic landscape around the base of the San Francisco Peaks is on **Red Mountain** (★), 33 miles north of Flagstaff off Route 180. A gap in the base of this thousand-foot-high volcanic cone lets you follow the **Red Mountain Trail** (1 mile) from the end of the national forest access road straight into the crater without climbing. Not often visited by tourists, this is a great place to explore with older children.

For maps and detailed hiking information on these and many other trails in Coconino National Forest, contact the **Peaks Ranger Station** (5075 North Route 89; 602-526-0866).

SEDONA/PRESCOTT AREA TRAILS While every visitor to Flagstaff or Sedona drives through often-crowded Oak Creek Canyon, one of central Arizona's "must-see" spots, few stop to explore the canyon's west fork, a narrow canyon with sheer walls hundreds feet high in places, which is only accessible on foot. The **West Fork Trail** (7 miles) starts at a chained-off road ten miles north of Sedona. There is a small parking area nearby, often full. The first three miles of the fairly level trail, which pass through a protected "research natural area," are heavily used and easy to hike. Farther up, the trail becomes less distinct and requires fording the creek repeatedly.

A very popular hiking spot in the Red Rock Country is Boynton Canyon, one of Sedona's four "Vortex" areas. According to Sedona's New Age community, Boynton Canyon is the most powerful of the Vortices, emanating an electromagnetic yin/yang psychic energy that can be felt for miles around. Whether you believe in such things or not, it is undeniably beautiful. From the trailhead on Boynton Pass Road—a continuation of Dry Creek Road, which leaves Route 89A in West Sedona—the nearly level **Boynton Canyon Trail** (1.5 miles) goes up the canyon through woods and among redrock formations. There are several small, ancient Sinagua Indian cliff dwellings in the canyon.

A right turn from Dry Creek Road on the way to Boynton Pass will put you on unpaved Sterling Canyon Road, which is rough enough in spots that drivers of low-clearance vehicles may want to think twice before proceeding. From this road, the **Devil's Bridge Trail** (1 mile) climbs gradually through piñon and juniper country to a long red sandstone arch with a magnificent view of the surrounding canyonlands. You can walk to the top of the arch. Three miles further, at the end of Dry Creek Road, is the trailhead for the **Vultee Arch Trail** (2 miles), which follows Sterling Canyon to another natural bridge.

There are many hiking trails in the national forest around Prescott. One of the most popular is the **Thumb Butte Trail** (1.7 miles), a loop trip that goes up a saddle west of town, through oak and piñon woods, offering good views of Prescott and Granite Dells. The trail starts from Thumb Butte Park. To get there, go west on Thumb Butte Road, an extension of Gurley Street.

More ambitious hikers may wish to explore the **Granite Mountain Wilderness**. Of its several trails, the one that goes to the summit of the 7125-foot mountain is **Granite Mountain Trail** (3.7 miles), a beautiful all-day hike with an elevation gain of 1500 feet. For information on this and other trails in the area, contact the Prescott National Forest—Bradshaw District ranger station just east of Prescott at 2230 East Route 69; 602-445-7253.

COLORADO RIVER AREA TRAILS **Hualapai Mountain Park**, 14 miles southeast of Kingman, has an extensive network of hiking trails from a single trailhead through piñon, oak, aspen and ponderosa forest teeming with bird and animal life. Six interconnecting trails branch from the **Aspen**

Springs Trail (1 mile) to let you custom-design your own hike, whether you want to take an easy walk to **Stonestep Lookout** (.5 mile) or a more ambitious hike to the summit of **Aspen Peak** (2.5 miles with a 3200-foot elevation gain) or **Hayden Peak** (2.75 miles with a 3400-foot elevation gain). The Aspen Springs Trail can be combined with the **Potato Patch Loop** (2 miles) for a great five-mile loop trip.

The **Mohave Sunset Walking Trail** in Lake Havasu State Park winds for two miles between Windsor Beach and Crystal Beach through a variety of terrains from lowlands dense with salt cedar to ridgelines commanding beautiful views of the lake. Signs along the sometimes hilly trail identify common Mohave Desert plant life.

A wonderful, little-known wintertime hike in the vicinity of Bullhead City/Laughlin is **Grapevine Canyon** (★) (1 mile). There is no clearly defined trail, but you will have no trouble tracing the tracks of other hikers up the wash along the canyon floor. Some rock scrambling is involved. At the mouth of the canyon are many petroglyphs that nomadic Native Americans scratched into the sandstone with their atl-atls, or throwing sticks, an estimated 1200 years ago. Farther up the canyon, a thin waterfall flows year-round. The presence of water attracts nocturnal wildlife, and you may see tracks of badgers, skunks, desert bighorn sheep and even mountain lions. The wild grapes that grow here give the canyon its name. Grapevine Canyon is in Nevada, 13 miles west of the Bullhead City-Laughlin bridge on Route 163 and one-and-a-half miles in on the clearly marked, unpaved road to Christmas Tree Pass. There is a parking area near the mouth of the canyon.

Transportation

BY CAR

Except for the Grand Canyon North Rim, all destinations covered in this chapter are within an hour's drive of **Route 40**, the major interstate route through northern Arizona and northern New Mexico.

The Grand Canyon's North Rim is at the end of **Route 67**, which forks off of **Route 89A** at the resort village of Jacob Lake. It is more than 150 miles from the nearest interstate highway—**Route 15**, taking exit 15 north of St. George, Utah—but is within an easy morning's drive of either Zion National Park or Bryce Canyon National Park (see Chapter Nine: Southwestern Utah) or Lake Powell (see Chapter Ten: Southeastern Utah).

Although only 12 miles of straight-line distance separate them, the shortest driving distance between the North Rim and South Rim visitors areas of the Grand Canyon is 216 miles around the eastern end of the canyon via

Route 67, Route 89A, **Route 89** and **Route 64**, crossing the Colorado River at Navajo Bridge. The only other alternative for driving from rim to rim is to go by way of Las Vegas, Nevada—a trip of more than 500 miles.

From Route 40, eastbound motorists can reach Grand Canyon Village on the South Rim by exiting at Williams and driving 57 miles north on Route 64 and **Route 180**. Westbound travelers, leaving the interstate at Flagstaff, have a choice between the more direct way to Grand Canyon Village, 79 miles via Route 180, or the longer way, 105 miles via Route 89 and Route 64, which parallels the canyon rim for 25 miles. These routes combine perfectly into a spectacular loop trip from Flagstaff.

Another scenic loop trip from Flagstaff goes south on Route 89A, descending through Oak Creek Canyon to the trendy town of Sedona in the magnificent Red Rock Country, a distance of 26 slow miles. From Sedona, Route 89A continues for 58 more miles through the historic mining town of Jerome, with a steep climb over Cleopatra Hill, to Prescott, the old territorial capital. From there, a 51-mile drive on Route 89 returns travelers to interstate Route 40 at Ash Fork, about 55 miles west of Flagstaff.

On Arizona's "West Coast" along the lower Colorado River, the Bullhead City-Laughlin resort area is reached by exiting Route 40 at Kingman and driving 26 miles on **Route 68** through the most starkly stunning scenery in the Mohave Desert, or by exiting Route 40 at Topock, 12 miles east of Needles, California, and driving 35 miles north on **Route 95**. The other major Colorado River resort, Lake Havasu City, is 21 miles south of Route 40 on Route 95. A fascinating back-road route connecting Route 95 with Route 40 at Kingman goes through the historic gold-mining town of Oatman on its steep climb over Sitgreaves Pass, a drive challenging enough to evoke amazement at the fact that this numberless road used to be part of Old Route 66, the main highway across the Southwest to Los Angeles in the days before the interstate was built.

BY AIR

Flights can be booked from most major cities to **Grand Canyon Airport**, which is located in Tusayan just outside the south entrance to the national park. America West Airlines services this stop, as do several smaller commuter airlines, such as Air Nevada, Air Vegas and National Executive Airlines. A shuttle service runs hourly between the airport and Grand Canyon Village.

Air Sedona provides commuter service between the **Sedona Airport** and Phoenix.

Mesa Airlines serves the **Bullhead City-Laughlin Airport, Mohave County Airport** in Kingman and the **Lake Havasu City Airport**. States-West Airlines also provides service to Bullhead City and Lake Havasu City.

BY BUS

Navajo-Hopi Xpress (399 South Malpais Lane, Flagstaff; 602-774-5003) provides bus service to the Grand Canyon South Rim, as well as Flagstaff, Sedona, Williams and Phoenix. **Trans Canyon Shuttle** (Grand Canyon; 602-638-2820) operates a daily shuttle bus service between the two rims of Grand Canyon National Park.

Greyhound/Trailways Bus Lines stops at the bus terminals in Flagstaff (399 South Malpais Lane; 602-774-4573), Prescott (820 East Sheldon Street; 602-445-54770), Kingman (303 Metcalf Road; 602-753-2522) and Bullhead City (1010 Route 95; 602-754-4655).

BY TRAIN

Amtrak's "Southwest Chief" (1 East Santa Fe Avenue, Flagstaff; 800-872-7245) serves Flagstaff and Kingman daily on its route between Chicago and Los Angeles. The westbound passenger train stops in Flagstaff late in the evening, so arriving passengers will want to make hotel reservations in advance with a deposit to hold the room late. Amtrak offers a complimentary shuttle bus service to the Grand Canyon for its Flagstaff passengers.

CAR RENTALS

Rental cars available at the Grand Canyon Airport are **Budget Car Rental** (602-638-9360) and **Dollar Rent A Car** (602-638-2625).

Flagstaff has about a dozen car-rental agencies, most of them located at the Flagstaff Municipal Airport. Among the airport concessions are **Avis Rent A Car** (602-774-8421), **Budget Car Rental** (602-779-0306) and **Hertz Rent A Car** (602-774-4452). Downtown at the corner of Humphreys (Route 180 North) and Aspen streets, more convenient for those arriving by train or bus, are **Sears Rent A Car** (602-774-1879) and a second **Budget Car Rental** (602-774-2763). **Admiral Car Rental** (602-774-7394), located in the lobby of the University Inn, will accept a cash deposit in lieu of a credit card. Also in Flagstaff is an office of **Cruise America** (824 West Route 66; 602-774-4797), a nationwide motorhome rental agency.

At the Sedona Airport, rentals are available from **Budget Car Rental** (602-282-4602).

Prescott Municipal Airport's car-rental agencies include **Hertz Rent A Car** (602-776-1399), **Sears Rent A Car** (602-778-4282) and **Toyota Rent A Car** (602-778-3806). Jeeps and vans can be rented by the day or week at **York Motors** (602-445-4970).

TAXIS

Flagstaff has more than its share of taxi companies because many public transportation travelers stop there en route to the Grand Canyon. These cabs will take you anywhere in central Arizona at any time of day or night. Sedona? Phoenix? No problem. Call **City Taxi & Tours** (602-779-2867), **Northland Taxi** (602-526-2338), **Alpine Taxi Cab Co.** (602-526-4123), **B&D Taxi Service** (602-779-2867), **Flagstaff Taxi & Limousine** (602-774-1374) or **Dream Taxi** (602-774-2934). Shop and compare—rates vary.

Sedona's local taxi service is **Twenty Eight Four A Cab** (602-282-7891). Prescott has two taxi companies—**Ace City Cab** (602-445-1616) and **Mile High Taxi** (602-778-7728); both offer discounted rates for senior citizens and physically challenged persons.

TOURS

There are many ways to see the Grand Canyon but the classic tour is by **mule**. Trips range from one-day excursions as far as Plateau Point to two- and three-day trips to the bottom of the canyon, which cost several hundred dollars a person including meals and accommodations at Phantom Ranch. Mule trips depart from both the North Rim and the South Rim. Reservations must be made well ahead of time—as much as a year in advance for weekends, holidays and the summer months. For South Rim departures, contact **Grand Canyon National Park Lodges** (P.O. Box 699, Grand Canyon, AZ 86023; 602-638-2631). For North Rim departures, contact **Grand Canyon Trail Rides** (P.O. Box 128, Tropic, UT 84776; in summer, 602-638-2292; the rest of the year, 602-679-8665).

Many "flightseeing" tours offer spectacular eagle's-eye views of the Grand Canyon. Among the major air tour companies are **Grand Canyon Airlines** (P.O. Box 3038, Grand Canyon, AZ 86023; 602-638-2407), **Air Grand Canyon** (P.O. Box 3399, Grand Canyon, AZ 86023; 602-638-2686) and **Windrock Aviation** (P.O. Box 3125, Grand Canyon, AZ 86023; 602-638-9591), all of which operate from Grand Canyon Airport near Tusayan.

Even more thrilling—and more expensive—flights by **helicopter** are offered by **Papillon Grand Canyon Helicopters** (P.O. Box 455, Grand Canyon, AZ 86023; 602-638-2419), **Kenai Helicopters** (P.O. Box 1429, Grand Canyon, AZ 86023; 602-638-2412) and **AirStar Helicopters** (Grand Canyon Airport; 602-638-2622).

CHAPTER THREE

Northeastern Arizona

East of the Grand Canyon stretches a land of sandstone monuments and steepwalled canyons that turns vermillion by dawn or dusk, a land of foreign languages and ancient traditions, of sculptured mesas and broad rocky plateaus, of pine forests and high deserts. This is the heart of the Southwest's Indian Country.

It is home to the Navajos, the biggest American Indian tribe, and the Hopis, one of the most traditional. To them belongs the top northeastern third of Arizona, 150 miles in length and 200 miles across the state. In addition to this impressive expanse, Navajoland spills into New Mexico, Utah and Colorado.

Here, by horseback or jeep, on foot or in cars, visitors can explore the stark beauty of the land, delve into its uninterrupted centuries of history, then dine on mutton stew and crispy blue-corn piki bread. You can watch dances little changed in centuries or shop for a stunning array of crafts in Native American homes, galleries and trading posts dating back to the end of the Civil War. And here, in the pit houses, pueblos and cliff dwellings of people who have occupied this land for 12,000 years, are more remnants of prehistoric Native American life than anywhere else in the United States.

Five generations of archaeologists have sifted through ruins left by the region's dominant prehistoric culture, the Anasazi—Navajo for "ancient ones." None are more beautiful or haunting than Betatakin and Keet Seel at Navajo National Monument, 45 miles due north of today's Hopi mesas.

Hopi traditions today offer insights about life in those older cities. Traditional and independent, most villages are run by their religious chiefs. Each maintains an ancient, complex, year-long dance cycle tied to the renewal and fertility of the land they regard with reverence. As one Hopi leader put it, the land is "the Hopi's social security." Their multistoried architecture, much of it set within the protection of caves, has influenced many 20th century architects.

Surrounding the Hopis is Navajoland, the largest Indian reservation in the United States. At 26,000 square miles, it is twice the size of Israel. Unlike the village-dwelling Hopis, most of the 150,000 Navajos still live in far-flung family compounds—a house, a hogan, a trailer or two, near their corrals and fields. (Some clans still follow their livestock to suitable grazing lands as seasons change.)

This is both an arid, sun-baked desert and verdant forested land, all of it situated on the southeastern quarter of the Colorado Plateau. At elevations of 4500 to 8000 feet above sea level, summer temperatures average in the 80s. July through September is monsoon season, when clear skies suddenly fill with clouds that turn a thunderous lightning-streaked black. These localized, brief, intense summer rains bearing wondrous smells have been courted by Hopi rituals for centuries and are crucial to the survival of their farms.

For the modern adventurer, September and October can be the most alluring months to visit—uncrowded, less expensive, sunny, crisp, with splashes of fall color.

The Colorado Plateau is famous for its rainbow-colored canyons and monuments that have been cut by rivers and eroded by weather. Erosion's jewels here are Monument Valley on the Arizona-Utah border, a stunning pocket of towering red spires, bluffs and sand dunes, and Canyon de Chelly, a trio of red-rock canyons that form the heart of Navajo country.

At Navajoland's southernmost boundary, the world's densest, most colorful petrified logs dot Petrified Forest National Park. They're located amid bare hills that look like they were spray painted by a giant artist and aptly named the Painted Desert.

This mesmerizing geography serves as a backdrop to the region's riveting history. Navajos probably began arriving from the north a century or two before the Spaniards rode in from the south in the 1540s. The conquistadors brought horses, sheep, peaches, melons, guns and silversmithing—all of which would dramatically change the lives of the indigenous Indians. The Navajos had arrived in small groups, nomadic hunters, primitive compared to their Pueblo neighbors.

Cultural anthropologists now believe the turning point in Navajo history followed the Pueblo Indian Revolt of 1680 when all the village-dwelling Indians of the Southwest united to push the hated Spanish out of what is now New Mexico. When the Spaniards returned a dozen years later, heavily armed and promising slavery for unyielding villagers, many Pueblo people from the Rio Grande fled west to the canyons of Navajo country, intermarrying and living as neighbors for three-quarters of a century.

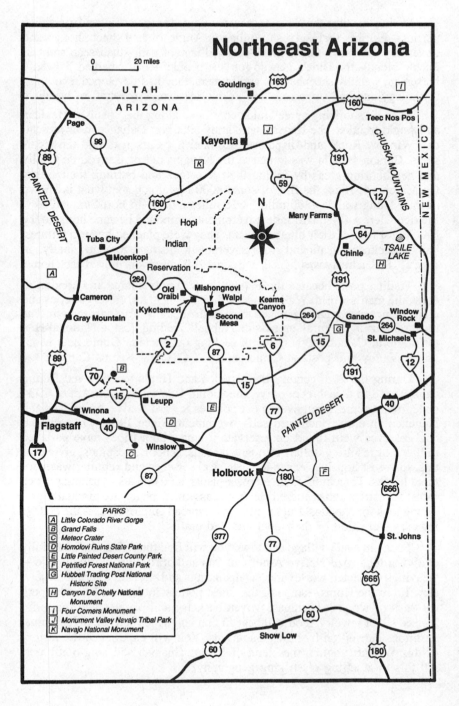

Northeast Arizona

0   20 miles

UTAH

ARIZONA

Gouldings [163]

Page

[160]

Teec Nos Pos

[98]

NEW MEXICO

[89]

Kayenta

[J]

PAINTED DESERT

[K]

[191]

CHUSKA MOUNTAINS

[59]

N

[12]

[160]

Hopi

Many Farms

Tuba City

Indian

[64]

Chinle

TSAILE LAKE

Moenkopi

Reservation

[191]

[H]

[264]

[A]

Old Oraibi

Mishongnovi

Cameron

Walpi

Keams Canyon

[264]

Window Rock

Kykotsmovi

Second Mesa

[G]

Ganado

Gray Mountain

[2]

[87]

[6]

[15]

St. Michaels

[264]

[89]

[15]

[191]

[12]

[70]

[B]

[15]

[15]

Leupp

[E]

[40]

Winona

[D]

[77]

PAINTED DESERT

Flagstaff

[40]

[17]

[C]

Winslow

Holbrook

[180]

[F]

[87]

[666]

PARKS

[A] *Little Colorado River Gorge*
[B] *Grand Falls*
[C] *Meteor Crater*
[D] *Homolovi Ruins State Park*
[E] *Little Painted Desert County Park*
[F] *Petrified Forest National Park*
[G] *Hubbell Trading Post National Historic Site*
[H] *Canyon De Chelly National Monument*
[I] *Four Corners Monument*
[J] *Monument Valley Navajo Tribal Park*
[K] *Navajo National Monument*

[377]

[77]

St. Johns

[666]

[60]

[60]

Show Low

[60]

[180]

During that time the Navajos grew in wealth due to their legendary raiding parties—helping themselves to Indian or Anglo-owned sheep, horses and slaves. By the late 1700s, a much-changed race of part Athabascan and part Pueblo blood—the Dineh, Navajo for "the people"—had emerged. Powerful horsemen, wealthy sheepherders and farmers, they had developed a complex mythology and had surpassed their Pueblo teachers at the craft of weaving.

Navajo "shopping spree" raids continued along the Spanish, Mexican and Anglo frontier. The United States army built Fort Defiance, near present-day Window Rock, and dispatched Colonel Kit Carson to end the incursions. Carson's tactic was to starve the Navajos out of Canyon de Chelly and neighboring areas by killing their livestock and burning their fields. On March 14, 1864, the first of some 8000 Navajos began what is known as their "long walk"—300 miles at 15 miles a day—to Fort Sumner, New Mexico. Here a 40-square-mile government compound became home to the Navajo for four of their bitterest years. They were plagued by crop failures, hunger, sickness, death and gross government mismanagement. Finally, on June 1, 1868, a treaty was signed, and some 7000 survivors moved back home.

Trading posts became the Indians' new supply source and conduit to the white man's world. While modern shopping centers, crafts galleries and convenience stores have replaced most of them, a few originals remain. The most famous is the rural, creek-side Hubbell Trading Post, a National Historic Site at Ganado. Others worth seeking out include Oljeto near Monument Valley and posts at Cameron, Tuba City and Keams Canyon.

During the 20th century the Navajos and Hopis have moved from a subsistence to a cash economy. The Indian Reorganization Act of 1934 ended overt repressive government policies toward Native Americans and launched an era of increased self-government. Since 1961, when oil and coal reserves were found on reservation lands, both tribes have parlayed millions of resulting dollars into paved roads, schools, hospitals, civic centers, low-cost housing, expanded electrical services and running water for more homes. Three mines, three power plants, a 60,000-acre farming project, forest industries and scattered electronic assembly plants are gradually providing jobs for Navajos. But the most widespread employment is the cottage industry—creation of their own arts and crafts.

Today in every village and town you will find the rich and wonderfully evolving legacy of Native American arts and crafts. From the Navajo—weavings respected worldwide, sandpaintings and silver and turquoise jewelry. From the Hopis—some of the finest pottery in the Southwest, superb carvings of wooden kachinas, woven basketry and plaques and masterful incised silver jewelry. You will hear Indian languages and see rich spiritual traditions carried on by new generations. You will experience the history of this Western region, the blend of Indian, Spanish and Anglo cultures. All this in a setting of striking geography.

Southern Navajo Country

Indian Country is a concept that barely does justice to the astonishing diversity of the southern Navajo realm. There is so much to see and do in this region, which also embraces the pastel realm of the Painted Desert, that you may be tempted to extend your stay. Ancient Anasazi ruins and colorful badlands are just a few of the highlights.

On the southwest corner of the Navajo Indian Reservation, during spring runoff—usually March and April—a detour off Route 40 brings you to the thundering, muddy **Grand Falls** of the Little Colorado River—plummeting 185 feet into the canyon of the Little Colorado River. A lava flow from Merriam Crater ten miles to the southwest created the falls about 100,000 years ago. Some years the falls are only a trickle, and even during the best years they dry up by May, resuming again briefly during abundant summer monsoons. It is wise to inquire in Winslow or Flagstaff about the level of the Little Colorado River before making the trip. To get there, turn off Route 40 either at Winona, 17 miles east of Flagstaff, or at the Leupp Junction (Route 99), ten miles west of Winslow to Route 15. Either way, ask at the turnoff for exact directions. The Winona route is the shortest from the highway—about 20 miles, the last eight unpaved.

Many locals contend the most colorful and dramatic concentration of Painted Desert hills in central Arizona is at **Little Painted Desert County Park (★)**, 13 miles northwest of Winslow on Route 87. A two-mile scenic rim drive, a hiking trail and picnic tables overlook this vast basin where clay and silt deposited by ancient rivers have eroded into gray, red, purple, ochre and white striped badlands—300 feet to 400 feet tall. Colors are most vivid at dawn and dusk.

The scattered broken pottery, rock drawings and crumbling walls speak with quiet eloquence of an ancient past at **Homolovi Ruins State Park** (Route 87; 602-289-4106) three miles east of Winslow. The park contains six major 14th-century pueblos of 40 to 1000 rooms, with over 300 identified archeological sites, a visitor center and museum where interpretive programs are presented. Nine miles of paved roads and a mile of hiking trails lead to the two largest village ruins, inhabited between 1150 and 1450 A.D. The park also includes petroglyphs and a pithouse village dating from 600 to 900 A.D. Hopis believe this was home to their ancestors just before they migrated north to today's mesas. They still consider the ruins—located on both sides of the Little Colorado River—sacred and leave *pahos* (prayer feathers) for the spirits. (At press time the park service hoped to move its visitor center from 523 West 2nd Street in Winslow to the park entrance.)

Winslow, the hub of Northeastern Arizona, is a railroad town and was an early trade center. Its current history goes back to Mormon pioneers who arrived in 1876 and built a small rock fort known as Brigham City, as well as a few other small settlements. The town grew, and soon a water system, stores and an opera house appeared, along with a school, saloons and, that harbinger of all frontier civilizations, sidewalks. The Aztec Land and Cattle Company purchased a million acres of land from the railroad in the late 1800s and thousands of head of cattle were brought in to be handled by local cowboys. The town was incorporated in 1900. For information contact **Winslow Chamber of Commerce** (300 West North Road; 602-289-2434).

The **Old Trail Museum** (212 Kinsley Avenue; 602-289-5861) houses changing exhibits related to Winslow's history, including Native American and pioneering artifacts.

To the east of Winslow on Route 40 you'll come to **Holbrook**. Headquarters for the Sitgreaves National Forest, Holbrook was named for H. R. Holbrook, first engineer of the Atlantic and Pacific Railroad, forerunner of the Santa Fe Line. It was once a tough cowboy town—the Aztec Land and Cattle Company drove cattle here, a rough-and-tough bunch that shot up everything and earned the name the Hashknife Posse. There are probably more people still wearing ten-gallon hats and cowboy boots here than in any other small town in the West.

The **Courthouse Museum** (100 East Arizona Street; 602-524-6558) is located in the historic Navajo County Courthouse, which flourished from 1898 until 1976. It's now a museum focusing on Holbrook's past, including the town's original one-piece iron jail. It also houses the Holbrook Tourism Information Center.

The signs advertising sale of "gems" and "petrified wood" on every other block in Holbrook offers a good clue that **Petrified Forest National Park** (602-524-6228) can't be far away. Entrances at the northern and southern gateways to this park are located 18 miles east of Holbrook—the northern entrance on Route 40, the southern one on Route 180. Either one launches you on the park's 28-mile scenic drive. Frequent pullouts let you walk amid two stunning marvels of nature. The park lies within the colorful, heavily eroded mudstone and siltstone known as the Painted Desert. The southern third is also home to the world's densest concentration of petrified forest— ancient logs that crystallized 200 million years ago now lie strewn along the surface; others yet unseen lie buried in 300 feet of silt.

Continue on the scenic drive from the Route 40 (north) entrance to the **Painted Desert Visitor Center** (602-524-6228). Here you'll see a 17-minute film on the mysteries of the making of the forest—silica crystals replacing wood cells in the cone-bearing trees—aricarioxylon pine. The center also offers cafeteria and gift-shop amenities.

North of Route 40, eight overlooks highlight different Painted Desert panoramas. Here you'll see bands of red, white and pink—the effect of the sun reflecting on mudstone and siltstone stained by iron, magnesium and other minerals. Colors are the most intense nearest sunrise, sunset or on cloudy days.

The **Painted Desert Inn Museum** (three miles north of the visitor center at Kachina Point on the scenic drive; 602-524-2550) is a 1930s pueblo-style building, once a Fred Harvey inn. Detailed hand-carved wood and tin furnishings were made by the Civilian Conservation Corps. Murals painted by the late Hopi artist Fred Kabotie depict scenes of Hopi life: a January buffalo dance to ensure return of buffalo each spring, the journey of two Hopis to Zuni lands to gather salt.

South of Route 40 on the scenic drive, the park's midsection contains prehistoric sites of the Anasazi, Sinagua and Mogollon peoples dating from 300 A.D. to 1400 A.D. Scientists have discovered petroglyphs here used as solar calendars. A trail at Puerco Indian Ruins, the first pullout south of Route 40, leads through Anasazi ruins occupied until about 1400 A.D. A few excavated rooms are partially restored, and an overlook with telescopes gives views of **Newspaper Rock**, a sandstone block covered with petroglyphs.

The first petrified wood occurs at Blue Mesa, where a trail leads through dramatic towering hills. The southern third of the park holds the greatest concentration of petrified logs. At **Jasper Forest Overlook** you'll see a petrified log jam, some logs complete with root systems indicating they had grown nearby. A trail at Crystal Forest leads you close to dense pockets of logs, many over 100-feet long and a foot or two in diameter. In 1886, on a $10 bet, a daring cowboy rode his steed across a treacherous divide spanned by petrified Long Log, now shored up with cement.

At **Rainbow Forest Museum** (near the park's southern entrance; 602-524-6822) photographs, drawings and samples tell the story of the area's geologic and human history. Outside, the half-mile long Giant Logs trail leads past enormous rainbow-hued trees. The scenic drive ends two miles farther south at Route 180.

Adjacent to Petrified Forest National Park's south entrance is a 6500-acre privately owned area where visitors, for a modest fee, can legally collect their own specimens of multicolored fossilized wood. Check in at **Petrified Forest Trading Post** (★) (on Route 180, 19 miles southeast of Holbrook; 602-524-3470) for a map to locate areas where the wood abounds. Here, too, you can rent hammer, chisel and carrying bags. Popular with commercial petrified-wood and gem buffs, some 200,000 pounds are collected here annually.

SOUTHERN NAVAJO COUNTRY HOTELS

The top two hotels in Winslow are both Best Westerns. The two-story **Adobe Inn** (1701 North Park Drive; 602-289-7638) has 72 rooms, each decorated in contemporary fashion. You'll find a café and an indoor pool on the premises. **Town House Lodge** (West Route 66; 602-289-4611) has 68 rooms with modern furnishings and a guest laundry. Both moderate.

Fifteen dazzling white stucco wigwams, the sort of kitsch old Route 66 was famous for, are found in Holbrook. They make up one of the world's most novel motels, and for budget prices yet! **Wigwam Motel and Curios** (811 West Hopi Drive, 602-524-3048) "is the funnest place I've ever slept," insisted our 3-year-old neighbor. We couldn't argue. Built in 1950 by Chester Lewis, (six other cities had wigwam motels of similar design; only one other survives), his children and grandchildren restored these and still operate them. Inside each, matching red-plaid curtains and bedspreads adorn original handmade hickory furniture. Scenes from Tony Hillerman's *Dark Wind* were filmed here in 1990. There's no extra charge for lulling vibrations as trains rumble by in the night.

For a more traditional resting spot there's the **Adobe Inn** (615 West Hopi Drive, Holbrook; 602-524-3948), a two-story, 54-room Best Western that has modern furnishings and a pool. Budget.

Another Best Western motel is the **Arizonian Inn** (2508 East Navajo Boulevard, Holbrook; 602-524-2611) with 70 rooms, contemporary furnishings and a pool. Moderate.

SOUTHERN NAVAJO COUNTRY RESTAURANTS

Dining out in the Southern Navajo Reservation area is not a very exciting experience. You can take a counter seat on one of the swivel stools or settle into a booth at **Falcon Restaurant** (1113 East 3rd Street, Winslow; 602-289-2342) where the menu includes steaks, chicken, roast turkey and seafood. This brown stucco establishment also features the only Greek mural we found in Navajo country. Moderate.

Celebrated in newspapers ranging from New York to San Francisco, the **Casa Blanca Café** (1201 East 2nd Street, Winslow; 602-289-4191) is known for its tacos, chimichangas, cheese crisps and burgers. Choose between booth and table seating at this ceramic-tiled establishment where cactus baskets grace the walls. The dining room is cooled by Casablanca fans but, alas, there's no trace of Bogie.

At **Gabrielle's Pancake and Steak House** (918 East 2nd Street, Winslow; 602-289-2508) photos of the Painted Desert and a quartet of pancake shaped clocks add a decorative touch. Inside this shake-shingle coffee shop you can enjoy burgundy booth or counter seating and dine on steaks, seafood and homemade pies. Moderate.

In Holbrook, **Aguilera's Restaurant** (200 Navajo Boulevard; 602-524-3806) serves huge portions of Mexican and American specialties in a small, carpeted dining room decorated with pictures of roaming buffalo and bulls. This adobe colored establishment is cooled by ceiling fans. Moderate.

Rock walls add an earthy note to **The Plainsman** (1001 West Hopi Drive, Holbrook; 602-524-3345). For casual dining try the coffee shop where there's booth seating. Enjoy meals such as liver and onions, veal cutlet and turkey sandwiches. The dining room is a favorite of the local Chamber of Commerce which meets here monthly. Popular items include châteaubriand, prime rib, frogs' legs and grilled trout. Moderate.

The **Roadrunner Café** (1501 East Navajo Boulevard, Holbrook; 602-524-2787) offers everything from grilled-cheese sandwiches to pot roast and steaks. The carpeted dining room has table and booth seating. Plants and wildflower photos bring the Southwest indoors. Budget to moderate.

SOUTHERN NAVAJO COUNTRY SHOPPING

Founded in 1903, **Bruchman's Gallery** (113 West 2nd Street, Winslow; 602-289-3831) features Indian art and handicrafts—fetishes, Hopi kachina dolls, Navajo jewelry, drums, baskets, wallhangings, saddle blankets, baskets and rare pottery.

Linda's Indian Arts and Crafts (405 Navajo Boulevard, Holbrook; 602-524-2500) is a small shop but offers a good selection of Native American jewelry and crafts.

For the biggest selection of top-of-the-line Indian arts and crafts, **McGee's Beyond Native Tradition** (2114 East Navajo Boulevard, Holbrook; 602-524-1977) sells everything from Hopi jewelry to Navajo blankets and drums.

Nakai Indian Cultural Trade Center (357 Navajo Boulevard, Holbrook; 602-524-2329), in business for over 25 years, also features top-quality Indian products as well as jewelry made on the premises.

More Native American jewelry, kachinas, baskets and crafts can be found at **Tribal Treasure** (1601 Navajo Boulevard, Holbrook; 602-524-2847), over 20 years in business.

Painted Desert Visitor Center Gift Shop (Route 40 entrance to the Petrified Forest National Park; 602-524-6228) sells polished and natural petrified wood, from tiny stones to great slabs, plus other gems as well as Southwest Indian crafts and curios.

In the basement of the restored pink 1930s lodge, **Painted Desert Inn Shop** (602-524-2550) has a bookstore and gift shop selling a good selection of books on the Southwest, plus a variety of Indian crafts and curios.

Fred Harvey Curios and Fountain (by the Route 180 entrance to Petrified Forest National Park; 602-524-6822) also sells a variety of petrified wood, gems, geodes and other treasures to rockhounders, plus some Southwestern Indian crafts and curios.

Behind general merchandise and video displays at **R. B. Burnham & Co. Trading Post** (Route 666, at Route 40 in Sanders; 602-688-2777) is one room lined with naturally dyed yarns. Behind that room is a shrine to

Hopi and Navajo crafts. Assembled with much care, and for sale, are gallery-quality Navajo rugs, carved furniture upholstered in Navajo weavings, plus the whole array of Indian arts and crafts. It's worth a stop just to look!

SOUTHERN NAVAJO COUNTRY NIGHTLIFE

It's pretty quiet out this way. For nightlife the choices are limited.

The **Tumbleweed Lounge** (1400 East 3rd Street; 602-289-5213) is the newest nightspot in Winslow and draws the biggest crowds, with guitars and country-and-western poetry put to music—Who's going to mend my broken heart?

All the action happens at **Young's Corral Bar** (865 East Navajo Boulevard, Holbrook; 602-524-1875) where weekends are filled with the sounds of live country-and-western music.

SOUTHERN NAVAJO COUNTRY PARKS

Little Painted Desert County Park—One of the nicest, most colorful chunks of the 40-mile-long Painted Desert is concentrated in this 900-acre park, at 5500-foot elevation near the southern boundary of the Navajo Indian Reservation north of Winslow. Large 300- to 400-foot-tall fragile mounds of mud slate in grays, reds, purples and yellows tend to change in color intensity throughout the day. Colors are most vivid at dawn and dusk.

Facilities: Two-mile rim drive, an overlook, two picnic ramadas, restrooms (no water). A strenuous, one-mile hiking trail descends some 500 feet into the mounds, from which you can explore on your own; information, 602-524-6161.

Getting there: Located 15 miles north of Winslow on Route 87.

McHood Park Clear Creek Reservoir—Once an important water source for Winslow, the deep canyon five miles from town is now a favorite boating, swimming and picnic area.

Facilities: Picnic area, restrooms, showers, boat ramp; information, 602-289-3082.

Camping: There are 11 sites (3 with RV hookups); $6 per night, $7 for hookups.

Getting there: Take Route 87 south to Route 99, and turn left.

Cholla Lake Park—One of the larger bodies of water in northeastern Arizona, the park is adjacent to a power station. This manmade lake offers swimming, boating, fishing and picnicking.

Facilities: Picnic tables, restrooms, showers, boat ramp; groceries and restaurants are located two miles away in Joseph City; information, 602-288-3717.

Camping: There are 20 sites (8 with RV hookups); $7 per night for standard sites, $10 for hookups. A group cam is also available.

Getting there: Take Route 40 east from Winslow for about 20 miles to Exit 274, then follow the power plant road to the park.

Petrified Forest National Park—Straddling Route 40 and abutting the southern boundary of the Navajo Indian Reservation, this 28-mile-long (north to south) park features rolling badlands of the Painted Desert—mainly red-hued hills—north of Route 40. South of Route 40 lies the densest concentration of petrified prehistoric forests in the world. Each section has a wilderness area.

Facilities: At each entrance is a visitor center with restaurant, restrooms and museum. A 28-mile road leads visitors past nine Painted Desert vistas and 13 Petrified Forest stops; information, 602-524-6228.

Camping: Back country only; get permit at visitor centers.

Getting there: Both park entrances are 18 miles east of Holbrook: the northernmost on Route 40, the southern one on Route 180.

Western Navajo Country

The Western Navajo Reservation, bordering such wonders as the Grand Canyon National Park and Lake Powell National Recreation Area, is a land of great beauty and ancient sights. President William McKinley signed an order January 8, 1900, deeding these one-and-a-half-million acres of land to the Navajos who had migrated westward 32 years earlier after outgrowing their original reserve. Where Routes 89 and 64 meet, the Navajos operate **Cameron Visitor Center** (602-679-2303), offering advice and brochures on tribal attractions.

Follow Route 64 west ten miles to an unpaved spur road and walk a few hundred feet to a dramatic overlook. At the bottom of hundreds of feet of sheer canyon walls is a muddy ribbon of the Little Colorado River. Upper limestone cliffs, layered like flapjack stacks, contrast with massive sandstone slabs below, evidence of a shallow sea 250 million years ago. This **Grand Canyon of the Little Colorado Gorge Tribal Park** is owned by the Navajos. From Memorial Day through Labor Day a festive air reigns as Indians set up their flag and banner-bedecked crafts booths in the parking area.

A mile north of the visitor center is **Cameron Trading Post, Motel and Restaurant** (Route 89; 602-679-2231), a stone pueblo-style complex built in 1916 by Hopis and Navajos, and recently restored. Long known as an oasis of hospitality, it's located by Tanner's Crossing, the last place wagons could cross the Little Colorado before the river enters gorges too deep to navigate. Quicksand pockets made this one especially treacherous.

Today this mini-city is a great place to people watch: old Navajo women in traditional velvet blouses, men in tall, black reservation hats and turquoise jewelry accompanied by youngsters in mod T-shirts and tennies. Inside the post, packed with curios and quality crafts, you'll often see a weaver at work. Next door, don't miss **Cameron Collector's Gallery (★)** offering antique Indian crafts and outstanding works of contemporary Native American art— rare chief's blankets, pottery, dolls, weaponry and ceremonial garb. Behind the gallery, **Mrs. Richardson's Terraced Garden**, recently revived, is a garden spot of vegetables and flowers.

North of Cameron, continuing on Route 89 to The Gap, lies the northernmost extension of the **Painted Desert**, a multihued ancient land of silt and volcanic ash hills barren of vegetation. Red sphynx shapes astride crumbling pyramids of eroded solidified sand, these badlands are red and white along some miles; gray and white along others. They're part of the Chinle Formation beloved by geologists for its dinosaur-era fossils.

At **Dinosaur Tracks** (the turnoff is five miles west of Tuba City on Route 160, then north one-eighth mile along a dirt road) jewelry shacks mark the spot where scientists believe 20-foot-long carnivorous Dilophosaurus left tracks. For a small tip locals escort you to the several impressions— three-toed footprints twice as big as adult hands. (Look for the reconstructed skeleton of this dinosaur in Window Rock at the Navajo Tribal Museum.)

Worth a stop in Tuba City, named for a 19th-century Hopi leader, is the hogan-shaped, two-story native stone **Tuba Trading Post** (Main Street and Moenave Avenue; 602-283-5441). Built in 1905 during a tourism boom, its door faces east to the rising sun; crafts, groceries and sundries are for sale. Next door, you can enter a built-for-tourists hogan replica. Now administrative and trade center for western Navajos, Tuba City was founded by Mormons in 1877.

WESTERN NAVAJO COUNTRY HOTELS

Lodging in Navajo and Hopi country can be summed up in one word: scarce. In an area about the size of Massachusetts, barely 600 rooms are available, so it's no wonder reservation motels claim 100 percent occupancy most nights from Memorial Day through Labor Day. If you get stuck, reservation border towns (Holbrook, Winslow and Flagstaff) usually have vacancies, though they too can sell out, especially on weekends of special events.

Padded headboards and blue bedspreads and drapes cozy up 100 simple, cementblock rooms in the **Anasazi Inn** (Route 89; 602-679-2214) in Gray Mountain. It boasts the Western Navajo Reservation's only swimming pool. Budget.

Cameron Trading Post and Motel (Route 89, 30 miles east of the Grand Canyon's east entrance, and 50 miles north of Flagstaff; 602-679-

2231) in Cameron is a favorite overnight stop in Indian Country. This tiny, self-contained, 112-acre, privately owned outpost sits on a bluff overlooking the eastern prelude to the Grand Canyon of the Colorado. From 6 a.m. until 10 p.m. or later, the trading post is a beehive of tourists and Navajos mingling to shop, dine or pick up everything from mail and tack to baled hay. It's mainly the tourists who stay overnight in 45 rooms priced budget to moderate. Built in 1916, the motel rooms are two story and of native stone and wood architecture (variously called Pueblo style or Victorian territorial) as is the rest of the compound. The rooms tend to be a little funkier than elsewhere on the reservation.

Adjacent to the historic octagonal-shaped Tuba Trading Post is the pleasant, lawn-studded **Tuba City Motel** (Main Street; 602-283-4545), furnished with tan rugs and furniture of Southwestern hand-carved fashion. It has 80 rooms. Moderate.

Students at Tuba City's Greyhills High School are learning the hotel management business by operating the 32-room **Greyhills Inn** (60 Warrior Drive, northeast of Bashas on Route 160; 602-283-6271) as an American Youth Hostel, open year-round to all ages. Rooms are comfy and carpeted, with hand-me-down Hyatt furniture. Guests share bathrooms, a television lounge, and room with pool table, and for a modest fee can share meals with Navajo students in their cafeteria. For security reasons, doors lock at 12 a.m. so guests should inform the Inn if they plan to be out past midnight. Budget.

WESTERN NAVAJO COUNTRY RESTAURANTS

Assuming you're not on a cholesterol-free diet you'll find Indian country food, as with everything else here, an adventure. Fry bread appears at lunch and dinner with taco trimmings as an Indian taco, or as bread for a sandwich, or as dessert dripping with honey. Other Indian Country favorites include mutton stew, usually served with parched corn, chili, Mexican food, burgers, steaks, and for breakfast, biscuits with gravy. Note that prohibition is still observed throughout the Hopi and Navajo country. It is illegal to bring or drink alcoholic beverages here.

Gray Mountain Restaurant (Route 89, Gray Mountain; 602-679-2214) fills its walls with Southwest kitsch including a turquoise-covered cow skeleton. Entrées (baked ham, chicken-fried steak, broiled halibut, pepper steak) come with soup or salad, hot rolls, baked potato, cowboy beans or french fries and salsa. Budget to moderate.

A nice surprise is the **Cameron Trading Post Restaurant** (Route 89; 602-679-2231). After walking through the typically low, open-beam ceiling trading post, you enter a lofty room lined with windows looking out onto the Little Colorado River. Tables and chairs are of carved oak and the ceiling glimmers silver from its patterned pressed tin squares. Forty-one breakfast choices include Navajo taco with egg, *huevos rancheros* and hot cakes; for dinner, try the deep-fried fish and chicken or steak entrées. Budget to moderate in price.

Poncho's Family Restaurant (Main Street, Tuba City; 602-283-5260) amid open-beam and wood decor, offers dinners of steak and shrimp, Virginia baked ham, breaded veal with gravy, plus the inevitable Navajo taco, and a variety of Mexican entrées. Look for the large historic photos of Charles H. Algert, pioneer Indian trader and founder of Tuba Trading Post, shown on horseback in 1898, and an 1872 photo of the Hopi leader Tuba, standing with arms folded. Moderate.

WESTERN NAVAJO COUNTRY SHOPPING

In business for more than half a century, **Sacred Mountain Trading Post** (23 miles north of Flagstaff on Route 89; 602-679-2255), is often a good outlet for museum-quality Navajo pitch-glazed pottery; also available are glass beads and bead-making materials, Hopi pottery, kachinas and Navajo baskets.

The 1916 stone **Cameron Trading Post** (Route 89; 602-679-2231) is like a department store of Indian crafts, crammed with a good selection of nearly everything—lots of Navajo rugs, cases of jewelry from all Southwestern tribes, kachinas, sandpaintings, baskets and pottery. Cameron Gallery (adjoining) offers the most expensive crafts including antique Indian weavings, Apache baskets, Plains beadwork, weaponry and ceremonial garb.

Tuba Trading Post Co. (Main Street and Moenave Avenue, Tuba City; 602-283-5441) emphasizes Navajo rugs, usually including large pictorials. Also for sale are kachinas, jewelry and the Pendleton blankets Indians like to give one another for births, graduations and other celebrations.

Hopi Indian Country

Three sand-colored mesas stacked and surrounded by a dozen ancient villages form the core of the Hopi Reservation. Completely surrounded by the Navajo Reservation, the villages are strung along 90 miles of Route 264. Home for several centuries to the Hopi, this fascinating high-desert place (about 4000-foot elevation) looks stark and poor one minute, then ancient and noble the next.

Looking for crafts to buy at the homes of Hopi craftsmakers or attending dances are good reasons to visit the villages. **Hopi Indian Dances**, nearly all of them involving prayers for rain for their dry-farm plots, occur year-round. Dates are rarely announced more than two weeks in advance. Whether or not you can attend will vary with the dance and the village. To ask, call the Hopi Tribe's Office of Public Relations (602-734-2441) or Second Mesa Cultural Center (602-734-2401). Don't miss a chance to attend one. Instructions for visitors will be posted outside most villages. In all cases, leave cameras, tape recorders and sketching pads in the car. Photography is not permitted in the villages or along Hopi roads.

Two miles southeast of Tuba City at **Moenkopi** ("the place of running water"), a village founded in the 1870s by a Hopi chief from Oraibi, note the rich assortment of farm plots. This is the only Hopi village that irrigates its farmland—water comes from a nearby spring. Elsewhere farmers tend small plots in several locations, enhancing their chance of catching random summer thundershowers. It's also the only one of 12 Hopi villages not situated on or just below one of the three mesas.

It's some 40 miles to the next two villages. **Bacavi**, comprised mostly of prefab homes, was built in 1909 following a political upheaval at Old Oraibi. **Hotevilla**, also a relatively new (built in 1906) village, with its mix of adobe and cinderblock homes at the edge of a mesa, is nonetheless a traditional village known for its dances and crafts. A few miles down the road, on the edge of Third Mesa, **Old Oraibi** is one of the oldest continuously inhabited villages in the United States. Hopis lived here as early as 1150. Try the ten-minute walk from the south edge of the village to ruins of a church built in 1901 by H. R. Voth, a Mennonite minister. It was destroyed by lightning. At Kykotsmovi, "mound of ruined houses," two miles east, then south one mile on Route 2, the **Hopi Tribal Council Office of Public Relations** (602-734-2441) provides visitor information.

Continue east on Route 264 a half dozen miles to **Shungopovi**, Second Mesa's largest village, built at a cliff's edge. It's two more miles to the **Hopi Cultural Center** at Second Mesa (on Route 264; 602-734-2401), the biggest social center for Indians and visitors. Hopi staffers of this white, pueblo-style museum-restaurant-motel-gift shop complex always know when and where dances are scheduled; ask at the motel desk. Tribally owned, it includes the Hopi Museum, exhibiting murals, pottery and historic photos of each mesa. Shop spaces usually house galleries of Hopi-made arts and crafts. Just 100 feet west of the complex at the **Hopi Arts and Crafts Cooperative Guild** (602-734-2463) silversmiths are at work amid the biggest assortment of Hopi-made crafts on the reservation.

East of the Cultural Center, the two weathered villages of **Shipaulovi** and **Mishognovi** (a steep climb north to both up an unnamed road from Route 264) are strikingly placed above the desert floor on Second Mesa, many of their dwellings carved from stone. Founded in the 1680s, both are known for their dances and are worth a visit for the views.

If you have time to make only one stop, visit the trio of villages on First Mesa—**Hano, Sichomovi** and **Walpi** (six miles east of the Secakuku Trading Post). Perched atop the flat oblong mesa, its sides dropping precipitously 1000 feet to the desert below, the village locations help you understand why the Hopis believe they live at the center of the universe. Accessible only by a thrilling curvy drive up a narrow road with no guardrails (signs off Route 264 point the way) all three villages seem to grow out of the mesa's beige-colored stone. Vistas are uninterrupted for miles amid an eerie stillness.

Most awesome is Walpi. Built some 300 years ago on a promontory with panoramas in all directions, Walpi's houses stack atop one another like children's blocks, connected with wooden ladders. From the parking lot (no cars are permitted in Walpi) the village resembles a great stone ship suspended on a sea of blue sky. Leaders keep the village traditional so that neither electricity nor running water are permitted. Shy schoolgirls lead **tours of Walpi** daily in summer. Sign up at Ponsi Hall (602-737-2262) or the Community Development Office (602-737-2670) in Sichomovi.

Here, as in the other villages, kivas, or ceremonial chambers dug into the earth, serve as they have since Anasazi days, a refuge where clan dancers fast and observe rituals for days prior to dances. Then on dance days, no longer farmers in denims, the Hopis slowly emerge through ladders on kiva roofs to the hypnotic rhythm of drums and rattles. Transformed in masks, feathers, bells and pine boughs, they appear as sacred beings.

Everyday activities include women baking bread out of doors in beehive ovens or tending clay firings. These are excellent pottery villages. Crude signs in windows invite you into homes of kachina and pottery makers, a wonderful chance to get acquainted with these hospitable people.

Hano resembles its neighboring Hopi villages, but in language and custom it remains a Tewa settlement of Pueblo Indians who fled Spanish oppression in the Rio Grande region in the late 1690s.

Continuing east on Route 264, Hopi Indian Country ends at Keams Canyon, the federal government administrative center, with tourist facilities (restaurant, motel, grocery) clustered around **Keams Canyon Trading Post**. Well-chosen crafts are for sale; the finest art is in a side room.

Follow the canyon northeast into the woods. About two miles in, on the left, near a ramada and a small dam, you'll find **Inscription Rock (★)** where Kit Carson signed his name on the tall sandstone wall about the time he was trying to end Navajo raiding parties.

HOPI INDIAN COUNTRY HOTELS

Designed by Arizona's award-winning architect Benny Gonzales, Second Mesa offers the only Hopi-owned tourist complex. Here are 33 moderately priced rooms of the **Hopi Cultural Center Motel** (Route 264; 602-734-

2401) with their white walls, blonde furniture, television, desk, vanity, dusty rose rug and Indian print-wall decor.

Old trailer home modules make up the **Keams Canyon Motel** (Route 264; 602-738-2297). The 20 units are a little depressing (with sagging curtains and scratches on wood walls and stains on the carpets), but clean; at budget rates, they are often sold out during summer.

HOPI INDIAN COUNTRY RESTAURANTS

Hopi's primary meeting place, the **Hopi Cultural Center Restaurant** (Route 264 at Second Mesa; 602-734-2401) with open-beam ceiling and sturdy, wood-carved furniture, offers Hopi options at all meals. Breakfasts include blue-corn pancakes, blue-corn cornflakes with milk and fry bread. For lunch or dinner, Nok Qui Vi—traditional stew with corn and lamb, served with fresh-baked green chilies and fry bread—as well as steak, chicken and shrimp entrées round out the menu. For dessert there's strawberry shortcake. Budget to moderate.

Second Mesa Nova-Ki (602-737-2525) next to the pueblo-style Secakuku Supermarket serves up burgers, grilled pork chops and Mexican plates amid mauve walls, blue tablecloths and Native American paintings. Budget in price.

Murals depicting Hopi mesa life decorate the exterior at **Keams Canyon Café** (Route 264 in Keams Canyon; 602-738-2296). This simple eatery has such dinner entrées as filet mignon, T-bone steak, roast beef and barbecued ribs, all served on formica tables. Meals fall in the moderate price range.

HOPI INDIAN COUNTRY SHOPPING

The number of roadside Hopi galleries and shops doubled in the early '90s. Owned by individual families, groups of artists or by craftsmakers with national reputations, all these Hopi crafts enterprises are on or near Route 264.

Third Mesa's **Monongya Arts and Crafts** has large rooms filled with Indian jewelry, some pottery and kachina doll sculptures.

Driving east a half-mile, follow the Old Oraibi signs south to **Old Oraibi Crafts** specializing in Hopi *dawas*—wall plaques made of yarn. This tiny shop with a beam ceiling also sells stuffed Hopi clown dolls.

Southbound on 264, **Calnimpetwa's Gallery** looks like a house. Spacious, white-walled rooms are lined with gallery-quality baskets, pots and

(Text continued on page 108.)

The Fine Craft of Shopping

While shopping for arts and crafts in Indian Country we've been invited into Hopi homes to eat corn fresh from the field, have discussed tribal politics with college-educated shopkeepers and met traditional basketmakers who spoke no English. At the same time we've longingly admired contemporary Indian-crafted jewelry that would dazzle New York's Fifth Avenue crowd.

Shopping can occur anywhere in Indian Country. Once we bought sandpaintings from the trunk of an Indian artist's car while camping in the Chuskas. But Indian Country's main shopping avenue is Route 264, from Tuba City to Window Rock where you'll find two fine old trading posts—**Tuba Trading Post** (Main Street and Moenave Avenue; 602-283-5441) in Tuba City and **Hubbell Trading Post** (602-755-3254) near the town of Ganado.

Throughout Hopi country, shopping is the best way to get to know the locals. Shops line entrances to all three mesas and most villages have at least a few signs in home windows inviting visitors in to look at family-made crafts. (*Note:* Tribal officials caution against making a deposit on any craft you can't take with you unless you know the craftsmaker or have a reliable personal reference.)

What should you be you looking for when shopping? Both the Hopi and Navajo offer crafts unique to their tribe.

HOPI CRAFTS

Baskets: Hopi wedding and other ceremonial baskets are still woven by Hopi women. Third Mesa villages are also known for their wicker plaques of colorfully dyed sumac and rabbit brush. Coiled yucca plaques are preferred at Second Mesa. Trays of plaited yucca over a willow ring serve as sifters and are made at First and Second Mesa villages.

Jewelry: The favorite Hopi jewelry form is overlay—designs cut from silver sheets, then soldered onto a second silver piece. Cut-out areas are oxidized black.

Kachinas: Kachinas are often carved in dancers' poses, then painted or dressed in cloth, feathers and bright acrylics. The newer trends feature

stylized, intricately detailed figures carved from one piece of cottonwood root, then stained. (Navajos now make kachinas too, to the irritation of Hopi carvers.)

Pottery: Nampeyo, a First Mesa woman inspired by ancient pottery shards, started the revival of yellow-to-orange pottery a century ago. First Mesa remains a major producer of pottery decorated with black thin-curved-line motifs.

Weaving: Hopi men do the weaving in this tribe—mostly ceremonial belts and some rugs.

NAVAJO CRAFTS

Baskets: The most popular basketry of the Navajos is the coiled wedding basket, with its bold-red, zigzag design. Other baskets found in Navajo trading posts are likely to be made by Paiutes who also live in the area. During the 1980s, a renaissance resulted in some large, intricately designed coil baskets—both plate and jug-shaped.

Jewelry: Since the 1860s, Navajos have engaged in the art of silver-smithing, shaping silver to fit turquoise stones. Other popular items are stoneless silver rings, bolos, earrings, necklaces— especially the squash blossom—made by handwrought or sand-cast methods.

Pottery: Navajo ceramics are simple, unadorned brown pieces glazed with hot pitch. The pieces look wonderful when made by a master; clunky and amateurish otherwise.

Sandpaintings: Medicine men sing curing ceremonies while assistants create elaborate pictures on the ground with sands and crushed minerals in an astonishing assortment of colors. Each is destroyed at the ceremony's end. Similar designs glued onto wood are sold as sandpaintings. Widely available, these are made mainly in the Shiprock, New Mexico, area.

Weaving: Thousands of Navajo women and a few dozen Navajo men weave rugs today on the reservation, but only a small percentage of them are considered masterweavers, commanding the highest prices. Still, even a saddle blanket can be a treasured memento.

jewelry made primarily by Hopi, Navajo and Santa Domingo Indians. Many of the crafts have a sleek contemporary look.

Continue east, then south a half-mile on the Kykotsmovi road to **Hopi Kiva Indian Arts and Crafts** (602-734-6667), specializing in Hopi overlay jewelry, kachinas, cradle dolls and gourd earrings.

The family-owned **Dawa-ki House of the Sun** (one-fourth mile west of the Hopi Cultural Center, Second Mesa; 602-734-9288) sells Hopi overlay silver work, kachina dolls, pottery and wicker baskets. Often you can see jewelers at work.

In Second Mesa, by the Hopi Cultural Center, the pueblo-style **Hopi Arts and Crafts Cooperative Guild Shop** (602-734-2463) sells work by more than 350 Hopi craftsmakers, often introducing new artists. You'll see fine, reasonably priced samples of all Hopi crafts—coil baskets, wicker plaques, kachina dolls—from traditional to the contemporary baroque and even the older-style flat dolls, plus silver jewelry, woven sashes and gourd rattles. Prices are good. Staff members are knowledgeable about who the best craftsmakers are in any specialty and where to find them. In the shop you'll also see Hopi silversmiths at work.

East of the Hopi Cultural Center one-and-a-half miles, on the left, stop at an unassuming-looking **Tsakurshovi** (602-734-2478) to find the funkiest shop en route, the only place you can buy sweetgrass, bundled sage, cottonwood root, fox skins, elk toes, warrior paint, dance fans and the oldest-style kachina dolls, amid a delightful hodgepodge of crafts and trade items adored by Hopi dancers. (Owners invented the "Don't Worry, Be Hopi" T-shirts.)

Phil Sekaquaptewa's Gallery (one mile east of the Hopi Cultural Center, next to Secakuku Supermarket, Second Mesa; 602-737-2211), has eight Hopi artists who share space devoted mainly to contemporary jewelry baskets, kachinas, Zuni fetishes and even edible paper-thin blue-corn Hopi *piki* bread.

Honani Crafts Gallery (five-and-a-half miles east of the Hopi Cultural Center; 602-737-2238) with its stained-glass windows of Hopi dancer designs, sells jewelry by 16 silversmiths from all three mesas plus kachinas, books and concho belts.

It's seven more miles to First Mesa, where Walpi residents welcome you to see pottery and kachinas they've made in Hopi's most picturesque village.

Twenty miles east, visit **McGee's Indian Art Gallery** (602-738-2295) at Keams Canyon Trading Post, distinctive for its Hopi village murals. For sale are a tasteful variety of Hopi and Navajo crafts—concho belts, silver jewelry, wicker plaques, kachinas, sandpaintings, moccasins and rugs. Be sure to look in the room housing their finest award-winning crafts.

Central Navajo Country

This is the heart, soul and capital of Navajoland—a strikingly beautiful land of canyons, red rocks, forests and mountains where the Navajos have recorded their proudest victories and most bitter defeats. The longer you stay and explore, the more you'll appreciate the ever-evolving culture that is The Navajo Way.

The ruins of ancient cities you'll see also remind us that long before the Navajo arrived this too was homeland to ancestors of the Hopis—the Anasazi.

Forty miles east of Keams Canyon on Route 264, near the small village of Ganado, follow a shaded road a half mile west along a creek to **Hubbell Trading Post National Historic Site** (602-755-3254) which still operates as it did when Lorenzo Hubbell, dean of Navajo traders, set up shop here last century. Now run by the National Park Service, Hubbell's remains one of few trading posts with the traditional "bullpen" design—shoppers stand outside a wooden arena asking for canned goods, yards of velvet, tack and such. Built in the 1870s, part museum and part gallery, these single-story stone rooms smell and look their age—the floors uneven from years of wear. Walls are jammed to their open-beam ceilings with baskets, books, rugs, historical photos, jewelry, postcards. Tack and tools still dangle from the rafters.

Self-guiding tours of the 160-acre complex and exhibits in the **Visitor Center** (602-755-3254) explain how trading posts once linked the Navajo with the outside world, and how Hubbell was not just a trader but a valued friend of the Indian community until his death in 1930. The Hubbell family continued to operate the post until it was given to the National Park Service in 1967. Also in the Visitor Center are a good selection of Indian related books. And for a tip, Navajo weavers and silversmiths demonstrating their crafts will pose for photos. Hour-long tours of the **Hubbell House**, with his excellent collection of crafts, give further insights into frontier life and the remarkable trader who lies buried on a knoll nearby.

Navajo-owned ponderosa pine forest lands comprise part of the 30-mile drive to Window Rock, eastward along Route 264. Picnickers may wish to stop a while at **Summit Campground** 20 miles east of Ganado, where the elevation reaches 7750 feet.

Seven miles east of Summit Campground, before entering Window Rock, stop in St. Michaels, on your right, at trailers labeled **Industrial & Tourism Department** (602-871-6436) for Central Navajo Country maps and tourism information.

Here you'll find **St. Michaels Historical Museum** (located by the post office; 602-871-4171) in the white, hand-hewn native stone building that in the late 1890s was four-bedroom living quarters and chapel for Franciscan friars from Cincinnati. (Sleeping must have been tough on such thin mattresses atop box crates!) Other displays—everything from uncomfortable-looking wooden saddles to vintage typewriters— include old photographs that depict their work and life. You'll see pages of the first phonetic systems they made to help create the written Navajo language. Outside, towering cottonwoods and a friar's three-quarter-acre flower garden create a park-like oasis.

East on Route 264 three miles, a rare Indian Country traffic light (at Route 12) marks "downtown" **Window Rock**, a growing, modern Navajo Nation capital. West of the Navajo Nation Inn, the **Navajo Tribal Museum** (east of Route 12 on Route 264; 602-871-6673 or 602-871-6675) and **Navajo Arts & Crafts Enterprise** share space. The former, with sophisticated exhibits, leads visitors through an overview of historic and contemporary Navajo life and traditions. Mannequins were created via plaster casts from real Navajos. One room is devoted to changing exhibits by noted and emerging Navajo artists. The crafts guild encourages innovation among its members and guarantees the quality of everything it sells.

A short distance east on Route 264 is the **Navajo Nation Zoological Park** (602-871-6573). In this natural setting roam domestic and wild animals that figure in Navajo culture and folk lore—everything from coyote, wolves, cougars, bears, deer, elk, bobcats, rattlesnakes and prairie dogs to goats. In all, 53 species live here. Look for the churro sheep, brought by the Spanish. Herds are being increased because of their proven resistance to disease and the excellent weaving quality of their wool. Displays include fork-stick and crib-log examples of hogan architecture. A modest botanical garden labels typical high-desert plants: Indian rice grass, Navajo tea, lupine, asters and junipers.

A row of towering red-sandstone pinnacles that resemble the **Haystacks**, for which they are named, forms the zoo's eastern boundary. The zoo and pinnacles are part of **Tse Bonito Tribal Park**, a primitive campground and shaded picnic area where the Navajos camped in 1864 on their "Long Walk" from their homeland.

When you arrive at the street light at the town of Window Rock, follow Route 12 north past Window Rock's shopping center, then drive right a mile to **Tseghahodzani**—"the rock with the hole in it." Here you'll find a sweeping wall, several stories tall, of vermilion-colored sandstone. Almost dead center is an almost perfectly circular "window" 130 feet in diameter eroded in it, offering views to the mountains beyond. John Collier, Commissioner of Indian Affairs in the 1930s, was so stirred by it, he declared it the site for the Navajo administrative center. Visitors can picnic and walk here.

Nearby, visit the octagonal stone **Council Chambers**, designed as a great ceremonial hogan. Murals painted by the late Gerald Nailor depict tribal history. It is here the 88-member Tribal Council meets four times a year to set policy. You'll hear Navajo and English spoken at all proceedings.

The prettiest route in Indian Country is **Route 12** from Route 40 through Window Rock and on north another 65 miles. The road hugs red-rock bluffs while skirting pine forests, lakes, Navajo homes and hogans surrounded by pasture, orchards and cornfields.

Follow signs to the pine-clad Navajo Community College's **Tsaile Campus** (Route 12, about 60 miles north of Window Rock) and its tall glass hogan-shaped Ned Hatathli Cultural Center with two floors devoted to the **Hatathli Museum and Gallery** (602-724-3311). From prehistoric times to the present—dioramas, murals, photographs, pottery, weaponry and other artifacts interpret Indian cultures including the Navajo. Wonderfully detailed murals tell the Navajo story of Creation, but you'll need to find someone to interpret it for you as there's little text. Books and crafts are sold in the adjacent gallery at this two-year college, established in 1957. Visitors are also welcome in the college's library and dining hall.

Route 64, to the left off of Route 12, leads to a favorite spot of tourists from around the world, **Canyon de Chelly National Monument** (access is also available off Route 191, six miles west of Ganado). By the time the Spanish arrived in the 1540s the Navajos already occupied this trio of slick, towering red-walled canyons that converge in a Y. The canyons and rims are still home to Navajo families, their sheep and horses grazing. Water near the surface moistens corn, squash and melon crops, apple and peach orchards.

It's hard to decide if Canyon de Chelly is most impressive from the rim drives, with their bird's-eye views of the hogan-dotted rural scenes, or astride a horse or an open-air jeep, sloshing (during spring runoff) through Chinle Wash. The best introduction for any adventure is the **Visitor Center** (along the main road through Chinle; 602-674-5436). Chinle, the shopping and administrative center for this part of the reservation, is as plain as its famed canyons are spectacular.

Be sure to stop at the visitor center museum where exhibits on 2000 years of canyon history, plus cultural demonstrations, local artists' exhibits and a ranger-staffed information desk will enlighten you about the area. Next door is a typical Navajo hogan; bring your cup and join rangers for coffee and questions most mornings. The center is also the place to hire Navajo guides—required if you hike, camp, or drive your own four-wheel-drive vehicle into the canyons.

Proud tales of the Navajos' most daring victories are retold daily by guides who also point out bullet holes in the walls from brutal massacres. Thousands of much older ruins leave haunting clues to a people who lived and died here from about 200 A.D. until the late 130Cs when prolonged drought throughout the Four Corners region probably caused them to move to the Rio Grande and other regions of Arizona and New Mexico. Each bend in the canyon reveals ever-taller canyon walls, more pictographs and petroglyphs (historic and prehistoric art drawn on rock walls). Each turn showcases vivid red walls and the yellow-green of leafy cottonwoods thriving along the canyon floor.

North and South Rim drives, each 21 miles one-way, take about two hours each to see. (It's a good idea to bring along brochures that point out geological, botanical and historical sites at each overlook.) **South Rim Drive** follows the Canyon de Chelly, which gives the monument its name. Highlights include: **White House Overlook** (located at 6.4 miles; the only non-guided hike into the canyon begins here), to view remains of a multistory masonry village where about 100 persons lived about 800 years ago; **Old Hogan and Sliding Rock Overlook** (at 11 miles) where you will see ruins of a hogan, and shallow basins eroded out of sandstone (at 12.9 miles). Navajos still sometimes gather fresh water from these basins. On a narrow ledge across the canyon, ancients built retaining walls to try to keep their homes from sliding off the sloping floor into the canyon.

Spider Rock Overlook (at 21.8 miles) is a vista of the steepest canyon walls, about a 1000-foot vertical drop. Look right to see Monument Canyon; left to see Canyon de Chelly. The 800-foot tall spire at their junction is **Spider Rock**, where Spider Woman is said to carry naughty Navajo boys and girls. Those white specks at the top of her rock, Navajo parents say, are the bleached bones of boys and girls who did not listen to mother and dad. Legend has it she also taught Navajos to weave.

North Rim Drive explores the **Canyon del Muerto**—"Canyon of the Dead"—named in 1882 by Smithsonian Institution expedition leader James Stevenson after finding remains of prehistoric Indian burials below Mummy Cave. Highlights include:

Antelope House Overlook (at 10.2 miles) which is named for paintings of antelope, probably made in the 1830s, on the canyon wall left of this four-story, 91-room ruin. Prehistoric residents contributed hand outlines and figures in white paint. Viewers from the overlook will see circular structures (kivas, or ceremonial chambers) and rectangular ones (storage or living quarters). Across the wash in an alcove 50 feet above the canyon floor is where 1920s archaeologists found the well-preserved body of an old man wrapped in a blanket of golden eagle feathers; under it was a white cotton blanket in such good shape it appeared brand new. It is believed he was a neighborhood weaver. Also here, at Navajo Fortress Viewpoint, the isolated high redstone butte across the canyon was once an important Navajo hideout from Spanish, American and perhaps other Indian raiders.

Mummy Cave Overlook (at 19 miles), is site of the largest, most beautiful ruins in Canyon del Muerto. The 1880s discovery of two mummies in cists found in the talus slope below the caves inspired this canyon's name.

Massacre Cave Overlook (at 21 miles) is site of the first documented Spanish contact with Canyon de Chelly Navajos. In the winter of 1805 a bloody battle is believed to have occurred at the rock-strewn ledge to your left, under a canyon rim overhang. Hoping to end persistent Navajo raiding on Spanish and Pueblo Indian villages, Antonio de Narbona led an expedition here and claimed his forces killed up to 115 Navajos, another 33 taken captive.

CENTRAL NAVAJO COUNTRY HOTELS

The Navajo Nation's only tribally owned motel, **Navajo Nation Inn** (at Window Rock's intersection of Routes 264 and 12; 602-871-4108) bustles with a mix of Navajo politicians and business people in suits and cowboys in black "reservation hats." The 56 rooms are pleasantly decorated with turquoise carpet, Southwestern-style wood furniture and matching bedspreads and curtains with traditional Navajo rural scenes. Moderate.

A park-like scene is the setting for the historic stone and pueblo-style **Thunderbird Lodge** (a quarter-mile southeast of Canyon de Chelly National Monument Visitor Center, Chinle; 602-674-5841). All 90 adobe-style rooms handsomely blend Navajo and Southwestern architectural traditions. Each features Native American prints and is an easy walk to the canyon entrance. There's a gift shop and cafeteria on the premises.

Canyon de Chelly Motel (a block east of Route 191 on Route 7, Chinle; 602-674-5875) makes up for its sterile architecture by providing Chinle's only swimming pool (indoor, for guests only); 68 rooms, some for nonsmokers. Moderate.

The only enterprise on the entire Navajo reservation letting you experience life with a rural Navajo extended family is **Tsosie's Bed and Breakfast** (★) (near Tsaile; 602-724-3383). Prices are moderate, accommodations primitive. Guests sleep in an authentic dirt-floor log hogan and use old-fashioned outhouses. Scholars, artists and folks eager for a rest from the predictable conveniences have found the Coyote Clan hospitality a refuge. Special tours to favorite backcountry haunts can be arranged.

CENTRAL NAVAJO COUNTRY RESTAURANTS

Café Sage (turn right a half-mile east of Hubbell's on Route 264), located in a two-story, brown stucco building, once the former Presbyterian College campus, welcomes tourists to dine in the Navajo Nation Health Foundation cafeteria where daily dinner specials might include tortellini and chicken with vegetables and garlic toast. Budget.

A trailer wide enough for two rows of sky-blue booths makes up **Tuller Café** (on the south side of Route 264 in St. Michaels; 602-871-4687). Here they dish up meat loaf, pork chops, fish and chips, Navajo sandwiches, Navajo stew and Homer's goulash (macaroni, meat, green pepper, tomatoes) with garlic toast; budget.

Navajo Nation Inn Dining Room (at Window Rock's intersection of Routes 264 and 12; 602-871-4108) in a modern, spacious room is the Navajo capital's biggest restaurant. Seating 250 and decorated with Navajo art, the menu includes a taco platter, chicken, steak, Navajo sandwich, Navajoburger, beef stew, vegetable stew and sometimes a mutton buffet for moderate prices. Lunch is always busy, the restaurant filled with politicians from nearby tribal headquarters offices.

Junction Restaurant (adjacent to Canyon de Chelly Motel—a block east of Route 191 on Navajo Route 7; 602-674-8443) is one of only two sit-down (non-buffet) restaurants in Chinle. A mix of peach and blue booths and blonde-wood tables and chairs seat patrons dining on everything from *huevos rancheros* or biscuits and gravy for breakfast to a crab Louis or hot sandwiches for lunch to Mexican specialties for dinner. Budget to moderate.

Located in the original 1902 trading post built by Samuel Day, **Thunderbird Restaurant** (part of Thunderbird Lodge, near Canyon de Chelly National Monument in Chinle; 602-674-5841) serves up half a dozen entrées cafeteria-style for each meal. The menu offers a good variety, and changes some each day. You sit in a choice of booths or tables surrounded by walls with top-quality, for-sale Navajo crafts. Moderate.

CENTRAL NAVAJO COUNTRY SHOPPING

Be sure to stop at the **Hubbell Trading Post** (Ganado; 602-755-3254), whose low stone walls, little changed in 90 years, contain the best Navajo rug selection en route, plus several rooms crammed with jewelry, dolls, books, baskets and historic postcards.

Navajo Arts and Crafts Enterprise (sharing a building with the Navajo Nation Museum, Window Rock; 602-871-4095) sells the work of some 500 Navajo craftsmakers. Selection is excellent and quantity is large—rugs of all styles, Navajo jewelry of all kinds, stuffed Navajo-style dolls.

Thunderbird Lodge Gift Shop (Chinle; 602-674-5841) provides a good selection of rugs, many of them made in the Chinle area, plus kachinas, jewelry, baskets and souvenirs. Some of the fine-quality crafts decorating the neighboring cafeteria walls are also for sale.

CENTRAL NAVAJO COUNTRY PARKS

Tse Bonito Tribal Park—Prior to their historic "Long Walk" to Fort Sumner, New Mexico, in 1864 the Navajo camped here among prominent red-sandstone hills called "Haystacks." The park encompasses the Navajo Nation Zoological Park housing native and domestic animals culturally important to the Navajos.

Facilities: Zoo visitor center with exhibits, restrooms; crib-log hogans; 53 species of animals, birds and other wildlife; information, 602-871-6573.

Camping: Primitive camping permitted; no fee.

Getting there: Located in Window Rock on Route 264.

Lake Asaayi Bowl Canyon Recreation Area—One of the prettiest of the Navajo fishing lakes, located in the Chuska Mountains known as the "Navajo Alps," Asaayi Lake is popular for fishing, picnicking and primitive camping. The 36-acre lake and creek are fishable year-round.

Facilities: Picnic areas, barbecue grills, pit toilets; information, 505-777-2741. *Fishing:* Rainbow trout.

Camping: Allowed in areas along the lake; the $2 permit is available at the recreation area.

Getting there: From Window Rock, take Route 12 to Route 134. Drive northeast about four miles then south seven miles on a graded dirt road to the lake.

Canyon de Chelly National Monument—The most famous and popular Navajo Reservation attraction is this 130-acre land of piñon and juniper forests cut by a trio of red-walled sandstone canyons. Extending eastward from Chinle to Tsaile, the canyon's rim elevations range from 5500 to 7000 feet while the canyon bottoms drop from 30 feet nearest Chinle to 1000-feet deep farther east. Cottonwood trees and other vegetation shade farms connected by miles of sandy wash along the canyon bottom. Two major gorges, 27 and 34 miles long, dramatically unveil walls of 250-million-year-old solidified sand dunes in a strata geologists call the Defiance Plateau.

Facilities: Motel, restaurant, gift shop, visitor center, museum, crib-log hogan, restrooms, jeep and horse tours, guided hikes; information, 602-674-5436.

Camping: There are 97 sites; no fee.

Getting there: Located in Chinle, via Routes 7 or 64.

Northern Navajo Country

There's something both silly and irresistible about driving to Four Corners to stick each foot in a different state (Colorado and Utah) and each hand in still two others (Arizona and New Mexico) while someone takes your picture from a scaffolding. But then, this is the only place in the United States where you can simultaneously "be" in four different states. The inevitable Navajo crafts booths offer up necklaces, bracelets, earrings, T-shirts, paintings, sandpaintings, fry bread and lemonade—a splendid way to make something festive out of two intersecting lines on a map.

To get there from the south, you'll have to pass by **Teec Nos Pos Arts and Crafts Center** (Routes 160 and 64), the usual roadside gallery of Southwestern Indian crafts, with an emphasis on area sandpaintings.

Heading westbound on Route 160, even before travelers reach Kayenta, amazing eroded shapes emerge on the horizon—like the cathedral sized and shaped Church Rock. Kayenta, originally a small town that grew up around John Wetherill's trading post at 5564-feet elevation, today is both Arizona's gateway to Monument Valley and a coal-mining center.

The 24 miles north to Monument Valley on Route 163 is a prelude to the main event, huge red-rock pillars. Half Dome and **Owl Rock** on your left form the eastern edge of the broad Tyende Mesa. On your right rise **Burnt Foot Butte** and **El Capitan**, also called Agathla Peak—roots of ancient volcanoes whose dark rock contrasts with pale-yellow sandstone formations.

A half-mile north of the Utah state line on Route 163 is a crossroads; left two miles to Gouldings Trading Post and Lodge, or right six miles to **Monument Valley Navajo Tribal Park Headquarters** (P.O. Box 93, Monument Valley, UT 84536; 801-727-3287) and Monument Valley Visitor Center. Inside you can see excellent views from a glass-walled observatory. This was the first Navajo Tribal Park, set aside in 1958. Within you'll see more than 40 named and dozens more unnamed red and orange monolithic sandstone buttes and rock skyscrapers jutting hundreds of feet. It is here that you can hire Navajo-owned jeep tours into the monument.

For a small fee, you can explore the **17-mile Loop Drive** over a dirt road, badly rutted in places, to view a number of famous landmarks with names that describe their shapes, such as **Rain God Mesa, Three Sisters** and **Totem Pole**. At **John Ford's Point**, an Indian on horseback often poses for photographs, then rides out to chat and collect a tip. A 15-minute round-trip walk from **North Window** rewards you with panoramic views.

The Navajos and this land seem to belong together. A dozen Navajo families still live in the park, and several open their hogans to guided tours. For a small fee, they'll pose for your pictures. A number of today's residents are descendants of Navajos who arrived here in the mid-1860s with Headman Hoskinini, fleeing Kit Carson and his round-up of Navajos in the Canyon de Chelly area. Hoskinini lived here until his death in 1909.

The ultimate cowboy-Indian Western landscape, Monument Valley has been the setting for many movies—*How the West Was Won, Stagecoach, Billy the Kid, She Wore a Yellow Ribbon, The Trial of Billy Jack* to name just a few. In all, seven John Ford Westerns were filmed here between 1938 and 1963.

Gouldings Trading Post, Lodge and Museum (two miles west of Route 163; 801-727-3231), a sleek, watermelon-colored complex on a hillside, blends in with enormous sandstone boulders stacked above it. The original Goulding two-story stone home and trading post, now a museum, includes a room devoted to movies made here. Daily showings can be seen in a small adjacent theater.

From Gouldings it's nearly eight miles northwest on paved Oljeto Road to the single-story stone **Oljeto Trading Post** (★), its Depression-era gas pumps and scabby turquoise door visible reminders of its age. Inside ask to see a dusty museum room filled with Native American crafts hidden behind the turquoise bullpen-style mercantile. Often you can buy a fine used Navajo wedding basket for a good price.

Back to Kayenta and Route 160, it's a scenic 18-mile drive northwest to the turnoff for the **Navajo National Monument** which encompasses some of the Southwest's finest Anasazi ruins. This stunning region showcases the architectural genius of the area's early inhabitants. To gain an overview of the monument, stop by the **Visitor Center and Museum** (nine miles north of Route 160 on Route 564, Black Mesa; 602-672-2366) featuring films and exhibits of the treasures tucked away beneath the sandstone cliffs. You'll be impressed by pottery, jewelry and tools created by the Kayenta Anasazi who lived in these exquisite canyons. There's also a craft gallery selling Zuni, Navajo and Hopi artwork.

From the visitor center you can hike an undemanding forest trail to **Betatakin Point Overlook**. Here you'll get an overview of Tsegi Canyon. One of the ruins here, **Inscription House**, is closed to protect it for posterity. However, it is possible to make the strenuous but rewarding hike to **Betatakin Ruin**, located in a dramatic alcove 500 feet above Tsegi Canyon. On this trip back in time, you'll see a 135-room ledge house that rivals the best of Mesa Verde. Also well worth a visit is remote **Keet Seel**. Even some of the roofs remain intact at this 160-room, five-kiva ruin. You can only reach this gem with a permit obtained at the visitor center. For more information on the ranger led walks to these two well-preserved ruins see "Hiking" at the end of the chapter.

Back on Route 160, it's about 28 miles southwest to **Elephant Feet**, roadside geologic formations that resemble legs and feet of a gigantic sandstone elephant.

NORTHERN NAVAJO COUNTRY HOTELS

Wetherill Inn (Route 163, a mile north of Route 160; 602-697-3231) in Kayenta has 54 spacious rooms sporting dark-brown furniture, upholstered chairs, black-and-brown spreads and matching curtains in Southwestern style. Moderate.

Tour buses full of French, German, Italian and Japanese guests frequent the 160-room **Holiday Inn Kayenta** (Route 160 just west of Route 163; 602-697-3221). All rooms in the two-story adobe brick buildings, at deluxe prices, offer floral carpets in hallways, cherry-wood furniture, upholstered chairs and spacious bathrooms. There's also an outdoor pool.

The only lodging right at Monument Valley, open since the 1920s, takes brilliant advantage of the views. Sliding glass doors lead to balconies for each of 62 rooms at **Gouldings Lodge** (six miles east of the tribal park; Monument Valley, UT; 801-727-3231) so guests can enjoy the eroded Mitten Buttes. The indoor pool is for guests only. Deluxe.

Anasazi Inn at Tsegi Canyon (ten miles west of Kayenta on Route 160; 602-697-3793), with 52 rooms and a view of the canyon, is the closest lodging to Navajo National Monument; moderate.

NORTHERN NAVAJO COUNTRY RESTAURANTS

A hogan-style doorway sets the Indian theme at Kayenta's **Holiday Inn Restaurant** (on Route 160 just west of Route 163; 602-697-3221), complete with Anasazi-style walls and sandpainting room dividers. Tables for four and matching chairs are of rattan. There's a continental breakfast buffet for diners in a hurry; a salad bar and burgers, sandwiches, Navajo tacos for lunch or dinner; meat and fish entrées for dinner. Moderate.

Navajo owned and staffed **El Capitan Café** (Route 160, just east of Route 163; 602-697-8560) is popular with the locals, including the Navajo police. Folks come for Indian tacos and mutton stew. Budget.

Old West saloon architecture signals Kayenta's **Golden Sands Café** (adjacent to the Wetherill Inn on Route 163, a mile north of Route 160; 602-697-3684). Inside, wagon-wheel lamps, miniature stagecoaches and other Old West memorabilia continue the theme. Breakfast specials include waffles with strawberries or blueberry pancakes; dinner entrées include rib steak, barbecued chicken, veal cutlets, liver and onions; budget.

Lively, crowded and cheery, **La Fiesta Café** (on the east side of Route 163, about a mile north of Route 160; 602-697-8513) serves very respectable Mexican entrées amid blue-and-white tablecloths. Moderate.

Three levels of dining stairstep a bluff so that the **Stage Coach Dining Room** (at Gouldings Lodge near Monument Valley; 801-727-8231) patrons can enjoy the panoramas of Monument Valley. Part of a late 1980s major expansion and remodel, this former cafeteria now offers sit-down service. The peach and burnt umber booths and tables compliment the stunning sandstone bluffs and views outside. A dinner favorite is the roast leg of lamb. Desserts worth a splurge include pecan and pumpkin pie or a fudge brownie with ice cream. There's a salad bar, and nonalcoholic wine and beer are offered. Moderate.

An all-American menu at **Canyon Inn Café** (on Route 160, ten miles west of Kayenta; 602-697-3793) offers burgers, steak and chicken at moderate prices.

NORTHERN NAVAJO COUNTRY SHOPPING

Lee's Trading Post (next to Bashas grocery store in Kayenta at the Tee h'indeeh Shopping Center; 602-697-8439) sells beads, dolls, raw craft materials, Pendleton blankets, sandpaintings, corn necklaces, kachinas and a great choice of jewelry.

Ask to see the crafts room at the 1921 **Oljeto Trading Post** (801-727-3210), ten miles northwest of Gouldings near Monument Valley, and you'll be led into a dusty museum-like space. The room is crammed with antique as well as recently made crafts, some for sale, some for admiring. Best buys here are Navajo wedding baskets popular with today's local brides and grooms. Simple, brown-pitch Navajo pottery made in this area is also sold here as well as cedar cradleboards, popular on the "res" as a baby's safety seat.

Yellow Ribbon Gift Shop (part of Gouldings complex at Monument Valley; 801-727-3231) provides Southwestern tribal crafts and souvenirs for all budgets; closed in winter.

NORTHERN NAVAJO COUNTRY PARKS

Monument Valley Navajo Tribal Park—Straddling the Arizona-Utah border is the jewel of tribally run Navajo Nation parks. With its 29,816 acres of monoliths, spires, buttes, mesas, canyons and sand dunes—all masterpieces of red-rock erosion—it is a stunning destination. With dozens of families still living here, it is also a sort of Williamsburg of Navajoland.

Facilities: Thers's a visitor center with museum and shops, showers, restrooms, picnic tables, Indian food booths (mainly summer months), arts and crafts; information, 801-727-3287.

Camping: Mitten View Campground has 100 sites; $10 per night up to six people.

Getting there: Located on Route 163, 24 miles northeast of Kayenta. The visitor center is east another four miles. The Gouldings complex is west three miles.

Navajo National Monument—Three of the Southwest's most beautiful Anasazi pueblo ruins are protected in the canyons of this 360-acre park, swathed in piñon and juniper forests at 6000-foot elevation. Inscription House Ruin is so fragile it is closed. Betatakin Ruin, handsomely set in a cave high up a canyon wall, is visible from an overlook. But close looks at Betatakin and the largest site, Keet Seel, require fairly strenuous hikes permitted between Memorial Day and Labor Day.

Facilities: Visitor center, museum, gift shop, restrooms, picnic areas and barbecue grills; information, 602-671-2366.

Camping: There are 24 sites; no fee.

Getting there: Take Route 160 west of Kayenta, turn right at Route 564 and continue nine miles.

The Sporting Life

FISHING

Fishing is permitted year-round with a one-day to one-year Navajo tribal license required at all lakes, streams and rivers in the Navajo Nation. Exceptions are **Whiskey** and **Long Lakes**, known for their trophy-size trout, located in the Chuska Mountains, a dozen miles south of Route 134 via logging routes 8000 and 8090. Their season is May 1 through November 30.

Popular all-year lakes stocked with rainbow trout each spring include **Wheatfields Lake** (44 miles north of Window Rock on Route 12) and **Tsaile Lake** (half-mile south of Navajo Community College in Tsaile). Tsaile Lake is also popular for bass and catfish. Other popular trout lakes include **Asaayi Lake** (11 miles east of Navajo, New Mexico, on a dirt road; 505-777-2255) and **Morgan Lake** (four miles south of Kirtland, next to Four Corners Power Plant), which produces trophy largemouth bass. Also for largemouth bass and channel catfishing try **Many Farms Lake** (three miles via dirt road east of Route 191 in Many Farms).

No fishing tackle or boats are for rent on the reservation. Boats are permitted on many of the lakes; most require electric motors only. Get fishing license and boating permits from the following locations. Try **Red Barn Trading Post** (Sanders; 602-688-2762), **CSWTA Inc. Environmental Consultant** (Tuba City; 602-283-4323), **Cow Springs Trading Post** (Tonalea; 602-283-5377), **Navajo Fish & Wildlife** (Window Rock; 602-871-6451), **Kayenta Trading Post** (Kayenta; 602-697-3541), **Lakeside Store Wheatfields** (Wheatfields Lake; 602-724-3262) or **Tsaile Trading Post** (Tsaile; 602-724-3397). Most of them also sell fishing gear.

JOGGING

Navajos and Hopis, who pride themselves on their long-distance-running traditions that date back to first contact with whites in the 1540s, host races at every tribal fair. Races are open to non-Indians as well. And it is common to see Native American joggers daily along virtually any route, so bring your togs and run too.

At Canyon de Chelly, try the White House Ruins trail or either of the rim trails; also the four-mile road leading into Monument Valley or roads to Oljeto and around Gouldings Lodge.

HORSEBACK RIDING

Horses have been an important icon of Navajo culture since the Spanish introduced them in the mid-16th century. They're a grand way to connect with a Navajo guide while seeing awesome country through his eyes. Most offer one-hour to overnight or longer options; there's flexibility on where you go and how long you stay.

In Canyon de Chelly, **Justin Tso's Tsegi Stables** (602-674-5678) offers tours to White House Ruins and elsewhere in and beyond the canyon. **Twin Trails Tours** (602-674-3466) depart from the North Rim of Canyon de Chelly, just past Antelope House turnoff.

In Monument Valley, **Ed Black's Horse Riding Tours** (located via a dirt road north from the visitor center a quarter-mile; 801-739-4285) can be an hour around The Mittens, or all day or longer into the valley. **Bigman's Horseback Riding** (along the four-mile park entrance road; 602-677-3219), offers one-and-one-half-hour to overnight rides into the monument's buttes, mesas and canyons.

Arrange for horse rides to Keet Seel Ruin in Navajo National Monument through the **National Park Service** (602-671-2366).

RODEO

Navajos love ropin' and bronco ridin'. Their statisticians claim Navajos host more rodeos per year than all other United States tribes combined. Rarely does a summer weekend pass without Navajo cowboys and cowgirls of all ages gathering somewhere on the reservation. To find one when you visit, call *The Navajo Nation Today Free Press*, a weekly, in Window Rock (602-871-4289); the Navajo Tourism Office (602-871-6659); or Navajo Radio Station KTNN (602-871-2666).

BICYCLING

Bicycling is permitted on any paved roads throughout Navajo Country, but only on the main paved highways on the Hopi Reservation.

While you'll find no designated bike paths or trails within either reservation, bicycles are well suited to both rim roads at Canyon de Chelly and along the paved, pine-clad nine miles of Route 564 into Navajo National Monument Visitor Center. Mountain bikes are particularly suited to the 17-mile rutted dirt loop open to visitors in Monument Valley. Cyclists from around the world are attracted to the uphill challenges of the Chuska Mountain Routes 134 (paved), 68 and 13 (partially paved). Petrified Forest National Park routes will often be too hot for daytime summer riding but offer a splendid way to sightsee in cooler spring and fall seasons.

HIKING

Because most of the land covered in this chapter is tribally owned or in national parks and monuments, hiking trail options are limited. Hopi back country is not open to visitors; it is, however, on the Navajo Indian Reservation. For the mountains, ask for suggestions from area trading posts, or hire an Indian guide by the hour or overnight or longer. Guides know the way and can share stories about the area; they're available through the Navajo Tourism Office (602-755-3254) near Window Rock; **Canyon de Chelly National Monument Visitor Center** (602-674-5436); or at the **Monument Valley Visitor Center** (801-727-3287).

A hat, sunglasses and drinking water are recommended for all hikes; add a raincoat during the July and August monsoon season.

SOUTHERN NAVAJO RESERVATION TRAILS   **Little Painted Desert County Park** has a strenuous one-mile hiking trail descending 500 feet into some of the most colorful hills in all the Painted Desert. Colors are most intense early and late in the day.

Homolovi Ruins State Park offers a one-mile hiking trail leading past two of the largest Anasazi Indian village ruins; at each you'll see skeletal walls outlining living quarters and kivas (ceremonial chambers) from villages thought to have belonged to the ancestors of today's Hopi Indians before they moved to their current mesas.

Petrified Forest National Park's summertime temperatures often soar in the 90s and 100s. Hiking is best early or late in the day. Water is available only at the visitor center at the north and south end of the park, so you're wise to carry extra with you.

A loop that begins and ends at the Crystal Forest stop on the park's 28-mile scenic loop, **Crystal Forest Interpretive Trail** (.5 mile), leads past the most concentrated petrified wood stands in the park. You can see how tall these ancient trees were (up to 170 feet), and the great variety of colors that formed after crystal replaced wood cells.

An introduction to the Chinle Formation, **Blue Mesa Hike** (1 mile) is a loop interpretive trail that leads past a wonderland of blue, gray and white layered hills. Signs en route explain how the hills formed and are now eroding.

The Flattops (unlimited miles) trailhead descends off sandstone-relic mesas several hundred feet into Puerco Ridge and other areas of the 10,000-acre Rainbow Forest Wilderness at the park's southeastern end. A quarter-mile trail leads into the area, and then you're on your own, exploring a vast gray and brown mudstone and siltstone badlands with wide vistas around every hill. The backcountry permits required to visit this remote portion of the park are free from the visitor center; you can stay up to 14 days.

Painted Desert Wilderness Area (unlimited miles) trailhead begins at Kachina Point at the park's north end. A brief trail descends some 400 feet, then leaves you on your own to explore cross-country some 35,000 acres of red-and-white-banded badlands of mudstone and siltstone, bald of vegetation. The going is sticky when wet. Get free backcountry permits at either visitor center.

CENTRAL NAVAJO COUNTRY TRAILS   **Canyon De Chelly's** only hike open to visitors without a guide is **White House Ruin Trail** (1.25 miles), beginning at the 6.4-mile marker on the South Rim Drive. The trail switch-back is down red sandstone swirls, crosses a sandy wash (rainy seasons you will do some wading in Chinle Creek; bring dry socks) to a cottonwood-shaded masonry village with 60 rooms surviving at ground level and an additional ten rooms perched in a cliff's alcove above.

Free 9 a.m. to noon, ranger-led hikes of varying lengths elsewhere in the canyon begin most mornings at the visitor center. Navajo guides can be hired at the visitor center to take you on short or overnight hikes into the canyon.

Hiking is not permitted in **Monument Valley** without a Navajo guide. Hire one at the visitor center (801-727-3287) for an hour, overnight or longer. Fred Cly (801-727-3283, or ask at the visitor center), is a knowledgeable guide especially good for photo angles and best times of day.

Navajo National Monument trails include **Sandal Trail** (.5 mile), a fairly level self-guided trail to Betatakin Ruin overlook; bring binoculars.

The ranger-led hike to **Betatakin Ruin,** or "ledge house" in Navajo (2.5 miles), is strenuous, requiring a return climb up 700 steps. But it's worth the effort for the walk through the floor of Tsegi Canyon. National Park Service guides lead three tours of 24 hikers each day, May through September. Tokens are awarded on a first-come, first-served basis at the visitor center beginning daily at 8.

The hike to **Keet Seel** (8 miles), the biggest Anasazi ruin in Arizona (160 rooms dating from 950 A.D. to 1300 A.D.) is open to hikers for long weekends, May through October. Much of the trail is sandy, making the trek fairly tiresome. You can stay only one night; 20 people a day may hike in. Reservations are made 60 days in advance, call 602-671-2366. Or take your chances and ask for cancellations when you get there.

Transportation

BY CAR

This is a land of wide-open spaces, but don't despair. Roads have vastly improved in the last decade, easing the way for travelers.

Bounded on the south by **Route 40,** two parallel routes farther north lead east and west through Indian Country: the southern Route 264 travels alongside the three Hopi mesas and Window Rock; the northern Route 160, en route to Colorado, is gateway to all the northern reservation attractions. **Route 89,** the main north-to-south artery, connects Flagstaff with Lake Powell, traversing the Western Reservation. Five other good, paved north-south routes connect Route 40 travelers with Indian Country. **Route 99/2** and **Route 87** connect the Winslow area with Hopi villages. **Route 191** leads to Ganado, Canyon de Chelly and Utah. **Route 12**, arguably the prettiest of all, connects Route 40 with Window Rock and the back side of Canyon de Chelly. This is desert driving; be sure to buy gas when it is available.

BY AIR

There is no regularly scheduled commuter air service to Hopi or Navajo lands. The nearest airports are Gallup, New Mexico; Flagstaff, Arizona; and Cortez, Colorado.

BY BUS

Navajo Transit System (based in Fort Defiance; 602-729-5449) offers weekday bus service between Fort Defiance and Window Rock in the east and Tuba City in the west. The system also heads north from Window Rock to Kayenta on weekdays with stops including Navajo Community College at Tsaile.

BY TRAIN

Amtrak's daily "Southwest Chief" (800-872-7245) connects Los Angeles with Chicago stops at three Indianland gateway cities: Flagstaff, Winslow and Gallup. Nava-Hopi Bus Tours (602-774-5003) out of Flagstaff offers people arriving on Amtrak bus tours to Indian Country.

JEEP TOURS

Jeeps, either with tops down or with air conditioning on (not all jeeps have air conditioning, so ask operators before you pay money) are a popular way to see Navajo Reservation attractions noted for occasional sand bogs and even quicksand pockets. Navajo guides often live in the region and can share area lore and Native American humor.

At Canyon de Chelly, **Thunderbird Lodge Tours** (Thunderbird Lodge, Chinle; 602-674-5443) offer half- or all-day outings in large, noisy, converted all-terrain Army vehicles.

Monument Valley tour operators all offer half-day and all-day tours of Monument and adjoining Mystery Valley. It's the only way visitors can see the stunning back country. Most tours include visits to an inhabited hogan. Some offer lunch or dinner. Licensed operators include **Gouldings Monument Valley Tours** (at Gouldings Lodge near Monument Valley; 801-727-3231); **Tom K. Bennett Tours** (801-727-3283); **Golden Sands Tours** (from the Golden Sands Café on Route 163, one mile north of Route 160 in Kayenta; 602-697-3684); **Bill Crawley Monument Valley Tours** (Kayenta; 602-697-3463); **Frank and Betty Jackson's Dineh Guided Tours** (Monument Valley Visitor Center; 801-727-3287); and **Navajo Guided Tour Service** (Monument Valley Visitor Center; 801-727-3287).

CHAPTER FOUR

Central Arizona

If your image of Arizona is cowboys, ranches and hitching posts, think again, partner. For while the flavor of the West is very much evident in the central band of the state, the trappings of the 20th century are every-where—indeed, flourishing and growing apace. Head to its major cities—including Phoenix, Scottsdale, Tempe and Mesa—and you'll find a vibrant arts community, professional sports galore, shopping centers and stores as far as the eye can see, a fine college campus, intriguing architecture, enough golf, tennis and other activities to satisfy anyone and everyone. But if you're hankering for a glimpse of the frontier or a taste of the outdoor life, well, they're here, too: miles of virgin desert, rivers to swim and sail, towns more in the past than the present, trails to roam. So saddle up, friend.

Phoenix takes its name from the legendary phoenix bird, and with good reason: The biggest metropolis between southern Texas and California and the eighth largest in the country, Phoenix is a city taking flight. The population of Phoenix proper is 1,036,000, which balloons to 2,100,000 when you include the 23 satellite towns that blend seamlessly along the valley of the Salt River. Some thousand families a month set up homes in the broad river valley as subdivisions and shopping centers mushroom.

Phoenix today is a far cry from the era of the Hohokam Indians. It was their disappearance that led early settlers to select the name Phoenix, taken from the symbol of immortality of the ancient Egyptians who believed the bird set itself afire every six centuries and then rose again from the ashes.

The Hohokam, meaning "those who vanished," built a network of ir-rigation ditches to obtain water from the Salt River, part of which is still in use today. Then, as now, irrigation was vital to Phoenix. So much water is piped in to soak fields, groves and little kids' toes that the desert air is actually humid—uncomfortably so through much of the summer. Lettuce, melons, alfalfa, cotton, vegetables, oranges, grapefruit, lemons and olives are grown in abundance in the irrigated fields and groves, lending a touch of green to the otherwise brown landscape. Boating, waterskiing, swimming and even surfing—in a gigantic, mechanically activated pool—are splendid byproducts.

Did we mention sports? Whatever your game, this is sports heaven. In professional competition, Phoenix has baseball (the Triple-A Firebirds), hockey (the Roadrunners) and basketball (the Suns). Plus, the Arizona State University Sun Devils play football, basketball and baseball. Still other spectator sports include rodeos and horse racing. For the active set, there are 125 golf courses and hundreds of tennis courts, as well as bike, jogging and horse-riding trails, and opportunities for all kinds of other pursuits.

The action here isn't all on the field. The downtown area is in the midst of a $1.1 billion redevelopment that began in 1988. Testimony to the effort are the glitzy Arizona Center, the Mexican-themed Mercado and the 18,000-seat America West Arena next to the Civic Center Plaza.

Phoenix is the most air-conditioned city in America. Make no mistake: This desert community and all Central Arizona gets hot despite the seemingly innocuous average annual temperature of 72 degrees. Winter is cool and clear, in the 60s; spring is breezy and warm, in the 90s; summer is torrid, often topping 100, and that's when the monsoons come, the swift summer rainstorms that often arrive late in the day with spectacular flashes of lightning and deep, rolling rumbles of thunder; autumn is marvelously dry and clear, in the 80s. Depending on your weather propensity, choose your time to visit accordingly.

Metropolitan Phoenix, or the Valley of the Sun, originated in 1850 on the banks of the Salt River and became the capital of the Arizona Territory in 1889. At one time, nearly 25,000 Indians were the exclusive inhabitants of Arizona. The earliest were the Hohokam who thrived from 30 A.D. until about 1450 A.D. Signs of their settlements remain intact to this day. Two other major tribal groups followed: the Anasazi in the state's northern plateau highlands, and the Mogollon People, in the northeastern and eastern mountain belt. Today there are 23 reservations in Arizona, more than any other state, with an estimated 50,000 Indians from 17 different tribes living in sad testimony to the white settlers' land grabs. Some 150 miles east of Phoenix in the White Mountain region of northern Arizona is the Fort Apache Reservation with a million and a half acres of land. Bordering it, with another two million acres, is the San Carlos Apache Reservation. The largest Indian reservation in North America, Navajoland, home to 150,000 Navajos, begins 76 miles north of Flagstaff and extends into northwestern New Mexico and southeastern Utah. Located almost in the center of the Navajo Reservation is the Hopi Reservation, 6500 members strong, who

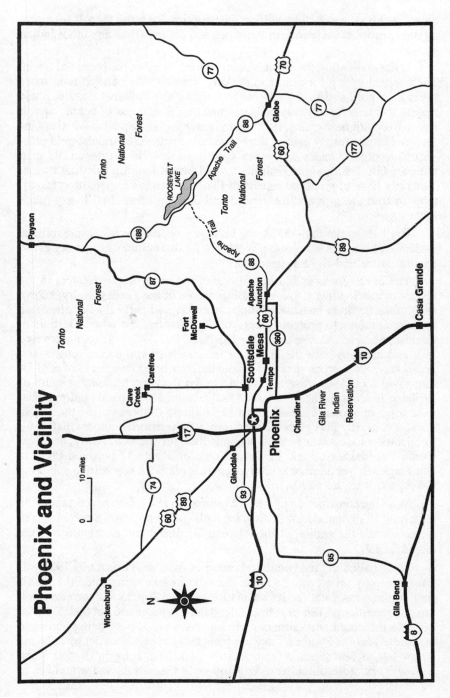

Phoenix and Vicinity

have lived on the same site without interruption for more than 1000 years, retaining more of their ancient traditions and cultures than any other Indian group.

In the mid-1500s, the conquistadors arrived, carrying the banner of Spain. They were looking for gold and seeking souls to save. They found more souls than gold and in the process introduced the Indians to cattle, horse raising and new farming methods, augmenting their crops of beans, squash and maize with new grains, fruits and vegetables. The Spanish-Mexican influence is still strongly evident throughout the Southwest. And the gold prospector eventually became the very symbol of the Old West—an old man with a white beard, alone with his trusted burro, looking to strike it rich. You only have to go 30 miles east of Phoenix into the Superstition Mountains to find the lore and the legend and the lure of gold still very much alive today.

Until about the mid-1880s, the Indians accepted the few white miners, traders and farmers who came West, but as the number of settlers grew, friction arose and fighting resulted.

The cavalry was called in and one of the most brutal chapters in the history of the Southwest followed. Black troops of the Tenth Cavalry, known as Buffalo Soldiers because of their dark skin and curly black hair, came in large numbers to protect citizens of the Arizona land where Geronimo, Cochise, Mangus, Alchise and other chieftains had dotted the cactus-covered hills and canyons with the graves of thousands of emigrants, settlers and prospectors. Numerous sites throughout the state bring those days of conflict into vivid focus—Cochise Stronghold in the Dragoon Mountains south of Willcox, hideout of the notorious Apache chief; Fort Bowie National Historic Site, an adobe ruin that was a key military outpost during the Indian wars, and nearby Fort Huachuca, an important territorial outpost that's still in operation today as a communications base for the U.S. Army; and Fort Verde State Historic Park, in Camp Verde on Route 17 between Phoenix and Flagstaff, yet another military base that played a key role in subduing the Apaches in the 1870s.

With the construction of the first railroad in 1887, fast-paced expansion took hold as Phoenix drew settlers from all over the United States. In 1889 it was named the capital of the Arizona Territory, and statehood was declared in 1912.

Once hailed as the agricultural center of Arizona, Phoenix by 1920 was already highly urbanized. Its horse-drawn carriages represented the state's first public transportation. Its population reached 29,053 and the surrounding communities of Tempe, Mesa, Glendale, Chandler and Scottsdale added 8636 to the count. As farmers and ranchers were slowly being squeezed out, these years of Phoenix's development saw a rugged frontier town trying to emulate as best it could famous cities back East. It had a Boston Store, a New York store, three New England-style tea parlors and a number of gourmet shops selling everything from smoked herring to Delaware cream cheese. The region's dry desert air also began to attract scores of "health-seekers." The advent of scheduled airline service and the proliferation of dude ranches, resorts and other tourist attractions changed the character of the city still further.

Today, high-tech industry forms the economic core of Phoenix, while tourism remains the state's number one job-producer. Not surprisingly, construction is the city's third major industry. But Phoenix retains a strong community flavor. Its downtown area isn't saturated with block after block of highrises and apartment houses. The city and all its suburbs form an orderly, 800-square-mile pattern of streets and avenues running north and south and east and west, with periphery access gained by soaring Los Angeles-style freeways. Beyond are the mountains and desert, which offer an escape from city living, with camping, hiking and other recreational facilities.

If the desert isn't your scene, neighboring Scottsdale just might be. Billing itself as "The West's Most Western Town," Scottsdale is about as "Western" as Beverly Hills.

Scottsdale's population of 134,000 appears to be made up primarily of "snow birds" who came to stay: rich retirees from other parts of the United States who enjoy the sun, the golf courses, the swimming pools, the mountains, the bolo ties and the almost endless selection of handicraft shops, boutiques and over 120 art galleries. Actually, retired persons account for only 20 percent of this fast-growing city, whose median adult age is 34. There are far more yuppies than grandmas.

Scottsdale was only desert land in 1888 when U.S. Army Chaplain Winfield Scott bought a parcel of land near the Arizona Canal at the base of Camelback Mountain. Before long, much of the cactus and greasewood trees had been replaced by 80 acres of barley, a 20-acre vineyard and 50 orange trees. Scottsdale remained a small agricultural and ranching community until after World War II. Motorola opened a plant in Scottsdale in 1945, becoming the first of many electronics manufacturing firms to locate in the valley.

Less than a quarter-mile square in size when it was incorporated in 1951, Scottsdale now spreads over 138 square miles. Its unparalleled growth would appear never-ending except that the city is now braced up against the 50,000-acre Salt River Indian Reservation, established in 1879 and home of the Pima and Maricopa Indians who haven't let their juxtaposition with one of the nation's wealthiest communities go unrewarded. The reservation boasts one of the largest shopping malls in the Southwest, a junior college, thousands of acres of productive farmland and future hotel sites.

The network of satellite communities that surrounds the Phoenix-Scottsdale area, like random pieces of a jigsaw puzzle, is primarily made up of bedroom communities. Tempe to the south is home of Arizona State

University. Burgeoning Glendale, to the northwest, was originally founded as a "temperance colony" where the sale of intoxicants was forever forbidden. Mesa, to the east, covering 100 square miles, is Arizona's third-largest city. Carefree and Cave Creek, to the north, are two communities sheltered by the Sonoran Desert foothills and surrounded by mountains. Carefree was planned for those who enjoy fun-in-the-sun activities like tennis, golf and horseback riding. Cave Creek, a booming ranching and mining center back in 1873, thrives on its strong Western flavor. A bit hokey, but fun. Like fallout from a starburst, these and other neighboring communities all revolve around the tempo, pace and heartbeat of the Phoenix-Scottsdale core. Beyond the urban centers, Arizona's broad central band sweeps across the state in what visiting English author J. B. Priestley once described as "geology by day and astronomy by night." You can pull up to a gas station that's the last one from anywhere, visit honkey-tonk saloons, skinny-dip in a mountain lake, pan for gold, meet dreamers and drifters. The best way to see the West is to be part of it, to feel the currents of its rivers or the steepness of its hills underfoot. Central Arizona certainly offers ample opportunity.

Phoenix

The history of Central Arizona unravels in smooth, easy chapters through Phoenix's museums and attractions, particularly highlighting its Indian heritage. But this is by no means all you'll find here. The city is also a bustling art mecca, evident from the moment visitors arrive at Sky Harbor Airport, with its array of contemporary and Western artworks on display. The airport's program of changing art exhibits, in conjunction with the Phoenix Art Commission, is a model for similar programs at airports throughout the country. Art is everywhere in the city. Along Squaw Peak Freeway, a ten-mile stretch that connects downtown Phoenix with the city's northern suburbs, you may think you're seeing things, and you are. The freeway is lined with 35 giant three- and four-foot sculptures—vases, cups, Indian-style pots and other utensils, all part of the city's public arts project "to make people feel more at home with the freeway." Not everyone in Phoenix loves the idea. Detractors have dubbed the freeway art project "Chamber Pots of the Gods."

Surely the last of the rugged Marlboro men can still be seen astride handsome, well-groomed horses in Phoenix, but they're not riding off into the sunset, never to be seen again. Chances are they're heading into the vast expanse of desert land that still surrounds the city proper to recharge their motors. Long considered a scourge of man, arid and untamable, the desert with its raw awesome beauty is now considered by many as the last vestige of America's wilderness. Numerous tour operators offer guided jeep and horseback tours into the desert, but as any Arizonian will tell you, the desert is best appreciated alone. Southwest Indians have long known the secrets of the desert. Now the settler man comes to turn his face skyward into the pale desert sun.

But whether the city proper or its environs are your scene, trying to take in all the sights and sounds in one trip is a bit like counting the grains of sand in a desert. We suppose it can be done, but who on earth has the time? To help you on your quest, here are some of this city's highlights.

Southwest anthropology and primitive arts are featured at **The Heard Museum** (22 East Monte Vista Road; 602-252-8840; admission). The 18 exhibition galleries on three levels include a Hopi kachina collection, Cochi story-teller figures, pottery by Maria Martinez, silver and turquoise jewelry, basketry, blankets and other Native American crafts. Indian art demonstrations are frequently presented.

Phoenix Art Museum (1625 North Central Avenue; 602-257-1222; admission) adjacent to the Phoenix Public Library, features exhibits on Western, contemporary and decorative arts. This Frank Lloyd Wright-style, two-story stucco building has an outstanding collection of Arizona costumes, accessories and textiles, as well as its Asia Gallery of Oriental paintings, ritual objects, porcelains and cloisonné. The research library includes over 32,000 books, monographs and art periodicals. Kids won't want to miss the junior museum downstairs where they can indulge their creativity in a variety of media.

Literally a museum piece of a museum, the state's first, **Phoenix Museum of History** (1002 West Van Buren Street; 602-253-2734) is housed in its original adobe building (circa 1927). Here you'll find a marvelous collection of curios and antiquities covering 2000 years of Arizona history all jammed into the museum's tiny confines. Highlights include prehistoric Native American artifacts and a display on the evolution of Phoenix through the 1930s. Paintings by early Arizona artists, the state's oldest railroad locomotive, instruments from the Phoenix band and political memorabilia are also found here. The gift shop has a good selection of Arizona history books.

Wander over to the **Arizona State Capitol Museum** (1700 West Washington Street; 602-542-4675), built in 1900 to serve as the Territorial Capitol. The building has been restored to the 1912 era when Arizona won statehood. Guided tours feature permanent exhibits in the Senate Chambers, the Governor's Suite and the Rotunda. A wax figure of the state's first Governor, George Hunt, is seated at his rolltop desk surrounded by period furnishings. Major artifacts include the original silver service taken from the *U.S.S. Arizona* before the battleship was sunk at Pearl Harbor and the roughrider flag carried up Cuba's San Juan Hill during the Spanish American War.

Mineral and ores from Arizona and the rest of the world are displayed at the **Arizona Mining and Mineral Museum** (1502 West Washington Street; 602-255-3791), one of the finest of its kind in the Southwest.

Over at the **Hall of Fame Museum** (1101 West Washington Street; 602-255-2110) you'll find exhibits dedicated to the women, territorial lawmen and cattle ranchers who made Arizona what it is today. Crammed with artifacts, each section offers insight on the colorful lives of pioneers who built this state. Among the highlights is Wyatt Earp's gun.

Painted in 35 colors, **The Mercado** (Van Buren Street between 5th and 7th streets; 602-256-6322) is composed of half a dozen commercial buildings patterned on a traditional Mexican village. This two-block-long complex includes shops offering Western wear, Indian jewelry and African American handicrafts. Beautiful courtyards add to the charm of this eclectic complex that features two restaurants.

A Mercado highlight, **Museo Chicano** (641 East Van Buren Street; 602-257-5536; admission) features changing exhibits ranging from local to international focus. Hispanic culture, arts and history are exhibited, as well as the work of well known and emerging artists. In addition, the museum offers a popular series of cultural programs and performing arts events, such as the city's Mexican Ballet Folklorico.

It seems appropriate—a museum of science and technology located in a parking garage! That's where you'll find the **Arizona Museum of Science and Technology** (80 North 2nd Street; 602-256-9388; admission) which features energy, physics and life sciences exhibits, and a hands-on young people's discovery arcade, all located on the main level of the Hyatt Regency parking garage. The focus is on subjects like gravity, momentum, energy, nutrition and infinity. Also on display are stars of the Southwestern desert such as the iguana, gila monster, python, vine snake and tortoise.

Heritage Square (7th and Monroe streets; 602-262-5071) is a Southwestern time warp featuring eight turn-of-the-century homes, the Arizona Doll and Toy Museum, an Artist's Cooperative, the Heart and Hand Tea Room and Jack and Jenny's Barn and Grill. The **Silva House**, a Victorian style-bungalow, has exhibits ranging from turn-of-the-century swimsuits to origami. At the **Rosson House**, an 1895 Eastlake Victorian, you'll see a beautiful collection of period furniture. Be sure to browse at the **Artist's Cooperative** for weavings, raku pottery, jewelry, wearable art and ceramics.

For a glimpse into the Hohokam tribe's past, visit the **Pueblo Grande Museum** (4619 East Washington Street; 602-495-0901; admission). The exhibits include a prehistoric Hohokam ruin, a permanent display on this legendary tribe and a changing gallery featuring Southwestern Indian arts and crafts. Of special interest is an outdoor trail that leads visitors to the top of a Hohokam platform mound. There is also an interactive exhibit for children.

Not far from the central Phoenix museums is the **Desert Botanical Garden** (1201 North Galvin Parkway; 602-941-1225; admission) where more than 15,000 plants from desert lands of Africa, Australia, North and South America are displayed. You can see this beautiful garden via a self-guided nature walk or a group tour. New is a three-acre showcase of native Sonoran desert plants, a saguaro forest, a mesquite thicket, a desert stream and an upland chaparral habitat, complete with historic Native American dwellings.

Nearby is the **Phoenix Zoo** (5810 East Van Buren Street; 602-273-1341; admission) which uses natural settings, including a four-acre African Savanna, to showcase over 1300 mammals, birds and reptiles. Phoenix newcomers are frequently startled to find themselves driving along busy Van Buren alongside a family of trumpeting elephants. For a convenient zoo overview take the Safari train. Popular highlights are the World Herd of Arabian Oryx, a rare Sumatran tiger exhibit and the Baboon Kingdom. Children will especially enjoy the hands-on participatory exhibit called Wildlife Encounters-Mammals. Be sure to visit the one-acre tropical rainforest, the home of 15 bird and animal species adopted from around the world.

The largest firefighting museum in the nation is the **Hall of Flame Museum** (6101 East Van Buren Street; 602-275-3473; admission). On display are more than 90 restored hand-drawn, horse-drawn and motorized fire engines and hundreds of artifacts. Special games, exhibits and programs, all stressing fire safety, are offered for children.

Tucked away in the foothills of South Mountain Park, the **Mystery Castle** (800 East Mineral Road, end of South 7th Street; 602-268-1581; admission) is an 18-room extravaganza fashioned from native stone, sand, cement, water, goat's milk and Stutz Bearcat wire-rim wheels. Warmed by 13 fireplaces, the parapeted castle has a cantilevered stairway, chapel and dozens of nooks and crannies and is furnished with Southwestern antiques. It's known as the "mystery" castle because the builder, Boyce Luther Gulley, thinking he was about to die from tuberculosis, ran away from his Seattle home in a Stutz Bearcat and devoted 15 years to the construction project. It was only after his death in 1945 that the missing builder's family learned of his whereabouts and inherited the castle.

Pioneer Arizona Living History Museum (Pioneer Road, exit off Route 17; 602-993-0212; admission) re-creates an Old West town using original buildings—a church, schoolhouse, printing shop and blacksmith shop—and featuring costumed interpreters. Living history exhibitions include cooking, gardening and sewing. At the opera house you'll see melodramas, music and dance performances all themed to the territorial period, 1858 to 1912. Of special interest is one of our nation's last remaining herds of colonial Spanish horses. You can also enjoy weekend wagon rides the picnic area and a restaurant specializing in barbecue.

PHOENIX HOTELS

As a major resort and convention center, the Valley of the Sun features some of the most spectacular hotel resorts in the country. It has had the rare distinction of having more *Mobil Travel Guide* Five Star resorts (three of the 12 top-rated resorts nationwide) than any other city in the United States (see "Spoil Yourself" below). Yet it's not without its share of budget- and moderate-priced hotels and motels, and proliferating bed and breakfasts.

An elegant scene of the past is mirrored in the glossy facade of the present with the rebirth of the **San Carlos Hotel** (202 North Central Avenue; 602-253-4121) in the heart of downtown. Built in 1927, the seven-story San Carlos was overhauled recently, but its charm was kept intact—a crystal chandelier and period furnishing in the lobby, original bathtubs, basins and furniture in the 120 guest rooms. Deep carpets line the hallways. There's even a London taxi (circa 1932) to pick guests up at the airport. Afternoon tea and lights snacks are served in the Palm Room. The San Carlos is one of the largest hotels listed in the National Register of Historic Places. Moderate.

The 24-story **Hyatt Regency Phoenix** (2nd and Adams streets; 602-252-1234) is across from Civic Plaza downtown. With 711 rooms, it's the city's largest hotel. It has a heated swimming pool, exercise equipment, a café, lounges and revolving roof-top dining room. Rooms are smallish but tastefully furnished in a light, Southwest style. Deluxe.

A find, price-wise, is the **Pyramid Inn** (3307 East Van Buren Street; 602-275-3691), an attractive two-story brick inn with 30 large, newly decorated rooms—mauve and green color themes predominating— and a swimming pool. Budget.

For those interested in meeting fellow budget-travelers try the **Hostel Metcalf House** (1029 North 9th Street; 602-254-9803). Here's what you get: two dormitory-style rooms (men's and women's) with bunk beds for ten in each. Guests may use the kitchen and community room.

The **YMCA** (350 North 1st Avenue; 602-253-6181) has 140 rooms in an eight-story downtown building. It's good old Y-style, nothing fancy, but it's clean. Budget.

If you want to can stay in shape while you're away, try the **City Square Hotel & Athletic Club** (100 West Clarendon Avenue; 602-279-9811), a full-service hotel with 171 rooms, restaurant and lounge along with a full-scale athletic club facility including sauna, steamroom and swimming pool. Rooms are standard Southwest decor, but the workout's great. Moderate.

If you're on a budget, you've come to the right place. **Warren House East** (2911 East Indian School Road; 602-956-1345) is a motel with a restaurant, swimming pool and tennis courts. Its 89 rooms are furnished in contemporary styles, with light desert colors. Best yet, most have kitchen units and refrigerators. Budget.

Desert Sun Hotel (1325 Grand Avenue; 602-258-8971) offers 100 rooms with modern furnishings and various color themes. It has a 24-hour restaurant, a lounge, swimming pool, and the price is right—budget.

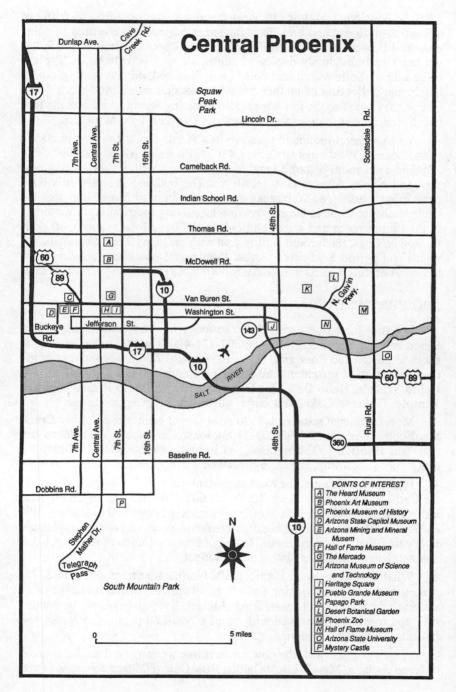

Central Phoenix

Dunlap Ave.

Cave Creek Rd.

Squaw Peak Park

Lincoln Dr.

7th Ave.

Central Ave.

7th St.

16th St.

Scottsdale Rd.

Camelback Rd.

Indian School Rd.

48th St.

Thomas Rd.

McDowell Rd.

Van Buren St.

Washington St.

Jefferson St.

Buckeye Rd.

N. Galvin Pkwy.

RIVER

SALT

Baseline Rd.

Rural Rd.

Dobbins Rd.

Stephen Mather Dr.

Telegraph Pass

South Mountain Park

N

0   5 miles

POINTS OF INTEREST
A The Heard Museum
B Phoenix Art Museum
C Phoenix Museum of History
D Arizona State Capitol Museum
E Arizona Mining and Mineral Musem
F Hall of Fame Museum
G The Mercado
H Arizona Museum of Science and Technology
I Heritage Square
J Pueblo Grande Museum
K Papago Park
L Desert Botanical Garden
M Phoenix Zoo
N Hall of Flame Museum
O Arizona State University
P Mystery Castle

The **Maricopa Manor** (15 West Pasadena Avenue; 602-274-6302) is a Spanish-style bed and breakfast situated in a garden-like setting of palm trees and flowers in the heart of north central Phoenix. Built in 1928, the inn has five individually decorated suites, all with private baths. Typical is the Library Suite with its canopied king-sized bed, private deck entrance, handsome collection of leather-bound books and an antique work desk. Guests may also use the inn's spacious Gathering Room as well as the formal living, dining, music rooms, patio and gazebo spa. Moderate.

Set in a desert mountain preserve in a serene foothill setting in northwest Phoenix, **Westways** (P.O. Box 41624, Phoenix, AZ 85080; 602-582-3868) is a six-room bed-and-breakfast mini-resort with its own swimming pool and nearby country club privileges. The building is styled in a contemporary Spanish Mediterranean design with interior furnishings that include leather and oak in the sunken-fireplace living room, antique Victorian in the dining room and rattan and oak in the large leisure room, all with vaulted ceilings. Each room is furnished with brass, wicker, oak, rattan, antiques and period Southwest pieces. Continental breakfasts are served in the summer, full American breakfasts during the rest of the year. Moderate.

PHOENIX RESTAURANTS

Looking for a quick snack? Go to toney new **Arizona Center** (Van Buren between 3rd and 5th streets; 602-271-4000) and take the elevator or stairs to the second floor and, viola! Here you'll find a whole array of attractive fast-food restaurants all sharing a mutual sit-down dining area— **Fajita Willy's, Hello Deli, Hot Dogs on a Stick, Scotto Pizza, Teriyaki Temple, Chinese Cake**, and more, all in the budget-price range.

More traditional restaurants in Arizona Center include the **Copper Creek Steakhouse and Grille** (602-253-7100), for steaks, rotisseries, chicken and fish, and **Hooters** (602-257-0000), as in owls, an unrefined, delightfully tacky spot for shrimp, clams, oysters and seafood salads. Both moderate.

It's said breakfast is the most important meal of the day, which makes the **Cadillac Café** (4540 North 7th Street; 602-266-2922) an important place indeed—fresh-baked breads, muffins, biscuits, pastries and cinnamon rolls and Kona coffee from Hawaii highlight breakfast specials served in this pleasant little café filled with antiques and fresh-cut flowers. Lunch of the soup, salad and sandwich variety is also served. Budget.

What it lacks in decor, **Ham's** (3302 North 24th Street; 602-954-8775) makes up for in great cooking and affordable prices. Specials change daily and include Yankee pot roast, fried chicken, liver and onions, barbecued beef and meatloaf, all served with heaps of mashed potatoes, veggies and biscuits. Budget to moderate.

A spot popular with the downtown office workers anxious for a touch of home cooking, **Mrs. White's Golden Rule Café** (808 East Jefferson Street;

602-262-9256) offers pork chops, chicken, cornbread and cobbler. Get there early for a table. Closed weekends. Moderate.

The French Corner (50 East Camelback Road; 602-234-0245) is a noisy brasserie with its own bakery and a live jazz band. On the menu are soups, salads, quiche, rich, heavenly omelettes and other French delights. The restaurant is small, two dining rooms with marble-top tables and overhead fans, à la Casablanca. The wine is fine. Deluxe.

A popular neighborhood restaurant, Lone Star Steaks (6003 North 16th Street; 602-248-7827) really looks like it was transferred over from Dallas with its neon beer signs, glowing jukebox, antique wall memorabilia (old Texas license plates and the like) and chalkboard menus. Seating is in booths and formica-topped tables. Steaks come in a variety of sizes, from an eight-ounce fillet to an 18-ounce Lone Star, but the biggest seller of all are the chicken-fried steaks served with heaps of mashed potatoes and buttermilk biscuits, just like in Texas. Moderate.

The Gold Room Bar & Grill (24th Street and Missouri Avenue; 602-954-2504) is the open, airy dining room at the Arizona Biltmore where its traditional grille menu includes mesquite-grilled steaks, seafood, veal and poultry as well as such bistro-style items as white bean casserole garlic herb sausage with duck confit, and braised osso buco and potato gnocchi. Pastas are also available. Deluxe.

With a dozen aquariums scattered around the lobby and dining room, the Golden Phoenix (1534 West Camelback Road; 602-279-4447) appears to have the largest tropical fish population of any restaurant in Arizona. While the decor of this stucco-style establishment offers few Asian touches, the kitchen does wonders with Mandarin dishes like *kung pao* shrimp, hot sizzling beef and chicken. Moderate.

Christopher Gross, the chef-owner of Christopher's (2398 East Camelback Road; 602-957-3214) was recently named one of the ten top chefs in the country and now you can hardly get into the place. It's located in the Biltmore Financial Center, which is good; wait 'til you see the bill. Contemporary French food is served in a small (16 tables) candlelit dining room, all new and gleaming. The attentive waiters really know their wines, so helpful advice is available if needed. Ultra-deluxe. Adjacent to Christopher's is The Bistro, same owner, same kitchen, different entrances, but far more casual, with a marble floor and open kitchen. Deluxe.

Known for its steaks and its bakery, Oscar Taylor's (2420 East Camelback Road, Phoenix; 602-956-5705) is a handsome oak paneled restaurant appointed with leaded glass and historic photos of the windy city, Chicago. There's booth and table seating as well as patio dining off the bakery and lounge. The menu features prime rib, barbecued specialties, pasta and veal. And then there's the excellent desserts and homemade breads. Moderate.

At **Ayako of Tokyo** (2564 East Camelback Road, Phoenix; 602-955-7009), Teppan Yaki chefs grill chicken, scallops, shrimp, filet mignon and lobster at your table. Each entrée comes with soup, salad, rice, vegetables and green tea. Rice paper screens add a Japanese touch to the decor of this restaurant graced with Oriental paintings and panels. There are also sushi and tempura bars, as well as a lounge. Moderate to deluxe.

Havana Café (4225 East Camelback Road; 602-952-1991) offers the not-too-spicy cuisine of Spain and Cuba in an atmosphere that's more a small, cozy café than in the style of Hemingway's Havana. *Chicharitas*, an appetizer of fried green plantain chips, will get the juices flowing. There's saucy chicken with blends of herbs, spices, rice, tomatoes, vegetables and olive oil and paella (for two), the house specialty, sausage, *sopa de ajo* (garlic soup), *escabeche*, *picadillo* and more. Moderate.

The moderately priced **Christo's** (6327 North 7th Street; 602-264-1784) specializes in Northern Italian cuisine, which means less pasta in favor of meatier fare—chicken *zingarella*, osso buco veal, rack of lamb—and fish dishes such as halibut topped with goat cheese, olive oil, garlic and sliced tomatoes. Sparkling stemware, crisp pink-and-white tablecloths and table flowers add a festive note.

With legions of regulars stopping by, **Chubb's** (6522 North 16th Street; 602-279-3459) is dimly lit and comfortable with fine decor (dark-wood paneling, columns, booths, tables and captain's chairs, ceiling fans and globed chandeliers). That sets the tone for hearty meals such as juicy prime rib, steak, pork chops and teriyaki chicken. Moderate.

And you thought diners went the way of the dinosaur. Step into **Ed Debevic's Short Orders Deluxe** (2102 East Highland Drive; 602-956-2760) and you'll find yourself back in the 1950s, complete with tabletop jukeboxes, photos of Marilyn, blue-plate specials, burgers, shakes and fries. The budget prices are right out of the past, too.

PHOENIX SHOPPING

Western wear would seem a natural when hitting the shopping scene—and you're right. There's a herd of places selling boots, shirts, buckles and whatever else you might want. If you're in the market for Western clothes, just to look the part or to get ready for your next rodeo appearance you might start with **Aztex Hats** (15044 North Cave Creek; 602-971-9090) offering the largest selection of Western hats in Arizona. **Frontier Boot Corral** (7th and Van Buren streets; 602-258-2830) has been in business for over 40 years with a complete line of Western wear. **Saba's Western Store** (2901 West Bell Road; 602-993-5948), in business since 1927, includes Barry Goldwater among its clientele. Saba's also has stores in Mesa, Chandler and Scottsdale. **Sheplers** (9201 North 29th Avenue; 602-870-8085) is part of the world's largest Western-wear chain.

If you like malls and shopping complexes, get ready. Phoenix has them in abundance. Some of the best are: **Park Central Mall** (Central Avenue and Earll Drive; 602-264-5575) is the city's best-known shopping center and the oldest. Fashionable **Dillard's** department store can be found here. **Metrocenter** (9617 Metro Parkway West; 602-997-2641) is an enclosed double-deck mall that includes **Robinson's, Dillard's** and **Broadway.**

One of the newest additions to downtown Phoenix is **The Mercado** (Van Buren Street between 5th and 7th streets; 602-256-6322) a festive mall and Mexican cultural center adjacent to the Phoenix Civic Plaza, with colorful buildings, brick-lined streets and outdoor dining. Mexican shops and restaurants feature arts, crafts, fashions and good things to eat of the hot and spicy persuasion.

For designer merchandise at legendary low prices head for **Loehmann's** (3135 East Lincoln Drive).

Located in a 90 year-old Heritage Square home, **Craftsmen's Gallery** (614 East Adams Street, Phoenix; 602-253-7770) is an intriguing art cooperative. Here 26 artists exhibit dolls, basket weaving, pottery, wearable art and wood-dried flowers.

Museum gifts shops also offer unique finds for selective shoppers. For instance, the **Phoenix Art Museum** (1625 North Central Avenue; 602-257-1222) offers books, posters, catalogs and art-replica gifts. It also has a special section for children.

The **Desert Botanical Garden** (1201 North Galvin Parkway; 602-941-1225) has a gift shop offering foods, spices and jellies made from desert plants, as well as nature books and Southwest souvenirs and crafts; plants are sold in an adjoining greenhouse.

Don't drop just yet. Because after all those malls and other stores, we come to the farmers' markets! Every Wednesday afternoon farmers from around the community sell their freshest produce at low prices in the courtyard at **Heritage Square** (Monroe and 7th streets; 602-262-5071).

For a kicker, **American Park N Swap** (3801 East Washington Street, Phoenix; 602-273-1258) is the largest open-air flea market in the Southwest, with over 2000 dealers selling or swapping everything from used office furniture and rare antiques to Indian jewelry and rare one-of-a-kind photos of Marilyn Monroe.

A small town south of Phoenix is the setting for the **Guadalupe Farmer's Market** (8808 South Avenida del Yaqui, Guadalupe) for fresh vegetables, exotic fruits and dried chili peppers. A few blocks north is **Mercado Mexico** (8212 South Avenida del Yaqui, Guadalupe; 602-831-5925) where Mexican *dulces* (sweets) are sold—*ates* (jellied fruit candies), sugared pecans, lightly dusted chocolate balls, jars of *cajeta*, a caramel sauce made from goat's milk, and other sticky delights. You'll find a good range of handicrafts and souvenirs from Mexico here as well.

PHOENIX NIGHTLIFE

Nightlife in Central Arizona is as diverse and far-reaching as the area itself, from twanging guitars of country-and-western bands to symphony strings. There are Indian ceremonials and sophisticated jazz as well. To find out what's happening, check the entertainment pages of the *Arizona Republic* and the *Phoenix Gazette*.

With its array of major resorts, much of the valley's nightlife centers around the hotel entertainment scene.

If you feel more adventurous, you might try some of the following: **Graham Central Station** (40029 North 33rd Avenue; 602-279-4226) where traditional and country-and-western music can be heard nightly, with big-name acts, concerts and live bands. Friday's happy hour is one of the best in town.

From the sound of things, **America's Original Sports Bar** (455 North 5th Street; 602-252-2502), on the ground level of the Arizona Center, might seem to newcomers like a place for nightly brawls. No way. There are miniature golf, basketball hoops to shoot at and even a volleyball court, all in the Valley's trendiest new bar. Food is served, and of course plenty of drinks. With all that action you can work up a thirst. Cover. Also in the Arizona Center, upstairs, is the **Cheyenne Cattle Company** (455 North 5th Street; 602-253-6255) a glitzy country-and-western nightspot with live music, cowgirl waitresses and a goodly share of business-expense-account types (the Convention Center is nearby) among the loyal crowd of hooters and honkers. Weekend cover.

A valley institution for the two-step crowd, **Mr. Lucky's** (3660 West Grand Avenue; 602-246-0686) has live country-and-western music upstairs and recorded Top-40 rock-and-roll downstairs. Weekend cover.

"Home of the Nashville Stars," **Toolies Country** (4231 West Thomas Road; 602-272-3100) is a 600-seat frontier Western cabaret with dinner and dancing nightly to the music of big-name country entertainers. Cover.

Acapulco Beach Club (3837 East Thomas Road; 602-273-6077) offers nightly live music, half Latin, half rock. With its south-of-the-border spirit and lively crowd, it's one of the most popular spots in town. Wednesday and weekend cover.

As the name suggests, everyone comes dressed in everything from Levi's to dinner jackets at **Denim and Diamonds** (3905 East Thomas Road; 602-225-0182). Both recorded and live country-and-western sounds, special events and surprise free buffets are offered.

Nightlife here isn't restricted to the bar and two-step scene. A more refined look at the arts flourishes here as well. **The Herberger Theater Center** (221 East Monroe Street, Phoenix; 602-252-8497) is an ultramodern theater complex housing two separate theaters, **Center Stage** and **Stage West**, where professional theater performances take place. The Center is also home to **Ballet Arizona,** the **Phoenix Little Theater,** the **Desert Dance Theater** and numerous traveling troupes. The 2500-seat **Phoenix Symphony Hall** (225 East Adams Street; 602-262-7272) is home to the Phoenix Symphony and stages entertainment ranging from opera and ballet to Broadway shows and name concert performers.

PHOENIX PARKS

South Mountain Park—With 15,000 acres, this is the largest metropolitan park in the United States, a vast rugged mountain range that was once Indian hunting ground. A spectacular view of Phoenix can be seen from Dobbins Lookout, 2300 feet above the desert floor. The park offers 40 miles of well-marked hiking and riding trails. Its steep canyons reveal evidence of ancient Indian artifacts and petroglyphs.

Facilities: Picnic areas, restrooms and a sunken concrete stage for park ranger lectures or impromptu sing-alongs; information, 602-495-0222.

Getting there: Located at 10919 South Central Avenue in Phoenix.

Papago Park—A part of the Phoenix parks network since 1959, Papago is a neat blend of hilly desert terrain, quiet lagoons and glistening streams. The former Indian townsite now offers golf, picnic sites, ballfields and fishing. Also within its boundaries is the Phoenix Zoo, the Desert Botanical Garden and the Hall of Flame Museum.

Facilities: Picnic areas, golf course, firepits, restrooms, softball fields, archery range, bike paths and running courses; information, 602-256-3220.

Fishing: Three lagoons stocked with bass, catfish, bluegill and tilapia. Free for kids 15 and under but a state fishing license is required for all others.

Getting there: Located at 6000 East Van Buren Street in Phoenix.

Squaw Peak Recreation Area—One of Phoenix's most familiar landmarks with its craggy, easily identifiable pinnacle, Squaw Peak is primarily known for its hiking trails. However, the rocky terrain has been moderately developed for more other recreational pursuits as well, whether picnicking or curling up in the shade of a towering saguaro with an Edward Abbey tome on the evils of overdevelopment.

Facilities: Picnic ramadas with electricity, drinking water, firepits, tables, benches and restrooms; information, 602-495-0222.

· *Getting there:* Located at 2701 East Squaw Peak Drive.

Estrella Mountain Regional Park—With 19,200 acres, Estrella offers abundant vegetation and spectacular mountain views, with peaks within the Sierra Estrella Mountains reaching 3650 feet. The park offers excellent areas for hiking and riding, camping, a rodeo arena and golf course. Horse and hiking trails abound.

Facilities: Picnic areas, restrooms, an amphitheater for lectures and gatherings, horse/rodeo arena and golf course; information, 602-506-2930.

Getting there: Located 18 miles southwest of Phoenix via the access road two miles south from Route 85, on Bullard Avenue. Cross the Gila River and then turn right on West Vineyard Avenue for one-quarter mile.

Scottsdale

Like neighboring Phoenix, Scottsdale is proud of its frontier heritage, which can be traced at a number of locations in and near the town. In the Old Scottsdale section, where only 35 years ago Lulu Belle's and the Pink Pony were the only two watering holes for miles around, the buildings all have falsefronts, hand-crafted signs and hitching posts, and horses still have the right of way. Many restaurants feature waiters and waitresses in period dress. The women have teased hairdos, and the men are all called Slim, Ace, Tex, Shorty and Stretch.

But that's about as *Western* as it gets. Otherwise, Scottsdale is chic, elegant and expensive. Amid its ties to the past, Scottsdale is a showplace of innovative architecture. The Frank Lloyd Wright Foundation is located here (at Taliesin West), as is the Cosanti Foundation, design headquarters for the controversial prototype town of Arcosanti where building and nature are being fused some 30 miles from Prescott.

Scottsdale is also the center of the Arizona art scene. Galleries flourish here. The **Southwestern Art and Cultural Adventures** (3533 North 70th Street, Suite 201/202; 602-946-8860) offers day and half-day visits to artists' studios, galleries, museums and architectural sites with art experts leading the groups.

Housed in a building made of adobe blocks mixed with desert plants (for strength), the **Hoo-Hoogam Ki Museum** (10000 East Osborn Road; 602-941-7379; admission: free to Native Americans) is located on the Salt River Pima-Maricopa Indian Reservation bordering the city. Here you will find displays of baskets, artifacts, pottery and historical photographs. Basket-weaving demonstrations are presented daily.

Also, don't miss **Rawhide-Arizona's 1880 Western Town** (23023 North Scottsdale Road; 602-563-5111; some attractions have charges) with its colorful variety of rides and attractions, shops, a steakhouse and a saloon—all mostly located along a rickety Main Street where visitors dodge real sheep and goats. Western shootouts, fiddlers, a gypsy fortuneteller, stunt shows, a full-size 1880s-style locomotive, a carriage exhibit, a covered-wagon circle and an Old West museum are all part of the fun.

Taliesin West/Frank Lloyd Wright Foundation (13201 North 108th Street; 602-860-2700; admission), a National Historic Landmark owned by the Frank Lloyd Wright Foundation, was the architect's Arizona home and studio. Situated on 600 acres of rugged Sonoran Desert, this remarkable set of buildings still astounds architectural critics with its beauty and unusual forms. A variety of guided tours are offered. There's also a lecture series.

Adams Arabians (12051 North 96th Street; 602-860-1218) is a world-renowned Arabian horse breeding and training ranch whose owners are receptive to occasional visitors checking out the scene and chatting with the trainers. As a private working ranch, it offers no organized programs or facilities, apart from a Coke machine in the tack room.

Fleisher Museum (17207 North Perimeter Drive; 602-585-3108) has rotating shows and permanent exhibits devoted to "American Expressionism, California School," with lots of ladies from that stylish period between the turn of the century and the 1940s, plus misty, dream-like landscapes, architectural and still-life paintings.

SCOTTSDALE HOTELS

Holiday Inn-Scottsdale (5101 North Scottsdale Road; 602-945-4392) lifts itself out of the ordinary chain motel category with a stunning landscape of desert palms and a mountain backdrop. It has 216 rooms and suites—lots of yellows and beige, with floral paintings on the walls and bright Southwest colors for the slipcovers—built around a large swimming pool, spa and patio. On-premise facilities include the Flamingo Dining Room, Versailles Lounge and a gift shop. Moderate.

Clarion Hotel at Scottsdale Mall (7353 East Indian School Road; 602-994-9203) is located in the heart of "Old Town," close to everything. Its 206 rooms have a Southwest motif. There are a lounge with nightly entertainment, a restaurant, swimming pool and tennis. Moderate.

The revamped **Scottsdale Plaza Resort** (7200 North Scottsdale Road; 602-948-5000) is a true find. Set within 40 acres, with 404 rooms and 180 suites, the resort features Spanish/Mediterranean-style villas throughout, accented with courtyard swimming pools. The rooms are large and styled with Southwest furnishing and art. Fountains, palm trees, earth-tone tiles, mauve carpeting, acres of fresh-cut flowers and potted greens add cooling touches. There are swimming pools, outdoor spas, tennis courts, indoor racquetball courts, a pro shop, gym and, if you need more, croquet. Ultra-deluxe.

If you're looking for a gem of a mini-resort, try the 58-room **Papago Inn & Resort** (7017 East McDowell Road; 602-947-7335). This Best Western property has a heated pool, sauna and hot tub, lounge and dining room. Guest rooms all overlook a treed and flowered interior courtyard and swimming pool. Moderate.

Camelview (701 East Indian Bend Road; 602-991-2400), a Radisson Resort located on 35 lushly landscaped acres in the heart of Scottsdale, has 200 guest rooms (including 17 one- and two-bedroom suites). All reflect the natural colors of the desert and are richly appointed with Southwest and

Indian art. Recreational facilities include tennis courts, nearby golf, jogging trails, horseback riding and a pool. Ultra-deluxe.

Scottsdale's Fifth Avenue Inn (6935 5th Avenue; 602-994-9461), a secluded retreat right in the heart of Scottsdale's premier shopping district, sprawls out around a central courtyard with a large heated swimming pool. Its 92 newly decorated guest rooms feature desert colors, king and double queen beds, and separate dressing areas. Rates includes a full breakfast. Moderate.

One of the oldest homes in the area, Hays House (5615 Lafayette Boulevard; 602-947-0488) is a former citrus ranch house turned into a bed and breakfast. It offers three suites in the main house and two adjoining apartments. All have private baths and are furnished with Persian rugs and an assortment of antique furnishings and paintings. "It's not quite museum status," says the English-born owner. The British background is reflected in the full sumptuous breakfasts served each morning. Two acres of orange and grapefruit trees surround the house. Moderate.

The Thunderbird Inn (7515 East Butherus Drive; 602-951-4000) may be a Best Western property, but don't let the chain-affiliation throw you. It's a four-story, all-suite, deluxe-category hotel designed in a courtyard setting with a heated pool and spa. Each of the hotel's two-room suites is styled in desert mauve and teals with light Southwestern contemporary furnishings.

SCOTTSDALE RESTAURANTS

The first thing seasoned travelers look for when staking out a new town is a good place to have breakfast. In Scottsdale, Boman's N.Y. Kosherstyle Restaurant & Deli (373 North Scottsdale Road; 602-947-2934) hits the spot. Small and nondescript, it has a deli counter on one side, separated from the blue formica tables and banquets by a white picket fence. Ceiling fans, an advertisement for Dr. Brown's Cream Soda and an indifferent waitress pretty much set the ambience. The focus is on good food at moderate prices—french toast, applejack pancakes, ham and eggs. It's also open for lunch and dinner (pastrami on rye, pickles, brisket, chicken in the pot, stuffed cabbage). A sign on the cash register says, "Shalom, Y'all."

Another traditional breakfast spot (it also serves lunch) is The Original Pancake House (6840 East Camelback Road; 602-946-4902), in business over 40 years, serving up steaming stacks of golden flapjacks, topped with melted butter, honey, maple syrup, berries or whatever's your pleasure. The restaurant is small—11 tables (including a huge one for that girl-getting-married-and-leaving-the-office party) and ten booths. The decor is Southwestern with light green and tan colors dominating. Large picture windows in front keep it bright and cheerful. Budget.

Any restaurant that combines American decor with traditional Greek flourishes (would you believe a bellydancing lounge?) has to be interesting. The food at Andros (8040 East McDowell Avenue; 602-945-95673) runs from chicken and burgers to rolled grape leaves, rice and olives, and there's all that great Greek music in the background. Moderate.

The **Marquesa** (7575 East Princess Drive; 602-585-4848) is one of the top restaurants in the valley. Even people who normally avoid hotel dining rooms flock to this one in the Scottsdale Princess Resort to soak up all of its Old World Spanish ambience and nibble on tapas before settling down to more serious pursuits. Roast grouse, in season, with brandy sauce and cranberries, for instance, or steaming Mediterranean-style paella for two. The Marquesa is also known for its excellent wine list. Deluxe.

Don't wear a necktie if you're going to the **Pinnacle Peak Patio** (10426 East Jomax Road; 602-967-8020) because they'll snip it off and hang it from the rafters. That's part of the appeal of this highly informal Western-style steak house where 16-ounce mesquite-broiled steaks, with all the beans and fixin's, top the menu and the walls reverberate with the sounds of live country-and-western bands nightly. Moderate.

You probably won't want to wear a necktie here, either. **Greasewood Flats** (27000 North Alama School Road; no phone) is a hot dog, chili and beer kind of place housed in an old graffiti-covered wooden shack in what appears to be a Western junk yard, with discarded school desks, wooden wagons, saddle frames, wagon wheels, milk cans and egg crates all around it. But folks line up to get in. Budget.

Malee's on Main Thai Gourmet (5641 East Lincoln Drive; 602-947-6042) is a charming little spot with a bar in one corner, tables inside and a patio, weather permitting, for dining outside. Attractive tableware is set against peach and green tablecloths. Popular with the art crowd (in Scottsdale that covers a wide swath), its extensive menu comes in various degrees of spicy intensity. Moderate.

House of Yang (14016 North Scottsdale Road; 602-443-0188) is small, only a few tables and chairs and it appears to do a large take-out business. But whether you eat in or take out, the House of Yang is a course in Chinese cuisine, serving Szechwan, Hunan, Mandarin and Cantonese. Shrimp with lobster sauce comes with shrimp, onions and peppers, stir-fried and topped with a black bean sauce, rice, wantons and egg roll. Mongolian beef is thinly sliced beef with egg roll, fried rice and wantons. Moderate.

The Spanish Colonial setting is spectacular, with high *viga* ceilings, white walls, antique furnishings and sweeping views of the valley. It's **La Relais** (8711 East Pinnacle Peak Road; 602-998-0921), very French and very fine. Both nouvelle and traditional French dishes fill the two-page menu—loin of lamb with garlic and basil, medallions of veil, poached stingray—all served by attentive, black-tied waiters. Ultra-deluxe.

Voltaire (8340 East McDonald Drive; 602-948-1005) is another bastion of French gastronomy, all candlelight and crystal. Boned chicken à la

Normande with apples, sautéed sand dabs, rack of lamb and sweetbreads sautéed in lemon butter and capers highlight the extensive menu. Deluxe.

Rawhide Steakhouse and Saloon (23023 North Scottsdale Road; 602-563-5600) is the place to belly up to the bar in Scottsdale's popular Old West frontier town. There's good things to eat, too—mesquite broiled steaks, prime rib, barbecued chicken, baby back ribs and even fried rattlesnake. The saloon section has an antique bar, gambling tables (but no gambling), "crooked" card dealers and live country music. Deluxe.

Julio's Barrio (7234 East Camelback Road; 602-423-0058), established in 1934, somehow manages to combine a '30s art deco, Santa Fe and Mexican truck-stop decor—ceiling fans, black-tile walls and framed vintage-Mexican advertisements—into a trendy contemporary look. The food is much more clearly defined—*pollo Mexicana*, beef tacos, bean tostadas, steaming bowls of rice and beans, chili con carne and tortillas. Prices are moderate, and the staff is friendly and attentive.

If you're looking for shades of the '60s, you'll find it at **The Soapbox Coffeehouse** (6208 North Scottsdale Road; 602-998-4766) where espresso, quiche, soups, homemade muffins, desserts and exotic teas and coffees are served in that quintessential ambience of chess, backgammon, poetry readings, hot-topic discussions and live jazz, blues and folk music. Moderate.

Shells Oyster Bar & Seafood (5641 East Lincoln Drive; 602-948-7111) is the best known of the four restaurants located at Marriott's Mountain Shadows Resort. Live miniature fish swim in an illuminated aquarium. The decor is bright and airy, with nautical touches, polished brass, etched mirrors and natural wood finishes. Seafood entrées come in a variety of preparations—flame broiled, steamed, sautéed, pan fried or blackened Cajun style, accompanied by a selection of special butters and sauces. Ultra-deluxe.

One of the oldest, and many consider the finest, Mexican restaurant in Scottsdale is **Los Olivos Mexican Patio** (7328 East 2nd Street; 602-946-2256). The restaurant was founded in 1945, but the adobe building in which it's located was built in 1928 and is officially listed as one of Scottsdale's historic landmarks. Large and rambling, with *viga* ceilings, it has several individual dining rooms inside and patio dining outside. The Mexican cuisine served is primarily Sonoran—enchiladas, seasonal green corn tamales, chimichangas, *chile rellenos* and steak picado. The decor is festive (clay pots, flowers and piñatas) and there's live music and dancing on weekends. Aficionados rate its margaritas among the best in the state. Moderate.

If a touch of old Boston at the turn of the century strikes your fancy, stop into the **American Grill** (6113 North Scottsdale Road; 602-948-9907) and you'll think you're there. Dark-wood paneling, polished brass and glass, exposed tile, ceiling fans whooshing over comfortable tables and booths, and a busy open kitchen. Made-to-order clam, Manhattan, corn, fish and cheddar chowders, served with sourdough bread, are the house specialties.

Grilled mustard shrimp, Cajun blackened rockfish, prime rib and hickory-smoked grilled chicken also get a big play. This place is popular with the after-work white-collar crowd and tends to be boisterous at times. Moderate.

SCOTTSDALE SHOPPING

Scottsdale lifts shopping malls and mall shopping to the realm of high art. The **Scottsdale Galleria** (4343 North Scottsdale Road; 602-951-1262), for instance, is a glitzy new shopping complex that breaks the mold with its musical fountains and million-gallon aquarium in the atrium where a tropical rain forest has been created. Oh, yes, there are 165 shops, boutiques, bookstores, galleries and restaurants, including: **Shakespeare and Beethoven** (602-945-2646) for all the latest best sellers and a full range of classical records and tapes, and **L'Escale Paris** (602-488-2123) for ladies' apparel with a French flair.

And **The Borgata of Scottsdale** (6166 North Scottsdale Road; 602-998-1822) may just be a harbinger of a striking new trend in shopping centers—mini-theme-park shopping malls—this one, a 14th-century-styled village with medieval courtyards. International fashions, fine jewelry, unusual gifts, a book and music store and a spate of art galleries await.

Despite the trendy intrusions, **Scottsdale Fashion Square** (7000 East Camelback Road; 602-990-7000) remains Scottsdale's most fashionable shopping complex. It features such top-quality stores as **Neiman Marcus** (602-990-2100), **Dillard's** (602-949-5869) and **Robinson's** (formerly Goldwater's) (602-941-0066). There's even a shop for the kiddies—**The Disney Store** (602-423-5008).

Fifth Avenue Shops (6940 East 5th Avenue; 602-947-5377) comprise the landmark shopping area in the heart of downtown Scottsdale, a sprawl of specialty shops, boutiques, bookstores, galleries, jewelry stores, Indian crafts shops and restaurants, over 70 in all by latest count. Among them: **Sewell's Indian Arts** (602-945-0962) for Indian jewelry, kachina dolls, Pueblo pottery and Navajo sandpaintings; **Lemonade Folk Art** (602-945-2219) for tole painting, howling cows and other country and Southwest folk art and gifts; **Oz Turkish & Oriental Handicrafts** (602-423-5026) for outstanding gifts and imports; **Gallery 10** (602-994-0405) for prints and posters galore, featuring contemporary, Native American and Western artists; and the **Brass Pelican** (602-949-7997) for bells, scrimshaw, lamps, portholes, sextants, binoculars and other things nautical.

Elsewhere, mystery lovers should seek out **The Poisoned Pen** (7100 East Main Street; 602-947-2974), a mystery bookstore specializing in crime, detective and suspense books from American and British publishers.

For you cowpolks, **Porters** (3944 North Brown Avenue; 602-945-0868) is one of the oldest names in Scottsdale cowboy gear and features top-of-the-line name brands.

After New York City and Santa Fe, Scottsdale is the busiest art center in the country, with over 200 galleries offering contemporary works, Indian art, Western and Old Masters.

If you're interested in the local art scene, the **Scottsdale Art Association** (602-941-0900) conducts art walks every Thursday, October through May, from 7 in the evening until 9 p.m., visiting many of the leading galleries. At other times of the year, the Art Walks are conducted on the third Thursday of each month. The Art Walks begin at the Scottsdale Center for the Arts (7383 Scottsdale Mall; 602-944-2787).

If you want to check out the art scene on your own, consider **Arizona West Galleries** (7149 Main Street; 602-994-3752) which specializes in American 19th- and 20th-century Western art, including works by Frederic Remington, Charlie Russell and Maynard Dixon.

The **Biltmore Galleries** (7113 Main Street; 602-947-5975) also features 19th- and 20th-century art, including works by early New Mexico master Nicolai Fechin, Joseph Sharp and Ernest Blumenschein.

Buck Saunders Gallery (2724 North Scottsdale Road; 602-945-9376) has long been the exclusive representative of Arizona's best-known, best-loved artist, Ted De Grazia.

Specializing in abstract and Southwest representational art is **Galerie Sloan** (4151 North Marshall Way; 602-945-8512). Work by currently much-in-demand Cherokee artist Bert Seabourn can be found here.

Glenn Green Galleries (6000 East Camelback Road; 602-990-91110) uses the elegant grounds of the posh Phoenician Resort (the gallery is located in the hotel's retail corridor) to display the mammoth bronze and stone sculptures of famed Indian artist Alan Houser.

J. R. Fine Arts (4151 North Marshall Way; 602-945-7856) handles serigraphs, lithographs, oils and sculpture, including those by top contemporary Indian painters R. C. Gorman and Earl Biss.

SCOTTSDALE NIGHTLIFE

For starters, try the big-band sounds at the Royal Palm Inn's **El Mirage Lounge** (5200 East Camelback Road; 602-840-3610), live contemporary dance music at The Phoenician Resort's **Charlie Charlie's** (6000 East Camelback Road; 602-423-2445), and jazz at the Scottsdale Hyatt Regency's **Lobby Bar** (7500 East Doubletree Ranch Road; 602-991-3388) or **JD's Lounge** (7220 North Scottsdale Road; 602-948-5000) at the Scottsdale Plaza Resort.

Lulu Belle's (7212 East Main Street; 602-994-9800) is the sole survivor of Scottsdale's two original bars (the Pink Pony burned down) and a live country-and-western band keeps a mostly older crowd tapping their toes.

Scottsdale Center for the Arts, located in the beautifully sculptured Civic Center Mall, hosts a variety of events, including the Scottsdale Symphony, guest performing artists, concerts, lectures classic cinema and art exhibitions. During the summer, music lovers flock to the concerts held outside on the grassy lawn at the east end of the mall. For a schedule, call 602-994-2787.

Actors Lab Theater Center (7223 East 2nd Street; 602-990-1731) is the home of Scottsdale's resident professional theater company. It has two stages offering a variety of Broadway productions.

East of Phoenix

Immediately east of Phoenix are the communities of Tempe and Mesa. Continuing out over the desert that stretches on to New Mexico are Apache Junction and Globe. It's as though, heading east, all the big-city sheen dissolves in degrees into the West of the Old West, the pace slows down and you can almost reach up and feel the sky in your hands.

Bordered by Scottsdale, Mesa, Phoenix and Chandler, **Tempe** was founded in 1872 by Charles Turnbell Hayden who established the Hayden Flour Mill that year, now the oldest continuously operating business in Arizona. **Old Town Tempe** (North of University Street along Mill Avenue; 602-894-8158) is where Tempe was originally founded, set up around the old Hayden Flour Mill. Today many of the early homes and buildings have been renovated and serve as restaurants, shops, offices and galleries. Stop by the **Tempe Convention and Visitors Bureau** (60 East 5th Street, Tempe, AZ 85281; 602-894-8158) for maps and information.

Forming the character of Tempe is **Arizona State University,** located in the heart of the city. Home of the Fiesta Bowl, it has the largest enrollment of any school in the Southwest. With its 700-acre main campus, where strikingly modern buildings rise from a setting of palm trees and subtropical plants, Arizona State provides the chiefly residential city with its main industry. A number of outstanding museums dot the campus and are open to the general public. **Arizona State University Art Museum** (602-965-2787) has an extensive collection of American paintings, prints and crafts as well as artworks from Africa, Latin America and the South Seas. The **Museum of Anthropology** (602-965-6213) includes archeological, physical and sociocultural anthropology exhibits. Highlight exhibits at the **Museum of Geology** (602-965-5081) focus on rare geologic specimens, seismographs and earthquake displays.

Tempe also houses the outstanding **Tempe Historical Museum** (809 East Southern Avenue; 602-350-5100; admission) which covers the history of Tempe from early Indian days to the present. Three changing galleries offer art exhibits of contemporary, Native American and Western artists. There are also hands-on displays for children.

For art buffs there is the **Tempe Arts Center and Sculpture Garden** (54 West 1st Street; 602-968-0888) which features eight changing gallery exhibits of contemporary arts, crafts and sculpture. Large-scale works are showcased in the adjoining Sculpture Garden, with many of the works for sale.

Just east of Tempe, you'll come to the town of **Mesa**. Situated on a plateau, Mesa in Spanish means "tabletop." The town was founded by Mormons in 1883 and was long a farming community. Irrigation canals built by the Hohokam Indians were still used in Mesa until fairly recent times. For information on sights and services in Mesa, stop by the **Mesa Convention and Visitors Bureau** (120 North Center Street; 602-969-1307).

Mesa Southwest Museum (53 North MacDonald Street; 602-644-2230; admission) covers the history of the Southwest from the time of the dinosaurs to the settlement of the West, with hands-on exhibits inside and a one-room schoolhouse and a gold-panning stream outside.

A find for aviation aficionados, the **Champlin Fighter Museum** (4636 Fighter Aces Drive; 602-830-4540; admission) has a collection of 30 restored fighters from World War I, World War II and the Korean and Vietnam wars. Historic weaponry is also displayed. An art gallery, video theater and pilot-memorabilia gift shop round out the bill.

Twenty minutes north of Mesa in Fountain Hills is the **Out of Africa Wildlife Park** (2 South Fort McDowell Road; 602-837-7779; admission) where lions, tigers, leopards and giant pythons do their things. There are shows, natural habitat viewing. cub-petting and a playground for the kids. There's also a gift shop and restaurant.

The meeting point of Routes 60, 80 and 89 (the Apache Trail) about 30 miles to the east of Phoenix is **Apache Junction**. Once only a sunburned babble of bars, motels and filling stations, it has grown so much of late that local dude ranch operators are complaining that there's no range left to ride. A statue of Jacob Walts in the center of the town honors the man believed to have discovered an elusive gold treasure but died with the secret of its location unspoken—the Lost Dutchman Gold Mine.

Seekers of the precious metal may want to head out to the **Superstition Mountains**. With blunted peaks reaching well over 6000 feet and razor-edged canyons plunging into the pit of the earth, they comprise an area 40 miles long and 15 miles wide—some of the roughest, rockiest, most treacherous terrain in the United States. Located about 30 miles east of Phoenix, the mountains are part of the National Forest Wilderness System. As such, the use of motorized equipment of any kind is forbidden. With the help of experienced guides, you can lash your gear to packhorses and mount up for a three-to-seven day—or longer—trip where you can pan for gold or search for the legendary Lost Dutchman Gold Mine, for which the mountains are most famous, or simply ride the wilderness trails, camp, cook, bathe in icy streams and sleep out under the stars. For information, contact **Peralta Riding Stables and Pack Trips** (Meridian Road; 602-982-5488), **Superstition Stables** (North Meridian Drive; 602-982-6353) or the **Superstition Mountain Guide Service** (602-982-4949), all in Apache Junction.

Superstition Mountain/Lost Dutchman Museum (Route 88; 602-983-4888; admission) displays historical artifacts pertaining to the legend of the Lost Dutchman Gold Mine, along with folk art, prehistoric Indian artifacts, Spanish and Mexican crafts and documents, pottery and relics of early cowboys, prospectors and miners. For more information contact the **Apache Junction Chamber of Commerce** (P.O. Box 1747, Apache Junction, AZ 85219; 602-982-3141).

Globe, at the eastern end of the Apache Trail, was originally named "Besh-ba-Gowah" by the Apaches, meaning "place of metal." It was silver that brought the first settlers—the town is named for a globe-shaped piece of silver whose surface resembled continents—but copper is what formed and sustained the economy. Cattle ranching also helped in its development. More information about the area can be obtained at the **Greater Globe-Miami Chamber of Commerce** (1450 North Broad Street, Globe, AZ 85502; 602-425-4495).

Besh-Ba-Gowah Archaeological Park (150 Pine Street; 602-425-0320; admission) was the home of the Salado people from 1225 A.D. to 1400 A.D., who built a great pueblo containing 300 rooms that once housed an estimated 1500 people. A period of excavation, restructuring and stabilization began in 1985, and three years later the park was open to the public. Along with the impressive ruins, the park has a visitor center and museum displaying artifacts, models and photographs relating to the site.

Continuing in Globe, **The Cobre Valley Center for the Arts** (101 North Broad Street; 602-425-0880), housed in the old Gila County Courthouse, is a showcase for local and regional artists and the courthouse building itself is a prize model of restoration.

The rip-roaring days of the early miners come to life at the **Gila County Historical Museum** (Route 60, Globe; 602-425-7385) with exhibits of early artifacts, mining equipment and Salado Indian relics. The museum is housed in the former Old Dominion Mine Rescue and First Aid Station.

About 30 miles northwest of Globe is **Roosevelt Lake** (off Route 88). Fed by waters of Tonto Creek from the north and the Salt River from the east, and impounded by Roosevelt Dam, the lake is 23 miles long and two miles wide. It offers a full range of recreational opportunities.

Globe is the commercial gateway to the **San Carlos Apache Reservation**, the two-million-acre expanse that's home to nearly 5000 Apache Indians. Rambling and remote, lush and rustic, the land is a natural habitat for javelina, elk, bear, waterfowl, grouse, quail, rabbits and a variety of fresh-water fish. Camping, hunting and fishing are permitted, with licenses. Contact the Recreation and Wildlife Department, 602-475-2343.

EAST OF PHOENIX HOTELS

Westcourt in The Buttes (2000 Westcourt Way, Tempe; 602-225-9000) is a dramatic 300-room, four-story resort built into the mountainsides, with Southwest styling and art throughout. All guest rooms feature a Southwest decor or rose and earth tones, cactus and wood furnishings. It has two restaurants, a nightclub, pools, tennis and all of the modern trim and trappings associated with luxury resort living in the valley, including cascading waterfalls and two romantic mountainside whirlpools. Ultra-deluxe.

A little bit of Ireland located within walking distance of the ASU campus is found at the **Valley 'o the Sun Bed and Breakfast, Tempe** (P.O. Box 2214, Scottsdale, AZ 85252; 602-941-1281). It has three rooms (two with connecting bath) located in a ranch-style home with a view of the Papago Mountains. The owner is from the Old Sod. The decor and decorations reflect a note of nostalgia. Full or continental breakfast, as desired, is included. Budget.

Cornerstone of downtown Mesa, **The Centennial Hotel** (200 North Centennial Way; 602-898-8300) has 280 rooms, contemporary furnishings, lounge, restaurant and swimming pool. Deluxe.

Buckhorn Mineral Wells (5900 East Main Street, Mesa; 602-832-1111) is a motel and natural hot water mineral springs bath house where massages and therapeutic hot soaks are offered. The motel has 14 rooms in contemporary Southwest decor. Budget.

In Apache Junction, **Meanwhile Back at the Ranch Guest Ranch** (6300 East Pioneer Street; 602-982-2112) is a bed and breakfast for both riders and horses set in the compound of a former working ranch. Its seven buildings accommodate 14 guests and as many horses, all of whom receive breakfast (continental plus for riders, feed for the horses). Guest cabins, all with private baths, are individually furnished, maintaining original Western trappings, colonial rockers, bed covers with Indian and Southwest designs and paneled walls. Moderate.

The 130-room **Superstition Grande Hotel** (201 West Apache Trail, Apache Junction; 602-982-7411), at the gateway to the Superstition Mountains, is set up in an old wagon-wheel style, a main building with a central courtyard and eight motel-type spurs running from it. The main building is red-brick tile and white stucco. The rooms, brightly colored in pink and green, have modern furnishings. The lobby is contemporary, the bar Western with copper appointments. A favorite of film crews shooting Westerns in the area, the hotel has hosted John Wayne, Ronald Reagan, Richard Boone and other Hollywood stalwarts. Rooms where they stayed bear their names. Moderate.

In Globe you'll find the **Copper Manor** (637 East Ash Street; 602-425-7124), a 62-room, two-story motel with contemporary furnishing, pool and all-night café. Budget.

Copper Hills Inn (Globe-Miami Highway; 602-425-7151) is another Globe caravansary—a 70-room Best Western with basically nondescript contemporary furnishing, a dining room, coffee shop and lounge, two swimming pools and guest laundry. Moderate.

A perfect lakeside retreat for water sports enthusiasts is the **Roosevelt Lake Marina Motel** (Route 88, Globe; 602-467-2245) with 21 rooms overlooking the lake. It's rustic (no television or telephone), but the staff couldn't be more folksy. Budget.

EAST OF PHOENIX RESTAURANTS

Mill Landing (398 South Mill Avenue; 602-966-1700) is a handsome restaurant housed in a historic building in the downtown Old Town section of Tempe offering a variety of light meals, salads, soups, sandwiches and seafood specialties. There's dining in the patio, weather permitting. Deluxe.

In a similar mold and in a similar building (the Andre, built in 1888), **Paradise** (401 South Mill Avenue, Tempe; 602-829-0606) specializes in prime rib and fresh fish. Moderate.

Casa Reynoso (3138 South Mill Avenue, Tempe; 602-966-0776) is one of the better Mexican restaurants in town, despite its modest appearance—vinyl booths and wrought iron. Try the *gollo burro* or *chile rellenos*. Moderate.

The Coffee Plantation (Mill Avenue and 6th Street, Tempe; 602-829-7878) is a Caribbean-style coffeehouse and retail store in a two-story plantation house. Beans are roasted daily in a rustic roasting shack. There's indoor and outdoor seating where espresso, cappuccino and specialty coffees are served, along with pastries and desserts, breakfast, light lunch and dinner. Budget.

A little bit of the Big Island went adrift and ended up in Tempe. **McGurk's of Hawaii** (909 East Elliott Road; 602-730-9009) is the place to go for ribs Kamehameha, Mai Mai and chicken *panido*, clams, lobster and hickory barbecued chicken, island style—all served in an atmosphere of early Trader Vic's and Gilligan's Island. Moderate.

The decor is plain and simple and the food is anything but at **Char's Thai Restaurant** (927 East University Drive; 602-967-6013) where an exotic touch the East comes to Tempe with such offerings as chicken soup with coconut milk, smoked beef salad, curried duck and seafood combinations in peanut sauce. There's also a good selection of Asian beers. Moderate.

Mother Tucker's (1457 West Southern Avenue, Mesa; 602-898-0880) is a clone of Mother Tucker's in Phoenix—informal atmosphere, Early

(Text continued on page 158.)

Spoil Yourself

The American West is big and grand: How inconsistent it would be if its great resort hotels were not just a reach beyond all expectation. And Central Arizona is home to some of the biggest and grandest around.

Designed by Frank Lloyd Wright and Albert Chase McArthur, the newly refurbished **Arizona Biltmore** (24th and Missouri streets, Phoenix; 602-955-6600) has maintained an aura of ease and luxury since its opening in 1929. From its palm-lined drive, elaborate high portico and immense lobby to its bright, handsomely furnished guest rooms, the 530-room Biltmore is as dramatic and visually exciting as it is comfortable. "Arizona's Grande Dame" provides a full range of activities: golf courses, tennis courts; pools; a health club; and nearby riding facilities.

Another ultra-deluxe establishment in Phoenix, to say the least, is **The Phoenician** (6000 East Camelback Road; 602-941-8200), the most prestigious and talked-about resort in the Valley of the Sun. Sprawled over 130 acres along the sun-dappled flanks of Camelback Mountain, it's set within a tiered oasis of waterfalls and pools, the largest of which is tiled entirely with mother-of-pearl. Its 442 guest rooms are large and lavish with most situated in the main hotel, others in surrounding casitas. There are also 107 casita units with parlor suites that have hand-carved travertine fireplaces. If you really want to make a night of it, there are two presidential and 29 luxury suites. Recreational facilities run the gamut— a golf course, lighted tennis courts, tournament croquet and a health and fitness spa.

The **Scottsdale Princess** (7575 East Princess Drive; 602-585-4848), an ultra-luxury resort in the pretty-in-pink tradition of Princess hotels everywhere, has 600 rooms. It's one of the Valley's largest hotels. Set on 48 elaborately landscaped acres with a central courtyard, waterfall and three swimming pools, the Princess is one of the most visually arresting of its kind. The rooms are large, decorated in Southwest furnishing, with a hint of Santa Fe.

With 423 rooms, **Marriott's Camelback Inn** (5402 East Lincoln Drive, Paradise Valley; 602-948-1700) outside Scottsdale is yet another glorious world-class retreat dramatically nestled in the foothills between the Camelback and Mummy mountains, where landscaped paths wind through gardens of cactus and desert palms. Its Southwest pueblo architecture and adobe-style casitas blend harmoniously into the stunning desert background. For the sportsminded there are championship golf and tennis, swimming, trail rides, weekly cookouts and fitness facilities.

Marriott's Mountain Shadows (5641 East Lincoln Drive, Paradise Valley; 602-948-7111) offers palm trees, waterfalls, sparkling streams and lakes, and that's just the golf course. At the foot of Camelback Mountain, with over a hundred acres of land, Mountain Shadows seems designed for the sports devotee. Along with its pro 54 holes of golf, it has lighted tennis courts, putting greens, and swimming pools. The hotel's 388 guest rooms are clustered over the entire property; each room, designed in muted Southwest colors, has a private lanai. The resort has four restaurants.

Who says the West is wild? The **Wigwam** (300 East Indian School Lane, Litchfield Park; 602-935-3811) west of Phoenix is an upper-upper-scale resort on 75 acres of what was originally virgin desert. The design is pueblo-style, with 331 desert-brown adobe casitas set in a lavish golf and country-club setting—towering palms, green lawns, cascading flowers and fragrant orange trees. Through the use of building materials native to the Southwest, architecture blends with nature. Slate, stone and wood surfaces are accented with Indian themes and desert colors. Championship courses, riding, tennis, swimming and other activities keep the body occupied while the mind relaxes.

American tables, hanging greenery, cozy booths and country-beamed ceilings. The house specialty is roast prime rib of beef. The chef slices it to order. The salad bar has over 50 items. Deluxe.

For a good solid breakfast or lunch, they don't come much better than the **Ripe Tomato Café** (745 West Baseline Road, Mesa; 892-4340) where it's always wall-to-wall people. It's a great find for breakfast, and the steak, sandwiches and Mexican specialty lunches aren't bad either. Moderate.

Lake Shore Restaurant (14011 North Bush Highway; 602-984-5311) is a rustic, casual dining facility on Saguaro Lake with a deck where you can dine while enjoying a view of the lake. Shaded by a giant awning, this outdoor eatery is cooled by a mist system and ceiling fans. Start with a frozen strawberry daiquiri and then order from the menu featuring burgers, salads, sandwiches and fried fish (all you can eat on Friday). The up-beat tempo is enhanced by reggae, oldies and classical music. Moderate.

Down Apache Junction way, **Mining Camp Restaurant and Trading Post** (on Apache Trail; 602-982-3181) is almost as famous as the Lost Dutchman Gold Mine—and it's easier to find. It's worth looking for, offering long wooden tables, planked floors, tin trays and cups, and family-style, all-you-can-eat dining—chicken, beef and barbecued ribs. Moderate.

Lakeside Canyon and Cantina (Route 88, Apache Junction; 602-380-1601) is a tri-level restaurant and lounge with a deck built out over the Canyon Lake. The decor—mauves and teal—is more Californian than Arizonan. Out of the kitchen comes burgers, sandwiches, chicken and grilled rib eye steaks with mushrooms and onions. Featured is an all-you-can-eat fish fry on Fridays. Moderate.

For true Western flavor, hitch your horse up at the always-crowded **Los Vaqueros** (101 West Apache Trail, Apache Junction; 602-982-3407) and settle down to a rib-eye or T-bone, baked potato, biscuits and beans. There's foot-stomping music and occasionally a brawl at the bar. Los Vaqueros means "the cowboys," and there are plenty of them here. Moderate.

El Rey Café (Route 60/70, Globe; 602-425-6601) is an authentic Mexican restaurant, small in size but big in flavor, with enchiladas, *chile rellenos*, green-corn tamales, tacos and chimichangas. Moderate.

Blue Ribbon Café (474 North Broad Street; 602-425-4423), located in the heart of Globe's old historic district, isn't called "blue ribbon" for nothing. A popular breakfast spot, it's also busy at lunchtime serving sandwiches, salads, burgers and pasta. Moderate.

EAST OF PHOENIX SHOPPING

In Tempe, **Chief Dodge** (601 South Mill Avenue; 602-967-9365) is an Indian jewelry store with a wide selection of turquoise and silver bracelets, squash bloom necklaces, bolas and belts, all made on the premises.

If you want to wear a souvenir home, try **The U Shop** (725 South Rural Road, Tempe; 602-829-1743) which has a large selection of Arizona State University clothing and gift items, as well as Phoenix Cardinal and Phoenix Sun merchandise.

For quality Indian arts, the **Warbonnet Gallery** (1234 West Madero Avenue; 602-733-6258) in Mesa offers modern Indian paintings, Navajo rugs, kachina dolls and sandpaintings. Represented here are Marina Martinez and Joseph Lonewolf, among other Native American artists.

The Lenox Factory Outlet (2121 South Power Road, Mesa; 602-986-9986) offers selected seconds on the company's famous china and crystal products, as well as candles, silver and other tabletop accessories.

If you plan to go looking for the Lost Dutchman Gold Mine, or even if you're not, **Pro-Mack South** (940 West Apache Trail, Apache Junction; 602-983-3484) sells mining equipment, gold pans, lanterns, picks, rope, boots, supplies and just about everything but the treasure map.

Pastime Antiques (1068 Adonis Street, Miami; 602-473-3791) is filled with antique furniture, paintings, Western memorabilia, historic photos, old magazines, postcards, posters and other relics and remnants of the past. Even the building is a treasure. It used to be the town library.

In Globe, **Bacon's Boots and Saddles** (290 North Broad Street; 602-425-2681) represents the last of the great saddle makers. Owner Ed Bacon has been hand-crafting saddles for more than 40 years. His store also features a full range of Western wear.

Globe's **F. W. Woolworth's** (127 North Broad Street; 602-425-7115), opened in 1916 and housed in the historic Sultan Building, is the oldest continuously operating Woolworth's west of the Mississippi.

EAST OF PHOENIX NIGHTLIFE

Grady Gammage Memorial Auditorium (602-965-3434), at the Arizona State University campus in Tempe, is a 3000-seat auditorium designed by Frank Lloyd Wright. Its entertainment features range from Broadway productions to symphony orchestra concerts and ballet. Guided tours of the center are offered on Monday and Saturday.

The Butte's swinging **Chuckwalla's** (2000 Westcourt Way; 602-259-9000) with its 24-foot video screen, karaoke bar and live entertainment is one of hottest spots in Tempe.

Bandersnatch (1253 East 5th Street, Tempe; 602-966-4438) is big with the ASU college crowd, which means lots of beer and a house special brew that may or may not be homemade. Live jazz and, for those so inclined, live volleyball. **Chuy's** (310 South Mills Avenue, Tempe; 602-967-2489) is another college hangout where alternate live sounds can be heard: blues, rhythm-and-blues, rock and jazz.

Bobby McGee's (1320 West Southern Avenue, Mesa; 602-969-4600) has a disk jockey, great sounds and big crowds.

For live dinner theater, it's the **Landmark** (809 West Main Street; 602-962-4652) in Mesa on Wednesdays and weekends—from melodramas to suspense and comedy—and the food is good, too.

In Apache Junction, a live Western band stomps away every night at **Los Vaqueros** (101 West Apache Trail; 602-982-3407) and that's where everybody goes.

EAST OF PHOENIX PARKS

McDowell Mountain Regional Park—This 21,099-acre wilderness expanse 15 miles northeast of Scottsdale is one of the region's most scenic parks with an abundance of vegetation and majestic mountain views. Elevation ranges from 1600 feet at the southeast corner to 3000 feet along the western boundary. The area is ideal for camping, picnicking, horseback riding and hiking.

Facilities: Picnic areas, restrooms, showers; information, 602-506-2930.

Camping: There are 76 sites (all with RV hookups); $8 per night. Also available is a backpacking camp (free).

Getting there: Located via McDowell Mountain Road, four miles northeast of Fountain Hills.

Usery Mountain Recreation Area—This 3324-acre wilderness area is just northwest of the Superstition Mountains. It has an extensive hiking and riding trail system. The Apache Trail (Route 88) weaves its way through mountain country leading to the Salt River chain of lakes—Canyon, Apache and Roosevelt lakes—which have been developed for fishing, boating, swimming, picnicking, hiking and camping.

Facilities: Picnic sites, restrooms, showers and horse-staging areas. The Apache Lake Marina (Route 88; 602-467-2511) offers boat rentals, storage and gas. A motel and restaurant are also located here. The Canyon Lake Marina (Route 88; 602-986-5546) 15 miles northeast of Apache Junction is also a full service marina, with a restaurant and camping facilities.

Camping: There are 73 sites, all with RV hookups; $8 per night; information, 602-834-3669.

Getting there: Located east of Phoenix via Apache Boulevard or Superstition Freeway (Route 360). Head east to Ellsworth Road and turn north. At McKellips Road, Ellsworth becomes Usery Pass Road. Continue north to park entrance.

North of Phoenix

From cactus flowers to remote mountain lakes, here is a region rich in scenic wonders. Best known for its dude-ranch resorts, mining towns, cool forests and desert playgrounds, this recreational paradise includes the Wild West town of Wickenberg—the Dude Ranch Capital of the World— the three-million-acre Tonto National Forest and some of the Southwest's better ghost towns.

Established in 1950, **Carefree** is a planned community situated in the scenic foothills of the Arizona desert. To the north and east stretches the immense Tonto National Forest. Next door you'll find an old-time town, **Cave Creek**. Once a booming mining camp in the 1880s (gold and silver), Cave Creek wasn't incorporated until a hundred years later. Sheep and cattle were raised here as well. Today Cave Creek leans heavily on its past, with its Frontier Town re-creation and annual spring rodeo. For additional information contact **Carefree/Cave Creek Chamber of Commerce** (748 East Street, Carefree; 602-488-3381).

Cave Creek Museum (6140 East Skyline Drive; 602-488-2764) offers a living-history exhibit of the desert foothills region, with a restored 1920s tuberculous cabin and a 1940s church, as well as displays of pioneer living, ranching, mining, guns and Indian artifacts.

To the northwest, on Route 89, you will come to the site of the richest gold strike in Arizona. Named after the Russian settler Henry Wickenburg, who discovered it, **Wickenburg** is primarily known today as a winter resort.

Frontier Street preserves Wickenburg's turn-of-the-century character with its old-time train depot now housing the **Wickenburg Chamber of Commerce** (602-684-5479) and a number of vintage wood and brick buildings. One, the Hassayampoa, was once the town's leading hotel. Maps for a self-guided historic walking tour are available at the chamber office. Before the town jail was built, the nearby **Jail Tree** (Tegner Street and Wickenburg Way) was used to chain criminals. Friends and relatives brought them picnic lunches. Today the tree is on the property of the Chaparral Ice Cream Parlor, and tykes eat their ice cream cones there now, probably none the wiser.

Venture over to the **Desert Caballeros Western Museum** (20 North Frontier Street; 602-684-2272; admission) which covers the history of Wickenburg and surrounding area with major exhibits divided into various rooms. "Period" rooms include the Hall of History and a Street Scene representing Wickenburg at the turn of the century. Others focus on 19th- and early-20th-century lifestyles. Its art gallery features Native American art and Western masters of the past and present. The Museum Park outside offers unique desert landscaping and plants.

Those interested in gold mines and ghost towns might want to visit **Vulture Mine** (Vulture Mine Road; 602-377-0803; admission). This is a historic gold mine and ghost town of sorts. The home of the town founder of Wickenburg can be seen, as well as an early assay office, blacksmith shop, stamp mill, a 3000-foot mine shaft and even a hanging tree.

To the northeast of Phoenix lies **Payson**, district headquarters for the Tonto National Forest. Payson provides a base camp for numerous scenic attractions within the forest primeval. Founded over a century ago as a tiny mining and ranching community, it now thrives on its recreation industry. **Payson Chamber of Commerce** (1006 South Beeline Highway; 602-474-4515) offers information on the area.

Ten miles north of Payson, **Tonto Natural Bridge** (602-476-3440) in the Tonto National Forest, is the largest natural travertine bridge in the world.

Payson Zoo (602-474-5435), six-and-a-half miles east of town, has 60 animals, many of them trained "movie stars" who have appeared in films shot in and around Payson.

A state historic monument, **Strawberry Schoolhouse** (village of Strawberry; 602-476-3547), is the oldest standing schoolhouse in Arizona. Built in 1884, its last class was held in 1916. The small mountain village at 6000 feet was named for the many wild strawberries that covered the area when pioneers first arrived.

NORTH OF PHOENIX HOTELS

Located just northeast of Scottsdale, **The Boulders** (34631 North Tom Darlington Drive, Carefree; 602-488-4118) is built directly against a stunning backdrop of 12-million-year-old granite boulder formations that soar hundreds of feet against the desert sky. Situated on 1300 acres, the resort consists of a main lodge and 136 adobe-style casitas, each individually designed to fit the sculptured contours of the desert and the rocks. The hotel is designed in broad architectural sweeps and makes dramatic use of Indian and regional art and artifacts—Navajo blankets, weavings, pottery, ceramics, paintings, stone sculptures and basketry. Guest rooms feature earth-tone furnishings, hand-hewn, *viga* ceilings, fireplaces, wet bars, ceiling fans and oversized windows for broad desert vistas. Ultra-deluxe.

Tumbleweed Hotel (6333 East Cave Creek Road; 602-488-3668) is a small downtown Cave Creek hotel made of white slumpstone brick, with 16 rooms in the main building and eight casita-style guest houses, all with modern Western-style furnishings and decor. The hotel has a swimming pool. Moderate, dropping to budget during the summer.

Flying E Ranch (2801 West Wickenburg Way, Wickenburg; 602-684-2690) is a working cattle ranch—and guest ranch—complete with trail rides, hay rides and chuckwagon dinners on its 21,000-acre spread. There are 16 rooms, plus a heated pool, sauna and whirlpool, along with tennis and shuffleboard. Four miles west of town, it's open November to May. Deluxe.

Another top-notch dude ranch in Wickenburg (this one's listed in the National Historic Register), the **Key El Bar Ranch** (Rincon Road; 602-684-7593) has room for 20 guests in hacienda-style adobe buildings beneath huge salt cedar trees. The lobby has a stone fireplace, and outside there's a pool for soaking after those long hours in the saddle. Open October 15 to May 1. Deluxe.

For those on a budget, **La Siesta** (486 East Wickenburg Way, Wickenburg; 602-684-2826) is a 17-room motel with a pool and café. Rooms are simply furnished, but pleasant enough. Budget.

The Rancho Grande Motel (293 East Wickenburg Way, Wickenburg; 602-684-5445) is a one- and two-story 80-room Best Western with a pool, whirlpool and playground. Rooms are furnished in contemporary motif. Budget to moderate.

Swiss Village Lodge (Route 87, Payson; 602-474-3241) is a handsome, two-story hotel with lots of Alpine flavor in the midst of a European-style village of shops and restaurants. Its 99 rooms are decorated in contemporary furnishings, plain and simple. Some have fireplaces. A café, bar and swimming pool are on the premises. Moderate.

NORTH OF PHOENIX RESTAURANTS

The Satisfied Frog (6245 East Cave Creek Road, Cave Creek; 602-488-3317) captures a bit of the Old West with wood tables, sawdust on the floor and weird things on the walls—animal heads, posters, old farm tools. House specialties include barbecued beef, pork and chicken. The Frog has its own micro-brewery and produces four house brands. Moderate.

Another amphibian-named eatery, **The Horny Toad** (6738 Cave Creek Road, Cave Creek; 602-997-9622) is a rustic, informal restaurant with wooden tables and booths, seating about 150 for lunch and dinner. Added touches are a small bar and lots of greenery. Moderate.

Still ready for more old time Wild West flavor? You'll find it at the **Gold Nugget** (222 East Wickenburg Way, Wickenburg; 602-684-2858), a bar and restaurant with red-flocked wallpaper, brass chandeliers and turn-of-the-century decor. Steaks, prime rib and chicken dominate the menu. Moderate in price.

Payson offers **Aunt Alice's** (512 North Beeline Highway; 602-474-4720), green and blue on the outside, down-home on the inside. Aunt Alice serves up fish, burgers and chicken-fried steak in a country-style setting. Budget.

La Casa Pequeña (911 South Beeline Highway, Payson; 602-474-6329) features chimichangas, burritos and chicken Acapulco in a pleasant, south-of-the-border atmosphere. There's music on weekends. Prices are in the moderate range.

To the west of Phoenix, check out **The Spicery** (7141 North 59th Avenue, Glendale; 602-937-6534) located in the Catlin Court Shops District, a downtown area where historic homes have been preserved. This eatery is in a charming, 1895 Victorian house. It offers tea service all day as well as food the way mother used to make it—homemade soups, salads, chubby sandwiches, fresh-baked bread and pies. Moderate.

NORTH OF PHOENIX PARKS

Tonto National Forest—Ranging from Sonoran Desert to sprawling forests of ponderosa pine, Tonto's nearly 2.9 million acres serves as an outdoor playground for area residents who can enjoy tubing, rafting and fishing on the Salt and Verde rivers. Forest lakes—Saguaro, Apache, Canyon, Roosevelt, Barlett and Horseshoe Reservoir—serve as watersheds, wildlife habitats and recreational sites for camping, swimming, fishing and boating. Tonto Natural Bridge, the largest known travertine bridge in the world, is a popular attraction, as was Zane Gray's cabin until it burned down in 1990. (The Zane Gray Society has plans for its restoration.) The famed Apache Trail is found here as well, via Routes 60 and 89 east. The scenic drive follows the trail originally used by Apache Indians as a shortcut through the Superstition Mountains.

Facilities: Picnic areas, restrooms, showers, boat rentals, snack stands, restaurant, hiking and riding trails; information, 602-225-5200.

Camping: There are 50 campgrounds; $5 to $12 per night. Primitive camping is also allowed. Reservations are available through MISTIX, 800-283-2267.

Getting there: Located via Route 87 north from Phoenix to the town of Payson, in the heart of Tonto National Forest.

White Tank Mountain Regional Park—Covering 26,337 acres of desert, canyons and mountains, White Tank is the largest park in the Maricopa County Park System. Elevations range from 1402 feet at the park entrance to 4083 feet at the park's highest point. White Tank contains an excellent hiking and riding trail system, a seasonal flowing waterfall (reached by a mile-long self-guided hiker's trail) and scattered Native American petroglyphs throughout.

Facilities: Picnic sites, restrooms, showers; information, 602-506-2930.

Camping: There are 38 sites; $5 per night. Backpack camping allowed (free). Information, 602-935-2505.

Getting there: The park is located on Dunlap Avenue, 15 miles west of Glendale.

South of Phoenix

Out beyond the metropolis, where the bright lights give way to Native American ruins you'll find the homeland of the Pima and Maricopa Indians, the site of Arizona's only Civil War battlefield and cotton fields that stretch for miles. Also, mountain peaks, great fishing and, for the born-to-shop crowd, factory-outlet malls. It is an intriguing blend of old and new Arizona.

Gila River Indian Center (602-315-3411) in the Gila River Indian Reservation has an Indian museum, gift shop and restaurant featuring authentic Indian fry bread and Southwestern food. Here, too, is **Heritage Park**, featuring about half a dozen mini Indian villages. The center is located off Route 10, via Route 93 (exit 175). The museum is free and you can also take an interpretive walking tour of Heritage Park conducted by Native American Joe Enos. Several tours are offered during the day, but it's best to call ahead to find out approximate times.

Further south is **Casa Grande**, named for the Indians ruins northeast of town. Casa Grande is known primarily for cotton-growing, industry and for the many name-brand factory-outlet stores that have mushroomed there in recent years. For additional information, contact **Casa Grande Chamber of Commerce** (575 North Marshall Street; 602-836-2125).

Casa Grande Ruins National Monument (602-723-3172) is about 20 miles east of Casa Grande on State Route 87. Originally built by the Hohokam Indians in the early 1300s, the village was abandoned by the end of that century. Four stories high, and covered recently by a large protective roof, the main structure is the only one of its size and kind in this area. (The monument grounds contain about 60 prehistoric sites.) The ruins are easily explored on well-marked self-guided tours. There is a visitor center and museum where ranger talks are presented.

For cowboy fans, the **Tom Mix Monument** (Pinal Pioneer Parkway out of the town of Florence; 602-868-9433), honors the silent-movie cowboy star near the spot where he died in an auto wreck in 1940. "In memory of Tom Mix whose spirit left his body on this spot and whose characterizations and portrayals in life served to better fix memories of the Old West in the minds of living men," reads the inscription.

SOUTH OF PHOENIX HOTELS

Francisco Grande Resort and Golf Club (26000 Gila Bend Highway; 602-836-6444) is where it's all at in Casa Grande. The tallest building in Pinal County (eight stories), the hotel's tower building contains most of its 112 rooms, while other rooms, motel style, are located around the patio. Furnishings are Southwest throughout including paintings on the guest-room walls—cowboys and Western landscapes. The hotel has a restaurant, lounge (with nightly entertainment), swimming pool and golf. Deluxe.

Holiday Inn (777 North Pinal Avenue, Casa Grande; 602-426-3500), a three-story, Spanish-style stucco building, has 175 rooms in contemporary styling, an outdoor pool and spa, restaurant and lounge. Moderate.

SOUTH OF PHOENIX RESTAURANTS

Gila River Arts and Crafts Restaurant (Gila River Reservation; 602-315-3411) features Indian fry bread along with burritos, tacos, hamburgers, homemade pies and coffee. Budget.

Mi Amigo Ricardo (821 East Florence Boulevard, Casa Grande; 602-836-3858) offers up hot and spicy Mexican specialties—chimichangas, enchiladas, frijoles, tamales, flautas and *posole*—with beer and wine to soothe the flames. The decor is Mexican, of course, and quite attractive. Moderate.

Bring a big appetite to the **Golden Corral** (1295 East Florence Boulevard, Casa Grande; 602-836-4630). It's a traditional Western steak house where owner Vicki Carlson cuts her steaks fresh daily and the salad bar has 150 items. Moderate.

Bedillon's (800 North Park Avenue, Casa Grande; 602-836-2045) is a restaurant and museum in two separate buildings. The museum features Indian artifacts and Western memorabilia. The menu offers a full range of American cuisine. Moderate.

A small, downtown Casa Grande bakery and café, **The Cook E Jar** (100 West 2nd Street; 602-836-9294) serves up breakfast and lunch as well as take-out bakery goods (even wedding cakes) and sandwiches. Budget.

SOUTH OF PHOENIX SHOPPING

Gila River Indian Center (Gila River Reservation; 602-315-3411) has a shop selling traditional Native American arts and crafts, silver and turquoise jewelry, sandpaintings, kachina dolls, baskets and blankets.

Gila River Arts and Crafts (Casa Blanca Road, Sacaton; 602-963-3981) sells quality Indian items, including jewelry, baskets, kachina dolls, rugs and baskets.

Casa Grande, the main town along Route 10 between Phoenix and Tucson, is the site of the largest number of factory-owned **outlet stores** in Arizona. More than 70 are located in two sprawling commercial malls off Route 10 (take Exit 149, Florence Boulevard). More than a million shoppers a year come to Casa Grande seeking bargains from such major represented firms as **Liz Clairborne, American Tourister, Bugle Boy, Royal Doulton** and **Westpoint Pepperell**. For information, contact Casa Grande Factory Stores at 602-421-0112.

The Sporting Life

Arizona's climate is ideal for recreational pursuits—most of the time. But during the summer scorchers, dry heat can be deceiving and you may think it's cooler than it actually is. So keep summer exertion to a minimum and play indoors, where there's air-conditioning, if you can.

RIVER RAFTING/TUBING

Three main rivers in Central Arizona, the Verde, the Salt and the Gila, all east of Phoenix, offer a wealth of recreational activities year-round. In summer, they provide a welcome reprieve from the desert heat. A number of companies provide half-day, day and overnight rafting and tubing expeditions, with pick-ups, meals and guides included. Among them are **Cimarron River Co.** (6925 5th Avenue, Suite E-6, Scottsdale; 602-994-1199); **Desert Voyagers Guided Rafting Tours** (P.O. Box 9053, Scottsdale, AZ 85252; 602-988-7238) and **Salt River Recreation Inc.** (Bush Highway and Usery Pass Road, Mesa; 602-984-3305).

JOGGING

The Valley's extensive network of canals provides ideal, often shaded tracks. If you want to jog during the hot summers stick to cooler early-morning hours. Phoenix's **Encanto Park**, three miles north of the Civic Plaza, is an excellent jogging trail. Scottsdale's **Indian Bend Wash Greenbelt** is a dream trail for joggers. It runs north and south for the entire length of Scottsdale, including 13 winding miles of jogging and bike paths laid out within the Greenbelt's scenic system of parks, lakes and golf courses.

SWIMMING

There are no beaches to speak of in the state, but have no fear: So many swimming pools are found in Central Arizona that gathering rain clouds, so it's said, are often colored green from all the chlorine. Numerous public pools are available, over 30 in Phoenix alone. To name just a few: **Cactus Pool** (3801 West Cactus Road; 602-262-6680), **Grant Pool** (701 South 3rd Avenue; 602-261-8728), **Starlight Pool** (7810 West Osborn Road; 602-495-2412) and **Washington Pool** (6655 North 23rd Avenue; 602-262-7198). For additional information and listings, call 602-258-7946.

More varied watery delights can be found at **Waterworld U.S.A.** (4243 West Pinnacle Peak Road, Phoenix; 602-266-5299; admission) which offers 20 acres of ridin', slidin', fun and sun with its Breaker Beach wave pool, six-and-a-half-story Avalanche Slide and other attractions.

The **Adobe Dam Recreation Area** (northwest of Adobe Dam, just south of Pinnacle Peak Road between 35th and 51st avenues, Phoenix; 602-581-6691) also has a Family Water Park featuring a wave pool and waterslides.

In Tempe, **Big Surf** (1500 North Hayden Road; 602-947-7873; admission) includes 20 acres of sandy beach, a 300-foot surf slide, swimming and raft-riding in a gigantic, mechanically activated fresh water pool.

Swimming is ideal at **Canyon, Apache and Roosevelt lakes**. (For more information, see "East of Phoenix Parks.")

GOLF

More than half of Arizona's 205 golf courses are located in Central Arizona, making Phoenix and environs the undisputed Golf Capital of the Southwest. Some of the country's finest courses can be found among its resorts, parks and country clubs. Two of the most spectacular are the **Wigwam Gold** (Litchfield and Indian School Road, Litchfield Park; 602-935-3808) and the **Gold Canyon Golf Club** (6100 South Kings Ranch Road, Apache Junction; 602-982-9449). The **Arizona Golf Association** (800-458-8484) can supply specifics. Among the top public courses in Phoenix: **Encanto Park** (2705 North 15th Avenue; 602-495-0333), **Papago Golf Course** (5595 East Moreland Street; 602-495-0555) and **Palo Verde Golf Course** (6215 North 15th Avenue; 602-249-9930).

In Scottsdale, top public courses include: **Continental Golf Course** (7920 East Osborn Road; 602-941-1585); **Coronado Golf Course** (2829 North Miller Road; 602-947-8364); **Tournament Players Club of Scottsdale** (17020 North Hayden Road; 602-585-3600); and the **Villa Monterey Golf Course** (8102 East Camelback Road; 602-990-7100). Tempe has a number of fine public courses, including **Ken McDonald Golf Course** (Western Canal and Rural Road; 602-350-5250), **Pepperwood Golf Course** (647 West Baseline Road; 602-831-9457) and **Rolling Hills Golf Course** (1415 North Mill Avenue; 602-350-5275). In Apache Junction try, **Gold Canyon Golf Club** (6100 South Kings Ranch Road; 602-982-9090).

TENNIS

The Valley of the Sun has even more tennis courts than it has swimming pools. Almost all of the parks in the Valley's vast network have a court; for information, call the **Parks and Recreation Department** (Phoenix, 602-262-6861; Scottsdale, 602-994-2408; or Maricopa County, 602-272-8871).

Among the numerous public courts in Phoenix are: **City Center Tennis Courts** (121 East Adams Street, atop the parking garage roof; 602-256-4120); the **Hole-in-the-Wall Racquet Club** (7677 North 16th Street, at the Pointe at Squaw Peak Resort; 602-997-2543); **Phoenix Tennis Center** (6330 North 21st Avenue; 602-249-3712); **Pointe Tapatio Cliffs Racquet Club** (11111

North 7th Street; 602-997-7237); and **Mountain View Tennis Center** (1104 East Grovers Avenue; 602-788-6088).

In Scottsdale try **Indian School Park** (4289 North Hayden Avenue; 602-994-2740), **Chestnut Park** (4565 North Granite Reef Road; 602-994-2408) and **Mountain View Park** (8625 East Mountain View; 602-994-2584). Outstanding in Tempe is the **Kiwanis Recreation Center** (611 South All-American Way; 602-350-5201).

HORSEBACK RIDING

Dozens of stables, dude ranches and equestrian outfitters are available for saddling up and heading off into desert wilderness for a few hours or a few days under the supervision of a crusty trail boss. If there was ever a place for horsing around, it's here. For information, contact the **Arizona Equestrian Center** (1750 Notton Lane, Litchfield Park; 602-853-0011) or **Westworld** (16601 North Pima Road, Scottsdale; 602-483-8800). Or check out any of the following: **All Western Stables** (10220 South Central Avenue, Phoenix; 602-276-5862); **North Mountain Stables** (25251 North 19th Avenue, Phoenix; 602-581-0103); **Hank's Horse World Stables** (16601 North Pima Road, Scottsdale; 602-941-4756); **Old MacDonald's Farm** (26540 North Scottsdale Road, Scottsdale; 602-585-8239); **Papago Riding Stables** (400 North Scottsdale Road, Tempe; 602-966-9793); **Don Donnelly Stables at Gold Canyon** (6010 North Kings Ranch Road, Apache Junction; 602-982-7822); and **Superstition Mountain Guide Service** (Apache Junction; 602-982-4040).

BALLOONING AND HANG GLIDING

Steady but manageable winds and constantly shifting updrafts and downdrafts make the Valley ideally suited for ballooning. For gliding enthusiasts, the surrounding mountains provide the perfect setting to let it all hang out. Dozens of firms will be happy to take you up, up and away, including, **Aerostats Inc.** (21632 North 7th Avenue, Phoenix; 602-252-2664); **Xanadu Balloon Adventures** (3745 West Columbus Drive, Phoenix; 602-938-9324); **Hot Air Affair** (2980 North 73rd Street, Scottsdale; 602-423-8551); **Unicorn Balloon Co.** (15001 North 74th Street, Scottsdale; 602-991-3666); and **Adventures Aloft** (6716 East Malcomb Drive, Paradise Valley; 602-951-2650).

For hang gliding, try **Sky Sail School of Hang Gliding** (2237 East Karen Drive, Phoenix; 602-493-1216) or **Arizona Windsports** (1327 East Bell De Mar Drive, Tempe; 602-897-7172). Both offer instructions.

BICYCLING

A basic bikeway system was set up for Phoenix in 1987, and since then more than 100 miles of bike paths have been added. Unfortunately, there's a lot of traffic, so be ever cautious. A free Phoenix Bikeway System map is available at most bike shops, or call the Parks, Recreation and Library Department (602-262-6861); for bicycling events call 602-262-6542. Also for special-event biking activities contact **Arizona Bicycle Association** (602-345-8747). Phoenix's **South Mountain Park** (10919 South Central Avenue), **Cave Creek** and **Carefree**, 30 miles northeast of town, offer excellent biking conditions. Also popular is **Papago Loop Bicycle Path** through the rolling hills that border the canal edging Papago Park. Scottsdale's **Indian Bend Wash Greenbelt** has miles of excellent bike paths.

BIKE RENTALS   Bike-rental shops include the following: **Bike Den** (3450 West Dunlap Avenue, Phoenix; 602-973-3450); **Landis Cyclery** (712 West Indian School Road, Phoenix; 602-264-5681); **Try Me Bicycle Shop** (1514 West Hatcher Road, Phoenix; 602-943-1785); **Airplane and Bicycle Works of Wilbur and Orville** (4400 North Scottsdale Road, Scottsdale; 602-949-1978); **Bicycle Warehouse Co.** (4420 North Miller Road, Scottsdale; 602-949-7106); **Fun on Wheels** (7607 East McDowell Road, Scottsdale; 602-945-2881); **Tempe Bicycle** (267 East Bell Road, Tempe; 602-375-1515); and **Baseball Bicycles** (825 West Baseline Road, Tempe; 602-491-3921).

HIKING

With all that elbow room and knockout scenery, Central Arizona is a hiker's paradise. Visitors, in fact, have been known to park their cars on the highway and impulsively hike up the side of a mountain. Many of the parks have excellent hiking trails. There are some wonderful trails in other areas. Be sure to take water with you when hiking these desert locations, and allow plenty of time to get there and back.

PHOENIX AREA TRAILS   The **Phoenix Mountain Preserve** has 200 miles of trails and almost pristine areas virtually in the center of Phoenix. It stretches from Lincoln Drive in Paradise Valley north to Bell Road, bordered on the west by 19th Avenue and on the east by Tatum Boulevard. The Phoenix Parks, Recreation and Library Department offers a free map of 45 marked trails within the preserve. Call 602-262-7901 or 602-262-7797.

Its most popular trail is the **Squaw Peak Summit Trail** (1 mile) that wraps its way up Squaw Peak, offering good lookout points along the way, and from its 2608-foot summit, a dramatic view of the city. (The only drawback is the number of fellow hikers you'll meet along the way.)

A more demanding trek, for experienced hikers only, is **Circumference Trail** (3.5 miles), beginning at the parking area at the end of Squaw Peak Drive and looping around the base of the peak in a northerly direction.

SCOTTSDALE AREA TRAILS   **Camelback Mountain** in the Scottsdale area is the valley's best known landmark, and serious hikers truly haven't hiked Arizona until they've conquered it. Part of the Echo Canyon

Recreation Area (602-256-3220), Camelback offers sheer red cliffs that in some places rise 200 feet straight up its side. An interpretive ramada near the parking area offers information about the various trails.

A relatively easy climb of about four-fifths of a mile goes from the ramada to **Bobby's Rock**, a landmark formation of rocks set aside from the cliff and perfect for rock climbers. Also beginning at the ramada, the route to **Praying Monk** is more difficult. A stone formation rises at its summit high above Echo Canyon cliffs. From Praying Monk, the trail continues to the tip of Camelback Mountain, 2704 feet above sea level, 1.3 ever-upward miles. Echo Canyon is off McDonald Drive east of Tatum Boulevard.

EAST OF PHOENIX TRAILS **Usery Mountain Recreation Area** offers the well-maintained **Wind Cave Trail** (1 mile) which is moderately challenging and popular with local climbers. **Pass Mountain Trail** (7 miles) takes about four hours to complete.

Transportation

BY CAR

Visitors driving to Phoenix by car are in for a treat. Arizona's highways are among the best in the country, gas is traditionally cheaper and the scenery in any direction is spectacular—lofty saguaros, magnificent mountains, a cowboy here, a pickup truck there, beer signs blinking faintly in the purple glow of evening. Along the way, small Western towns unfold like storybook pop-ups. **Route 10** traverses the city from the east (El Paso) and west (Los Angeles). From the northwest, **Route 40**, once the legendary Route 66, enters Arizona near Kingman; **Route 93** continues on from there to Phoenix.

BY AIR

With the recent completion of the Barry M. Goldwater Terminal 4 and a new four-gate international concourse, **Sky Harbor International Airport**, four miles from downtown Phoenix, is served by Aero California, Air Sedona, Alaska Airlines, America West Airlines, American Airlines, Continental Airlines, Delta Airlines, Mesa Air, Northwest Airlines, Skywest Airlines, Southwest Airlines, Trans World Airlines, United Airlines and USAir.

A variety of ground transportation options are available from Sky Harbor Airport. **SuperShuttle** (602-244-9000) offers airport-to-door service 24 hours a day. **Courier Transportation** (602-244-1818) also provides transfers to and from the airport. **Arizona Shuttle Service** (602-795-6771) has service to and from Tucson. **Air Coach** (602-882-7661) provides shuttle service between Sky Harbor and Tucson. If you're heading north to red rock country, the **Sedona/Phoenix Shuttle Service** (602-282-2066) departs three times daily from Sky Harbor, making stops in Cottonwood and Sedona.

BY BUS

Greyhound/Trailways Bus Lines has service to Phoenix from all around the country. The main Phoenix terminal is at 525 East Washington Street (602-248-4040). Other stations are found in Mesa (1423 South Country Club Drive; 602-834-3360) and Tempe (502 South College Avenue; 602-967-4030).

CAR RENTALS

If you arrive by air, you'll find plenty of car-rental agencies with counter space at the airport. These include **Advantage Rent A Car** (602-244-0450), **Alamo Rent A Car** (602-244-0897), **Avis Rent A Car** (602-273-3222), **Avon Rent A Car** (602-257-7777), **Budget Rent A Car** (602-267-4000), **Dollar Rent A Car** (602-275-7588), **Hertz Rent A Car** (602-267-8822), **National Car Rental System** (602-275-4771), **Resort Rent A Car** (602-220-0122) and **Superior Rent A Car** (602-275-5177). Agencies with pick-up service are **American International Car Rental** (602-273-6181), **Courtesy Rent A Car** (602-273-7503), **Enterprise Leasing and Rent A Car** (602-225-0588), **General Rent A Car** (602-273-0991), **Thrifty Car Rental** (602-244-0311) and **Value Rent A Car** (602-273-7425). For others in Central Arizona, consult the local yellow pages.

PUBLIC TRANSPORTATION

The **Phoenix Transit Bus System** (602-253-5000) covers Phoenix and Scottsdale and provides express service to and from other districts within the Valley. It also serves the Phoenix airport. Express buses access Phoenix from Mesa, Tempe and other suburbs. **The Molly Trolley** (602-941-2957) offers rubber-tire trolley service from 22 Scottsdale resorts and 12 shopping areas on day-pass basis; rides are free within the downtown shopping area. **Downtown Dash** (602-253-5000) serves the downtown Phoenix area with free shuttles that depart every ten minutes and loop the downtown area between the State Capitol, Arizona Center and the Civic Plaza weekdays.

TAXIS

Taxis are expensive in Phoenix since the city sprawls out in all directions. Going from Point A to Point B, at times, may seem like you're crossing the entire state. Some of the major companies in Central Arizona are **AAA CAB** (602-253-8294), **ACE Taxi** (602-254-1999), **All American Cab** (602-252-1277), **American Cab** (602-941-0007), **ABC Cab** (602-254-8022 or 602-375-5079), **Courier Cab** (602-232-2222), **Quick Silver Taxi** (602-437-9063) and **Yellow Cab** (602-252-5252). AAA, Courier and Yellow are contracted with the airport in Phoenix.

AIR TOURS

Because Arizona is big-sky country, a great way to see it is by air. Several firms, all based out of Scottsdale's Airpark, offer tours of the Grand Canyon, Sedona, Monument Valley, Lake Powell and other scenic destinations. Among them are **Arizona Air** (602-991-8252), **Flight Quest Aviation** (602-991-5557) and **Sky Cab** (602-998-1778). **Corporate Jets** (602-948-2400) offers sunset champagne tours (none for the pilot) and Grand Canyon tours.

CHAPTER FIVE

Southern Arizona

The ultimate insult to a Tucson resident is to say their town is just like Phoenix. Like bickering siblings, the two cities have never gotten along well and each is proud of their different personalities. Whereas Phoenix is a vast, sprawling city that welcomes booming development, Tucson would just as soon stay the same size and keep developers out—especially those that would alter the environment. Phoenix thrives on a fast past; Tucson is informal, easygoing and in no great rush to get anywhere.

Basically, Tucson is an affable, unpretentious town that feels comfortable with itself. There's no need to impress anyone here with high fashion—blue jeans are good enough for most places. Nor do wealth and conspicuous consumption have a large following. Most Tucsonans don't come here to make lots of money, but instead to live in a beautiful, natural area that's within driving distance to more of the same.

Surrounded by five mountain ranges and sitting in a cactus-roughened desert, Tucson is an arid, starkly beautiful place with wide-open skies and night silences broken by howling coyotes. The highest mountains are powdered with snow in winter; the desert is ablaze with cactus blooms in spring.

Most of Tucson's 11.4 inches of annual precipitation arrives during the late summer monsoon season when afternoon thunderstorms roll through the desert with high winds and dramatic lightning shows. Despite the monsoons, Tucson has more sunshine than any other city in the United States—about 350 days each year. During summer, average highs are 98. In winter, average highs hover around 65, making it a popular spot for winter visitors who come to golf and relax in the balmy weather.

175

The Hohokam Indians were the first in the area. Father Eusebio Francisco Kino, a Jesuit priest, came to work with the Indians and establish a chain of missions, including Tucson's famous Mission San Xavier del Bac.

Later, the Spanish flag flew over the city, as did the Mexican, Confederate and United States flags. In 1867, Tucson was the capital of the Arizona Territory. But when the capital moved north, disgruntled Tucson was given the University of Arizona as compensation. This increased the population, and it jumped again just before World War II when Davis-Monthan Air Force Base began training pilots to fly B-17 bombers. Today, 700,000 people call Tucson home and live within the metro area's 500 square miles. The university has grown to 35,000 students, and Davis-Monthan is still an active military base with more than 7500 military personnel and civilians. Other employment opportunities in Tucson include a number of high-tech firms, including IBM and Hughes Aircraft.

The cultural heritage in Tucson is a mix of Spanish, Mexican and Native American. The city is only 60 miles from the Mexican border in Nogales, but you don't have to go that far to find Mexican food, artwork and culture. And the red-tiled adobe homes spread across the valley reflect the love of Spanish and Indian architecture.

Southern Arizona is a vast region of grasslands and desert punctuated with mountains. Four ranges have peaks higher than 9000 feet—the Santa Catalinas, Santa Ritas, Huachucas and Chiricahuas. Southwest of Tucson is a large, scarcely populated area containing the Papago Indian Reservation, Cabeza Prieta National Wildlife Refuge and Organ Pipe Cactus National Monument. In the westernmost corner of this area is Yuma, a historic town on the Colorado River that attracts people with its lush, subtropical climate that supports farmlands fertile with vegetables, citrus trees and groves of date palms.

Scattered east of Tucson are portions of the Coronado National Forest, while south of the city is the most populated portion of Southern Arizona. Off Route 19 is Tubac, an artists' community with about 50 studios and galleries. Further south is the border town of Nogales, where you can bargain for Mexican crafts and sample authentic cuisine. The rolling grass and woodland hills around Patagonia are some of the state's best cattle and horse land, and further north near Elgin spread acres of green vineyards where local wines are produced. Further east is Sierra Vista, whose claim to fame is Fort Huachuca, a historic military base whose troops defeated Apache leader Geronimo and where 11,400 soldiers and civilians are still based.

Tombstone and Bisbee are old mining towns. Tombstone, the town too tough to die, survives by selling its history. There are historic museums and exhibits on every corner—each, of course, charging for the pleasure of your company. Visitors flock here to relive the rowdy life of the Old West, from the shootout at O.K. Corral to the gambling at Birdcage Theater. Bisbee has become a quiet artists' colony with a more bohemian flavor. Visitors

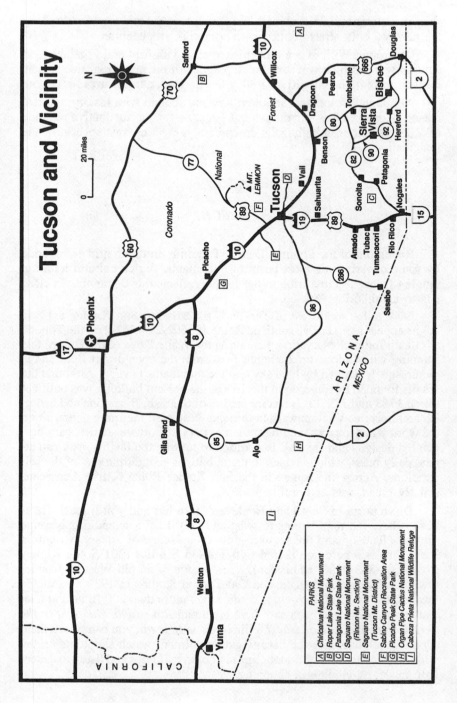

Tucson and Vicinity

N

0   20 miles

Phoenix

Safford

Willcox

10

70

B

A

Forest

Dragoon

Pearce

Tombstone

666

Douglas

Bisbee

Sierra
Vista

80

Benson

Hereford

92

National

77

MT.
LEMMON

Coronado

Vail

D

Tucson

F

Sahuarita

82

90

Patagonia

Sonoita

Nogales

C

60

89

19

89

Picacho

10

E

Amado
Tubac
Tumacacori

Rio Rico

15

G

Sasabe

286

86

10

8

Gila Bend

85

Ajo

H

2

ARIZONA

MEXICO

17

10

8

Wellton

I

Yuma

CALIFORNIA

PARKS

A Chiricahua National Monument
B Roper Lake State Park
C Patagonia Lake State Park
D Saguaro National Monument
   (Rincan Mt. Section)
E Saguaro National Monument
   (Tucson Mt. District)
F Sabino Canyon Recreation Area
G Picacho Peak State Park
H Organ Pipe Cactus National Monument
I Cabeza Prieta National Wildlife Refuge

shop in historic buildings along Main Street, tour old mines and walk along the narrow, hilly streets dotted with Victorian architecture.

Up around Willcox are orchards teeming with fruit and vegetables. In autumn you can pick your own or stop at one of the many roadside stands. Further north in the Gila River Valley lies Safford, a fertile area for cotton.

Although Tucson and Southern Arizona abound with history, the real reason people visit is for the natural beauty—for the meditative solitude of a desert that seemingly rolls on endlessly, creating vast spaces for the imagination.

Tucson

Rising out of the Sonoran Desert, Tucson is an urban grid surrounded by some of Arizona's most beautiful mountains. A rich cultural tradition ranging from the Pima tribe to the Jesuits reflects this community's close ties to neighboring Mexico.

Nine miles southwest of Tucson is the **Mission San Xavier del Bac** (signs appear as you drive south on Route 19; 602-294-2624) on the Tohono O'odham Indian Reservation. Known as the White Dove of the Desert, this stunning white adobe brick church rises from the open desert floor and is picturesquely framed by blue sky and the mountains beyond. Although the Jesuits founded the mission in the 1600s, the present building was built between 1783 and 1797. It is a combination of Spanish, Byzantine and Moorish architecture. Visitors walk in through weathered mesquite doors, sit on the worn wooden pews, and feast their eyes on the ornate statues, carvings, painted designs and frescos. In addition to touring the facility, you can attend daily mass, which is open to the public, or visit during one of the celebrations. Across the square in the **San Xavier Plaza** Native Americans sell fry bread, arts and crafts.

Drive north to Speedway Boulevard, turn left and you'll reach Gates Pass, where the road begins to twist and you'll have splendid panoramic views of Tucson and the saguaro-dotted landscape of Tucson Mountain Park. This is where you'll find **Old Tucson Studios** (201 South Kinney Road; 602-883-0100; admission), a re-creation of an old Western frontier town. Columbia Pictures created Old Tucson Studios in 1939 as a movie location for the film *Arizona*, and since then more than 200 films and television episodes have been shot here including *Rio Bravo*, *Gunfight at the O.K. Corral* and *El Dorado*. If a film crew is in town, you can watch them shoot. Otherwise, ride the narrow-gauge railroad, watch shootouts on the wide dirt streets, enter the adobe and slatboard buildings and listen to dance-hall music, or indulge in shopping.

Just a few minutes down Kinney Road is **The Arizona-Sonora Desert Museum** (2021 North Kinney Road; 602-883-2702; admission), a cross between a zoo and botanical garden with more than 200 different animals and 400 plant species indigenous to the Sonoran Desert. Visitors can inspect the aquatic exhibits and the animals in their desert habitats, or walk inside an aviary and a re-created limestone cave. Definitely worth a visit.

Another place to find plants indigenous to the area is the **Tucson Botanical Gardens** (2150 North Alvernon Way; 602-326-9255; admission) which contains a small field of Native American crops, a cactus and succulent garden, tropical greenhouse, and a xeriscape (arid landscaping) demonstration garden. Perhaps most unusual is the historic garden—lush foliage and flowers that surround and reflect the era of the 1920s Porter House.

For a panoramic view of Tucson from 3100 feet, drive to the top of **A Mountain** (take Congress Street exit west off Route 10 to Cuesta Street, then go south onto Sentinel Peak Road). Settlers of territorial days used it as a lookout for Apache raiders. The latest raiders are students from the University of Arizona, who have been whitewashing the A on it before the first football game of the season since 1915.

A big part of Tucson is the **University of Arizona**, a 298-acre campus dotted with red-brick buildings. If you decide to explore the campus there are a few worthwhile stops. One is **Flandrau Science Center & Planetarium** (corner of University and Cherry avenues; 602-621-7827; admission to laser shows) with its laser light shows, science store, public observatory with a 16-inch telescope available for public use and science exhibits such as a walk-through model asteroid and night skies exhibit. The **Center for Creative Photography** (★) (1030 North Olive Street; 602-621-7968) has a collection of more than 50,000 photographs, along with galleries, a library and research facilities. Photography exhibitions from the permanent collection and traveling exhibitions are displayed in the galleries. The **University of Arizona Museum of Art** (Olive Street near Speedway Boulevard; 602-621-7567) has Renaissance and later European and American art, including works by Rembrandt, Picasso, Rothko and O'Keeffe. The collection includes more than 3000 paintings, sculptures, drawings and prints.

El Presidio Historic District (Church Avenue to Alameda Street) was once the Presidio of San Augustin del Tucson, which the Spanish army enclosed with a 12-foot-high adobe wall in 1783. Today, the main attraction in El Presidio is the **Tucson Museum of Art** (140 North Main Avenue; 602-624-2333; admission), a complex specializing in pre-Columbian, modern American and Southwestern art, along with several historic houses and the Plaza of the Pioneers—a showplace for the museum's sculpture collection.

Fort Lowell Museum (★) (2900 North Craycroft Road; 602-885-3832) is a reconstructed commanding officers' quarters from the days when it was a key military post during the Apache Indian wars of the 1870s and 1880s.

Life on a military post in frontier Arizona is revealed through furnishings, artifacts and displays of military equipment.

The late Ted De Grazia gained fame painting impressionistic-style portrayals of the Southwest and its people. Today his home and galleries, the **De Grazia Gallery in the Sun** (6300 North Swan Road; 602-299-9191; admission), are open to the public. Skylights in the adobe structures bathe his paintings in light. Walking through, you pass underneath brick archways and go through landscaped courtyards that he so lovingly tended when he lived here. The unusual architecture, including an iron gate inspired by the historic Yuma Prison, is worth a visit in itself.

Pima Air Museum (6000 East Valencia Road; 602-574-0462; admission) contains one of the largest collections of historic aircraft in the world. Among the 160 aircraft are the Boeing B-29 Superfortress, the type of plane that dropped the first atomic bomb on Japan, and the first jet fighter to exceed the speed of sound in level flight.

For a truly unusual experience, stop by **Biosphere 2** (Route 77 Mile Marker 96.5, Oracle; 602-896-2108; admission) a three-acre miniature replica of the earth with a tropical rainforest, savannah, marine, marsh and desert. The airtight structure is home to a research team of eight men and women who entered the biosphere in the fall of 1991 and supposedly won't leave it until fall of 1993. They grow their own food, raise animals and are totally self-sufficient. Although you can't go inside the structure, you can see the outside of this high-tech, space-age glass and steel monolith, look through its glass walls and stop by the visitor center.

TUCSON HOTELS

Although Tucson is known for its upscale, full-service resorts—a haven for those escaping cold winters elsewhere—it also has a number of budget and mid-range accommodations.

Built in the 1930s, the **Arizona Inn** (2200 East Elm Street; 602-325-1541) is a historic gem. Although it's in the middle of town, it feels like a lush oasis with 14 acres of lawns and gardens thick with orange trees, native cypress and date palms. No two of the resort's 80 rooms are alike, but all are decorated to the 1930s period and some have antiques. This deluxe-priced inn also has a swimming pool, tennis courts, a restaurant and a cocktail lounge decorated with 19th-century Audubons.

Hotel Congress (311 East Congress Street; 602-622-8848) is a piece of Tucson's history. The block-long classical brick and marble structure was built in 1919 to serve Southern Pacific railroad passengers, and John Dillinger's gang were among its guests. Geometric Indian designs add character to the lobby, which also provides seating for the tiny Cup Café and overflow from the nightclubs. The renovated hotel rooms are decorated with black-and-white-tile bathrooms, black headboards and salmon-colored walls. The hotel's 40 rooms are budget-priced, and seven are hostels with bunk or single beds and private baths. None of the rooms have televisions, but they *do* have a rarity nowadays—windows that open.

Bed and breakfasts are proliferating in Tucson. Built in 1905, the **Peppertrees Bed and Breakfast** (724 East University Boulevard; 602-622-7167) is a Territorial home dominated by two large California pepper trees. There are two Southwestern-style guest houses, and two main rooms furnished with period pieces from England. French doors lead outside to a beautifully landscaped patio. Moderate.

La Posada del Valle (1640 North Campbell Avenue; 602-795-3840) is a stucco-and-adobe inn built in 1929. A novelty is afternoon tea, served in a living room furnished with art deco antiques from the '20s and '30s. The 1920s theme carries over to the five guest rooms, and each is named after famous women of that era. Zelda's Room is a favorite with a 1920s inlaid queen-size bedroom set. Moderate.

Centrally located, **North Campbell Suites Hotel** (2925 North Campbell Avenue; 602-323-7378) offers four-room suites with kitchens at budget prices. The 11 rooms aren't fancy, but are homey and functional with adequate furnishings and a hide-a-bed in the living room for extra sleeping space. A swimming pool and trees help soften the look of the motor court.

Tanque Verde Inn (7007 East Tanque Verde Road; 602-298-2300) is an 89-room, hacienda-style inn with rooms overlooking a lush courtyard dotted with Mexican fountains. Rooms are clean and comfortable; some are kitchenettes. Breakfast is complimentary at this moderately priced inn that also boasts a pool and local health club privileges.

For an assortment of budget motels, drive down Miracle Mile, once the main thoroughfare through the city. The area is a bit seedy with several strip joints, but there are a few decent places. One is the **Best Western Ghost Ranch Lodge** (801 West Miracle Mile; 602-791-7565). The lodge sits on what was once a working cattle ranch. Today, the property has 81 rooms housed in brick buildings surrounded by grassy lawns, palm trees and cactus gardens. The theme is Western, with a cow skull over the lobby fireplace and Western memorabilia throughout. There's also a restaurant, pool and whirlpool.

The Lodge on the Desert (306 North Alvernon Way; 602-325-3366) is a garden resort hotel with 40 adobe-colored villas grouped around patios that open to lawns and gardens. Rooms have beamed ceilings, hand-painted Mexican tile accents, Monterey furniture, and many have mesquite-burning beehive fireplaces. Other amenities include a restaurant and pool with mountain views. Moderate.

A bit north of Tucson on Mount Lemmon is the **Alpine Inn** (12925 East Sabino Canyon Road, Summerhaven; 602-576-1500). It's part-pub, part-country store, part-six-room bed and breakfast. Rooms are plainly furnished with light-brown carpet, a card table with chairs, a dresser and shower/bathroom. Moderate.

The resorts are expensive during winter high season, but most slash prices during the hot summer months. Among the best resorts is the **Westin La Paloma** (3800 East Sunrise Drive; 602-742-6000). The 487 Southwestern-style rooms have private balconies or patios, a sitting area, oversized closet and a stocked fridge. Many of the suites have woodburning fireplaces and sunken spa tubs. For recreation, there's a large swimming pool with swim-up bar, Jack Nicklaus golf course, tennis and racquetball courts, a health center and, for tired parents, day care for the small fry! Ultra-deluxe.

Located in the foothills of the Santa Catalina Mountains, **Loews Ventana Canyon** (7000 North Resort Drive; 602-299-2020) is another 93-acre, ultra-deluxe-priced resort. Highlights are an 80-foot waterfall cascading down into a lake, and secluded paths lined with mesquite, squawbush and blue palo verde. Many of the 398 Southwestern-style rooms have original artwork, burnished-pine furnishings, private balconies and bathrooms with marble floors. Amenities include five restaurants and lounges, tennis, golf, fitness trails, pools, a health club and shops.

Just north of town is **The Triangle L Ranch** (★) (2805 Triangle L Ranch Road, Oracle; 602-623-6732), an 1880s homestead on an 80-acre ranch. The four private cottages include an ivy-covered adobe cottage with a clawfoot tub in the bathroom and screened sleeping porch, and one with a stone fireplace, rose arbor entry and private patio. A woodburning stove warms the kitchen for breakfast, which consists of eggs from the owner's chickens and other homemade treats. Moderate.

Picacho Motel (6698 Eisenhower Street, Picacho; 602-466-7500) has been around since the 1930s. Waitresses in the lobby restaurant often double as receptionists to check guests into this casual, budget-priced motel. Just outside the 17 rooms are palm and fruit trees, while inside is somewhat worn wood paneling hung with country pictures, along with bureaus and desks.

TUCSON RESTAURANTS

There is an eclectic mix of cuisine in Tucson, but Southwestern and Sonoran-style Mexican fare are the specialties. For Southwestern food, try **Café Terra Cotta** (4310 North Campbell Avenue; 602-577-8100). The outdoor patio is lit by miniature white lights at night, while the indoor section is decorated in turquoise and terra cotta colors. Entrées include large prawns stuffed with herbed goat cheese and Southwestern tomato coulis, stuffed red and green chilies, and innovative pizzas that are cooked in the woodburning oven and topped with ingredients such as chorizo, herbed mozzarella, lime and cilantro. Moderate.

Although Key lime pie is on the menu, most of the other dishes at the **Presidio Grill** (3352 East Speedway Boulevard; 602-327-4667) are Southwestern in flavor. Try an appetizer of Anaheim chili stuffed with chorizo, fresh corn, cilantro and *havarti*, followed by innovative pizzas, pastas and grilled meats. Decor here is postmodern with an unusual color scheme of black, green, orange and yellow. And for those booth aficionados among us, it's nice to find a place with more booths than tables. Priced in the moderate range.

You can't beat **Janos** (150 North Main Avenue; 602-884-9426) for American nouvelle cuisine with a Southwestern twist. The adobe house shares a courtyard with the Tucson Museum of Art, and inside displays of original art hang below ocotillo ceilings on 20-foot-high walls. Menus change with the seasons, but typical entrées are lobster with papaya and champagne, or a meal of hickory smoked duck, chestnut mousse and cranberry butter. Ultra-deluxe.

Central Tucson

POINTS OF INTEREST
A Mission San Xavier del Bac
B Tucson Mountain Park
C Tucson Botanical Gardens
D University of Arizona
E El Presidio Historic District
F Fort Lowell Park
G Gene C. Reid Park

Café Magritte (254 East Congress Street; 602-884-8004) is an intimate, artsy café located in the heart of the arts district. The two-story eatery has brick walls hung with local artwork and wood floors. The food is eclectic, but has a hint of the Southwest. Specialties include brie melted over crabmeat tortilla rolls, and chicken simmered in garlic, mixed with cheese, corn, green chilies and red peppers. Budget.

Just down the road is **Bentley's House of Coffee & Tea** (121 East Congress Street; 602-798-1715). Here, you choose the ambience. One dining room is sophisticated with black tables and chairs and modern artwork, while the other room is cozier and contains shelves lined with books. Food is typical café fare—soups, sandwiches, quiches—while beverages include espresso, gourmet coffee and a wide range of Italian cream sodas. Budget.

Tucsonans also love Mexican food, and there are no lack of choices. Rosita Sinbres presides over **El Arte de Rosita** (★) (1944 East Prince Road; 602-881-5380), cooking all of their tasty Mexican food. On the walls hang photographs of Rosita with the late artist and friend Ted De Grazia, along with some of his prints. Handmade crocheted curtains cover the windows, and outside Christmas lights line the porch year-round and plants take root in clawfoot tubs. Eclectic homestyle best describes the atmosphere, while the prices are in the budget range.

Mi Nidito Café (★) (1813 South 4th Avenue; 602-622-5081) is a tiny, tacky, crowded Mexican joint with great food, from enchiladas to menudo. Portions are generous and there are always plenty of locals lining up to fatten their waistlines. Walls are covered with murals of palm trees and lighted plastic flowers. Budget.

Micha's (★) (2908 South 4th Avenue; 602-623-5307) is a larger restaurant owned by the Mariscal family for many years and whose portrait is just inside the door. On weekends mariachi bands stroll through the restaurant. You won't leave here hungry—even the flour tortillas are about a foot in length. Don't miss the chimichangas, topopo salad or grilled shrimp fantasia. Budget.

Walk into **Café Poca Cosa** (88 East Broadway Boulevard; 602-622-6400) and you're bombarded with festive color. Green paint covers the ceilings, red chili peppers dot the walls, lights hang on indoor trees, and purple, green and red tiles cover the tables. The menu changes two or three times daily, and is written on a blackboard that's brought to the table. Dishes are homestyle Mexican. Specialties include chicken breast in mango sauce, *pollo en chitotle* (chili) sauce and pork marinated in beer. Breakfast is also served. Budget to moderate.

Located in the warehouse district, **Tooley's** (★) (299 South Park Avenue; 602-798-3331) is little more than a glorified taco stand with good food. Customers order food at an outdoor window, then sit at one of the handful of tables on the sidewalk or perch on the curb. The menu boasts that Tooley's is home of the turkey taco, and turkey is used instead of chicken on all their entrées. If you're watching your wallet, you can't beat the super budget prices here.

Although it gets few points for ambience, **El Taco** (2825 North Country Club Road; 602-326-0580) is credited for good Mexican fast food at budget prices. The green chili and bean burros are especially tasty, and they also offer taco salads, enchilada dinners and other typical favorites. There's a drive-through window, and inside the A-frame building are four vinyl booths.

If you'd rather stay away from high-calorie Mexican food, try **The Good Earth** (6366 East Broadway Boulevard; 602-745-6600), the local choice for health foods. The extensive menu has salads, hot and cold sandwiches, pasta, seafood, chicken, vegetarian dishes and breakfast items that are served all day long. Although spacious, the atmosphere is nevertheless cozy with earth toned decor, solid wood tables, lots of hanging plants, and a cactus garden to add a touch of the Southwest. Budget.

Tork's Café (★) (1701 North Country Club Road; 602-325-3737) is a tiny, family-run place with only a handful of tables and delicious Middle Eastern food. The *shawerma* plate with beef, chicken or lamb contains strips of meat cooked with onions and bell peppers. Other choices are the vegetarian falafel plate, hummus dip, tabuli and kabobs. Budget.

Buddy's Grill (4821 East Grant Road; 602-795-2226) is a white-collar hangout. The narrow, blue-and-white room consists mainly of booths. Here you'll find fajita salads, sandwiches, burgers cooked on a mesquite-wood grill and delicious baked French onion soup. You might also take a peek at the exhibition kitchen. Budget.

As the name suggests, diners at **Van Gogh's Ristorante Italiano** (7895 East Broadway Boulevard; 602-722-5518) eat Italian food amid reproductions of Van Gogh's artwork. Along with traditional, moderately priced fare, you'll find more imaginative specials such as roast duck stuffed with smoked oysters and pine nuts, served with a Grand Marnier sauce. In addition, diners can hear live jazz music on the enclosed patio.

For the innovative in pizza, try **Magpies Pizza** (605 North 4th Avenue; 602-628-1661). Examples of their fare include The Greek with spinach, basil, garlic, piñon nuts, feta cheese, cheese and sundried tomatoes, or Cathy's with garlic, stewed tomatoes, mushrooms, artichokes, roasted red peppers and Romano cheese. Located in a small strip center, Magpies has a contemporary look with a black-and-white-tile floor, red chairs and modern art on the walls. Budget to moderate.

In the next block is **Delectables** (533 North 4th Avenue; 602-884-9289) where waiters with ponytails often hover over tables. Inside are wood-beamed ceilings and curving windows that look out onto 4th Avenue, while outside are somewhat rundown green metal tables with matching chairs. Moderately priced salads and sandwiches, such as turkey breast with havarti and avocado, are the choices here.

Walk through antique, hacienda-style doors and you're inside **Tohono Chul Tearoom** (★) (7633 North Paseo Del Norte; 602-797-1711), located in a rustic, 50-year-old house in the midst of Tohono Chul Park. Unless the weather is bad, opt for outdoor dining on a patio that sits amid palo verde trees and cactus, and offers free entertainment from the birds and other critters that come to nibble. For lunch, innovative sandwiches are served on croissants or sourdough bread. Other choices are breakfast, Sunday brunch and afternoon tea complete with finger sandwiches, scones and pastries. Budget.

The two boulevards boasting the largest concentration of restaurants in town are Broadway and Speedway. Here you'll find almost any type of local or ethnic food. The **Olympic Flame** (7970 East Broadway Boulevard; 602-296-3399) offers something rare in a Greek restaurant—white tablecloths and fresh flowers. They serve flaming *saganaki* at the table amid a chorus of opas, as well as pastitsio, moussaka, gyro, steaks and Greek-style salads. Moderate.

Jamaica Bay Café (6330 East Speedway Boulevard; 602-296-6111) has, as one would expect, a tropical setting with high ceilings, plants and colorful carpeting. Specialties of this moderately priced Caribbean restaurant include tomato-based Jamaican stew with sirloin and potatoes, Jamaican black bean soup and, for dessert, *tembleque* (Jamaican coconut custard pudding).

Further down the road is **Szechuan Omei Restaurant** (2601 East Speedway Boulevard; 602-325-7204), a Chinese restaurant where you can choose from more than 130 entrées, including lunch specials. Decor is nothing fancy, just red tablecloths and chairs and the usual Chinese lanterns and paintings. Budget.

Meat lovers may want to pull up a chair at **The Ranchers Club** (5151 East Grant Road; 602-797-2624), where you can order aged prime beef and seafood grilled over your choice of mesquite, hickory, wild cherry or sassafras wood. There is also a variety of sauces, butters and condiments including wild-mushroom sauce, onion marmalade and Cajun rémoulade. A harpist plays while diners eat on tables set with pink tablecloths and candles, but this elegant setting has a Western twist with cow horns and other Western paraphernalia. Deluxe.

Webb's Old Spanish Trail Steak House (★) (5400 South Old Spanish Trail; 602-885-7782) specializes in delicious barbecue ribs and chicken, as well as steaks. The moderately priced restaurant is casual with a few picnic tables thrown into the seating plan. At night, settle down by the picture window and you're likely to see javelinas stop by to feed.

At the **Arizona Inn** (2200 East Elm Street; 602-325-1541), you choose the ambience: formal dining room, casual patio or courtyard ablaze with tiny lights in the trees. The fare includes Continental, Southwestern, nouvelle and traditional selections. One treat is the fresh steamed fish, enhanced with ginger and leeks, and served at your table from a bamboo steamer. Or how about trying those buffalo burgers? Moderate.

The **Gold Room** (245 East Ina Road; 602-297-1151) is at the Westward Look resort. Dine with a stellar view of the city. Meats and seafood are prepared with a French twist, such as veal Oscar with crab meat, roast rack of lamb and châteaubriand. A few entrées are Mexican in style, such as a broiled New York steak sandwich served on toast with green chilies, cheese and red onions. Deluxe.

At the **Blue Willow Restaurant** (2616 North Campbell Avenue; 602-795-8736) you can either dine inside the house with its light blue walls and artsy posters, or opt for the brick, vine covered courtyard. Either choice is a winner. Although they serve sandwiches and salads at lunch and dinner, breakfast is the most popular meal here with 24 omelettes, including one with spinach, tomatoes and onions, or one with avocados, jack cheese and green chilies. Budget.

Two minutes away is **Coffee Etc.** (2700 North Campbell Avenue; 602-795-5305) where it's best to skip the entrée and go straight for the dessert and coffee. Favorites are the Snicker cheesecake served with Danish nutcream or cocoa almandine coffee. Resembling an open air café, the restaurant has umbrellas over the tables and clouds painted on the ceilings. Budget.

The **Alpine Inn** (★) (12925 East Sabino Canyon Road, Summerhaven; 602-576-1500) offers Eastern European cuisine such as beef stroganoff, and an alpine Bavarian grill served with grilled knockwurst, smoked wurst, German-style potato salad and cabbage. To really get decadent, top it off with Swiss white-chocolate fondue laced with frangelica and piñons. Moderate.

Although it's in the lobby of the Picacho Motel, the **Picacho Restaurant** (6698 Eisenhower Street, Picacho; 602-466-7500) is a cozy affair with dark-wood ceilings and booths and a Southwestern flavor with cow skulls and Indian rugs on the wall. People come mainly for the oversized hamburgers, although they also serve sandwiches, steaks and Mexican food. Budget.

TUCSON SHOPPING

If you want anything with a Southwestern flair, Tucson is where you'll find it. In addition, you'll find shops catering to almost every need, with the majority of the artsy and antique shops downtown and various specialty shopping plazas scattered throughout the town.

For shopping mixed with entertainment, head for the **Tucson Arts District** (located downtown roughly between Congress and Cushing streets, and Main and 4th avenues; 602-624-9977) on the first and third Saturday of the month. Stores and restaurants stay open late, musicians perform in the streets, and the area becomes a hot night spot for entertainment-seekers and shopaholics. There are 28 galleries, in addition to antique, novelty and specialty shops.

B&B Trading Co. (300 East Congress Street; 602-798-3906) carries Southwestern antiques and collectibles, including cowboy saddles and spurs. **Berta Wright Gallery** (260 East Congress Street; 602-882-7043) has a wide range of high-quality Mexican imports. For the tykes, there's **Yikes!** (278 East Congress Street; 602-792-9505), a toy store with unusual gifts, small toys and books. **Periwinkles** (266 East Congress Street; 602-624-9941) specializes in children's footwear—one whole wall is devoted to unusual socks!

Nearby is **4th Avenue** with about 70 shops and restaurants. Shops in this older neighborhood contain vintage clothing, unique fashions, jewelry, books and art. Don't be surprised to find touches such as incense burning in the shops.

Antigone Books (600 North 4th Avenue; 602-792-3715) specializes in books for and about women. **The Jewel Thief** (557 North 4th Avenue; 602-623-7554) offers a huge selection of earrings, with most hanging on large boards around the shop and priced at under $10. For clothing, try **Jasmine** (423 North 4th Avenue; 602-629-0706) with its natural fiber clothing, some handwoven in Morocco, or **Del Sol** (435 North 4th Avenue; 602-628-8765) with its Southwestern clothes, scarves and jewelry, and a huge selection of Indian rugs. On the vintage side, stop by the **Tucson Thrift Shop** (319 North 4th Avenue; 602-623-8736) which specializes in vintage clothing from the 1960s, or **Loose Change** (417 North 4th Avenue; 602-622-5579), a funky place with clothes from different eras that you try on in rooms closed off with refrigerator doors.

In the El Presidio Historic District downtown is **Old Town Artisans** (186 North Meyer Avenue; 602-623-6024), an 1850s restored adobe structure with surrounding shops that fill an entire city block. In the outdoor courtyard hang chili peppers and handmade hummingbird feeders, along with Mexican fireplaces. Inside the 13-room marketplace is Southwestern folk art made by Arizona artisans, Native American tribal art and imports from Latin America. Another worthwhile stop in this area is the **Tucson Museum of Art gift shop** (140 North Main Street; 602-624-2333) with contemporary pottery and other artistic gifts.

Many Hands Courtyard of Artisans (★) (3054 North 1st Avenue) is styled after a Mexican village and sells handmade works by local artists. Shops include **The Artist's Threads** (602-798-3454) with handwoven clothing and accessories, **Anni's Ears Galleria** (602-299-0523) with Southwestern furniture, turquoise jewelry and oxidized copper jewelry, and **This and That Crafts** (602-623-3260) with kachina dolls, paintings, stitchery and wooden crafts.

For Mexican imports, check out what is unofficially called the Lost Warehouse District—a group of shops located in old, red-brick warehouses. **Rustica** (★) (200 South Park Avenue; 602-623-4435) sells Southwestern and Mexican furnishings and accessories at wholesale prices, while **Magellan Trading** (★) (228 South Park Avenue; 602-622-4968) has great buys on Mexican glassware and handcrafted imports from Mexico and the Pacific Rim that include antique furniture, wood carvings and folk art.

St. Philips Plaza (corner of River Street and Campbell Avenue) is a cluster of Southwestern-style shops with red-tile roofs that include art galleries, clothing stores and restaurants. **Bahti Indian Arts** (602-577-0290) offers Native American crafts such as drums, jewelry, rugs and kachina dolls, while **Mercado de las Americas Gallery** (602-577-0640) has imports from Mexico, Peru, Chile and Ecuador including pottery, masks and folk art. Check out the bridge and pond in the back of the store. For pricey Italian shoes, stop by **Espada Footwear** (602-299-6650).

Drive further down River Road and you'll see **River Center** (corner of River Street and Craycroft Road) a Southwestern-style shopping plaza. The stores surround a brick courtyard with a fountain and waterway. **Totally Southwest** (602-577-2295) has Southwestern gifts while **Gift Alternatives Inc.** (602-299-8121) has unusual items for gift baskets from prickly pear erasers to chocolate caramel-covered tortillas. **The West** (602-299-1044) has cookbooks, cards, kids gifts and needlework supplies, with proceeds going to local women's and children's charities.

Built in 1932, **Broadway Village** (corner of Broadway Boulevard and Country Club Road) was one of the first shopping centers in Arizona. It houses a variety of shops in whitewashed red brick buildings. The more unusual includes a tiny mystery bookshop called **The Footprints of a Gigantic Hound** (★) (16 Broadway Village; 602-326-8533) where a huge Irish wolfhound is often found sprawling across most of the floor space. There are also two expensive, fashionable children's boutiques called **Boomers** (602-323-2441) and **Angel Threads** (602-326-1170), and a fun, unusual children's toy store called **Mrs. Tiggy-Winkle's** (602-326-0188).

B&B Cactus Farm (11550 East Speedway Boulevard; 602-721-4687) has more than 600 varieties of cacti and succulents from around the world.

For antiques outside the downtown area, browse through **Unique Antique** (5000 East Speedway Boulevard; 602-323-0319), a 75-dealer antique mall that owners claim is the largest in Southern Arizona, or **Sandy's Antiques** (4500 East Speedway Boulevard, Suite 78; 602-327-0772), which specializes in gold and silver jewelry from Navajo and Zuni Indians, as well as furniture, collectibles, clocks and dolls.

Casas Adobes Shopping Center (7051 North Oracle Road) is yet *another* Southwestern-style shopping plaza with a variety of specialty shops. A favorite is **Antigua de Mexico** (602-742-7114), a Latin American import store with Mexican Colonial and Southwestern furniture, folk art, pottery, glassware, tinware, sterling silver and jewelry from Taxco. North Campbell Avenue has a number of shopping venues. One of the most popular, judging by the ever crowded parking lot, is **Bookman's** (1930 East Grant Road; 602-325-5767)—*the* place for bibliophiles to browse. The owner claims the largest selection of used books and new magazines in the Southwest. Bookman's also has a rare book room and sells used magazines, records, tapes and CDs. As an added bonus, classical guitarists or jazz pianists perform live every day. Although less popular, there's also **African Arts Ltd.** (3025 North Campbell Avenue, Suite 151; 602-795-1997) with traditional and contemporary African items, from beer pot covers to baskets made of banana leaves.

TUCSON NIGHTLIFE

THE BEST BARS

Bum Steer (1910 North Stone Avenue; 602-884-7377) is a casual place in a large, barnlike building containing a restaurant, several bars, a video arcade, volleyball court and small dancefloor. Inside, everything from cannons to airplanes hang from the vaulted roof. The campus crowd flocks to the place.

Even if you don't plan to eat or drink, the **Solarium Restaurant and Lounge** (6444 East Tanque Verde Road; 602-886-8186) is worth a visit just to see the architecture. The best description defies description, but the three-story wood structure is a cross between a ship and a greenhouse. Enter through large floral iron doors, and inside are lots of windows, plants and wood planks. An acoustical guitarist performs Tuesday through Saturday.

The Chicago Bar (5954 East Speedway Boulevard; 602-748-8169) offers a heady mix of music. There's rock-and-roll on Monday and Tuesday, reggae on Wednesday and Thursday, blues on Friday and Saturday, and Motown on Sunday. Chicago memorabilia covers the walls, from White Sox parking signs to hometown banners. Cover.

Berkey's Bar (5769 East Speedway Boulevard; 602-296-1981) is another good place to hear the blues with live music all week long. An older crowd hangs out here, ordering drinks from the glass block bar, dancing and shooting pool.

Gentle Ben's Brewing Co. (841 North Tyndall Avenue; 602-624-4177) is a microbrewery near campus with delicious European-style ales, the most popular being Red Cat Amber and Tucson Blonde. If you're there at the right time of month, you can actually see workers brewing. Inside, the wooden floors and tables have obviously been much worn by the campus crowd, and outside is a big patio to see and be seen. There's live reggae and rock-and-roll on Friday and Saturday.

Laffs Comedy Nightclub (2900 East Broadway Boulevard; 602-323-8669) hosts everything from national to local acts. Tuesday is open mike night, Wednesday is ladies night and Thursday is college and military I.D. night.

The smell of money is thick in **The Board Room** (5350 East Broadway Boulevard; 602-750-7555), where lawyers and other professionals meet. Pictures of courtrooms adorn the place, along with lots of oak and brass. While you're there, don't forget to try Dave's Electric Beer brewed in Bisbee, Arizona.

Follow the cowboy hats and neon lights and you'll end up at **Cactus Moon** (5470 East Broadway Boulevard; 602-748-0049), a huge place specializing in country music. Western artwork hangs on the walls and rodeos roll on movie screens. A glittering, colored light shines on the dancefloor, which is big enough for two-steppers not to be toe-steppers. Cover on weekends.

Cactus Moon is tiny compared to **Wild Wild West** (4385 West Ina Road; 602-744-7744), a music hangout that sprawls over an entire acre. Inside are a country and a rock-and-roll bar, each with their own dancefloors. Around the perimeter of the Wild Wild West are stores selling items from cowboy hats to photographs, and in the middle is the only racetrack dancefloor in Tucson. There's no live music; cover on weekends.

A green neon sign announces the **Green Dolphin** (95 North Park Avenue; 602-622-6099), a college hangout with green walls, graffiti on the ceilings, lots of beer posters, beer mirrors and assorted other clutter. Although there's live music occasionally, people mainly come here to drink and shoot pool.

For salsa and traditional jazz music, stop by **Café Sweetwater** (340 East 6th Street; 602-622-6464), a narrow bar squeezed next door to the restaurant.

Graffiti on the tables and walls is the decor at **Bob Dobbs' Bar & Grill** (★) (2501 East 6th Street; 602-325-3767), a local hangout for the college and older crowd. A bright, noisy place, it has indoor and outdoor seating and plenty of televisions for catching the latest sports coverage.

For alternative music—and alternative crowds—peek into **Club Congress** (311 East Congress Street; 602-622-8849) adjoining the Hotel Congress. Tucson's unconventional set mixes with the college crowd at this cavern-like place with a red-and-brown-tile floor and dark walls. Cover.

Once a blacksmith shop, store and nightclub in the 1930s, today **Cushing Street Bar and Restaurant** (343 South Meyer Avenue; 602-622-7984) is a popular bar featuring live blues, jazz, rock and reggae. Diners swill drinks in turn-of-the-century tables and chairs amid antiques such as a floor-to-ceiling, 1880s legal bookcase and a circa-1850 cut-glass globe above the bar. There's also an outdoor patio. Cover.

Tucson McGraws (4110 South Houghton Road; 602-885-3088) is a Mexican cantina with a bar and dining room. Step outside, walk down the steps and you'll land on the terrace ramada that looks towards the Santa Rita Mountains and Tucson's beautiful sunsets. An outdoor fireplace warms customers on cold evenings, and a guitarist entertains on weekends.

If you're a beer lover, don't miss **The Shanty** (★) (401 East 9th Street; 602-622-7107) with more than 100 different beers from around the world, including Peru and Tahiti. Push a heavy copper door and you'll enter a room with a copper-topped bar and tables. Outside diners drink on a brick-paved patio surrounded by vine-covered wrought iron walls. The place has been around since 1937, but it's in a somewhat seedy area of town so watch your step.

THEATER

Arizona Theater Company (330 South Scott Avenue; 602-884-4875) has been unofficially called the State Theater of Arizona and performs six varied productions in Phoenix and Tucson from October to June. Plays by the Arizona Theater Company and other groups are performed in the restored Spanish Colonial Revival **Temple of Music and Art,** built in 1927.

Gaslight Theatre (7000 East Tanque Verde Road; 602-886-9428) offers corny musical melodramas. Patrons eat free popcorn while hissing at the villains and cheering for the hero or heroines. Many of the comedies are original, written especially for the theatre.

Invisible Theatre (★) (1400 North 1st Avenue; 602-882-9721) has classics, musicals and Off Broadway plays by Arizona playwrights and contemporary dramatists. During the lunch hour they offer brown-bag play festivals.

OPERA, SYMPHONY AND DANCE

Ballet Arizona (602-882-5022) is the state's professional ballet company that performs in both Tucson and Phoenix. They perform a repertoire of classical and contemporary works including world and national premieres.

Southern Arizona Light Opera Company (908 North Swan Road; 602-323-7888) performs four Broadway musicals a year at the Tucson Convention Center Music Hall.

Arizona Opera (3501 North Mountain Avenue; 602-293-4336) serves both Tucson and Phoenix and produces Grand Opera. The Tucson season runs from October through March, and productions have included *Don Giovanni, Otello* and *Madame Butterfly.*

For classical, pops and chamber concerts there is the **Tucson Symphony Orchestra** (443 South Stone Avenue; 602-792-9155).

Centennial Hall (University of Arizona, Building 29; 602-621-3341) hosts a full lineup on an international scale, from Chinese acrobatics to African dances. Past performers include Itzhak Perlman, Prague Symphony Orchestra and George Winston.

A professional modern dance company, **Tenth Street Danceworks** (738 North 5th Avenue; 602-628-8880) performs about four times a year and specializes in mixed media videography, or projecting video images on a screen or the dancers.

TUCSON PARKS

Gene C. Reid Park—This 130-acre park is a lush oasis in the desert with grassy expanses dotted with mature trees. There are a wide variety of recreational facilities here, including two golf courses, a swimming pool, pond, tennis and racquetball courts and Hi-Corbett field where major league baseball teams come for Spring training. Other attractions are Reid Park Zoo and a rose garden with more than 2000 plants.

Facilities: Picnic tables and ramadas, restrooms, zoo, recreation center, paddleboat rentals. *Fishing:* Allowed with urban fishing license; information, 602-791-4560.

Getting there: The park is between Broadway Boulevard and 22nd Street, Country Club Road and Alvernon Way.

Tucson Mountain Park—Winding, hilly roads take you through this 18,000-acre, high-desert area brimming with ocotillo, palo verde, mesquite and saguaros and punctuated by mountains with rugged volcanic peaks. A popular spot is the Gates Pass overlook just past Speedway where you can pull off the road and get a panoramic view of Tucson, Avra Valley, Kitt Peak and watch Arizona's renowned sunsets. The park also includes the Arizona-Sonora Desert Museum and Old Tucson.

Facilities: Picnic sites, archery and rifle ranges. *Hunting:* Allowed in season with proper permit; information, 602-740-2690.

Camping: Gilbert Ray Campground has 34 tent sites and 116 RV hookups; $6 per night for tent sites and $9 per night for hookups; information, 602-883-4200.

Getting there: Located about ten miles west of the city limits off Gates Pass Road (no recreational vehicles are allowed on the road). Another entrance is on Kinney Road off Ajo Way.

Fort Lowell Park—With its blend of history and recreation, Fort Lowell Park is an ideal family getaway. Fort Lowell was once a major military post and supply depot. Stroll between the trees on Cottonwood Lane, and you'll see a number of ruins, including that of the adobe post hospital built in 1875. Further down is a museum in the reconstructed officers' quarters.

The 59-acre park also has a pond with a fountain and plenty of hungry ducks around the perimeter, and a trail with marked exercise stops along the way.

Facilities: Tennis and racquetball courts, pool, picnic areas, lighted ball fields, shade ramadas; information, 602-791-4873.

Getting there: Located at 2900 North Craycroft Road.

Saguaro National Monument—Established to protect the saguaro cactus, found mainly in Arizona, the monument is divided into two segments on opposite sides of Tucson. The most popular is the Rincon Mountain Unit east of town, a 66,336-acre chunk established in 1933. Begin your tour at the visitor center, with dioramas and other exhibits of the geological and botanical history of the monument. Then drive along Cactus Forest Drive, a scenic eight-mile-loop showing off tall saguaro cactuses with their splayed arms.

The 20,738-acre Tucson Mountain District to the west features the six-mile-long Bajada Loop Drive that passes dense saguaro forests and Indian petroglyphs. Overall, the monument has more than 100 miles of hiking trails.

Facilities: Picnic areas, restrooms, barbecue grills; information, 602-296-8576.

Getting there: Drive east on Old Spanish Trail about three miles beyond city limits to get to the Rincon Mountain Unit, and the Tucson Mountain District is two miles beyond the Arizona-Sonora Desert Museum off Kinney Road.

Sabino Canyon—One of the most scenic spots in the region is a route that cuts through the Santa Catalina Mountains in the Coronado National Forest. You can either hike or take the shuttle on a seven-and-a-half-mile round trip that climbs a road lined with cottonwoods, sycamores, ash and willow trees. Along the route flows Sabino Creek with its pools and waterfalls that tumble underneath arched stone bridges. The shuttle makes nine stops along the way, so you can jump on or off as you go. For the romantically inclined, the shuttle has moonlight rides during the full moon from April to June and September to December. The shuttle will also take you on the two-and-a-half-mile trip to Bear Canyon Trail, where you then hike two more miles to Seven Falls, which cascade almost 500 feet down the side of a hill.

Facilities: Restrooms, visitor center; general information, 602-749-3223 or shuttle information, 602-749-2861.

Getting there: Sabino Canyon is at the north end of Sabino Canyon Road shortly before it dead-ends near the intersection with Sunrise Drive.

Mount Lemmon—In the hour's drive from Tucson to the top of Mount Lemmon, you travel from a lower Sonoran Desert zone to a Canadian zone forest, or from cactuses to pine forests. For this reason, Tucsonans flock there in summer to escape the heat, and in winter to ski at Mount Lemmon Ski Valley, the southernmost ski area in the United States. If you take Catalina Highway to the top, the steep and winding mountain road will pass

Rose Canyon Lake stocked with trout, and the town of Summerhaven with its handful of shops and restaurants. Once on Mount Lemmon, you can hike on about 150 miles of trails.

Facilities: Restrooms, picnic areas; information, 602-749-8700.

Camping: There are numerous sites at Rose Canyon, Spencer Canyon, Molina Basin and General Hitchcock campgrounds; $6 per night.

Getting there: Located within the Coronado National Forest, drive east on Tanque Verde Road to Catalina Highway, then head north 30 miles to Summerhaven.

Tohono Chul Park (★)—Few tourists seem to know about this treasure hidden in northwest Tucson. But walk down the winding paths of the 35-acre park and you'll discover about 400 species of arid climate plants, many of which are labeled, along with water fountains, grotto pond areas and a greenhouse with plants for sale. In addition, you'll find an art gallery, two gift shops and a tea room.

Facilities: Picnic tables, ramada, restrooms, drinking fountains; information, 602-575-8468.

Getting there: Located off Route 89 at 7366 North Paseo del Norte, about six miles north of the Tucson city limits.

Catalina State Park—This 5500-acre preserve sits in the foothills of the Santa Catalina Mountains. Highlights include Romero Canyon, a beautiful area with clear pools shaded by sycamore and oak trees, and adjacent Pusch Ridge Wilderness, home to desert bighorn sheep. The Hohokam once farmed the area, and as you walk through the park you can still see some of the pit houses and ball court ruins.

Facilities: Restrooms, showers, picnic tables and grills; information, 602-628-5798.

Camping: There are 48 sites; $7 per night, per vehicle.

Getting there: Located off of Route 89, about eight miles north of the city limits at 11570 North Oracle Road.

Picacho Peak State Park—The most dramatic part of the park is Picacho Peak, a landmark formation that rises 1500 feet above the desert floor and can be seen for miles around. The peak is believed to be 22 million years old—or four times as old as the Grand Canyon—and was used as a landmark by early explorers. It was also the site of the battle of Picacho Pass during the Civil War. The 3400-acre park has hiking trails that wind past saguaro cactuses.

Facilities: Picnic areas, shade ramadas, restrooms; information, 602-466-3183.

Camping: There are 85 sites ($7 per night) plus 12 RV hookups ($12 per night).

Getting there: Located 40 miles north of Tucson just off Route 10.

East of Tucson

The Wild West comes to life in this area of Arizona where murder and lynching were once considered leisure activities, poker was more popular than Sunday church services and whiskey was king. While this region is best known for infamous spots like Boot Hill and the O.K. Corral, it's also the home of historic mining towns like Bisbee, mineral spas and a cowboy hall of fame.

Get on Route 10 heading east and one of the first attractions you'll pass is **Colossal Cave** (off Old Spanish Trail in Vail; 602-791-7677; admission), one of the largest dry caverns in the world. Set in the Rincon Mountains, it was once home for Indians and outlaws. During 50-minute tours, hidden lights illuminate formations such as the Frozen Waterfall and Kingdom of the Elves.

Further east on Route 10 is Benson, where the **Arts & Historical Museum (★)** (180 South San Pedro Street; 602-586-3070) tells the story about how Benson grew along with the arrival of the railroad. Inside are antiques, artifacts and a huge mural running down one wall depicting the Pony Express from Dragoon to Benson. A gift shop offers local arts and crafts.

On your way to the Old West towns of Bisbee and Tombstone, take a detour towards Elgin. You will enter what at first seems an oxymoron—Arizona **wine country**. But there are several wineries out here, and it's a pretty drive through the vineyards. In the town of Elgin you'll find **The Chapel of Santa Maria (★)**, a small chapel set amid grasslands, vineyards and cottonwood trees that is open for contemplation and administered by the Monks of the Vine, a Wine Brotherhood of area vintners.

Head south on Route 90 and you can't miss **Fort Huachuca** (Sierra Vista; 602-538-7111) a National Historic Landmark founded in 1877 to protect settlers from Apache raiders. The Fort Huachuca soldiers eventually tracked down and defeated Apache leader Geronimo. Today, 11,400 people are garrisoned or working at this 73,000-acre installation. One highlight is the Fort Huachuca Museum, located in a turn-of-the-century building first used as a bachelor officers' quarters. Inside are military artifacts, dioramas and the history of the fort. For a panoramic view of the fort and town, drive up Reservoir Hill Road. If you'd prefer picnicking, there are plenty of scenic spots amid large, old trees on base. For a map, stop at the visitor center at the entrance.

Hop on Route 90 again for the quick trip to **Bisbee** near the Mexican border. An old mining town and now an artists' enclave, the town is full of Victorian architecture perched on hillsides, along with funky shops and restaurants. For the full history of the town, start at the **Bisbee Mining & Historical Museum** (5 Copper Queen Plaza; 602-432-7071; admission) located in the former General Office Building of the Copper Queen Consolidated Mining Co. On the front lawn is old mining equipment, while inside the 1897 red-brick building are photo murals, artifacts and walk-in environments that highlight Bisbee's history.

For a firsthand view of mining history, put on a slicker, hard hat and battery-pack light and hop on the underground train at the **Queen Mine Underground Tour** (118 Arizona Street; 602-432-2071; admission). An ex-miner narrates as he takes you through the Copper Queen Mine, which prospered for more than 60 years before it closed in 1943. The journey is a cool one, so bring a jacket. From here you can also take the **Lavender Open Pit Mine Tour**, a narrated, 13-mile bus tour around a 300-acre hole where more than 380 million tons of ore and waste have been removed.

Continue your time travel to the Old West at **Slaughter Ranch** (★) (Geronimo Trail; 602-558-2474; admission), located near the Mexican border in the small town of Douglas. Now a National Historic Landmark, it was once the home of John Slaughter, a former Texas Ranger, sheriff of Cochise County and one of the founders of Douglas. He bought the fertile grassland in 1884 and developed it into a cattle ranch. Slaughter's house and half a dozen other buildings furnished to reflect the era are still on the 140-acre site.

Northwest of Douglas is **Tombstone**, the town too tough to die. Prospector Ed Shieffelin staked a silver claim there in 1877 and it became a Wild, Wild West town with saloons and gambling halls reputedly making up two of every three buildings. Unfortunately, today the town is extremely touristy and every attraction is out to make a buck, but there are a few worthwhile stops. The **Tombstone Courthouse** (219 Toughnut Street; 602-457-3311; admission) has a restored courtroom and two floors of historic exhibits that reflect the ups and downs of this once rowdy town. Now part of the Arizona State Park system, the red-brick building was the town's courthouse from 1882 until 1931.

Allen Street is the heart of Tombstone. At one end is the **Bird Cage Theatre** (6th and Allen streets; 602-457-3421; admission), a famous night spot in the late 1800s. Overlooking the gambling casino and dance hall are birdcage-like compartments where prostitutes plied their trade. Never a dull place, the theater was the site of 16 gunfights. If you bother to count you'll find 140 bullet holes riddling the walls and ceilings. Also, the longest poker game in the history of the West reputedly unfolded here . . . it lasted more than eight years. Is this an ace attraction or what?

The most famous of Tombstone's numerous gunfights occurred in 1881 at **O.K. Corral** (Allen Street; 602-457-3456; admission) just down the street from the Bird Cage Theatre. Lifesize figures stand in the corral as a narrator describes the shootout. An adjacent building showcases old Tombstone photographs and other historic items.

The losers of the shootout and other gunslingers lay buried at **Boot Hill Graveyard** (Route 80 West; 602-457-3348). Enter the graveyard through the gift shop to see rows of graves—little more than piles of rocks with white metal crosses to mark them—as well as a spectacular view of the area.

A huge rose bush that spreads across 7000 feet of supports is the main attraction at the **Rose Tree Inn Museum** (4th and Toughnut streets; 602-457-3326; admission). Planted in 1885, the bush is an especially awesome sight if you come in Spring when it's covered with white blossoms. You can also tour the historic adobe home with local artifacts and period rooms.

Founded in 1880, the **Tombstone Epitaph** (9 South 5th Street; 602-457-2211) is still being published. In one corner of the newspaper office is the original press and other printing equipment. As residents say, Every Tombstone should have an Epitaph.

After looping off Route 10 to see Sierra Vista, Bisbee and Tombstone, get back to Route 10 and go east to Dragoon, home of the **Amerind Foundation** (★) (Triangle T Road; 602-586-3666; admission) and little else. This is a real treasure tucked away amidst the rock formations of Texas Canyon. The research facility and museum have been devoted to Native American culture and history since they opened in 1937. Visitors walk through the Spanish Colonial Revival-style buildings to see Native American pieces, such as beadwork, costumes, ritual masks and weapons, as well as Western artwork, including works by Frederic Remington and William Leigh.

More Western history is further east on Route 10 in Willcox at the **Museum of the Southwest and Cowboy Hall of Fame** (1500 North Circle I Road; 602-384-2272) adjoining the Cochise Information Center. Highlights include portraits by cowboy artist Carl Clapp and photographs of the cowboys who pioneered the area. There's also a bust of Chief Cochise, Indian artifacts, a horse-drawn carriage and a mineral and rock collection.

The most famous cowboy of the area was Rex Allen, born in Willcox in 1920. **The Rex Allen Arizona Cowboy Museum** (155 North Railroad Avenue; 602-384-4583; admission) features mementos of Rex Allen's life, from his homesteading and ranch life in Willcox to his movies and television shows. Another section features the pioneer settlers and ranchers of the West.

Lying low in the Gila River Valley and surrounded by mountains is **Safford**, where cotton is still king. The **Safford Valley Cotton Growers** (★) (120 East 9th Street; 602-428-0714) has one of a handful of gins in the area that you can tour during season, typically September through January. Call ahead for reservations.

Underground hot springs are another natural resource in Safford. To take a dip, stop by **Kachina Mineral Springs Spa** (★) (Cactus Road just off Route 666; 602-428-7212; charge for services) where you can soak in springs funneled into tiled, Roman-styled tubs. Other amenities include massages, sweat wraps and reflexology (therapeutic foot massage). Although it's a tacky, run-down place, the baths are wonderful and the tubs are clean.

Archeology buffs can check out the **Museum of Anthropology** (★) (345 College Avenue, Thatcher; 602-428-1133) on the Eastern Arizona College campus. Artifacts of southeastern Arizona are the focus. Exhibits include pottery and jewelry, a stratigraphic depiction of Gila Valley prehistory, replicas of Indian weaponry and a diorama of late Ice Age Arizona.

EAST OF TUCSON HOTELS

You won't find any ritzy accommodations in Benson, but some of the budget-priced motels aren't too bad. The **Oasis Court** (363 West 4th Street; 602-586-9784) is a family-run motor court that has been around since the 1920s. All five units are kitchenettes, and each has covered parking. Rooms are clean and comfortable.

The majority of accommodations in Sierra Vista are located along Fry Boulevard—the main commercial thoroughfare through town—and on South Route 92. **Sierra Suites** (391 East Fry Boulevard; 602-459-4221) is a two-story, red-brick hotel that lures guests with complimentary breakfast and cocktails. The 100 rooms face courtyards, and inside are mirrored sliding glass closet doors, small glass tables and a chest of drawers. Most even have refrigerators. The moderate price includes use of the pool and whirlpool.

Thunder Mountain Inn (1631 South Route 92, Sierra Vista; 602-458-7900) is a two-story, beige-colored brick building with 102 rooms, a dining room and lounge. Lower-level rooms facing the pool have sliding-glass doors. Most accommodations have double beds and a desk. Budget.

For a really secluded getaway, venture out to **Ramsey Canyon Inn** (★) (31 Ramsey Canyon, Hereford; 602-378-3010) located in the Huachuca Mountains along a winding mountain stream and adjacent to the Nature Conservancy's Mile Hi/Ramsey Canyon Preserve and the Coronado National Forest. Accommodations consist of three cabins and six rooms furnished with country antiques. Moderate.

Built in 1917, **The Bisbee Inn** (45 OK Street, Bisbee; 602-432-5131) overlooks Brewery Gulch, once one of the Southwest's wildest streets. Each of the 18 rooms has handmade quilts on the beds, antique dressers with mirrors, and its own sink. Guests share bathrooms in the hall. This red-brick inn is budget-priced and offers an all-you-can-eat breakfast.

Petra Bed & Breakfast (818 Tombstone Canyon, Bisbee; 602-432-2996) is a large, restored, 1917 red-brick schoolhouse just above Garfield Playground. The ten rooms are fairly large and each has a private bath with a large tub. A Southwestern breakfast is served family style in the dining room. Budget to moderate.

(Text continued on page 202.)

Calling All City Slickers!

Fueled by romantic images of Western heroes and desert sunsets and indulging in the fantasy of an escape to simpler times, more people than ever are opting to hang their saddles at dude ranches. In Southern Arizona, cowpokes have more than their fair share of choices. Guest ranches here range from resorts where you're more likely to overheat in the jacuzzi than the saddle, to working ranches where wranglers round 'em up and dine on beans and burgers. Whatever the orientation, most have horseback riding, a whole range of outdoor activities, and a casual, secluded atmosphere. Some are closed during the hot summer months, so call ahead.

One of the most luxurious getaways is **Tanque Verde Ranch** (14301 East Speedway Boulevard, Tucson; 602-296-6275). It comes complete with indoor and outdoor swimming pools, tennis courts, an exercise room and, of course, horseback riding. Guests stay in one of 60 casitas and patio lodges, some with beehive fireplaces, antiques and Indian bedspreads. Sliding glass doors offer stunning desert views. To relax, cozy up in the lounge with a good Western novel by the stone fireplace. The ultra-deluxe ranch has been around since the 1880s.

White Stallion Ranch (9251 West Twin Peaks Road, Tucson; 602-297-0252) sprawls across 3000 acres—grazing land for their herd of Longhorn. Guests take breakfast rides, watch rodeos every Saturday afternoon, and pet deer, sheep and pygmy goats at the on-site zoo. Rooms at this deluxe-priced ranch are rustic with Western decor.

Don't look for televisions or telephones inside the 20-room **Lazy K Bar Ranch** (8401 North Scenic Drive, Tucson; 602-744-3050), because here you're meant to leave the outside world behind. Ranch-style meals are served in a dining room, and Saturday night is set aside for steak cookouts beside a ten-foot waterfall. Afterwards, you can relax in the comfortable library with wood paneling and beams, bookshelves, a fireplace and card table. Rooms are rustic. Deluxe.

Price Canyon Ranch (★) (Route 80 to 400-mile marker, go left at cattle guard into dirt road and drive seven miles, Douglas; 602-558-2383) in the Chiricahua Mountains is a working cattle ranch with one-

and two-room bunk houses with baths. Meals are served in the 100-year-old main ranch house. Visitors can either ride on short trips or go on longer overnight pack trips for two to ten nights. Accommodations are moderate with meals and horseback riding included.

Grapevine Canyon Ranch (★) (Highland Road, Pearce; 602-826-3185) offers deluxe-priced accommodations in rooms with country-ranch furnishings and Native American touches. Visitors also lounge in the sitting room, a cozy place with a wood-beamed ceiling, Indian blankets and steer horns over the fireplace. At this working cattle ranch, horseback riding is the main attraction.

Rancho Santa Cruz Guest Ranch (★) (off the Route 19 frontage road, Tumacacori; 602-281-8383) is a 112-acre working ranch that opened in the 1920s. The eight adobe and stucco rooms are modest, but comfortable, and the three suites have fireplaces. A grassy courtyard with chairs beckons visitors to relax, as does the outdoor pool. Budget to moderate in price.

Circle Z Ranch (★) (Patagonia; 602-287-2091) in the foothills of the Santa Rita Mountains is a colorful, unpretentious place built in the early 1920s. Teddy Roosevelt was just one of the many famous visitors here. The deluxe-priced ranch accommodates no more than 45 people at a time. The ranch's adobe cottages are decorated with brightly painted wicker furniture and Mexican crafts, but don't have televisions or telephones. Instead, evening recreation centers around the lodge with its massive stone fireplace and bookshelves filled with classics, including Zane Grey titles.

Sitting in the foothills of Baboquivari Peak near the Mexican border, **Rancho De La Osa** (28201 West La Osa Ranch Road, Sasabe; 602-823-4257) is a 200-year-old Territorial-style ranch. Made of handmade adobe block, rooms have fireplaces and Indian and Spanish furnishings. Activities here include riding pure-bred quarterhorses and swimming, or sampling cocktails in the Cantina, an old Spanish/Indian mission. Moderate.

Other ranches include: **Hacienda del Sol** (5601 North Hacienda del Sol Road, Tucson; 602-299-1501), **Triangle T Guest Ranch** (★) (Dragoon; 602-586-3738) and **Rex Guest Ranch** (★) (Amado; 602-398-2914).

The Copper Queen Mining Co. built the **Copper Queen Hotel** (11 Howell Avenue, Bisbee; 602-432-2216) just after the turn of the century when it was a gathering place for politicians, mining officials and travelers, including the young Teddy Roosevelt. A plaque on one door marks the room where John Wayne stayed. The hotel is in the midst of an ongoing restoration, so ask for the restored rooms when you go. These are decorated Victorian style with floral wallpaper and tile bathrooms. The four-story building contains 45 budget-to-moderate-priced rooms, along with the Copper Queen Saloon and Dining Room.

The **Bisbee Grand Hotel** (61 Main Street, Bisbee; 602-432-5900) is ideally located in the main shopping area in town. The original hotel was built in 1906, and the 11 rooms reflect the era with floral wallpaper, red carpeting, brass beds and antiques. They also have sinks and ceiling fans. The rooms are upstairs, while downstairs is the old saloon, Victorian Ladies Parlor and a theater for melodramas. Moderate.

The **Jonquil Motel** (317 Tombstone Canyon, Bisbee; 602-432-5761) is a small motor court with seven clean, comfortable rooms at budget rates. The rooms have televisions but no telephones.

The **Gadsden Hotel** (1046 G Avenue, Douglas; 602-364-4481) is a National Historic Monument that opened in 1907 as a hotel for cattlemen, miners and ranchers. Although the 160 rooms are plain, the lobby is magnificent. It contains a solid white Italian-marble staircase, four marble columns with capitals decorated in 14K gold leaf, and vaulted stained-glass skylights that run the length of the lobby. Several Hollywood movies have been filmed here. Other amenities include the Saddle and Spur Lounge, El Conquistador Dining Room and The Cattleman's Coffee Shop. Budget.

If you're a John Wayne fan, ask for room #4 at the **Hacienda Huachuca Motel** (★) (320 Bruce Street, Tombstone; 602-457-2201). It's where the Duke himself stayed when he shot one of his movies in town. The seven kitchenettes face a small pool, and all have a rustic feel with wood-beam ceilings and overstuffed chairs. All the rooms have a small patio area, and some have mountain views. Be sure to say hello to Scooter, the talking cockateel, when you check in. Budget.

The seven-room **Tombstone Boarding House** (108 North 4th Street, Tombstone; 602-457-3716) is housed in an adobe building constructed around 1879. Rooms are tastefully decorated in pastel colors with lacy curtains and Victorian-era furnishings. A full breakfast is served in the parlor, and guests that know how to play the piano are welcome to entertain. Budget to moderate.

Olney House (★) (1104 Central Avenue, Safford; 602-428-5118) of Western Colonial Revival home has three guest rooms, all with original oak fireplaces and antiques. Scattered throughout are Asian decorations from the owners' travels, and in the dining room is a mural painted by an Indian artist. Guests start the morning with a Western breakfast. Before leaving, be sure to see the pecan tree, which they claim is the tallest in Arizona. Moderate.

EAST OF TUCSON RESTAURANTS

Horseshoe Restaurant & Lounge (★) (154 East 4th Street, Benson; 602-586-3303) is a family-owned restaurant that has been around for more than 50 years. On the walls are Western murals by artist Vern Parker, and the posts in the café display cattle brands of Southern Arizona. A neon horseshoe on the ceiling helps light the room. Entrées include chili, sandwiches, omelets, burgers, steaks and Mexican specialties. Budget.

Peking Chinese Cuisine (1481 East Fry Boulevard, Sierra Vista; 602-459-0404) is located in a small strip center with neon signs in the windows. The best deal here is an all-you-can-eat lunch buffet. The place is casual with red booths and tables, and Chinese-type lanterns and fans hanging from the ceiling. Budget.

Speaking in relative terms, the **Thunder Mountain Inn Restaurant** (1631 South Route 92, Sierra Vista; 602-458-7900) is one of the more expensive places in town. Diners eat moderately priced prime rib and seafood atop pink tablecloths in booths divided by etched glass.

Bisbee has a number of small eateries that almost defy description. One is **18 Steps (★)** (41½ Main Street; 602-432-3447). Just as the name implies, you must climb 18 steps to get to this tiny, budget-priced restaurant. Three tables are in one room, while in another room is a table and a small sitting area with a couch and bookshelves. If you'd prefer to eat on the couch, it's perfectly okay with the owners. The menu is on a blackboard and features delicious homemade specialties such as brie crêpe with raspberry sauce and tomato cheese pie.

Just underneath 18 Steps is **The Wine Gallery Bistro** (41 Main Street, Bisbee; 602-432-3447) with seating in the sunny, open street level room or the more intimate basement. Victuals here include gulf shrimp with roasted garlic, sundried tomatoes and almond pasta, and orange roughy with macadamia nuts. Moderate.

The Renaissance Café (★) (10 A Lyric Plaza, Bisbee; 602-432-4020) is a tiny, no-frills place where the locals hang out. Local artists' works hang on the walls, bulletins paper the front window, and a radio station plays in the background. There are a few tables inside, and a few out on the sidewalk. Offerings include sandwiches, hot bagel melts, quiche, pizza, salads and desserts as well as tasty coffee, espresso and herbal teas. Budget.

At **Golden China** (15 Brewery Gulch, Bisbee; 602-432-5888), the bargain is the big lunch buffet. Some favorite menu items are beef with scallops on a sizzling platter and lobster Szechuan style. Along with the standard

Chinese decor is a splashing rock fountain in the back of the restaurant. Budget.

The **Nellie Cashman Restaurant** (121 South 5th Street, Tombstone; 602-457-2212) is housed in an 1882 building with decor to reflect the era including a stone fireplace, high wood ceilings and photos of bygone years. Although they serve sandwiches and burgers, they're best known for their homemade berry pies. Budget.

Known for their ribs, **The Lucky Cuss Restaurant** (414 East Allen Street, Tombstone; 602-457-3561) serves their meat after smoking it for 14 hours on a mesquite-wood fire. The walls of this moderately priced place are falsefronts of historic Tombstone buildings, such as the Bird Cage Theatre and Tombstone Epitaph newspaper.

If you're in the mood for the biggest hot dog in Cochise County, weighing in at half-pound and measuring a foot long, then saunter over to the **Longhorn Restaurant** (501 East Allen Street, Tombstone; 602-457-3405) and order a Longhorn Dog. If that's not what you crave, they offer a wide selection of Italian, Mexican and American food. The decor is Western with longhorns hanging over the door and yellowing wanted posters of characters such as Billy the Kid laminated on the tables. Budget.

El Charro Restaurant (628 Main Street, Safford; 602-428-4134) is a local hangout with formica tables and local artwork on the wall. Mexican specialties include cheese crisps with green chili con carne, green or red chili burros and Sonora enchiladas. Budget.

The **Country Manor House** (420 East Route 70, Safford; 602-428-2451) is open 24 hours a day and is adjacent to the Country Manor Motel. Old farm implements hang on the walls and you're likely to see a table of old timers in here shooting the breeze and eating home-cooked meals such as chicken fried steak, liver and onions and meatloaf. Budget.

EAST OF TUCSON SHOPPING

Singing Wind Bookshop (★) (Ocotillo Road, two-and-a-quarter miles north of Route 10, Benson; 602-586-2425) is in the *really hidden* category. No signs announce it, only the name on a mailbox. Don't let the chained green cattle gate stop you—just open it and drive on in and down to the ranch house. Here, there are two huge rooms full of new books about the Southwest, Western Americana and other categories. If you're friendly, the owner just may give you some coffee, food, or spin a yarn or two.

In downtown Benson, **Zearings Mercantile Store** (★) (305 East 4th Street; 602-586-3196) is a narrow, high-ceilinged place that has been around as long as anyone can remember. Inside you'll find guns, gifts, relics and every imaginable kind of knickknack. For trendier items, stop in **Kiva Gifts** (363 West 4th Street, Benson; 602-586-9706) next to the Chamber of Commerce where they sell Southwestern, Native American and Mexican arts, crafts and clothing.

Head south to Sierra Vista and you'll discover **Misty's Gift Gallery** (228 West Fry Boulevard; 602-458-7208), one of the largest collectors' galleries in the Southwest with names that include Goebel, Hummel, Lladro, Gorham, De Grazia and Perillo. There is also a gallery with original artwork, lithographs and bronzes.

Bisbee is a real shopping mecca, especially for art lovers. Pick up a map at the Chamber of Commerce to aid in navigating the spending trail. The majority of shops are on Main Street, including **The One Book Bookstore** (★) (38 Main Street; 602-432-5512). You can literally buy only one book here (you don't expect us to give away the title, do you?) But here's a hint: Author Walter Swan sits in the bookstore window wearing overalls and a black cowboy hat, ready to spin tales and talk about the book that describes his childhood in Cochise County. Next door is **The Other Book Bookstore** which, you guessed it, houses his other books.

Across the street is the **Johnson Gallery** (69 Main Street; 602-432-2126), a huge place with a variety of imports including Native American serigraphs, lithographs and etchings, Mexican and Indian masks, Tarahumara Indian artifacts, Native American arts and Quezada family pottery.

Curves (55 Main Street, Bisbee; 602-432-4694) is a fine art gallery and eclectic shop featuring what they claim are handmade clothing and art from everywhere in the world except Antarctica. For local stuff, jump **Into the Fire** (45 Main Street, Bisbee; 602-432-4690) with its contemporary pottery and porcelain. Or stop by **The Gold Shop** (9 Howell Avenue, Bisbee; 602-432-4557) which features innovative, contemporary jewelry created by about a dozen craftspeople from Bisbee and the Southwest.

Jack a Lope (★) (9 Naco Road, Bisbee; 602-432-7833) has used, rare and out-of-print books as well as records, cassettes and CDs.

Allen Street is the heart of shopping in Tombstone, where you'll find lots of souvenir shops mixed in with higher-quality jewelry and clothing stores. **Arlene's Southwest Silver & Gold** (404 Allen Street; 602-457-3344) is a large place with Indian jewelry and artwork including pottery, baskets, kachina dolls and rugs. **Gabe's Dolls & Museum** (312 Allen Street; 602-457-3419) is one of the oldest shops in Tombstone. The place is crammed full of dolls, dollhouse pieces, Victorian cards, collectibles and more than 150 paper dolls. In the back of the shop is a museum with dolls dating back to the 1830s.

Looking for antique African clam shell discs, camel bone beads or yak bone beads handcarved in Pakistan? Even if you aren't, the **Bovis Bead Co.** (220 East Fremont Street, Tombstone; 602-457-3359) has them, and one of the largest selections of beads in the country. They import from all over the world, and also make their own beads.

Eagle's Nest Leathers (509 Allen Street, Tombstone; 602-457-3805) has leathers and Western wear including handmade belts, moccasins, hats, buckles and knives.

The time to travel out to the Willcox area is fall, when farms and roadside stands are selling their produce. The Willcox Chamber of Commerce has a brochure listing 27 orchards and mills where you can stop. One is **Stout's Cider Mill** (1510 North Circle I Road; 602-384-3696) where you can pick your own produce or buy apples, cider, dried fruit, nuts, peaches, apple pies, chili peppers and Arizona desert preserves.

Unless you're in the market for jewelry or rocks, there's not much shopping in Safford. **Arizona Gems & Crystals** (414 5th Street; 602-428-5164) offers custom-designed jewelry, jewelry-making supplies, lapidary equipment and a variety of rough rock, minerals and crystals. It's also one of the largest retailers of green peridot—80 percent of it is mined from the local Apache reservation. **Brown's Turquoise Shop Inc.** (2248 1st Street, Safford; 602-428-6433) has rough and cut natural Morenci turquoise and handmade Indian jewelry.

EAST OF TUCSON NIGHTLIFE

Arena Bar & Rodeo Grounds (★) (250 North Prickly Pear Street, Benson; 602-586-9983) overlooks the rodeo grounds—a plus when there's something to watch, but that's not too often. Inside a Western theme dominates. A lasso hangs on the door, cow skulls decorate walls, and you can warm yourself by the big rock fireplace. There are also a pool table and dancefloor, along with outdoor picnic benches.

Established in 1902, **St. Elmo Bar and Grill** (15 Brewery Avenue, Bisbee; 602-432-2775) in historic Brewery Gulch is a tradition around here. Memorabilia such as old maps hang on the walls, and seating is mainly stools at the counter. On weekends there's live music and dancing. Entertainment during the week is supplied by change in the jukebox or pinball machines.

Adjoining the Copper Queen Hotel, the **Copper Queen Saloon** (11 Howell Avenue, Bisbee; 602-432-2216) is a small, dark, intimate place with some turn-of-the-century furnishings and live music on weekends.

At the **Stock Exchange Bar** (15 Brewery Avenue, Bisbee; 602-432-2775), almost one whole wall is covered with an original board from the New York stock exchange. This historic building has a pressed tin roof, worn wooden floors and copper topped tables.

Walk through swinging doors of **Big Nose Kate's Saloon** (417 East Allen Street, Tombstone; 602-457-3134) and you step back into the Old West. Waitresses dressed as saloon gals serve drinks in the same place where Lily Langtry and Wyatt Earp once tipped their glasses. Lighted, stained-glass panels depict Tombstone's characters, and old photos hang on the walls. On weekends you'll find live country music and skits of Western brawls.

The **Crystal Palace** (420 East Allen Street, Tombstone; 602-457-3611) has been restored to look like it did when it was built in the 1880s. The long, narrow room has old wood tables and red drapes underneath a pressed-tin ceiling. Live music is performed Wednesday through Sunday.

Johnny Ringo's Saloon (404 Allen Street, Tombstone; 602-457-3101) is a historic, intimate bar where the main attraction is the collection of more than 600 military patches on the walls.

The **Saddleman Steakhouse & Lounge** (★) (400 East Route 70, Safford; 602-428-2694) offers country-and-western music on weekends along with free dance lessons.

EAST OF TUCSON PARKS

Chiricahua National Monument—The Chiricahua Apaches called this area the Land of the Standing-Up Rocks because throughout the park are huge rock spires, stone columns and massive balanced rocks perched on small pedestals. Geologists believe that these formations were created as a result of explosive volcanic eruptions. For an overview of the park, drive up the winding, eight-mile-long Bonita Canyon Drive. You'll pass pine and oak-juniper forests before reaching Massai Point at the top of the Chiricahua Mountains where you can see the park, valleys and the peaks of Sugarloaf Mountain and Cochise Head. You can also explore the park on foot via about 20 miles of trails. Other attractions include historic Faraway Ranch and Stafford Cabin.

Facilities: Picnic tables, restrooms, visitor center with exhibits; information, 602-824-3560.

Camping: There are 26 sites; $6 per night. No backcountry camping is allowed within the monument.

Getting there: Take Route 666 south from Tucson, then go east on Route 181.

Mount Graham—The highest peak of the Pinaleño Mountains at 10,720 feet is Mount Graham. Drive the 35-mile-long Swift Trail to the top and you'll leave the cactus and mesquites at the base and travel to a forest of ponderosa pine, aspen and white fir. At the top is 11-acre Riggs Lake, which is stocked with rainbow trout and also available for boating (electric motors only).

Facilities: Water faucets, restrooms, picnic areas; information, 602-428-4150. *Fishing:* License plus trout stamp required.

Camping: There are seven developed campgrounds; $5 per night except at Riggs Flat ($6 per night). Primitive camping is allowed free anywhere in the area.

Getting there: Go south from Safford for seven miles on Route 666 and turn west at the Mount Graham sign. The first 28 miles of the Swift Trail are paved; the last seven are gravel.

Roper Lake State Park—In addition to swimming in a 30-acre lake with a beach, you can soak outside in a rock tub filled with hot springs bubbling up from the ground. The 240-acre park also includes a refuge for endangered fish in two ponds. For meals, sit out on the peninsula's grassy picnic area under a grove of shade trees.

Facilities: Restrooms, picnic ramadas, boat launch ramp; information, 602-428-6760. *Fishing:* You can fish from the shady dock for catfish, bass, bluegill and crappie.

Camping: There are 75 sites, 20 with RV hookups; $7 per night for standard sites and $10 per night for hookups.

Getting there: Located six miles south of Safford off Route 666.

Aravaipa Canyon Wilderness (★)—Aravaipa Creek flows through an 11-mile-long canyon bordered by spectacular cliffs. Lining the creek are large sycamore, ash, cottonwood and willow trees, making it a colorful stop in fall. You may spot javelina, coyotes, mountain lions and desert bighorn sheep, as well as nearly every type of desert songbird and more than 200 other bird species.

Facilities: None.

Camping: Primitive camping allowed. The maximum stay is three days/two nights. Permits are required and can be obtained from the Bureau of Land Management's Safford District Office (425 East 4th Street, Safford; 602-428-4040) or the visitor information stations at either end of the canyon.

Getting there: To get to the East Trailhead, drive on Route 70 about 15 miles northwest of Safford, then turn off on Klondyke Road. Or follow Route 666 19 miles south of Safford and turn on the Fort Grant Road, then follow the signs.

South/West of Tucson

Far off the beaten track, southwestern Arizona is home to the world's leading astronomical center, remote ghost towns, wildlife preserves and a sanctuary dedicated to the unusual Organ Pipe Cactus. This is also where civilization disappears and the desert blooms.

Heading south on Route 19, you will pass the retirement community of Green Valley and arrive at the **Titan Missile Museum** (1580 Duval Mine Road; 602-791-2929; admission), the only intercontinental ballistic missile complex in the world that's open to the public. Here you'll be taken to the bowels of the earth, experience a countdown launch of a Titan missile (actually a movie soundtrack) and view a silo. It's an eerie excursion.

To get away from the high-tech missiles and delve deeper into the area's history, continue further south on Route 19 to Tubac. Here, the Spanish founded a presidio in 1752 to protect settlers from the Indians. At **Tubac Presidio State Historic Park** (602-398-2252; admission) visitors can see the remains of the original presidio foundation and wall, an 1885 schoolhouse and a museum detailing the history of Tubac.

A few more minutes down Route 19 are the adobe ruins of a Spanish frontier mission church at the **Tumacacori National Monument** (Route 19 at exit 29, Tumacacori; 602-398-2341). Along with the museum, visitors walk through the baroque church, completed in 1822, and the nearby ruins, such as a circular mortuary chapel and graveyard. Since little has been built in the vicinity, walking across the grounds feels like a walk back in time.

Continuing south, Route 19 hits the Mexican border. Nogales, Mexico, is a border town offering bargain shopping, restaurants and some sightseeing. On the other side is Nogales, Arizona. Photographs and artifacts detail the town's history at the **Pimeria Alta Historical Society Museum** (★) (223 Grand Avenue; 602-287-4621), a 1914 mission-style building that once housed the city hall, police and fire departments.

Just off of Route 82 you'll pass by some **ghost towns** (★), including Harshaw and Duquesne. Duquesne was a mining center established around the turn of the century with a peak population of 1000 residents, including Westinghouse of Westinghouse Electric. Harshaw was settled around 1875 and operated about 100 mines. Today all that's left are ruins and graveyards. Some of the roads en route are extremely rugged and bumpy, so be prepared.

Tucson and the surrounding area is known as the Astronomy Capital of the World with more astronomical observatories than anywhere else. One of the most famous is the **Kitt Peak National Observatory** (50 miles southwest of Tucson off Route 386; 602-325-9200; admission). Drive up a mountain road and you'll come across the observatory's gleaming white domes and its 21 telescopes. During tours you can step inside some of the telescopes, including the 19-story-high Robert R. McMath solar telescope. There's also a Visitor Center with exhibits on the observatory. If you're planning on staying awhile, bring food—it's a long haul up the mountain and there's nothing to nibble on at the top.

Continuing to the west about 100 miles on Route 86 you'll come to **Ajo**, a small scenic town whose center is a green plaza surrounded by Spanish Colonial-style buildings. It is also an old copper mining town and as such shows its scars. The **New Cornelia Copper Mine** (La Mina Road; 602-387-5631) is one of the largest open-pit copper mines in the world, stretching a full mile in diameter. Although operations ceased in 1984, you can go to the pit lookout and learn about mining operations at the adjacent Mine Lookout Visitor Center.

From the mine you can see the **Ajo Historical Society Museum** (★) (160 Mission Street; 602-387-7105) located in St. Catherine's Indian Mission, a stucco church built in the 1940s. Inside are artifacts from Ajo's history, including a blacksmith ship, dentist's office, printing shop and Native American artifacts such as old saddles found on graves.

From Ajo, drive north on Route 85 until you reach Route 8; proceed west and you'll eventually hit Wellton. Don't blink, or you'll miss the **McElhaney Cattle Company Museum** (★) (Avenue 34; 602-785-3384) with its amusing collection of antiquities including buggies, carriages, a popcorn wagon, an old hearse, several stage coaches, a fire wagon and antique cars.

Much further west, near the California border, is **Yuma**. Once a steamboat stop and major crossing on the Colorado River, today it is a bustling city that supports farming and basks in a sub-tropical climate. The first major construction here was the **Yuma Territorial Prison** (209 North Penitentiary Avenue; 602-783-4771; admission), a penitentiary between 1876 and 1909 and now a state historic park. Known as the Hell-hole of Arizona, life inside the walls were rough, and prisoners who escaped were faced with hostile deserts and the currents of the Colorado River. Today visitors walk through the gloomy cells and climb the guard tower, where one can see the Colorado River and surrounding area.

Just across the river from the prison is **The Quechan Indian Museum** (Indian Hill Road, Yuma; 619-572-0661; admission), one of the oldest military posts in the area. Currently it is headquarters for the Quechan Indian Tribe and houses their artifacts.

The military supply hub for the Arizona Territory was the **Yuma Quartermaster Depot** (North 2nd Avenue, Yuma; 602-329-0471; admission), which served the Southwest until it closed in 1883. Several of the original buildings remain, including the commanding officer's quarters and Office of the Quartermaster Depot. Costumed interpreters provide tours of the complex.

More of Yuma's history comes to light in the **Arizona Historical Society Century House Museum** (240 South Madison Avenue; 602-782-1841). Once the home of pioneer merchant E. F. Sanguinetti, it now has artifacts, photographs and furnishings of Arizona's territorial period. Just outside are colorful gardens and aviaries with exotic birds.

The **Yuma Art Center** (281 Gila Street; 602-783-2314; admission) is in the restored Southern Pacific Railroad Depot and features changing exhibits by contemporary and traditional artists.

For an excursion on the Colorado River, try a jetboat tour. **Yuma River Tours** (1920 Arizona Avenue; 602-783-4400; admission) offers rides past petroglyphs, homesteads, steamboat landings, mining camps and other landmarks left by Native Americans and pioneers.

SOUTH/WEST OF TUCSON HOTELS

Located in Madera Canyon, **Santa Rita Lodge Nature Resort** (★) (Sahuarita; 602-625-8746) is a perfect birders getaway. Just outside the large windows in each of the 12 rooms are feeders that attract a number of bird species. Inside the rooms, charts hang with pictures of different types of hummingbirds. The lodge also offers nature programs that meet in the patio area, and staff birders will take guests on birding walks. Moderate.

Bing Crosby founded the **Tubac Golf Resort** (1 Otero Road, Tubac; 602-398-2211) back in 1959. The 32 rooms and suites have wood-burning fireplaces, Mexican furniture, tiled bathrooms and patios facing the mountains. The resort has a golf course, tennis court, pool and spa, hiking trails and a full service restaurant and bar. Moderate.

Rio Rico Resort & Country Club (1069 Camino Caralampi, Rio Rico; 602-281-1901) is a beautiful resort in the Cayetano Mountain range. Many of the rooms have wood beamed ceilings, sliding glass doors overlooking the pool or mountains, and contemporary Southwestern decor in pastel colors. Amenities include a golf course, horse stables, jacuzzi, exercise room, restaurant and lounge. Moderate.

The Stage Stop Inn (303 Mckeown Avenue, Patagonia; 602-394-2211) is a 43-room hotel with a restaurant and clean, comfortable rooms facing the pool in the middle. Movie casts and crew often stay here while filming in the area. The Western lobby showcases a moose skull above the fireplace, cattle brands on the tile floor and Western paintings on the walls. Budget.

A tiny treasure, **The Little House** (★) (341 Sonoita Avenue, Patagonia; 602-394-2493) is an adobe home with two rooms. Each has a sitting area with corner fireplace, a private bath and patio, and contemporary Southwestern furnishings. Guests are invited for complimentary continental or full breakfasts with eggs, sausage, fruits and breads. Moderate.

Looking like a miniature dollhouse, **The Guest House Inn** (3 Guest House Road, Ajo; 602-387-6133) is a charming, white house with blue trim and a long front porch dotted with white wicker furniture for lazing away the hours. Phelps Dodge built it in 1925 to entertain dignitaries, and breakfast is now served on the 20-foot-long walnut dining table where these guests once ate. Inside the setup is unusual, with a living room in the middle and guest rooms lining either side of the house. Each of the four bedrooms has a private bath and its own decorating scheme, such as Santa Fe or Victorian. Moderate.

Located atop the highest hill in Ajo, **The Mine Manager's House Inn** (1 Greenway Drive; 602-387-6508) was built in 1919 for the mine manager's family. You can see the mine from the house, and inside old photos of the mine hang in the cozy living room. Instead of reflecting the house's history, room furnishings are modern. But breakfast is served at the huge pecan table original to the house. During free time, stop in the reading room or soak in the outdoor hot tub. Moderate.

A number of Gila Bend's motels were built in the 1960s and their decor reflects that era. For instance, the **American Western Inn** (1046 East Pima Street; 602-683-2248) is a throwback from the '60s with an orange and yellow exterior and red doors. The 60 rooms have full-length windows, whitebrick walls and odd furniture. Amenities include a pool, restaurant and lounge. Budget.

Built during the space races with the Russians, the theme at the **Best Western Space Age Lodge** (401 East Pima Street, Gila Bend; 602-683-2273) is obvious. Sputniks are perched on the roof, and rooms have pictures of rockets blasting off into space. The rooms contain whitewashed wood furniture, pastel colors and large, well-lighted mirrors above the counter. This moderately priced motel also has a pool and coffee shop.

La Fuente Travelodge (1513 East 16th Street, Yuma; 602-329-1814) has 96 Southwestern-style rooms decorated in pastels. Some rooms face the grassy interior courtyard and pool. Prices include a complimentary continental breakfast, happy hour and use of the fitness room. Moderate.

SOUTH/WEST OF TUCSON RESTAURANTS

Even though there's not much in Amado, it's worth a stop to eat at **The Cow Palace** (★) (28802 South Nogales Road; 602-398-2201), a local landmark that has been around since the 1920s. While in town to shoot movies, Western stars have frequented the place and their photos hang on the walls. Decor is rustic Western, with a wagon wheel for a chandelier and red tablecloths, carpet and curtains. Entrées carry on the theme with names such as The Trail Boss porterhouse steak and Chuck Wagon burger. Budget.

If you've never dined in a 150-year-old horse stable, stop in at **The Montura** (1 Otero Road, Tubac; 602-398-2211) restaurant at The Tubac Golf Resort. Actually, the place is quite nice. Inside are arched windows, cobblestone floors and pottery made by Mexicans and Native Americans. Look closely and you might find Apache Indian arrowheads embedded in the restaurant's adobe walls. Dinner focuses on steak, pasta, seafood and Mexican specialties with a Southwestern twist. Moderate.

Finding a good German restaurant in Tubac was quite a surprise, but **Johanna's Café International** (★) (192 Tubac Road; 602-398-9336) fits the bill. It's homey and airy with lots of windows covered by lace curtains and German music playing in the background. The owner, Edith Bobbitt, once owned a famous Munich restaurant. Entrées include *Schweine Kotelett*, or a pork chop prepared like a schnitzel (dipped in egg, breaded and pan fried), potato pancakes, bratwurst and German-style bread. Moderate.

Sergeant Grijalva's Restaurante y Cantina (257 Camino Otero, Tubac; 602-398-2263) adjoins and partially merges with the Misty Mountain

Gallery, lending a feel of sophistication to this otherwise typical Mexican restaurant. You can also dine in the covered, outdoor patio. Budget.

Opened in the 1940s as a coffee shop in someone's home, **Wisdom's Café** (★) (Route 19 service road, Tumacacori; 602-398-2397) is now a restaurant crammed with old photographs, farming tools, velvet paintings, patchwork rugs and other odds and ends. You can spot it on the road by the two gigantic imitation chickens in front. If you can get by the chickens, try some of their Mexican food. Budget.

La Cima (1069 Camino Caralampi, Rio Rico; 602-281-1901) in the Rio Rico Resort & Country Club offers American and Mexican cuisine as well as a Sunday champagne brunch at moderate prices. Two walls have floor to ceiling windows with panoramic views of the mountains. The interior is rustic with wood beams, lanterns and wicker chairs.

Home Plate (★) (277 McKeown Avenue, Patagonia; 602-394-2344) is a greasy spoon where the locals meet to chow down on burgers and hot and cold sandwiches. Civic-club banners circle the room and partially cover the brick walls. Budget.

The Stage Stop Inn (303 Mckeown Avenue, Patagonia; 602-394-2211) has the hotel's Western theme with cattle brands on the floors, a chuckwagon containing a salad bar, and a Cowboy Steak Sandwich. Other offerings here are hot and cold sandwiches, burgers, Mexican food and homemade desserts. Budget.

The name is fancier than the place, because basically the **Territorial House Restaurant & Deli** (100 Estrella, Ajo; 602-387-7322) is a budget-priced deli with counter service. There's ample seating, inside and out, at plastic-covered tables underneath hanging plastic plants. The sandwiches are decent, as are the side orders.

Although the exterior of **Dago Joe's** (2055-A North Route 85, Ajo; 602-387-6904) is rather plain, the owners have livened up the interior with contemporary decor—framed posters, plants, and a peach-accent wall with matching tablecloths. The menu is varied, but they're known for moderately priced steaks.

A Yuma tradition for more than a decade, **Hensley's Beef Beans and Beer** (2855 South 4th Avenue; 602-344-1345) is the place for prime rib, lobster, seafood and hamburgers. Moderately priced dishes are served amid walls covered with cowboy pictures, cow horns and Indian blankets.

SOUTH/WEST OF TUCSON SHOPPING

About 50 shops and restaurants make up the town of **Tubac**. Although it's geared to tourists, they've managed to avoid the rubber-tomahawk syndrome and you'll find high-quality artwork. All of the shops are within walking distance, but the bulk are along Tubac Road, which is off to the right as you enter from the frontage road beside Route 19.

Highlights along this road include **Tortuga Books** (190 Tubac Road; 602-398-2807) known throughout the Southwest and specializing in philosophy, psychology, children's books, greeting cards and Southwestern literature. **The Pot Shop Gallery** (166 Tubac Road; 602-398-2898) features R. C. Gorman signed lithographs, prints, pottery and clay artwork created by Arizona artisans. **Chile Pepper** and **Chile Pepper, Too** (201 Tubac Road; 602-398-2921) offer Southwest gourmet foods, chili food products, chili wreaths, coffees and teas. Victorian **Tubac House** (602-398-9243) has Southwestern art by more than 50 Arizona artists. For handcrafted Indian jewelry, kachinas, sand paintings, baskets and pottery, stop in **Old Presidio Traders** (27 Tubac Road; 602-398-9333).

To shop in the older, more historic section of town, go to Calle Iglesia. In this area you'll find **Hugh Cabot Studios & Gallery** (Calle Iglesia, Tubac; 602-398-2721) housed in a 250-year-old adobe building that used to be a hostelry for Spanish soldiers. This nationally known artist creates Western and general interest works in several mediums and makes his home in Tubac. At **VIDA de la TIERRA** (★) (Calle Iglesia; 602-398-2936) you can sometimes catch artisans Penny and John Duncklee at work creating pottery and mesquite wood furniture. For authentic Navajo, Santo Domingo and Hopi Indian art made by old-timers, stop next door at the **Peck Gallery El Nido** (★) (Plaza de Anza; 602-398-2683).

Also in town you'll find **Tubac Ironworks** (217 Plaza Road, Tubac; 602-398-2736) with its metal arts including copper bird feeders and fountains, metal bells and wind chimes by Southwestern artisans.

A handful of shops line the main street in Patagonia, including **J. Nickerson Gold & Silver Smith** (★) (602-394-2690). His specialty is silver jewelry, including earrings somehow made out of snowflakes using silver as a medium. He also designs jewelry with local materials such as turquoise, malachite, azurite and Patagonia red jasper.

If you drive through Sonoita, stop by **La Pradera** (★) (Route 82; 602-455-5612). The owner of the racehorse Secretariat built it to look like his barn, and the original Triple Crown trophy awarded to Secretariat is displayed in the hall. Inside are five shops, including the **Turquoise Tortoise Gallery** (602-455-5853) with paintings, jewelry, pottery and sculptures by Native American.

Housed in a long, narrow, 1916 building on the Plaza, **Kliban's Variety Store Inc.** (29 Plaza, Ajo; 602-387-6421) offers an eclectic mix of hardware, clothing, baby stuff and old knickknacks. Another Ajo stop is the **Ajo Art Gallery** (671 North 2nd Avenue; 602-387-7525) with a mixture of contemporary paintings by California and Arizona artists.

SOUTH/WEST OF TUCSON NIGHTLIFE

Scenic mountain views from picture windows draw people to **La Cantina** (1069 Camino Caralampi, Rio Rico; 602-281-1901) at the Rio Rico Resort & Country Club. The contemporary, Spanish-style bar has live Top-40, jazz and dance music on weekends.

Luts Casino (221 Main Street, Yuma; 602-782-2192) is one of the oldest continually owned and operated pool and domino parlors in the state. Open since 1920, the place is crammed full of farm implements, paintings and historic memorabilia.

SOUTH/WEST OF TUCSON PARKS

Patagonia Lake State Park—The largest recreational lake in Southern Arizona (275 acres) is located in this park. Patagonia Lake, nestled amid rolling hills, was created by the damming of Sonoita Creek in 1968. A small, sandy beach lures swimmers. Because of its elevation of 3750 feet, the 600-acre park offers moderate temperatures throughout the year.

Facilities: Picnic areas, restrooms, showers, boat launch, marina with boat rentals; information, 602-287-6965. *Fishing:* Good, stocked with bass, crappie, bluegill and catfish. *Waterskiing:* Fair. *Swimming:* Good.

Camping: There are 100 sites, including ten RV hookups and 12 accessible by boat only; hookups are $12 per night, all other sites $7 per night.

Getting there: Located off Route 82 about 12 miles north of Nogales. Follow the signs to the park.

The Patagonia Sonoita Creek Sanctuary (★)—Nine miles north of Patagonia Lake State Park is a 312-acre sanctuary in a narrow flood plain between the Santa Rita and Patagonia mountains. It encompasses a one-and-a-half mile stretch of Sonoita Creek lined with large stands of cottonwoods—some a hundred feet tall—as well as Arizona walnut, velvet ash, willows and Texas mulberry. Birdwatchers from all over the world come here because more than 200 species of birds have been seen. It is also home to white-tailed deer, bobcat, javelina, coyotes and the most endangered fish in the Southwest, the Gila Topminnow.

Facilities: None; groceries are available in nearby Patagonia; information, 602-622-3861.

Getting there: From Patagonia, turn northwest off Route 82 onto 4th Avenue, then go left on Pennsylvania Avenue. When the pavement ends you'll cross a creek, and then you're in the sanctuary. An information board is inside the gate.

Coronado National Forest—The Coronado National Forest in Arizona has 1.7 million acres of public land in 12 sky islands, or mountain ranges that jut above the surrounding desert. Following are three of the highlights:

Madera Canyon—This spot is a great place for birdwatching, with more than 200 species including several varieties of woodpeckers, hawks, wrens and vultures. Driving up through the canyon the desert changes from grassland to forest. Trees on the lower slopes of the Santa Rita Mountains are mesquite, and farther up are live oaks, alligator junipers, cottonwoods and sycamores along Madera Creek. There are more than 70 miles of trails.

Facilities: Restrooms, picnic areas, grills, telephones; information, 602-281-2296.

Camping: There are 12 sites at Bog Springs Campground; $6 per night.

Getting there: It's located 35 miles south of Tucson. Take Route 19 south from Tucson to Green Valley's Continental Road, then go southeast for 13 miles.

Pena Blanca Lake (★)—This is a 57-acre lake surrounded by oak, cottonwood and mesquite trees and light-colored bluffs. The lake is at 4000 feet—making it higher and somewhat cooler than Tucson. A trail leads around it.

Facilities: Picnic areas, restrooms, picnic tables, boat launch; information, 602-281-2296. Pena Blanca Lake Resort (602-281-2800) has a lodge, restaurant, fishing supplies and boat rentals. *Fishing:* Good for bass, bluegill, crappie, catfish and rainbow trout.

Camping: There are 13 sites at White Rock Campground (a quarter-mile from the lake), although there are no lake views; $5 per night.

Getting there: Located five miles north of the Mexican border. Take Route 19 south from Tucson to Ruby Road, then go west for about nine miles.

Parker Canyon Lake (★)—Parker Canyon Lake is an 80-acre fishing lake east of the Huachuca Mountains and surrounded by grassy, rolling hills.

Facilities: Picnic areas, boat launch and rentals, grocery store (open weekends and holidays), fishing bait, fishing dock, restrooms; information, 602-378-0311. *Fishing:* Good for bluegill, bass, perch, trout and catfish.

Camping: There are 64 sites and an overflow area in the summer that accommodates 50 to 75 self-contained vehicles; $8 per night.

Getting there: From Sonoita, take Route 83 south for 30 miles until it runs into the park.

Organ Pipe Cactus National Monument (★)—This 330,000-acre refuge became a national monument in 1937 to protect the Sonoran desert plants and animals and the unique Organ Pipe Cactus. Start at the visitor center 17 miles south of the northern entrance. Here you can see exhibits and pick up a self-guided tour pamphlet. A good tour is the Puerto Blanco Scenic Drive, a 53-mile graded dirt loop with numbered stops described on the tour. The only paved road through the park is Route 85. While exploring the monument, you'll pass mountains, plains, canyons, dry washes and a pond surrounded by cottonwood trees.

Facilities: Restrooms; groceries are available in Lukeville, five miles south; information, 602-387-6849.

Camping: There are 208 sites in the main campground; $8 per night. Primitive camping is allowed at four sites; permits available at the visitor center.

Getting there: The monument is located 35 miles south of Ajo, and the visitor center is at the 75-mile marker on Route 85.

Cabeza Prieta National Wildlife Refuge (★)—Established in 1939 to protect the desert bighorn sheep, the 860,000-acre refuge is an arid wilderness rife with cactus and mountains. Passing through the park is the 250-mile El Camino del Diablo (Highway of the Devil) that was pioneered by Spanish Conquistador Captain de Anza in 1774—and stretches from Mexico to California. Along the way you pass Cabeza Prieta Mountain with its lava-topped granite peak, and Mohawk Valley with sand dunes and lava flows. Since roads here are rugged and unimproved, four-wheel-drive vehicles are required. Also, beware of the six species of rattlesnakes.

Facilities: None. The closest groceries are in Ajo, seven miles east of the refuge. The refuge is sometimes closed for military use; call ahead to see if it is open. You can't enter without a valid Refuge Entry Permit, so stop by the refuge office in Ajo (1611 North 2nd Avenue; 602-387-6483).

Hunting: Limited hunting for desert bighorn sheep. Contact refuge office.

Camping: There are three primitive campgrounds with no facilities; no wood fires allowed; no water. Permit required.

Getting there: You'll need explicit directions, which you can get when you pick up the entry permit in Ajo.

The Sporting Life

BOATING, CANOEING, WATERSKIING

Although water isn't plentiful in Southern Arizona, there are a few lakes. Boat rentals are available at **Patagonia Lake State Park** (Patagonia; 602-287-6965), **Parker Canyon Lake** (off Route 83 near Sierra Vista; 602-670-6483) and **Pena Blanca Lake** (off Route 289, Nogales; 602-281-2800). You can also rent paddle boats at **Gene C. Reid Park** (between Broadway Boulevard and 22nd Street, Country Club and Alvernon Way, Tucson; 602-791-4560).

SWIMMING

For a retreat from the heat take a plunge! Tucson public pools include **Fort Lowell Park** (2900 North Craycroft Road; 602-791-2585), **Himmel**

Park (1000 North Tucson Boulevard; 602-791-4157), **Morris K. Udall Park** (7200 East Tanque Verde Road; 602-791-4004), **Northwest District** (1400 North Silverbell Road; 602-791-4752) and **Jacobs Park** (1010 West Lind; 602-791-4358.

East of Tucson, try **Safford City Government** (Firth Park, Safford; 602-428-6666).

HORSEBACK RIDING

A Western town like Tucson wouldn't be the same without opportunities to go horseback riding. Dudes and dudettes can saddle up at **Desert-High Country Stables Inc.** (6501 West Ina Road; 602-744-3789), **El Conquistador Stables** (10000 North Oracle Road; 602-742-4200), **Pusch Ridge Stables** (11220 North Oracle Road; 602-297-6908), **Tucson Trailrides DBA Pantano Stables** (4450 South Houghton Road; 602-298-9076) and **Wild House Ranch Resort** (6801 North Camino Verde; 602-744-1012)

Elsewhere, you can ride at **Rio Rico Stables** (320 Stable Lane, Rio Rico; 602-281-7550) and **Equi-Sands Training Center** (5706 South Kino Road, Sierra Vista; 602-378-1540).

BALLOONING

There's nothing like floating above it all. To see Tucson from on high, call **A Balloon Experience** (602-747-3866), **A Southern Arizona Balloon Excursion** (602-624-3599), **Balloon America** (602-299-7744) and **Desert Breezes Balloon Adventures** (602-299-6308).

SKIING

There's only one place to ski in these parts—the **Mount Lemmon Ski Valley** (Mount Lemmon; 602-576-1400). The southernmost ski-area in North America, Mount Lemmon Ski Valley offers 15 runs, equipment rental, ski school and restaurant.

GOLF

Mild winters make most of Southern Arizona ideal for golfers, and aficionados can choose between a wide range of private and public courses. In the Tucson area, these include **Tucson National Golf Club** (2727 West Club Drive; 602-575-7540), **Tournament Players Club At Star Pass** (3645 West 22nd Street; 602-622-6060), **Sun City Tucson** (1495 East Rancho Vistoso Boulevard, Catalina; 602-825-3110), **Randolph Golf Course** (600 South Alvernon Way; 602-791-4161), **El Conquistador Country Club–Sunrise Course** (10555 North La Canada Drive; 602-742-7300), **Dorado Golf Course** (6601 East Speedway Boulevard; 602-885-6751), **Arthur Pack Desert Golf Course** (9101 North Thornydale Road; 602-744-3322), **Ventana Canyon Golf & Racquet Club** (6200 North Club House Lane;

602-577-1400), **Cliff Valley Golf Course** (5910 North Oracle Road; 602-648-1880), **El Rio Golf Course** (1400 West Speedway Boulevard; 602-791-4229), **Fred Enke** (8215 East Irvington Road; 602-296-8607) and the **Silverbell Golf Course** (3600 North Silverbell Road; 602-791-5235).

Other prime golfing spots include **Coyote Hills** (800 East Country Club Road, Benson; 602-586-2323), **Fort Huachuca** (Fort Huachuca, Sierra Vista; 602-538-7160), **Turquoise Valley** (Naco Highway, Bisbee; 602-432-3091), **Douglas Municipal Golf Course** (Leslie Canyon Road, Douglas; 602-364-3722), **Rio Rico Golf Course** (1410 Rio Rico Drive, Rio Rico; 602-281-8567, **Tubac Valley Country Club** (Tubac; 602-398-2211), **Mount Graham Golf Course** (Golf Course Road, Safford; 602-428-1260) and **Mesa Del Sol Golf & Tennis Club Ltd.** (10583 Camino Del Sol Avenue, Yuma; 602-342-1817).

TENNIS

When it's not too hot to serve, try the public tennis courts in Tucson. Call **Fort Lowell Park** (2900 North Craycroft Road; 602-791-2584), **Himmel Park** (1000 North Tucson Boulevard; 602-791-3276), **Jesse Owens Park** (400 South Sarnoff Drive; 602-791-4821), **Randolph Tennis Center** (100 South Randolph Way; 602-791-4896) and **Pima Community College** (2202 West Anklam Road; 602-884-6005).

In Yuma, play at the **Mesa Del Sol Golf & Tennis Club Ltd.** (10583 Camino Del Sol Avenue; 602-342-1817).

BICYCLING

Tucson is a very popular area for bicycling. Some favorite routes include riding on **Oracle Road** north of Ina Road where cyclists find wide shoulders and beautiful mountain views. Ride about 15 miles to Catalina, where the road narrows and is best left to experienced riders. On the way back turn into Sun City Vistoso, a large retirement community where the roads are wide and the scenery pretty.

Another popular ride is parallel to the Santa Catalina Mountain foothills along **Sunrise Drive** to Sabino Canyon, where you can climb up a challenging, four-mile road through the mountains. Because of the trolley, Sabino Canyon is only open to bicyclists before 9 a.m. and after 5 p.m.

Starting on North Campbell Avenue and running along the banks of the dry Rillito River is a hike-and-bike trail. Currently it's about three miles long, although it's still under construction and more trails are added annually.

The **Saguaro National Monument**, both east and west, also offers a number of good trails, both for mountain and road bikes, as does the hilly **Tucson Mountain Park**. Both are in scenic areas studded with cactus and mountains. Another enjoyable route is along the **Old Spanish Trail** from Broadway Boulevard to Colossal Cave.

For more information and maps on bicycling in the area, contact the City of Tucson bicycling coordinator at 602-791-4372.

Good areas for bicycling can also be found elsewhere. Take Route 83 from Colossal Cave, past Sonoita and Patagonia to Nogales. This road has little traffic and wide shoulders. Other bikeable roads are Route 90, which you can take to Sierra Vista and then on to Bisbee, and Route 80 through Tombstone.

BIKE RENTALS   There are a handful of places in Tucson where you can rent bicycles, including The Bike Shack (835 North Park Avenue; 602-624-3663), Broadway Bicycles (140 South Sarnoff Drive; 602-296-7819), Desert Pedals (2131 East 5th Street; 602-884-8838) and Southwest Cycle & Sport (818 East University Boulevard; 602-791-0818).

HIKING

TUCSON TRAILS   In the Rincon Mountain District in Saguaro National Monument is the Freeman Homestead Nature Trail (1 mile), a loop that starts off the spur road to the Javelina picnic area and descends from a saguaro forest to a small wash filled with mesquite trees. Along the way you pass the ruins of an adobe house built in the 1920s.

The Cactus Forest Trail (2.5 miles) takes you though a saguaro forest between Broadway Boulevard and Old Spanish Trail. You also pass the remains of the first ranger station built in the monument, and two kilns used to manufacture lime around the turn of the century.

For a trek on Mount Lemmon follow the Wilderness of Rocks Trail (5.2 miles). It starts at the Marshall Gulch Picnic Area. On the way are pools along Lemmon Creek and thousands of eroded and balanced rocks.

Pima Canyon Trail (7.1 miles) in the Santa Catalina Mountains is a difficult trail that climbs from 2900 to 7255 feet through a bighorn-sheep management area. Along the way you'll pass Pima Canyon Spring and good views of Tucson and A Mountain. To get there, follow Christie Drive north until it dead-ends at Magee Road. Go right and park.

In the Tucson Mountain District the King Canyon Trail (3.5 miles) begins off Kinney Road across from the Arizona-Sonora Desert Museum, then climbs up to a picnic area and beyond to the top of Wasson Peak (elevation 4687), the highest point in the area.

The short Signal Hill Petroglyphs Trail (.25 mile) goes up a winding path along a small hill off Golden Gate Road. At the top are rocks with ancient Indian petroglyphs on them.

The Valley View Overlook Trail (.75 mile) on the Bajada Loop Drive descends into two washes and ends on a scenic ridge overlooking most of Avra Valley.

Hunter Trail (2 miles) in **Picacho Peak State Park** offers scenic lookouts as it climbs from 2000 to 3374 feet in height. It was named for Captain Sherod Hunter, a Confederate officer who placed lookouts at Picacho pass and was involved in the battle that occurred here in 1862.

EAST OF TUCSON TRAILS To find **Lutz Canyon Trail** (2.9 miles), drive 12 miles south of Sierra Vista on Route 92 to Ash Canyon Road. Hikers walk past old mine workings in a narrow, deep canyon with oak, juniper and Douglas fir.

Crest Trail (10.6 miles) in the **Coronado National Memorial** runs along the crest of the Huachuca Mountains which affords a great view of northern Mexico on clear days.

Within the **Chiricahua National Monument** you'll find **Massai Point Nature Trail** (.5 mile), which starts at the geology exhibit at Massai Point and takes you past a large balanced rock, a board with a description of the park's geologic story and views across Rhyolite Canyon.

Natural Bridge Trail (2.5 miles) begins at the Bonita Canyon scenic drive, then passes a natural rock bridge and climbs through oak and juniper woodlands to a pine forest.

Heart of Rocks Trail (3.5 miles) winds through pine and fir forests and some of the park's most impressive rock formations, including Big Balanced Rock, Punch and Judy and Totem Pole.

Built as a supply artery for fire fighters stationed in the high Chiricahuas, **Greenhouse Trail** (3.75 miles) ascends 3000 feet. Along the way you'll pass Cima Cabin, the fire fighters' headquarters, and Winn Falls, which flows at a peak during the summer. To get there, go north off Cave Creek Spur Road onto Greenhouse Road and drive half a mile.

The **Coronado National Forest** offers the **South Fork Trail** (7.25 miles). Beginning off Cave Creek Road at the road end in South Fork Forest Camp 3.5 miles above Portal, Arizona, it passes South Fork Cave Creek, one of the most famous bird-watching canyons in the Chiricahua Mountains, and a 70-foot-tall finger of red rhyolite called Pinnacle Rock. It starts in a forest of sycamores, maples and black walnut trees and leads to huge Douglas fir trees and the small bluffs above the South Fork Cave Creek.

Arcadia Trail (5.1 miles) on **Mount Graham** passes through a forest of Douglas fir, aspen and pine trees, along with wild raspberry vines. As the highest range in Southern Arizona, hikers will see a panoramic view of the area.

SOUTH/WEST OF TUCSON TRAILS **Kent Springs-Bog Springs Trail Loop** (5.7 miles) within the Santa Rita Mountains climbs from 4820 feet to 6620 feet. Along the way are three springs, which create an unusually lush area with large sycamore and walnut trees. Exit off Route 19 at Madera Canyon and park near Bog Springs campground.

Transportation

BY CAR

From Tucson, **Route 10** runs north toward Phoenix, then crosses **Route 8** which heads west toward Gila Bend and Yuma. **Route 85** from Gila Bend goes south, turns into **Route 86**, cuts through the Papago Indian Reservation and goes to Tucson. South of Tucson is **Route 19** to Nogales, while the main thoroughfare east from Tucson is Route 10 toward New Mexico. Jutting south off Route 10 are **Route 83** to Sonoita, **Route 90** to Sierra Vista, **Route 666** to Douglas and **Route 186** to Chiricahua National Monument.

BY AIR

Tucson International Airport is served by America West Airlines, American Airlines, Delta Air Lines, Northwest Airlines, Trans World Airlines and USAir.

Yuma International Airport is served by America West and Skywest, and **Sierra Vista Municipal Airport** by Mesa Airlines.

BY TRAIN

Amtrak (800-872-7245) has train service to the area on both the "Texas Eagle" and the "Sunset Limited." Train depots are found in Tucson (400 East Toole Avenue), Benson (4th and San Pedro streets) and Yuma (281 Gila Street).

BY BUS

Greyhound/Trailways Bus Lines services Tucson from around the country. The downtown terminal is at 2 South 4th Avenue, 602-792-3475. Other stations in Southern Arizona include Nogales (35 North Terrace Avenue; 602-287-5628) and Yuma (170 East 17th Place; 602-783-4403). There are also terminals in Benson, Sierra Vista, Bisbee, Douglas, Willcox and Safford.

CAR RENTALS

At Tucson International Airport are **Avis Rent A Car** (602-294-1494), **Dollar Rent A Car** (602-573-1100), **Hertz Rent A Car** (602-294-7616) and **National Car Rental** (602-573-8050).

Car-rental agencies at the Yuma International Airport are **Avis Rent A Car** (602-344-5772), **Budget Rent A Car** (602-344-1822), **Hertz Rent A Car** (602-726-5160), **National Car Rental** (602-726-0611) and **Sears Rent A Car** (602-344-1824).

Enterprise Rent A Car (602-458-2425) and **Rent A Ride** (602-459-1296) serve the Sierra Vista Municipal Airport.

PUBLIC TRANSPORTATION

For extensive bus service throughout Tucson, call **Sun Tran** (602-792-9222).

Local bus service in Nogales is **Dabdoub Bus Service** (602-287-7810).

TAXIS

Leading cab companies in Tucson include **ABC Cab Co.** (602-623-7979), **Allstate Cab Co.** (602-888-2999), **Checker Cab Co.** (602-623-1133) and **Yellow Cab Co.** (602-624-6611).

In Sierra Vista call **Call A Cab** (602-458-5867) or **Cochise Cab Co.** (602-458-3860).

CHAPTER SIX

Northern New Mexico

Native cultures scoff at the notion that Columbus discovered this continent. When the Europeans were just treading through the Dark Ages, the Anasazi Indians were well into their building of intricate Chaco Canyon in Northern New Mexico.

The Pueblo Indians are thought to have come to Santa Fe around 1200 or 1300 A.D., although they were preceded for centuries by the Anasazi, well before Europeans dreamed of a New World. Taos Pueblo alone was constructed almost 1000 years ago.

The first Spanish settlers claimed this aptly named "Kingdom of New Mexico" in 1540 and the Spanish made Santa Fe a provincial capital in 1610; Taos was founded less than a decade later. Over the next seven decades, Spanish soldiers and Franciscan missionaries sought to convert the Pueblo Indians of the region. Tribesmen numbered nearly 100,000 calling an estimated 70 multistoried, burnt-orange adobe towns (or pueblos) home.

In 1680, the Pueblo Indians revolted, killing 400 of the 2500 Spanish colonists and driving the rest back to Mexico. The Pueblos sacked Santa Fe and burned most of the structures, save the Palace of the Governors. For 12 years, the Pueblos remained in Santa Fe, until Don Diego de Vargas reconquered the region.

When Mexico gained independence from Spain in 1821, so too did New Mexico. But it wouldn't be until the Mexican-American War that an American flag flew over the territory. In 1848, Mexico ceded New Mexico to the United States and by 1912 New Mexico was a full-fledged state.

Why have people always flocked to this land of rugged beauty? There are open panoramas in Farmington and the Four Corners region, in the very northwestern corner of the state, that are surprisingly ripe for farming and quite habitable for living. The high plateau of Taos, 7000 feet above sea level, bordered by the Sangre de Cristo mountains on one side and the raging Rio Grande River on the other, seems to have a calming effect on the soul. The absolute isolation provided by the fortress-like hills in Los Alamos appealed first to the Native Americans, later to scientists. The natural barriers surrounding sky-high Santa Fe, coupled with its obvious beauty, have always made it a desirable city and deserving capital, located at the crossroads of north and south.

There's also the magic light and intense colors that artist Georgia O'Keeffe captured so accurately on her canvasses. It is indeed the light which is so different about this area, from the subtle morning hues to evenings that can be so bold and empowering.

The high-altitude sun beaming on the earth tones helps to create shadows and vibrancies not to be believed. In fact, before New Mexico adopted the moniker of Land of Enchantment, it was known as the Sunshine State. Supposedly the sun shines 70 percent of the year. Even on the coldest days of winter, the sun keeps temperatures from being unbearable. Summers rarely overheat either, again because of the region's altitude.

Watching a New Mexico sunset unfold over the Sangre de Cristo and Jemez mountains can be a spiritual experience as oranges, pinks and violets, chalk-colored pastels and lightening bolt streaks of yellow weave together a picture story with no plot. Color even emerges in everyday life, as blood-red chili *ristras* line highway stands against a big blue sky.

Some maintain the lands of Northern New Mexico are sacred. Each year there's a pilgrimage to the modest Santuario de Chimayo church, said to be constructed on sacred and healing ground. The Indians, who successfully rejected white man's attempts to force feed them organized religion, have their blessed grounds and rituals which remain secret to all outsiders. The spirituality takes many forms. For example, in Taos a radio station offers daily astrological forecast, and semifrequent supernatural occurrences are reported as straight news.

Many newcomers, like the region's tourists, come because of the climate. These high, dry mountain towns are pleasingly warm during spring and fall. Summer can bring intense heat and the winters are cold enough to make Santa Fe and Taos viable ski areas. Summer and fall are particularly popular among vacationers.

Northern New Mexico's cultural mix is as colorful and as varied as the weather with the co-existence of Anglo, Indian and Spanish peoples. The strength of the Indian nations remains today in different and expanded forms and each group has grown more accepting of others' beliefs while still holding on strong to their time-honored traditions.

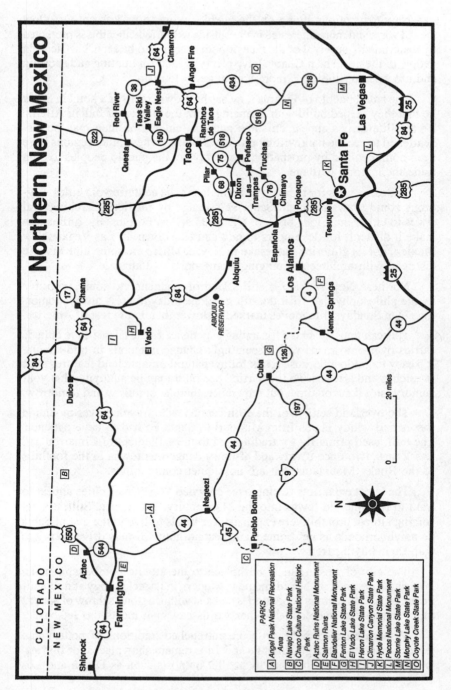

Northern New Mexico

PARKS

A Angel Peak National Recreation Area
B Navajo Lake State Park
C Chaco Culture National Historic Park
D Aztec Ruins National Monument
E Salmon Ruins
F Bandelier National Monument
G Fenton Lake State Park
H El Vado Lake State Park
I Heron Lake State Park
J Cimarron Canyon State Park
K Hyde Memorial State Park
L Pecos National Monument
M Storrie Lake State Park
N Morphy Lake State Park
O Coyote Creek State Park

New generations living on the pueblos seem to be less apt to follow the old ways and more interested in the outside world. Whether this is prompted by materialism, survival of the race or both, remains to be seen. The Jicarilla people of the north near Chama have plenty of land for hunting and sporting and are opening the door more and more to tourism.

The small pueblo of Picarus now has half-ownership of a hotel in Santa Fe that they helped build with financing from the Bureau of Indian Affairs. As satellite dishes appear on some pueblos, elder tribesmen may be disheartened to see the handwriting on the wall. Still, where other regions have been homogenized by prosperity, in no way are the pueblo peoples tossing aside their proud heritage.

The same goes for the physical remains in the centuries-old cities. Rigorous zoning laws maintain Santa Fe's image by restricting architectural styles to either the adobe brick or territorial styles. Fortunately, ordinances make it difficult for developers to raid and tear-down. In Las Vegas (New Mexico, not its glittering namesake in Nevada) there are some nine historic districts, with architecture ranging from adobe to Italianate.

Northern New Mexico is still a land of "mañana" to some, who live by the philosophy that "if it doesn't get done today, there's always tomorrow." On Sundays, life moves markedly slower than in the rest of America.

This can translate into a frustrating experience as the laissez-faire attitude carries over onto roads which seemingly change numerals in mid-stream. It's easy to get lost because roads follow natural organic land features such as ditches and arroyos. To the hurried person it may be annoying that your laundry isn't done on time, but remember, there's tomorrow and tomorrow.

The overland settlers of the 19th century who traveled over mountain passes and windy plains from Missouri to Santa Fe had to have patience. The trail, used primarily for trading, led to the settlement of Cimarron and Las Vegas, two once-rowdy and at-times dangerous towns in the foothills of the Rocky Mountains that are now quiet communities.

The latest expatriots fleeing over-crowded West Coast cities appear to want to rush the old towns into the 21st century. Fat chance. Still, it's becoming almost prohibitively expensive for locals to live in the quaint Santa Fe neighborhoods as newcomers and second-home owners drive up prices with their buying frenzy.

The city of Los Alamos, birthplace to the atomic bomb, remains an interesting contrast of the old and new. Modern in its technology and scientific findings, Los Alamos' laboratories co-exist within a stone's throw of ancient ruins and Indian pueblos—in other words caveman meets the Jetsons.

Modern art also melds with the entrenched traditions of pottery and jewelry-making. Though Santa Fe and Taos remain showplaces for fine artistry, the creators are moving to smaller outposts such as Dixon and Los

Alamos, Tierra Amarilla and Chimayo. And of course, let's not forget all the work that's created within the pueblos.

Early Taos art founders Ernest Blumenschein and Bert Phillips were dazzled by the town's beauty and started the tradition of artists flocking to Taos. By 1915, they had convinced others of Taos, "brilliant light" and formed the now-famous art colony known as the Taos Society of Artists.

New York heiress Mable Dodge Lujan, a flamboyant fireball and ardent patroness of the arts, attracted writers and artists like D. H. Lawrence, Georgia O'Keeffe, Willa Cather and Aldous Huxley here as well, leaving a lasting legacy of writers and painters inspired by the region's artistic soul.

New styles of cooking in many of the exciting restaurants of the regions rely upon old recipes, with a twist. Piquant food is distinctive and uses homegrown chilies and family recipes, blue-corn tortillas and Navajo bread. Rejection of Anglo-izing has made the area unique. Whether it's in the names, lifestyles or biting scents of sage and piñon, in Northern New Mexico, everything has an accent to it.

Santa Fe Area

A trivia game asks what's the oldest state capitol in the United States. The answer of Santa Fe, which has been home to a government seat since 1610, is always a stumper. Not only does the "City Different," as Santa Fe's commonly called, defy the stereotypical governmental center with a domed capital building and proper tree-lined streets, but unlike most state capitols, it's not easy to get to.

You can't take a commercial jet into Santa Fe or even a train. Albuquerque, an hour's drive south, is the closest large airport, and the city of Lamy, about 17 miles south, is the nearest Amtrak stop. But the independent Santa Feans seem to like it this way. And once you arrive, you'll find it's well-worth the trouble.

Strict guidelines mandate the now well-known Santa Fe-style look of territorial and Spanish Colonial architecture. Thanks to city codes, there are no high-rises blocking the mountain views or the ever-changing colors at dawn and dusk. This attractive capital, situated at 7000 feet elevation and backdropped by the spectacular Sangre de Cristo Mountains, is becoming desirable to more and more people who are fleeing their city homes for Santa Fe's natural beauty and culture.

Those in a rush to relocate there either part or full time have driven housing prices to outer-space levels. Fledgling artists aren't being represented in galleries, as owners can only afford to stock their high-rent shops with proven names. Chain stores are sneaking into the commercial core and around the popular Plaza area looking for the all-too-important tourist dollar.

There are worries that Santa Fe may become victim to its own success, but a city that has survived numerous invasions and changes of flag can surely endure a massive influx by former city dwellers.

By digging a little deeper, it's still possible to find a soul amid Santa Fe's slickening veneer. Avoiding summer holiday weekends, such as Memorial Day or Labor Day, will find favorite tourist spots less crowded and Santa Feans more willing to have a chat. The city is quite beautiful in the fall, when the leaves are changing, and days still balmy.

A good way to start any visit to this region is with a stop at **"Footsteps Across New Mexico"** (211 Old Santa Fe Trail, inside The Inn at Loretto; 505-982-9297; admission). This multimedia presentation recounts about one million years of history in 30 minutes and helps orient visitors to the geology, history, social and economic forces at work in New Mexico.

There is plenty to see in Santa Fe, from palaces of worship to galleries to the Indian Market, but save time for the aforementioned **state capitol** (Paseo de Peralta and Old Santa Fe Trail; 505-984-9589) one of the only round capitol buildings in the United States. Built in 1966 in the shape of the Pueblo Indian Zia, the structure symbolizes the circle of life—four winds, four seasons, four directions and four sacred obligations.

The oldest continuously used church in the United States is the **San Miguel Mission** (401 Old Santa Fe Trail; 505-983-3974). The Tlaxcala Indians from Mexico built this church around 1610. But this was probably considered sacred ground before that as there is evidence of human occupation dating back to 1300 AD. San Miguel is an amazing archive of everything from pyrographic paintings to buffalo hides. Included in the collection is a bell that dates back to 1356!

Not surprisingly, the oldest church is located near the earthen **Oldest House in U.S.** (215 East DeVargas Street; 505-983-3883) which is believed to have been built 800 or more years ago. Two small adobe rooms contain boxes, bowls, chairs and a spinning wheel. An adjacent Oldest House gift shop sort of detracts from the historical structure, but then again, it probably pays for it, too.

Meander up the Old Santa Fe Trail through the park-like setting and over the mountain-runoff fed Santa Fe River. Pass by traditional irrigation ditches called *acequias* that carry moisture from the hills found throughout the city.

Continue up the Santa Fe Trail to the **Plaza**, built in 1610 by Don Pedro de Peralta. There's always plenty of excitement revolving around this town square, which was built as an end to the Santa Fe Trail and today is the center of activity in this capitol city. A marker in the Plaza commemorates its completion. Native Americans roll out their blankets and hawk their wares to tourists on the sidewalks surrounding the Plaza. Their prices have been adjusted to meet Santa Fe's ever-increasing popularity. Groups of young Hispanic men crowd into big cars and slowly cruise the square's perimeter. If you're lucky, there will be live music and dance starting in the city's center.

For serious shoppers, the Plaza offers little in the way of bargains. A Plaza department store's transformation into boutiques bothered many Santa Feans. **Woolworth's Five and Dime** (58 East San Francisco Street; 505-982-1062) sells wool Indian blankets and Santa Fe souvenirs in addition to its usual inventory, but with rising rents and a lease coming up for renewal, there are fears this landmark could go, too.

America's oldest public building, the **Palace of Governors** (on the Plaza; 505-827-6483; admission) may be more historically significant than the artifacts it houses. The adobe fortress, built by the Spanish in 1609-1610, served as capital of Nuevo Mexico, Spain's northernmost colony in the New World, before the Pilgrim's landed at Plymouth Rock. Once held by Pueblo Indians, the Palace has been used as governmental headquarters for Mexico, the Confederacy and the territorial United States. Today, the Palace houses exhibits of regional history. There's also a working exhibit of antique printing presses, as well as a photo archive, history library and gift shop.

Situated west of the Palace of Governors, the **Museum of Fine Arts** (on the Plaza; 505-827-4455; admission) is a prototype of the architectural revival style called Spanish-Pueblo. The building is a reproduction of the New Mexico exhibit at the 1915 Panama-California Exposition in San Diego. Two years later, "The Cathedral of the Desert" rose again, this time in Santa Fe. It embodies aspects of the Spanish mission in the region. Notice the ceilings of split cedar latillas and hand-hewn *vigas*. Housing more than 7000 pieces of art, the museum is a repository for works of early Santa Fe and Taos masters, as well as contemporary artists.

Before leaving the Plaza area, you'll want to pop into the **La Fonda Hotel** (100 East San Francisco Street; 505-982-5511), which calls itself the inn at the end of the trail, for a drink in the popular bar or meal in its impressive dining room. You can glean as much information about what's going on at La Fonda as at the chamber of commerce.

If you're interested in attending church services, then stop by the beautiful Santa Fe **Cathedral of St. Francis of Assisi** (131 Cathedral Place; 505-982-5619), whose cornerstone was laid in 1869 by Archbishop Lamy. With its stained-glass windows, bronze panels and smaller Sacrament Chapel, it's certainly the grandest church in the Southwest. In a corner is the sacred La Conquistadoria, "lady of the conquest," the oldest representation of the Madonna in the United States. Devotion has been maintained to the wood-carved statue, located in her own section of the chapel, for more than 300 years. In the early morning light, La Conquistadoria appears positively heavenly.

Those who believe in miracles must make a point of stopping by the tiny **Loretto Chapel** (211 Old Santa Fe Trail; 505-988-5531; admission), patterned after France's La Chappelle, which holds the beautiful wood "magic staircase." When the chapel was built, craftsmen failed to install any way to reach the choir loft. Short on funds, the nuns prayed for a solution to the problem. The story goes that a man came armed with only a saw, hammer and hot water to shape the wooden staircase. He worked for months and built a staircase that makes two 360-degree turns but has no visible means of support. When it came time for payment, the man mysteriously disappeared.

The **Museum of International Folk Art** (706 Camino Lejo; 505-827-8350; admission) houses 125,000 artifacts—the world's largest collection of folk art—from around the globe. Toys, textiles, ritual and religious art are colorfully displayed in the Girard Wing. The Hispanic Heritage Wing looks at the traditions of New Mexico's Hispanic folk culture including a huge Spanish colonial collection. Video interaction monitors help visitors learn more about the history and craft of various artifacts. The museum parking lot also affords a spectacular view of the Jemez Mountains, southwest of Santa Fe and the Sangre de Cristos to the north.

The Pueblo, Navajo and Apache Indian peoples are the focus of the **Museum of Indian Arts & Culture** (710 Camino Lejo; 505-827-8941; admission). Exhibits are drawn from extensive collections of the museum's Laboratory of Anthropology. For a treat spend time in the Resource Center, where you can weave on an authentic Navajo loom, use a Pueblo drum, card wool and touch various artifacts.

Impressive is a good term to describe the privately owned **Wheelwright Museum of the American Indian** (704 Camino Lejo; 505-982-4636). Though the collection has a lot of Navajo weavings, there's also historic and contemporary Native American art including sandpaintings, jewelry, basketry and pottery.

Wandering up to **Canyon Road** (see "Santa Fe Area Shopping" below), you'll pass by historic haciendas and witness first-hand the center of Santa Fe's burgeoning arts community.

The **Downs at Santa Fe** (Route 25; 505-471-3311; admission) hosts quarter-horse and thoroughbred racing on Wednesdays, Fridays and weekends in-season. For a more uptown experience, pay a few extra dollars for entrance to the Jockey Club.

Settle into a private hot tub under the starlit night. Enjoy a full-body massage, facial or snack on a healthy treat. At the authentic Japanese health spa **Ten Thousand Waves** (Ski Basin Road, Santa Fe; 505-982-9304; admission) step into the rehabilitative powers of the Far East ways.

To take in the whole picture of Santa Fe, hoof it up to the **Cross of the Martyrs** in the city's Marcy Park section. There are stairs by Paseo de Peralta and Washington Avenue which you climb to earn the bird's eye view of the city.

HIGH ROAD TO TAOS   When it comes time to leave Santa Fe, drive up Bishop's Lodge Road through the upscale village of Tesuque and connect with Route 76 to take the High Road to Taos.

En route, if you can keep from being intrusive, stop and visit Archbishop Lamy's private chapel at the **Bishop's Lodge** (Bishop's Lodge Road, Tesuque; 505-983-6377). Small, private and very holy describes this retreat along the Little Tesuque Stream. *Vigas* have replaced the former rafters in this intimate chapel, but the archbishop's cloak, hat and crucifix remain. Enter this sanctuary by way of an old church key! It's quite possible a visit here will inspire you to read Willa Cather's classic, *Death Comes for the Archbishop*.

In Tesuque, visit the **Shidoni Foundry** (Bishop's Lodge Road; 505-988-8001) on Saturdays for bronze pourings. The art foundry, gardens and contemporary gallery are world-renowned for purveyors of fine art.

Just outside the village is the **Tesuque Pueblo** (Route 285, Tesuque; 505-982-2667; admission). Considered one of the most traditional of the pueblos, Tesuque continues to have a strong agricultural emphasis, which results in natural food products for sale. Bright designs characterize their pottery. The pueblo also hosts bingo games.

At Pojoaque, go left on Route 502 to **San Ildefonso Pueblo** (Route 502, Pojoaque; 505-455-2273; admission) where you'll see beautiful burnished black matte pottery in the tradition of the late Maria Martinez. Current potters continue to create artistic wonders. There's a museum on site and tours of the pueblo's nearby Black Mesa.

The **Pojoaque Pueblo** (Route 285; 505-455-2278) hosts special fiesta days and has a tourist center where handcrafted items are sold. Pojoaque is the smallest of the Tewa pueblos. Pojoaque has an RV park on site.

Through Pojoaque to Route 503 turn right and wind past the cottonwoods to **Nambe Pueblo** (Route 503, Nambe; 505-455-7752; admission) and sparkling Nambe Falls picnic area. This area was once a Spanish province where early settlers developed their communal land grants. Many Nambe residents are descendants of those early settlers.

Turn left on Route 520 to **Chimayo,** where you begin a sacred tour of three of the most amazing and legend-filled churches in North America. The Chimayo Valley between the Sangre de Cristos and the Rio Grande Valley is a fertile area at the confluence of three streams.

Within the village of Chimayo is the **Santuario de Chimayo** (★) (Route 520; 505-351-4889), also known as Lourdes of America, which has been the place of countless miracles. Legend has it that back in the early 1800s, a man saw a shining light coming from the ground. He dug and found a crucifix. The cross was moved to a church nearby and placed on the altar.

The next morning the crucifix was gone, and found in its original location. The crucifix was moved again to the church, but again disappeared and ended up in its original location. This kept happening until people realized, someone or something wanted it to remain at this site. So, a church was built in Chimayo between 1814 and 1816. This is probably one of the reasons why people believe the Santuario's dirt is blessed.

El Santuario, "The Shrine," remains a magic place where people with ailments come to feel God's healing touch. There's an annual pilgrimage to the church beginning on Good Friday. Testaments to its healing powers are everywhere, as discarded crutches, braces and *retablos* (Christ drawings) fill the church's side rooms.

For eight generations, the Ortega family has been weaving brilliant sashes, vests and purses, jackets all done on the premises of its wonderful little shop, **Ortega Weaving** (Route 76, Chimayo; 505-351-4215). The outpost also has a great selection of regional books.

After visiting Chimayo, turn right to Route 76 and the town of **Truchas**, a burgeoning little arts center whose people are undoubtedly inspired by the splendid scenery of the Sangre de Cristos and the second highest mountain, 13,102-foot Truchas Peak. The tough little village was home to John Nichols' *The Milagro Beanfield War.*

Stop by the **Hands Artes Gallery** (Route 76, Truchas) and the other gift shops that seem to keep popping up in homes along the main drag.

Continue north on Route 76 to **Las Trampas**. Once a walled adobe village—to protect it from "wild" Indians—Las Trampas is home to the 18th-century **Church of San Jose** (Route 76), a much-photographed mission church with mud plastering and early paintings.

After passing through Las Trampas you'll come to Peñasco. Turn on Route 75 through the **Picuris Pueblo** (Route 75, Peñasco; 505-587-2519; admission) to see the native pottery, museum and remains of the old pueblo that was built in the 1770s in the Spanish Colonial style. Picuris, with its standing round house, remains the smallest of New Mexico's pueblos.

From Picuris, rejoin Route 76 for a few miles until you connect with Route 3 and pass over the landmark U.S. Hill Vista, an early, tortuous trading route. After driving over hill and dale, when Route 3 meets with Route 68, head straight to the Ranchos de Taos.

There you'll find **San Francisco de Asis** (★) (Route 68, Ranchos de Taos; 505-758-2754), a Spanish Colonial adobe church that was the favorite of artists Georgia O'Keeffe and Ansel Adams. It's home to Henri Ault's amazing painting, "The Shadow of the Cross," which some say is miraculous. The painting depicts Christ carrying a cross when observed from one angle. In different light, however, the cross cannot be seen.

RIVER ROAD TO TAOS   If you opt not to take the High Road to Taos and want to continue north out of Santa Fe on Route 285, you'll come

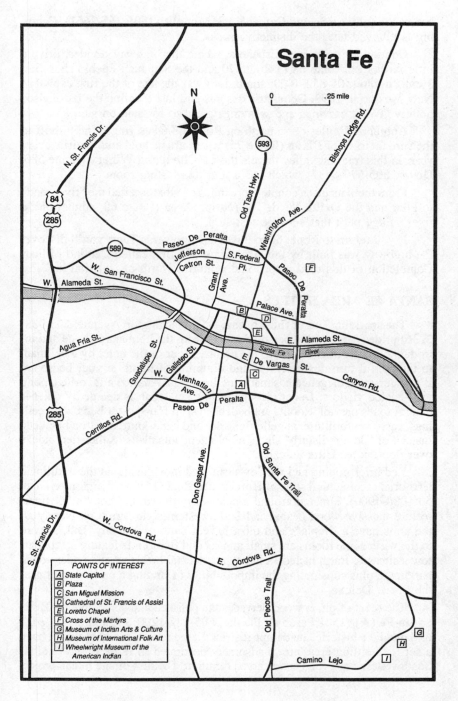

Santa Fe

N

0 .25 mile

N. St. Francis Dr.

Bishops Lodge Rd.

593

Old Taos Hwy.

84

285

589

Paseo De Peralta

Jefferson

Catron St.

S. Federal Pl.

Washington Ave.

Paseo De Peralta

F

W. San Francisco St.

W. Alameda St.

Grant Ave.

Palace Ave.

B

D

E

E. Alameda St.

Agua Fria St.

Guadalupe St.

Galisteo St.

W.

Santa Fe River

E. De Vargas St.

C

Canyon Rd.

Manhattan Ave.

A

Paseo De Peralta

285

Cerrillos Rd.

Don Gaspar Ave.

Old Santa Fe Trail

S. St. Francis Dr.

W. Cordova Rd.

E. Cordova Rd.

Old Pecos Trail

POINTS OF INTEREST
A State Capitol
B Plaza
C San Miguel Mission
D Cathedral of St. Francis of Assisi
E Loretto Chapel
F Cross of the Martyrs
G Museum of Indian Arts & Culture
H Museum of International Folk Art
I Wheelwright Museum of the
    American Indian

G

H

I

Camino Lejo

across the jolly sandstone **Camel Rock Monolith** (505-455-2661). Camping is allowed near the distinctive rock.

Continuing north past Española, where the highway divides, drive a little farther on Route 68 to Route 70 and the San Juan Pueblo sign. **San Juan Pueblo** (505-852-4400; admission) was the site of the first capital of New Mexico in 1598. Geometric designs and lustre define the red-incised pottery. Wood carvings and weavings are also for sale on site.

Another 15 miles or so north on Route 68 takes you to the turnoff to the verdant town of **Dixon** (Route 75) where artists hold studio visits every year. In this fragrant valley there's the **La Chiripada Winery** (Route 580, Dixon; 505-579-4437) which has a tour and tasting room.

From there its just a couple more miles on what's called the "river road" to Pilar and the **Orilla Verde Recreation Area** (Route 68; admission), a river's edge park that's a nice rest stop.

If you return to Route 68 to travel north towards Taos, you'll discover the highway was built by the U.S. Army and first called Camino Militar. Completion of this road helped end centuries worth of isolation in Taos.

SANTA FE AREA HOTELS

The sparkling **Inn of the Anasazi** (113 Washington Avenue; 505-988-3236) prides itself on the personal touch, from the homemade juice and introduction letter at check-in, to the escorted tour of the hotel by a bellman, to thoughtful turn-down service and dimming of lights in your bedroom. It's understated elegance has made the Inn of the Anasazi a favorite among well-heeled visitors. Decor throughout the small inn is decidedly quiet—neutral tones prevail. Rooms are bedecked with four-poster beds, *viga* ceilings, cast-iron furniture, angelic figurines and hand-knitted cotton blankets. Instead of "do not disturb" signs, hotel attendants place leather-tied blocks over doorknobs. Ultra-deluxe.

Red brick coping and windows trimmed in white signal the traditional territorial architectural style of **Hotel Plaza Real** (125 Washington Avenue; 505-988-4900). Situated around a central courtyard, the hotel's 56 rooms feature massive wood beams and Southwestern-style furniture. Nearly all the units have a fireplace and most have a patio or balcony. But, a word to the wise: some rooms are small and second floor units feature steep, narrow staircases. Rates include a hearty continental breakfast and underground parking, a plus considering the impossibility of finding a parking spot near the Plaza. Deluxe.

The scent of piñon wood pervades the polished and contemporary **Hotel Santa Fe** (★) (1501 Paseo de Peralta; 505-982-1200) located on the edge of Santa Fe's historic Guadalupe district. Large rooms, many of which have a separate sitting area, are handsomely decorated in those oh-so-familiar Southwestern colors and hand-carved furniture. The first-offsite Indian project in the state, the hotel is half-owned by the Picuris tribe. Its Pat'Ate gift shop is run by the Picuris; other Native Americans work in the rest of the hotel. Moderate to deluxe.

Literally, "the inn at the end of the Santa Fe Trail," **La Fonda Hotel** (100 East San Francisco Street; 505-982-5511) is a Santa Fe institution. Though the original 1610 adobe hotel is gone, the latest incarnation still caters to weary travelers in search of pleasant lodging and fine food. Each room is unique with hand-painted wooden furniture and room accents, many with balconies and fireplaces. A central meeting spot for area sightseeing tours and recreational activities, La Fonda hums with excitement. A newsstand, art gallery, shops, restaurant and cantina all add to the bustle. Deluxe.

Considering the noise on the street it fronts, rooms at the **Inn on the Alameda** (303 East Alameda; 505-986-2121) are surprisingly quiet. Everything seems sunny and clean—from the white adobe walls to blue and pink bathroom tiles to the clean, modern lines of artwork. Many rooms are decorated with wicker and wood-cane furniture; all come with fluffy robes for guest use. Breakfast is included. Deluxe to ultra-deluxe.

Romance blooms at **La Posada de Santa Fe** (330 East Palace Avenue; 505-986-0000). Lush grounds burst forth with tulips and sweet peas; flower fancy decor mimics the natural setting. Wood floors and *viga* ceilings adorn the cozy casitas, many of which have kiva fireplaces. The hotel's Victorian bar is a natural place for whispering sweet nothings. Moderate to deluxe.

If you find bigger is always better, then be sure to book a room at the looming, yet lovely, 218-room **Eldorado Hotel** (309 West San Francisco Street; 505-988-4455). Lovers of classic Santa Fe architecture about choked when this monolith was constructed. Yet few who venture inside find fault with the brass and chrome fixtured lobby bar, heated rooftop pool, cocktail lounge and adjacent shops. Medium-sized double rooms are done in mauves and earth tones. Those with bucks to burn might opt for the Presidential Suite with five rooms, two fireplaces, a wet bar and balcony. Even non-Gold Card holders will appreciate the rooms with fireplaces—a valet lights the fire for you. Deluxe to ultra-deluxe.

Afternoon tea attracts a high tone crowd to the **Hotel St. Francis** (210 Don Gaspar Avenue; 505-983-5700), one of the prettiest properties in town. Each of the 81 rooms and suites is unique with high ceilings, casement windows, brass and iron beds and cherrywood furniture. Original hexagonal tile and porcelain pedestal sinks give the bathrooms a lush, yet historic feel. A spacious lobby hosts the famous afternoon tea, complete with finger sandwiches and scones. Deluxe.

On the northern edge of town are two rather rural alternatives to the city lodging experience. **The Bishop's Lodge** (Route 22; 505-983-6377) is the better of the two primarily because of its rich history. The property along the Little Tesuque Stream was once the private retreat of Archbishop

Jean Baptiste Lamy. The bishop's sacred, private chapel still stands behind the main lodge and can be entered by borrowing a special key from the front desk. Since 1917, the 1000-acre ranch has hosted guests who choose from horseback riding, meditative hikes, tennis or on-site fishing. Rather simple, but well-kept, rooms are bedecked with older furnishings. Deluxe to ultra-deluxe.

A similar resort experience is offered at the more modern **Rancho Encantado** (Route 4, Tesuque; 505-982-3537) which has fancier accommodations but less overall ambience and attention to service than the Bishop's Lodge. Handsome tree-lined grounds are criss-crossed with cobblestone paths linking the main building to the casitas, corral, tennis courts and cantina. Victorian touches prevail in some of the spacious and thoughtfully furnished rooms and cottages, the latter which feature fireplaces. Deluxe to ultra-deluxe.

Lions and tigers and bears, oh my! At the **Inn of the Animal Tracks** (★) (707 Paseo de Peralta, Santa Fe; 505-988-1546) each of the five rooms uses a different animal theme. In the Playful Otter quarters for example, stuffed dolls keep the guests company as platform feather beds envelope tired bodies. There's a choice library of books from which to choose. All breakfast and high tea delectables are baked on premises. Not surprisingly, there's a resident dog, two cats and bird. Moderate to deluxe.

How many different ways can you say sweet? The **Grant Corner Inn** (122 Grant Avenue, Santa Fe; 505-983-6678) is a turn-of-the-century restored Colonial manor transformed into a wonderful bed and breakfast famous for its morning repasts. Looking more like a New England inn than a Southwestern abode, the Grant Corner is filled with gorgeous white wicker furnishings, brass beds, quilts, hand-drawn paintings and a collection of oh-so-cute bunny art. Moderate.

In the heart of Santa Fe's historic district lies **Pueblo Bonito** (138 West Manhattan; 505-984-8001). The compound, once a private estate, still boasts beautiful courtyards, narrow brick paths and adobe archways. Rooms in the bed and breakfast all feature private bath, fireplace, Navajo rugs and other regionally crafted art. Moderate to deluxe.

Not to be confused with the neighboring Hotel Santa Fe, the **Santa Fe Motel** (510 Cerrillos Road; 505-982-1039) has bungalow-style dwellings, standard lodge rooms as well as a large adobe home for rent. Each unit has its own personality; some are peppy while others are a little on the shady side. Given its prime location, within walking distance of the plaza, the Santa Fe Motel is probably the best value for the money. Budget to moderate.

Typically, the farther you move away from Santa Fe's plaza, the more hotel prices drop. But one must guard against a few of the 1950s-style hotels lining Cerrillos Road—some are dives!

The **El Rey Inn** (1862 Cerrillos Road; 505-982-1931), with its lush garden property filled with fountains and patios, stands tall against neighboring hotels. Decor varies between Indian pueblo, Victorian and Spanish. Some rooms have oriental rugs. In others you'll find wood floors. Omnipresent in all units is an attention to detail and cleanliness. Moderate.

Just down the road there is a standout in the chain hotel department. **Quality Inn's** (3011 Cerrillos Road; 505-471-1211) predictably decorated rooms are spacious and spotless. All top floor rooms have balconies. Formica showers and tile floors are found in the bathrooms. Budget to moderate.

SANTA FE AREA RESTAURANTS

Homemade granola and goat's milk yogurt start the day at the **Inn of the Anasazi** (113 Washington Avenue; 505-988-3030). The innovative kitchen creates indescribable cuisine that blends many elements, flavors, exotic grains and organic ingredients. Homemade breads, seafoods and wild game feature prominently in the menu. The Inn's beautiful 96-seat dining room alone is worth a visit. Deluxe.

Though the wait for a table can be long, don't pass up the opportunity to breakfast or brunch at **Grant Corner Inn** (122 Grant Avenue; 505-983-6678). Locals flock to this intimate restaurant (it only seats 30) located within one of the city's most popular bed and breakfasts. While the regular menu has first-rate fare (waffles, egg dishes, soufflés), best bet is the full brunch special which includes a fruit frappe, choice between two entrées, pastries and fresh ground Colombian coffee or Crabtree & Evelyn tea. Fresh flowers adorn every table and service is extremely attentive. Irish harp music adds to the soothing atmosphere. Reservations a must! Moderate.

Breakfast lovers head to the **Tecolate Café** (1203 Cerrillos Road; 505-988-1362) for omelettes bursting with gooey filling, thick flapjacks and baskets of biscuits and muffins. Budget.

Get the scoop on the world with your café mocha and dessert at the **Galisteo News** (201 Galisteo; 505-984-1316). A sophisticated selection of newspapers, including the *International Herald Tribune*, fill the racks. Galisteo is a fine, fine place for people watching. Budget.

Caffe latte never tasted so good as in the Bohemian atmosphere of the **Aztec Street Café** (317 Aztec Street; 505-983-1316), where you'll find lively conversation, tasty bagels, art worthy of discussion but alas, too much cigarette smoke. Budget.

Pontchartrain Restaurant (319 South Guadalupe, 505-983-0626) puts a Cajun and Caribbean twist on seafood, steaks and pastas to create dishes like crabmeat Louisiana, chicken mamou and boeuf aux champignon. Ponchartrain is a delicious little corner for a candle-lit evening. Deluxe.

Modern American cuisine in a hip setting makes **Zia Diner** (326 South Guadalupe; 505-988-7008) a fine place to come on your own. Sit at the counter or come with pals and the kids and grab a big table. There's food here for everyone, like capellini with prawns, meatloaf, hamburgers, pizza and a Mount Everest-size pile of french fries. Zia moves a good crowd through and provides a "window of reading" for delay times. The adjacent Zia bar hops, too. Budget to moderate.

Tongues smile at the thought of the **Santacafe** (★) (231 Washington Avenue; 505-984-1788) where herbs are exalted and only the freshest of foods find their way to the table. The combination of flavors never disappoints, from the starter to the grand finale. What's best about Santacafe is it doesn't try too hard when delivering its modern American/New Mexican cuisine. It doesn't have to. Deluxe.

You can smell the sizzling steak about a block away from the 150-year old adobe that houses the **Bull Ring** (414 Old Santa Fe Trail; 505-983-3328), a favorite hang-out for legislators and other influential types. Deluxe.

One of Santa Fe's most romantic restaurants is found in, surprise, surprise, an old convent! **La Tertulia** (★) (416 Agua Fria; 505-988-2769) never disappoints. A Spanish art collection bedecks the walls of this former Dominican order house turned parochial school turned eatery. The nuns must be watching over their former residence because from the chips to soups to main courses and rich desserts, the food is heavenly. A pitcher of sangria is a must as is the steak smothered in green chili. Moderate.

La Traviata (95 West Marcy Street; 505-984-1091) serves pastas with clams, great salads and other, simple honest, delicious meals in a whitewashed bistro. If only the noise level could be tamed by a decibel. Moderate to deluxe.

While the addition of a second Japanese restaurant in Santa Fe has given **Shohko Café** (321 Johnson Street; 505-983-7288) a run for the money, it still has the freshest food and best sushi bar. Sake and tempura ice cream are very viable accompaniments. Moderate to deluxe.

The **Coyote Café** (132 West Water Street; 505-983-1615) made a big splash when it first opened and was soon ranked among the top 100 restaurants in the country. The ever-evolving menu typically includes duck quesadillas and chili shrimp. Some locals feel the Coyote is overrated but it remains a favorite among the visiting crowd. Deluxe.

The Compound (653 Canyon Road; 505-982-4533) is where you'll probably want to go for a very special evening. Foie gras, lamb, caviar, fresh fish and daily specials are attentively served in this restored hacienda. The impressive wine cellar has some rare vintages. Ultra-deluxe.

Southwestern cuisine and Continental-style entrées with a tangy Creole snap dominate the menu at **Pink Adobe** (406 Old Santa Fe Trail; 505-983-7712) where the emphasis is on seafood. Moderate to deluxe.

Considered one of Santa Fe's finest restaurants, **La Casa Sena** (125 East Palace Avenue, Sena Plaza; 505-988-9232) boasts both a main dining room and smaller cantina. The restaurant is part of a restored 1860 adobe casa and fills its walls with paintings by early Santa Fe masters. Fine, fresh ingredients are used (even the water is from their own well), resulting in fabulous dining adventures. Entrées take regional favorites and give them a creative twist like roasted quail with blue-corn dressing, trout baked in clay or medallions of antelope with salsa. Don't miss the avocado-lime cheesecake with piñon crust. Outrageous! Deluxe.

Lines form early at the accompanying **La Casa Sena Cantina** (125 East Palace Avenue; 505-988-9232) because no reservations are accepted. But, in this bustling crowded space, everything is artistically presented from food to song. In fact, nowhere in Santa Fe does the roasted poblano chili come with a rousing rendition of "Phantom of the Opera." The limited menu includes such specialties as fresh *tilapia*, *chile rellenos* and *carne adovada* burrito. Waiters and waitresses perform excerpts from popular musicals, then follow with a sampling of show tunes. Patrons come and go between sets, making their way among the tiny butcher block tables and baby grand piano. Moderate to deluxe.

Locals still love **El Farol** (808 Canyon Road; 505-983-9912) which serves hot and cold Spanish tapas. Try the house specialty—scallops in white wine with peppers—for an inexpensive and filling meal. El Farol's ambience is as good as its food. Moderate.

If an old Mexico-style huge lunch followed by a siesta are what you're after, then seek out the venerable **Shed** (133½ East Palace Avenue; 505-982-9030), where wise eaters come before noon to avoid the awesome lines. Blue-corn tortillas served on sizzling plates wrap around cheese and pork specialties as corn meal-like posole sits comfortably on the side. Consider starting your meal with some fresh mushroom soup and ending it with lemon soufflé. Budget to moderate.

Another restaurant where waiting for a table is almost a given is tiny **Josie's Casa de Comida** (225 East Marcy Street; 505-983-5311). A sign even warns the anxious that preparation of fresh foods takes time. Burritos hold their own next to liver and onions entrées and chicken fried steak. Red raspberry shortcake and peach cobbler make it tough to "just say no." Budget to moderate.

Friday is a favorite time to visit **Rincon del Oso** (639 Old Santa Fe Trail; 505-983-5337) because that's when the popular specials such as sour cream enchiladas are served at this New Mexican café. Budget.

Somewhere you'd definitely not think to stop for a snack is **Woolworth's** (58 East San Francisco Street; 505-982-1062). But this particular franchise store sells a tasty, though messy, chip and bean concoction called Frito pie that is fun to munch on while sitting in the Plaza. Budget.

In the old railroad station is **Tomasita's** (500 South Guadalupe, Santa Fe; 505-983-5721) which on the surface looks like a tourist trap. But the food—Tomasita's wins raves for its green chili and *chile rellenos*—and its margaritas wipe away any disparaging thoughts. Moderate.

With the unlikely name of **Dave's Not Here** (1115 Hickox Street; 505-983-7060), this great little neighborhood spot serves typical Mexican food and a yummy Greek salad. But it's the burgers that keep people coming back. You can have them with guacamole, green chili, onions or just plain naked. By the way, namesake Dave really isn't here—he sold the restaurant a long time ago. Budget.

When you gotta have a pizza fix, head for **Il Primo Pizza** (234 North Guadalupe; 505-988-2007) for some cheesy, Windy City-style deep dish. Budget.

HIGH ROAD TO TAOS RESTAURANTS   Before it gets too trendy, check out the **Tesuque Market** (★) (Route 591 and Bishop's Lodge Road, Tesuque; 505-988-8848) and its casually chic atmosphere. The Tesuque chili-cheeseburger, stir-fry veggie plate and salads are highly recommended. There's a full wine cellar and good choices by the glass. Budget.

Tucked into the mountains 20 minutes north of Santa Fe, **Restaurante Rancho de Chimayo** (Route 520, Chimayo; 505-351-4444) serves up authentic New Mexican meals in an adobe home. Bill of fare includes tamales, enchiladas, tacos and flautas plus specialties like marinated pork cutlets served in a red-chili sauce and chicken breasts topped with chili sauce and melted cheese. Leave room for the homemade sopapillas and honey. During summer months, ask for the outdoor patio seating. Budget to moderate.

SANTA FE AREA SHOPPING

In a city known for its history and architecture, what everyone remembers about Santa Fe is . . . the shopping. A myriad of arts and crafts shops, plus 200 galleries crowd the Plaza and nearby Canyon Road, a two-mile street lined with fine art stores.

For silver jewelry, pottery and hand-woven blankets of exquisite detail, look no further than beneath the portal of the Palace of Governors on the Plaza where Indian artisans gather to market their wares.

Always exciting images by well-known and obscure shooters alike can be viewed at **Andrew Smith Fine American Photography** (★) (76 East San Francisco Street; 505-984-1234).

Fenn Gallery (10775 Paseo de Peralta; 505-982-4631) has New Mexican classics, folk art and plenty of regional treasures. Fenn's sculpture garden and fountains only add to the atmosphere. The late **Elaine Horwitch's Gallery** (129 West Palace Avenue; 505-988-8997) is modern, hooked into "the scene" and always worth your time.

Laura Carpenter (531 East Palace Avenue; 505-986-9090) is the place for contemporary art. Carpenter's gallery is quite well-regarded, internationally. **Gerald Peters** (439 Camino del Monte Sol; 505-988-8961) and **Allene Lapidus** (225 Johnson Street; 505-984-0191) are other purveyors of collectable art.

Stunning Southwestern scenes of adobes and more are found at **Ventana Fine Art** (211 Old Santa Fe Trail; 505-983-8815).

Well-priced Southwestern flavor casual clothing makes **Chico's** (328 South Guadalupe; 505-984-1132) a good place to purchase souvenirs.

Bodhi Bazaar (500 Montezuma; 505-982-3880) has natural clothing, vintage items and T-shirts. Earth-toned natural garments fill the shelves at **Pinkoyote** (315 Old Santa Fe Trail; 505-984-9911). Hand-appliqued shirts at fair prices are found at **Three Sisters** (211 Old Santa Fe Trail; 505-988-5045), one of several good shops located at the Inn at Loretto.

An unusual bookstore, **The Ark** (133 Romero Street; 505-988-3709) is found well-off the beaten track in a hideaway hacienda. Books on healing and UFOs, crystals and incense fill this New Age haven.

Find gold jewelry and brilliant earth stones like sugilite at **Spirit of the Earth** (211 Old Santa Fe Trail; 505-988-9558). Ear cuff king and master jeweler **Ross LewAllen** (★) (105 East Palace Avenue; 505-983-2657) has branched out into safari bracelets, Aloha spirit jewelry and wildlife-theme wearables.

Custom-made silver buckles shake hands with serpent and leather belts. Snazzy western boots can also be found at **Tom Taylor** (★) (100 East San Francisco Street; 505-984-2231).

For outrageous greeting and post cards, try the **Marcy Street Card Shop** (85 West Marcy Street; 505-982-5160). **The Chile Shop** (109 East Water Street; 505-983-6080) has wreaths, *ristras* and cookbooks.

Step into a whole 'nother world of beads and baubles at **Worldly Possessions Shop & Gallery** (330 Garfield; 505-983-6090), located in the up-and-coming Historic Guadalupe District.

For tribal arts there are numerous choices, including **Casa Hopi** (114 Old Santa Fe Trail; 505-984-9114), **La Fonda Indian Shop** (La Fonda Hotel; 505-988-2488), **Tin-Nee-Ann** (923 Cerrillos Road; 505-988-1630) and **Sky Mesa Traders** (235 Don Gasper; 505-982-5473).

CANYON ROAD While art abounds everyday in the City Different, from public sculpture to stylishly dressed Santa Feans, one of the greatest concentrations of galleries can be found on Canyon Road. High rents have made the old-artist-working-in-the-backroom an anomaly and turned Canyon Road into a rather exclusive enclave. There are plenty of beautiful things to be viewed here—from clothing and jewelry to furniture and paintings—satisfying most palettes if not every pocketbook.

Start your Canyon Road journey out at **Mabel's** (201 Canyon Road; 505-986-9105), a cat lover's paradise. There are kitties on slippers and bathrobes and puddy-tats emblazoning door knockers. From stationery to wool mittens, the feline set rules.

Slightly more serious is **Chris O'Connell Spider Woman Designs** (225 Canyon Road; 505-984-0136). Santa Fe women are known as stylish dressers. At O'Connell's shop you too can find one of those smart and timeless hand-woven jackets that everyone seems to be wearing.

Lovers of bronze sculpture should check out **Meyer Gallery** (225 Canyon Road; 505-983-1434) and its huge selection by well-known artists. **Mariposa Santa Fe** (225 Canyon Road; 505-982-3032) displays the marquetry and inlaid boxes of New Mexico artists Stan and Shirley Giser. In the same building is one of the country's oldest galleries, **Munson** (225 Canyon Road; 505-983-1657), featuring paintings, sculpture and graphics.

Contemporary Southwest and Native American art is well-represented at the **Galeria Capistrano** (409 Canyon Road; 505-984-3024). One of the longest-living galleries on the block, **Linda McAdoo** (503 Canyon Road; 505-983-7182) showcases representational and impressionistic painters and sculptors from the United States and abroad.

Important American regionalists and contemporary painters are shown at **Wiggins Fine Art** (526 Canyon Road; 505-982-5328). Splendid hand-woven tapestries, rugs and textiles inspired by South American and Far East designs are found at the **Market-Alice Kagawa Parrott's Fabrice** (634 Canyon Road; 505-982-0794).

Bellas Artes (653 Canyon Road; 505-983-2745) is an intriguing gallery featuring significant works in painting, clay and primitive medium. **Quilts Ltd.** (652 Canyon Road; 505-988-5888) sells just what it's name promises. Some are traditional, others are contemporary.

Weavings, kachinas and Native American art are among the artifacts found at **Kania-Ferrin Gallery** (662 Canyon Road; 505-982-8767). A working studio and gallery that's located in an old adobe, **Phil Daves Studio/Gallery** (669 Canyon Road; 505-982-4867) offers landscapes, figurative paintings and nudes.

Carol LaRoche Gallery (708 Canyon Road; 505-982-1186) has monotypes, abstract and representational art that was created by LaRoche herself. Adjacent is the **Leaping Lizard Gallery** (708 Canyon Road; 505-984-8434) featuring the artwork of a children's book illustrator.

Natural-fiber clothing designs and handmade garments are what have made **Judy's Unique Apparel** (714 Canyon Road; 505-988-5746) popular.

When light shines through colored glass, wonderful things happen. The **Dunbar Stained Glass Studio and Gallery** (801½ Canyon Road; 505-984-8515) sparkles with glasswork. You could get blinded by the glare from the gold and silver jewelry that's created on the premises at **Crystal Mesa Gallery** (821 Canyon Road; 505-983-3704).

American Indian art, folk art and vintage photos are found at **Alan Kessler** (836 Canyon Road, Santa Fe; 505-986-0123).

When you're writing a guidebook it's hard to decide whether the **Santa Fe Flea Market** (★) belongs in the shopping or sightseeing section. Just as every flea market reflects its surrounding community, this Northern New Mexico gathering place contains Spanish, Anglo and Native American traders alike. Pull your pick-up truck over to the side of the road, shuffle through the dust and you'll find everything from pinto beans to auto parts to fine turquoise jewelry. The flea market is open every Friday, Saturday and Sunday. To get there head six miles north from Santa Fe on Route 84; go left after the opera house.

SANTA FE AREA NIGHTLIFE

For a nightcap, try the gracious Victorian bar in **La Posada de Santa Fe** (330 East Palace Avenue; 505-986-0000) with its chandeliers and leather chairs and cushy couch by the fireplace. In the summer, take a sip on the outdoor patio.

A mix of politicians, tourists and just plain old working folks can be found at **The Pink Adobe** (406 Old Santa Fe Trail; 505-983-7712), a handsome watering hole around the corner from the state capitol.

Club West (★) (213 West Alameda; 505-982-0099) is regarded as the best nightclub in town, showcasing national and regional acts, blues and country to rock and jazz. Depending on the evening's act, the club can be a place to break out your fancy duds or the casual clothing.

Get ready to kick up your heels at **Rodeo Nites** (2911 Cerrillos Road; 505-473-4138), a rowdy nightclub for lovers of country and western.

El Farol (808 Canyon Road; 505-983-9912) is where locals love to hang out in the dark cantina and drink. With a spirit all of its own, El Farol attracts real people.

Even more down home is the macho **Evangelina's** (200 West San Francisco Street; 505-982-9014) where the beer is cheap, cheap, cheap.

The lounge in the **La Fonda Hotel** (100 East San Francisco Street; 505-982-5511) during happy hour gurgles with the energy of locals and visitors. Hot hors d'oeuvres and music are fine accompaniments to La Fonda's loaded margaritas.

The Palace Restaurant (142 West Palace Avenue; 505-982-9891) offers piano music, well-poured drinks and reliable service.

O solo mio: **La Casa Sena** (125 East Palace Avenue; 505-988-9232) has singing waiters and waitresses and one heck of a great wine list. For a more relaxed atmosphere, ease into the jazz piano at the **Ore House** (50 Lincoln Avenue; 505-983-8687).

OPERA, THEATER, SYMPHONY AND DANCE

Music and moonlight fill the **Santa Fe Opera** (Route 84-285; 505-982-3855), one of America's most famous (and finest) summer opera companies. Blending seasoned classics with exciting premieres, the Opera runs from late-June through August inside the open-air theater auditorium. Though some seats are sheltered, warm clothing and raingear are suggested, since evenings can be cold and/or wet.

New Mexico Repertory Theatre (1050 Old Pecos Trail; 505-983-2382) draws both national and local talent for its October to May season of contemporary and classic American and European plays.

From Greek tragedies to contemporary drama, **Santa Fe Actors' Theatre** (430 West Manhattan Street; 505-982-8309) is a treat. Performances are held in a historic warehouse converted into a 100-seat, modular space.

Community theater of the highest order is found at **Santa Fe Community Theater** (142 East De Vargas Street; 505-988-4262) which produces musical comedies, avant garde plays, a Fiesta Melodrama and a one-act series.

The beautiful Paolo Soleri Outdoor Amphitheatre of the Santa Fe Indian School campus serves as home to the **Santa Fe Summer Concert Series** (Cerrillos Road; 505-256-1777), which brings big-name acts to town.

The **Santa Fe Symphony** (505-983-3530) performs both classical and contemporary works at Sweeney Center (201 West Marcy Street).

Founded in 1974, the **Orchestra of Santa Fe** (505-988-4640) performs from September through May at the Lensic Theater.

Saint Francis Auditorium (inside the Museum of Fine Arts) plays host to the **Santa Fe Concert Association** (505-984-8759) and **Santa Fe Chamber Music Festival** (505-983-2075).

The sizzling, rapid-stepping **Maria Benitez Spanish Dance Company** (505-982-1237) returns to Santa Fe each summer for a series of flamenco dance concerts. Performances are held at the Picacho Plaza Hotel (750 North St. Francis Drive).

SANTA FE AREA PARKS

Hyde Memorial State Park—A small (350 acres) park in the foothills high above Santa Fe, Hyde Park's woodsy and sheltered feeling gives one the impression they're light years away from the city. A good base for cross-country skiing or hiking in the Santa Fe National Forest.

Facilities: Picnic areas, restrooms, general store with limited supplies; information, 505-983-7175.

Camping: There are 75 tent sites ($6 to $7 per night) and seven RV hookups ($11 per night).

Getting there: The park is located on Route 475, seven-and-one-half miles northeast of Santa Fe.

Morphy Lake State Park—A scenic mountain lake and park that's a popular fishing spot for everyone and swimming hole for only the very hearty. Unspoiled barely describes this little jewel.

Facilities: Boating, hiking, restrooms; information, 505-387-2328.

Camping: There are 25 standard sites ($7 per night) and 25 primitive sites ($6 per night).

Getting there: Located on Route 94, four miles south of Mora.

Coyote Creek State Park—Fishing and camping are the main attractions in this compact 80-acre park.

Facilities: Picnic sites, restrooms, playground; information, 505-387-2328.

Camping: There are 73 sites including ten RV hookups and 23 primitive sites. Fees per night are $6 for primitive sites, $7 for standard sites and $11 for hookups.

Getting there: Located on Route 434, 14 miles north of Mora.

Las Vegas Area

Coming into Las Vegas, New Mexico, for the first time, you may think it looks very familiar. That's probably because this charismatic town, the country's original Las Vegas, has been featured in countless silent movies. Located about an hour's drive east of Santa Fe, Las Vegas' modern-day roots go back to railroad's heyday, when it was an important mercantile center.

By driving the back road (Routes 84 and 85), which follows the Santa Fe Trail, between the capital city and Las Vegas, you'll first pass by the **Glorieta Battlefield**, where a decisive skirmish of the Civil War was fought at the summit of Glorieta Pass in 1862 between Union volunteers from Colorado and Texas Mounted volunteers.

It's a beautiful area, full of spotted, rolling hills all around. The next stop is the **Pecos Monument** (Route 63, Pecos; 505-757-6414), thought to once stand four to five stories back in 1451 when it had a population of 2000. By the 17th century the Spanish had taken it over and built a pair of mission churches. Rampant disease, coupled with Indian raids in the 1800s, led to its abandonment.

As you drive into the city of Las Vegas, you'll want to first head to the historic **Plaza district**, the center of Old Town which goes back to the 1600s with the Spaniards, although archeological digs in Las Vegas show that the Paleo Indians lived here as early as 8000 B.C.

The Mexican government granted 29 individuals land grants in 1835. Las Vegas was soon to become a major port of entry for supply wagons on the Santa Fe Trail.

By 1879, railroad tracks were laid east of the Gallinas River in "New Town;" not surprisingly, Railroad Avenue and the neighborhood boomed. But by 1905, railroad traffic was diverted south and the once expanding city, whose population in the late 1800s rivaled Denver's, dwindled.

The diverse origins of people who came during Las Vegas' heyday left an architectural legacy of everything from Territorial and Italianate styles to Victorian designs. In fact, Las Vegas has nine historic districts and more than 900 historically designated buildings.

Stop at the excellent **visitor center** (727 Grand Avenue; 505-425-8631), where maps of walking tours, hiking trails and information on Las Vegas' history are abundant. Next door is the **Rough Rider's Museum** (729 Grand Avenue; 505-425-8726) which has mementos of the Spanish-American War, Indian artifacts and other historical items, many of which were donated by Teddy Roosevelt and his cohorts.

Pretty buildings line the street of **New Mexico Highlands Campus** (National Avenue; 505-425-7511), which was established in 1893 bridging the rivaling Old and New Towns. The school is known for its fine arts and performing arts programs.

Yet the pride of the area is the **United World College** (Montezuma; 505-454-4248), near the former spa of Montezuma, which draws gifted students from around the world in a unique setting and approach to learning. The beautiful red slate turret-adorned structure looks like a castle.

Find it by driving up the pretty **Hot Springs Canyon** past painted barns, a picturesque little church and a couple of colorful wall murals. Well-marked natural hot springs baths are right off the highway in view of the college and are offered in varying temperatures.

It's a splendid drive on Route 65 through Gallinas Canyon past the college into the heart of the Sangre de Cristos and on up to the hiker's paradise of 10,263-foot **Hermit's Peak**.

Backtracking to Las Vegas and then north on Route 518 takes the traveler to boardsailing haven **Storrie Lake State Park**. A short drive farther north on scenic Route 518 delivers you in **Mora**, once known as the breadbasket of the area, as it grew wheat during the heyday of the Santa Fe Trail. At the nearby town of Cleveland, is the **Cleveland Roller Mill Museum** (505-387-2645; admission), a National Historic Landmark that has original mill equipment. The flour mill operated between 1892 and the early 1950s.

East of Las Vegas via Route 25 is **Fort Union** (Route 161, Watrous; 505-425-8025; admission), which beginning in 1851 and throughout most of the 19th century was the largest military post in the region and headquarters for soldiers who protected Santa Fe Trail travelers from Indian raids. A self-guided trail and visitor center explains its rich history.

LAS VEGAS AREA HOTELS

Victoriana is alive in the center of Las Vegas at the historic **Plaza Hotel** (230 Old Town Plaza, Las Vegas; 505-425-3591). Originally built (1882) in the Italianate bracketed style, the Plaza was the first major inn built after the railroad's arrival. A century later, original features such as tin ceilings and window bracketing were uncovered. Rooms are decorated in period furniture, antiques and floral accents typical of the late-19th-century buildings in the West. Moderate.

Or drive a few miles to the "new" section of town to the hacienda-style **Inn on the Santa Fe Trail** (★) (1133 Grand Avenue, Las Vegas; 505-425-6791) for the best rooms for the price in Northern New Mexico. Completely gutted and redone in 1991, the property is handsomely decorated in oak and whitewashed pine furniture crafted by a Las Vegas artisan. Chili and coyote-style Southwestern paintings cover pink walls. New fiberglass tubs are found in the linoleum-floored bathrooms. Budget.

LAS VEGAS AREA RESTAURANTS

For a real slice of Americana, wander into the formica-filled **Spic and Span Bakery and Café** (713 Douglas Avenue; Las Vegas; 505-425-6481) where homemade donuts and sweet rolls jam the glass cabinets. Mexican specialties are served in the café. A natives' hangout, heads swivel when a newcomer enters the sanctum. Budget.

Don't be deterred by the shabby exterior of **Estella's Café** (Bridge Street, Las Vegas; 505-454-0048). Thoughtfully prepared American and Mexican cuisine dominate the menu. The green chili comes highly recommended. Budget.

Get your pasta fill at **Gustavo's Italian Restaurant** (236 Mills Avenue, Las Vegas; 505-425-7080). Desserts like fuzzy navel peach pie and French chocolate Chambord are sure to keep you from overdoing it on the early courses. Moderate.

LAS VEGAS AREA SHOPPING

On the historic Plaza in Las Vegas is the **La Galeria de los Artesanos Book Store** (220 North Plaza; 505-425-8331) where you'll find books on the West, guidebooks and local literature housed in a former law office.

LAS VEGAS AREA NIGHTLIFE

In Las Vegas, try a saloon that was named after a ghost, **Byron T's in the Plaza Hotel** (230 Old Town Plaza; 505-425-3591) for a selection of libations.

LAS VEGAS AREA PARKS

Storrie Lake State Park—A pretty mountain lake in a jewel of a setting that's favored by gung-ho boardsailers who like the consistent winds and families that enjoy the jewel-like setting for a nice day outing.

Facilities: Visitor center, picnic area, toilets, showers, boat ramp; information, 505-425-7278.

Camping: There are 54 sites (22 with RV hookups); tent sites are $7 per night and hookups are $11 per night. Primitive camping is allowed along the lake's shore; $6 per night.

Getting there: Located on Route 518, six miles north of Las Vegas.

Taos and Enchanted Circle Area

A step down in the frenetic category from hustle-bustle Santa Fe is the casually sophisticated atmosphere of Taos. Galleries and working artists flourish because rents aren't nearly as suffocating as in New Mexico's capital city. The tri-cultures of Anglo, Indian and Spanish co-exist in Taos within the main city, the Taos Pueblo and south of the town in the relatively rural Ranchos de Taos.

Surrounding the city are the Sangre de Cristo (Blood of Christ) mountains and expanse of Carson National Forest, making recreational pursuits easily accessible for the many sports-minded people who are drawn to Taos' world-class ski slopes. At the turn of this century it was aesthetes, not athletes, who settled here to form a colony of artists, writers and critical thinkers.

The Sangre de Cristos abut the town, which sits at an altitude of nearly 7000 feet above sea level, on the east. The Rio Grande River forms the city's western boundary. Given its superb natural setting, it's ironic that in all but the slowest seasons, gridlock and auto pollution on Taos' main artery, Paseo del Pueblo, can be stifling. But there's really no other way to get to Taos, and given the large local opposition to any airport expansion, it could remain this way for awhile. So be ecologically minded, leave your car at your residence and hoof it around the compact commercial core.

Taos Plaza, as is true in so many Southwestern towns, is its lifeblood. The Plaza has for centuries remained the commercial center for tourism and throughout the centuries, three flags—Spanish, American and Mexican— have flown over the stucco buildings. Plaza galleries and shops merit at least a day's visit. Pick up sightseeing information at the **Taos Chamber of Commerce** (314 Paseo del Pueblo Norte; 505-758-3873).

Kit Carson Memorial Park (Route 522, Taos; 505-758-8234) is a 22-acre verdant park in the center of town that houses the grave of frontiersman Kit Carson. There are picnic areas, a playground and restrooms.

Two miles north of the city, the distant past endures at the **Taos Pueblo** (Route 522; 505-758-8626; admission; camera and artist sketching fees), largest of the New Mexican Indian pueblos open to the public. This complex houses ancient ruins that appear much as they did when Spanish explorers first viewed them in 1540. Five stories of adobe structures tower over the site, which allows no electricity or running water for its 50 or so remaining families.

Traditional ways are followed—food is cooked in an outdoor *horno* (oven) and water is drawn from the stream that breeches the heart of the pueblo. Local artisans sell mica-flecked pottery, silver jewelry, moccasins, boots and drums here. Authentic Indian fry bread, hot and drizzled with honey, is a firsthand way to sample Indian cooking.

Just north of the pueblo turn right on Route 150 for a trip to the **Taos Ski Valley**. The road rises and rolls past churches and tiny hotels through the sleepy towns of Arroyo Seco and Valdez to the Taos Ski Valley. Making the dozen-mile trip at dusk, when the light reflects from the aspen trees in ever-changing hues, can be a magical experience.

South of Taos, at the **Martinez Hacienda** (Ranchitos Road, Route 240; 505-758-1000; admission) you might discover craftsmen chinking the dark wooden walls of a sheep barn to ward off winter's cold. One of the only fully restored Spanish Colonial adobe haciendas in New Mexico, the fortress-like home is constantly being replastered to maintain its structural integrity. Inside, area artisans perpetuate century-old skills through a living history program and demonstrate folk arts like weaving, quilting and wood carving.

Mountain man and scout Kit Carson purchased a 12-room adobe home in 1843 as a wedding gift for his bride. Today, the **Kit Carson Home** (Kit Carson Road; 505-758-0505; admission) showcases the Old West through gun and mountain man exhibits. The living room, bedroom and kitchen re-create the period when Carson's family lived there.

Native American and Hispanic art fill the **Millicent Rogers Museum** (four miles north of Taos off Route 522; 505-758-2462; admission), a memorial to the late Standard Oil heiress. Within the 11 galleries are rare examples of jewelry, textiles, basketry, paintings and pottery, as well as contemporary exhibits by new artists.

Blending the sophistication of European charm with a classic Taos adobe, the **Ernest L. Blumenschein Home** (Ledoux Street; 505-758-0330; admission) showcases the paintings of Blumenschein (co-founder of the Taos Society of Artists), his wife Mary Greene Blumenschein, their daughter Helen and other Taos artists. The fully-restored home, built in the late 1700s, is filled with original furnishings, plus European antiques.

Two blocks southwest of the Plaza, at the west end of historic Ledoux Street is the **Harwood Foundation Museum** (238 Ledoux Street; 505-758-3063), a Pueblo-revival-style adobe compound. New Mexico's second-oldest museum, the Harwood showcases the brilliant work of the Taos Society of Artists, core of the Taos artists' colony. A collection of 19th-century *retablos* (religious paintings on wood) will also fascinate.

The **Fechin Institute** (227 Paseo del Pueblo Norte; 505-758-1710; admission) is full of handcarved woodwork in the former adobe of Russian artist Nicolai Fechin. Open odd hours so call first.

Governor Bent's House and Museum (117 Bent Street; 505-758-2376) has unusual knick-knacks and war era memorabilia from the first governor of New Mexico after it became a U.S. territory. It's worth about 15 minutes of your time.

You'll likely see a lot of art while in New Mexico, but as gallery rents continue to rise, finding locally produced art becomes more difficult. That's why the **Stables Art Center** (133 Paseo del Pueblo Norte; 505-758-2036), with its accent on local artists, is so refreshing.

ENCHANTED CIRCLE   After you've "done" Taos and want to tour the area known as the "Enchanted Circle," drive south of downtown to Route 64 and cruise over scenic Palo Flechado Pass which was used by Native Americans and Spaniards who came from the plains via the Cimarron River. Along the way there are several places to pull over for a picnic or snapshot.

Upon reaching the intersection of Route 434, turn south for a quick visit to the resort town of **Angel Fire**. In the winter it's a favorite destination for intermediate skiers, while in the summer, golfers, hikers and lovers of chamber music flock to Angel Fire.

Back on Route 64 you'll soon come to **Eagle Nest Reservoir**, a fine sailing, surfing and fishing lake that affords a spectacular lookout from which you can see the state's highest peak, Wheeler, which stands at 13,161 feet above sea level.

At the lake's north shore is the village of Eagle Nest that has a handful of restaurants and shops. From there it's 24 windy miles to Cimarron through the Cimarron Range (one of the eastern-most ranges of the Sangre de Cristo mountains), the Colin Neblett wildlife area and Cimarron Canyon.

The settlement of **Cimarron**, where plain and pasture meet rugged mountains, was founded in 1848 with entrepreneur Lucien Maxwell's land grant. Life was cheap back at this outpost on the mountain branch of the Santa Fe Trail and death from a gunfight was not uncommon. Cimarron the town and Cimarron the river certainly lived up to the Spanish translation of their name—wild and untamed. While that may have described it a century ago, these days it's a pretty mellow small town. The rambling river waters too have been calmed by the establishment of Eagle Nest Reservoir.

A trip to present-day Cimarron wouldn't be complete without a peek inside the historic **St. James Hotel** (Route 1; 505-376-2664) with its partly renovated interior and completely authentic funkiness. Built in 1875 by one of Abraham Lincoln's chefs, some say the St. James is haunted by outlaw ghosts of the past. If you think real hard you can imagine crusty old wild westerners like Billy the Kid bellying up to the bar or betting the house on a card game at the St. James.

More down to earth, Cimarron is also home to the **Philmont Scout Ranch** (about four miles south of Cimarron on Route 21; 505-376-2281), a huge camp that's been donated to the Boy Scouts of America. A small attached museum has local artifacts and work from Ernest Seton, one of the original scouts.

See the **Old Mill Museum** (Route 21, Cimarron; 505-376-2913; admission), which was originally built as a grist mill, for a look at mementos of traders and saloon keepers, ranchers and homesteaders who came here to seek their fortunes.

Continuing another 38 miles northeast of Cimarron on Routes 64 and 25, you'll come to **Raton**, a small New Mexican city located on the original Santa Fe trail. Raton, with its scenic mesas, sits at the foot of Raton Pass and was first founded as a railroad outpost.

During the summer months, families head to **La Mesa Park** (Route 64, Raton; 505-445-2301) for quarter horse and thoroughbred racing.

The most worthwhile area attraction is the **Capulin Volcano National Monument** (30 miles east of Raton on Route 64, Capulin; 505-278-2201). Now dormant, the mile-wide cone of the volcano rises 1400 feet above the flat plains. There is a visitor center and small museum providing information on the natural wonder.

Returning back west on Route 64 to the heart of the Enchanted Circle, you'll pass through the high walls of **Cimarron Canyon State Park** (505-377-6271). Be sure and watch your speed, and at nighttime be on the lookout for deer, as you travel through the narrow wall-lined canyon.

Between Eagle Nest and Red River (where Route 64 becomes Route 38) is an open and pretty valley ringed with high mountains. Drop down Bobcat Pass into another wild west village named **Red River**. Though touristy, this turn-of-the-century gold mining town retains a certain charm from its rip-roaring gambling, brawling and red light district days. A ski area rises out of its center and the town is completely surrounded by national forest land.

Continuing east on the Enchanted Circle, which hugs gurgling Red River, you'll drive past plenty of forest and camping spots until you reach the honey-producing town of Questa.

When Route 38 intersects with Route 522, turn south for 13 miles until you come to then **D. H. Lawrence Ranch** (San Cristobal; 505-776-2245), a retreat for writers. Public access is restricted. The shrine to British writer Lawrence, who lived for three years in Taos, can be readily visited during the daytime hours.

Another 13 miles south is Route 64 and the exit to the **Rio Grande Gorge Bridge** where you may want to hold your breath while crossing this suspension bridge, 650 feet over the Rio Grande.

After sitting in the car all day, one's neck tends to stiffen and the shoulders develop knots. It's time for a soak in some mineral hot springs and maybe a massage. About one-hour southwest of Taos is the no-frills spa called **Ojo Caliente Mineral Springs** (Route 285; Ojo Caliente; 505-583-2233; admission). Soak in the springs or perhaps take an herbal wrap. Five minerals—iron, soda, lithia, sodium and arsenic—bubble from the ground. One of the oldest health resorts in the country, Ojo Caliente still looks as it did oh-so-many years ago.

TAOS AND ENCHANTED CIRCLE AREA HOTELS

Epicenter of Taos activity is the enormously popular **Historic Taos Inn** (125 Paseo Norte; 505-758-2233). A National Historic Landmark, the inn is comprised of several separate houses from the 1800s. Forty rooms are decorated in a Southwestern motif with Mexican tile, locally designed furniture and hand-loomed Indian bedspreads; most have hand-painted fireplaces. If the inn is booked, which it may very well be, set aside an evening to enjoy a drink in the living room atmosphere of the lobby. A favorite hangout for locals, also known as "Taosenos," the inn's lobby is showplace to the recurring "Meet the Artist Series." Moderate to deluxe.

The **Laughing Horse Inn** (729 Paseo del Pueblo; 505-758-8350) is a 100-year old hacienda transformed into a European-style pension. As the name implies, it helps to have a sense of humor when staying here. For example, a hallway features a mini "shrine" to John Lennon. One guest room has hot chili pepper-motif lights and the inn's floor varies between old wood and varnished dirt. The communal kitchen offers light snacks available for next-to-nothing prices. Budget.

A hermit could easily hole up for an extended period of time in the **Sonterra Condominiums** (206 Siler Road; 505-758-7989), a special little side-street retreat. Quiet, comfortable and decorated in light, bright contemporary New Mexican style, most of Sonterra's units have fireplaces, separate sitting space and private, fenced patio. Moderate.

From the friendly "welcome home" greeting by the front desk clerk to the hearty skillet breakfasts, the **Ramada Inn Taos** (615 Paseo del Pueblo Sur; 505-758-2900) is big on comfort and warmth. Refurbished in nouvelle-adobe style and pastel colors, the Ramada capably handles groups—even in the hot tub, which après ski is often shoulder to shoulder—but is careful not to neglect individuals. Moderate to deluxe.

The exterior of the **Sagebrush Inn** (1508 Paseo del Pueblo Sur; 505-758-2254) looks just like that of any other Pueblo-style hotel. But open the hefty front door and it's a totally different world. Rooms are dark and romantic, usually furnished with fireplaces, Navajo rugs and pottery. For sports fans, there's probably no better place than the inn's lobby, with its big-screen television and rowdy crowd. A pool, tennis courts and hot tubs are nice amenities. Breakfast is included in the room price. Moderate.

Set among the cottonwood trees in a park-like setting is the **El Monte Lodge** (317 Kit Carson Road; 505-758-3171). Refrigerators are standard issue in the traditionally appointed Southwestern-style rooms. Some of the units sport kiva fireplaces and kitchenettes. Moderate.

Taos bed and breakfasts are extraordinary and becoming ever-more popular. Hidden on a lovely lane about five blocks south of the Plaza is **Casa des Chimenas** (405 Cordoba Road; 505-758-4777), a guest-house for those who love being pampered. The largest of the three units has a study and living room, with a collection of books and magazines. Oak furniture, tiled bathrooms and views of the formal garden and fountains are standard issue. There's a hot tub on site and a large common area. Deluxe.

Every room at **Casa Benavides Bed & Breakfast Inn** (★) (137 Kit Carson Road; 505-758-1772) is different, but they share one common quality—luxury. Several meticulously restored buildings, including an old trading post and artist's studio make up the 22-room complex. This crème de la crème property is elegantly furnished with tile floors, handmade furniture, kiva fireplaces, down comforters and a bevy of unusual antiques. Less than one block from the Plaza, Casa Benavides is also noted for its sumptuous breakfasts all served in the airy, bright breakfast room. Deluxe to ultra-deluxe.

One of the area's original bed and breakfast's, **La Posada de Taos** (309 Juanita Lane; 505-758-8164) provides a homey atmosphere in its huge book-filled living room and open, sunny dining room. The 100-year-old house has been lovingly remodeled with five guest units each with tiled baths and antique furnishings. Four of the units are inside the inn itself, the fifth is a separate, honeymoon cottage across the adobe-walled courtyard. All, except the Taos Room, have wood-burning stoves or adobe fireplaces. Moderate to deluxe.

A distinctive Pueblo-style architecture marks the **Holiday Inn Don Fernando de Taos** (1005 Paseo del Pueblo Sur; 505-758-4444). Rooms are designed around central courtyards and connected by walkways that meander through landscaped grounds. Standard rooms are oversized, while suites have living rooms, fireplaces and hospitality bars. All feature Southwestern styles including hand-carved New Mexican furniture. A large heated swimming pool, hot tub, tennis court and on-site restaurant and lounge add to the friendly ambience. Moderate to deluxe.

Still think "there's no place like home?" Then visit **The Ruby Slipper** (416 La Lomita; 505-758-0613) bed and breakfast where even Dorothy, Auntie Em and the Cowardly Lion could find a room to suit their very needs. Choose from a room with a water bed or one with willow furniture. Oak floors, kiva fireplaces, traditional *viga* ceilings and private entrances also characterize some of the seven, quiet rooms. Afternoons can be spent reclining in hammocks and munching on the ubiquitous snacks baked by the innkeepers. The Ruby Slipper is about a ten-minute walk from the Plaza. Moderate.

Close to the Taos Ski Area, with outrageous views of the Sangre de Cristo Mountains, is luxurious **Salsa Del Salto** (Route 150, El Prado; 505-776-2422). Goose-down comforters warm the king-size beds. Leather couches in the common area are in front of the stone fireplaces—a good place for getting horizontal after a long day on Taos' tough slopes. The pool, tennis courts and hot tub help take the edge off, as well. Deluxe to ultra-deluxe.

Skiers, hikers and other adventuresome spirits looking for an ultracheap experience have two hostels, located right next door to each other, from which to choose. The **Abominable Snowmansion** (Taos Ski Valley Road, Arroyo Seco; 505-776-8298) has six dorm rooms with large closets and dressing areas. A piano, fireplace and conversation area are also available to the guests. Budget. Neighboring **Indian Country International Hostel** (Taos Ski Valley Road, Arroyo Seco; 505-776-8298) offers visitors the choice of laying their head inside Indian tepees or a bunkhouse. Showers, use of the solar kitchen and the opportunity to play with barnyard animals are included in the price. Budget.

It's hard not to get lost while walking around the compound known as the **Quail Ridge Inn** (Taos Ski Valley Road; 505-776-2211). Low-slung buildings containing fully equipped apartment-size rooms dot the landscape. A casual, yet country-club variety clientele clogs the outdoor pool, tennis and squash courts and fitness center. The self-contained resort offers so many on-site amenities and diversions that you need not ever leave the complex, which would be a crying shame considering all there is to see in Taos. Deluxe to ultra-deluxe.

If long days of skiing and multicourse meals are enough to satisfy you, consider staying in the Taos Ski Valley at one of the European-flavored lodges like the simple but comfortable **St. Bernard Hotel** (Taos Ski Valley Road; 505-776-2251). There you'll find location, location, location and a family atmosphere prevailing in this 28-room chalet-style dwelling. All meals are included. Moderate to deluxe.

About one mile from the ski area is the **Austing Haus Hotel** (Taos Ski Valley Road; 505-776-2649). As the name implies, this wood-beamed hotel has an Austrian ambience. Largest and tallest timber-frame building in America, this charming 14-unit bed and breakfast features an elegant glass dining room. Moderate.

ENCHANTED CIRCLE HOTELS   Bring the family to the full-service **Legends Hotel and Conference Center** (Lodge Drive, Angel Fire; 505-377-6401) where ultraspacious rooms, bedecked in pastel colors and Southwestern styles, have plenty of room for rollaways and closet space to accommodate all your ski needs. Moderate to deluxe.

The Inn at Angel Fire (Route 62, Angel Fire; 505-377-2504) offers 28 clean and sensible motel rooms plus on-site restaurant, game room, sauna and kennels. Budget to moderate.

Prices drop even more just 12 miles north of Angel Fire on the pretty road to Eagle Nest at the **Laguna Vista Lodge** (P.O. Box 65, Eagle Nest, NM 87718; 505-377-3522). Motel rooms and suites are available. Budget.

Best bet in Cimarron is by far the spooky **St. James Hotel** (Route 21; 505-376-2664) where famous residents such as Buffalo Bill Cody and Annie Oakley hung their Wild West duds. Originally built in 1880 and then lovingly restored and reopened a century later, this landmark has rooms with cast iron beds, period furniture and wild cat rugs. Each unit is unique and ghosts haunt the hallways, so you may ask to inspect your room before renting. Moderate.

For something a little more Southwestern, seek out the charming white adobe bed and breakfast **Casa del Gavilan** (Route 21, Cimarron; 505-376-2246). Period antiques are omnipresent; a full country breakfast provides plenty of fuel for sightseeing. Moderate.

At Red River is the **Alpine Lodge** (Main and Malette streets; 505-754-2952) on the river bank by the ski lifts. Standard issue rooms and apartments are well-maintained, all with porch or balcony. On-site restaurant and ski rental make the Alpine a convenient one-stop spot for skiers. Moderate.

The Lodge at Red River's (Copper King Trail and Main Street; 505-754-6280) 18 rooms could be considered rustic, although they were recently renovated. Its central location is appealing. Budget to moderate.

TAOS AND ENCHANTED CIRCLE AREA RESTAURANTS

Delicious whole-grain breads, fresh-squeezed juices, plus tarts and pies to undo all the good you've put in your body are common at the **Main Street Bakery** (211 Donaluz; 505-758-9610). If you're shy about garlic, don't order the home-style potatoes. This is a great place to catch up on local gossip. Budget.

The funky sign on the local institution **Michael's Kitchen** (304 Paseo del Pueblo Norte; 505-758-4178) might grab you, but the donut and sweets' cabinet could lock you into a stranglehold. Spill-off-your-plate size breakfasts pack 'em in on ski mornings; diner-type meals are served the rest of the day. Budget.

If the sun gods are with you, sit outside on the patio of **La Cigale** (★) (223 Paseo del Pueblo Sur; 505-751-0500), sample the lovely wine list, nibble on a baguette and pretend you're in France. Crepes and fondue, poulet sauce Forestiere, salmon *poche*, ratatouille and vegetable mousse top the menu. Given Taos' international following, you may hear only French spoken here. Moderate.

You could eat three meals a day in the Taos Inn's award-winning restaurant **Doc Martin's** (★) (125 Paseo del Pueblo Norte; 505-758-1977) and never get bored. Blue corn and blueberry hotcakes at breakfast make the mouth water, as do New Mexican-style onion rings and shrimp burritos for lunch. But it's dinner when the kitchen really shines. Savor the roasted pheasant breast, venison or wild mushroom and spinach lasagna and try and save room for dessert. Moderate to deluxe.

The emphasis is on fresh at the **Apple Tree** (123 Bent Street; 505-758-1900), a charming house converted to a restaurant. The Apple Tree offers innovative interpretations of old standard poultry, fish and meat dishes. Killer desserts top off the menu. Moderate.

Pizza Emergency (316 Paseo del Pueblo; 505-758-8665) has great New York style pizza and a name you won't quickly forget. They have delivery in the Taos area, but only until 10 p.m.—well before the pizza bug typically strikes. Budget.

Located on the north side of Taos Plaza, **La Cocina de Taos** (505-758-2412) specializes in authentic Northern New Mexico cuisine at affordable prices. No fancy decor—this is a true locals hangout—but hearty, home-cooked fajitas, *chile rellenos* and enchiladas. Budget.

Taos has no shortage of newsstand cafés. **Caffe Tazza** (122 Kit Carson Road; 505-758-8706) and **Dori's** (402 Paseo del Pueblo Norte; 505-758-9222) are nice places to sip espresso and munch on a sweet or just hang out and read. Budget.

For outstanding *chile rellenos*, blue-corn tortillas and other regional food in a fun and rowdy atmosphere, try the **Chile Connection** (Taos Ski Valley Road; 505-776-8787). Moderate.

Those looking for a special evening in an intimate atmosphere would be well-advised to try **Casa Cordova** (Taos Ski Area Road, Arroyo Seco; 505-776-2200) where regional food speaks with an Italian accent. R. C. Gorman prints decorate the walls, big Mexican chairs seem to suck you up when the tequila and Sangria start doing their number. Deluxe to ultra-deluxe.

After a steady diet of New Mexican food you might start yearning for something completely different. Try **Carl's French Quarter** (in the Quail Ridge Inn, Taos Ski Valley Road; 505-776-8319) for Cajun and Creole treats like scampi and oysters Rockefeller. Deluxe to ultra-deluxe.

Amid an Old World kind of atmosphere, the **Rathskeller Restaurant** (in the Hotel St. Bernard, Taos Ski Area; 505-776-2251) features beer, bratwurst and hearty sandwiches. Budget to moderate.

Seatings for nonguests are tough to come by at **St. Bernard's** (Taos Ski Area; 505-776-2251) set-menu restaurant but well worth the cajoling to enjoy a typical dinner such as rack of lamb or bouillabaisse, topped off by raspberry melba. Deluxe.

For après-ski nibbles, mosey on down the hill to **Tim's Stray Dog Cantina** (Taos Ski Valley; 505-776-2894). Quaff multiple varieties of margaritas while chowing down on Tim's rich tequila shrimp, yummy green-chili french fries and mud pie to push your cholesterol count off the Richter scale. Moderate.

ENCHANTED CIRCLE RESTAURANTS   Try fresh trout with piñon nuts or a double-decker pizza at the **Coyote Creek Café** (Route 434, Angel Fire; 505-377-3550) after you've worked up an appetite on the slopes. Budget to moderate.

The **St. James Hotel** (Route 1, Cimarron; 505-376-2664) offers everything from sandwiches to escargots in its coffee shop and dining room. Moderate.

Corny as it may sound, you won't waddle away hungry from **Texas Red's Steakhouse** (Main Street, Red River; 505-754-2964), which specializes in slabs of beef, big burgers and other hearty Western-style meals. Moderate.

TAOS AND ENCHANTED CIRCLE AREA SHOPPING

The Taos "mystique" has always lured artists and craftsmen, so expect to find lots of shops and galleries around the Plaza and surrounding streets.

Foot fetish? For a cheap deal on moccasins, stop by the **Taos Moccasin Co. Factory Outlet** (216 Paseo del Pueblo Sur; 505-751-0032). **Old Mexico Shop** (McCarty Plaza; 505-758-1133) is a traditional favorite for Indian prints and native clothing.

Find chilies, china and more at **Taos Cookery** (113 Bent Street; 505-758-5435).

Antiques and beautiful oriental rugs fill the front yard of **Patrick Dunbar** (222 Paseo del Pueblo Norte; 505-758-2511), which is interesting to visit even if you can't afford a single thing.

(Text continued on page 262.)

Colorful Cuisine

Chances are the one question you'll be asked after a New Mexico vacation is, "How was the food?" Like Cajun cooking in Louisiana or spicy Szechuan dishes in China, authentic New Mexican cooking can delight the senses as much as any scenic panorama. Odds are, long after you've left the state, your palate will still savor the flavorful (sometimes fiery) tastes of New Mexico.

Bottom line . . . New Mexican cooking is not Mexican or Tex-Mex. It is distinctive cuisine with strong roots in the state's Indian culture as adapted by Spanish and Anglo settlers. From flavors to cooking techniques, all are delicately balanced, with the result a literal feast of tastes, textures, smells and colors: green chilies, yellow cheese, blue corn.

This mélange dates back hundreds (maybe even thousands) of years. New Mexico's early inhabitants dined on rabbit and venison. But these meats were quickly replaced by beef, *chorizo* (a spicy pork sausage) and mutton after the Spanish arrived. Corn, beans, squash and nuts originated with Native Americans. Europeans brought wheat, rice, fruit, onions, garlic and grapes. From Mexico came tomatoes, avocados and chocolate.

Today's New Mexican cooking uses such unusual fruits and vegetables as jicama, chayote (or vegetable pear), *nopales* (the flat green pads of the prickly pear cactus), tomatillos (with their tart lemon flavor) and plantains. Cumin is the predominant spice, though oregano, cilantro, *epazote*, mint, cinnamon and coriander are also utilized.

Traditionalists will tell you there are four basic elements to a true New Mexican meal—chili, corn, cheese and beans. If all four aren't served, you aren't getting an authentic dinner.

Ah, yes, the chili: heart and soul of New Mexican cooking. Politics, religion, who'll win the Super Bowl, no topic generates more dispute than red versus green and hot versus mild. New Mexicans consume more chilies per capita than any other state and it's the state's second-largest cash crop. If you compared chilies to grapes, New Mexico would be the champagne capital of the world. Local experts estimate more than 35,000 tons are exported within a single year.

The chili (not to be confused with chili powder or chili in a bowl) may have existed as early as 700 B.C. Columbus found "chili" (the Aztec name for the wrinkled, fiery pods) in the West Indies in 1493 and brought

them to the New World. Pueblo Indians were growing a mild version along the banks of the Rio Grande when the Spanish arrived in the 1500s. Two centuries later, some people used red chili as a meat preservative, while others rubbed it on their gums for a toothache.

Nowadays, some still believe a hot dose of chilies will clear the sinuses. True or not, chilies are high in vitamins A and C. Most of us recognize at least a few of the many varieties—green bell pepper, *poblano* (a large, dark green chili), jalapeño, serrano and *chipotle* to name a few. Almost everyone quickly recognizes the New Mexico red chili strung in wreaths and chains called *ristras*.

Part of the nightshade family (which includes tomatoes and potatoes), chilies used before they are ripe are green. Once ripe, they're red. They can be picked and eaten in both stages. Not all chilies are "hot." The amount and variety of chili and whether it is fresh, dried or ground determines the hotness.

One of the best ways to learn all there is about New Mexican cooking is at the **Santa Fe School of Cooking** (116 West San Francisco Street, Upper Level, Plaza Mercado, Santa Fe; 505-983-4511). Here, expert chefs demonstrate the history and techniques of New Mexico cuisine. Best of all, students get to sample the finished product.

If enrolling in a two-and-a-half hour class isn't your idea of a vacation, it's at least a good idea to master a few Spanish terms for the basic dishes. For example, *carne asada* means roasted meat (though it now sometimes includes grilled meat). *Carne adovada* refers to meat marinated in red chili. Chicken in chili sauce is known as *mole*.

A traditional tamale is minced meat and red pepper rolled in corn meal, wrapped in corn husks and baked or steamed. The ever-popular *chile rellenos* refers to a large, battered, fried green chili, stuffed with either cheese, avocado, shrimp, pork, etc. *Chile con queso* is a chili and cheese pie. A side order of *frijoles* will get you a plate of pinto beans. *Sopapilla* translates to "pillow," an apt description for light, puffy fried dough served with honey. And *flan* is smooth, creamy caramel custard.

Tortillas are the "bread" of New Mexico. Usually made of white cornmeal, they come hot and fresh with almost every dish. Some cooks favor flour or blue cornmeal for preparing tortillas. And yes, blue corn is really "blue." Finally, never be embarrassed to ask questions or request your chili on the side. New Mexicans take great pride in their cooking and want you to enjoy all the flavors (and surprises) it holds.

Touristy, yes, but wonderful too, is **R. C. Gorman's Navajo Gallery** (210 Ledoux Street; 505-758-3250), where you'll find paintings and sculpture of the master's zaftig ladies.

Rod Goebel's Gallery (117 Camino de la Placitas; 505-758-2181) features interpretive portraiture, landscapes and still lifes. **The Clay and Fiber Gallery** (135 Paseo del Pueblo Norte; 505-758-8093) has beautiful bowls and clothing and pricey sculpture.

Stables Art Center (133 Paseo del Pueblo Norte; 505-758-8093) carries the work of many area artists, while the **New Directions Gallery** (204 North Plaza; 505-758-2771) specializes in contemporary art. Other galleries worthy of a visit include **Wade Gallery of Taos** (208 Paseo del Pueblo Norte; 505-758-7500), **Taos Traditions Gallery** (221 Paseo del Pueblo Norte; 505-758-0016) and **Burke Armstrong** (121 North Plaza; 505-758-9016).

Taos has great bookstores and if you're not careful, it's possible to spend a huge chunk of your sightseeing time just browsing among the tomes. A favorite is **Moby Dicken's Bookshop** (124-A Bent Street; 505-758-3050), where there are plenty of places to sit and read. A watch cat guards the door. **Brodsky Bookshop** (218 Paseo del Pueblo Norte; 505-758-9468) has some unusual and hard-to-find volumes, while the **Taos Book Shop** (122D Kit Carson Road; 505-758-3733) purports to be the oldest book shop in the state.

Taos Artisans Gallery (107-A Bent Street; 505-758-1558) is an impressive cooperative of silk and weaving. Another gem of an art cooperative is **Open Space Gallery** (103-B Taos Plaza East; 505-758-1217), where you can find plenty of handmade gifts for yourself or someone special.

Wonderful masks, ceramic birds and other colorful items from Old Mexico are found on the **Plaza at Tesoros** (110 North Plaza; 505-758-4848). Nearby **Magic Mountain Gallery** (107-A North Plaza; 505-758-9604) features contemporary ceramics, inlaid boxes, bronze sculpture and oil paintings.

Though not the sexiest name, **Buffalo Gal** (16 Bent Street; 505-758-7571) does have gorgeous and exotic clothing for women without too outrageous prices. The same owners run a trendy store called **10 1/2 for Men** (109 Bent Street; 505-758-1226) featuring casual and out-on-the-town duds for dudes.

LaLana Wools (136 Paseo Norte; 505-758-9631) uses fine natural fibers to make sweaters and coats, yarns and jackets. **Taos Mountain Outfitters** (114 South Plaza; 505-758-9292) sells garb and equipment for your treks into the high country.

Nativa (215 Paseo del Pueblo Norte; 505-758-1339) has contemporary clothing at reasonable prices.

Fabrique Unique (Taos Ski Valley Road, El Prado; 505-776-1642) sells luscious silks and hand-made paper clocks.

TAOS AND ENCHANTED CIRCLE AREA NIGHTLIFE

Movies, live theater and visiting performers use the **Taos Community Auditorium** (Paseo del Pueblo Norte; 505-758-4677).

To taste the local flavor, swing by the **Taos Inn's Adobe Bar** (125 Paseo del Pueblo Norte; 505-758-2233) to catch up on local gossip or to take a gander at the recurring local artists' series.

Hot times on weekends are had at the **Sagebrush Inn Bar** (1508 Paseo del Pueblo Sur; 505-758-2254). Live music can frequently be heard at the **Ramada Inn** (615 Paseo del Pueblo Sur; 505-758-2900).

A true sports bar, the **Chile Connection** (Ski Valley Road; 505-776-8787) has a lively atmosphere and boisterous crowd.

After a long day of skiing, mustering enough energy for a drink can sometimes be more than you can handle. If you want to go out in the Taos Ski Valley, check out the different flavored margaritas at **Tim's Stray Dog Cantina** (Taos Ski Valley; 505-776-2894). The **Thunderbird Lodge** (Taos Ski Valley; 505-776-2280) is another good bet.

On the road back to Taos, **Casa Cordova** (Ski Valley Road, Arroyo Seco; 505-776-2200) is a natural stop for après ski drinks.

ENCHANTED CIRCLE NIGHTLIFE   Over the mountain in Red River, stop in at **Bull o' the Woods** saloon (Main Street; 505-754-2593), the **Motherlode** (West Main Street; 505-754-6240) or the **Red River Mining Company** (Main and Mallette streets; 505-754-2488). Melodramas are staged in season at the **Red River Inn** (Main Street; 505-754-2930).

TAOS AND ENCHANTED CIRCLE AREA PARKS

Orilla Verde Recreation Area (formerly Rio Grande Gorge State Park)—Situated on the banks of an ultrascenic stretch of the Rio Grande River in the Wild River Recreation Area, the park is popular for day outings and weekend camping. The park is renowned for its trout fishing.

Facilities: Picnic areas, restrooms; information, 505-758-8851.

Camping: There are four campgrounds; $7 per night.

Getting there: Located on Route 68, 16 miles southwest of Taos.

Cimarron Canyon State Park—Granite formations tower above a sparkling stream where brown and rainbow trout crowd the waters and wildlife congregates. Rock-climbing is permitted within these environs and there are some hiking trails; however, the most popular park activity is fishing.

Facilities: Picnic area, restrooms; information, 505-377-6271.

Camping: There are 104 developed sites ($7 per night) and 9 primitive sites ($6 per night).

Getting there: Located on Route 64, eight miles east of Eagle Nest.

Los Alamos Area

Los Alamos was developed in the early 1940s for scientists and their families working on the highly secretive Manhattan Project, a project that would change the course of history. Isolated in the high-altitude Jemez Mountains, the U.S. government chose a town that housed the private Los Alamos Ranch School for Boys and little else. Amid spectacular scenery of dense forest and Indian pueblos, with an extinct volcano forming a natural barrier on the other side, the school was closed and the Manhattan Project set underway.

Bright young minds were imported to create the first atomic bombs—nicknamed "Fat Man" and "Little Boy"—that eventually helped end World War II. But alas, the inventors were forced to live behind a wall of secrecy where passes were needed for leaves and mail was subject to a censor's pen. It was physicist Robert Oppenheimer, architect of the atomic bomb, who once said: "The notion of disappearing into the New Mexico desert for an indeterminate period disturbed a good many scientists."

Los Alamos National Laboratory remains the major presence in the city and accounts for the lion's share of Los Alamos' jobs. The Department of Energy still owns the laboratory that employs more than 7000 for national security studies, metallurgy, genetics information, geothermal and solar research. Los Alamos, obviously, still attracts the intelligencia.

No matter how you feel about the introduction of the atomic age, a visit to the **Bradbury Museum** (★) (Diamond Drive, Los Alamos; 505-667-4444) is a must. Three dozen exhibits are interspersed with photographs, a timeline, films and letters like the one from Albert Einstein to President Roosevelt. The Robert Oppenheimer story is detailed and fission and fusion are discussed in layman's terms. The museum is alternatingly frightening and enlightening.

To understand a little more about this unique town, be sure to stop at the **Los Alamos County Historical Museum** (1921 Juniper Street; 505-662-6272) which covers pre-bomb history dating back to the 13th century, artifacts from the defunct boy's school and items from the World War II era.

Adjacent to the historical museum is a 1928 log building that's home to the **Los Alamos Chamber of Commerce** and **Fuller Lodge Art Center** (2132 Central Avenue; 505-662-9331). This national landmark, which once was the recreation hall for ranch school students, hosts exhibits by native and visiting artists.

Nearby is the gleaming **Larry R. Walkup Aquatic Center** (2760 Canyon Road, Los Alamos; 505-662-8170), the highest-altitude indoor Olympic-size pool in the United States, serving athletes and recreational swimmers who enjoy a splash.

Los Alamos is warming (no pun intended) to visitors after decades as an ultra-insular community. The bomb was invented under a veil of secrecy, where even in Santa Fe (about 35 miles away) people didn't know what was going on "up there."

The earth is hot around Los Alamos less because of radioactivity than its volcanic history, and hot springs bubble forth to the delight of those who enjoy a refreshing and relaxing dip. In their natural state are the **Spence Hot Springs** (Route 4, about seven miles north of Jemez Springs) and **Battleship Rock Warm Springs** (Route 4, about five miles north of Jemez Springs). Short, well-trod foot paths take off from the respective parking areas.

At the more developed **Jemez Springs Bathhouse and Pool** (Route 4 near town of Jemez Springs, about 40 miles southwest of Los Alamos; admission) nudity is not an option.

One mile north of the city of Jemez Springs is the **Jemez State Monument** (Route 4, Jemez Springs; 505-829-3530; admission). The monument, officially recognized in 1935, honors pre-Columbian Indian ruins and the remains of a Spanish mission, the Church of San Jose, that was built in the 17th century. A tiny museum explains some of the Jemez tradition.

Valle Grande (Route 502, 14 miles west of Los Alamos) was created about a million years ago when a volcano's summit seemingly crumbled and spewed ash as far east as Kansas. It left a broad basin called a caldera that stretches about 15 miles in diameter. It is thought this caldera is the largest of its kind.

An estimated 7000 archeological sites surround the Los Alamos area but really this is just a rough guess. Centuries before white men arrived, the Anasazi Indians settled in the Jemez Mountains for a time period that's thought to be between 1100 to 1580 A.D. The Pajarito Plateau, the eastern flank of the Jemez hills, was named for the prehistoric settlements that existed here so long ago.

Bandelier National Monument (Route 4, Los Alamos; 505-672-3861; admission) encompasses 32,737 acres of scenic wilderness. The Anasazi Indians, who left symbols on the canyon walls, were thought to have farmed this comparatively lush area in Frijoles Canyon. Most of Bandelier, named for ethnologist Adolph Bandelier, is wild backcountry, a riparian oasis. Steep cliffs mean strenuous climbs are required to observe many of the ruins.

Start your perusal of the park at the Visitor Center with a ten-minute slide show of "The Bandelier Story." A self-guided and short Ruins Trail takes off from the Visitor Center near the Frijoles River and passes the impressive circular ruin known as **Tyuonyi** (meaning meeting place) thought to once stand three stories high. Its single entrance has led to speculation that this large and impressive room was used as a lookout for enemies.

Behind Tyuonyi is **Talus House,** which amazingly still has standing stone walls. The trail continues to **Long House Ruin,** nestled under a cliff that's suspected to have been the largest settlement at Bandelier. It's full of ancient pictographs and petroglyphs that tell many stories.

By scrambling up a cliff face and climbing several somewhat scary ladders, you can continue on the trail to the **Ceremonial Cave** which affords a great overall view of the ruins. Backtracking to the Visitor Center, hike down Frijoles Canyon across the river to the Upper Waterfall and then view yet another waterfall about a half-mile down the path.

Bandelier has miles of maintained hiking trails in a wilderness area known as **Tsankawi,** which are in a separate section of the monument. Largely unexcavated, a trail to the top of the mesa passes by some interesting Anasazi drawings. North of Tsankawi a few miles are the **Otowi ruins,** where stair-step rooms and cliff dwellings have been partially unearthed.

If your appetite is whet for ruins, then drive a few dozen miles northwest to the **Puye Cliff Dwellings** (Route 5, 11 miles west of Route 30, Española; 505-753-7326; admission), a fascinating little ancient city. Once inhabited by up to 1500 people between the years of 1250 to 1577, Puye is currently operated by the neighboring Santa Clara Pueblo, who are probably descendants of the original settlers. The Santa Clara hold a celebration here each summer.

The excavated ruins of the ancient apartment-like complexes are evident from miles away as you approach the site. Upon arrival, the visitor has two choices for exploring, either the Cliff Trail or the Mesa-Top Trail.

The **Cliff Trail** takes off from above the parking lot and offers the visitor a chance to walk through cave-like rooms and past petroglyphs and the outlines of buried masonry dwellings for over a mile along the south face of the Puye mesa. Rock inscriptions of spirals and masks, serpents and humans are carved along the caves and cliffs. You'll also see outlines of buried masonry dwellings that are also known as talus rooms. Stepping places and hand grips lead to kivas and the grand Community House from the cave, or cavate, rooms below. Near the base of the cliffs are two subterranean ceremonial chambers called kivas. But there may be more kivas and other treasures lying undiscovered, well-beneath the earth's surface.

It's possible to drive up to the second trail, appropriately called **Mesa-Top,** by following the road past the Visitor Center. From there, the Puye's 740-room pueblo, with its restored room, can be examined. Historians imagine the structure loomed as high as three stories tall. When perusing the building remains, stop and take a look around at the splendid views of the Rio Grande region. Puye villagers of so long ago likely enjoyed a similar panorama.

After exploring the cliff dwellings, drive six miles farther west to a nice place for a picnic or fishing stop, gorgeous Santa Clara Canyon.

Returning to Route 30 and continuing north toward the city of Española takes one to the **Santa Clara Pueblo** (Route 30, Española; 505-753-7330), which is known for its highly polished black and red pottery. A stream, several lakes and picnic areas are open to the public. There is no admission fee but paid permits are required for photography and filming.

Passing through **Española**, founded in the 1880s as a railroad stop, (although it was discovered by the Europeans as early as 1598) you'll notice the community remains true to its Hispanic heritage in everything from culture to churches. Although it has evolved into a bedroom community for Santa Fe, Española's claim to fame has always been as the "Low Rider Capital" of the world. Cruise Main Street on a Saturday night to see the spiffed-up vehicles and macho young men.

Turning west on Route 84 takes the traveler through the ink spot of a town called Hernandez. Stop at **Romero's Fruit Stand** (Junction of Routes 84 and 285; 505-753-4189) to pick up authentic chili *ristras*, local honey and tart apple cider before continuing your trip north.

The scenery of sage-filled hills and open vistas will probably start to look more and more familiar as you continue north on Route 84. This is Georgia O'Keeffe country with its blue-bird skies, yucca plants and red-brushed hills in the high desert. The muddy, red-tinged Rio Chama sidles along the highway.

Abiquiu, the small town at the river's bend which was settled in the 1700s on the site on an Indian ruin, was O'Keeffe's home for many years. When steep, pastel-colored cliffs, part of the shifting formation called the Gallina Fault Zone, come into view, you'll know you're nearing the **Ghost Ranch Living Museum** (★) (Route 84, Abiquiu; 505-685-4312; admission). Subtle environmental education is a theme at this unique learning center. Operated by the U.S. Forest Service, the living museum's short walking tours showcase the native plants. The outdoor zoo of wildlife is just plain fun. Those who object to the caging of animals will be pleased to know that only the orphaned, injured and zoo-born remain in captivity. A new Rio Chama Information Center at the museum provides current and useful facts on the river.

A handful of miles north again on Route 84 takes you to the trails and natural wonder of Echo Canyon Amphitheater. Years of erosion have hollowed out this gargantuan sandstone theater. A picnic area and campground is available.

Los Ojos (Route 84, ten miles south of Chama) is the site of the **Tierra Wools Cooperative Showroom** (Route 84; 505-588-7231) where artisans try to revitalize the once thriving native tradition. The town was founded about 1860 and plenty of original houses remain standing. The architecture combines traditional adobe construction with turn-of-the-century pitched roofs, Victorian influences and gingerbread trim.

The **Brazos Cliffs** abut the skyline south of Chama (Route 512, seven miles east of Route 84) and for about three weeks each spring during snow runoff time, a waterfall cascades off 11,288-foot Brazos Peak.

The tribal members residing on the unspoiled Jicarilla Apache reservation open their lands up for hunting, fishing and camping on the mountain lakes. The Jicarilla's commercial center of **Dulce** (Route 64, 25 miles west of Chama) is where you'll find a tribal arts and crafts shop and a small museum.

At an altitude of 8000 feet, **Chama**, located in the southern San Juan Mountains just nine miles from the Colorado border, is becoming more and more popular as a recreation area. Summer is still high time but with over 300 miles of trails in the Carson National Forest, snowmobile safaris are common in the little town that bills itself as the snowmobile capital of the Southwest.

Tourism, ranching and lumbering are the lifeblood of Chama, which experienced its first population explosion in the early 1880s with the building of the railroad. The train served mining camps that were digging into this rich region. Records show those were wild times as saloons and gambling halls lined the main drag.

Like most Wild West towns, Chama had its bust, too. But in 1974, the governments of Colorado and New Mexico decided to purchase 64 miles of rail and restore the coal-fired steam train as a tourist attraction. The "double-header" (twin engine) historic narrow gauge **Cumbres and Toltec Scenic Railroad** (★) (Main Street, Chama; 505-756-2151; admission) leaves Chama daily between Memorial Day weekend and mid-October, to chug over hill and dale, through meadows and past groves of piñon, oak, aspen and juniper, nestling against the river's edge, fording a trestle and hugging high passes.

The train makes a one-way, 64-mile trip to Antonito, Colorado, (you ride a van back) or shorter round-trips to Osier, Colorado. It travels through the valley of Los Pinos River that bursts with iris and sunflower and Indian paintbrush. The steam train moves along up the four percent grade of 10,015-foot Cumbres Pass and burrows through two tunnels to the Toltec Gorge.

Autumn is a nice time to see the aspen trees alight the forest. No matter what the season, the ride may be chilly and snow always a possibility. It's not a ride for anyone in a hurry. The one-way, 64-mile trip takes six-and-a-half hours.

LOS ALAMOS AREA HOTELS

They'll loan you golf clubs or bikes, recommend hikes and heap up plenty of free advice at the **Orange Street Inn** (3496 Orange Street, Los Alamos; 505-662-2651) bed and breakfast, a quiet alternative to Los Alamos' hotel scene. The suburban-looking house—one almost expects to see June Cleaver at the door—is bedecked with antiques, quilts and large wooden beds. Four of the six rooms have shared baths. Not only is the morning meal included, but the fridge is open for frozen yogurt during the day and wine in the afternoon. Budget to moderate.

At the recently renovated **Los Alamos Inn** (2201 Trinity Drive, Los Alamos; 505-662-7211), the 115 rooms are bright and pleasant with pastel spreads and art class-variety paintings. The Inn is located in a wooded area of town. Sitting by the outdoor swimming pool and sauna gives one the feeling they are miles away from the city. Moderate.

A dwelling of the same variety is the **Hilltop House Hotel** (Trinity Drive and Central Street, Los Alamos; 505-662-2441) which caters to the business person with on-site secretarial services and special amenities for female travelers. Mini-suites and executive suites with full kitchens are available as well. Moderate.

Train buffs holing up in the Chama area for a few days would be wise to make their nest at the homey **Demasters Lodge** (★) (Route 17, Chama; 505-756-2942). Five enormous rooms with private baths are clean as a whistle and appointed with down quilts that help cut the chill of Chama's nights. During hunting season or winter, a huge fire roars in the shared family room that's watched over by a den of animals—bear, elk and mountain lion—bagged locally. Hearty, made-to-order country breakfasts are included in the room price. Moderate.

Just a few steps out the back door from the **Oso Ranch and Lodge** (Seco Drive, Chama; 505-756-2954) bed and breakfast is the Chama River and ranch lakes for trout fishing. The log lodge has a real outdoorsy feel, from the leather and pine bedrooms to the free roaming goats on property. Guests can choose from lodging only or full meal plans. Moderate.

LOS ALAMOS AREA RESTAURANTS

Satisfy all kinds of taste demands by dining at **De Colores** (820 Trinity Drive, Los Alamos; 505-662-6285) where the menu features native cuisine, mesquite grilled chicken and steaks. Moderate.

Seafood and veggie dishes are offered along with Italian cuisine at **Boccacio's** (4244 Diamond Drive, Los Alamos; 505-662-7204). Start your meal with homemade bread and soups. Moderate.

For lighter fare like croissants, sandwiches, pastries and espresso, pay a visit to **Café Allegro** (800 Trinity Drive, Los Alamos; 505-662-4040). Budget.

Let your nose lead you: The spicy, peppery smell of native cuisine grabs you upon entering **Vera's Mexican Kitchen** (Route 84, Chama; 505-756-2557) where rellenos, burritos and enchiladas await. Budget.

Standard American cuisine and, best of all, a salad bar are offered at the **High Country Restaurant and Store** (Route 84, Chama; 505-756-2384). Budget to moderate.

LOS ALAMOS AREA SHOPPING

Attempting to revitalize the timeless art of weaving are the wool growers and craftspersons of **Mountaineer At Tierra Wools** (Route 84, Los Ojos; 505-588-7231) who gladly offer their wares through a cooperative showroom.

The **Narrow Gauge Gift Shop** (Main Street, Chama; 505-756-2963) sells engineers caps (naturally!) and T-shirts at fair prices.

LOS ALAMOS AREA NIGHTLIFE

They roll up the sidewalks early in Los Alamos; a big night out may consist of a brew at the corner pub (which are admittedly few and far between).

Chama has melodramas during the summer and winter season on weekends with a gun show and 100 year-old soap opera at **Foster's Hotel, Restaurant and Saloon** (4th and Terrace streets; 505-756-2296). The historic hotel, where you'll want to stop for a beverage on any other night, has been in business since 1881.

LOS ALAMOS AREA PARKS

Bandelier National Monument—Nestled in the Jemez Mountains are cave and cliff dwellings and Pueblo ruins abandoned about 800 years ago by Indians thought to be hunters and farmers. A system of ancient volcanic craters located within Bandelier's 36,971 acres is believed to be the largest of its kind in the world. Hiking trails lead the curious visitor around this secret honeycombed world.

Facilities: Visitor center, food service, general store; information, 505-672-3861.

Camping: There are 94 sites during the summer, about 30 sites during the off-season; $6 per night for individual sites, $10 per night at group sites. Closed December through February.

Getting there: Take Route 502 to Route 4, about 15 miles south of Los Alamos.

Fenton Lake State Park (★)—Sheltered in a ponderosa pine forest below 1000-foot red cliffs, the park surrounds a 28-acre trout lake that allows no motorboats or swimming. In the winter, nordic skiers enjoy gliding around the frozen lake through deep snow. Campsites fill early in the summer, in spite of the fact that Fenton Lake's 7600-foot elevation makes for cool, cool nights.

Facilities: Picnic areas, restrooms, boat access; information, 505-829-3630.

Camping: Permitted in the 30 sites; $7 per night.

Getting there: Take Route 4 to Route 126, 45 miles west of Los Alamos.

Abiquiu Reservoir—An Army Corps of Engineering project, all water sports are permitted in this 4000-acre reservoir that was created by damming the Rio Chama. The colors of the day, especially sunsets, are splendid in the wonderfully pastel-colored country that artist Georgia O'Keeffe loved so much.

Facilities: Boat ramp, picnic areas; information, 505-766-2738.

Camping: There are 63 sites; $4 per night ($2 for tent-only sites).

Getting there: On Route 84, seven miles northwest of Abiquiu.

El Vado Lake State Park—This is a beautiful mountain lake that's ideal for waterskiing and where fishing is popular year-round. A fishing derby is held here in the summer; during the winter ice fishermen head for the frozen waters.

Facilities: Picnic areas, boat ramp, marina and playgrounds; information through State Parks Department, 505-827-7465.

Camping: There are 43 developed sites ($7 per night) and 41 primitive sites ($6 per night).

Getting there: On Route 112, 14 miles southwest of Tierra Amarilla.

Four Corners Area

Farmington is the natural base camp for sightseeing in the Four Corners area, the sole hub in the continental United States where four states—New Mexico, Arizona, Colorado and Utah—meet. Three rivers, the San Juan, Animas and LaPlata also converge here, dispelling the notion this is dry, dusty desert country. In fact, Farmington was founded on farming, hence its name, although the still laid-back town now has industry and mining at its financial base.

Start your sightseeing tour of the region on Route 550, about 30 miles west of Farmington at the **Shiprock** pinnacle, which the Native Americans call a "rock with wings." Solidified lava and igneous rock comprise this neck of a volcano, which can be seen by air from more than 100 miles away. The towering Shiprock rises from a great stretch of nothing but sand and rock. The site has a roadside picnic area available, but little else in the way of services.

Get your fill of literature at the very helpful **Farmington Visitor Center** (203 West Main Street; 505-326-7602) and peruse your options at **Vietnam Veterans Memorial Park** (Main and Orchard streets) in the center of downtown.

For an overview of the area's cultural and outdoor offerings, check in at the **Farmington Museum** (302 North Orchard Street; 505-599-1066), where there's a replica of how New Mexico's fifth largest city looked during frontier days, a natural history exhibit and a children's gallery.

The **Kokopelli Center** (615 West Main Street; 505-327-0675; admission) is wholly committed to the area's archaeology and features tours, exhibits and Native American arts and crafts.

Meanwhile, the **McKee Carson Collector's Memorial Museum** (309 West Main Street; 505-327-1347; admission) is a privately funded international cultural museum that is jam-packed with fossils and artifacts.

Not all of Farmington's sights are found indoors.The season at **San Jose Race Track** (593 Route 64; 505-326-4551) runs weekends from spring through Labor Day. Thoroughbreds and quarter horses compete here. At San Jose there's also the opportunity for inter-track wagering with four other regional parks.

Near the race track you'll find **Salmon Ruin** (975 Route 64, Farmington; 505-632-2013) which has remains from an 11th century pueblo, including a large kiva, that were built by the Chaco Indians. Ongoing excavation of the site, which was mysteriously abandoned after only 60 years of occupation, continues to this day.

At Salmon Ruin is **Heritage Park,** a re-creation of habitation units representing man's occupation in the San Juan Valley, from sand dune campgrounds to tepees and hogans. The on-site museum houses regional artifacts, too.

Less than 30 minutes' drive north of Farmington on Route 550 brings the traveler to the charming town of **Aztec,** with its ancient Indian ruins and turn-of-the-century buildings. Aztec's modern-day renaissance took place in the 1890s and Victorian influences and flavor of that era live on. Evidence is found in the neighborhoods surrounding downtown.

Your first stop on a whirlwind tour of Aztec should begin at the old City Hall where the **Aztec Museum** (125 North Main Street; 505-334-9829; admission) is filled with all kinds of bric-a-brac, like minerals and rocks, pioneer home settings, Victorian fashions, sleighs and buggies, tools used by the early settlers and an oilfield exhibit.

Strolling along Aztec's Main Street, you'll see plenty of turn-of-the-century buildings, including the landmark **Odd Fellows Hall** (107 South Main Street) and one which houses the **Aztec Resident Hotel** (300 South Main Street). On a side street is the **Presbyterian Church** (201 North Church Street) which was built of adobe brick in 1889.

Another building worth a look-see is the **Denver & Rio Grande Western Railway Depot** (408 North Rio Grande). No tracks remain on the site of this commercial building turned residence, but the 1915 structure is a classic reminder of the railway's heyday.

Aztec's buildings seem perfectly modern in comparison to the ancient **Aztec Ruins National Monument** (Aztec Ruins Road; 505-334-6174; admission), a major prehistoric settlement chock full of 12th century pueblo ruins and a restored great kiva. The Chaco civilization to the south and the Mesa Verde settlement to the north, probably both influenced Aztec's development. But despite its misleading name, no Aztec Indians ever inhabited this area.

A visit to Aztec is a must, not only because of its wonders but it's sheer accessibility. First take the self-guided trail that begins outside the visitor center. You'll come upon the **West Ruin** and the magnificently restored **Great Kiva**. West Ruin could be compared to a present-day apartment building because as many as 300 people may have lived there at a single time.

The kiva, or underground chamber that's traditionally used for religious ceremonies, was carefully constructed of sandstone blocks from materials that were hand carried from quarries miles away. Most unusual is a line of green sandstone on one outer wall. Few doors and openings exist, probably so interlopers would have a harder time of breaking into this main building. The kiva was excavated in 1921 and reconstructed about a dozen years later.

The open plaza area was the center of daily life in Aztec. Wandering north out of the main ruins takes you to the **Hubbard Site**, a kiva that's unique in that it has three concentric circular walls. It's presumed this building was used for religious ceremonies. Another tri-walled kiva, largely unexcavated, exists in a nearby mound.

Off the beaten path is the **East Ruin** and its annex, thought to be the second and later civilization at Aztec. Both are largely unexcavated. Adjacent to the Aztec ruins is a shady, tree-lined park, a nice place for a snack or repose after wandering through the ancient playground.

To return to ruin sightings like desolate Angel Peak, you must backtrack to Aztec or take Route 64 east to Bloomfield and then turn south on Route 44 for 17 miles to the turnoff.

Angel Peak is a multimillion-year-old geologic formation and sacred dwelling place to the Navajos. A five-mile road along the rim allows great views of the pastel-hued mesas and buttes. Camping and picnicking are allowed, though no water is available. After Angel Peak, continue on to Chaco Canyon, the epicenter of Anasazi life, but first consider stopping at the **Navajo trading posts** along Route 44 that definitely have something to offer, including jewelry, rugs, necessary supplies and plenty of local gossip.

There are two roads, Route 57 and Route 45, leading from Route 44 to **Chaco Culture National Historic Park** (★) (505-988-6716); both are rough going. A debate continues on whether the road should be upgraded, but so far, those who believe Chaco remains in better shape because of its inaccessibility, have prevailed. Unless you're driving an expensive sports car or the road is slippery from rain, it's worth the bumpy ride to view 13 major ruins and the remains of a culture suspected to have begun in Chaco around 900 A.D.

The fascinating civilization of 1000 years ago, with its developed road and city network, has left traces of advanced art forms like pottery and weaving in its wake. The Chaco Anasazi were farmers who probably fled the drought-stricken area in the 13th century. Chaco is considered to be the center of Anasazi culture—the road network tells us that—and religious ceremony because of all the kivas left behind. Site excavation began in the late 1890s and continues today through the University of New Mexico's Chaco Research Institute.

Park rangers conduct informational walks through Chaco Canyon, or you can grab a map from the visitor's center and chart your own path through this eerily-silent land. Self-guided trails are found at Pueblo Bonito, Chetro Ketl and Casa Rinconada.

Closest to the visitor center is the partially excavated **Una Vida** ruin, with its five kivas and 150 rooms. Because it was built on a mound, Una Vida appears higher than it actually is. Petroglyphs and remains from hogans huddle in the surrounding rock. From the paved park road, there is the **Hungo Pavi** ruin, an easy trek from the car. Farther down the road is **Chetro Ketl**. With its estimated 500 rooms and 16 kivas it was one of the largest Chacoan villages. Chetro Ketl's expansive plaza section is thought to be typical of great houses from this time.

A short jaunt in the other direction from the same trailhead brings you to the amazing **Pueblo Bonito**, which was probably the heart and soul of Chaco. The four-story, stone masonry complex is obviously the product of painstaking craftsmanship. Consider it to have been the New York City of its day with multiple rooms and kivas crammed into a relatively tight space.

Pueblo del Arroyo, a D-shaped, high-standing house, with its 280 rooms and 20 kivas, is found nearby along the paved road. **Kin Kletso** was built in two stages and the pueblo had 100 rooms and five kivas. It may have risen as high as three stories. Take the trail that begins here to the prehistoric **Jackson Stairs**, one of the more impressive stairways in the Anasazi world, and try to figure out the farming terraces of the Anasazi.

Past Kin Kletso is Casa Chiquita, where the hike to the unexcavated great house of **Peñasco Blanco** from central canyon is well-worth the effort. On the south side of paved park road is **Casa Rinconada**, one of the largest kivas in the Southwest. A trail that begins here winds to the South Mesa and the seven-rooms strong great house of **Tsin Kletsin**.

The more adventurous and archeological-minded can wander in search of what are called "outlier" sites of Chaco Canyon like Pueblo Pintado and Kin Ya-ah. Free backcountry permits are required before setting out and directions are available from the visitor center.

FOUR CORNERS AREA HOTELS

Reflecting the simplicity of lifestyle and slower pace of the region's people, the lodging choices in the Four Corners region are characterized by their cleanliness and efficiency, without a lot of fuss.

Cast iron sculptures honoring the "ancient ones," decorate the walls of the newly remodeled pink-hued rooms at the **Anasazi Inn** (903 West Main Street, Farmington; 505-325-4564). Handsome quilt prints in the Southwestern scheme and spotless bathrooms are reason enough to try this centrally located lodge. Moderate.

If bigger is better, then **Best Western the Inn** (700 Scott Avenue, Farmington; 505-327-5221) has something over its chain competitors on the same street. Extra large rooms are great for families and help give The Inn a leg up. A sizeable indoor pool in a tropical setting almost makes you forget this is desert country. Moderate.

With just 34 rooms, the **Farmington Lodge** (1510 West Main Street, Farmington; 505-325-0233) falls into the small, no frills category. Most of the well-maintained rooms have refrigerators; a heated pool operates during the summer. Budget.

Its location on a busy highway is definitely a drawback, but you can shut out most of the world's noise in the tidy rooms of the **Enchantment Lodge** (1800 West Aztec Boulevard, Aztec; 505-334-6143). Budget to moderate.

Most visitors come to Aztec for the mysterious ruins. But a visit to its historic Main Street is well worth your time. Smack in the middle of the main drag is the **Aztec Resident Hotel** (300 South Main Street; 505-334-3452). Built around 1905, the woodsy rooms—some with partial kitchens, others with kitchenettes—are large enough for multiday living. Weekly rates are a bargain. While this palace of funk is not for everyone, it is a good place to hang your hat if you plan on thoroughly exploring the Four Corners. Budget.

On the edge of the road leading to the mysterious Chaco Canyon ruins is a welcome respite from the dust and heat. The **Chaco Inn at the Post** (★) (Route 44, Nageezi; 505-632-3646), a bed and breakfast, promotes a family-style atmosphere—the innkeepers live on the premises and pride themselves in keeping the guests well-satiated. Rooms are quaint, with clean lines and wooden floors. In the shared space, guests can use a pool table, if there's time away from sightseeing. Moderate.

FOUR CORNERS AREA RESTAURANTS

Spinach and feta cheese croissants that come piping hot out of the oven, raspberry granola bars and multigrain breads are a few of the healthy, homemade delectables found at **Something Special Bakery & Tea Room (★)** (116 North Auburn Avenue, Farmington; 505-325-8183). It's open for breakfast and lunch. Budget.

Among the standard family restaurants offering wholesome "American cuisine" that dot downtown Farmington, **TJ's Downtown Diner** (119 East Main Street; 505-327-5027) is just a little bit better. Budget.

How hot do you like your green chili? For authentic Mexican cuisine, try the **El Charro Café** (737 West Main Street, Farmington; 505-327-2464) or the **Los Rios Café** (915 Farmington Avenue, Farmington; 505-325-5699). Budget to moderate.

While the name suggests a trip back to merry old England, the menu is closer to south-of-the-border. Still, **Chelsea's London Pub** (4601 East Main Street, Farmington; 505-327-9644) is a nice place for an ale and sandwich, steak or enchilada. Sorry, no kidney pie. Moderate.

A lunch buffet brings in local nine-to-fivers, but specialties such as Peking duck and sweet and sour pork are favored by diners frequenting the **China House** (104 South Main Street, Aztec; 505-334-8838).

FOUR CORNERS AREA SHOPPING

Try the **Foutz Trading Co.** (Route 550, Shiprock; 505-368-5790) for splendid Navajo and Hopi arts and crafts such as silver jewelry, weaving supplies and beaded barrettes.

After you've been on the road for awhile and need some "herbal fitness," you might want to stop in at **Herbs and Stuff** (6510 East Main Street, Farmington; 505-327-3205) and pick up natural remedies, vitamins and supplements for all that ails you.

Aztec-made ceramics, earrings and old and new goodies are found at **Gifts of the West** (300 West Chaco, Aztec; 505-334-1094).

FOUR CORNERS AREA NIGHTLIFE

Farmington is not exactly a late night town. But if you want to go out and hear some live music, check out the **Top Deck Bar** (515 East Main Street; 505-327-7385) for country music and the **Lariat** (1835 East Main Street; 505-327-9193) for rock bands.

The **San Juan Stage Company** holds court at the Totah Theatre (317 West Main Street, Farmington; 505-327-7477) for a six-play season.

A lively and colorful musical drama, "Anasazi, the Ancient Ones," is performed each summer at the **Lions Wilderness Park Amphitheater** (College Boulevard, Farmington; 505-326-7602).

FOUR CORNERS AREA PARKS

Navajo Lake State Park—New Mexico's largest lake offers boating, fishing, swimming and even scuba diving fun from three recreation areas—Pine, Sims Mesa and the San Juan River. Navajo Lake's sparkling waters and nearly 200 miles of shoreline is chock full of cold and warm water species of game fish, including trophy trout, catfish, pike and bass.

Facilities: Visitor center, boat ramps, marinas, picnic sites; information, 505-632-2278.

Camping: There are 178 sites at Pine (including 48 hookups), 46 at Sims Mesa (including nine hookups) and 47 at San Juan River. Fees are $7 per night for standard sites, $11 per night for electrical hookups and $13 per night for full hookups.

Getting there: Take Route 173 to Route 511, 23 miles east of Aztec.

Angel Peak National Recreation Site—A heavenly looking 40-million year-old geologic formation appears to be suspended within a lovely colored canyon. The five-mile-long road around the canyon rim offers fine vistas of the buttes and badlands in this land of the "sacred ones."

Facilities: Picnic tables, parking lot; information, 505-327-5344.

Camping: There are eight sites; no water.

Getting there: Take Route 44 to Angel Peak turnoff, about 19 miles southeast of Bloomfield.

Bisti Wilderness Area—Nearly 4000 acres of unusual eroded shale, clay and sandstone spires, mesas and sculpted rock that defy description were naturally sculpted in this former inland sea. Large reptiles and mammals were thought to walk these lands about 70 million years ago; fossils and petrified wood are all that remain in the desolate area of badlands. No developed trails or signs mar this protected wilderness.

Facilities: None; information, 505-327-5344.

Camping: Primitive camping allowed; no water.

Getting there: Located on Route 371, 36 miles south of Farmington.

Chaco Culture National Historical Park (★)—Prehistoric life existed grandly in this high desert settlement as evidenced by the most amazing ancient buildings and art forms in the region. An intricate highway system, irrigation ditches and 13 great house ruins have led archaeologists to speculate that at one time Chaco was a center for the Anasazi civilization. Chaco Canyon has remained in a comparatively pristine state largely because ac-

278 Northern New Mexico

cess is difficult on rutted dirt roads. Visitors must come fully prepared with food, water and gas because on-site services are virtually non-existent.

Facilities: Visitor center, restrooms; information, 505-988-6716.

Camping: Campers in Chaco Canyon must come equipped with plenty of provisions, especially water. The Gallo campground is located about one mile east of the visitor center. There are 64 sites; $5 per night.

Getting there: Located 54 miles south of Bloomfield via Route 44 and Route 57.

The Sporting Life

HORSEBACK RIDING

Trail rides, lessons and outfitting are available through: **B Bar C Training & Boarding Stables** (Route 10, Santa Fe; 505-471-3331), **Bishop's Lodge** (Bishop's Lodge Road, Santa Fe; 505-983-6377), **Camel Rock Ranch** (Route 285, Tesuque; 505-986-0408), **Mountain Mama** (Santa Fe; 505-986-1924), **Turquoise Trail** (Rocking S Ranch, Santa Fe; 505-438-7333), **Enchanted Journeys** (Mineral Hill Road, Las Vegas; 505-425-3324) and **The Panavista Equestrian Centre** (Las Vegas; 505-425-6190).

Ride with the Native Americans on the Great Spirit's property at the **Taos Indian Horse Ranch** (1 Miller Road, Taos Pueblo; 505-758-3212). Also try **Shadow Mountain Guest Ranch** (Taos Canyon Road, Taos; 505-758-7732) for horse riding in the Sangre de Cristo Mountains. Trail rides and pack trips can be taken through the **Llano Bonito Ranch** (129 Upper Llano Road, Peñasco; 505-587-2636), **Roadrunner Horseback Tours** (Route 434, Angel Fire; 505-377-6416) and **Blue Skies Outfitters & Guide Service** (Tenderfoot Trail, Red River; 505-754-2518). **Round Barn Ranch** offers trail rides and archeological horseback tours (Route 285, Ojo Caliente; 505-583-2233).

Get picked up at a train stop with horses and camp for a day or two. Hang out in a high meadow camp for as long as you like. Take a pack trip in the "red rim country" and rent an entire lodge, Chavez Creek, in the wilderness through **Western Outdoor Adventures** (Main Street, Chama; 505-756-2194). For day trips, fishing excursions and pack trips try **S/D Stables** (Chama; 505-588-7225).

BOATING/WINDSURFING

On the shores of Storrie Lake north of Las Vegas are the **North Shore Windsurfing Centre** and **G&G Sailboards** (no phone or permanent building), ready to supply you with boards and wet suits. On the edge of Eagle

Nest is the **Lakeshore Marina** (Route 64, Eagle Nest; 505-377-6966). In the Los Alamos area, hire vessels from **J. R.'s Boat Rental & Storage** (Chama; 505-588-7436) and the **Stone House Lodge** (Heron Lake Road, Rutheron; 505-588-7274).

RIVER RAFTING

Get your feet wet on a tame or tumultuous guided tour of the Rio Grande and Chama River through Santa Fe outfitters ready and willing to help immerse you in the fun of wave riding. They include: **Rocky Mountain Tours** (1323 Paseo de Peralta, Santa Fe; 505-984-1684), **New Wave Rafting Co.** (107 Washington Street, Santa Fe; 505-984-1444), **Rio Bravo Rafting** (1412 Cerrillos Road, Santa Fe; 505-988-1153) and **Santa Fe Rafting** (710 Columbia Street, Santa Fe; 505-988-4914).

In the Taos Area are rafting guide services like: **Los Rios River Runners** (Taos Ski Valley; 505-758-1880), **Far Flung Adventures** (109 Brooks Street, Taos; 505-758-2628) and **Native Sons Adventures** (813 Paseo del Pueblo Sur, Taos; 505-758-9342).

FISHING

In the Santa Fe area, the fish are probably biting at Morphy Lake State Park and Storrie Lake, as well as the Pecos River. Try **High Desert Angler** (435 South Guadalupe, Santa Fe; 505-988-7688) for your fly fishing guide service.

For tackle, advice and guide services try **Los Rios Anglers** (2268 Paseo del Pueblo Norte, Taos; 505-758-2798), **Sierra Sports** (207 Paseo del Pueblo Sur, Taos; 505-758-2822), **Taylor Streit Flyfishing Service** (El Salto Road, Taos; 505-776-8698) and **Dos Amigos Trading Co.** (Route 64, Eagle Nest; 505-377-6226).

The San Juan River at the base of the **Navajo Dam** (about 20 miles west of Aztec on Route 511) is the site of quality waters that teem with trout. One of the largest lakes in New Mexico, Navajo provides angling opportunities for bluegill, bass, trout, pike and catfish. Try **Born-n-Raised on the San Juan River** (Route 173, Navajo Dam; 505-632-2194) or **Rizuto's Tackle** shop (807½ East Main Street, Farmington; 505-326-0664).

SWIMMING

Take a Santa Fe splash at the **Salvador Perez Pool** (601 Alta Vista Street, Santa Fe; 505-984-6755), **Tino Griego Pool** (1730 Llano Street, Santa Fe; 505-473-7270) and the **Alto/Bicentennial pool** (1121 Alto Street, Santa Fe; 505-984-6773). **New Mexico Highlands University** (2118 8th Street, Las Vegas; 505-425-7511) has an Olympic-size pool that's open to the public on a limited basis. **The Don Fernando Pool** (Civic Plaza Drive; 505-758-4160) is the only public place to get wet in Taos. **The Larry Walkup**

Aquatic Center (2760 Canyon Road, Los Alamos; 505-662-8170) has the highest altitude indoor Olympic-sized pool in the nation that's used by athletes for endurance training. It's open to the public for lap swimming.

WINTER SPORTS

Don't be fooled by the seeming dryness of the New Mexico landscape: the mountains are situated in a moisture belt that in an average year receives more snow than the Colorado Rockies. When storm clouds part, be prepared for warm, sunny days in the high desert.

How many capital cities have a full-service ski area within a 30-minute drive? **Santa Fe Ski Area** (Route 475, Santa Fe; 505-982-4429) is located up a winding, twisting road, approximately 15 miles northeast of downtown.

Granddaddy of New Mexico's alpine ski resorts is **Taos Ski Valley** (Route 150/Taos Ski Valley Road; 505-776-2291), with a summit elevation of nearly 12,000 feet above sea level. Taos boasts more than 1000 acres of bowls and chutes, served by eight chairs and two surface lifts. For backcountry adventures and guided yurt (mountain shelters) tours, consult the **Southwest Nordic Center** (Taos; 505-758-4761).

Novice skiers will find a lot to like at **Angel Fire** (Route 434, Angel Fire; 505-377-6401). Skiers who prefer the peaceful sounds of nature will enjoy gliding through the **Enchanted Forest** (Route 38, Red River; 505-754-2374) cross-country area. There are no services save for a warming hut. For rentals, lessons or a moonlight ski tour, check in at **Miller's Crossing** (West Main Street, Red River; 505-754-2374).

Just a mountain away from Taos as the crow flies is **Red River Ski Area** (Route 38, Red River; 505-754-2382), towering above a funky little Western-style town of the same name. Between Taos and Santa Fe is the modest **Sipapu Ski Area** (Route 518, Vadito; 505-587-2240).

In the Jemez Mountains overlooking Valle Grande volcano is the surprisingly challenging **Pajarito Ski Area** (Route 4, Los Alamos; 505-662-5725). Located eight miles from Los Alamos, Pajarito is open to the public only on a very limited basis—weekends, Wednesdays and federal holidays.

In Chama, the community-trail system maintains nearly four miles of groomed tracks in the Rio Grande National Forest. Ski rentals, backcountry supplies and maps to exciting telemarking terrain are available through **Chama Ski Service** (Main Street, Chama; 505-756-2492).

SKI RENTALS   In Santa Fe, **First Powder** (Hyde Park Road; 505-982-0495) has alpine, nordic and snowboarding equipment; also try **Alpine Sports** (121 Sandoval; 505-983-5155) and **Gardenswartz Sportz** (2860 Cerrillos Road; 505-473-3636).

To rent your sticks, visit **Taos Ski Valley Sportswear** (Taos Ski Valley; 505-776-2291) and **Terry Sports** (314 Paseo del Pueblo Norte, Taos;

505-758-8522). Get cross-country equipment from **Taos Mountain Outfitters** (114 South Plaza, Taos; 505-758-9292).

In Angel Fire try **Angel Fire Ski Rentals** (505-377-2301) located at the mountain base or **Ski Tech** (Angel Fire Road; 505-377-3213). Get your gear in Red River at **River City Sports** (505-754-2428) near the mountain base and **Miller's Crossing** (Main Street; 505-754-2374).

Near Los Alamos, try **Trail Bound Sports** (771 Central Avenue; 505-662-3000). For backcountry supplies and repairs, check in with **Chama Ski Service** (Chama; 505-756-2492).

GOLF

Believe it or not, the New Mexico desert harbors great golfing. Lush courses provide a cool respite from summer heat and ideal playing conditions even in the dead of winter. Plus, there's no charge for the fabulous scenery. Practice your swing at the **Santa Fe Country Club** (Airport Road, Santa Fe; 505-471-0601), **Quail Run Golf Course** (3101 Old Pecos Trail, Santa Fe; 505-986-2255), **Cochiti Golf Course** (5200 Cochiti Highway; 505-465-2239) and **New Mexico Highlands University Golf Course** (2118 8th Street, Las Vegas; 505-425-7711).

Also try the **Los Alamos Golf Club** (Los Alamos; 505-662-8139), **Angel Fire Resort** (Route 434, Angel Fire; 505-377-6401), **Piñon Hills Golf Course** (2101 Sunrise Parkway, Farmington; 505-326-6066), **Civitan Municipal** (2200 North Dustin Street, Farmington; 505-599-1194) or **Hidden Valley Country Club** (Aztec; 505-334-3248).

TENNIS

Santa Fe vacationers can take a swing at the **Galisteo Tennis Courts** (Camino Capitan and Galisteo), **Dr. Richard Angle Tennis Courts** (Old Pecos Trail and St. Michael's Drive), the **Fort Marcy Complex** (Old Taos Highway and Morales Road) and **Larrigoite Park** (Agua Fria and Avenida Cristobal Colon). Tennis court information is available at 505-662-8036.

In Taos try the **Fred Baca** (Ranchitos Road and Middle Street) and **Kit Carson** (Paseo del Pueblo Norte) parks in town. The **Quail Ridge Inn** (Taos Ski Valley Road, Taos; 505-776-2211) has bubble-covered courts.

In Los Alamos, try **Urban Park** (48th and Urban streets) and **East Park** (East Park Road near the Tewa Loop); in Farmington the **Lions Club Pool** (Apache and Wall streets). For general information call 505-599-1184.

BICYCLING

From the Santa Fe Plaza, pedal to **Ski Area Basin Road** that takes cyclists up a windy and at times steep 15-mile, two-lane road through heavily wooded National Forest land to Santa Fe Ski Area. To enjoy a shorter trip at a more forgiving altitude (the ski area is at 10,400 feet), just ride the eight miles to Hyde State Park.

A less-arduous trip that's packed full of rollers and hills, but no major mountain passes, follows the old Pecos Trail southeast of town 18 miles out to Glorieta.

A killer ten-mile ride for mountain bikers starts north of the Picacho Hotel on St. Francis Drive, crosses Dead Man's Gulch and Camino La Tierra before heading into the foothills of La Tierra. Circle back via Buckman Road to the hotel.

La Jara Canyon is a meandering two-mile climb to an alpine meadow that is especially appealing to those new in the (bike) saddle. Find it at the horseshoe between Taos and Angel Fire on Route 64.

Overlook the town of Taos on a relatively difficult two-and-one-half-mile loop trail called Devisadero. Start across from the El Nogal picnic area on Route 64 and get ready to climb 1300 vertical feet of elevation.

Wait until late afternoon to take the three-mile-long Cebolla Mesa Trail, for the sunsets are splendid. Pedal near the rim of the 800-foot Rio Grande Gorge at Cebolla Mesa, located about 18 miles north of Taos on Route 522. Start the trip at the intersection of Cebolla Mesa road and Route 522 and ride to the campground.

About five miles south of Jemez Springs, take Route 485 which cuts northwest for about ten miles through the hills and two narrow-gauge railroad tunnels. Join the Crimson Rock dirt road which follows the river up to Fenton Lake State Park and its headwaters. Once you get to Fenton Lake, there are miles of dirt roads within these environs.

The only signed mountain bike trail in Farmington is north of San Juan College (College Boulevard north of 30th Street). The brown trail markers leading to the area are somewhat unobtrusive. There are innumerable dirt roads across the 40 miles of trail, 25 miles of which have signs.

There's just a single trail where you can ride non-motorized bikes in Chaco Canyon, and that's the mile-and-a-half Wijiji. Keep your eyes peeled for petroglyphs.

BIKE RENTALS   To get rolling in Santa Fe, try the Downtown Bike Shop (719 Paseo de Peralta; 505-983-2255), First Powder (Hyde Park Road; 505-982-0495) or Santa Fe Schwinn (1611 St. Michael's Drive; 505-983-4473). In the Enchanted Circle area, try Gearing Up Bicycle Shop (129 Des Georges Mall, Taos; 505-751-0365) or Taos Mountain Outfitters (114 South Plaza, Taos; 505-758-9292). Trailbound Sports (771 Central Street; 505-662-3000) is Los Alamos' biking center. In Farmington mountain bikes are available from Bicycles Unlimited (915 Farmington Avenue; 505-326-3407) and Pedal Sports (201 West Main Street; 505-326-7553).

HIKING

SANTA FE AREA TRAILS   Just outside the city limits of Santa Fe, national forest land beckons and the hiker can disappear almost immediately into the dozens of trails that dip around peaks and to mountain lakes.

The **Winsor Trail** (2 to 9 miles) meanders at 11,000 feet, sidling along Big Tesuque Creek and the Nambe River. Start at the top of Ski Basin Road and traipse through stands of aspen and evergreen and finally, above timberline to 12,000-foot-plus Santa Fe Baldy. If you prefer a longer hike, begin in Tesuque along the creek. The gentle Borrego Trail branches off of Winsor.

A trail to **Hermit's Peak** (4 miles) gains nearly 3000 vertical feet after starting at an elevation of 7500. A narrow and rocky path, the view from atop the peak is spectacular. Find it by following Route 65 to the parking lot at El Porvenir, about 15 miles northwest of Las Vegas.

ENCHANTED CIRCLE AREA TRAILS   In the **Carson National Forest** near Taos are more than 20 marked trails of varying difficulty that wind in and around some of the state's more magnificent scenic spots.

Yerba Canyon Trail (4 miles) begins in the aspens and willows, but snakes through fir and spruce tress as you approach the ridge. As its name would suggest, the trail follows Yerba Canyon for most of its length and climbs some 3600 feet in elevation before reaching Lobo Peak. The trailhead is located on Taos Ski Valley Road one mile up the hill from Upper Cuchilla Campground.

From roughly the same access point is the **Gavilan Trail** (3.5 miles). The colorful hike is located primarily along Gavilan Creek. Steep in its early section, the trip flattens out as it opens into meadows near the ridge.

In the Red River area is the trail to **Middlefork Lake** (2 miles) which climbs 1200 vertical feet to a glacier lake. **Wheeler Peak Trail** (7 miles) to New Mexico's highest peak is for conditioned hikers only.

LOS ALAMOS AREA TRAILS   The vast majority of Bandelier Monument is considered undisturbed backcountry. Stone Lions Shrine is about six-miles from the visitor center, on the edge of Hondo Canyon.

Plenty of gratification without a whole lot of effort is found on the **Ruins Trail** (1 mile) in Frijoles Canyon at Bandelier National Monument. Start from the visitor center and walk past the big kiva, and the condominium-style dwelling built into the canyon wall that's known as Long House.

Trail to the Falls (2.5 miles) crosses Rio de los Frijoles and passes the Rainbow House ruin and Tent Rocks before arriving at the falls.

The trail to the detached **Tsankawi Ruins** (1.5 miles) starts from a trailhead near the intersection of Routes 4 and 502 and winds through lush piñon-juniper woodland, past petroglyphs to a high mesa and the unexcavated Tsankawi Ruins and cliff dwelling, yet another condo-style ruin. The trail provides spectacular views of the Española Valley.

FOUR CORNERS AREA TRAILS   At Chaco Canyon, hikers should take precautions—such as starting out early in the day or at dusk—to avoid the scorching sun. Because of Chaco's sheer remoteness, a first-aid kit is recommended, as is an oversupply of water.

In an attempt to retain Chaco's pristine beauty, trails are marked with rock piles called cairns. Beware of rattlesnakes and plague-carrying rodents. Though these creatures aren't aggressive, they will respond to provocation or a wandering pet that disturbs their slumber.

A nice hike for late afternoon is **Tsin Kletzin Trail** (1.5 miles) which begins at Casa Rinconada ruin. Head south up the rocky slope to the top of the mesa; en route you'll find sparse vegetation and some interesting natural storage holes used by Indian tribes. The two kivas of Tsin Kletzin were thought to reach two stories high and contain more than 70 rooms.

The rather flat **Peñasco Blanco Trail** (2.5 miles) follows a wagon road from the Casa Chiquita trailhead down the Chaco Wash. Hikers pass assorted petroglyphs and an Anasazi art panel. There is a side loop to the colorful "supernova" pictograph that's well worth the hike. By following the cairns you'll end up at Peñasco Blanco, an unexcavated great house.

Transportation

BY CAR

Route 25 is the favored north-south road through New Mexico, accessing Las Vegas and Santa Fe. **Route 68** heads south from Taos to Santa Fe, while **Route 285/84** heads north from Los Alamos through Española, all the way to Chama and the New Mexico/Colorado border.

Route 64 skirts across the northern edge of New Mexico passing through the Four Corners Area and across to Chama. Parts of the highway that cross high through Carson National Forest are closed during the winter, but back down at lower elevations, Route 64 also leads to Taos and on east through Cimarron.

BY AIR

Most visitors to Northern New Mexico fly into Albuquerque (see "Transportation" in Chapter Seven). **Santa Fe County Municipal Airport** has daily flights via Mesa Airlines from Albuquerque. Mesa Airlines and United Express offer a flights into Farmington's **Four-Corners Airport**.

Both **Faust's Transportation** (505-758-3410) and **Pride of Taos** (505-758-8340) provide shuttle service to Taos from the Albuquerque airport.

Shuttlejack (505-982-4311) departs the Albuquerque airport on a regular basis for Santa Fe.

BY BUS

Greyhound/Trailways Bus Lines services Santa Fe (858 St. Michael's Drive; 505-471-0008) and Taos (South Santa Fe Road and Raton Bypass; 505-758-1144).

BY TRAIN

Amtrak's "Southwest Chief" (800-872-7245) serves Santa Fe via the village of Lamy, 17 miles from town. The Lamy Shuttle (505-982-8829) can take you into Santa Fe, as can Faust's Transportation (505-758-3410).

CAR RENTALS

Car rental agencies in Santa Fe include **Adopt A Car Rentals** (505-473-3189), **Agency Rent A Car** (505-473-2983), **Avis Rent A Car** (505-982-4361), **Budget Rent A Car** (505-984-8028), **Enterprise Rent A Car** (505-473-3600), **Hertz Rent A Car** (505-982-1844), **Snappy Car Rental** (505-473-2277) and **Thrifty Car Rental** (505-984-1961).

Firms located at Four-Corners Airport include **Avis Rent A Car** (505-327-9864), **Budget Rent A Car** (505-327-7304), **Hertz Rent A Car** (505-327-6093) and **National Car Rental** (505-327-0215).

PUBLIC TRANSPORTATION

You need a car in Northern New Mexico because public transportation is nearly non-existent. In Los Alamos, the **Los Alamos Bus System** (505-662-3492) provides regularly scheduled bus service on a variety of routes.

TAXIS

In Santa Fe try **Capital City Cab Co.** (505-989-8888) or **Village Taxi** (505-982-9990). **Faust's Transportation** (505-758-3410) is the only game in town in Taos. Taxicab service in Farmington is provided by **Roadrunner Taxi** (505-327-1909).

WALKING TOURS

Perhaps the most down-to-earth method of touring cities like Santa Fe and Taos is via a walking tour. Locals guides provide rich historical and personal insight to their communities as you stroll ancient streets and narrow lanes. Most tours last about two to three hours and may include visits inside area museums. Call **Santa Fe Walks** (La Fonda Hotel lobby, Santa Fe Detours Desk, 100 East San Francisco Street; 505-983-6565) or **Taos Walking Tours** (505-758-3861).

GLENN KIM '12

CHAPTER SEVEN

Central New Mexico

Billy the Kid once roamed this area. Now you can, too. The vast ranch-land plains east of the Rocky Mountains haven't changed much since the Kid rode into legend more than a century ago. But Albuquerque is another story. Just another small town on the banks of the Rio Grande downriver from Santa Fe in the heyday of the Wild West, it has been transformed into a bustling metropolis boasting a unique mosaic of lifestyles and cultures. This is the Central New Mexico that intrigues the traveler: A mixture of the wild and the sublime, the cowboy and the Indian, the small town and the big city, the past and the present.

Route 40 is the ribbon that ties together the diversity of Central New Mexico. At the knot is Albuquerque. With 500,000 residents in the greater metropolitan area, Albuquerque accounts for a quarter of the population of the entire state. Developing into a crossroads thanks to the railroad and highways, the city mixes Indian, Spanish, Mexican and Anglo cultures into a delightfully tasty stew.

History is part of the enchantment of Albuquerque and its environs. Geography is another. In fact, the setting is one of the things the residents love most about this area. Sandia Peak towers a mile above the eastern city limit. Rural farmland follows the Rio Grande south. And to the west is a vast and beautiful emptiness. Visitors are often surprised by the abruptness with which the city gives way to wilderness at Albuquerque's edge. Route 40 plunges into a parched, overgrazed, alkaline high-desert wasteland that gradually reveals its stark beauty in twisting arroyos and jagged black-lava fields, fortresslike rock mesas and solitary mountains that rise like islands from an arid sea.

287

Central New Mexico is a neat combination of the high, cool forests of the Rocky Mountains to the north and the rocky, sunbaked Chihuahuan Desert stretching a thousand miles to the south. As a result, if you don't like the weather, you can just change it. In June, the hottest month of the year, when air-conditioning becomes essential in Albuquerque, a short drive into the mountains offers shade, cool streams and occasional patches of un-melted snow. In January, skiers can enjoy nearby slopes and then return to lower elevations where snowfalls are infrequent and light.

The mix of mountain coolness, desert dryness and southern latitude produces evening temperatures that drop to about 50° even in mid-summer and daytime highs above freezing in the dead of winter. In autumn, people watch the month-long procession of bright-gold foliage gracefully descend-ing from the mountain heights to the cottonwood bosque along the rivers. In springtime, new greenery spreads slowly up the slopes toward the sky.

Cultural contrasts are equally dramatic. This is a melting pot of Navajo and Pueblo Indians whose lifestyles were upset by the Spanish exploration that began in the 1500s. Also mixed in are Norteño descendants of Spanish and Mexican colonists (New Mexico was a province of Mexico from 1821 until the 1848 treaty that ended the Mexican War with the United States) and Anglos who began settling here in the early 1800s. All these cultures come together in modern-day Albuquerque, a polyglot of a city where an-cient ceremonies and futuristic technological research, fiestas and balloon races, cowboys and entrepreneurs, exist side-by-side.

Outside Albuquerque's city limits, equally fascinating sights await the traveler. The eastern plains, where most travelers stop only to exit the inter-state for gasoline and a bite to eat, offer beaches and watersports on several large, manmade lakes along the Pecos and Canadian rivers. You'll find the gravesite of Billy-boy himself in the town of Fort Sumner. There are sites abandoned to wind, weather and wildflowers but which are just aching to be explored.

Near the small town of Mountainair at the foot of the Manzano Moun-tains, sightseers can explore Spanish and Indian ruins from centuries past, one-time Native American trade centers and headquarters for missionary efforts during the colonial era. Outside Socorro, just off the interstate, nature-lovers visiting between November and March can witness the spectacular congregation of snow geese, Canadian geese and sandhill cranes by the tens of thousands.

The area of Grants and Gallup, close enough that it could be glimpsed as a day trip out of Albuquerque, offers such a rich tapestry of experiences that it can serve as a primary vacation destination on its own. Visitors can explore the Indian pueblos of Acoma and Zuni, where Native American peo-ple have lived continuously since long before Christopher Columbus sighted land. The Pueblo Indians have been here so long that their legends, passed on by spoken word from each generation to the next, contain eyewitness

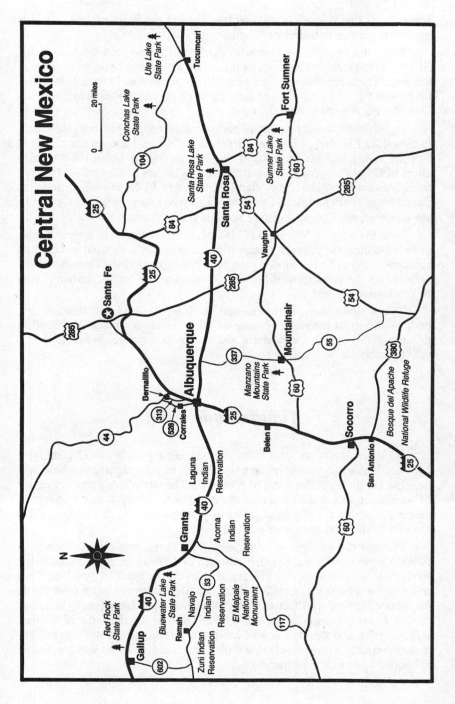

Central New Mexico

20 miles

0

N

Santa Fe

Tucumcari
Ute Lake State Park
Conchas Lake State Park
104
25
Fort Sumner
Sumner Lake State Park
84
Santa Rosa Lake State Park
Santa Rosa
84
40
54
25
60
285
Vaughn
285
54
Albuquerque
Bernalillo
313
528
Corrales
44
337
Mountainair
Manzano Mountains State Park
55
60
25
Belen
Socorro
380
Bosque del Apache National Wildlife Refuge
San Antonio
25
Laguna Indian Reservation
40
Acoma Indian Reservation
60
Grants
53
Navajo Indian Reservation
El Malpais National Monument
117
Ramah
Gallup
Red Rock State Park
Bluewater Lake State Park
Zuni Indian Reservation
40
602

accounts of the volcanic eruptions that created the huge malpais, or lava badlands, on the outskirts of Grants.

From the Spanish soldiers who explored Central New Mexico in the first half of the 16th century, faint remnants of conquest can be found throughout the area. These reminders of the past include the site of Coronado's bridge near Santa Rosa and the ruins of the massacred pueblo of Kuaua at Coronado State Monument near Albuquerque.

But nowhere is the memory of early exploration as vivid as in the mountains south of Route 40 between Grants and Gallup. Here, in the poor and isolated villages of the Zuni Reservation, is the reality behind the "golden cities of Cibola" legend that lured the first explorers northward all the way from Mexico City. Here, too, stand the cliffs of El Morro where Indians, Spanish explorers and Anglo settlers alike carved messages in stone to create a permanent "guest register" spanning 800 years.

Near the western boundary of New Mexico, Gallup is the largest border town adjoining the Navajo Reservation. It presents a cultural contrast as striking as any to be found along the Mexican border, as the interstate highway brings the outside world to the doorstep of the largest Indian nation in the United States.

This sounds like a lot to see and do. It is. But amid all this activity, perhaps the most astonishing thing of all is that every place described in this chapter is within three hours' drive of Albuquerque. What more can you possibly be waiting for?

Albuquerque Area

Albuquerque is an ideal hub for exploring the sights of Central New Mexico. Make this your starting point. Much of your sightseeing here will be rooted in the past. But don't be dismayed. The city offers a fine collection of such amenities as art museums and nightspots. Many scenic wonders of nature are within the city limits or nearby. And when the day is done, there are plenty of good places to eat and sleep.

Perhaps the best place to begin is **Old Town**, the original center of Albuquerque during the Spanish colonial and Mexican eras. West of the modern downtown area, this low-rise district can be reached by taking Central Avenue west from Route 25 or Rio Grande Boulevard south from Route 40. Situated around an attractive central plaza with a bandstand, many buildings in Old Town date as early as 1780. After 1880, when the railroad reached Albuquerque and the station was built at a distance from the plaza, businesses migrated to the present downtown area and Old Town was practically abandoned for half a century.

Revitalization came when artists, attracted by bargain rents, established studios in Old Town. Galleries followed, as did gift shops, boutiques and restaurants. Today, it's easy to while away half a day exploring the restored old adobe (and more recent "pueblo-ized" stucco) structures, hidden patios, brick paths, gardens and balconies of Old Town, browsing at the handmade jewelry and pottery offered by Native American vendors and just people-watching from a park bench.

Two of the city's best museums are on opposite sides of Mountain Road three blocks north of Old Town Plaza. The **Albuquerque Museum** (2000 Mountain Road Northwest; 505-243-7255; admission) contains art, science and history exhibits, including the permanent "Four Centuries: A History of Albuquerque" display that features the largest collection of Spanish colonial artifacts in the United States. Visitors can see conquistadors' armor and weapons, medieval religious items brought by early missionaries and ordinary household items that evoke the lifestyle of early settlers along the Rio Grande.

Nearby, the **New Mexico Museum of Natural History** (1801 Mountain Road Northwest; 505-841-8836; admission) is the newest major natural-history museum in the United States. It features unique and imaginative exhibits that let visitors walk through time, explore an Ice Age cave, stand inside an erupting volcano and sit on the back of a dinosaur.

East of the downtown area on Central Avenue, the **University of New Mexico** (505-277-3729) offers a varied choice of on-campus museums as well as cultural events. The **Maxwell Museum of Anthropology** (Redondo Drive and Ash Street; 505-277-4404) displays selections from the university's huge collection of pre-Columbian Indian artifacts from all over the Southwest. Its "People of the Southwest" exhibit simulates an archeological dig in progress. Current-events information and a campus map are available at the **Fine Arts Center** (Cornell Street and Redondo Drive; 505-277-4001). Besides performing-arts facilities, the Fine Arts Center contains the **University Art Museum.** Although the museum's exhibition space is not large, its collection is outstanding, featuring works by such well-known Southwestern visual artists as Georgia O'Keeffe and Ansel Adams. The university has a separate small art museum, the **Johnson Gallery** (1909 Las Lomas Boulevard Northeast; 505-277-4967), which displays selections from a 2000-piece collection of the works of early-20th-century New Mexico artist Raymond Johnson. Northrop Hall (505-277-4204), the geology building, has a **Geology Museum** and a **Meteoritics Museum,** and next door in the Biology Annex is the university's **Museum of Southwestern Biology** (505-277-5340).

A small, privately owned museum near the university, the **Spanish History Museum** (2221 Lead Avenue Northeast; 505-268-9981) shows the genealogy and heraldry of the first 250 Spanish families who colonized New Mexico and contains drawings, documents and other memorabilia of the

Spanish presence in North America from Columbus' arrival through the Spanish role in the American Revolution. This is the only museum in the United States devoted entirely to the Spanish-American heritage.

Across the street from the International Nuclear Weapons School at Kirtland Air Force Base is Albuquerque's scariest tourist attraction. The **National Atomic Museum** (Wyoming Boulevard and K Street; 505-845-6670) traces the development of nuclear weapons through exhibits including Albert Einstein's original letter to President Franklin D. Roosevelt suggesting the possibility, replicas of various atomic bombs from the 1940s and '50s and videos of nuclear tests, as well as an outdoor exhibit area with missiles and a B-52 bomber. The museum also covers the development of atomic-power plants, experiments with nuclear fusion and contemporary problems of nuclear-waste disposal.

The clean, imaginatively designed **Rio Grande Zoological Park** (900 10th Street Southwest; 505-843-7413; admission) is expanding fast. Enclosures are designed to resemble the animals' natural habitats as much as possible. The most unusual inhabitants are a pack of Mexican lobos, a small wolf subspecies that is extinct in the wild. Of the two dozen lobos that survive in a federal captive-breeding program, the majority live at the Rio Grande Zoo.

The **Indian Pueblo Cultural Center** (2401 12th Street Northwest; 505-843-7270; admission), jointly owned and operated by all 19 of New Mexico's pueblos, has one of the finest Indian museums in the state. Through artifacts and dioramas, it traces the history of New Mexico's native population over a span of 20,000 years. Exhibits of traditional pottery and other arts and crafts show the stylistic differences between the various pueblos. The museum also features an excellent collection of photographs from the Smithsonian Institution taken of Pueblo people in the late 19th century. The cultural center has retail galleries, a restaurant serving Native American food, an indoor theater and an outdoor plaza where special events such as dance performances and craft demonstrations are staged almost daily during the summer and most weekends the rest of the year.

Along the dark volcanic escarpment on Albuquerque's western perimeter, visitors can find perhaps the largest assemblage of ancient Indian rock art in the Southwest—over 10,000 specimens in all. The drawings were chipped into the patina of rock surfaces 800 to 1000 years ago. Some are representational pictures of animal, human and supernatural figures, and others are abstract symbols, the meanings of which have provided generations of archaeologists with a fertile topic for speculation. A portion of the petroglyphs can be viewed along a short, steep trail in **Indian Petroglyphs State Park** (6900 Unser Boulevard Northwest; 505-823-4016). A larger area around the state park has been earmarked for preservation as a future national monument. To reach the park, take the Atrisco exit from Route 40 West and follow the signs.

For many visitors, the ultimate experience is a trip up **Sandia Peak** (elevation 10,400 feet) east of the city. The mountain rises so sharply on the city's eastern boundary that from either bottom or top it looks as if a rock falling from the cliffs along the top ridgeline would land in someone's yard in the fashionable Northeast Heights neighborhood a mile below. On a typically clear day, you can see almost half the state from the summit.

While the summit can be reached by car (see "Turquoise Trail" below) or on foot (see "Hiking" at the end of the chapter), the most spectacular way to climb this mountain is the **Sandia Peak Tramway** (10 Tramway Loop Northeast; 505-298-8518). The world's longest aerial tramway takes just 15 minutes to ascend the 2.7-mile cable, offering eagle's-eye views of rugged canyons in the Sandia Wilderness Area and sometimes a glimpse of Rocky Mountain bighorn sheep grazing on a distant promontory. At the summit are an observation deck and a deluxe restaurant at the tram station, a gift shop and snack bar a short walk away at the end of the auto road and breathtaking views wherever you look.

OUTSIDE ALBUQUERQUE   Thirteen miles south of Albuquerque on Route 25 in the South Valley, **Isleta Pueblo** (505-869-3111) is a labyrinthine mixture of old and new houses comprising one of New Mexico's larger pueblos. Visitors who wander the narrow streets of the town will eventually find their way to the mission church, one of the oldest in the United States. The pueblo operates a fishing lake, campground and bingo parlor. Several small shops around the plaza sell the local white, red and black pottery.

Traveling north of Albuquerque on Route 25, motorists can explore a number of ancient and modern Indian pueblos. The two nearest to Albuquerque—**Santa Ana Pueblo** (505-867-3301) and **Sandia Pueblo** (505-867-3317)—are so small that they often go unnoticed. Santa Ana Pueblo has about 500 tribal members, but nearly all live away from the old pueblo. It comes to life for feast-day dances. The tribe owns a golf course nearby and operates an arts-and-crafts cooperative. Just up the road, Sandia Pueblo owns the land on which the Sandia Peak Tramway is situated and also has an arts-and-crafts market and a "Las Vegas-style" bingo operation. The Sandia people number about 300 and speak Tiwa, a different language from that spoken at other pueblos in the area. They claim descent from the inhabitants of Kuaua at nearby Coronado National Monument.

Founded beside the Rio Grande around the year 1300, Kuaua was a thriving pueblo when a Spanish expedition consisting of 1100 men led by Francisco Vasquez de Coronado arrived in 1540. The explorers spent the winter there and found the people of Kuaua hospitable at first, but as supplies ran short and the Spanish demands on the pueblo increased, the Indians became uncooperative, and Coronado destroyed the pueblo.

Today, the ruins of Kuaua are preserved as **Coronado State Monument** (505-867-5351) 15 miles north of Albuquerque on Route 25 near the town of Bernalillo. The unique feature of this ruin is a round ceremonial kiva which, when excavated, was found to have intact painted murals around its interior—the only pre-Columbian pueblo kiva paintings that have survived the centuries. Archaeologists carefully removed the painted layers and mounted them. The original paintings are displayed in a room adjoining the visitor center along with diagrams that explain their meanings. The kiva itself has been fully restored and ornamented with replicas of the paintings, and visitors are welcome to climb down into it. The visitor center contains exhibits about both the pueblo people and the Spanish conquistadors.

Tradition is strong at **San Felipe Pueblo** (505-867-3381), ten miles north of Bernalillo on Route 25. Photographs and sketching are strictly prohibited. The pueblo is known for large, spectacular dances, and the bowl-like central plaza has actually been worn down three feet below ground level by centuries of ceremonies. The pueblo's artisans do beadwork, specializing in *heishi* (disc-like beads used for necklaces).

Adventuresome motorists will find an unpaved road running between San Felipe Pueblo and **Santo Domingo Pueblo** (505-465-2214). Each pueblo is within a few miles of Route 25, but the road between them seems a world apart from the interstate as it winds through tribal farmland unchanged by time. Santo Domingo is the largest of the Rio Grande Indian pueblos and one of the most conservative. After admiring the horses and other ornate designs painted on the church facade, visitors may wish to stroll through the narrow, old streets and hear the residents speaking in the native Keresan language. The pueblo has a small museum and outdoor arts-and-crafts market near the interstate.

A few miles from the pueblo is the picturesque **Santo Domingo Trading Post**, the granddaddy of Indian curio shops. The storefront, brightly painted back in the 1940s, now faded and peeling, proclaims the trading post to be one of the Southwest's top attractions—as seen in *Look* magazine.

The mission church at **Cochiti Pueblo** (★) (505-465-2244) dates back to 1628 and is among the oldest on the Rio Grande. Cochiti artisans originated the pottery storyteller figures that now are popular collectibles. The pueblo leases the tribal real estate on which Albuquerque's water supply and recreational reservoir, Cochiti Lake, as well as the town of Cochiti Lake, is situated. It operates the campground and other lake services and permits fishing in the Rio Grande for a fee. Cochiti Pueblo is farther removed from the interstate than any of the other pueblos between Albuquerque and Santa Fe. To get there, travel north on Route 25, then take the marked tribal road for about 15 miles.

TURQUOISE TRAIL   A more relaxed and less congested route between Albuquerque and Santa Fe, the Turquoise Trail (Route 14) takes just 15 minutes more driving time than the interstate. To find it, take Route 40 eastbound from Albuquerque to the Tijeras/Cedar Crest exit, a distance of about ten miles from the city center, and turn north.

At Cedar Crest, a few miles from the interstate exit, a well-marked paved road, steep in places, forks off from the Turquoise Trail and leads up the

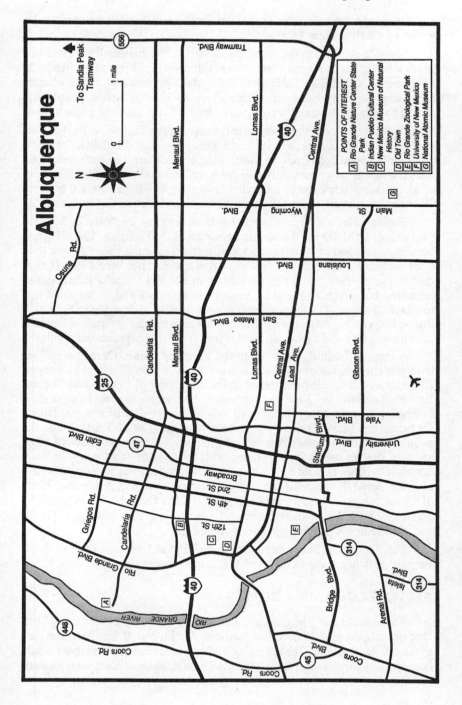

Albuquerque

To Sandia Peak Tramway

N

0   1 mile

POINTS OF INTEREST

A   Rio Grande Nature Center State Park
B   Indian Pueblo Cultural Center
C   New Mexico Museum of Natural History
D   Old Town
E   Rio Grande Zoological Park
F   University of New Mexico
G   National Atomic Museum

eastern slope of the Sandias to **Sandia Peak** summit with its spectacular views of Central New Mexico.

About a mile from the Turquoise Trail on the Sandia Peak road is a small wonder for those traveling with children—the **Tinkertown Museum** (★) (Route 536; 505-281-5233; admission), which exhibits a miniature Western community entirely hand-carved from wood with mechanical people and moving vehicles. It is easily recognized by its fence made of glass bottles.

Midway between Albuquerque and Santa Fe, the Turquoise Trail crosses the San Pedro Mountains, a small but rugged range that was the site of major gold-mining operations from the 1880s to the 1920s. Once the area's residential hub, **Golden** is now practically a ghost town. Beside the highway, the ruins of an old stone schoolhouse and other collapsing buildings can still be seen. There is also a small, beautifully restored mission church dating back to 1830.

Eleven miles away, on the other side of the pass, the town of **Madrid** (pronounced "MAD-rid") owes its existence to coal mining. The all-wood buildings, atypical of New Mexico architecture, give the community a look reminiscent of Appalachian coal towns. Abandoned after World War II, Madrid has since been partly repopulated by artists and historic-district entrepreneurs, but much of the town remains dilapidated and unoccupied due to a lack of water. The town's water supply used to be brought in by a train that no longer runs. Attractions in Madrid include a mining museum, a summertime melodrama and a baseball field where concerts are presented regularly.

A third old mining town along the Turquoise Trail, **Cerrillos** still retains the appearance of an old Spanish village. While silver, gold, copper, zinc and lead have all been mined in the hills north of town—and Thomas Edison once built a $2 million laboratory here in an unsuccessful attempt to develop a method for refining gold without water—Cerrillos is best known for turquoise. Indians mined turquoise here as early as 500 A.D. Later, the people of Chaco and other Anasazi pueblos traveled from hundreds of miles away to dig pit mines for the stone, which was their most precious trade commodity. Others from Spanish colonists to modern-day prospectors have also wandered the maze of the Cerrillos hills in search of turquoise. Tours of the old turquoise mines can be arranged at **Casa Grande** (505-438-3008), a 21-room hacienda in town that has been converted into a bed and breakfast and also features a petting zoo and museum.

The Turquoise Trail intersects Route 25 at the western edge of Santa Fe, where it becomes Cerrillos Road, a busy main street.

ALBUQUERQUE AREA HOTELS

As New Mexico's largest city, Albuquerque has lodgings for every taste. One downtown grand hotel that predates World War II has been restored to the height of luxury. The emerging bed-and-breakfast scene features small, homey places that range from Victorian mansions to contemporary suburban guest houses. Rates for Albuquerque accommodations are much lower than the cost of comparable lodging in Santa Fe or Taos.

Native New Mexican Conrad Hilton started his hotel chain in Albuquerque. The second Hilton hostelry, built in 1939, has been lovingly restored as the city's showpiece downtown historic hotel, **La Posada de Albuquerque** (125 2nd Street Northwest; 505-242-9090). The lobby, with its vaulted ceiling and Indian murals, sets the tone—a blend of old-fashioned grand hotel elegance and unique New Mexican style. Handmade traditional New Mexico furniture graces the modern guest rooms, which range from moderate to deluxe.

The contemporary **Albuquerque Hilton** (1901 University Avenue Northeast; 505-884-2500) is the finest of several major hotels that cluster northeast of the Route 25 and Route 40 interchange. Moderate to deluxe.

On the east edge of town, near the Central Avenue/Tramway Boulevard exit from Route 40, is another concentration of franchise lodgings, from the moderately priced **Best Western American Motor Inn** (12999 Central Avenue Northeast; 505-298-7426) to the budget-priced **Econo Lodge** (13211 Central Avenue Northeast; 505-292-7600). Although this area is a long way from central destinations like Old Town and the university, it is a convenient location from which to ride the tramway or drive up Sandia Peak.

The deluxe-priced **Holiday Inn Pyramid** (5151 San Francisco Road Northeast; 505-821-3333) is easy to spot by its stepped pyramid shape alongside Route 25 in the industrial/commercial zone north of the city. Inside is an atrium with a 50-foot waterfall, a glass elevator and Mayan and Aztec motifs. The 312 rooms are of the standard hotel variety.

Also on the city's north side off Route 25, the **Howard Johnson Plaza Hotel** (6000 Pan American Freeway Northeast; 505-821-9451) bears little similarity to the orange-and-blue Ho-Jos of yesteryear. This moderately priced hotel offers some surprising touches of class, from the sunny atrium lobby to the bright, contemporary guest rooms, not to mention the indoor-outdoor swim-through pool.

Families traveling together who appreciate the extra space and amenities of a suite can find weekend bargain rates at several of Albuquerque's all-suite hotels. For example, the moderate-priced **Barcelona Court All-Suite Hotel** (900 Louisiana Boulevard Northeast; 505-255-5566) off Route 40 has suites with separate bedrooms and kitchen facilities that include microwave ovens.

Visitors looking for budget accommodations should take Central Avenue east beyond the University of New Mexico Campus. Central used to be Route 66, the main east-west highway through Albuquerque before the interstates were built. Although the old two-lane highway has become a wide, busy commercial thoroughfare, several tourist courts dating back to that earlier era still survive along Central between Carlisle and San Mateo boulevards.

The budget-priced **De Anza Motor Lodge** (4301 Central Avenue Northeast; 505-255-1654) is a prime example. Something about its pueblo styling and teepee-shaped sign recalls that small town, halfway-from-home-to-California mystique that many people nostalgically associate with Old Route 66. Caution: This part of Central Avenue is considered a "bad neighborhood" because a few of the old motels are frequented by prostitutes.

Strolling among the low-rise, territorial-style buildings of Old Town, it would be easy to imagine yourself in an earlier century were it not for the towering presence of the 11-story **Sheraton Old Town** (800 Rio Grande Boulevard Southwest; 505-843-6300) a block away. The grounds preserve natural desert landscaping. The large lobby bursts with Southwestern designs and colors, and the restaurant features improbably nautical decor. Views from the upper floors of this deluxe-priced hotel may be the most spectacular in town.

Casas de Sueños (310 Rio Grande Boulevard Southwest; 505-247-4560) is a unique bed and breakfast three blocks from Old Town Plaza. The cluster of small houses and duplexes surrounding courtyard gardens began as an artists' colony in the 1940s. Each living unit is individually designed and furnished, and many have kitchen facilities or fireplaces. Rates range from moderate to deluxe. Over the entrance to the main house is a large protuberance, which the innkeepers refer to as "the snail." The sight of this architectural curiosity stops cars on the street as drivers gawk. It was originally designed as a nonlinear law office by then-struggling young architect Bart Prince, who is now known worldwide. The snail is available as a conference space. Visitors can tour it on request.

Did we say bed and breakfast? Until recently, the bed-and-breakfast trend seemed to have bypassed Albuquerque. The moderately priced downtown **W. E. Mauger Estate** (701 Roma Street Northwest; 505-242-8755), a Queen Anne home with high ceilings, flowered wallpaper and hardwood floors, was just about the only bed and breakfast in the city. Happily, the W. E. Mauger has some company now.

The **Old Town Bed & Breakfast** (707 17th Street Northwest; 505-842-6401) is east of Old Town within easy walking distance of the New Mexico Museum of Natural History and the Albuquerque Museum. It features adobe and *viga* architecture, a patio and a hot tub. Closer to the plaza, the **Böttger Mansion Bed and Breakfast** (110 San Felipe Street Northwest; 505-243-3639) is in a 1910 Victorian home listed on the National Register of Historic Landmarks. Only three guest rooms share the house with a coffee house, gift shop and beauty salon. Both moderate.

Also in the downtown area, the **W. J. Marsh House and Snyder Cottage** (301 Edith Street Southeast; 505-247-1001) offers deluxe-priced accommodations in an 1895 home complete with a resident ghost. A minimum stay of three nights is required.

Several more first-rate, moderately priced, suburban bed and breakfasts are located in the Paseo del Norte area of Albuquerque and on the other side of the Rio Grande. **Adobe and Roses** (1011 Ortega Street Northwest; 505-898-0654) rents a guest house and a suite. The traditional New Mexico architecture features brick floors, Mexican tiles and *vigas*. Both units have fireplaces as well as private entrances and kitchenettes.

Nearby, **Casa del Granjero** (100 C de Baca Lane Northwest, Albuquerque; 505-897-4144) is a huge, old adobe house from the territorial era with a lovely enclosed courtyard. It has two rooms. Amenities include a hot tub and horses.

Casita Chamisa (850 Chamisal Road Northwest, Albuquerque; 505-897-4644) also has two units, each with private bath, in a 19th-century adobe home. The shady, forested acreage that is the Casita Chamisa's setting is also an archeological site, and the innkeepers are happy to show a video that explains all about it.

A number of the Albuquerque area's best small bed and breakfasts are in Corrales, a rural North Valley community near Bernalillo and Coronado State Monument. **Yours Truly Bed and Breakfast** (160 Paseo de Corrales; 505-898-7027) offers two guest rooms in a modern adobe house with fireplaces, a spa and nearby hiking trails. The **Corrales Inn Bed & Breakfast** (Corrales Road; 505-897-4422) has six rooms, private baths and a cozy library. And **La Mimosa Bed & Breakfast** (505-898-1354) with one room is a private adobe guest house secluded in a shady courtyard. All have rates in the moderate range.

For those who seek an even more remote setting, still within easy commuting distance of Albuquerque's attractions, **Elaine's** (★) (72 Snowline Estates; 505-281-2467) is a bed and breakfast in a three-story log home among the ponderosa pines. Elaine's is on four acres adjoining Cibola National Forest near Cedar Crest where the auto road up Sandia Peak turns off from the Turquoise Trail. The house has big balconies, a huge country fireplace, European antiques everywhere you look and two rooms. Moderate.

Reservations are advised for all bed and breakfasts.

ALBUQUERQUE AREA RESTAURANTS

As every visitor discovers immediately, New Mexico boasts a distinctive culinary style. The two regional specialties that set it apart from Mexican food familiar in other regions are blue corn, grown by the Pueblo Indians and considered sacred in their traditions, and green chili. New Mexico produces virtually all the chili peppers grown in the United States, and while it is exported to the rest of the country in the form of red chili powder, the local preference is to pick the chilies while green, roast, peel and eat them as a vegetable—chopped as a stew, breaded and fried as *rellenos* or poured as a sauce over just about any entrée. Contrary to many visitors' misconceptions, green chili is *not* milder than red chili.

Albuquerque has great New Mexican restaurants in all price ranges.

New Southwestern cuisine—traditional New Mexican ingredients imaginatively used in Continental dishes or New Mexican specialties prepared with improbable ingredients—is appearing in quite a few Albuquerque restaurants these days. For example, the menu at **McGrath's** (330 Tijeras Avenue Northwest; 505-766-6700), the deluxe-priced restaurant at the Hyatt Regency Hotel, features a filet mignon brushed with Hatch red chili, a roast duck quesadilla and oysters with guacamole salsa.

A popular, moderately priced Mexican restaurant is **La Hacienda** (1306 Rio Grande Boulevard Northwest; 505-243-3709). The Spanish colonial atmosphere, with *ristras* and a big kiva fireplace, and lots of Southwestern art on the walls, fits right into the Old Town experience. The menu includes steak and seafood dishes as well as local cuisine. There is a second location in Old Town at 302 San Felipe Street Northwest (505-242-4866).

Another excellent Mexican restaurant in Old Town is **Maria Teresa** (618 Rio Grande Boulevard Northwest; 505-242-3900). Arguably Albuquerque's most beautiful restaurant, it is in the Salvador Armijo House, a National Historic Landmark dating back to the 1840s and elegantly furnished with Victorian-era antiques. Besides local specialties, the menu includes fine contemporary American and Continental dishes. Moderate.

In one of Old Town's oldest buildings, circa 1785, **High Noon** (425 San Felipe Street Northwest; 505-765-1455) serves fajitas, enchiladas and burritos as well as Continental cuisine and a few Southwestern specialties like New Mexican stir fry (beef or chicken stir-fried with vegetables and smothered in red or green chili sauce) at moderate prices to the strains of live flamenco guitar music.

A place where the green chili will knock your socks off (or maybe burn them off) is **Sadie's Dining Room** (6230 4th Street Northwest; 505-345-5339). This budget-priced establishment is as local as it gets, with a view of a bowling alley.

A different kind of local cuisine can be found at the restaurant in the **Indian Pueblo Cultural Center** (2401 12th Street Northwest; 505-843-7270). Open for lunch only, this budget-priced restaurant serves traditional Pueblo Indian dishes such as fry bread, Indian tacos and *posole.*

At **Nicole's** (2101 Louisiana Boulevard Northeast; 505-881-6800), a restaurant in the Marriott Hotel, offerings include salmon *rellenos* with green chili and cheese and grilled swordfish in a green chili-piñon sauce. Deluxe.

New Southwestern cuisine is also the specialty at **Casa Chaco** (Albuquerque Hilton, 1901 University Boulevard Northeast; 505-884-2500). Formerly the hotel's coffee shop, Casa Chaco has become a moderately priced, full-scale restaurant featuring such delicacies as chili lobster sausage, sea scallops marinated in New Mexico white wine with green-chili cream sauce, tornedos of pork loin with a prickly pear cactus glaze and pâté seasoned with cilantro, jalapeño and piñon nuts. The Albuquerque Hilton's deluxe-priced restaurant, the **Ranchers Club**, lives up to its name as a quintessential steak house. Entrées include a 40-ounce T-bone and a 48-ounce porterhouse. You can choose which wood will be used to grill your steak—mesquite, hickory, sassafras or wild cherry.

Firehouses seem to be a popular theme for Albuquerque restaurants. The **Monte Vista Firestation** (3201 Central Avenue Northeast; 505-255-2424) is located in what was once a real fire station and today stands as one of the city's finest surviving examples of the "Pueblo Deco" architecture that sprang up along Old Route 66 in the 1930s. The fare at this moderately priced restaurant is highly imaginative. The menu changes daily. A typical dinner might include an appetizer of chicken rolls with prosciutto and fresh mango and an entrée of grilled parrot fish with linguini and julienne vegetables.

For budget-priced fare in a lively student environment blending intellectual conversation, video games and general rowdiness, a long-time favorite spot is the **Frontier Restaurant** (2400 Central Avenue Northeast; 505-266-0550) across the street from the main entrance to the University of New Mexico campus. Food choices include burgers, spicy dishes such as *huevos rancheros* (served any time of day) and giant, sticky, delicious cinnamon rolls.

Farther out on Central, you can get a green-chili cheese dog, a rich, thick chocolate shake and a big dose of nostalgia at the **66 Diner** (1405 Central Avenue Northeast; 505-247-1421) a budget-priced, 1950s-style roadside diner designed with Historic Route 66 buffs in mind.

For what many consider the best homemade green-chili stew in Albuquerque, visit the budget-priced, 180-seat **Sanitary Tortilla Factory** (403 2nd Street Southwest; 505-242-4890).

Don't be put off by the unpretentious exterior of the **Adobe Rose** (6724 Central Avenue Southeast; 505-255-7673), located near the state fairground. This longstanding local favorite featuring New Mexican and Tex-Mex food in the budget range is renowned for its great fajitas.

If seafood is your preference, try the **Café Oceana** (1414 Central Avenue Southeast; 505-247-2233). Entrées are moderately priced and served in a friendly neighborhood atmosphere. Shrimp comes prepared in any of a half dozen different ways. The menu also features a daily fresh catch—for example, mahi mahi sautéed with garlic, ginger, bell peppers, jalapeños and red chili.

Our favorite Albuquerque restaurant for unusual food at moderate prices is the **Artichoke Café** (424 Central Avenue Southeast; 505-243-0200) where the menu changes frequently to take advantage of fresh, seasonal ingredients. The choices are wide ranging: veal osso buco, venison medallions, smoked-duck sausage, grilled sea scallops in red-pepper sauce over angelhair pasta or an array of pâtés served with french bread and cornichons. As one might expect, the first item on the menu is an artichoke—steamed and served with three dipping sauces. The walls carry paintings by local artists.

One of the finest restaurants in these parts is the **High Finance** (Sandia Crest; 505-243-9742). It's the setting that makes this deluxe-priced restaurant so special. At the top of the Sandia Peak Tramway, the restaurant affords an incomparable view of Albuquerque glistening in a vast, empty landscape a mile below. Entrées include prime rib, steaks and lobster. Guests with dinner reservations here receive a discount on their tramway fares.

Steaks and seafood are also served at the lower end of the tramway in the **Firehouse Restaurant at the Tram** (38 Tramway Road; 505-292-3473). Other specialties at this moderately priced restaurant include mesquite-barbecued ribs and chicken. The view of the city is spectacular even from the foot of the mountain, and those with dinner reservations at the Firehouse receive discounts on tram tickets. The Firehouse has a converted antique fire engine for a bar.

An Indian-owned restaurant is the elegant **Prairie Star** (★) (Jemez Dam Road, Bernalillo; 505-867-3327), located 15 minutes north of the city off Route 25 and operated by the Santa Ana Pueblo in a sprawling, mission-style adobe house. Menu items range from moderate to deluxe in price and include entrées such as marinated flank steak flambéed with bourbon as well as New Southwestern dishes like Pasta Sudoeste (spaghetti with green chili and cream).

ALBUQUERQUE AREA SHOPPING

The **Indian Pueblo Cultural Center** (2401 12th Street Northwest, Albuquerque; 505-843-7270) has a series of galleries surrounding the central dance plaza. All operated by the cultural center, the galleries differ by price ranges from curio items to museum-quality collectors' objects. Because the cultural center is owned by a coalition of Indian pueblos, authenticity is assured, making this one of the best places to shop for Native American pottery, sculpture, sandpaintings, rugs, kachinas and traditional and contemporary jewelry.

Shoppers can buy directly from Indian craftspersons along San Felipe Street across from the plaza in **Old Town**, which is also Albuquerque's art gallery and boutique district. Almost 100 shops can lure visitors into making Old Town an all-day expedition.

The **Santo Domingo Indian Trading Post** (two Old Town locations: 2049 South Plaza Northwest, 505-766-9855; and 401 San Felipe Street Northwest, 505-764-0129), specializing in jewelry, is owned and operated by the people of Santo Domingo Pueblo—a bit ironic since the trading post at the pueblo is operated by non-Indians.

The **Santa Fe Store** (2041½ South Plaza Northwest; 505-242-4707) shows works by Santa Fe-area folk artists, many of whom are not exhibited in Santa Fe. There are excellent examples of traditional and contemporary northern New Mexico arts including pictorial quilts, hand-carved wooden saints and fanciful wooden animals.

The **Chili Pepper Emporium** (328 San Felipe Street Northwest; 505-843-6505) has the largest and most complete selection in New Mexico—and the world, probably—of chili items, ranging from spices, sauces and jellies to chili-motif T-shirts and chili-shaped Christmas tree lights.

The **Good Stuff** (2102 Charlevoix Street Northwest; 505-243-5790) displays an outstanding array of Southwestern antiques, **Rosebud and Olive** (304 San Felipe Street Northwest; 505-247-2979) sells hand-painted "Wild West artwear" and **Old Town Perfume and Candle** (206½ San Felipe Street Northwest; 505-243-0859) carries unusual perfumes blended locally using desert-flower scents.

For more practical shopping needs, Albuquerque's major shopping malls are **Winrock Center** (Louisiana Boulevard Southeast and Indian School Road Southeast, near the Louisiana Boulevard exit from Route 40) and **Coronado Center** (Louisiana Boulevard Southeast and Menaul Boulevard Southeast).

ALBUQUERQUE AREA NIGHTLIFE

Albuquerque has a full range of after-hours entertainment, from rock-and-roll bars like **Confetti** (9800 Montgomery Boulevard Northeast; 505-298-2113) with a mixed crowd of University of New Mexico students and military personnel from Kirtland Air Force Base, to **Player's Sports Bar and Grill** (1520 Tramway Boulevard; 505-296-5926) where patrons come to watch sporting events daily from the lunch hour to the wee hours of the morning on 22 television sets.

The most popular bar in the university district is the **Fat Chance Bar and Grille** (2216 Central Avenue Southeast; 505-296-5653) where both students and professors come to socialize and listen to live music.

The top comedy club in town is **Laffs** (3100 Juan Tabo Boulevard Northeast; 505-296-5653), featuring local and national stand-up comedians as well as Tuesday open-mike amateur nights. A favorite disco frequented by singles from the uptown business district is **Nicole's Lounge** (2101 Louisiana Boulevard Northeast; 505-881-6800).

The **Sundance Saloon & Dance Hall** (12000 Candelaria Boulevard Northeast; 505-296-6761) features big-name country-and-western bands nightly and offers dance lessons on weeknights.

Albuquerque has a lively performing-arts scene, most of which centers around the University of New Mexico. Productions at the university's **Popejoy Hall** (505-277-3824) include plays by Broadway roadshow companies, performances of the **Albuquerque Civic Light Opera** (505-345-6577), concerts by the New Mexico **Jazz Workshop** (505-255-9798) and the **New Mexico Symphony Orchestra** (505-842-8565). Other theaters on campus include the Theatre Arts Department's **"X" Theatre** in the basement of the Fine Arts Center and the **Rodey Theater** adjoining Popejoy Hall. For schedule information on both theaters, call the Fine Arts Center box office (505-277-4402).

Another important performing-arts venue in Albuquerque is the historic **KiMo Theater** (423 Central Avenue Northwest; 505-848-1370), which hosts performances by groups including the **Albuquerque Ballet Company** (505-265-8150), the **New Mexico Repertory Company** (505-243-4500) and the unique bilingual **Compania de Teatro** (505-242-7929).

ALBUQUERQUE AREA PARKS

Paseo del Bosque—The bosque, or cottonwood forest, lining the banks of the Rio Grande is protected for future park development all the way through the city of Albuquerque. Most of this area remains wild, undeveloped and inaccessible to motor vehicles. A five-mile paved trail for joggers, cyclists and horse riders leads through the woods, following the river north from the Old Town vicinity to the city's edge in the North Valley where an unpaved river trail continues 12 more miles to Bernalillo and Coronado State Monument.

Facilities: Paved trail.

Getting there: Trail access from Campbell Road, Mountain Road or Rio Grande Nature Center on Candelaria Boulevard Northwest.

Rio Grande Nature Center State Park—The easiest access to the bosque and riverbank is this urban wildlife refuge. The visitor center has exhibits on the river's ecology. Observation windows on one side of the building overlook a shallow lake frequented by ducks, geese and herons, especially during migration seasons—November and April. The park is a favorite spot for birdwatching in all seasons. Two nature trails, each a mile-long loop, wind through the bosque, and one of them leads to several peaceful spots along the bank of the Rio Grande.

Facilities: Restrooms, trails, visitor center and gift shop; information, 505-344-7240.

Getting there: It's at 2901 Candelaria Boulevard Northwest, where Candelaria ends at the river a few blocks west of Rio Grande Boulevard.

Coronado State Park—Below the visitor center for the pueblo ruins at Coronado State Monument are pretty camping and picnic areas set amid stands of cottonwood, tamarisk and cholla cactus along the bank of the Rio Grande. Sandia Peak provides a spectacular backdrop.

Facilities: Picnic area, restrooms, showers, visitor center, playground and trails; restaurants and groceries nearby in Bernalillo; information, 505-867-5589. *Fishing:* Good.

Camping: There are 36 sites (15 with RV hookups); $7 per night for standard sites, $11.50 per night for hookups.

Getting there: Located 15 miles north of Albuquerque. Take the Bernalillo exit north from Route 25 and cross the bridge over the Rio Grande.

Cochiti Lake—At the confluence of the Santa Fe and Rio Grande rivers, Albuquerque's water reservoir and also its local recreation beach. Windsurfing on the lake is popular, and some people paddle kayaks. Power boating is permitted but restricted to no-wake speed.

Facilities: Picnic area, restrooms and boat ramp; groceries nearby in town of Cochiti Lake. *Fishing:* Good for large- and smallmouth bass, catfish and walleye. *Swimming:* Good.

Camping: Operated by the Cochiti Pueblo, the two campgrounds overlooking the lake are open year-round. Cochiti has 55 sites (34 with RV hookups) and Tetilla Peak has 50 sites (34 with RV hookups); $6 per night for standard sites, $8 per night for hookups.

Getting there: Located 36 miles north of Albuquerque on Route 25 and then 15 miles northwest on Route 22.

Santa Rosa Area

Lakes and some intriguing Wild West history invite you here. Of particular interest to history buffs, this is where the Billy the Kid legend is rooted, and indeed, this is where the Kid is buried. Located along the Pecos River, this town of 4600 population lies 110 miles east of Albuquerque at the junction of Routes 40 and 54. While Spanish farmers settled the town during the 1860s, its historic roots extend much deeper in time.

Spanish explorer Vasquez de Coronado built a bridge across the Pecos River in 1541, according to legend, ten miles south of present-day Santa Rosa at **Puerto de Luna**. Although the bridge no longer exists, the almost-ghost town makes for an interesting short excursion away from the interstate. In the 1880s, Puerto de Luna was the largest community in the southeastern quarter of New Mexico Territory. Today the stone county courthouse is beginning to crumble. Other historic buildings include a rock-faced church and a saloon where Billy the Kid hung out from time to time.

Santa Rosa's main vacation attractions are lakes, to the point that it calls itself "The City of Natural Lakes." Those who find the claim improbable for a town in the arid high plains of New Mexico will be even more surprised to learn that Santa Rosa is a mecca for scuba divers. (See "Santa Rosa Area Parks" below.)

If you want to Kid around, drive 46 miles south to **Fort Sumner**, whose claim to fame is that Billy the Kid was shot to death at a ranch outside of town in 1881. You might expect that "Billymania" would be more prevalent in the outlaw's home town of Lincoln, 100 miles to the south, where most of his escapades took place. But the fact is, the Billy the Kid capital of the Southwest is the town of Fort Sumner. It was here that he happened to be hiding out when the law caught up with him for the final time.

Two privately owned museums show Billy the Kid's life and legend. Each is good enough to occupy the curious for an hour or two and spur speculations about whether Billy was a frontier Robin Hood, a psychopathic killer or a product of media hype. There is some duplication between the two museums, since a number of the documents on exhibit are photocopies of originals in the state archives.

The **Billy the Kid Museum** (1601 East Fort Sumner Avenue; 505-355-2380; admission), which has a large collection of ranch antiques and a jail cell in which Billy is said to have been locked up once, is located near the east edge of town on the way to Fort Sumner State Monument.

The **Old Fort Sumner Museum** (Billy the Kid Road, Fort Sumner; 505-355-2942; admission) displays letters written by Billy to the governor to negotiate a pardon, letters from Sheriff Pat Garrett to his wife describing his search for the outlaw, a history of impostors who have claimed to be the real Billy the Kid, and a chronology of more than a dozen motion pictures about his brief, violent career. **Billy the Kid's Grave**, in the Maxwell family cemetery behind the Old Fort Sumner Museum, is locked securely behind iron bars because the headstone has been stolen twice.

Just down the road from Billy the Kid's grave, **Fort Sumner State Monument** (505-355-2573) marks the site of the army outpost for which the town was named. By the time Billy the Kid came to town, the fort had been converted to a ranch headquarters, and it was here that Garrett killed him. Just a few years earlier, the fort was the scene of larger and more infamous events. Colonel Kit Carson, after forcing the entire Navajo tribe to walk 300 miles from their homeland to this place, ordered them to build Fort Sumner as a concentration camp. More than 11,000 Indians lived in captivity here for six years, and 3000 of them died of starvation and disease. Finally the government concluded that keeping the Navajo at Fort Sumner was too expensive and that their homeland was without value to the white man. Then the surviving Navajo people were allowed to walk back home. Today, no trace remains of the original fort. Low adobe walls mark the location of the main fort buildings. The most moving part of the monument is a simple shrine of stones brought from all over the Navajo Reservation and left here by Native Americans in memory of those who lived and died here.

SANTA ROSA AREA HOTELS

Santa Rosa has over a dozen motels. Most of them are locally owned and operated, and all but one offer budget rates. The exception is the **Best Western Adobe Inn** (Will Rogers Drive at Route 40 exit 275; 505-472-3446), which straddles between the budget- and moderate-price ranges for its spacious, modern rooms.

A trip down the main street, Will Rogers Drive, reveals that close to half the commercial buildings in Santa Rosa are motels. A good bet is the **Shawford Motel** (1819 Will Rogers Drive; 505-472-3494), which has double-room units for families and operates one of the town's best restaurants next door.

Billy the Kid fans might consider spending the night in Fort Sumner. It is quiet. The town has two motels, both budget-priced. **The Oasis Motel** (1704 East Sumner Avenue; 505-355-7414) and the **Coronado Motel** (309 West Sumner Avenue; 505-355-2466) are standard roadside facilities with the basic amenities of motels everywhere.

Motels have been an important industry in Tucumcari since the 1940s, when the town was a natural evening stop along Old Route 66 because it was the only place for many miles. Today, billboards along Route 40 for hundreds of miles in each direction tout the fact that Tucumcari has 2000 beds for rent. A number of motels in town still offer the authentic flavor of roadside America half a century ago. Even their names—Buckaroo, Lasso, Palomino, Apache—evoke a notion of the West in an earlier era.

The finest motor inn in Tucumcari is the moderately priced **Ramada Inn** (1302 West Tucumcari Boulevard; 505-461-3140), which has in-room movies, phones and a laundromat. Among the best budget bargains is the **Sahara Sands Motel** (315 East Tucumcari Boulevard; 505-481-0330).

SANTA ROSA AREA RESTAURANTS

The **Club Café** (561 Parker Avenue; 505-472-3631) in Santa Rosa is a true Route 66 classic. This rather dark, very air-conditioned little eatery with its red-vinyl booths has been serving up enchiladas, chicken-fried steaks and the like since 1935. The present owner is an enthusiastic promoter of Old Route 66 nostalgia, and books on the subject are on sale at the cashier counter.

Santa Rosa also has a dozen other restaurants of more recent vintage, most of them either nationwide franchises or motel restaurants. For good Mexican food, try **Mateo's Family Restaurant** (Old Route 66; 505-472-5720). The best salad bar in town, along with steaks and seafood, are to be found at **Joseph's Restaurant** (865 Will Rogers Drive; 505-472-3361). Prices are in the budget range at all Santa Rosa restaurants.

In Fort Sumner, an all-around good place to eat is the family-style **Rio Pecos Restaurant** (309 Sumner Avenue; 505-355-7778). In the mood for Mexican food? Try **Tito's Burritos** (505 Sumner Avenue; 505-355-7820). Both are budget-priced.

Practically all the roughly 30 eating establishments in Tucumcari are familiar fast-food franchises. The nicest restaurant is the moderate-priced **Piñon Tree** (1302 West Tucumcari Boulevard; 505-461-3140), serving steak and seafood dinners. The breakfast menu features on-the-road fare such as biscuits and gravy, breakfast burritos and steak and eggs with grits on the side.

SANTA ROSA AREA PARKS

Blue Hole—This spot attracts dive-club caravans from Texas, Oklahoma and Colorado on most warm weekends. Formed by a collapsed cave and fed by a subterranean river, the lake is deeper than it is wide—81 feet in depth. The water is amazingly clear. Carp live in the dark reaches far below the surface. Swimming is popular, and on hot summer days teenagers can often be seen cannonballing into Blue Hole from the cliffs above even though the water temperature is a very chilly 60°.

Facilities: Restrooms and dive shop.

Getting there: Located at the southeast edge of Santa Rosa on Blue Hole Road. Follow the signs from Will Rogers Drive (the business loop from Route 40).

Janes-Wallace Memorial Park—This park is really no more than a local fishing hole. But don't be put off. It's a great place to drop a line and is stocked with what may just be your dinner.

Facilities: Restrooms. *Fishing:* Good for bass, catfish and rainbow trout.

Camping: Allowed anywhere in the park.

Getting there: Follow 3rd Street, which becomes Route 91, south from Will Rogers Drive.

Santa Rosa Lake State Park—A flood-control reservoir along the Pecos River, Santa Rosa Lake provides so much irrigation water to the surrounding farmlands that some years it can practically disappear in late summer. Phone ahead to make sure the lake has water in it. In wet years, the extensive shallows make for some of the best fishing in the state. Especially known for walleye pike, the lake is also stocked with catfish and bass. Most fishing here is done from boats. Waterskiing is also popular. A short "scenic trail" starts from the state park's Rocky Point Campground. There is no shade anywhere around the lake.

Facilities: Picnic tables, restrooms, showers, boat ramp, playground, trails, visitor center; information, 505-472-3110. *Fishing:* Good for walleye pike, catfish and bass.

Camping: Rocky Point has 50 sites (16 with RV hookups) and Juniper has 25 sites; $7 per night for standard sites, $11 per night for hookups.

Getting there: From Santa Rosa, drive out 8th Street and continue north for seven miles.

Sumner Lake State Park—On the way from Santa Rosa to Fort Sumner, this irrigation reservoir on the Pecos River is one of New Mexico's most underused fishing lakes. It is Y-shaped, with several quiet side canyons and a little village of summer cabins. The lake offers good spots for fishing from the shore in shallow, medium or deep water. State park areas below the dam provide access to both banks of the river.

Facilities: Picnic tables, restrooms, showers, boat ramp, playground; information, 505-355-2541. *Fishing:* Good for crappie, catfish, bluegill and northern pike. *Swimming:* Permitted.

Camping: There are 23 tent sites ($7 per night) and 18 RV hookups ($11 per night).

Getting there: Located six miles off Route 84. The marked turnoff is 35 miles south of Santa Rosa and ten miles north of Fort Sumner.

Bosque Redondo—This Fort Sumner city park consists of a series of small lakes on 15 acres. The grassy shore, shaded by cottonwood trees, is a nice picnic spot. Ducks live on the lakes year-round.

Facilities: Restrooms. *Fishing:* Good.

Getting there: Located two miles south of Fort Sumner on a marked road from the east edge of town.

Conchas Lake State Park—Conchas Lake, on the Canadian River north of Tucumcari, is one of the most popular recreation lakes in New Mexico. Most of the 50-mile shoreline is privately owned, so the only easy public access to the lake is the state park, which includes developed areas on both sides of the dam.

Facilities: Picnic tables, restrooms, showers, playground, boat ramp, marinas and groceries; restaurants, lodging, golf course and air strip nearby; information, 505-868-2270. *Fishing:* Good. *Swimming:* Permitted.

Camping: There are 100 sites (33 are full RV hookups). Primitive camping available. Fees per night are $6 for primitive sites, $7 for standard sites and $11 for hookups.

Getting there: It's 25 miles north of Route 40 from the Newkirk/Route 129 exit, which is 27 miles east of Santa Rosa, or 31 miles northeast of Tucumcari on Route 104.

Gordon Wildlife Area—Tucumcari has a municipal wildlife refuge on the edge of town. The 770 acres of wetlands provide a rest stop for migrating ducks and geese. Eagles are sometimes seen here.

Facilities: Auto road and hiking trails.

Getting there: Located just east of town, marked by a sign on Tucumcari Boulevard (Route 40 Business Loop).

Ute Lake State Park—This reservoir was created in 1963 specifically for recreational purposes to bring tourism dollars to the Tucumcari area. Records have been set here for the largest bass ever caught in New Mexico. The marina has boats for rent.

Facilities: Picnic tables, restrooms, showers, boat ramps, marina and hiking trails; restaurants, lodging and groceries in the lakeshore community nearby; information, 505-487-2284. *Fishing:* Good.

Camping: There are 23 standard sites (18 with RV hookups) and three primitive camping areas. Fees per night are $6 for primitive sites, $7 for standard sites and $11 for hookups.

Getting there: It's 25 miles northeast of Tucumcari on Route 54.

Mountainair Area

East of Route 25, 39 miles from Belen via Routes 47 and 60, the quiet, little town of Mountainair used to call itself the "Pinto Bean Capital of the World." Today it serves the local ranching community and provides travelers a base for exploring the widely separated units of **Salinas Pueblo Missions National Monument** (505-847-2585). Although the Mountainair area is sparsely inhabited now, it was one of the most populous regions of New Mexico for several centuries. The national monument preserves the ruins of three large Anasazi pueblos that date back to the 1200s.

The occupants gathered salt from nearby dry lakebeds and prospered by trading it to other pueblos as well as plains Indian tribes. The communities still flourished in 1598, when the first Spanish soldiers and priests arrived. Massive, crumbling walls of Franciscan mission churches adjoin each pueblo site. The Spanish colonial presence lasted less than 80 years before famine, drought, disease and Apache raids forced priests and Indians alike to abandon all the pueblos in the area, moving to Isleta and other Rio Grande pueblos.

The **Abo** unit of the national monument is just off Route 60, nine miles west of Mountainair. Unexcavated pueblo ruins and the remains of the Mission of San Gregorio de Abo fill the small park area sandwiched between private farms. A traditional Anasazi ceremonial kiva built within the church *convento* at Abo puzzles archaeologists, since elsewhere in the Salinas pueblos priests destroyed kivas to halt native religious practices.

The red-walled mission at **Quarai** eight miles north of Mountainair on Route 55 was the headquarters for the Spanish Inquisition in New Mexico during the 17th century. Today, in its tranquil setting alongside big cottonwoods at the foot of the Manzano Mountains, Quarai is perhaps the most photogenic of the three Salinas mission ruins. The adjoining pueblo ruins are thoroughly buried and difficult to see. A small museum displays relics found at the site.

The **Gran Quivira unit** (★) 25 miles south of Mountainair via Route 55 presents the national monument's most extensively excavated Anasazi ruins. One of the largest pueblos in New Mexico, the limestone complex was home to about 2000 people at its height. Facilities include a visitor center with interpretive displays and a picnic area. There is no camping at any of the Salinas Pueblo Missions National Monument sites.

In Mountainair, the **Shaffer Hotel** (505-847-9911) stands as a monument to the whimsical imagination of Clem "Pop" Shaffer, the town's blacksmith in the 1920s and 1930s. Inside and out, the hotel's unique handcrafted ornamentation continues to make visitors smile. Indian symbols are everywhere, and colored stones have been set into concrete walls to form animal shapes. The Shaffer Hotel now operates as a bed and breakfast, café and gift shop.

Those who would like to see more of "Pop" Shaffer's work can do so at **Rancho Bonito** (★) (505-847-2832), south of Mountainair on the road to Gran Quivira. The ranch is owned by Shaffer's heirs, who are working to restore it gradually. Walking tours are available in the summer months whenever the "open" sign hangs on the front gate. In the original ranch cabin, visitors can see examples of the fanciful animals Shaffer carved from tree roots. The state of New Mexico used to make an official gift of one of his wooden animals to each newly elected U.S. president. Both the Shaffer Hotel and Rancho Bonito are on the National Register of Historic Places.

MOUNTAINAIR AREA HOTEL

The place to stay in Mountainair is the **Shaffer Hotel** (505-847-9911). Originally built as a hardware store in 1923, it was converted into a hotel soon afterward by renowned local folk artist "Pop" Shaffer for his wife. Shaffer spent the next ten years ornamenting the hotel with his unique, self-taught designs in paint, wood and stone. It closed in 1943 due to lack of help and remained closed for 40 years. Restoration of the hotel began in 1982 and is now 90 percent complete. The Shaffer offers simple, pleasant rooms reminiscent of an Old West hotel. Guests order breakfast from the 1935 menu and pay 1935 prices—5 to 25 cents. Room rates, too, are budget. You can't miss the place—it's the biggest building in town.

MOUNTAINAIR AREA RESTAURANT

The **Pueblo Café** (505-847-9911) in Mountainair's Shaffer Hotel serves sandwiches and tasty full meals at budget prices. The unique decor alone

(Text continued on page 314.)

Be a Road Warrior

Albuquerque residents know it as the "Big I"—the congested freeway interchange in the middle of the city where two famous routes of bygone eras meet.

Interstate Route 25 follows the path of the oldest highway still in use in the United States. Originally known as El Camino Real de Tierra Adentro ("the Royal Road to the Inner Land"), it was established in 1598 to link Mexico City with New Mexico, the northernmost province of the Spanish empire in America. El Camino Real spanned a distance of 1700 miles, crossing brutal expanses of desert and venturing through lands guarded by hostile Apache warriors. Spanish soldiers in armor traveled its length, as did hooded monks on foot. Horses, cows and *vaqueros*—cowboys—first came to the American West via the old Royal Road.

Interstate Route 40 traces Old Route 66, the first paved highway connecting the eastern United States and the West Coast. Route 66 was the kind of highway dreams are made of. It ran across vast, sunbaked, brightly colored desert inhabited by cowboys and Indians all the way to Hollywood, capturing America's imagination as it went. John Steinbeck wrote about it. Glenn Miller immortalized it in song. The television series "Route 66" was one of the most popular programs of the 1960s. Old Route 66 became practically synonymous with the mystique of the open road.

Before the two-lane, blacktop road was replaced by today's high-speed, limited-access highway, travelers had no alternative to driving down the main street of each small town along the route—places like Tucumcari, Santa Rosa, Laguna and Gallup. Today, chambers of commerce in these towns enthusiastically promote Route 66 nostalgia, and what used to be cheap roadside diners and tourist traps are now preserved as historic sites.

While both El Camino Real and Old Route 66 have been paved and straightened into modern interstate highways, travelers willing to take the extra time can still experience much of what it must have felt like to travel either of these roads in times past.

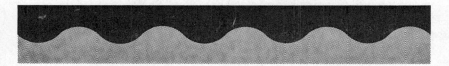

Alternate highways, usually traffic-free and often out of sight of the busy interstate, parallel Route 25 almost all the way from the Indian pueblos north of Albuquerque to El Paso and the Mexican border. These secondary highways trace El Camino Real more exactly than the interstate does, and the New Mexico state government has put up historical markers along them to identify important landmarks from Spanish colonial days such as the stark landscape of the Jornada del Muerto ("Journey of Death").

Good Camino Real alternatives to the interstate include Route 313 from Albuquerque north to San Felipe Pueblo; Routes 47 and 304 south of Albuquerque on the opposite side of the Rio Grande from the interstate, serving old rural communities such as Bosque Farms, Valencia and Belen; Route 1 from San Antonio through Bosque del Apache Wildlife Refuge to Elephant Butte Reservoir; Route 187 from Truth or Consequences to Las Cruces; and Route 28 from La Mesilla, just west of Las Cruces, to El Paso and the border.

Most of Old Route 66 has been obscured by interstate Route 40. Only a few sections of frontage roads and old secondary highways—notably Route 124 from Mesita through the villages of the Laguna Indian Reservation to Acoma—give any hint of the road that used to carry travelers across the desert. The place to look for remnants of Old Route 66 is along the main streets of towns that the interstate has bypassed. Deco-style diners, quaint ma-and-pa motels and old-fashioned curio shops with concrete Indian teepees out front and signs like "Last Chance Before the Desert!" and "See the Baby Rattlers!" can still be found on Route 40 business loops all across New Mexico, from Tucumcari to Albuquerque's Central Avenue to Gallup where the main street was recently renamed Historic 66.

Traveling any of these alternate routes takes twice as long as driving straight down the interstate. The rewards are several—avoiding busy truck routes, discovering the offbeat charm of small-town New Mexico and sampling what cross-country travel used to be like in the American Southwest.

makes it worth planning a meal stop here. "Pop" Shaffer painted the ceiling panels with bright Indian designs, each one different. The furniture is hand-painted, and old newspaper and magazine articles telling the hotel's history are framed on the walls.

MOUNTAINAIR AREA PARK

Manzano Mountain State Park—This small state park in the foothills near the village of Manzano and the Quarai Unit of Salinas Pueblo Missions National Monument provides the most convenient camping for visitors to the monument. The forest road that continues past the state park turnoff leads to the Red Canyon trailhead at the Manzano Mountain Wilderness boundary.

Facilities: Picnic tables, restrooms, playgrounds and nature trails; information, 505-847-2820.

Camping: There are 20 sites (5 with RV hookups); $7 per night for standard sites, $11 per night for hookups.

Getting there: It's 13 miles northwest of Mountainair off Route 55.

Socorro Area

Just off Route 25, the town of Socorro is so small that its distinctive character is overshadowed by the strip of motels and gas stations along the interstate business loop. But take the time to look around; it will be worth it. This sleepy municipality of 9000 souls is actually one of the oldest towns in the state. Located along the Rio Grande Valley 75 miles south of Albuquerque, it dates to 1615 when Franciscan priests began building a mission.

Socorro has a small, attractive historic district that surrounds the plaza a short distance west of California Street on Manzaneras Avenue. Noteworthy are the restored **San Miguel Mission** (403 Camino Real; 505-835-1620) built in 1820 on the site of the earlier church that was destroyed during the Pueblo Revolt of 1680, the **Garcia Opera House**—one of two opera houses in town during the 1880s—and the old **Valverde Hotel** (203 Manzaneras Avenue East). The **Hilton Block**, near the opera house, is named for a relative of hotel tycoon Conrad Hilton who operated a drug store there in the 1930s. Conrad Hilton was born and raised in San Antonio, a town about nine miles south of Socorro that is so tiny it has no hotel or motel.

Northwest of Socorro's downtown area is the New Mexico School of Mines. The school's museum has been combined with specimens donated by prominent mining speculator C. T. Brown to form the **New Mexico Mineral Museum** (School of Mines Road; 505-835-5420), housing one of the largest rock collections on earth with over 10,000 pieces including gems and fossils as well as mining artifacts.

An 18-mile drive south of Socorro on Route 25, **Bosque del Apache National Wildlife Refuge** (505-835-1828) is especially worth visiting between November and March when it presents one of the most spectacular birdwatching opportunities around. The refuge was established during the 1930s to protect the sandhill crane, which had nearly vanished along the Rio Grande. Local farmers grow corn on refuge land during the summer months and leave one-third of the crop for the birds. Today, more than 12,000 cranes spend the winter at the refuge. Besides the four-foot-tall sandhill cranes and a couple of rare whooping cranes that were introduced into the flock in an unsuccessful breeding experiment, the refuge provides a winter home for about 40,000 snow geese. The white geese often rise en masse from the manmade wetlands to fill the sky in a noisy, dazzling display.

Of several ghost towns in the Socorro area, perhaps the most interesting is old **San Pedro** (★), across the river from San Antonio where visitors exit the interstate to go to Bosque del Apache. To get to San Pedro, drive east from San Antonio for 1.4 miles on Route 380 and turn south on an unpaved road. Ruins of several adobe houses in Mexican and early Territorial styles remain from this town where people used to grow grapes and produce champagne. Tamarisks have grown up through the floors of the houses to conceal much of the village. An abandoned mission church still stands.

Fifty miles west of Socorro on Route 60 is the unusually named **National Radio Astronomy Observatory Very Large Array** (505-772-4011). These 27 giant parabolic dish antennas, each weighing 100 tons, are used to search deep space for faint radio waves emitted by celestial objects. Together, the antennas can "see" as well as a telescope with a lens 20 miles in diameter. The Very Large Array is also used in combination with other radio observatories around the world to explore the far limits of the universe. A visitor center at the site explains how it works, and a one-hour, self-guided walking tour lets visitors see the antennas up close.

SOCORRO AREA HOTEL

Every motel in Socorro falls within the budget range. Accommodations are found in two clusters along California Street, the business loop from Route 25. The best in town is the **Best Western Golden Manor Motel** (507 North California Street; 505-835-0230) about a block from Mission San Miguel. Representative of the good, clean independent motels in Socorro is the **Motel Vagabond** (North California Street; 505-835-0276).

SOCORRO AREA RESTAURANTS

Socorro has several small budget restaurants that serve excellent New Mexican food. Try **Armijo's Mexican Restaurant** (1010 South Route 85; 505-835-1917) or **Don Juan's Mexican Food** (118 East Manzaneras Avenue; 505-835-9967). For a wider selection, **Steve's Restaurant** (400 North California Street; 505-835-1259) offers an eclectic menu of Italian, Greek, Mexican and American dishes. The **Valverde Steak House** (203 East Manzaneras Avenue; 505-835-3380) serves moderately priced steaks and seafood. It is in an old hotel listed on the National Register of Historic Places.

One of the most interesting restaurants in the Socorro area is the **Owl Bar & Café** (505-835-9946) in the center of the small town of San Antonio nine miles south of Socorro. Not as budget-basic as its name suggests, this restaurant offers everything from inexpensive sandwiches to moderately priced seafood dinners such as Alaskan King crab. Their claim to serve the best green-chili cheeseburgers in the world may well be accurate.

Grants/Gallup Area

Just over an hour's drive west of Albuquerque on Route 40, Grants is situated at the center of an intriguing array of places—the most ancient continuously inhabited pueblos in New Mexico, a vast and forbidding lava bed with ice caves, a landmark where centuries of explorers left their marks and solitary, massive Mt. Taylor, a sacred mountain in Navajo tradition.

Midway between Albuquerque and Grants, **Laguna Pueblo** is home to more than 6000 native people. The old pueblo, situated on a hillside overlooking the interstate, dates back to 1699. The centerpiece of Old Laguna is San Jose de Laguna church, a mission church in use since the pueblo's founding. Most Laguna residents live in modern villages scattered across the reservation.

Travelers in no particular hurry and tired of dodging trucks on the interstate can catch a remnant of **Old Route 66** at Laguna. The road parallels Route 40 and plays peekaboo with it all the way to the Acoma reservation.

Acoma Sky City, 15 miles east of Grants on Route 40 and another 15 miles south on a marked tribal road, was built on a solitary mesa top above a valley of stone pillars in the 12th century—earlier than the pueblos at Salinas, Bandelier or Pecos. It has been inhabited continuously ever since. New houses are still being built on the roofs of houses centuries old. There is no school bus service, electricity or running water on the mesa, so today only 15 families live in the Sky City year-round. All of them work as potters or pottery painters. More than 400 well-maintained homes in the old pueblo are used as spiritual retreats and summer houses by their owners who live in modern reservation towns near the interstate. Shuttle buses carry visitors up the steep road, built by a motion-picture crew in 1969, for an hour-long, guided tour of the pueblo. Those who choose to can hike back down on the short, steep trail used by Acoma residents for at least 800 years before the road was built. For schedule information, call 505-252-1139.

Grants got its start as a railroad stop back when the region's major industry was carrot farming. In 1950, a Navajo sheepherder discovered a strange, yellow rock that turned out to be radioactive, and Grants suddenly became the center of a uranium mining boom. The mines have been closed since the 1970s. Today, despite its prime location amid many of western New Mexico's best sightseeing highlights, Grants is a low-key highwayside town with few of the trappings of a tourist mecca. Those who wish to learn more about the uranium era can do so at the **New Mexico Museum of Mining at Grants** (100 Iron Street; 505-287-4802). Visitors ride an elevator down from the museum's main floor to explore an underground mine replica.

Route 53, a quiet, secondary highway, leads south and west of Grants to two national monuments—the first ever established in the United States and one of the newest. The highway continues across the Ramah Navajo and Zuni reservations. Near the pueblo of Zuni, Route 602 goes north and returns to Route 40 at Gallup.

Since **El Malpais National Monument** was created in 1988, federal funding has not been available for facilities such as campgrounds, interpretive exhibits or paved roads. The visitor center is in a former service station (620 East Santa Fe Street; 505-285-5406) in Grants. Malpais is Spanish for "bad land," and the 115,000-acre national monument protects one of the largest lava beds in New Mexico. Two highways—Route 53 on the north and Route 117 on the east—border the lava flow. They are connected by a rugged dirt road that runs along the west and south perimeters and should only be attempted in a high-clearance vehicle. Hiking opportunities in El Malpais National Monument are discussed in the "Hiking" section below.

The most rewarding stop on a quick visit to El Malpais is **Bandera Crater and Ice Cave** (505-783-4303), a privately owned tourist concession that eventually will be acquired as part of the monument. Separate easy trails take visitors to the crater of one of the volcanoes that made the lava field and to a subterranean ice cave, a lava tube where the temperature stays below freezing even on the hottest summer days.

At **El Morro National Monument** (505-783-4226), a 15-minute drive west on Route 53 from Bandera Crater, a high, white-sandstone bluff marks the location of a 200,000-gallon waterhole. Atop the bluff are the ruins of Atsina, a 13th-century pueblo where about 1500 people lived. The Indians carved petroglyphs along the trail between the pueblo and the waterhole, starting a tradition that would last 800 years. When conquistador Don Juan de Oñate camped by the pool in 1605, returning after his discovery of the Gulf of California, he scratched an inscription in the sandstone to memorialize his passing. Spanish explorers added their often-lengthy messages to the rock face until 1774. The absence of inscriptions for 75 years bears mute witness to the social turmoil surrounding the Mexican Revolution and the Mexican War. The first English inscription appeared in 1849, and soldiers, surveyors and pioneers continued to carve their names in the cliff until 1904. Two years later, President Theodore Roosevelt declared El Morro the nation's first national monument, and defacing the rock with its historical graffiti has been prohibited ever since.

Zuni Pueblo, situated on Route 53 about 30 miles west of El Morro and 40 miles south of Gallup, is the largest pueblo in New Mexico with a population of about 7000. The Zuni people speak a language unlike any other known Native American dialect. The modern town of Zuni has evolved from a pueblo called Halona, which had already been established for centuries when Coronado arrived in 1540, believing it to be one of the fabulously wealthy, mythical "Seven Golden Cities of Cibola." The town does not look like anything special at first glance, but the more you wander the back streets, the more antiquity reveals itself. Stone foundations 800 years old support many modern buildings in Zuni Pueblo, and crumbling stone storage sheds in people's yards may have been built long before Christopher Columbus first set sail.

Gallup, numbering about 20,000 population, rests astride old Route 66 just 22 miles from the Arizona border. Located near both the Navajo and Zuni reservations, this historic town bills itself as the "Gateway to Indian Country." Pawn shops, bars and a row of neon motels lend a hard edge to the local ambience, but the annual Inter-Tribal Ceremonial and large concentration of Native Americans make it a prime place to view native crafts.

GRANTS/GALLUP AREA HOTELS

Motels are a mainstay of the fragile economy in Grants. There are about 20 of them in town. The more modern franchise motels, located near the easternmost Grants exit from Route 40, include the modern **Best Western The Inn** (1501 East Santa Fe Avenue; 505-287-7901) with large guest rooms as well as amenities like an indoor swimming pool and sauna. Moderate.

Farther west along the busy main street, Santa Fe Avenue, is a number of independent motels, all budget. Several of them formerly belonged to national chains, still recognizable under fresh coats of paint. The **Sands Motel** (112 McArthur Street; 505-287-2996) is a block off the main route and offers a little more peace and quiet.

An hour's drive to the west, Gallup has more motels comparable in quality and price to those in Grants. It also has one unique historic hotel that is both rustic and elegant. The **El Rancho Hotel** (1000 East Historic 66; 505-863-9311) was built in 1937 by the brother of film producer D. W. Griffith. It was the place where movie stars stayed while shooting Westerns in the spectacular red-rock canyon country around Gallup. Ronald Reagan (surely you remember him before he was president) stayed here half a century ago. Other illustrious guests included John Wayne, Humphrey Bogart,

Spencer Tracy, Katharine Hepburn, Alan Ladd and Kirk Douglas. Rich, dark wood polished to a gleam predominates in the larger-than-life, two-story lobby. Mounted elk heads decorate massive wood beams, and Navajo rugs hang above the stone fireplace. Room rates in the old hotel are moderate, and budget-priced motel rooms are available in a modern annex next door.

Accommodations are almost nonexistent in Zuni country. One delightful exception is the **Vogt Ranch** (Ramah; 505-783-4362), a budget-priced bed and breakfast operated by an innkeeper from England. The bright, airy rooms are in a modern ranch house set well away from the highway. The turnoff is just east of Ramah, midway between El Morro National Monument and Zuni Pueblo.

GRANTS/GALLUP AREA RESTAURANTS

Grants has several budget-priced restaurants that serve good New Mexican food. The family-style **Monte Carlo Café** (721 West Santa Fe Avenue; 505-287-9250) serves a great sheepherder sandwich—a steak sandwich on a tortilla with chili and cheese. **Jaramillos Mexi-Catessen** (213 North 3rd Street; 505-287-9308), a hole-in-the-wall local favorite, offers a choice of eating on the premises or ordering take-out for a spicy picnic lunch. Fancier, but still in the budget-price range, is **El Jardin** (912 Lobo Canyon Road; 505-285-5231), featuring more sophisticated Mexican entrées such as chimichangas, flautas and machaca burros.

For plain old good food and plenty of it, consider the budget-priced **Iron Skillet** (Route 40 at Horizon Boulevard; 505-285-6621) at the Petro Truck Stop in Milan west of Grants. This is one of the largest truck stops along the length of Route 40, and the restaurant confirms the adage that the best food is to be found where the most semi trucks are parked out front. Open 24 hours daily, the Iron Skillet offers both full family menus and an impressive all-you-can-eat buffet and salad bar. Each booth has a telephone.

In Gallup, an unusual eatery is the restaurant in the historic **El Rancho Hotel** (1000 East Historic 66; 505-863-9311). The food is fairly conventional budget-to-moderate-priced American fare, but movie stars like John Wayne, Humphrey Bogart and Ronald Reagan once ate here and now have menu items named after them as well as publicity photos on the walls—a little bit of old Hollywood in Indian country!

Budget-priced New Mexican food is served at **Genaro's** (600 West Hill Avenue; 505-863-6761), a well-hidden, little café specializing in stuffed sopapillas. Also good is **Peewee's Place** (2206 East Historic 66; 505-722-5159), a family-style restaurant serving both Mexican and American dishes as well as huge cinnamon rolls.

In the moderate-price range, New Mexican beef dishes such as *carne adovada* and green-chili steak are on the menu alongside Italian food at **Panz Alegra** (1201 East Historic 66; 505-722-7229). Another popular mid-range restaurant is the **Ranch Kitchen** (3001 West Historic 66; 505-722-2537), where waiters in Native American garb serve American and Mexican fare in an atmosphere defined by Indian art and motifs.

GRANTS/GALLUP AREA SHOPPING

Indian jewelry is said to be the leading industry in Gallup. The number of wholesalers, Indian galleries and pawn shops specializing in rugs and jewelry supports this claim, as does the presence of buyers and collectors from all over the world. As the biggest town on the edge of the Navajo Reservation and the nearest town to Zuni, the largest of New Mexico's Indian pueblos, Gallup is the natural location for trading companies that deal directly with Native American artists and craftsworkers.

Prices for Indian items are normally lower in Gallup than in Santa Fe or Albuquerque, but quality is more variable. While state law protects Indians and collectors alike from fraud in the sale of Indian-made goods, it can require an experienced and discerning eye to tell handmade craft items from those made in factories that employ Indians or to tell genuinely old items from newly made ones "antiqued" to appear old. Still, the region has been a major Indian arts-and-crafts trading center for more than a century, and it is possible to find valuable, turn-of-the-century Germantown blankets and forgotten pieces of "old pawn" turquoise and silver jewelry.

The largest concentration of Indian traders is along Historic 66 between 2nd and 3rd streets. The oldest shop on the block is **Richardson's** (222 West Historic 66; 505-722-4762), where the small, modest facade gives little hint of the treasures in several large rooms inside. This is one of several downtown pawn shops that serve as "banks" for the Navajo people, continuing the tradition whereby the Indians store their individual wealth in the form of handmade jewelry, use it as needed to collateralize loans and redeem it for ceremonials.

Another large, highly reputable Indian trading company is **OB Enterprises** (3330 East Historic 66; 505-722-5846). Visitors interested in the materials and techniques of Indian jewelry making can learn about them on a visit to **Thunderbird Jewelry Supply** (1921 West Historic 66; 505-722-4323). Recently, galleries have been appearing along Coal Street, downtown Gallup's main drag a block south of Historic 66. Several of them emphasize contemporary Indian and Southwestern arts including painting and sculpture.

Zuni Pueblo has several well-stocked Indian galleries, including **Shiwi Trading Post** (505-782-5501) and **Turquoise Village** (800-748-2405).

GRANTS/GALLUP AREA PARKS

Bluewater Lake State Park—Secluded in a valley halfway between Grants and Gallup, this picturesque reservoir dates back to the 1920s. The lake is said to have one of the highest fish-catch rates of all New Mexican lakes. Near the state park campground, a trail leads down to a lush side canyon.

Facilities: Picnic tables, restrooms, showers, boat ramp, marina, playground and hiking trails; groceries near the entrance; information, 505-876-2391. *Fishing:* Good; the lake is stocked trout.

Camping: There are 150 sites (15 with RV hookups); primitive camping is allowed near the lake. Fees per night are $6 for primitive sites, $7 for standard sites and $11 for hookups.

Getting there: Located on Route 412, seven miles south of the exit from Route 40, which is 19 miles west of Grants.

Ramah Lake—Mormon settlers created this small lake in the 1880s for irrigation. It operated for generations as a private fishing lake and has been open to the public since 1987.

Facilities: None. *Fishing:* Good; bass and bluegills are the most common fish in the lake. There are also a few trout.

Getting there: Located just north of Ramah on Route 53. Ramah is near the eastern boundary of the Zuni Reservation, 55 miles southwest of Grants.

Zuni Lakes—The Zuni tribe operates nine fishing lakes in the hills of the reservation. A fishing permit must be obtained from tribal headquarters in the town of Zuni. Boating is allowed on all lakes, though gasoline motors are prohibited.

Facilities: Blackrock Lake has picnic facilities and a playground. *Swimming:* Permitted at Ojo Caliente, Nutria Lakes, Bolton Lake and Eustace Lake. *Fishing:* Good at all lakes.

Camping: Primitive campsites are available at Blackrock Lake, Ojo Caliente, Nutria Lakes, No. 2 and No. 4, Bolton Lake and Eustace Lake. Campgrounds at six of the lakes are open all year; $3 overnight or $8 for a stay up to eight days.

Getting there: Blackrock Lake is located three miles east of Zuni off Route 53. Bolton Lake and Eustace Lake are also just east of Zuni. Galestino Lakes are eight miles south of Route 53 on an unpaved road. Nutria Lakes are seven to 11 miles north of Route 53 on an unpaved road. Ojo Caliente is ten miles south of Zuni on Tribal Route 2. Pescado Lake is 17 miles east of Zuni just of Route 53.

Red Rock State Park—The park's main feature is its rodeo grounds nestled in a sheer-walled canyon. It is the site of several important Indian events, including the annual Inter-Tribal Ceremonial, the largest powwow in the United States. The small museum exhibits ancient, historic and contemporary Indian arts and crafts, including pottery, kachinas, baskets, masks and oil paintings, by artists from various tribes in the region. Named for the red sandstone cliffs that lend an austere beauty to the surrounding descent, this 640-acre park also contains archaeological sites that date back over a thousand years.

Facilities: Picnic tables, restrooms, showers and trails; information, 505-722-3839.

Camping: There are 145 sites with hookups; $8 to $12 per night.

Getting there: Located just off Route 40 east of Gallup.

The Sporting Life

BALLOONING

Hot-air balloons are one of Albuquerque's greatest claims to fame. Those who want to try ballooning for themselves and see what it's like to float above the city on the breeze can do so by contacting any of several local companies that offer rides. Contact **Cameron's Balloons** (2950 San Joaquin Avenue Southeast; 505-265-4007) or the **World Balloon Corp.** (4800 Eubank Boulevard Northeast; 505-293-6800).

HORSEBACK RIDING

Albuquerque has two popular areas for horseback riding—the Rio Grande bosque and the foothills of Sandia Peak. Near the river, **Los Amigos Stables** (10600 4th Street Northwest; 505-898-8173) rents horses and offers guided tours. Individual rentals and group tours are also available at **Tramway Riding Stables** (25 Tramway Boulevard Northeast; 505-293-1270) in the hills overlooking the city and **Turkey Track Stables** (Tijeras; 505-281-1772) east of the city near Route 40 in Tijeras Canyon.

SKIING

An average annual snowfall of 183 inches make Sandia Peak one of the most popular ski slopes in New Mexico. **Sandia Peak Ski Area** (505-296-9585) can be reached either by car or by the Sandia Peak Aerial Tramway. Sandia Peak also offers great cross-country skiing, especially on the Crest and 10-K trails, which begin near the Sandia Crest House at the top of the auto road.

Primitive roads on **Mt. Taylor** in the Grants/Gallup Area are also used for cross-country skiing. For information on routes and conditions, contact the Cibola National Forest—Mt. Taylor District Ranger Station (201 Roosevelt Street; 505-287-8833) in Grants.

SKI RENTALS   In Albuquerque, cross-country skis are available for rental at the **Sandia Crest House** (505-243-0605) and at **The Bike Coop Ltd.** (3407 Central Avenue Northeast; 505-265-5170). Downhill skis are rented by several sporting-goods stores, including **Sport About** (North Towne Plaza, Wyoming Boulevard at Academy Boulevard; 505-821-8402), **New Mexico Ski Systems** (Foot Hill Shopping Center, Juan Tabo and Menaul boulevards; 505-299-9593) and **Competitive Spirit** (9800 Montgomery Boulevard Northeast; 505-275-2600).

SAILBOARDING

For a glide across one of New Mexico's lakes, take your board in hand and hoist the sail. The sport is most popular at Cochiti Lake between Albuquerque and Santa Fe. Windsurfing is also permitted at Bluewater Lake in the Grants/Gallup Area and on Santa Rosa, Conchas and Ute lakes in the eastern part of the state. Sailboards can be rented in Albuquerque at **Action Sports** (7509 Menaul Boulevard Northeast; 505-884-5611).

TENNIS

Match point. Albuquerque has several municipal tennis courts where you can swing a racquet, including **Arroyo del Oso Park** (Wyoming Boulevard and Spain Street Northeast), **Los Altos Park** (10300 Lomas Boulevard Northeast), the **Jerry Cline Tennis Complex** (Constitution Boulevard at Louisiana Boulevard Northeast; 505-256-2032) and the **Albuquerque Tennis Complex** (1903 Stadium Boulevard Southeast; 505-848-1381). Tennis courts are very rare outside of Albuquerque in Central New Mexico.

GOLF

Tee off in Albuquerque at the **University of New Mexico South Course** (Yale Boulevard at George Street Southeast; 505-277-4546) or **Arroyo del Oso Golf Course** (7001 Osuna Road Northeast; 505-884-7505). Many Albuquerque golfers travel 40 miles north to play in a lovely setting below the rugged volcanic canyons of the Jemez Mountains at the Indian-owned **Cochiti Lake Golf Course** (505-465-2239).

In the Santa Rosa area, try your hand at the **Santa Rosa Golf Club** (505-472-3949) or **Tucumcari Municipal Golf Course** (505-461-1849)or the **Conchas Lake Golf Course** (505-868-2228). In Socorro, tee off at the **New Mexico Tech Golf Course** (1 Canyon Road; 505-835-5335). In the western part of the state, try **Grants/Milan Municipal Golf Course** (505-287-9239) or **Gallup Municipal Golf Course** (505-863-9224).

For more information on golf courses throughout New Mexico, contact the **Sun Country Golf Association** (10035 Golf Course Lane Northwest, Albuquerque, NM 87114; 505-867-0864).

BICYCLING

Albuquerque has a well-developed system of bike trails throughout the city. **Paseo del Bosque** is a paved bike and horse trail running for five miles along the Rio Grande from the Old Town area to the northern edge of town, passing through the Rio Grande Nature Center. **Paseo de las Montañas** is a 4.2-mile biking and jogging trail between Tramway Boulevard Northeast and the Winrock Shopping Center on the northeast side of the city. It offers grand views of Albuquerque. **Paseo del Noreste**, a six-mile trail, allows residents of the fashionable Northeast Heights area to commute downtown by bicycle. For complete information about these and other bike trails and bike routes, contact the **Albuquerque City Parks and Recreation Department** (505-768-3550).

A favorite mountain biking area is the series of five extinct volcanos that make up a city-owned open space on **West Mesa**, the western skyline of the city. Dirt roads ramble all around the volcanoes and lead to the edge of the West Mesa Escarpment where petroglyphs can be found.

Outside of Albuquerque, popular cycling trips include the level, unpaved 15-mile tour loop at **Bosque del Apache National Wildlife Refuge** near Socorro and, for mountain bikes only, the roads in the vicinity of **Fourth of July Campground** in the Manzano Mountains.

BIKE RENTALS **Two Wheel Drive** (1706 Central Avenue Northeast, Albuquerque; 505-243-8443) rents ten-speeds and mountain bikes. The staff there can provide information about bike routes, local clubs and the group rides they sponsor. Another good place to rent bikes is **The Bike Coop Ltd.** (3407 Central Avenue Northeast, Albuquerque; 505-265-5170).

HIKING

ALBUQUERQUE AREA TRAILS **Sandia Peak**, the 10,400-foot mountain that fills Albuquerque's eastern skyline, offers hiking trails for every preference, from gentle strolls to ambitious ascents. Temperatures on the crest of the mountain run about 20° cooler than the downtown streets.

The easiest way to hike Sandia is to either drive or take the aerial tramway to the crest of the mountain and walk the well-worn trail between the restaurant at the top of the tramway and the gift shop at the end of the auto road, a distance of about a mile with continuous views of the city below. The **Crest Trail** continues along the top ridge through the Sandia Wilderness Area all the way down to Canyon Estates, 14 miles to the south near Route 40, and Placitas, a similar distance to the north near Route 25.

The **10-K Trail** (6 miles) starts at a trailhead two miles down the road from the crest and reaches the top ridge at the broadcast towers north of the gift shop. The hike to the summit leads through shady forests of Douglas fir, aspen and spruce with a 1000-foot elevation gain. A continuation of the trail follows the road back down to the trailhead to close the loop.

A trailhead midway up the Sandia Peak road marks the **Tree Spring Trail** (2 miles), which climbs to the top ridge, joining the Crest Trail a mile south of the tram station. It is a 1400-foot climb from the trailhead to the crest.

The most challenging trail on Sandia Peak is **La Luz Trail**, which takes expert hikers up the seemingly sheer west face of the mountain from Juan Tabo Picnic Ground to the tram station on the crest. It is a 7.5-mile climb from 7060 feet elevation at the foot of the mountain to 10,400 at the summit. You can ride the tram to the top and hike back down La Luz Trail.

On the north side of Sandia Peak, lush **Las Huertas Canyon** is accessible by the road that leads from Route 25 through the village of Placitas or by a steep, narrow road that descends from the Sandia Crest auto road. Near the upper end of the canyon, an easy .75-mile trail takes hikers along the canyon wall to **Sandia Man Cave** where University of New Mexico archaeologists found artifacts left by hunting and gathering Indians during the last Ice Age. A flashlight is needed to reach the inner recesses of the cave.

A profusion of bigtooth maple trees makes Fourth of July Campground near Tajique, about 30 miles south of the Tijeras exit from Route 40, a favorite for fall hiking. Two trails leave from the campground. The **Fourth of July Trail** (5 miles) makes a loop to the south, along the edge of the Manzano Mountain Wilderness, affording great views of the Rio Grande and Estancia valleys. The **Albuquerque Trail** runs north to the Isleta Indian Reservation boundary and turns back south to make a 6-mile loop.

MOUNTAINAIR AREA TRAILS   The southern Manzano Mountains offer excellent hiking opportunities. Two of the best trails start from the unpaved road past Manzano Mountain State Park near the town of Manzano, 12 miles north of Mountainair and just north of the Quarai unit of Salinas Pueblo Missions National Monument.

The **Red Canyon Trail** follows a creek with small waterfalls into the Manzano Mountain Wilderness for three miles to within scrambling distance of the summit of Gallo Peak, elevation 10,003 feet. It is a strenuous climb with a 2000-foot altitude gain.

The **Kaiser Mill Trail** climbs 2000 feet in two miles to intersect the **Manzano Crest Trail**, which runs along the top ridge of the Manzanos. Hikers can reach the summit of Manzano Peak, elevation 10,098 feet, by following the Crest Trail for about a mile south of the intersection. Those who plan to hike only the lower portion of one of these trails should choose the Red Canyon Trail, since the first part of the Kaiser Mill Trail, outside the wilderness boundary, has been heavily logged.

SOCORRO AREA TRAILS   From the upper ridges of the Magdalena Mountains, you can see Sandia Peak in the distance. Notice the difference. While hiking any of the Sandia trails on a summer day can be a very social experience, few people visit the Magdalenas. **North Baldy Trail** (6 miles), the best hiking access, is a challenge to reach. Beyond Water Canyon Campground, which is off Route 60 about 16 miles west of Socorro, eight miles of unpaved, narrow, often rocky road lead to the trailhead. The trail starts near the summit where the state operates a laboratory to study thunderstorms. After a short, steep climb, the main trail runs along a ridgeline of high mountain meadows to the North Baldy summit (elevation 9858 feet).

GRANTS/GALLUP AREA TRAILS   Unpaved roads lead through **Cibola National Forest** to within a mile of the summit of **Mt. Taylor**, the 11,300-foot mountain that dominates the skyline north of Grants. A trail that starts near the junction of Forest Roads 193 and 501 climbs more than 2000 feet up the southwest side of the peak to the mountaintop in three miles. Another begins near La Mosca Peak Overlook and ascends the north ridge to reach the summit of Mt. Taylor in a mile.

In the spring and fall months, **El Malpais National Monument** south of Grants presents some unusual hiking possibilities. The **Zuni-Acoma Trail** (7.5 miles one-way) crosses the lava fields between Routes 53 and 117. Said to be part of a trade route that linked Zuni and Acoma pueblos in ancient times. The trail is level, but the lava is so rough and uneven that even a short walk from either trailhead will prove strenuous.

Other trails into El Malpais start along unpaved Route 42, which skirts the western and southern edges of the monument. The road requires a high-clearance vehicle. The **Big Lava Tubes Trail** (.5 mile) leads to Big Skylight Cave and Four Window Cave, both entrances to the same immense lava tube, which is 17 miles long.

Transportation

BY CAR

Two major interstate highways, **Route 25** and **Route 40**, cross near the center of Albuquerque. The intersection is known locally as the "Big I." Santa Rosa is on Route 40, two hours east of Albuquerque, and Tucumcari is another hour east of Santa Rosa. To the west of Albuquerque on Route 40, it is a two-hour drive to Grants and another hour to Gallup.

Driving south of Albuquerque on Route 25 will bring you to Socorro. The most direct way to reach Mountainair from Albuquerque is by exiting Route 25 at Belen and taking **Route 6**, which merges into **Route 60** and runs through Mountainair. Route 60 parallels Route 40 across eastern New Mexico and runs through Fort Sumner. A straight and very empty two-lane highway through pronghorn antelope country, **Route 41** is the most direct route between Santa Fe and the Mountainair area.

BY AIR

Albuquerque International Airport is the only major commercial passenger terminal in the state. Carriers include American Airlines, Continental Airlines, Delta Airlines, Southwest Airlines, United Airlines and USAir.

Taxis and hotel courtesy vans wait for passengers in front of the airport terminal. The **Shuttlejack** (505-243-3244) provides bus transportation to major Albuquerque hotels and continues to Santa Fe. **Sun Tran** (505-843-9200). Albuquerque's public bus system, also serves the airport.

BY TRAIN

Amtrak's (800-872-7245) "Southwest Chief," which chugs between Chicago and Los Angeles, stops at the Albuquerque passenger station (314 1st Street Southwest; 505-842-9650) daily. The trains also stop in Gallup at the Santa Fe Station (201 East Historic 66; 800-872-7245).

BY BUS

Greyhound/Trailways Bus Lines provides service to the Albuquerque Bus Transportation Center (300 2nd Street Southwest; 505-243-4435) as well as to depots in Tucumcari (118 East Center Street; 505-461-1350), Fort Sumner (1018 Sumner Avenue; 505-374-9300), Socorro (202 South California Street; 505-835-1930), Grants (1801 West Santa Fe Avenue; 505-285-6268) and Gallup (105 South Dean Street; 505-863-3761). **TNM&O Coaches** (505-243-4435), a regional carrier, also serves Albuquerque.

The **Pueblo Shuttle Service** (505-863-3761) operates a daily shuttle between Gallup and Albuquerque, and the **Socorro Shuttle Service** (505-835-0040) runs daily between Socorro and Albuquerque. The **Shuttlejack** (505-243-3244) travels between Santa Fe and Albuquerque every two hours.

CAR RENTALS

Rental agencies at Albuquerque International Airport include **Budget Car Rental** (505-884-2666), **Alamo Rent A Car** (505-842-4057), **Sears Car & Truck Rental** (505-883-8787) and **Ugly Duckling Rent A Car** (505-243-0285). Any of the more than 60 agencies listed in the Albuquerque yellow pages can arrange car pick-ups and drop-offs at the airport or a hotel.

PUBLIC TRANSPORTATION

Sun Tran (601 Yale Boulevard Southeast; 505-843-9200), Albuquerque's metropolitan bus system, has routes covering most parts of the city, including the airport, the bus depot, Old Town, the University of New Mexico and all major shopping malls.

TAXIS

Taxi services in Albuquerque include **Albuquerque Cab Co./Duke City Cab Co.** (505-883-4888), **Checker Cab Co.** (505-243-7777) and **Yellow Cab Co.** (505-247-8888).

CHAPTER EIGHT

Southern New Mexico

Southern New Mexico has little in common with the northern part of the state. In pre-Columbian times, when the Anasazi were building cities in the Four Corners region, Mimbres people occupied the southern region, living in small cliff-dwelling communities. Their pottery is famed for the imaginative artistry of its animal motifs, and scientists are only now realizing what a sophisticated knowledge of astronomy the Mimbres possessed. They vanished without explanation centuries before the first European settlers arrived, and nomadic Apaches moved into the region.

The Spanish colonists who settled Santa Fe avoided the south, where the land was parched and arid, and Apache Indians terrorized any outsider who set foot in their territory. Most of the development in the region has come in the 20th century, from air force bases to ski resorts and huge boating reservoirs. Today the same Indians' descendants operate exclusive recreation facilities at the edge of the Mescalero Apache Reservation near Ruidoso.

With the exception of Carlsbad Caverns National Park, Southern New Mexico is less visited by vacationers than other parts of the state. That's surprising, and somewhat disappointing, for this region offers enough outdoor sports and roadside sightseeing to fill a two-week vacation easily. Cool islands of high mountain forest offer relief from the scorching summers of the Chihuahuan Desert. On top of this, they're great for winter skiing. The lowlands enjoy a much longer warm season for spring and fall outdoor activities than Albuquerque, Santa Fe or Taos, making the entire region an attractive year-round destination.

Southern New Mexico is divided into several geographic regions. The area east of the mountains is, for all practical purposes, indistinguishable from west Texas. Carlsbad Caverns is closer to the Texas state line than to any New Mexico town. Ruidoso, the horse racing and skiing town in the mountains west of Roswell, caters almost exclusively to visitors from Texas. South of Ruidoso, memories of the Wild West live on in Lincoln, once among the most lawless towns on the frontier, now a low-key historic district.

South Central New Mexico encompasses several barren mountain ranges and the vast, unpopulated desert area known as the Jornado del Muerto ("Journey of Death") so desolate that the United States government chose it as the place to test the first atomic bomb. Today, the population of this region lives along two main north-south routes separated from each other by the huge White Sands Missile Range, which is off-limits to all nonmilitary persons.

Driving on interstate Route 25 or the older highway that parallels it, motorists find an empty landscape flanking a series of large recreational lakes. Taking Route 52 through the Tularosa Basin, the sights are more unusual—a giant lava field, many ancient Indian petroglyphs, and miles of pure white sand dunes. In the mountains just west of Alamogordo, charming little Cloudcroft is a bustling ski town in the winter and a cool, quiet haven the rest of the year.

The southwestern part of the state is filled with national forest. Driving to the boundary of the roadless Gila Wilderness, the largest wilderness area in the lower 48 states, you won't find any gas stations or grocery stores along the route, but you will discover many scenic lookouts, mountain lakes and hiking trails. Travel within the Gila Wilderness is restricted to horseback riders and hikers. A driving trip skirting the edge of the wilderness, from Gila Cliff Dwellings National Monument in the canyonlands at the heart of the wilderness to the Catwalk on the western perimeter and then north through the ghost town of Mogollon to Snow Lake on the high mountain slopes, can take several scenic, pleasurable and adventurous days.

Southeastern New Mexico

Best known for Carlsbad Caverns and the legacy of Billy the Kid, Southeastern New Mexico is a land filled with new discoveries for the traveler. Lincoln National Forest's White Mountain Wilderness, Sierra Blanca, New Mexico's highest peak, Bitter Lake National Wildlife refuge and a living memorial to that firefighting icon Smokey the Bear are some of Southeastern New Mexico's primary attractions. Technicolor sunsets, secluded mountain lakes, great skiing and mountain biking are just the extra added attractions.

Carlsbad Caverns National Park (505-785-2232; admission) takes you 750 feet underground inside a limestone mesa in the foothills of the Guadalupe Mountains, where ancient underground rivers shaped a spectac-

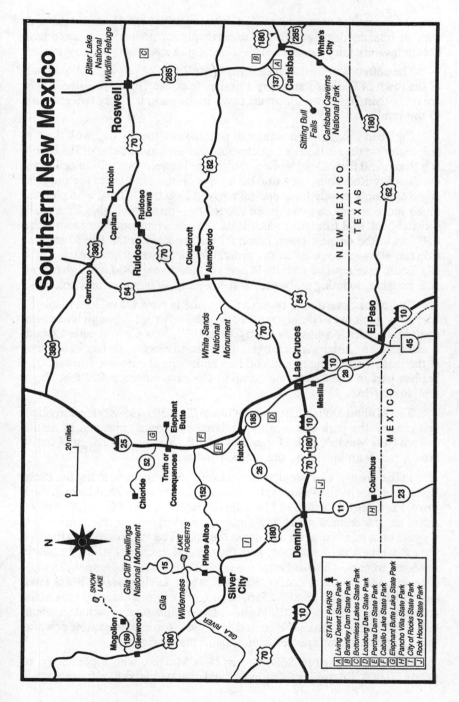

Southern New Mexico

Bitter Lake National Wildlife Refuge

Roswell

285

180

285

White's City

137

Carlsbad

Sitting Bull Falls

Carlsbad Caverns National Park

180

NEW MEXICO

TEXAS

62

Lincoln

Capitan

Ruidoso Downs

Ruidoso

70

380

Carrizozo

Cloudcroft

Alamogordo

82

54

54

White Sands National Monument

70

Las Cruces

El Paso

10

380

45

28

Mesilla

MEXICO

185

D

10

Elephant Butte

G

F

E

180

70

Chloride

52

Truth or Consequences

Hatch

26

152

J

Columbus

23

H

11

Piños Altos

LAKE ROBERTS

I

180

Deming

10

15

Gila Cliff Dwellings National Monument

Silver City

70

SNOW LAKE

Mogollon

159

Glenwood

180

Gila

Wilderness

GILA RIVER

N

20 miles

0

25

STATE PARKS
A Living Desert State Park
B Brantley Dam State Park
C Bottomless Lakes State Park
D Loasburg Dam State Park
E Percha Dam State Park
F Caballo Lake State Park
G Elephant Butte Lake State Park
H Pancho Villa State Park
I City of Rocks State Park
J Rock Hound State Park

ular honeycomb of caves and eons of dripping dampness decorated the cave with an amazing display of natural mineral spires, curtains, crystals and lace. Bottomless pits, fairy temples and alien landscapes challenge your imagination.

The entrance to Carlsbad Caverns is off Route 285. It is 20 miles south of the town of Carlsbad and only 17 miles from the Texas state line. There are more than 70 known limestone caves in the park, but only two are open to the public.

Carlsbad Cavern is the one most people visit, the big one with the visitor center on the surface and an elevator that runs to a corner of the cave's Big Room 750 feet below. Visitors can choose between two self-guided tours. On the easy Red Tour, they ride both ways on the elevator to see only the Big Room on a mostly level one-mile paved loop trail. Those who pick the much more strenuous—and more rewarding—three-mile Blue Tour walk a switchback trail from the mouth of the cave down to a depth of more than 830 feet at the deepest point, climb 80 feet back up to the Big Room and ride the elevator back up to the ground level. However you reach it, the Big Room inspires awe with its 14 acres of floor area, 200-foot-high ceiling and massive, looming stalactites and towering stalagmites and columns.

The other cave that is open to the public is **New Cave**, in an isolated part of the park back country reached via a county road. Though it has been open for exploration since its discovery in 1937, New Cave is undeveloped. It can only be toured with a ranger, tours must be booked a day in advance at the main visitor center, and children under age six are not allowed. The hardest part of the tour is the climb to the cave entrance 500 feet above the parking lot.

The **Million Dollar Museum** (White's City; 505-785-2291; admission), just outside the park entrance, is the largest historical museum in Southeastern New Mexico, with 11 rooms of exhibits including dolls, guns, music boxes, ranch antiques and mummified Indians.

In the town of **Carlsbad**, a marked auto tour route runs along the Pecos River, which is partially dammed to form long, narrow Carlsbad Lake through town. **President's Park** (711 Muscatel Avenue; 505-887-0512) has carnival rides, an 1890s main street and a sternwheeler riverboat that carries passengers on a minicruise up and down the lake. The tour route runs through the town's best neighborhood, past the mineral springs that inspired early residents to name Carlsbad after the famous spa resort in Germany, and finally into the hills overlooking the town, where **Living Desert State Park** (just off Route 283; 505-887-5516; admission) offers a close-up look at the animal and plant life of the Chihuahuan Desert. Inhabitants include a mountain lion, a bear, wolves, bison and javelinas. An indoor exhibit contains giant tropical cactus species from around the world.

The largest town in Southeastern New Mexico, with a population of nearly 50,000, **Roswell** is the shipping and commercial center for thousands of square miles of ranchlands in the region. At first glance, Roswell does not look like the kind of place that would have much to offer vacationers. Explore a bit and you'll discover some little-known sightseeing treasures. Bottomless Lakes State Park and Bitter Lake National Wildlife Refuge are described in the "Southeastern New Mexico Parks" section below.

The **Roswell Museum and Art Center** (100 West 11th Street; 505-624-6744) is one of the best in the state, with collections ranging from Western art and Indian artifacts to early rockets. The museum's highlight is a collection of paintings by famed landscape painter and portraitist Peter Hurd, who was born in Roswell and spent most of his life on his ranch nearby. Other artists represented here include Georgia O'Keeffe and Marsden Hartley.

Ruidoso is a year-round resort. Its main claims to fame are skiing and horse racing. The race track, **Ruidoso Downs** (505-378-4431), is located five miles east of town on Route 70. Quarter horses and thoroughbreds run here each afternoon during the summer season, which climaxes with the All-American Futurity, the world's richest horse race with a $3 million purse. At the end of the racing season, mule races and high-priced horse auctions provide a last burst of excitement.

The village of **Lincoln** would have faded from the map generations ago had it not been the scene of an infamous "war" between two competing groups of storekeepers and ranchers in 1878. After the leader of one faction was assassinated, one of his employees, a professional gunman known as Billy the Kid, avenged him by killing all the participants in the ambush and their bosses. The Lincoln County War ultimately brought down the territorial government of New Mexico and made Billy the Kid a legend.

The whole village and its surrounding area are now a historic district, giving Lincoln the authentic feel of a late 19th-century town. The focal points of a walking tour of Lincoln are several units of **Lincoln State Monument** (505-653-4372; admission) as well as other structures. The Old Courthouse contains exhibits explaining the Lincoln County War and an actual bullet-hole made by Billy the Kid during a jailbreak. The Historical Center Museum displays Victorian-era frontier artifacts and has exhibits about "buffalo soldiers" (black troops stationed in the West after the Civil War) and the Apaches they fought.

A few miles west of Lincoln on Route 380, the sightseeing highlight in the small town of Capitan is **Smokey Bear State Historical Park** (505-354-2748; admission). A must for kids and anyone interested in the history of advertising, this small museum traces the career of America's best-known bear from early artist's sketches through more than 40 years of forest service propaganda, children's comics and commercial kitsch. A film tells the story of the "real" Smokey the Bear (1950-1976), who was rescued by rangers from a fire in Lincoln National Forest and sent to live in a Washington, D.C. zoo. The live bear was named after the imaginary character, not vice-versa as legend suggests.

SOUTHEASTERN NEW MEXICO HOTELS

Visitors to Carlsbad Caverns may choose to stay at White's City by the national park entrance or in the town of Carlsbad, a 20-minute drive away. In White's City, rates are moderate at the **Best Western Cavern Inn**, the **Walnut Canyon Inn** and the **Guadalupe Inn** (505-785-2291 for all three inns), fairly standard motel accommodations.

In the town of Carlsbad, the **Park Inn** (3706 National Parks Highway; 505-887-2861) offers spacious rooms surrounding a courtyard patio and pool at budget to moderate rates. For more homelike accommodations, try **La Casa Muneca Bed & Breakfast** (213 North Alameda; 505-887-1891), a pleasant, modern residence in Carlsbad's best neighborhood. Moderate.

Roswell's lodging scene is unexceptional. The top of the line is the moderate-priced **Best Western Sally Port Inn** (2000 North Main Street; 505-622-6430) with its tropical atrium, spa facilities and guest rooms with tall picture windows and refrigerators. One of the better budget-priced motels is the **Frontier Motel** (3010 North Main Street; 505-622-1400).

The ultra-deluxe-priced **Inn of the Mountain Gods** (Carrizo Canyon Road; 505-257-5141) near Ruidoso is one of the most exclusive resorts in New Mexico. It is owned by the Mescalero Apache Indians, whose mountainous reservation extends from Ruidoso south to Cloudcroft. Guest rooms are in several buildings scattered through the ponderosa pine forest above a manmade lake used for fishing, canoeing, sailing and motorboating. Other facilities include an outstanding golf course, indoor and outdoor tennis courts, a horseback riding stable, archery and skeet shooting ranges and a spa. Many activities are open to nonguests for a fee.

Other accommodations in Ruidoso range from condos to cabins and come in all price ranges. The moderate-priced **Carrizo Lodge** (Carrizo Canyon Road; 505-257-9131) is a historic inn featuring Spanish-style stucco architecture in a canyon setting shaded by old trees. Amenities available to guests include art and exercise classes.

Several complexes near the Ruidoso River rent cabins in the pines with kitchens and fireplaces in the moderate-price range. Among them are **Story Book Cabins** (Upper Canyon Road; 505-257-2115) and **Whispering Pines Cabins** (Upper Canyon Road; 505-257-4311).

Lower-priced motels in the Ruidoso area cluster east of town on Route 70 near the Ruidoso Downs horse racetrack. Also in the Upper Canyon is the town's best bed-and-breakfast inn, **Kearney's Rest & Relaxation** (110 McCarty Drive; 505-257-2940). For budget lodging, try the **Stagecoach Motel** (East Route 70; 505-257-2610) or the nearby **Timberline Motel** (East Route 70; 505-378-4706). Both are clean and simple and have color televisions.

In Alto, six miles north of Ruidoso on Route 37 at the turnoff to Ski Apache, is an attractive bed and breakfast in the mountains—the moderately priced **Monjeau Shadows Bed & Breakfast Establishment** (505-336-4191).

A four-story Victorian farmhouse, this seven-room inn is furnished with antiques and heirlooms. Located on ten wooded acres with walking paths, there's a big gameroom on the premises and the owners can arrange historic tours of Billy the Kid country, skiing, horseback riding and golf.

Lincoln has a small selection of memorable places to stay. Advance reservations are essential at all of them. The moderately priced, state-owned **Wortley Hotel** (505-653-4500) dates back to the days of the Lincoln County War. Open seasonally from May to September, the Wortley is a neat, unimposing Territorial adobe building with eight guest rooms restored in frontier Victorian style.

There are also three small bed and breakfasts in town. Two of them, **Casa de Patron Bed & Breakfast** (505-653-4676) and **Ellis Store Bed & Breakfast** (505-653-4609), are in carefully restored Territorial-period adobes, while the third, **Old Lincolntown Bed & Breakfast & Gallery** (505-653-4185), is in a modern building. All three are in the moderate price range and open all year.

SOUTHEASTERN NEW MEXICO RESTAURANTS

Carlsbad Caverns Restaurant (505-785-2281) serves budget-priced fare cafeteria-style in the national park visitor center. It is often crowded enough to make hungry sightseers wish they'd brought a picnic lunch. Inside the cave, near the elevators that carry visitors back to the surface at the end of the tour, the lunchroom serves box lunches containing fried chicken or ham-and-cheese sandwiches.

In the town of Carlsbad, the pub-style **Full House Bar & Grill** (834 South Canal Street; 505-887-9996) serves steaks and Italian food. Prices are moderate. **Cortez** (506 South Canal Street; 505-885-4747) has been a local favorite for over 50 years with its budget-priced Mexican dishes.

An unusual dining possibility is the **Flying X Chuckwagon** (7505 Old Carlsbad Highway, Carlsbad; 505-885-6789), where cowboys serve barbecued beef chuckwagon style on tin plates to a crowd of hundreds of people nightly during the summer months. The moderate price includes after-dinner entertainment.

In the Roswell area, one of the most elegant restaurants is the **Club House** (ten miles west of Roswell, on Route 70; 505-622-1158), serving moderately priced American favorites such as prime rib in a country club atmosphere. The best budget bargain in town is catfish and homemade pie at **Hazel's Cajun Kitchen** (5800 South Main Street; 505-623-7441).

Ruidoso has an abundance of good places to eat. Of the three restaurants at the exclusive Inn of the Mountain Gods (Carrizo Canyon Road; 505-257-5141), the finest is **Dan Li Ka**, the main dining room, whose wide-ranging menu offers everything from wild game to enchiladas. Most prices are in the moderate range, and the lake and mountain view is incomparable.

Guests are seated in metal captain's chairs painted blue-green and served on peach linen. Dan Li Ka decor features Native American weavings, baskets and modern paintings.

An even more elegant possibility is the deluxe-priced **La Lorraine** (2523 Sudderth Drive, Ruidoso; 505-257-2954). Located in an adobe building with green canopies, the chandeliered dining room has upholstered chairs, fine silver, white linen and a good collection of regional art. During the summer months you'll enjoy dining on the patio on such entrées as rack of lamb, scallops and roast duck in an atmosphere of casual elegance.

At the other end of the dining spectrum, the budget-priced **Texas Café** (East Route 70, Ruidoso; 505-378-5466) serves a mean bowl of red chili con carne or your choice of hamburgers named after Texas cities.

Ruidoso has the **Flying J Ranch** (Route 37; 505-336-4330), a cousin of the Flying X near Carlsbad, featuring the same summer evening combination of barbecue beef and singing cowboys at a moderate price.

Lincoln has very little in the way of places to eat. The town's only full-service restaurant is the dining room in the historic **Wortley Hotel** (505-653-4500). Open during the summer season only, the restaurant's biggest claim to fame is that a sheriff once ate there just before being gunned down by Billy the Kid. The cuisine includes steak and other standard American fare at moderate prices.

SOUTHEASTERN NEW MEXICO SHOPPING

In Carlsbad, the gift shop at **Living Desert State Park** (505-887-5516) sells a nice assortment of cactuses that make good souvenirs.

Ruidoso has an impressive number of art galleries, which seem to keep a lot of race track winnings from leaving town. More than a dozen of them can be found along Mechem and Sudderth streets. Take a look at the horse racing art in the **Sunbird Studio** (2615 Sudderth Drive; 505-257-5331) and the cowboy art at **Gray Fox Gallery** (2301 Sudderth Drive; 505-257-5427).

The museum shop at the **Lincoln County Historical Center** (Lincoln; 505-653-4025) sells a remarkable array of Billy the Kid books, comics, posters and motion picture videos. How the outlaw's legend has endured!

SOUTHEASTERN NEW MEXICO NIGHTLIFE

Near the front gate of Carlsbad Caverns National Park, melodrama is presented nightly during the summer season at **Granny's Opera House** (White's City; 505-785-2291).

For evening entertainment nothing can compete with the sunset flight of almost half a million Mexican freetail bats from the entrance of **Carlsbad**

Caverns. The bats put on their show nightly from April through October. They migrate to the tropics for the winter.

Both the **Flying X Chuckwagon** (7505 Old Carlsbad Highway; 505-885-6789) near Carlsbad and the **Flying J Ranch** (Route 37; 505-336-4330) near Ruidoso represent a traditional Western genre of tourist entertainment. After a barbecued beef dinner served "chuckwagon-style" (that is, in a chow line), singing cowboys take the stage to perform classics like "Red River Valley" and "Git Along, Little Dogie." Corny and lots of fun.

Ruidoso is the liveliest town after dark in this part of the state. You'll find live music, Texas-style, at the **Great American Land and Cattle Company** (East Route 70 East; 505-378-8009), as well as at the **Bull Ring** (Mechem Street at White Mountain Drive; 505-258-3555) and **Nottingham's Pub** (2535 Sudderth Drive; 505-257-2495), among other places.

SOUTHEASTERN NEW MEXICO PARKS

Carlsbad Municipal Park—This large park runs through town for more than a mile along the west bank of Lake Carlsbad, a portion of the Pecos River which has been dammed to make it wider and deeper. It is used for waterskiing, swimming, fishing and sailing. On the shore, the park has broad lawns and shade trees.

Facilities: Picnic area, restrooms, playground, golf course, tennis and handball courts.

Getting there: Take Greene Street east several blocks from Route 285 to the river.

Sitting Bull Falls—Although it is a long drive on unpaved roads through uninhabited backcountry, Sitting Bull Falls is a locally popular spot, likely to be crowded on summer weekends. It is one of the largest falls in New Mexico—130 feet high—and practically the only running water in the arid foothills northwest of Carlsbad. Swimming is permitted in the pool at the bottom of the falls, and three miles of hiking trails lead around the oasis.

Facilities: Picnic area, restrooms, trails. *Swimming:* Permitted.

Getting there: From Route 285 about 12 miles north of Carlsbad, take Route 137 southwest for 25 miles and watch for a sign to Sitting Bull Falls. The falls are at the end of the eight-mile unpaved road.

Brantley Lake State Park—This irrigation reservoir on the Pecos River north of Carlsbad is in the early stages of recreational development for boating and sportfishing use.

Facilities: Boat ramp, picnic area, restrooms, showers, volleyball, horseshoe pits, nature trail; information, 505-457-2384.

Camping: There are 49 sites with RV hookups; $11 per night. Primitive camping is allowed; $6 per night.

Getting there: It's 15 miles north of Carlsbad, just off Route 285.

Bottomless Lakes State Park—New Mexico's oldest state park, Bottomless Lakes consists of seven natural lakes, small in surface area but as much as 90 feet deep, formed by collapsed underground salt caves. The largest, Lea Lake, is the only one where swimming is allowed. It also has a public beach and sailboat and paddleboard rentals and is a popular site for scuba diving. From the visitor center near Cottonwood Lake, a half-mile nature trail leads through a dry sinkhole that will become a lake in future centuries and up to an overlook above beautiful Mirror Lake, surrounded by red cliffs. Ducks, geese and other waterfowl abound on the lakes during spring and fall migration seasons.

Facilities: Picnic area, restrooms, showers, boat rentals; information, 505-624-6058. *Swimming:* Permitted at Lea Lake.

Camping: There are 18 sites (ten with RV hookups; $7 per night for standard sites, $11 for hookups.

Getting there: From Roswell, take Route 380 for 12 miles east, then turn south on Route 409 for two miles to the park entrance.

Bitter Lake National Wildlife Refuge—Small wetlands along the Pecos River attracts a lot of migrating waterfowl as they cross this arid region, though few winter here. As many as 65,000 snow geese, 70,000 sandhill cranes and 100,000 ducks stop at Bitter Lake each year. Visitors can hike anywhere in the refuge except for an off-limits research area.

Facilities: Restrooms, automobile-tour route, hiking trails; information, 505-622-6755.

Getting there: From Route 285 two miles north of Roswell, turn northeast on Route 70 and follow the signs for nine miles to the refuge headquarters. There is also a road to the refuge from Route 380, midway out to Bottomless Lakes State Park.

South Central New Mexico

Birthplace of the atomic age, a favorite resting place of Apache rebel Geronimo and a bonanza for petroglyph buffs, South Central New Mexico is famous for its gypsum dunes and lava fields. Juxtaposing desert and mountains, this Rio Grande region offers a number of popular dammed lakes ideal for outdoor enthusiasts. Home of the only city in America renamed for a game show, this region is also a must for ghost town buffs.

The northern part of the Tularosa Basin, which begins north of Carrizozo and extends 80 miles to the south, is a jagged wasteland of black lava. At **Valley of Fires Recreation Area**, off Route 380 just east of the town of Carrizozo, a self-guided nature trail leads across a portion of the

10,000-year-old lava field for a closeup look at this strange and forbidding landscape.

From Carrizozo to Alamogordo, Route 54 runs along the western edge of **White Sands Missile Range**, a vast area used by the military to test weapons. It has been off-limits to the public since World War II, when it was the site of the first atomic bomb test. A tour of the Trinity Site where the original bomb was exploded is conducted once a year in October.

Halfway between Carrizozo and Alamogordo, just off Route 54, the **Three Rivers Petroglyph Site (★)** contains thousands of pictures chipped into the dark patina of boulders by artists of the Mimbres people, an Indian culture centuries older than the Anasazi of the Four Corners region. A three-quarter-mile, often steep trail follows the crest of a high hill to let visitors see the mysterious pictures of animals, humans and magical beings as well as abstract symbols whose meanings can only be guessed at. There is a pleasant picnic area at the foot of the trail.

In Alamogordo, the **International Space Hall of Fame** (Indian Wells Road at Scenic Drive; 505-437-2840; admission) houses one of the world's largest collections of space exploration artifacts. The gleaming five-story gold cube on the hillside contains antique rockets, space suits, Apollo and Gemini capsules, moon rocks, satellites and lots more. An outdoor park displays larger rockets and the Sonic Wind Rocket Sled, which was used to test the effects of rocket acceleration on humans. Adjoining the museum is the **Clyde W. Tombaugh Space Theater,** a planetarium that presents laser light shows and Omnimax movies as well as educational astronomy programs. It is named after the man who discovered the planet Pluto.

To learn more about the exploration of space, drive up to the Sacramento Peak Solar Observatory on the crest of the mountains to the east. First, take the 16-mile drive on Route 82 from Alamogordo to the village of **Cloudcroft**. Nestled in the pines near the crest of the Sacramento Mountains, Cloudcroft has seen little of the rampant resort development evident at Ruidoso on the other side of the Apache Reservation, and it retains the weathered charm of a little Rocky Mountain logging town.

From there, take Forest Road 64 for 15 miles, following the signs to "Sunspot." Maintained by the National Science Foundation for the use of various universities, the **Sacramento Peak Solar Observatory** has several solar telescopes. The main one extends from 20 stories below ground level to 13 stories above. Visitors on self-guided tours of the facility can view solar flares on a video screen in the small lobby and often watch scientists studying the sun on similar screens. The panoramic view of the Tularosa Basin, White Sands and the Valley of Fires from the observatory's lookout point is worth the drive by itself.

A trip to this area would not be complete without a stop at **White Sands National Monument** (505-479-6124; admission), located off of four-lane

Route 70 between Alamogordo and Las Cruces. The monument protects the southernmost part of White Sands for public use. A 16-mile round-trip scenic drive takes visitors into the heart of the big, white-as-snow gypsum dunes, where you can park and step out into this strange landscape. The juxtaposition of pristine white sand and bright blue sky can make you feel like you're walking on clouds. When you return to earth you'll realize that this is the world's largest gypsum dunefield, encompassing 300 square miles of sand.

As beautiful as it is unusual, the landscape is ever-changing: Desert winds constantly reshape the dunes, creating pure-white sculptures in the air that disappear with each fresh gust. Surrounded by a spectacular wasteland, with an occasional yucca plant the only sign of life, it's difficult to decide whether this is heaven, hell or simply the end of the earth. Hiking is allowed without limitation, but camping is only permitted at a single backcountry tent site available by reservation. Rangers conduct morning and evening nature walks during the summer months.

Las Cruces (population 50,000) is the largest city in South Central New Mexico. In addition to being the county seat, Las Cruces is noteworthy for the Organ Mountains that loom east of the city. Vaulting 5000 feet above the valley, they derive their name from the spires and minarets that are like a pipe organ cast in stone.

A short distance west of Las Cruces on Route 10, the village of **Mesilla** is one of the prettiest and best-preserved historic districts in the state, dating back to 1598. Mesilla achieved further historical significance as the Confederate capital of the Arizona Territory for a short period during the Civil War. The downtown plaza and some of its surrounding Territorial-style buildings have been designated as **La Mesilla State Monument**. Points of interest around the plaza include the **Gadsden Museum** (Barker Road; 505-526-6293; admission), with folk art and artifact collections representing the Anglo, Spanish and Indian cultures of the region and the **San Albino Church**, the oldest in the area, built in 1853.

Fifteen miles north of Las Cruces via Route 25, **Fort Selden State Monument** (505-526-8911; admission) includes the ruins of an adobe fort used by the Army from 1865 to 1891. It was a base for troops guarding the Mesilla Valley and providing protection for wagon trains and later the railroad. A small museum recalls life at the fort during the Territorial era.

Farther north along Route 25, the main point of interest in the town of **Truth or Consequences**, a sprawling retirement community just south of Elephant Butte Lake, is the **Geronimo Springs Museum** (325 Main Street; 505-894-6600; admission). It is a fairly large museum with 12 exhibit rooms full of Mimbres pottery, ranch antiques, fossils and petrified wood, works by local artists, awards for wool production and other curiosities from all over Sierra County. The highlight of the museum is the Ralph Edwards Room, commemorating the television show that inspired Hot Springs, New Mexico, to change its name to Truth or Consequences in 1950.

Truth or Consequences' popularity as a spa resort has long since faded, but the hot springs themselves remain. A 115° natural spring where Apache resistance leader Geronimo is said to have relaxed is next to the museum. Several others are well hidden around the downtown area. Springs that are open to the public for bathing include **Sierra Natural Healing Baths and Massage** (710 Broadway; 505-894-3619), **Dave's Cloverleaf Baths and Health Foods** (207 South Daniels Street; 505-894-3350) and **Sierra Grande Lodge and Health Spa** (603 McAdoo; 505-894-6976). Natural-flowing hot pools can be found at **Indian Springs Apartments and Pools** (200 Pershing Road; 505-894-3823).

There are several ghost towns in the Truth or Consequences vicinity. The most interesting is **Chloride** (★), 29 miles off the interstate on Route 52 and then two-and-one-third miles on a marked, unpaved forest road. This is one of the few New Mexico ghost towns that looks the way you expect a Western ghost town to look, with about a dozen falsefront buildings still standing along a deserted main street. In its heyday during the late 19th century, Chloride was a center for silver mining and had a population of about 500.

SOUTH CENTRAL NEW MEXICO HOTELS

Virtually all Alamogordo accommodations are standard highway motels and with few exceptions their rates are in the budget range. Representative of the type is the **Satellite Inn** (2224 North White Sands Boulevard; 505-437-8454), which has phones, cable color televisions and an outdoor heated pool.

A more interesting option is to spend the night in Cloudcroft, high in the mountains and just 16 miles from Alamogordo. The most elegant hotel in town is the **Lodge at Cloudcroft** (Lodge Road; 505-682-2566), with moderately priced rooms as well as suites in the deluxe range. The three-story lodge has been in operation since the turn of the century and has been completely refurbished and modernized. Rooms have high ceilings and some antique furnishings.

The lodge also operates the **Lodge Pavilion Bed & Breakfast** (Curlew Street at Chipmunk Avenue; 505-682-2566), offering moderately priced accommodations in the town's oldest building. Both the Lodge and the Pavilion are listed on the national register of historic places.

For more modest, quiet and cozy lodgings, Cloudcroft has numerous cabins for rent. For example, **Buckhorn Cabins** (Route 82; 505-682-2421), located in the center of town, has rustic-style cabins ranging from budget-priced rooms with kitchenettes to moderate-priced two-bedroom cabins with living rooms and fireplaces.

(Text continued on page 344.)

On the Trail of Billy the Kid

No other character in New Mexico's history captures visitors' imagination like Billy the Kid. He was the west's enigmatic "live fast, die young" character, a sort of 19th-century James Dean who has lived on in novels and movies. More than a century after his violent death at the age of 21, Billy the Kid's legend seems stronger than ever. Travelers can explore throughout Southern New Mexico, from Lincoln to Mesilla to Silver City and beyond, following historical markers that recall the outlaw's exploits.

Lincoln is where the foundation was laid for Billy the Kid's immortality. There, visitors learn about the 1878 Lincoln County War, a violent conflict between a naive newcomer and a ruthless cattle baron that spread to involve the whole county in gunfights and arson for months and finally toppled the government of territorial New Mexico. Billy the Kid was on the side of the "good guys," legally deputized to capture the gunmen who had murdered his employer. Instead of arresting them, however, he shot them to death, causing modern scholars to believe that he was a violent sociopath.

After ridding Lincoln County of its nest of cattle rustlers, robber barons and corrupt politicians, Billy was granted amnesty by the new governor of New Mexico, Lew Wallace. Many people throughout the county reputedly saw him as a Robin Hood character. Yet he became the region's leading cattle rustler himself before he was hunted down for the murders of two sheriffs and a deputy and shot to death by the newly appointed Lincoln County sheriff, his old friend Pat Garrett.

One of the things Billy the Kid was best at was escaping. Lincoln was the site of two of his most daring escapes—one from a burning house under siege by a local posse and federal troops, the other from a makeshift jail cell in the old courthouse that houses the Lincoln State Monument headquarters today.

South of Lincoln, in Ruidoso, visitors can see the water wheel of Dowlin's Mill, where gunmen cornered Billy the Kid seeking revenge

for a friend he had shot. Billy escaped by hiding in a flour barrel. South of Ruidoso, Blazer's Mill near Mescalero was the site of a furious gunbattle during which the leader of the band of gunmen known as the Regulators was killed, after which Billy, the youngest and wildest member of the gang, took command.

Billy the Kid enthusiasts—and Southern New Mexico sees many of them—can find traces of the outlaw and his legend all across the state. On the outskirts of Fort Sumner (see Chapter Seven for more information) is the site of Billy the Kid's grave near the ranch where Pat Garrett caught up with him. Fort Sumner also has the two biggest Billy the Kid Museums in the state. An outdoor theater production recounting Billy's exploits is presented during the summer months.

On Route 70 east of Las Cruces, a state sign marks the spot where Garrett himself was later killed in a dispute over goat grazing. In old Mesilla, just outside of Las Cruces, visitors can see the courthouse where Billy was convicted and sentenced to hang for murdering a lawman. (He escaped.)

North of Carrizozo on the way to the town of Corona, a marker tells of yet another siege in which Billy and his gang were trapped by a posse inside a burning stagecoach station but escaped in the confusion after a deputy sheriff was killed in the crossfire while trying to negotiate a surrender.

Before the Lincoln County War began, Billy the Kid worked in a general store at Seven Rivers. The townsite is lost beneath the waters of Brantley Dam, but details can be found in the small historical museum in Artesia. Earlier, Billy spent part of his boyhood and attended school briefly in Silver City. His boyhood cabin and his mother's grave are there, along with the first jail he ever escaped from—at the age of 15 while in custody for robbing a Chinese laundry.

Populist hero or psycho killer? Historians and Hollywood scriptwriters are still guessing. But one thing's for sure: Billy the Kid wandered far and wide across some mighty pretty country.

In Las Cruces, the most luxurious hotel is the **Las Cruces Hilton** (705 South Telshor Boulevard; 505-522-4300), situated in the foothills on the east edge of town off interstate Route 25 and across the street from Mesilla Valley Mall. The modern seven-story hotel features bright, attractive guest rooms with refrigerators, and the swimming pool has palm trees around it. Rates are moderate for most rooms, with suites in the deluxe range.

Budget motels cluster along West Picacho Avenue. Try the large, fairly new **High Country Inn** (2160 West Picacho Avenue; 505-524-8627), which offers all standard amenities including outdoor pool, phones and cable color televisions.

More unusual lodging can be found at the **Inn of the Arts Bed & Breakfast** (618 South Alameda Boulevard; 505-526-3327), a small establishment with moderate rates that has one of Las Cruces's best art galleries on the premises.

Nearby, historic Mesilla has a large, elegant bed and breakfast, the **Meson de Mesilla** (1803 Avenida de Mesilla; 505-525-9212). All rooms in the modern adobe inn have private baths and Victorian-period decor. Amenities include a private courtyard, a putting green and complimentary bicycles for guests' use. Moderate.

In Truth or Consequences, all accommodations are in the budget range, from quality contemporary motor inns such as the **Elephant Butte Resort Inn** (Route 25 Exit 83; 505-744-5431) to a scattering of very low-priced older independent motels. One of these, the **Charles Motel and Bath House** (701 Broadway; 505-894-7154) has simple rooms with kitchenettes and offers mineral baths, sauna and massage at an extra charge.

SOUTH CENTRAL NEW MEXICO RESTAURANTS

In Alamogordo, fast-food places are the norm, along with family-style restaurants such as the budget-priced **Chuckwagon Restaurant** (604 1st Street; 505-434-0069), which specializes in steaks and barbecue. In the moderate price range, **George's** (607 South White Sands Boulevard; 505-437-2851) includes American, Mexican and Chinese dishes on its menu.

Cloudcroft has a number of good restaurants, many featuring Texas-style cuisine. In the middle of town, the moderately priced, cafeteria-style **Texas Pit Barbecue** (Route 82; 505-682-2307) offers mesquite-smoked beef and great chili con carne.

For deluxe-priced dining, there is **Rebecca's** (Lodge Road; 505-682-2566), the dining room at the Lodge at Cloudcroft, where Continental selections are served in an atmosphere of Victorian elegance with a view of the pine forest. The eatery's picture windows overlook White Sands. White linen, wicker furniture, historic portraits and a pianist make this a romantic spot.

In Las Cruces, **Nellie's Café** (1226 West Hadley Avenue; 505-524-9982) is a long-time local favorite serving good New Mexican and Old Mexican dishes like *carne adovada* and menudo at budget prices.

Fine restaurants surround the plaza in Mesilla. The most elegant of them is the **Double Eagle** (East Plaza; 505-523-6700), with a Continental menu and museum-quality period decor in a restored Territorial adobe listed on the National Register of Historic Places. Moderate.

Other plaza restaurants are **El Patio** (South Plaza; 505-524-6982) and **La Posta de Mesilla** (South Plaza; 505-524-3524). Both serve traditional New Mexican food at moderate prices in historic buildings.

Most Truth or Consequences restaurants present standard interstate highway exit fare. One exception is the **Damsite Restaurant** (Englestar Route; 505-894-2073), six miles north of town on the dam road. In an old adobe overlooking Elephant Butte Lake, the restaurant serves moderately priced Mexican food.

SOUTH CENTRAL NEW MEXICO SHOPPING

Eight miles northeast of Alamogordo via Route 70 and Route 545, local artists and craftsmen show their works at galleries around the small plaza in the old Spanish village of **La Luz**.

Las Cruces has a lavishly landscaped **downtown mall**, where a farmers' market and arts-and-crafts fair are held each Wednesday and Saturday through most of the year. At other times, visitors to the Las Cruces area will find the most interesting shopping in the shops around the old plaza in Mesilla.

Hatch, midway between Las Cruces and Truth or Consequences off Route 25, has a reputation for producing the best-tasting chili in New Mexico, and most of the stores in the little town are **chili shops**. In September, they sell fresh roasted green chili. The rest of the year, they sell it dried, canned, powdered, shaped as Christmas tree lights and as a T-shirt motif (we'll save a little surprise for you on that last one).

SOUTH CENTRAL NEW MEXICO NIGHTLIFE

In Alamogordo, the best bet for fun after dark is the laser light show presented by the **Clyde W. Tombaugh Space Theater** (Indian Wells Road at Scenic Drive; 505-437-2804; admission) at the International Space Hall of Fame.

Up in the mountains, the **Lodge at Cloudcroft** (Lodge Road; 505-682-2566) has a mellow piano bar and a saloon with live entertainment.

Las Cruces, a lively college town, has night spots that range from disco at **Popcorn's** (2205 South Main Street; 505-525-0991) to urban cowboy at the Holiday Inn's **Billy the Kid Saloon** (210 University Boulevard; 505-

526-4411). **New Mexico State University** provides a steady flow of cultural activities, notably the continuing New Mexico State University Film Series (505-646-3235).

SOUTH CENTRAL NEW MEXICO PARKS

Several dams on the lower Rio Grande form lakes used for recreation, ranging from little Leasburg Lake—hardly more than a wide spot in the river—to huge Elephant Butte Lake, one of the largest bodies of water in New Mexico. From south to north, these lakes are:

Leasburg Dam State Park—This park is on a small lake on the Rio Grande, set in a desert of creosote bushes and cholla cactus near Fort Selden State Monument. It is a popular area for swimming and boating.

Facilities: Picnic areas, restrooms, showers, playground, nature trails; information, 505-524-4068. *Fishing:* Permitted.

Camping: There are 50 sites (18 with RV hookups); primitive camping is allowed. Fees are $6 for primitive sites, $7 for standard sites and $11 for hookups.

Getting there: Located 15 miles north of Las Cruces, off Route 25 at Radium Springs.

Percha Dam State Park—Another small dam widens the river at this park, which is primarily a campground and riverbank fishing area with sandy beaches. Unlike Leasburg Dam, Percha Dam has tall old cottonwoods to provide shade on hot summer afternoons.

Facilities: Picnic area, restrooms, showers, playground, trails. Information, 505-743-3942. *Fishing:* Permitted.

Camping: There are 106 sites (six with RV hookups); $7 per night for standard sites, $11 for hookups. The camping area features green lawns—a rarity in Southern New Mexico.

Getting there: Located off Route 25 near the village of Arrey, 53 miles north of Las Cruces (21 miles south of Truth or Consequences).

Caballo Lake State Park—The name, Spanish for "horse," comes from the days when wild horses used to live in Caballo Canyon before it was dammed in the 1930s to form Caballo Lake. The lake is over a mile wide and 12 miles long, with more than 70 miles of shoreline. It is popular, especially in the spring, with fishermen angling for channel catfish, bass and walleye pike. The visitor center and main campground, picnic area and marina are across the dam and half a mile north on the east shore of the lake. From there, Route 85 follows the lakefront all the way to the upper end of the lake. Below the dam is a river fishing area with drinking water and campsites shaded by cottonwood trees.

Facilities: Picnic area, restrooms, showers, boat ramps, marina, boat rentals, visitor center; information, 505-743-3942. *Fishing:* Good.

Camping: There are 348 sites (48 with RV hookups) and primitive camping along the shoreline. Fees are $6 for primitive sites, $7 for standard sites and $11 for hookups.

Getting there: Located off Route 25, 60 miles north of Las Cruces (14 miles south of Truth or Consequences).

Elephant Butte Lake State Park—The dam creating this 40-mile-long reservoir, the second-largest lake in New Mexico, was originally built in 1916 to impound irrigation water for the whole Rio Grande Valley downriver. Today, it is New Mexico's most popular state park. Recreational activities include boating, waterskiing, windsurfing, sailing and even houseboating. The lake also has miles of sand beaches and several protected swimming areas. On display at the visitor center are dinosaur and early mammal fossils found in the area, including a tyrannosaurus rex jawbone. A network of unpaved roads provides access to a series of remote points along the west shore of the lake, but the upper half of the lake and all of the east shore can only be reached by boat.

Facilities: Picnic areas, restrooms, showers, boat ramps, marinas, boat rentals, playground, nature trails, visitor center; information, 505-744-5421. *Fishing:* Permitted.

Camping: There are 234 sites (103 with RV hookups) and an area for primitive camping. Fees are $6 for primitive sites, $7 for standard sites and $11 for hookups.

Getting there: The dam is due west of Truth or Consequences about six miles on Route 51. From there, Route 195 goes north to Elephant Butte Estates, and smaller roads, unpaved but suitable for passenger cars, follow the shore north for about 15 miles.

Southwestern New Mexico

Geronimo's base, Southwestern New Mexico is home to one of the state's finest ghost towns (Mogollon) as well as the Gila Wilderness, cliff dwellings and the frontier boom town of Silver City. If you like to pack in to high-country lakes, cycle through national forests or explore cliff dwellings, this remote area is your kind of place. While here you can learn about the legend of Pancho Villa who made the mistake of invading this area in 1916.

Gila Cliff Dwellings National Monument, 44 slow miles north of Silver City on Route 15, preserves seven natural caves which were inhabited by people of the Mogollon culture about 700 years ago. Visitors who have seen the Southwest's great Indian ruins, such as those at Chaco Canyon, Mesa Verde or the Jemez Mountains, sometimes find Gila Cliff Dwellings a disappointment because they consist of only 40 rooms, which housed a total of 10 to 15 families. But the small scale of these ruins and nearby pit houses, representative of the many communities scattered throughout the Gila country, is marvelous in the context of the vast surrounding canyonlands.

The real reason a national monument exists at Gila Cliff Dwellings is to administer the central trailhead for one of the nation's most important wilderness areas. Encompassing much of the 3.3 million-acre Gila National Forest, the rugged mountain and canyon country of the **Gila Wilderness** and adjoining **Aldo Leopold Wilderness** comprise the largest roadless area in the United States outside of Alaska. The Gila was the nation's first designated wilderness area, established by act of congress in 1924.

An **overlook** on Route 15 just before the descent to Gila Cliff Dwellings gives a good idea of the Gila's extent and complexity. Three forks of the Gila River join near the cliff dwellings. One of the three main hiking and horse trails into the Gila Wilderness follows each fork through a desert canyon that meanders between mountains for many miles. A treacherous tangle of side canyons off the main ones defied all pioneer efforts at settlement and provided a stronghold for renegade Apache leaders including Geronimo.

Today, mounted rangers take a full week to cross the wilderness patrolling on horseback, and hiking from boundary to boundary is practically impossible without a horse, mule or llama to carry your food supply. The rugged mountains visible from the overlook—the Black, Diablo, Mogollon, San Francisco and Tularoso—are also included in the wilderness area. Of the many hot springs in the area, the most popular is a series of natural springs a short hike up the Middle Fork from the forest service visitor center.

While the main roads are paved, visitors should not underestimate the trip to Gila Cliff Dwellings. The 44-mile drive from Silver City on Route 15 will take two hours; for the 99-mile trip via Routes 152 and 35 from exit 63 on interstate Route 25 south of Truth or Consequences, allow half a day. There are no gas stations or other travelers' services along the way. Even if you're not planning to hike into the wilderness, it is wise to allow a full day for any trip to the Gila.

Also rewarding is a drive around the **western perimeter** of the Gila Wilderness, taking Route 180 west from Silver City, 63 miles to the little town of Glenwood. Just outside of Glenwood, to divert water for a small hydroelectric generator in the 1890s, a mining company suspended a water pipeline from the sheer rock walls of Whitewater Canyon. To maintain the pipeline, workers had to balance on it 20 feet above the river. Today, the mining company and its pipeline are gone, but the Forest Service has installed a steel mesh walkway, known as **The Catwalk**, along the old pipeline route, affording visitors a unique look at this wild canyon. The upper end of **Whitewater Canyon** is a wilderness trailhead.

Three miles north of Glenwood, Route 159 turns off to the east and takes visitors four miles to **Mogollon** (★), one of New Mexico's most interesting and beautifully located ghost towns. A silver and gold mining boom town in the 1890s, Mogollon had a population of more than 2000—larger than any town in the area today. It boasted a theater, several stores and saloons, two churches and two separate red light districts (one Anglo and the other Spanish). Today, many of Mogollon's historic wood and stone buildings still stand in various states of disrepair. One portion of the street was spruced up for use as a motion picture location in the 1970s, and since then a few people have taken up residence in Mogollon during the summer months to restore old buildings, do art work and engage in low-key tourist enterprises. However, fewer than a dozen people live here year-round.

Past Mogollon, the road turns to dirt, passable by regular automobiles but not by long motor homes or vehicles with trailers and winds along the northern wilderness boundary through the **Mogollon Mountains**, the highest in the Gila with four peaks over 10,000 feet high, giving access to several hiking trails, forest service campgrounds and fishing streams and lakes.

Seven miles north of Silver City on the way to Gila Cliff Dwellings via Route 15, the historic town of **Piños Altos** also offers a look at life in southwestern New Mexico a century ago. While this "ghost town" has never been completely abandoned, it is a mere shadow of its glory days. Among the points of interest in Piños Altos today are a replica of Fort Webster—the original was built to protect residents from marauding Apaches who lived in the Gila Wilderness—and a turn-of-the-century opera house. Also here are a store owned by Judge Roy "Law West of the Pecos" Bean before he moved to Texas, and the Hearst Museum, dedicated to the memory of William Randolph Hearst's father, who struck it rich in Piños Altos mining.

Silver City is a pretty hillside town of 11,000 people, a quarter of them college students. Located in the Piños Altos foothills, the city's Victorian commercial district turns back the clock to frontier days. Bisected by a steep canyon, this town could easily be a set for a Hollywood Western. It's also the jumpoff point for one of the state's most picturesque mountain ranges, the Mogollon.

The best sightseeing highlight in town is the **Western New Mexico University Museum** (on campus, Silver City; 505-538-6386). The museum has the world's largest collection of 700- to 1000-year-old Mimbres pottery, painted with the distinctive animal designs that have been revived as a popular decorative motif throughout Southern New Mexico in recent years. One exhibit shows how symbols in some pottery pieces reveal that the Mimbres people had advanced knowledge of astronomy. Not easy for visitors to find, the museum is located in a two-story white building with peach-colored trim in the center of the campus, which is on the hillside on the west side of town.

Silver City also has an interesting downtown historic district. While quite a few of the old buildings are vacant, others provide space for art galleries and student-oriented stores. **Big Ditch Park**, a tree-lined 50-foot-deep arroyo with a small promenade, runs right through the center of town. In fact, it was originally Silver City's main street, but floods washed it away to its present depth, which explains why some of the original storefronts face the ditch instead of the street.

In the downtown area, the **Silver City Museum** (312 West Broadway Street; 505-538-5921) displays Victorian-era frontier artifacts collected from ghost towns and ranches throughout the county.

Silver City was home for a time to young **Billy the Kid**, as several minor historical sites attest. Downtown are the Antrim cabin, where Billy lived with his mother and stepfather, as well as the first jail Billy ever escaped from—at the age of 15, while under arrest for robbing a Chinese laundry. His mother's grave is located on the east side of town. For information and tour maps contact the **Silver City/Grant County Chamber of Commerce** (1103 North Hudson Street; 505-548-9378).

The sleepy little town of **Columbus** lies 32 miles south of Deming on Route 11. Its main claim to fame is that in 1916, Mexican revolutionary leader Pancho Villa invaded the United States with 1000 soldiers, intent on robbing a train carrying a gold shipment. His information was bad, and the train turned out to be carrying coal. After a battle in which 18 Americans and over 100 Mexicans died, Villa and his men retreated into Mexico with General Pershing and 6000 United States soldiers with motor cars and airplanes in hot pursuit.

The story is recalled at the **Columbus Historical Society Museum** (505-531-2708) in the restored train station at the crossroads in the center of town and in the smaller state park museum in the old customs house building across the street.

Cooperation between the United States and Mexico in the decades since is commemorated by a monument at nearby **Pancho Villa State Park**, a desert botanical garden where cholla, ocatillo, large prickly pears, century plants, tall yuccas and other plants of the Chihuahuan Desert grow in profusion on the slopes of the only hill around. Visitors may wish to drive the three miles to the border and walk across to the Mexican village of Palomas.

SOUTHWESTERN NEW MEXICO HOTELS

On the west side of the Gila Wilderness, there are a few accommodations in the little town of Glenwood. **Los Olmos Guest Ranch** (505-539-2311) has stone cabins scattered across several acres of lawn with shade trees. The moderate in-season rates include breakfast and dinner. The 13 stone and wood cabins are furnished with Western-style furniture. Wood-frame beds, upholstered couches and chairs and original Western paintings make these units inviting. The larger cabins offer sitting areas. There are a swimming pool and hot tub on the premises, and bicycles are available for those who want to explore the village. This ranch also has horseshoe pits, a volleyball court and gameroom.

Besides conventional motels, Silver City has a couple of special, surprisingly affordable places to stay. The **Palace Hotel** (106 West Broadway Street; 505-388-1811) is a bed and breakfast in a former bank building (circa 1882) on the main street of the downtown historic district. The guest accommodations, which range from bath-down-the-hall bedrooms to small streets, feature Territorial period furnishings and open onto a central sitting room where continental breakfast is served each morning. Budget.

The **Carter House** (101 North Cooper Street, Silver City; 505-388-5485), a dormitory-style AYH hostel, also has five private budget-priced bed-and-breakfast rooms, each with its own bath. The ambience is young and lively, and guests can use the fully equipped kitchen.

Deming, an agricultural and mining community on an interstate highway, holds no surprises where lodging is concerned. Every motel in town is budget-priced, from the top-of-the-line **Grand Motor Inn** (1721 Spruce Street; 505-446-2632) to older independent motels with rock-bottom rates such as the **Mirador Motel** (501 East Pine Street; 505-546-2795).

Columbus, a little town about as far off in the middle of nowhere as any place that can be reached by highway, has a few unexpected touches of sophistication. One is **Martha's Place** (★) (Main and Lima streets; 505-531-2467), a moderate-priced bed and breakfast. The four elegant second-floor guest rooms have four-poster beds, cable color televisions and balconies overlooking the rooftops of this one-story town.

SOUTHWESTERN NEW MEXICO RESTAURANTS

Silver City being a college town, most restaurants are budget priced. The most atmospheric, the **Main Street Grill** (108 East Broadway Street; 505-388-3320) serves Mexican and American fare in several small dining rooms decorated with lots of plants and paintings by local artists in a historic building overlooking the Big Ditch, the narrow park that was once Silver City's main street.

An irresistible breakfast spot is **Schadel's Bakery** (212 North Bullard Street, Silver City; 505-538-5392), serving a tasty assortment of baked goods café-style or to go.

The fanciest dining in the area is to be found at the **Buckhorn Saloon** (505-538-9911) in the historic town of Piños Altos, seven miles north of Silver City on Route 15. The restaurant and saloon are in a beautifully restored adobe building from the 1860s with big stone fireplaces and elegant place settings. Steaks are the specialty. Prices are moderate.

In between the chain fast-food places, Deming has a number of local restaurants that feature Mexican food. **La Fonda Restaurant** (601 East Pine Street; 505-546-8731) serves fajitas and has a good salad bar. Prices are in the budget range. **Sí Señor** (Pine and Silver streets; 505-546-3938) has stuffed sopapillas and red or green *huevos rancheros* at budget prices. In the moderate range, the **Grand Restaurant** (1721 East Spruce Street; 505-546-2632) has a comprehensive menu of steak, seafood and Mexican food.

In Columbus, the **Gallery Tea Room** (Broadway Street; 505-531-2208) in the Two-Sha Gallery compound was started by a retired professional restaurateur. The little "tea room" also serves complete meals with gourmet touches. Prices are in the budget range.

Speaking of budget-priced food, an unpretentious little diner called **Norma's** (Route 11, Columbus) serves Mexican food, hamburgers and a full breakfast menu at the lowest prices we've seen in the United States in years.

Even more authentic is the Mexican food at any of the nameless hole-in-the-wall taquerias across the border in Palomas—nothing fancy, but certainly foreign.

SOUTHWESTERN NEW MEXICO SHOPPING

The gift shop at the **Western New Mexico State University Museum** (on campus, Silver City; 505-538-6386) has a good selection of Mimbres design sweat shirts, coffee cups, tote bags, stationery and everything else these unique animal motifs from ancient pottery can be printed on.

A number of local artists have studios in Silver City's downtown historic district. Many of them are well-hidden in the residential blocks north of Broadway. More than a dozen artists participate in monthly Saturday afternoon open **studio tours** organized by the San Vicente Group (505-388-2007).

The best art gallery in Southern New Mexico is the **Two-Sha Gallery** (25 Broadway Street; 505-531-2468) in the little border town of Columbus. The owners dropped out of the sophisticated art scenes in Santa Fe and Denver to establish their dream gallery here—several large rooms of paintings, sculpture and decorative items by many of Southern New Mexico's best artists.

SOUTHWESTERN NEW MEXICO NIGHTLIFE

Near Silver City, the historic **Buckhorn Saloon** (505-538-9911) in Piños Altos is as authentic as Old West saloons come, complete with a collection of paintings of nude women.

Down in Columbus, the favorite nighttime entertainment is to cross the border to Palomas, where **mariachi bands** perform on the plaza on weekend evenings.

SOUTHWESTERN NEW MEXICO PARKS

Lake Roberts—Gila National Forest has a number of pretty, little mountain lakes. Lake Roberts is the best known and most accessible of them. Boating and rainbow trout fishing are popular on the 70-acre lake. The southeast shoreline is only accessible by foot trail or by boat. There are two campgrounds, one with full hookups on a mesa overlooking the lake and the other without hookups at the upper end of the lake. The shoreline has some summer cabin development.

Facilities: Picnic area, restrooms, boat rental; information, 505-536-2250. *Fishing:* Seasonally good.

Camping: Mesa Campground has 24 sites ($7 per night). There are ten additional sites at the upper end of the lake ($5 per night).

Getting there: Located just off Route 35 about three miles east of the intersection with Route 15, which is 25 miles north of Silver City on the way to Gila Cliff Dwellings.

Snow Lake—This beautiful 100-acre mountain lake is at the north boundary of the Gila Wilderness at the foot of the Mogollon Mountains. Anglers consider it a great trout lake, especially in the springtime. Some people also catch, boil and eat the abundant crawfish. Use is limited to canoes, rowboats and other small boats without gas motors.

Facilities: Picnic area, restrooms, boat ramp; information, 505-538-2771. *Fishing:* Seasonally good.

Camping: There are 40 sites overlooking the lake ($7 per night). No-fee primitive camping is allowed at the south end of the lake.

Getting there: Follow unpaved Route 78 from Mogollon for 30 miles. This is a slow, sometimes narrow, winding and quite scenic unpaved mountain road. It is passable by passenger cars when dry, but tight curves pose problems for long motor homes and towed vehicles. An alternate route is the 40-mile gravel Forest Road 141 from Reserve.

City of Rocks State Park—South of Silver City on the way to Deming, this park makes an extraordinary spot for a picnic stop. At first sight, the small park appears to be a no-big-deal rockpile in an otherwise featureless desert marred by open-pit copper mines. As you approach, the strangeness of this little geological park becomes apparent. Picnic sites surround a rock dome that has been fractured and eroded into a fantastic maze of oddly shaped stone monoliths and passages that form a natural playground that children and the young at heart can explore for hours. It is impossible to get lost in the maze, since the park road surrounds it on all sides.

Facilities: Picnic area, restrooms, showers, visitor center; information, 505-536-2800.

Camping: There are 56 sites; $7 per night.

Getting there: Located several miles off Route 80, 20 miles south of Silver City and 24 miles north of Route 10 at Deming.

Rock Hound State Park—Mainly of interest to rock collectors in search of the garnets and other semiprecious stones found here, the park has the best public campground in the Deming-Columbus area and offers a close-up look at the arid, rocky slopes of the Florida Mountains.

Facilities: Picnic area, restrooms, showers, playground, trails, visitor center; information, 505-546-6182.

Camping: There are 33 sites, 27 with hookups; $7 per night for tent sites, $11 per night for hookups.

Getting there: Located 14 miles southeast of Deming off Route 143.

The Sporting Life

HORSEBACK RIDING

Although the Roswell region is full of horse-breeding ranches, southeastern New Mexico offers surprisingly little in the way of public horse rentals or tours. In Ruidoso, horses can be rented at the **Inn of the Mountain Gods** (505-257-5141), **Buddy's Stable** (Gavilan Canyon Road; 505-258-4027) and **Cowboy Stables** (1764 West Route 70; 505-378-8217). In Las Cruces, **Circle S Stables** (Baylor Canyon Road; 505-382-7708) offers guided part-day and full-day trips into the Organ Mountains from November through April. North of Silver City, **Whiskey Creek Outfitters** (Arenas Valley; 505-538-2102) and **Lake Roberts Outfitters** (Lake Roberts; 505-536-9393) conduct one- to three-day pack trips into the Gila Wilderness.

SKIING

Ski Apache (505-336-4356), 16 miles northwest of Ruidoso on the slopes of 12,000-foot Sierra Blanca, is one of New Mexico's most popular downhill ski areas. Owned and operated by the Mescalero Apache Indians, Ski Apache has 40 runs and trails. Numerous trails and primitive roads in **Lincoln National Forest** outside Ruidoso are used for cross-country skiing in the winter. For current trail information and snow conditions, contact the Smokey Bear Ranger Station (Ruidoso; 505-257-4095).

Ski Cloudcroft (505-682-2333) has one chairlift and two surface lifts serving 27 runs. It is at a lower elevation than Ski Apache, and snow conditions can vary despite nightly snow making. Lift tickets cost considerably less than at Ski Apache. There are well-groomed cross-country tracks at the **Lodge at Cloudcroft Nordic Ski Center** (505-682-2566), where ski rentals and lessons are available.

GOLF

To tee off in Southern New Mexico head to the **Lake Carlsbad Municipal Golf Course** (901 Muscatel Avenue, Carlsbad; 505-885-5444), **Spring River Golf Course** (1612 West 8th Street, Roswell; 505-622-9506), **Inn of the Mountain Gods** (Ruidoso; 505-257-5141), **The Links at Sierra Blanca** (Ruidoso; 505-258-5330), **Carrizozo Golf Course** (Route 380, Carrizozo; 505-648-2451), the **Alamogordo Municipal Golf Course** (2351 Hamilton Road; 505-437-0290), **The Lodge Golf Course** (Lodge Road, Cloudcroft; 505-682-2098), **Ponderosa Pines Golf Course** (Route 130, Cloudcroft; 505-682-2995), **New Mexico State University Golf Course** (on campus; 505-646-3219), **Truth or Consequences Golf Course** (Truth or Consequences; 505-894-2603) or **Scott Park Memorial Municipal Golf Course** (Silver City; 505-538-5041).

TENNIS

Tennis is pretty scarce in this neck of the woods. Courts are available at **Carlsbad Municipal Park**. In Ruidoso, there are facilities at **Cahoon Park** (West 8th Street) and **Spring River Park** (East 12th Street). For a fee, nonguests can use the courts at **Inn of the Mountain Gods** (505-257-5141) near Ruidoso. In Las Cruces, public courts are located in **Apodaca Park** (Madrid Road at Solano Drive) and **Lions Park** (Picacho and Melendres streets).

BICYCLING

The nine-and-a-half-mile unpaved scenic drive that begins near the visitor center in **Carlsbad Caverns National Park** makes for a good mountain bike ride during the spring or autumn. (In the summer months, it is too hot and often has too much car traffic for enjoyable biking.)

In the Roswell area, cyclists ride the back roads in the ranchlands east of town, particularly the paved roads through **Bitter Lakes National Wildlife Refuge** and **Bottomless Lakes State Park**.

Mountain bikers around Ruidoso use the six-mile unpaved forest road from the Ski Apache road up to Monjeau Campground or any of several jeep roads into the national forest around Bonito Lake.

Mountain bikes are not allowed within the Gila Wilderness, but several jeep roads in the **Piños Altos** area lead into other parts of the national forest. Ambitious cyclists may wish to tackle unpaved Route 78, which skirts the northern boundary of the wilderness beyond Mogollon.

BIKE RENTALS   In Ruidoso, **Wild West Ski Shop** (North Route 48; 505-258-3131) rents mountain bikes and can provide information on area bike trails.

In Silver City, the place for mountain bike rentals is **Gila Hike & Bike** (103 East College Street; 505-388-3222), which offers free information sheets on day hikes, road rides and mountain-bike rides in Gila National Forest.

HIKING

SOUTHEASTERN NEW MEXICO TRAILS   Three-fourths of **Carlsbad Caverns National Park** is a wilderness area restricted to horse and foot travel only, with an extensive trail system. Some are accessed from the scenic drive that starts near the visitor center, while others start from inconspicuous dirt roads off Route 62/180.

One of the more interesting hikes is **Yucca Canyon** (2.5 miles), which leads through piñon and oak forest and past old cabins to cool Longview Spring, with a magnificent view of the Carlsbad Caverns Wilderness.

Near the Yucca Canyon trailhead, another trail leads up to **Goat Cave** (3 miles). The cave is not long—only about a quarter of a mile—but the size of its single room is impressive. Persons wishing to enter the cave must first obtain a permit from the ranger desk at the Carlsbad Caverns visitor center, which is also the place to ask for up-to-date information on these and numerous other hikes in the national park.

Lincoln National Forest has a network of more than 50 miles of trails throughout the **White Mountain Wilderness** northwest of Ruidoso.

From the Ski Apache ski area, a five-mile trail leads to the summit of **Sierra Blanca**, the highest mountain in Southern New Mexico. This is a strenuous hike with an elevation gain of 2100 feet. In the summer and fall, the ski lifts carry people to the summit to enjoy the spectacular view and then hike down.

Another great hike is up **Argentina Canyon** (3.5 miles) with its lush ancient forest and streams fed by mountain springs. The trail starts at the end of the road past Bonito Lake, which leaves Route 48 twelve miles north of Ruidoso.

SOUTH CENTRAL NEW MEXICO TRAILS   A favorite hiking trail in this part of the state is **Three Rivers Trail** (★) (6 miles), which starts at the national forest campground at the end of the unpaved road beyond Three Rivers Petroglyph Site, midway between Carrizozo and Alamogordo. Eventually the trail climbs up to Elk Point on the north side of Sierra Blanca, where it intersects several other major trails leading to all parts of the wilderness area. Many more hikers enter the wilderness from the other side, near Ruidoso, than from Three Rivers.

The main feature of **Oliver Lee Memorial State Park** (505-437-8284), ten miles south of Alamogordo, is Dog Canyon, a hidden oasis in the barren-looking foothills of the Sacramento Mountains. The easy **Dog Canyon Interpretive Trail** (.5 mile) runs from the visitor center up along a small creek between steep slopes covered with ocatillo and giant prickly pear cactuses to a lovely little spring seeping out of the canyon wall.

The steeper, longer **Dog Canyon National Recreation Trail** follows a different route and, in about two-and-a-half miles, reaches a higher spring. The trail continues, climbing out of the canyon to a high ridgeline, where it joins a primitive road that runs about 60 miles from the Carlsbad area.

In the Organ Mountains just east of Las Cruces, the easy **Ice Canyon Trail** (1.5 miles) leads up a steep-walled canyon to Dripping Springs, the former site of a stage stop, a major turn-of-the-century resort and a tuberculosis sanitarium.

The **San Mateo Mountains** (★) west of Truth or Consequences are probably the least-visited mountains in New Mexico. This is a beautiful area characterized by rugged, narrow canyons. It is hot for summer hiking but far enough south to be relatively snow-free in the early spring.

The heart of the San Mateos is the 45,000-acre Apache Kid Wilderness, named for a renegade who made his hideout here in the late 19th century. The main route through the wilderness is the **Apache Kid Trail** (13 miles), an ambitious hike which follows Nogal Canyon for about a mile from the trailhead at Cibola National Forest's Springtime Campground and then climbs steeply to the upper ridge of the mountains. Several side trails lead to hidden canyons and midway along the trail is the Apache Kid's gravesite, where he was shot down by local ranchers.

SOUTHWESTERN NEW MEXICO TRAILS   The **Gila Wilderness** is restricted to foot and horse travel, and over 400 miles of trails extend to all areas of the wilderness. Several guidebooks devoted to hiking trails in the Gila Wilderness are locally available in Silver City. Here are a few of the top hiking options in the Gila:

The **West Fork Trail** (33.5 miles) is the longest trail in the Gila Wilderness, and for the first five miles the most-used trail. For an adventurous day hike, follow the trail upriver about three miles to a narrow, deep section of canyon where caves containing ancient cliff dwellings can be seen high on the sheer rock faces. The trail fords the cold river six times in the three-mile trip.

Those planning longer backpacking trips should note that the trails following the river forks from the Gila Cliff Dwellings area all eventually climb several thousand feet from canyon floors to mountain slopes. A less-strenuous approach to the Gila high country is to hike one of the numerous trails that cross the unpaved forest route from Mogollon to Snow Lake on the north boundary of the wilderness. The trails there start at higher altitudes so that less climbing is involved.

Nine different major side trails branch off the **Crest Trail** (12 miles), which starts at the marked Sandy Point trailhead, 14 miles up the road from the ghost town of Mogollon. Through lush ancient forest, the main trail climbs to the crest of the mountain range and follows it to the 10,770-foot summit of Mogollon Baldy, where an old fire-lookout station affords a panoramic view of boundless wilderness. It is a moderate two- to three-day backpacking expedition. For a one-day hike, take the first four miles of the trail to Hummingbird Spring.

Another major Gila hiking area, the **Aldo Leopold Wilderness**, is accessible from the top of 8100-foot Emory Pass on Route 152, the most direct way from interstate Route 25 to the Gila Cliff Dwellings. The main trail runs north from the pass through stately ponderosa and Douglas fir forest up 10,011-foot **Hillsboro Peak** (5 miles). On the way up the mountain, it intersects six other major trails that go to all corners of the wilderness.

Transportation

BY CAR

Carlsbad and Roswell are on **Route 285**, a two-lane highway that crosses unpopulated plains from Santa Fe, New Mexico, all the way to Del Rio, Texas. The distance from either Santa Fe or Albuquerque is about 200 miles to Roswell and another 100 miles to Carlsbad Caverns National Park. From El Paso, it is a 150-mile drive to Carlsbad Caverns via **Route 62/180**.

Ruidoso and Lincoln are both about 60 miles west of Roswell via **Route 70/380**. The highway forks 47 miles west of Roswell at Hondo, with Route 70 going to Ruidoso and Route 380 going to Lincoln.

Two highway corridors run north-and-south through south central New Mexico: interstate **Route 25** along the Rio Grande through Truth or Consequences and Las Cruces, and the more interesting and isolated **Route 54** down the Tularosa Valley through Carrizozo and Alamogordo. Both highways lead to El Paso, Texas. Four-lane **Route 70/82** links Alamogordo with Las Cruces, making a weekend loop tour of the south central area an enjoyable possibility.

Southwestern New Mexico is the most remote, undeveloped part of the state. The most convenient hub for exploring this area is Silver City, 52 miles north of **Route 10**. An apparent shortcut, **Route 90** from Route 25 south of Truth or Consequences over the Mimbres Mountains to Silver City, saves many miles but not much time compared to driving south to Deming and then north again.

BY AIR

Mesa Airlines provides passenger service to Carlsbad's **Cavern City Air Terminal** and the **Roswell Industrial Air Center** from Albuquerque.

Many visitors to Carlsbad Caverns fly in to the international airport at El Paso, Texas, and rent cars for the trip to the caverns. Mesa Airlines also serves **Alamogordo Municipal Airport** as well as **Las Cruces Municipal Airport** and **Silver City-Grant County Airport.**

Dart-El Paso Limousine Service (505-546-6511) shuttles passengers from Deming to the international airport in El Paso. In Alamogordo, airport transportation is available from **Alamo-El Paso Shuttle Service** (505-437-5124). In Las Cruces call, **Las Cruces Shuttle Service** (505-525-1784).

BY BUS

In the southeastern part of the state, **TNM&O Coaches** has daily bus service to the terminals in Carlsbad (1000 South Canyon Street; 505-887-1108), Roswell (515 North Main Street; 505-622-2510), Ruidoso (138 Service Road; 505-257-2660) and Alamogordo (601 North White Sands Boulevard; 505-437-3050). **Greyhound/Trailways Bus Lines** serves Las Cruces (415 South Valley Drive; 505-524-8518),Truth or Consequences (311 Broadway Street; 505-894-2369), Deming (300 East Spruce Street; 505-546-3881) and Silver City (315 South Hudson Street; 505-388-4086).

CAR RENTALS

In Carlsbad, **McCausland Rent A Car** (505-887-1500) has its agency at the Cavern City Air Terminal. **Independent Auto Rental** (505-887-1469) offers free airport pickup and delivery. In Roswell, most car rental agencies are located at the Roswell Industrial Air Center, including **Budget Car and Truck Rental/Sears Car & Truck Rental** (505-347-2284).

In Alamogordo, car-rental agencies operating from the airport include **Dollar Rent A Car** (505-258-5666) and **Hertz Rent A Car** (437-7760). In Las Cruces call **Avis Rent A Car** (505-522-1400) or **Hertz Rent A Car** (505-521-4807).

Grimes Car Rental (505-538-214) services the Silver City-Grant County Airport. Rental agencies offering pickup and delivery from the airport include **Taylor Car Rental** (505-388-1800) and **Ugly Duckling Rent A Car** (505-388-5813).

TAXIS

Local transportation is provided in the Carlsbad area by **Cavern City Cab Co.** (505-887-0994) and in Roswell by **City Cab Service** (505-624-1111). In Las Cruces **Yellow Cab/Checker Cab** (505-524-1711) supplies citywide service. **Dart-El Paso Limousine Service** (505-546-6511) provides taxi service throughout the Las Cruces-Deming-Lordsburg-Silver City area. **Silver City-Grant County Taxi** (505-538-5376) also serves Silver City.

CHAPTER NINE

Southwestern Utah

A child's jumbo-size crayon box couldn't contain all the pastels, reds, violets, greens and blues found in the unspoiled lands of Southwestern Utah. What's most striking about this country is not only that it has managed to avoid the grasp of developers but also that it's been seemingly skipped by the hands of time. This place puts the letter "p" in pristine.

For starters, consider national parks like Zion, established in 1919, and Bryce, declared a park in 1924. Ever popular, these facilities draw hoards of visitors who go away satisfied without even realizing that the wild beauty of Capitol Reef National Park is close by. Added to this hidden treasure, not more than a few hours away are state parks like Goblin Valley, Kodachrome Basin, Escalante Petrified Forest and the Anasazi Indian Village.

The area we call Southwestern Utah is bordered roughly by the Henry Mountains to the east, Vermilion Cliffs and Beaver Dam Mountains to the south and the arid Great Basin to the west. A unique topographic variety is contained within these lands, as high mountain lakes and forests overlook the twisted rock found in Capitol Reef and Goblin Valley. Ever-evolving sculptured rock pinnacles in Bryce coexist adjacent to bristlecone pines, thought to be the oldest living things on earth.

Generally low humidity and rainfall in the lower elevations provide a favorable growing climate for the rare Joshua trees, sagebrush and yucca, while up high the aspen and pine trees, oaks and juniper flourish.

Until recently, the powers in charge appeared to be in no hurry to sell this land. That is really no surprise. Despite being a primary connector, scenic Route 12 between Escalante and Torrey was paved only in the late 1980s. The rugged Henry Mountains, which abut Capitol Reef National Park, were the last range in this country to be charted, and herds of buffalo still roam freely as do bighorn sheep, antelope and bear. The little town of Boulder, hometown to Anasazi State Park, was the very last place in the 45th state to switch over to modern carriers after having its mail delivered by mule team for half a century.

Promotional efforts have begun to expand the possibilities for "Color Country," yet even the construction of skyscrapers couldn't detract from the rainbow-hued rocks, endless forests, lush gardens and those many, many waterways.

Southwestern Utah offers lakes and creeks like Panguitch, Gunlock and Quail brimming with fish not fishermen, hiking trails crying out for someone to traipse over them, ski areas with volumes of snow and biking areas that aren't freeways. Ghost towns have probably stayed that way for a reason.

Working ranches have not yet disappeared, and some towns appear to have more horses than people. The area has managed to remain true to its Western heritage as rodeos are a popular diversion in the summertime. The rugged terrain is well suited to these sturdy beasts. Probably the most famous quote about the area was made by 19th-century pioneer Ebenezer Bryce who said, "It's a hell of a place to lose a cow."

Among the landowners there's still a certain genuine country courtesy that can be traced to their Mormon traditions and culture rooted in a strong work ethic and family values. The accommodations and places to eat reflect this same simplicity in which clean air and water, a good church community and schools are reason enough to celebrate life. But don't be concerned that everything here is rustic. In the resorts and larger cities such as St. George and Cedar City, there are plenty of comfortable places to stay and a range of decent eateries. And while Utah's liquor laws are still a bit confusing and the number of clubs and taverns is limited, the state has made progress in simplifying the process of getting a drink. One unique practice here is the state's "private" nightclubs, which actually are open to the public but require dues (essentially a cover charge) for the evening.

Mind you, in the outlying areas, at times you're better off sleeping under the stars and using the local grocery for main meals. But isn't there a certain beauty in this contrast?

Nor should you fear that this is a cultural wasteland. The Utah Shakespearean Festival, based in Cedar City, draws thousands of theater-lovers to the region each summer. And the internationally acclaimed American Folk Ballet calls Cedar City home as well. Concerts, plays, dance companies and more are booked into large convention complexes and tiny high school auditoriums alike. Both Dixie College in St. George and Cedar City's Southern Utah University are known for their academic excellence.

Still, it's the church that remains the heart of the area. Brigham Young, the Mormon prophet himself, sent 309 families to colonize this corner of

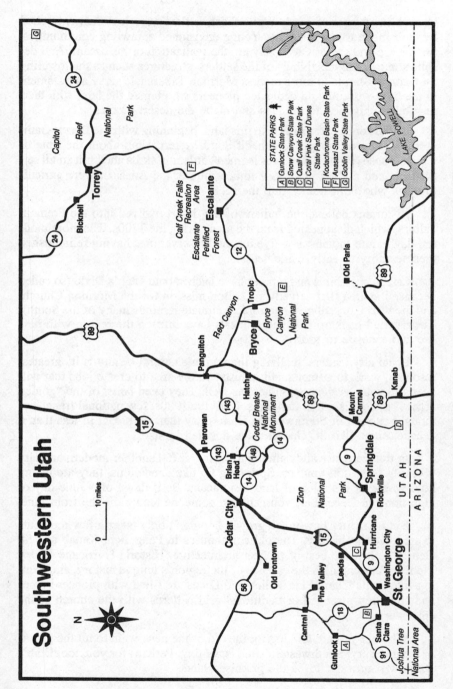

Southwestern Utah

STATE PARKS

A Gunlock State Park
B Snow Canyon State Park
C Quail Creek State Park
D Coral Pink Sand Dunes State Park
E Kodachrome Basin State Park
F Anasazi State Park
G Goblin Valley State Park

Utah in the winter of 1861. While those settlers were less than enthralled by their move to a wilderness, Young envisioned sprawling communities. St. George and Cedar City today are the realization of his dream. And despite some of the misgivings of the settlers, structures such as the towering St. George Temple or more modest Mormon Tabernacle serve as testament to the hard-working and dedicated pioneers who tamed the land with their newfound-irrigation techniques and made the desert bloom.

Indians once claimed title to this land, beginning with the Desert Gatherers, who were thought to inhabit Southwestern Utah about the time of Christ. These Native Americans learned gardening skills and built small settlements and crafted pottery. Another culture, the Anasazi, were agriculturalists who built homes into the rock.

Historians believe the Indians of the desert evolved into the Fremont culture, which disappeared from the area during the 1200s. The more modern-day Paiute Indians now live in small reservations, having relinquished their territory to early white settlers.

Lately, snowbirds and retirees have latched onto Utah's Dixie (so called because the area first served as a cotton mission for the Mormon Church, and the warm, dry, almost subtropical climate reminds many of the South). Their varied backgrounds and interests have infused the region with new life and a desire to grow.

Local city leaders, realizing the region's natural beauty is its greatest resource, work to attract small industry to the area to create jobs that will keep the younger generation here as well. They even *boast* of the "golden arches" along main thoroughfares. Until the 1980s, few national franchises thought enough of Southwestern Utah to try their luck. But in less than a decade, cities like St. George have doubled in size.

In this verdant valley among towering cliffs, another modern amenity is taking root: golf courses. Springing up like dandelions, they are taking hold wherever a stretch of land lies vacant. Be it dawn of a June day or high noon in December, you can find someone teeing off the front nine.

But no matter how much growth booms, it only takes a few moments to step back in history. The old courthouses in Panguitch, Kanab and St. George reflect the best of pioneer architecture. Historic Hurricane Valley Pioneer Park captures the essence of the region's unique history, and hamlets like Santa Clara, Pine Valley and Leeds are filled with pioneer homes and churches, arranged in traditional grid patterns with the church as the epicenter.

Whether you are looking for the old or the new, want to hit the greens or the greenery, Southwestern Utah is waiting. Perhaps for you, too, Utah's Dixie will turn out to be the promised land.

St. George Area

St. George is not only a winter resort for snowbirds and retirees but also a key gateway to Zion National Park, Cedar Breaks National Monument and Snow Canyon State Park. The area is also a historical gold mine, full of restored homes, buildings from the 1800s and fascinating ghost towns.

The city began when Brigham Young sent some 300 families from the lush land of northern Utah to the southern Utah desert. Young envisioned a huge cotton mission that could supplement the West's supply during the Civil War, which had cut off shipments from the South.

Though initially successful, the cotton mission (and one to grow silkworms as well) ultimately failed because of an inability to compete in the marketplace after the end of the Civil War. However, a warm climate and bevy of recreational activities eventually made St. George the fastest-growing city in the state.

Any tour of the city should begin at the **St. George Chamber of Commerce**, in the Old Washington County Courthouse (97 East St. George Boulevard; 801-628-1658). The brick-and-mortar building, completed in 1876, contains panels of original glass alongside the entrance doors, original wall paintings of Zion and Grand Canyons in the upper assembly room, an old security vault and much more.

The courthouse serves as first stop on the **St. George Walking Tour**. The three-square-block trek points out 22 sights including some of the city's finest pioneer buildings. Pick up a map at the Chamber of Commerce.

Some of the more notable walking-tour sights include **Pioneer Museum** (145 North 100 East; 801-628-7274), a vast collection of community artifacts overseen by the Daughters of the Utah Pioneers, and the **Brigham Young Winter Home** (89 West 200 North; 801-673-5181), where a guided tour showcases beautiful furnishings and memorabilia owned by the second president of the Mormon Church. Fruit and mulberry trees (fodder for those silkworms) still cover the grounds.

Stop 13 on the walking tour is **Judd's Store** (62 West Tabernacle; 801-628-2596), a turn-of-the-century mercantile that stocks candy, dolls, stuffed animals and the like. A working soda fountain dishes up welcome treats on those hot Utah days.

It took 13 years to complete the **Mormon Tabernacle** (Main and Tabernacle; 801-628-4072). Tour guides show off the building with pride telling how the limestone for three-foot-thick basement walls was hand quarried and the red sandstone blocks were hand cut stone by stone from a nearby site. Take special note of the intricate, plaster-of-Paris ceiling and cornice work, all shipped to California by boat and then hauled by wagon team to St. George.

Only card-carrying members of the Mormon Church may tread through the sparkling-white **St. George Temple** (450 South 300 East; 801-673-5181), but an on-site visitor center does provide a pictorial history of the temple's construction and other background on the Church of Latter Day Saints. Free guided tours of the grounds are also available.

Is it real or is it . . . ? That's the prevailing question at the **St. George Art Museum** (175 East 200 North, lower level of the St. George City office building; 801-634-5800; admission), which houses a collection of purported old masters such as Rembrandt, Van Gogh and Degas. While the work can't be authenticated, it is nevertheless intriguing.

Also located within St. George is the **Washington County Travel & Convention Bureau** (425 South 700 East, Dixie Center; 801-634-5747), which can provide information on the entire region.

If you're a real history buff, you might want to venture out to **Old Fort Pierce**, east of St. George. The adobe fort was built in 1866 to protect settlers. Only a few remnants and partial walls remain at the site, but there is a nice monument explaining the history of the fort. While there, you can also explore a series of **dinosaur tracks** (three-toed impressions left in the mud millions of years ago). Getting to Old Fort Pierce and the tracks requires a high-center vehicle and dry roads. Follow 700 South to the east until it becomes River Road and take an immediate left on Stake Farm Road. Then follow the signs.

Twenty-five miles north of St. George on Route 18 is the town of Central and the turnoff to **Pine Valley**, a mountain hamlet with a picturesque, satin-white chapel that's believed to be the oldest Mormon chapel still in continuous use. Nestled in the Dixie National Forest, surrounded by 10,000-foot peaks and ponderosa pine, is the Pine Valley campground and reservoir with numerous picnicking areas.

Just north of the Pine Valley turnoff is a stone marker for the **Mountain Meadows Massacre Site and Memorial**. Here, in 1857, a group of emigrants—120 men, women and children—en route to California was slaughtered by Mormons and Indians. The event is considered a dark period in Mormon history and one the church has tried to live down ever since.

After visiting Pine Valley, backtrack to Route 18 and travel 12 miles south to the **Snow Canyon State Park** (801-628-2255) turnoff. Along the way are numerous extinct volcanic cones and lava fields, many beckoning to be explored. A small park, the canyon itself is a white-and-red mix of Navajo sandstone covered with black lava beds. Elevations range from 2600 to 3500 feet atop the cindercones. Snow Canyon has served as movie location for several films including *Butch Cassidy and the Sundance Kid*. Grasses, willows, cacti and other shrubbery peer through cracks. Evidence of early man's impressions of Snow Canyon can be seen at several pictograph sites within the park.

Leaving the canyon, you'll pass through Ivins and then connect with the rural community of Santa Clara three miles west of St. George. Settled by Swiss immigrants, Santa Clara lays claim to the house built by noted missionary, Indian agent and colonizer Jacob Hamblin. Built in 1862, the rough-hewn, red sandstone **Jacob Hamblin Home** (Route 91; 801-673-2161) clearly demonstrates the sturdiness of frontier construction designed to withstand Indian attack and showcases a number of furnishings and tools from that period.

Backtrack from Gunlock to Route 91 and head south over the summit to the Beaver Dam Slope. As you drive toward the Arizona border you'll pass the 1040-acre, desert-like **Joshua Tree Natural Area,** claimed to be the farthest north these picturesque trees grow.

Route 91 connects with Route 15 at Beaver Dam. Head north back toward St. George and drive through the Virgin River Gorge, a giant gash in the rocky earth where the Virgin River heads out of Utah through Arizona and into Nevada. It took 12 years to build this 23-mile stretch of spectacular highway.

Center of the cotton mission, the **Washington Cotton Mill** (375 West Telegraph, Washington City; 801-673-0375; admission) is a long, rock building constructed in 1865. You can still tour the historic, two-and-a-half-story structure, which is now used for weddings, family reunions and club meetings.

In search of prehistoric creatures? A short (200-yard) walk takes adventurous souls to more **dinosaur tracks(★)**. Drive to the center of Washington City and turn north on Main until you pass under Route 15. Follow the dirt road north and turn right at the road that goes up the hill to the pink water tank. Park here, then walk up the road to a chained cable gate. Turn right and walk northeast to a deep wash. Go down into the wash and follow it downstream until you find a flat, greenish slab of rock. Here you'll find the foot-long tracks from another age.

Halfway between St. George and Zion National Park on Route 9 lies the town of Hurricane (pronounced hur-i-kun), a rural community that often attracts the overflow from Zion into its motels and restaurants. In the center of town lies **Pioneer Heritage Park** (West State Street). The museum and information center stands amid a grassy lawn filled with pioneer-era wagons and farm machinery. Within the museum are many pioneer items including an authentic kitchen.

A relaxing break from the rigors of the road may be found at **Pah Tempe Hot Springs** (825 North 800 East 35-4, Hurricane; 801-635-2879) a large grouping of eight soaking- and swimming-pool areas. Rustic but congenial, Pah Tempe resembles a '60s commune with a tiny bed and breakfast, lodge, campsites and boutique. Bathing suits required. Massage therapy programs, facial packs and other services may be arranged.

ST. GEORGE AREA HOTELS

The mid-point between Salt Lake City and Los Angeles, St. George is awash in hotels, motels and bed and breakfasts. Virtually every chain is represented, making it simple to find one that meets your requirements and pocketbook.

No one walks away unsatisfied from the **Seven Wives Inn** (★) (217 North 100 West; 801-628-3737), perhaps some of the nicest accommodations in St. George. Deluxe in every way except price, the 13-room bed and breakfast is graciously decorated in Victorian antiques. Some rooms boast fireplaces or woodburning stoves, and most have outside doors to porches or balconies. All have private bath. Rates include a huge gourmet breakfast in the elegant dining room and use of the swimming pool. Budget to moderate.

There's a lot of bang for the buck at **Ranch Inn** (1040 South Main; 801-628-8000). More than half the 53 units are classified "kitchenette suites," meaning they house a microwave oven, refrigerator, conversation-and-dining area, plus fully tiled bath with mirrored vanity. Indoor jacuzzi, sauna, guest laundry and heated pool round out the amenities. Budget.

Situated off the main drag, **Ramada Inn** (1440 East St. George Boulevard; 801-628-2828) offers quiet refuge. An expansive lobby provides portal to 90 rooms, each with desk and upholstered chairs. The hotel also has one of the prettiest swimming-pool settings with palm trees surrounding the site. Free continental breakfast is included. Moderate.

The streamlined architecture of **Best Western Coral Hills Motel** (125 East St. George Boulevard; 801-673-4844) is reminiscent of "The Jetsons," but the 98 rooms are more down-to-earth with turquoise carpeting, upholstered chairs and dark woods. Indoor and outdoor swimming pools, spas, putting green and exercise room are bonuses. Moderate.

Holiday Inn Resort Hotel (850 South Bluff; 801-628-4235) likes to think of itself as a complete recreational facility. Besides the well-appointed rooms, restaurant and atrium-style lobby (with mini-waterfall), guests are treated to a large indoor/outdoor heated swimming pool (you can actually swim in and out of the hotel), whirlpool, tennis court, putting green, mini-gym, gameroom, video arcade, gift shop and special children's play area. Moderate to deluxe.

The Bluffs Motel (1140 South Bluff; 801-628-6699) seems to offer two of everything: double queen suites, two televisions, two telephones, even two king suites with private jacuzzi. The 33 rooms are exceptionally well decorated in soft tones and enjoy large bathrooms and a living-room area. There's also an outdoor heated pool and jacuzzi. Complimentary continental breakfast is offered in the sunny lobby. Budget to moderate.

A collection of pioneer homes makes up **Greene Gate Village** (62-78 West Tabernacle; 801-628-6999), a unique bed-and-breakfast complex designed to intrigue and delight. Surrounded by a flower-laden courtyard, manicured lawns, swimming pool and garden hot tub, the village boasts elegant decor—wallpapered rooms, duvets, antique furnishings, plump pillows—and a conscientious staff. A delicious country breakfast completes the picture. Moderate.

ST. GEORGE AREA RESTAURANTS

St. George doesn't lack for choices when it comes to places to eat. Besides the requisite chains (and none are missing), there are plenty that offer a hearty meal at a reasonable cost. At least this side of Utah has heard of the salad bar.

A friendly, casual pit stop for breakfast, lunch or dinner is **Sil's** (939 East St. George Boulevard; 801-634-9910). The most popular choice on the eclectic menu is the soup, salad and hot-food buffet. Budget.

Perched on the third floor of the Tower Building in Ancestor Square, **J. J. Hunan Chinese Restaurant** (2 West St. George Boulevard; 801-628-7219) appears to be the area's choice for Oriental cuisine. Seafood, chicken, beef, duck, pork—it's all here presented in a gracious manner. Budget to moderate.

Fajitas are tops at **Pancho & Lefty's** (1050 South Bluff; 801-628-4772), a busy, fun Mexican restaurant. The menu of tostadas, burritos and tacos is priced in the budget-to-moderate range.

Grab a shaded table outside and enjoy a tall glass of iced strawberry tea at **Libby Lorraine's** (2 West St. George Boulevard; 801-673-0750). The bistro-style café features an array of sandwiches (like the Caribbean—crab and bay shrimp in sour cream and dill dressing on a croissant) and pastas, plus a delightful breakfast menu. Budget.

Fireplaces, greenery galore and waitresses dressed in early English garb lend a cozy, historic air to **Andelin's Gable House** (290 East St. George Boulevard; 801-673-6796), unequivocally St. George's finest dining establishment. Patrons choose from an elegant, five-course dinner or a more moderate menu. Regardless, all are served with pewter mugs and plates and taste delicious. Noteworthy are the roast brisket of beef, orange roughy and chicken pot pie. Save room for dessert. Moderate to deluxe.

For a refreshing lunch in the heart of St. George try **Rene's Restaurant** (430 East St. George Boulevard; 801-628-9300). Huge windows allow sunlight to stream across the booths and tables surrounded by lush greenery and white overhead fans. Home cooking and courteous service are watchwords as you choose from burgers, pastas, chicken, sandwiches and steaks.. Breakfast fans will appreciate the homemade breads and muffins. Budget.

Service is erratic, but **The Palms Restaurant** (850 South Bluff, inside the Holiday Inn; 801-628-4235) can be a good choice for family dining in a pleasant setting. Besides an extensive salad bar with homemade soups and breads, dinner choices range from roast turkey to mountain trout to chicken teriyaki. Sandwiches, hamburgers and salads comprise the lunch menu, while breakfast includes omelettes and griddle items. Budget to moderate.

ST. GEORGE AREA SHOPPING

Shopping in this region is pretty much designed with locals in mind. You'll find a few shopping malls and strip centers but little else. One place of note is the **Artist Co-Op Gallery** (#5 Ancestor Square, St. George Boulevard and Main, St. George; 801-628-9293), which carries works by more than a dozen regional artists.

ST. GEORGE AREA NIGHTLIFE

World-class entertainers are spotlighted through the **Celebrity Concert Series** at Dixie Center (425 South 700 East, St. George; 801-628-7003).

The **Southwest Symphony**, a community orchestra, performs throughout the year in the M. C. Cox Auditorium at Dixie Center (425 South 700 East, St. George; 801-628-7003), as does the **Southwest Symphonic Chorale.**

Dixie College (225 South 700 East, St. George; 801-628-3121) offers a year-round season of plays and musicals utilizing the talents of the Pioneer Players.

The **Blarney Stone** (800 East St. George Boulevard; 801-673-9191) is a beer bar serving a lively crowd. There's live music on weekends running the gamut from country to pop.

It's members only at **Chapter Eleven** (195 South Bluff; 801-673-0055), but anyone can gain temporary membership for a small fee. A bit more upbeat and affluent crowd frequents this establishment known for its live entertainment on weekends and good-sized dancefloor.

ST. GEORGE AREA BEACHES AND PARKS

Snow Canyon State Park—Black lava rock crusted over red Navajo sandstone make for a striking visual effect in this colorful canyon. Several volcanic cones welcome visitors to the northern end of the 65,000-acre park, considered a treat for photographers.

Facilities: Picnic areas, restrooms, hot showers, electrical hookups, sewage disposal station and covered group-use pavilion; information, 801-628-2255.

Camping: There are 31 sites (including 14 with partial hookups) and a hiker camp. Hiker campsites are $7 per night, standard sites $9 per night and hookups $11 per night. Reservations recommended.

Getting there: On Route 18 five miles northwest of St. George.

Gunlock State Park—This 240-acre reservoir is noted for its superb year-round boating, bass fishing, waterskiing and picnicking. Nestled in the rugged ravine of the Santa Clara River, the reservoir's waters abut redrock hills dotted with green shrubbery.

Facilities: Restrooms and boat ramp; information, 801-628-2255.

Camping: Primitive camping allowed within the camp.

Getting there: On old Route 91, 16 miles northwest of St. George.

Quail Creek State Park—Stark rock escarpments surround the 590-acre reservoir with a state park set on its west shore. Quail Creek attracts anglers eager to reel in bass, trout and catfish. Besides being an ideal site for camping and picnicking, Quail Creek is noted for its waterskiing, boating and windsurfing.

Facilities: Picnic areas and restrooms; information, 801-879-2378.

Camping: There are 23 sites; $7 per site.

Getting there: Located on Route 15, 14 miles north of St. George.

Red Cliffs Recreation Site—Maintained by the Bureau of Land Management, this camping area is a red-rock paradise at the foot of Pine Valley Mountain. Desert trees and plants crowd every campsite.

Facilities: Picnic tables, pit toilets and drinking water; information, 801-628-4491.

Camping: There are ten sites; $4 per night.

Getting there: From St. George go north on Route 15 about 17 miles to the Leeds exit. From there, it's four-and-one-half miles south.

Zion Area

If you've got rocks in your head, you've come to the right place. This is not to question your sanity but rather to underline the spectacular rock formations found here. From canyon walls to monuments to cliffs, the Zion Area has it all. Coupled with this are some neat historic buildings and movie-set towns that have been featured in hundreds of films.

It's easy to see why the popularity of **Zion National Park** (Route 9, Springdale; 801-772-3256; admission) has zoomed in the past few years. Extremely accessible year-round, with an endless variety of hiking trails geared to all abilities, this "heavenly city of God" is a park for all people.

Grandfather of Utah's national parks, Zion is packed with precipitous canyon walls and massive stone monoliths. Vividly colored cliffs, sheer-rock walls and unique formations make this park one of the state's most popular attractions.

This 147,000-acre park was carved almost singlehandedly by the Virgin River, which flows along the canyon floor. Cottonwoods, willows and velvet ash trees line the river, providing an ever-changing kaleidoscope of colors as one season follows another. To really avoid the crowds and traffic, gear your visit to November through April. Otherwise expect lots of cars, nonexistent parking and lots of other travelers.

Standing guard over the park entrance is **The Watchman**, a 2600-foot monolith of sandstone and shale. Some believe early Native Americans may have considered the massive stone formation a symbol of Zion's power.

Be sure to stop at the **Visitor Center** where rangers are happy to provide maps, brochures and backcountry permits. Naturalist guided walks, evening programs and patio talks are scheduled from late March to November. Specific dates and times are posted at the center.

Youngsters ages six through 12 can get down and dirty with nature at the **Zion Nature Center** through the Junior Ranger Program. From June through Labor Day, park rangers and the Zion Natural History Association conduct a variety of outdoor-adventure and environmental-science programs that acquaint the younger set with everything from the flight pattern of a golden eagle to the difference between a Utah beavertail cactus and a maidenhair fern.

Depending on time and specific interest, you can drive, bicycle or take a guided tram tour through Zion. But don't miss out on the fabulous sights that await just off the roads. Zion is best appreciated close-up, and you'll miss the true majesty of the park if you don't wander around.

Zion Canyon Scenic Drive takes visitors about six-and-a-half miles into the heart of Zion Canyon and its 2000-to-3000-foot-high walls carved inch-by-inch by the Virgin River cutting through the Markagunt Plateau. Just past the entrance you're likely to spot **West Temple**, highest peak in Zion's southern section. Notice the delineated strata of rock as it rises 4100 feet from base to peak.

One of the first places you might want to pause is **Court of the Patriarchs** viewpoint. From here you can see reverently named monuments like the Streaked Wall, the Sentinel, the Patriarchs (a series of three peaks called Abraham, Isaac and Jacob), Mt. Moroni, the Spearhead and the sheerwalled sandstone monolith Angels Landing, perched 1500 feet above the canyon bed. To the east and above are two other monuments, Mountain of the Sun and the Twin Brothers.

Emerald Pools parking area, two-and-a-half miles up the Scenic Drive, offers access to a trail network serving both the Upper and Lower pools. A creek from Heaps Canyon sends water cascading down waterfalls into pools below. Yucca, cacti and scrub oak line the trail to the upper pool, and the path affords views of shaded, north-facing slopes rich with ponderosa pine, aspen and Douglas fir. If you happen to visit Zion in the fall, this is a prime spot to see the changing colors.

The **Grotto Picnic Area** is the perfect spot to take a break from exploring the park. Here in the cool shade of broadleaf trees and gamble oak you'll find fire grates, picnic tables, water and restrooms.

Driving the road you'll spot **The Great White Throne** on the east side. Notice how this 2400-foot megalith ranges in color from a deep red at the base to pink to gray to white at the top. The color variations arise because the Navajo sandstone has less iron oxide at the top than the bottom.

A bit farther is a short, paved walk that leads to **Weeping Rock** where continuous rain "weeps" across a grotto. Even on a hot day, the spot remains cool. Like other parts of Zion, you should see lush, hanging cliff gardens thick with columbine, shooting-stars and scarlet monkeyflower. Pay close attention and you might spot the Zion snail, a creature found in the park and nowhere else.

The end of the road, so to speak, comes at **Temple of Sinawava**, perhaps the easiest area in the park to access. This huge natural amphitheater swarms with visitors enthralled by the sheer, red cliffs that soar to the sky and two stone pillars—the Altar and the Pulpit—in the center. There's a large parking area at the temple, but it fills quickly, so you may be forced to park up to a mile away alongside the Canyon Drive and hoof it in.

Route 9 branches off of Zion Canyon Drive and heads east from Zion National Park on what is called the **Zion-Mount Carmel Highway**. Considered an engineering marvel for its day (1930), the road snakes up high precipices and around sharp, narrow turns before reaching the high, arid plateaus of the east. And, if you've ever ridden Disneyland's Matterhorn, you'll love the mile-long, narrow, unlit tunnel. Rangers control traffic through the darkened tube, stopping drivers when an oversized truck or recreational vehicle is passing through. Even with some delays, the tunnel is a treat with huge, window-like openings allowing sunlight to stream in every so often, affording unparalleled views of the vermillion cliffsides. And was that the Abominable Snowman behind that rock?

On the other side of the tunnel lies the park's "slickrock" territory. It's almost like a time warp from one country to another.

Canyon Overlook is an easy, half-mile self-guided walk on the Zion-Mt. Carmel Highway just east of the long tunnel. Unlike the lush Zion Canyon floor, this area showcases plants and animals that make rock and sand their home. The overlook itself provides views of lower Zion Canyon including the Streaked Wall with its long, black marks sharply contrasting with the red canyon walls; West and East Temples, giant stone monoliths with temple-like edifices perched on top; and the massive, multicolored cliff called Towers of the Virgin.

Don't miss **Checkerboard Mesa**, a prime example of sandstone etched over time with horizontal lines and vertical fractures to resemble a mountainous playing board. You stay on Route 9 out of Zion National Park to connect with Route 89 and head south toward the Arizona border.

All that's missing is the surf at **Coral Pink Sand Dunes State Park** (12 miles off Route 89 between Springdale and Kanab; 801-874-2408). This is Mother Nature's sandbox just aching to be frolicked in by young and old alike. Some of the dunes reach several hundred feet in height. A resident park ranger is on hand to answer questions about this unusual area, and there are a few interpretive signs as well. But those who prefer sand to water will revel in the inviting dunes.

Continuing on Route 89, you'll pass what looks like a giant dinosaur jutting out of a mountainside. That's **Moqui Cave** (admission) which claims the largest collection of dinosaur tracks in the Kanab area. Other displays include Indian artifacts, foreign money and fluorescent minerals. Open only from April through October.

Farther south, Route 89 heads toward the base of the colorful Vermillion Cliffs and **Kanab**, a town known as "Little Hollywood" for the more than 200 movies, most of them B-grade Westerns, filmed in the area. Today, Kanab is a crossroads for travelers headed to Lake Powell, the Grand Canyon or Bryce and has numerous motels and restaurants.

Some movie-set towns are still evident throughout the area. Because most sit on private property, it's safest to check with the **Kane County Travel Council** (41 South 100 East, Kanab; 801-644-5033) for the latest information on which are open to the public. In Kanab, a bit like the Universal Studios tour is **Lopeman's Frontier Movie Town** (297 West Center; 801-644-5337), a replica of a Wild West movie set that caters to groups but lets individuals tag along. Here, marshals in white hats battle black-hatted villains during mock gunfights. You can walk along the boardwalk and peer into the false store fronts. Shops, a snack bar and historic exhibits are also on-site. The town is only open from April through October, and hours are intermittent. It's best to call ahead.

Heritage House (100 South Main; 801-644-2542) is an 1886, restored pioneer mansion built of brick and red rock and one of 13 homes making up the Kanab walking tour. You can find brochures at the house or at Kanab's city offices (40 East 100 North; 801-644-2534).

Thirty miles east along Route 89 takes you to the **Old Paria** turnoff. Here, fans will find the West of their imaginations come alive on a falsefront movie-set town that's open to the public and was once used for the "Gunsmoke" television series. Some also use Route 89 as a backdoor entrance to Lake Powell, with the highway continuing into Page, Arizona.

ZION AREA HOTELS

Massive vermillion cliffs surround **Zion National Park Lodge** (801-586-7686), located in the heart of the park. A huge, manicured lawn and shade trees welcome guests to the property, which includes motel-style rooms, suites and cabins. While standard furnishings are the norm, location is everything. Cabins afford more privacy and feature fireplaces and private porches. Dining room, snack bar and gift shop are on-site. Moderate to deluxe.

Rooms at **Flanigan's Inn** (428 Zion Park Boulevard, Springdale; 801-772-3244) range from okay to very nice indeed. Those on a budget might opt for the smaller, somewhat plain rooms. If you place a value on spaciousness, splurge on the larger, suite-like spaces done in oak furnishings with tile baths, bentwillow wall hangings and ceiling fans. Regardless of room, hotel guests can partake of the swimming pool and excellent restaurant. Budget to moderate.

American and English antique furniture fills **Under the Eaves Guest House** (980 Zion Park Boulevard, Springdale; 801-772-3457). Constructed of sandstone blocks from nearby canyon walls, the home resembles a cheery English cottage. Three rooms have private baths, another two share. Full breakfast is served each morning, and guests can sip a cup of tea in the outdoor gazebo that fairly bursts with flowers or soak in the soothing outdoor spa. Moderate.

Located in a quiet neighborhood, **Harvest House Bed and Breakfast** (★) (29 Canyon View Drive, Springdale; 801-772-3880) is sure to please even the most demanding. All four rooms are exquisitely decorated in what the owners term "urban eclectic." Expect bright, airy spaces full of wicker furniture, private baths, plush carpeting and balconies with an unparalleled view of Zion National Park. Beverages are available anytime from the dining room wet bar, and there's an extensive library of art and cookbooks. Moderate to deluxe.

Tree-shaded lawns and gardens mark the **Driftwood Lodge** (1515 Zion Park Boulevard, Springdale; 801-772-3262). Forty-eight oversized rooms bring the outdoors inside with oak furniture and gray-blue accents. A dining room, gift shop and outdoor swimming pool are nice pluses. Priced in the moderate range.

Nothing fancy, but good home cooking and warm hospitality are hallmarks of **Zion House Bed and Breakfast** (801 Zion Park Boulevard, Springdale; 801-772-3281). Two rooms offer private baths, two others share. Guests can swap tales of park adventures in the comfortable living room. Family-style breakfast is served. Budget to moderate.

Just a short drive to Zion National Park, **Weston's Lamplighter Motel** (280 West State, Hurricane; 801-635-4647) is a good alternative when Springdale accommodations fill. Thirty-two units are attractively furnished with small sitting areas, and a pool/jacuzzi provides respite after a day of touring. Moderate.

If you must overnight in Kanab, plan to stay at the **Shilo Inn** (296 West 100 North; 801-644-2562). The 118 mini-suites are nicely decorated in soft blues and pinks; most include microwaves and refrigerators. Extra amenities including free continental breakfast and fresh fruit raise the complex well above the motel crowd. Plus, there's a swimming pool and spa, gift shop, video-game room and guest laundry. Moderate.

ZION AREA RESTAURANTS

Right in the heart of Zion National Park, **Zion Lodge Restaurant** (801-772-3213) satisfies every appetite with bountiful breakfasts, hearty lunches and gourmet dinners. Hamburgers, salads, seafood and steak are pleasantly presented amid the beauty of Zion. Reservations required for dinner. Budget to moderate.

The rustic appearance of **Bit and Spur Saloon and Mexican Restaurant** (★) (1212 Zion Park Boulevard, Springdale; 801-772-3498) belies what many consider Utah's best Mexican restaurant. Besides standard favorites like *chile rellenos* and tostada supreme, the menu features deep-dish specials such as sour-cream enchilada and chicken enchilada, plus pasta diablo. Dinner only. Moderate.

You can't miss with breakfast, lunch or dinner at **Flanigan's Inn Restaurant** (428 Zion Park Boulevard, Springdale; 801-772-3244). The bright, airy establishment serves up healthy portions of everything from Rocky Mountain trout to Dixie ham steak, as well as pasta, chicken and beef dishes. Reservations recommended for dinner. Budget to moderate.

Consistently good is the **Driftwood Restaurant** (1515 Zion Park Boulevard in the Driftwood Lodge, Springdale; 801-772-3224) with its wrap-around windows providing a glorious view of Zion. Utah mountain trout, crispy chicken and flame-broiled steaks top the dinner menu. For dessert there's a bountiful selection of homemade pies and cheesecake. Breakfast fare includes eggs, pancakes, muffins and the like. Budget to moderate.

ZION AREA NIGHTLIFE

The **Grand Circle Multimedia Sound and Light Show** is a treat for the senses at the O.C. Tanner Amphitheater (Springdale; 801-673-4811; admission), May through September. The production takes viewers on an odyssey through Zion National Park and other nearby national gems. The amphitheater also provides other top entertainment.

There are dances every Saturday night and talent shows during the week at the **Old Barn Theater** (50 North 100 East, behind Parry Lodge; 801-644-2015) in Kanab.

ZION AREA BEACHES AND PARKS

Zion National Park—A true gem. Sheer, towering cliffs surround the verdant floor of Zion Canyon as lush hanging gardens and waterfalls stand in marked contrast to the desert-like terrain of stark rock formations and etched redrock walls.

Facilities: Picnic areas, restrooms, restaurant and snack bar and gift shop. Guided walks and a hiker shuttle service can be arranged through the on-site visitor center; information, 801-772-3256.

Camping: There are about 400 sites in two campgrounds; $7 per night. Primitive camping allowed with permit.

Getting there: Main entrance is one mile north of Springdale via Route 9. The east entrance is 25 miles west of Mt. Carmel Junction along Route 9. A one-mile tunnel connects Zion Canyon with plateaus on the east. Buses and many recreational vehicles are too large to navigate the tunnel in two-way traffic, so traffic may be temporarily halted.

Coral Pink Sand Dunes State Park—The beach comes to Utah at this expansive site of coral-pink sand dunes. Visitors are encouraged to play in the six square miles of sand, ride off-road vehicles or build a sand castle or two.

Facilities: Restrooms and showers; information, 801-874-2408.

Camping: There are 22 sites; $9 per night.

Getting there: On Route 89 about 35 miles northwest of Kanab.

Cedar City Area

Though now called "Festival City" because of its ties to the Utah Shakespearean Festival, it was iron that initially brought Mormon pioneers to Cedar City. Early Utah settlers worried about the lack of iron ore, and when deposits were discovered in the mountain 15 miles west of what is now Cedar City, an iron mission was established in 1851. Despite initial success, the foundry closed a mere seven years later, but Cedar City managed to survive and today hosts numerous cultural and sporting events.

The **Cedar City Chamber of Commerce** (286 North Main; 801-586-4022) can supply brochures, an interactive information video and helpful advice on what to do in the area. One of the best ways to fully explore Cedar City is via the **Historical Tour**. Fourteen sites spread throughout the city are featured, giving visitors a true sense of the entire community. Grab a tour map at the Chamber of Commerce.

Iron Mission State Park (585 North Main; 801-586-9290; admission) gives a comprehensive look at early Cedar City and the original foundry.

But the park's real showstopper is the Gronway Parry Horse-Drawn Vehicle Collection. Spanning 1870 to 1930, there are buggies, surreys, mail carts, sleighs, a bullet-scarred stagecoach, a white hearse and a water-sprinkling wagon. All are in tip-top shape and a real kick to explore.

Rock Church (Center and 100 East; 801-586-8475) was built by Cedar City residents during the Depression with native materials and donated labor. Red cedar adorns the interior and benches of the chapel, while the colorful stones (including iron, copper and gold ore) on the exterior were carefully matched.

Those lucky enough to visit Cedar City between late June and early September shouldn't miss an opportunity to see a performance at the renowned **Utah Shakespearean Festival**. Six plays rotate afternoons and evenings at two theaters on the campus of **Southern Utah University** (351 West Center; 801-586-7700), a four-year educational institution with 3000 students. Even if you can't attend the Shakespearean Festival, an authentic re-creation of the Tiring House Theater of Shakespeare's era shows Shakespearean displays and costumes during the festival season in the foyer of the Southern Utah University Auditorium. The theater sits just behind the auditorium.

Also on the campus is the **Braithwaite Fine Arts Gallery** (801-586-5432), which hosts art exhibits of all types throughout the year.

Sixteen miles north of Cedar City on Route 15, the small community of **Parowan** (southern Utah's oldest town) evokes a Western atmosphere with a strong heritage. Gateway to Brian Head Ski Area and Cedar Breaks, Parowan has a few motels and restaurants among many examples of original pioneer architecture.

Just over ten miles northwest of Parowan are the **Parowan Gap Petroglyphs**, a bountiful example of ancient Indian rock art etched on a canyon wall. The crude drawings of animals and men date back more than 2000 years to a time when the canyon was a major passageway for the Indians. Head north on Main and turn left at 400 North for ten and one-half miles to get there.

Old Irontown, 21 miles west of Cedar City on Route 56, still displays remnants of open-pit mining operations of the 1800s. A coke oven, foundry and blast furnace are on-site.

In sharp contrast to the manic crowds at the main section of Zion National Park, the **Kolob Canyons** (801-772-3256) entrance is virtually deserted. This section of the park is just off Route 15 at exit 40, 17 miles south of Cedar City. Arches, cliffs and mountains point like fingers to the sky in this part of the park, which claims the world's largest free-standing arch. A small visitor center offers backcountry permits and information including an invaluable interpretive auto-drive pamphlet that guides you to 14 stops along the five-and-one-half mile road into the Finger Canyons of the Kolob. Deeply colored cliffs of vermillion and goldenrod mark Kolob Canyon, a markedly different section of Zion. A huge rock scar just left of Shuntavi Butte is the result of a cataclysmic break of the cliff from the rock face in 1983.

Kolob Canyons Viewpoint (end of Kolob Canyons Road) provides the ideal spot from which to view the canyon walls of massive Navajo sandstone laid down as windblown dunes 150 million years ago that now extend as fingers into the edge of the high terrace.

Though a product of the same natural forces that shaped Zion and Bryce, Cedar Breaks National Monument (Route 148; 801-586-9451) clearly holds its own. You head east from Cedar City along Route 14 then turn north on Route 148. The drive through huge glades of evergreen forest doesn't adequately prepare the viewer for the grandeur of the brilliant rock amphitheater. The jaded may surmise they've driven to 10,350 feet for nothing until they look out the huge glass windows of the Visitor Center.

Like the coliseum of ancient Rome, Cedar Breaks is expansive and wide. Only here, visitors gaze upon a natural gallery of stone spires, columns and arches instead of warring gladiators. The sheer cliffs reveal a candy store of colors—lavenders, saffrons and crimsons—all melted together and washed across the rocks.

In marked contrast to the flowers are the bristlecone pines, called the "Methuselah" of trees. Small stands grow on the relatively poor limestone soil that is within and along the rim of the amphitheater. One gnarled and weatherbeaten pine that can be seen from the Wasatch Ramparts Trail near Spectra Point on the breaks' rim is estimated to be more than 1600 years old.

A five-mile road (Route 148) accesses the park's main attractions. Four scenic overlooks, trailheads and all visitor services are on or near the road. Heavy snows close the road during the winter, but the park is open for cross-country skiing and snowmobiling via Brian Head Resort.

Continuing east on Route 14 past the Cedar Breaks entrance, you'll come to Navajo Lake and Duck Creek Reservoir, splendid spots both known for their trout fishing. Formed by lava flows that left no drainages, Navajo Lake drains through sinkholes that sit beneath the surface and feed water into Duck Creek.

The grassy meadows and groves of aspen also surround Duck Creek Village, a hamlet best known as the film location for *My Friend Flicka* and *How the West Was Won*. Duck Creek is often frequented by cross-country skiers anxious to lay tracks on the extensive trails.

CEDAR CITY AREA HOTELS

Paxman Summer House (170 North 400 West; 801-586-3755) is a turn-of-the-century, two-story, brick farmhouse with three porches. Taste-

(Text continued on page 382.)

Ghost Towns of Color Country

While much of Utah's history is neatly preserved in museums and restored homes, a more fascinating (and sometimes poignant) look can be found in the ruins of towns eroded by time, nature and man. Golf courses and condominiums cover most of the region's early settlements, but a few sites remain where you can let your imagination run wild.

Two of the most popular and representative ghost towns of Southwest Utah are Silver Reef and Grafton, as diverse as two cities can be while both paying homage to the pioneers who forged a wilderness state.

"Silver!" was the cry that brought more than 1000 fortune-hunters to the town of **Silver Reef**. According to newspaper accounts, Silver Reef was the only spot in the United States where silver was discovered in a sandstone reef. John Kemple is credited with the 1866 find, and the town boomed into a notorious camp of 1500 (non-Mormon) miners. Citizens of nearby Mormon communities were warned not to mix with the rowdy populace rumored to participate in brawls, shootings and lynchings. With 29 mines scattered over two square miles, Silver Reef proved bountiful, yielding $8 million in silver before shutting down in 1910.

Today little remains, although area historians are slowly working to restore the community. Fittingly, the **Wells Fargo & Co. Express Building,** constructed in 1877 of sandstone blocks and metal doors, survived the ravages of time. It now houses the **Silver Reef Museum** (801-879-2254). Authentic mining tools, maps, clothing and other historic paraphernalia fill shelves and glass cases. Old newspapers recount Silver Reef's heyday, and town plats show how vast the boomtown spread. Visitors can even walk into the original Wells Fargo bank vault.

Half the Wells Fargo building is used by Western bronze sculptor Jerry Anderson as a **studio and gallery** (801-879-2359). Both his work and that of other prominent local artists are displayed and sold, along with a good assortment of books recounting Utah's ghost towns.

Nearby is a small structure that once served as Powder House (for a fun exercise, have your traveling companions guess what this was). Today, Powder House functions as the Silver Reef information center with models of the original township and more original plats. The bank building is home to the **Olde Rice Bank Craft Shop** (801-879-2482), a gift store with dolls, cards, shirts and the like.

It only takes a few minutes to drive around and look at the nearby stone ruins scattered among a new neighborhood development. At the site of the Barbee and Walker Mill, which began operating in 1887, all that remains are rock walls; likewise the drugstore and Chinese laundry.

While most Utah ghost towns lie in a stark desert environment, **Grafton** is an exception. Amid vast fields, mulberry trees and rambling cattle, the abandoned settlement sits beside the Virgin River near the redrock cliffs of Zion National Park.

Five Mormon families settled Grafton in 1859, naming the town after a Massachusetts community. Assisted by then-friendly Paiute Indians, the families dammed the Virgin River for irrigation hoping to plant cotton. In 1862, a flood ravaged the entire area and swept away homes, barns and fields. Survivors moved their settlement to higher and safer ground, digging a system of canals and ditches. Besides cotton, they planted corn, wheat and tobacco. By 1865, 200 acres were cultivated.

Later, Indian attacks disrupted community life. Settlers were killed in alarming numbers, and Grafton residents were forced to work the fields in armed bands. Occasionally, the entire town was evacuated. After the Indian threat eased in the 1870s, the settlers obtained Brigham Young's permission to plant mulberry trees and grow silkworms.

Grafton headed toward ghost town status after 1907, as persistent problems became too much for the settlers to face. But the quaint village charmed Hollywood, and since 1950 many films, including scenes from *Butch Cassidy and the Sundance Kid*, have been filmed here. Several of the buildings still stand, including a few woodframe homes and the one-room, brick schoolhouse with small belltower. All are open for exploring.

Victims of Indian attacks and other Grafton settlers are buried in the well-maintained Mormon cemetery that lies on the road southeast of town. The cemetery is also open to the public.

To get to Silver Reef, go north on Route 15 about 17 miles to the Leeds exit. Head east one mile through town to a sign marked "Silver Reef." Turn north under the freeway and drive about two miles.

For Grafton, take Route 9 (the road to Zion National Park) to the town of Rockville. Turn south on Bridge Lane, which crosses the Virgin River. After crossing the bridge, head west and backtrack along a rutted, dirt-and-gravel road several miles. Note that in some sections you are crossing or bordering private land so don't abuse the privilege.

fully decorated with antiques, the upper floor has a small sitting room surrounded by three bedrooms, each with private bath. A main-floor master bedroom is available during the summer. Homemade baked goods are featured every morning. Moderate.

The **Quality Inn** (18 South Main; 801-586-2433), a three-story, brick building, has 50 rooms furnished in typical hotel fashion—one or two queen beds, small sitting area, dark-wood dresser and headboards. A large swimming pool and complimentary continental breakfast (November to May only) are nice touches, and the staff is extremely cordial. Budget to moderate.

Holiday Inn Cedar City (1575 West 200 North; 801-586-8888) is one of the area's prettier properties with amenities including restaurant and lounge, pool, sauna, whirlpool and exercise room. As Cedar City has no taxi service, the van shuttle service to the airport is especially handy. Moderate.

Cedar City's largest hotel is the **Best Western Town & Country Inn** (200 North Main; 801-586-6518). The hotel is split into two parts, the main motor inn and a newer annex across the street. Rooms are outfitted with typical Best Western aplomb, and guests can use either of the two swimming pools (one enclosed during the winter), spa and gameroom. Moderate.

French provincial meets nouveau Southwest at the **Brian Head Hotel** (Route 143, Brian Head; 801-677-3000), Brian Head ski resort's premier property. Well-appointed, large rooms decorated in warm desert colors give skiers plenty of places to hang their hat . . . and their goggles and gloves and other accoutrements. Jacuzzi baths help work out the après-ski kinks. Or visit the on-site exercise room. Deluxe.

Neighboring **Brian Head Royale Motel's** (100 Hunter Ridge Court; 801-677-2800) rooms aren't as plush but are certainly no less spacious. Rooms have a Southwestern feel; the bathrooms could use a little work. Moderate to deluxe.

Brian Head, like all ski resorts, has many, many condominiums of all shapes and sizes for rent. Call **Brian Head Condominium Reservations** (801-677-2045) for information.

CEDAR CITY AREA RESTAURANTS

Though only open during the summer season, the **Black Swan** (164 South 100 West; 801-586-7673) is one of the busiest restaurants in Cedar City. In keeping with the town's Shakespearean bent, The Black Swan features "ye olde luncheon fare" and seven-course dinners. Châteaubriand is available nightly along with fish, poultry and lamb or pork selections. Even if you can't get a reservation, stop by for after-performance cake and coffee. Moderate to deluxe.

You wouldn't expect quality grub inside a livestock market, but the **Market Grill** (2290 West 400 North; 801-586-9325) delivers just that. From hearty country breakfasts to ribeye steaks and Texas toast, the grill is a taste of the West, all at budget prices.

An extensive menu geared to family dining makes **Sullivan's Café** (86 South Main; 801-586-6761) a popular choice. Sandwiches, soups, salads, steaks, egg dishes and pancakes are among the bountiful selections. The upscale La Tajada Room offers steak, seafood and Italian dishes in a more intimate atmosphere. Budget to moderate.

Like their St. George counterparts, **Pancho & Lefty's** (2107 North Main; 801-586-7501) and **J. J. Hunan Chinese Restaurant** (502 South Main; 801-586-8952) provide tasty Mexican and Chinese fare respectively. Budget to moderate.

A real find is **Yogurt Junction** (★) (911 South Main, in Cedar South Mall; 801-586-2345). Diners snuggle in booths, while a model train encircles the room from above. Besides the requisite yogurt treats, the café serves up hearty soups in a bread bowl, sandwiches and yummy, fresh-baked rolls. Budget.

At the Brian Head ski area, Brian Head Hotel's **Summit Dining Room** (Route 143, Brian Head; 801-677-3000) offers plenty of pasta dishes, fish and fowl of the day and an impressive wine list. While the dining room is open for dinner only, the hotel's **Columbine Café** serves breakfast and lunch. Moderate.

Innovative chicken dishes find their place amid steaks and beef brochettes at the **Edge Restaurant** (Route 143, Brian Head; 801-677-3343), which features hearty meals and a nice après-ski ambience. Moderate.

CEDAR CITY AREA SHOPPING

Catch ski fever just by walking into **George's Ski Shop** (by chairlift 1, Brian Head; 801-677-2013) where you've probably never seen so much merchandise crammed into a single chalet. Past season's gear is discounted for those who really don't care about this year's colors. A variety of skis plus knowledgeable advice make this the ski shop of choice at Brian Head.

For nordic gear and maps in the wintertime, try the shop in the **Brian Head Hotel** (Route 143; 801-677-2012). It becomes biking central during the rest of the year, with excellent service, books and technical support.

CEDAR CITY AREA NIGHTLIFE

The renowned **Utah Shakespearean Festival** stages six plays on the Southern Utah University campus (351 West Center, Cedar City; 801-586-7878) from late June through the first week of September. Plays are performed both in the Adams Theater, an authentic open-air re-creation of a Shakespearean stage, and the modern indoor Randall L. Jones Theater. Those wishing to really get in the spirit of the evening may dine in the tradition of the Old English great halls at the King's Pavilion located across the street north from the Festival Box Office. The **Renaissance Feast** (801-586-7878; reservations required) offers entertainment, fanfares, lively humor and winsome serving wenches. Tickets are available at the Box Office.

Southern Utah University (351 West Center, Cedar City; 801-586-5483) plays host to a variety of cultural attractions year-round. The **University Theater Arts Department** (801-586-7876) schedules plays in the fall and spring. **American Folk Ballet** (801-586-7278), a dance troupe that combines ballet with folk dancing, annually performs at the SUU Centrum. Plus, SUU books national and international talent spanning dance, opera, classical music, country and more.

In Cedar City, the college crowd likes to hang out at **Sportsmen's Lounge** (900 South Main; 801-586-9036), while the country-music set two-steps at **The Playhouse** (1027 North Main; 801-586-9010). Both bars feature live music on the weekends.

Quality bands come from near and far to play at the **Brian Head Hotel** (Route 143, Brian Head; 801-677-3000) during summer and ski seasons. Or, people amuse themselves by singing along with a karaoke machine. The club is free to hotel guests.

Live tunes are also featured at the **Club Edge** (406 South Route 143, Brian Head; 801-677-3343), another "private" nightspot where "dues" get you in the door.

CEDAR CITY AREA BEACHES AND PARKS

Zion National Park–Kolob Canyons—Less widely known than Zion Canyon, Kolob remains relatively untrodden yet provides as much colorful scenery as its more famous counterpart.

Facilities: Restrooms, visitor center and picnic area; information, 801-586-9548.

Camping: Backpack camping only with permit.

Getting there: Located off exit 40 on Route 15, 17 miles south of Cedar City.

Cedar Breaks National Monument—Millennia of erosion and uplift have carved one of the world's greatest natural amphitheaters filled with stone pinnacles, columns, arches and canyons of soft limestone three miles from rim to rim and 2500 feet deep. Some call it a Bryce Canyon in miniature. Surrounding Cedar Breaks is a sub-alpine environment with evergreen forest of bristlecone pine, spruce and fir trees, flower-laden meadows and tall grasses. Sorry, no cedars. The Mormon settlers confused them with the gnarled juniper trees found throughout.

Facilities: Restrooms, visitor center, picnic area and outdoor amphitheater; information, 801-586-9451. Services and roads usually closed from mid-October through March due to heavy snows, though snowshoeing, cross-country skiing and snowmobiling are allowed.

Camping: There are 30 sites; $6 fee.

Getting there: Located 21 miles east of Cedar City via Route 14 or take Route 143 south two miles from Brian Head.

Bryce Area

A couple of wonderful parks (surprise) await you here along with historic towns and one of the prettiest byways in the West. And for a bonus you can see the log cabin of Ebenezer Bryce.

If you opt to head northeast from Cedar Breaks along Route 143, you might want to check out the bubbling **Mammoth Creek Hot Springs**, about four miles south of Panguitch Lake and two miles east on a marked gravel Forest Service road.

In addition to this crystal clear spring also consider visiting **Mammoth Cave (★)** (located 14 miles south of Panguitch Lake), a network of lava tubes that include a two-tiered section of tunnel.

The handsome architecture in the historic town of **Panguitch**, settled in 1864, is evidence of its early pioneering spirit. Around the turn of the century, a communal brick factory was supervised by an English potter who was sent here by Brigham Young to be the company's craftsman. Part of the workers' weekly salaries were paid in bricks!

That accounts for the great number of stately, brick homes still found in Panguitch. English and Dutch influences are also evident in the buildings' Dixie dormers, delicate filigree and Queen Anne windows.

A short walking tour through the center of town gives you a chance to see the best of what's left. Begin the tour at the **Garfield County Courthouse** (55 South Main), built for just over $11,000 in 1907. Cross to the **Houston home** (72 South Main), which was constructed of extra-large brick fired in a Panguitch kiln. The home's lumber and shingles also came from a local sawmill. Two blocks north you'll find the town's **first jail** (45 South Main), built in 1890 under the supervision of a probate judge. The tiny, one-room structure was constructed of 2 × 4s.

The building on the corner of 1st North and Main is a classic bit of architecture called the **Garfield Exchange**. It has housed just about every kind of business you can think of, from general merchandise to furniture, groceries and now a gift shop.

Prominent on Center (none of this region's main thoroughfares, like Center, Main and Tabernacle, go by the name Street. Why? Ask the locals—

you may just make a friend in the process) is the **Panguitch Social Hall Corporation** (35 East Center), which was first built in 1908 but burned shortly thereafter. On the same spot, using some original materials, another social hall was built. Now it houses the Panguitch Playhouse. Next door is a library that was built in 1908 thanks to a generous donation from Andrew Carnegie.

Finally, the city's **Daughters of the Utah Pioneer Museum** (Center and 1st East), is a lovely, brick monolith on the site of the old bishop's storehouse. Back in the mid-19th century, members of the Mormon Church paid their tithes with cattle and produce that were kept on this lot. Now, visitors trace the region's history here.

Driving south from Panguitch on Route 89 takes you to the start of one of the most scenic byways in the West. After passing a few souvenir shops and cafés, Route 12 starts to wind through rock tunnels. That's when you know you're in **Red Canyon**. A visitor center on the road's north side offers information about the small park that's usually bypassed by people hurrying toward Bryce Canyon. Pink and red rocks stand amid huge pines in this compact and user-friendly park.

It's another ten miles on Route 89 to the **Bryce Canyon National Park** (801-834-5322; admission) turnoff. Bryce is a national park on the jagged edge of the Paunsaugunt Plateau that really does defy superlatives. Even the gigantic summertime crowds can't distract from the natural amphitheaters (which are 50 million to 60 million years old) in the Pink Cliffs layer of the earth. Who'd have ever thought there were this many shades of red or shapes of rock? The sands and shales of Bryce, some softer than others, are the result of eons of erosion wearing away the limestone.

Bryce offers 12 huge bowls of spires and pinnacles. Located at nearly 8000 feet above sea level, the 35,000-plus acres of Bryce receive more than their fair share of snow during the wintertime. Some say that the rocks covered with dollops of snow are at their most beautiful in winter.

Bryce was once covered by an inland lake, and geologists figure the rivers and streams carried silt and sediment from throughout the region to the lake. Material brought in these layers became compacted, making even more layers, until forces within the earth caused the lake bottom to rise. As the different levels of earth emerged they took shape and turned colors as the layers became exposed. Red and yellow hues were due to iron oxides. The purples came from manganese. White reveals an absence of minerals in that part of the rock.

At sections of the park like Silent City and other natural amphitheaters, the rock figures resemble chess pieces, a preacher, a woman playing the organ or faces that belong on Easter Island.

Sculptured rock forms come in countless profiles, the most famous of which have been named "hoodoos." These, too, are ever-changing because of rainwater and snow seeping into the cracks of the rock, melting and thawing to wear away the layers.

Bryce Canyon's nooks and crannies are best explored on foot. If time is a factor, it's wise to drive to the overlooks on the 21-mile park road for a sweeping look at the big picture. Start at the **Fairyland Point** lookout about two miles north of the visitor center to see the imaginary creatures, the looming **Boat Mesa** and mysterious **Chinese Wall** in Fairyland Canyon. The rather-strenuous Fairyland Loop Trail also begins here.

For a concentrated collection of formations, travel to the park's nucleus and either the **Sunrise** or **Sunset Point** lookouts to view the chess set-like people in **Queen's Garden**.

Walking along the Rim Trail, which skirts the canyon edge for a total of 11 miles, takes you to **Inspiration Point** and the eerie army of stone "people" called the **Silent City**. From the Rim Trail at this point it's possible to see the **Wall of Windows** and the majestic **Cathedral**.

Continuing south for another two-and-one-half miles takes you to **Bryce Point**, which allows breathtaking views of the whole Bryce Amphitheater. Three hiking trails, the Rim, Under-the-Rim and Peekaboo Loop, may be accessed from here. Horses share the Peekaboo Loop and take riders past profiles such as the **Alligator** and **Fairy Castle**.

From the main park road continue south for seven miles to **Farview Point** to gaze at the natural wonders stretching hundreds of miles outside of Bryce. The flat-topped mesa to the north is the **Aquarius Plateau**. South of the park are the distinctive **White Cliffs**.

Natural Bridge, with a huge opening in a rock, stands distinctly about two miles south of the Farview lookout. It's another two miles to **Ponderosa View Point**, where you can pick up the Agua Canyon connecting foot trail while seeing the lovely pink cliffs.

Drive the final two miles to **Rainbow Point** and **Yovimba Point**, and end up at the park's highest points, towering at over 9000 feet above sea level. A little more barren and rugged than other sections of Bryce, these two overlooks serve as trailheads for several hiking paths. It's worth the short jaunt on the **Bristlecone Loop Trail** to see the rare, gnarled trees up close and personal.

To fully explore the multimillion-year-old wonders of Bryce, begin the at-times arduous 22-mile **Under-the-Rim Trail** from here and travel north on a two- or three-day excursion. Camping in the park's backcountry is especially rewarding, as the stars tend to put on quite a show in this rarefied, high altitude air.

The closest real town to the park is **Tropic**—hometown to Ebenezer Bryce, the early park landlord who chose not to lose a cow here. There is a back route to Bryce from Tropic for foot travelers only, off the Peekaboo Loop trail. The easier way to go is by returning to Route 12 and traversing the ten miles or so through lovely **Tropic Canyon**. A recently discovered natural bridge is on the east side of the highway about three-tenths mile north of the Water Canyon Bridge.

Once in Tropic, stop for a snack or to stretch your legs in this special village that remains true to its name. Flowers seem to dance in the gardens, and old trees stretch their limbs languorously. At the south end of town is **Ebenezer Bryce's old log cabin**, which houses Indian artifacts.

Another few miles east on Route 12 is **Cannonville**, a town about half the size of Tropic that offers travelers basic services. Best known as gateway to Kodachrome Basin, Cannonville is also the jumping-off point for little side trips to a handful of caves and the narrow Bull Valley Gorge. Look for signs on the gravel road south of Cannonville.

Heading south on the only road out of Cannonville, you'll travel seven miles to **Kodachrome Basin State Park** (801-679-8562; admission), another wonderful Utah park with red-rock figures and slender chimneys. Stop at the Trail Head station, a little store, for maps and advice. Kodachrome is chock full of petrified geyser holes, 65 at last official count, believed to be freaks of nature and unique to this area. Spires, or "sand pipes," jut toward the sky, and natural arches beckon. Is it a surprise that Kodak is the park's official film? Quiet beauty and serenity are abundant in this out-of-the-way gem. Utah's most recently discovered arch, a 90-footer named **Shakespeare**, can be seen by taking a ten-minute hike on Chimney Rock Trail, one of six in Kodachrome.

An amazing feat of nature about ten miles south of the park boundary via a rough, unnamed road is the **Grosvenor double arch**. The delicate colors of the monolith, coupled with a bluebird sky, must be seen to be believed. Petrified wood may be found in the arch's vicinity.

Those with sturdy vehicles can continue south on the road to Cottonwood Canyon past two manmade circles of alabaster stones named **Gilgal**. Vaguely reminiscent of Stonehenge, the concept for Gilgal is biblically rooted and meant to symbolize the modern-day pilgrims who make an annual trek to this area in celebration of the summer solstice.

The entire stretch of road south of Cannonville to Route 89 crosses the Kanab fault several times and offers unusual scenery and fossils plus opportunities for exploring on foot. The road then continues a few miles to the western boundary of Lake Powell. Or return to Route 12 and drive west toward Escalante.

BRYCE AREA HOTELS

Cheap, clean and very basic describes the **Color Country Motel** (526 North Main, Panguitch; 801-676-2386) with its flowered bedspreads and scenic vistas on the walls. Budget.

A step up in quality and price is the **Best Western New Western** (180 East Center, Panguitch; 801-676-8876), natty and renovated in paisley patterns and scalloped carpeting with spotless housekeeping and a cool pool for those toasty summer days. Moderate.

The only one of the original trio of National Park Service properties that hasn't been devastated by fire, the **Bryce Canyon Lodge** (Bryce Canyon Park; 801-586-7686) is listed on the National Register of Historic Places. The three types of rooms—suites, cabins and doubles—fit most budgets and tastes. Splurging on a suite is a treat. These rooms ooze romance, from the white-wicker decor to Cleopatra chairs to the makeup mirror. Quaint log cabins have gas fireplaces, porches and dressing areas. Regular rooms are furnished in Southwestern style. Open only from spring until late fall, the lodge tends to book well in advance. Moderate to deluxe.

There's nothing like a full-service resort when you really feel like getting away from it all. **Best Western Ruby's Inn** (Route 12, Bryce Canyon; 801-834-5361) operates as a world of its own, with a general store, liquor store, campground, helicopter pad, riding stables, even its own post office on site! An international clientele can be found anytime. Rooms are decorated in Southwestern decor, and the staff remains friendly even after a long tourist season. Moderate to deluxe.

A kitchen and fireplace is what the **Bryce Canyon Pines** (Route 12, near Bryce Canyon; 801-834-5361) can offer its guests within cozy, knotty-pine rooms. The hotel's 50 rooms are open for groups as well as individuals. Moderate.

Another very comfortable residence is the **Bryce Point Bed and Breakfast** (61 North 400 West; 801-679-8629), found about eight miles east of Bryce in the perpetually flowering little town of Tropic. Guests enjoy a private entrance and private baths. Each of the four rooms features handmade oak cabinets and picture windows to the garden. Moderate.

BRYCE AREA RESTAURANTS

You expect country cooking at a place named **Foy's Country Corner** (80 North Main, Panguitch; 801-676-8851), and that's just what you get. Good juicy hamburgers, chicken-fried steaks, halibut and a salad bar highlight the menu. Budget.

When the urge for Mexican hits, locals head for the nearby **Old Towne Restaurant** in Hatch (244 South Route 89; 801-735-4314) for a chimichanga or two or three. Budget.

When it comes time to settle down and have a semifancy meal, there's little doubt that the top choice in this area is the beautiful old log restaurant in the **Bryce Canyon Lodge** (801-834-5361), the National Park Service concession. Service is quick and attentive though hardly fussy, the cuisine Continental but not generic. Homemade breads and Levi-busting desserts complement the generously portioned entrées. Moderate.

Equipped to serve and satisfy large groups, the **Best Western Ruby's Inn** (Route 12, Bryce Canyon; 801-834-5341) presents satisfying meals, though surely not imaginative fare at budget-to-moderate prices, in its spacious dining room. A menu of Continental cuisine features steaks and chops for dinner. The dining room can be a little noisy when large groups converge. During the busy summer months, the adjacent **Red Canyon Room Deli** is a convenient spot for quick and tasty on-the-go budget meals.

The booths are inviting, the coffee steaming and the pies and soups fresh and delicious at **Bryce Canyon Pines** (Route 12, northwest of Bryce Canyon entrance; 801-834-5536), which also offers specials every evening. Budget to moderate.

Had a local not made the recommendation, we'd have never stumbled onto the very modest **Pizza Place** (★) (North Main, Tropic; 801-679-8888). A wise-cracking chef kept the starving wolves at bay, appeasing our ravenous hunger with an order of wonderfully gooey and stringy mozzarella cheese sticks, before the main event—a hefty, generously topped, sweet-crusted pizza that could be the tastiest pie this side of Chicago. Budget.

BRYCE AREA SHOPPING

An enticing smell of potpourri tickles the nose upon entering **Favorite Pastimes** (415 East Center, Panguitch; 801-676-2608). Quilts and wreaths, bookends and knickknacks are carefully selected, if not handmade themselves.

It may seem corny, but you gotta love the **Old Bryce Town** (Route 12, across from Ruby's Inn; 801-834-5337), filled with shops and services. Among them, the **Canyon Rock Shop** (801-834-5337) has a huge selection of polished stones, fossils and petrified wood, plus a place to pan for gold! Step into the past at the **Old Time Photo Studio** (801-834-5337) and become a gangster, dance hall girl or town sheriff. The **Western Store** (801-834-5337) has a great selection of pseudo-Stetsons so you can set out on the range and not feel like a total city slicker.

Windchimes line the front porch, and Navajo rugs are omnipresent inside the **Bryce Canyon Trading Post** (Routes 12 and 89; 801-676-2688), a good place to pick up the requisite postcard, T-shirt or turquoise.

Hometown folks have also gotten together to create gifts for **Gerry's Creative Cottage** (221 West 100 South, Tropic; 801-679-8553). Craft supplies are available if you'd rather make it yourself.

BRYCE AREA NIGHTLIFE

The **Panguitch Playhouse** (Center) hosts summer musicals and special events.

Don't be surprised if angry Indians come a'chasing when you're riding in the covered chuck wagon train en route to a hoedown and sing-along. The **B-Bar-D Covered Wagon Company** (Route 12, Bryce Canyon; 801-834-5202) operates out of the Ruby's Inn complex during the summer season. Expect a huge country supper served on a dutch oven amid the pines before kicking up your heels in the foot stompin' hoedown. It's a hoot.

Rodeos featuring local talent are held nightly except Sunday throughout the summer at the **Rodeo Grounds** (801-834-5341) across from Ruby's Inn in Bryce Canyon. Barrel racing, bull wrasslin', roping and riding make for a full evening. During winter weekends **Ruby's Inn** (801-834-5341) offers live music in its Red Canyon Room.

BRYCE AREA BEACHES AND PARKS

Panguitch Lake—One of the top fishing areas in the region, Panguitch Lake offers fishing along its ten-mile shoreline and in boats for rainbow, cutthroat and brown trout.

Facilities: Two public boat ramps, boat rentals, tourist cabins, general store and snack shop; information, 801-865-3700.

Camping: Evergreen and Bluegreen campgrounds on the north side have 31 sites; Whitebridge and Vermillion campgrounds on the south side offer 45 sites; $7 per night. There are also several privately owned campgrounds in the area.

Getting there: On Route 143 about 17 miles south of Panguitch.

Tropic Reservoir and King's Creek Campground—This recreation site is a nice place for a picnic, a walk past sawmill remains or just a place to fish and relax.

Facilities: Restrooms, drinking water; information, 801-676-8815.

Camping: There are 40 sites; $6 per night.

Getting there: Located on an unmarked road off Route 12, about three miles west of Bryce Canyon junction.

Red Canyon—A lovely collection of sculptured pink, red and scarlet rocks in the shadow of Bryce Canyon. Because its neighbor is so well known, Red Canyon tends to be overlooked by visitors. Take advantage and explore the trails of this scenic but compact park.

Facilities: Visitor center and restrooms; information, 801-676-8815.

Camping: There are 40 sites; $7 per night.

Getting there: On Route 12 about four miles east of Route 89.

Bryce Canyon National Park—Famous for its stupendous rock formations that seem to change color within the blink of an eye, Bryce contains a maze of trails that wind in and around its many wonders.

Facilities: Lodging, restrooms, showers, restaurant, visitor center, nature walks, campfire programs, general store and laundry; information, 801-834-5322.

Camping: Permitted at either North Campground or Sunset Campground. More than 200 campsites are open during the summer, with fewer in the winter; $6 per night. There are also several backpacking campsites (permit required).

Getting there: Located two miles south of Route 12 on Route 63, eight miles northeast of the town of Tropic.

Kodachrome Basin State Park—Vividly colored sandstone chimneys, towering rock spires and arches fill this untouched, 2240-acre park that the National Geographic Society named for its photographic value.

Facilities: Picnic area, restrooms, hot showers, visitor center, general store; information, 801-679-8562.

Camping: There are 24 sites; $9 per night.

Getting there: Located seven miles south of Cannonville on the only road out of town.

Escalante Area

Nature's beauty, wildlife, prehistoric reminders and a region rich in the Indian and Mormon heritage await you in this region along scenic Route 12. Here you'll find a petrified forest, intriguing rock formations, orchards, dinosaur fossils and, for a wonderful surprise, buffalo.

Route 12 climbs from red rock to lush forest and back again to a semi-arid setting. Begin just south of the town of Escalante, which was settled in 1876 by Mormon ranchers, in the **Escalante Petrified Forest State Park** (801-826-4466; admission). It's a showcase for petrified wood, fossilized dinosaur bones and remnants from the Fremont Indian Village thought to be 1000 years old. You don't have to be an athlete or even reasonably fit to find and appreciate the petrified wood in this small park, which has trails to suit everyone.

Huge petrified logs in a spectrum of colors, dinosaur bones and nature trails help to explain the evolution of the 140 million-year-old wood turned to stone that became rainbow colored by the earth's minerals. It is thought that ancient trees were buried in the sand, causing the logs to become petrified. Millions of years later the natural weathering process exposed the wood from its rough outer shell. One word of warning: Don't nick any pieces as souvenirs because legend has it that bad things come to those who do. Instead, buy a piece of wood at one of the rock shops in Escalante.

Hole in the Rock Road, a Mormon pioneer passage, zigs and zags its way to Lake Powell from its starting point just north of Escalante. Along the historic, 62-mile road you'll see landmarks such as Chimney Rock, Dance-hall Rock and the Broken Bow Arch. An annual pilgrimage retraces the steps of the first settlers.

It's only been during the past few years that Route 12 has been paved between Boulder and Torrey. The high-altitude road linking Bryce to Cap-itol Reef has been called one of the most **scenic drives** in America. There are several campgrounds and dirt roads leading to mountain lakes along the way, plus opportunities to view vistas of the Henry Mountains, San Rafael Reef and distant shale deserts.

In tiny Boulder, the last town in the United States to receive its mail by mule team, is **Anasazi Village State Park** (Route 12; 801-335-7308; admission). It's located on the site of a former Anasazi community said to have been nearby between 1050 A.D and 1200 A.D. before mysteriously disappearing. Here you'll find excavated village Indian artifacts, a self-guided trail through the site and a museum showing informative movies and film-strips.

When Route 12 meets Route 24, it's less than a dozen miles east to the entrance of **Capitol Reef National Park** (801-425-3791; admission). Domed cliffs reminiscent of the rotunda in Washington, D.C. prompted early explorers to give Capitol Reef its unusual name. Another explanation for the moniker's origin is that maritime men were reminded of barrier reefs. Long before white men arrived, Native Americans were said to have grown corn, beans and squash along the Fremont River.

Wrinkled earth that was formed by the forces of nature, Capitol Reef is a mélange of domes and cliffs, spires and other amazing rock formations tossed together in a beautiful jumble. The cliffs of Waterpocket Fold, a 100-mile bulge in the earth's crust, slice through the park's epicenter. The **visitor center** offers a slide show exploring the formation of Capitol Reef.

Capitol Reef was established as a national monument in 1937 and be-came a national park in 1971. Elevations range from 5300 feet to 7000 feet, and summers can be quite warm. To beat the heat, take a dip in the famous Fremont River and its waterfalls seven miles east of the visitor center. But guard against the river's deceiving undertow.

Capitol Reef has several aspects. To the south, white sand upfolds. Near the center is lush Fruita, with its gardens and orchards. At Capitol's north end is the grandeur and peacefulness of Cathedral Valley.

When the Mormons came a century ago they planted beautiful orchards on the banks of the Fremont and Sulfer Creek in a settlement first called Junction, later renamed the more fragrant Fruita. Apples, pears, peaches, cherries and apricots are still harvested in **Fruita** orchards, which are administered by the National Park Service. Fruita is also home to a historic reminder of the past, a one-room log schoolhouse built in 1896.

Step back in time at **Behunin Cabin**, six miles east of the visitor center, a sandstone structure with a dirt floor that was built in 1882.

Exploration of Capitol's wild beauty continues along the park's 25-mile round trip scenic drive south of the visitor center where there are numerous opportunities for excursions in the rock. Branch off onto either the dry Grand Wash or Cassidy Arch hiking trails, located east of the road. Stay on the route until its conclusion and access **Capitol Gorge**, a sinuous canyon, and the yellow sandstone monoliths of the Golden Throne Trail.

Petroglyph panels have never been so easy to find as at a pullout on Route 24 about a mile east of the visitor center along the Fremont River.

Backtrack at day's end to a few miles west of the visitor center and cruise by **Sunset Point** where the light is kind to the mummy-like formations and landmark Castle Rock.

Not far from here you can walk up the short **Goosenecks Trail** (.1 mile) overlooking the gurgling Sulpher Creek below or sit on the bench and gaze at Boulder Mountain and the Aquarius Plateau. At day's end, a tiny trek from the car to **Sunset Point** (.2 mile) yields a view of the amazing Waterpocket Fold that reaches southward toward Lake Powell. With the Henry Mountains to the east, this is when Capitol's wild beauty bursts in all its splendor.

It's a rather bleak landscape between Capitol Reef and Hanksville, but before making the turn north on Route 24 to Goblin Valley, stop at the historic **Wolverton Mill** (100 West) in Hanksville, a log structure once used to cut wood and crush ore.

Looking south from Hanksville, the lush Henry Mountains come into view. Home to the only free-roaming buffalo herd in the country, towering **Mt. Helen** rises from the barren rock.

Heading north on Route 24 toward Route 70 and Green River, there are few roads and diversions. But on the western part of the road halfway between Hanksville and Green River is the entrance to **Goblin Valley State Park** (801-564-3633; admission). On the rough road leading to the park, you'll be stunned by the rock sculptures of Wild Horse Butte and Molley's Castle before entering the park itself. It's an enchanted land of countless standing rocks and troll-like figures. The park is divided into two relatively small sections, Carmel Canyon and the Curtis Formation. Gravel roads lead to beautiful Little Wild Horse Canyon, where there are two-and-one-half miles of narrows to explore.

The effects of wind, rain and sand on rock play tricks on the imagination to where it appears there are goblin-like faces staring from every corner of this small—just two miles by three miles—wonderland. Remote, yet not inaccessible, Goblin Valley would make a great setting for an episode of the "Twilight Zone." Photographers find many models in the Valley of Goblins.

ESCALANTE AREA HOTELS

A sign sporting a priest fishing marks the **Padre Motel** (20 East Main, Escalante; 801-826-4276). Most rooms feature a wall mural of regional landscape, linoleum-floored bathrooms and a desk. Small but tidy. Budget.

New and very clean is the **Wonderland Inn** (Routes 12 and 24, Torrey; 801-425-3775), which sits atop a hill on the edge of town. Cheerful local art dresses up 30 sunny, second-floor rooms (all with views). Fake-wood furniture is the only detractor. Budget to moderate.

Capitol Reef Inn & Café (360 West Main, Torrey; 801-425-3271) provides more than its simple facade would suggest. Spacious rooms with two double beds and working area are welcome to those toting a lot of high-country gear. But the walls can seem a little thin, depending on who your neighbors are. Budget to moderate.

Rustic best describes the **Rim Rock Resort Ranch** (2523 East Route 24, Torrey; 801-425-3843), a woody sort of Western place that continues the theme with its on-site restaurant, the Stagecoach Inn. Simple rooms have pine walls and small bathrooms. Rim Rock is the closest hotel to Capitol Reef. Budget to moderate.

ESCALANTE AREA RESTAURANTS

Fancy meals you won't find, but hearty American food is in abundance at two restaurants with similar menus in Escalante—the **Circle D** (475 West Main; 801-826-4297) and **Golden Loop Café** (39 West Main; 801-826-4433). For decent sandwiches, try the seasonal **Mary's Frosty Shop** (Route 12, Escalante; 801-826-4488). All are priced in the budget range.

Torrey, the gateway to Capitol Reef, has two very good restaurants. Specializing in locally raised foods, the **Capitol Reef Inn & Café** (360 West Main; 801-425-3271) surprises with its fresh approach to cooking in a land where expectations rarely exceed deep-fried, breaded concoctions. Utah rainbow trout, vegetarian dishes, homemade soups and heaping gardens of salad are the order of the day, along with hearty breakfasts. Espresso and café au lait are nice added touches. Moderate.

La Buena Vida (599 West Main; 801-425-3759) is a funky spot with mucho character. Homemade chips and salsa with a kick are served upon arrival, a prelude to menudo, turkey enchiladas, chile Colorado and darn good tacos. A stack of classic *National Enquirers* and *People* magazines helps pass the time when service is painfully slow. Budget to moderate.

For a quick snack, try **Brink's Burgers** (165 East Main, Torrey; 801-425-3710). Budget.

Prime rib and steaks highlight the dinner menu at the **Wonderland Inn Restaurant** (Routes 12 and 24, Torrey; 801-425-3775). Breakfast features fluffy hotcakes and the usual egg dishes. Budget to moderate.

Pies are the specialty of the house at the **Sunglow Café** (91 East Main, Bicknell; 801-425-3701). Pinto-bean pie, fruit pies and a renowned pickle pie outclass the other standard diner fare at this friendly eatery. Budget.

Surrounded by a moon-like landscape, the **Lunar Mesa Café** (Route 24, Cainville) is worth a stop if for nothing but its rooftop spaceship. Fajitas are a special favorite. Sip European coffees while reclining in the midst of this stark land. Budget.

ESCALANTE AREA SHOPPING

For jeans and T-shirts, but more important, to stock up on camping supplies and maps before meeting the wilderness, stop at **Escalante Outfitters** (310 West Main, Escalante; 801-826-4266).

The store at the **Capitol Reef Inn** (360 West Main, Torrey; 801-425-3271) has plenty of good guidebooks, maps and trinkets of the area.

ESCALANTE AREA BEACHES AND PARKS

Escalante Petrified Forest State Park—Trails in this well-known park lead to outcroppings of petrified wood that date back 140 million years. Wide Hollow Reservoir, which is included within the park boundaries, is a good fishing and picnicking spot.

Facilities: Restrooms, interpretive trail; information, 801-826-4466.

Camping: There are 22 sites; $9 per night.

Getting there: Located one mile west of Escalante on Route 12.

Calf Creek Falls Recreation Area—Gorgeous gorges and a waterfall that rushes down 126 feet over sandstone cliffs are reached after a moderate walk. Visitors can choose from an easy or difficult hiking trail. The lush setting of cottonwood trees makes Calf Creek a cool place to dine outdoors. The kids will love the playground.

Facilities: Restrooms, hiking trails; information, 801-826-4291.

Camping: There are 11 sites; $5 per night.

Getting there: On Route 12 about 15 miles east of Escalante.

Capitol Reef National Park—Covering almost a quarter-million acres, this national treasure is veined by roads and hiking trails. They lead past the region's sculptured rock layers to vista points, deep canyons and remote waterfalls.

Facilities: Restrooms, campfire programs, paved scenic road, orchards, developed and undeveloped hiking trails, visitor center; information, 801-425-3791.

Camping: There are 72 sites; $6 per night.

Getting there: The park is located on Route 24, 37 miles west of Hanksville.

Goblin Valley State Park (★)—This unusual locale features thousands of eerie rock formations. Several trails lead into the heart of the park to canyons, arches and balanced rocks.

Facilities: Restrooms, solar-heated showers and the only fresh water for 30 miles. Helpful rangers can be found roaming the park during the daytime hours, but plan ahead for maps and other information by contacting Green River State Park at P.O. Box 93, Green River, UT 84525; 801-564-3633.

Camping: Goblin Valley has 50 sites and Green River has 40; $9 per night.

Getting there: Head west on road off Route 24 halfway between Hanksville and Green River until the Goblin Valley turnoff (about four-and-one-half miles). The park is approximately seven miles south.

The Sporting Life

SPORTFISHING

Rainbow, German brown and brook trout are plentiful throughout Southwestern Utah. More than a dozen reservoirs plus natural lakes, creeks and rivers are stocked for fishing. Besides trout fishing, you can try your luck luring bass in Gunlock and Quail Creek reservoirs. Or there are Fish Lake, where mackinaw and trout are the catch of the day, and Panguitch Lake, which is nearly as popular in the winter for ice fishing as it is as a summer resort.

Boats, bait, tackle and licenses can be secured through the **Beaver Dam Lodge** (Shore Road, Panguitch Lake; 801-676-8339) or **Deer Trail Lodge** (Panguitch Lake; 801-676-2211).

For more specific locations of prime fishing spots and information on fishing licenses, you might try **Hurst Ben Franklin** (160 North 500 West, St. George; 801-673-6141), **McKnight's Sporting Goods** (968 East St. George Boulevard, St. George; 801-673-4919), **Ron's Sporting Goods** (138 South Main, Cedar City; 505-586-9901), **Wayne's Sporting Goods** (263 South 100 East, Kanab; 801-644-8100) or **The Outfitter** (310 West Main, Escalante; 801-826-4207).

SWIMMING

Southwestern Utah doesn't lack for refreshing water holes, natural and chlorinated. City swimming pools include the **St. George City Swimming Pool** (250 East 700 South; 801-634-5867), the **Cedar City Municipal Pool** (400 Harding Avenue; 801-586-2869), **Hurricane City Swimming Pool** (345 West 100 South; 801-635-2397), **Kanab Swimming Pool** (44 North 100 West; 801-644-5870), **Panguitch Swimming Pool** (250 East 1st South; 801-676-8806) and the **Wayne County Swimming Pool** (460 West 200 North, Bicknell; 801-425-3275). The swimming pools at **Dixie Center Fitness Center** (425 South 700 East, St. George; 801-673-8368) and **Southern Utah University** (351 West Center, Cedar City; 801-586-7815) are also open to the public, as are both swimming and soaking pools at **Pah Tempe Hot Springs Resort** (825 North 800 East 35-4, Hurricane; 801-635-2879).

JEEP TOURS

For a backcountry adventure you might tour **Kolob Terrace Road**, a two-lane, paved path along the fringes of Zion National Park's west side. The route provides overviews of the Left and Right Forks of North Creek, climbing through dense evergreen forests past Tabernacle Dome and Firepit Knoll. North Creek canyons, Pine Valley Peak and the Guardian Angels are just a few of the other scenic sights. Kolob Terrace Road starts at the town of Virgin, 14 miles from Zion's main entrance on Route 9.

The 9200-foot Boulder Mountain, south of Route 24, has many excellent four-wheel-drive roads. Over the back of **Thousand Lake Mountain** from Loa is the scenic, 25-mile ride to Capitol Reef's Cathedral Valley.

Burr Trail from Boulder to the Circle Cliffs of Capitol Reef is a gorgeous, 30-mile scenic drive on a chip-and-seal road across Deer Creek, Steep Creek and into the breathtaking Long Canyon. At the junction of Notom Road in Capitol Reef, travelers have the option of driving another 25 miles southeast to Bullfrog Marina at Lake Powell.

Hole-in-the Rock Road from Escalante to Lake Powell is not to be missed. First forged by Mormon pioneers looking for a "shortcut" to southeast Utah to establish new settlements, the famous and now vastly improved gravel road (54 miles) skirts along the Straight Cliffs and sandstone markers to landmark Dance Hall Rock, a natural amphitheater where the pioneers were said to have held a party and dance. Just past this point are the Sooner Tanks, potholes that often fill with water. Beyond the holes is a set of natural bridges. But this is where the route really deteriorates; just imagine how tough the trail would have been 100 years ago when you were riding in a covered wagon! From the end of the road there is a steep foot trail down to the lake.

Hell's Backbone Road from Escalante to Boulder straddles the mountain ridge with the daunting drop of Death Hollow keeping drivers alert. The road winds around Slickrock Saddle Bench, Sand Creek canyons, creeks, hills and vistas.

JEEP RENTALS **Hondoo Rivers & Trails** (90 East State, Torrey; 801-425-3519) offers backcountry tours and rents four-wheel-drive vehicles.

WINTER SPORTS

While primarily a summertime destination, more and more people are discovering how beautiful Southwestern Utah is once the snow flies.

Brian Head Ski Resort (329 South Route 143; 801-677-2035), 12 miles southeast of Parowan, is renowned for the volumes of light, dry snow it receives. Catering to both alpine and nordic skiers, Brian Head's seven chairlifts serve mostly intermediate terrain. Cross-country skiers like to glide to colorful Cedar Breaks and beyond.

Elk Meadows Resort (801-438-5433) in the Tushar Mountains 17 miles east of Beaver on Route 153 is the region's other full-service ski area with three chairs and 18 miles of marked and groomed cross-country ski trails.

Cross-country trails also are groomed on the rim of **Bryce Canyon**. But within the park skiers can break trail and wander through literally thousands of acres of wilderness, beyond the red-tipped fantasyland of rock spires and figures. Rentals and maps may be secured through Ruby's Inn (Route 12, Bryce Canyon; 801-834-5341).

Fish Lake on Route 25 attracts snowmobilers, while sledding and tubing fans head toward **Red Canyon** on Route 12 along with neighboring Bryce Canyon and **Coral Pink Sand Dunes** near Kanab.

HORSEBACK RIDING AND PACK TOURS

Riding through the sometimes rugged Color Country on leisurely horseback trips is one of the best ways to explore steep canyons. The horses are likely to be as sure-footed as mules at the Bryce and Zion National Park concessions, the only horse rides allowed into the park—the others are relegated to its periphery.

For trail rides contact **Diamond Valley Guest Ranch** (650 North Diamond Valley Road, St. George; 801-574-2281), **Snow Canyon Riding Stables** (at Snow Canyon State Park, Route 18; 801-628-6677), **Bryce-Zion Trail Rides** (Zion Lodge, 801-772-3967; or Bryce Lodge, 801-834-5219), **Best Western Ruby's Inn** (Route 12, Bryce Canyon; 801-834-5341), **Color Country Outfitters** (2523 East Route 24, Torrey; 801-425-3598) or **Hondoo Rivers & Trails** (90 East State, Torrey; 801-425-3519).

GOLF

Scenic and uncrowded best describe the golf courses here. Temperate weather, even in winter, means year-round play. In fact, many believe it's golf that has put St. George on the map. The city's seven area golf courses are **St. George Golf Club** (2190 South 1400 East; 801-634-5854), **Sunbrook** (Dixie Downs Road; 801-634-5866), **Twin Lakes** (660 North Twin Lakes Drive; 801-673-4441), **Green Spring** (588 North Green Spring Drive; 801-673-7888), **Dixie Red Hills** (1000 North 700 West; 801-634-5852), **Southgate** (1975 South Tonaquint Drive; 801-628-0000) and **Bloomington** (Bloomington Exit; 801-673-2029).

Other courses include **Cedar Ridge** (200 East 800 North, Cedar City; 801-586-2970) and **Coral Cliff** (700 East Route 89, Kanab; 801-644-2606).

TENNIS

Where there's golf, there's usually tennis. Though Southwestern Utah isn't packed with tennis courts, there are a few spots for lobbing the ball. St. George holds court at **Vernon Worthen Park** (400 East 200 South; 801-634-5850) and **Dixie High School** (350 East 700 South; 801-628-0441). Extensive courts for guests can be found at **Green Valley Resort** (1515 West Canyon View Drive; 801-628-8060). Tennis courts at **Southern Utah University** (351 West Center, Cedar City; 801-586-7815) are open to the public. And there's plenty of tennis action at **Cedar City's Municipal Tennis Courts** (Cedar Canyon Park, Route 14 three blocks east of Main; 801-586-8065) and at **Panguitch City Park** (Route 89).

BICYCLING

Cyclists are starting to discover this region for its sights, interesting topography and varied terrain. While mountain bikers overrun Moab at certain times of the year, these trails are just being discovered.

An intermediate loop ride is **Pine Valley Loop**, a 35-mile trek across dirt road and pavement. Best ridden between April and October, the route is mostly gentle, although hills sneak in on occasion. Give yourself three to five hours. Take Route 18 north 25 miles to the town of Central. Turn right (east) toward Pine Valley recreation area. The loop begins on Forest Road 011, six miles from the Route 18 junction.

Snow Canyon Loop takes riders about 24 miles, passing through the towns of Santa Clara and Ivins before climbing through Snow Canyon State Park. Start the loop at the northwest end of St. George along Bluff. Go west at the Bluff and Sunset Boulevard intersection. Route 91 takes you to Santa Clara, veer north to Ivins, then climb six miles to the park. Route 18 is downhill all the way home.

Both beginners and advanced will enjoy **New Harmony Trail**, one of southern Utah's finest single-track rides. The 3.6-mile trail offers a view point of Kolob Canyons, then a gradual uphill climb to Commanche Springs. Take Route 15 to the town of New Harmony and park your car at the far outskirts of town.

An easy ride is Route 9 from **Springdale through Zion National Park** (11 miles). In fact, a bicycle is one of the best ways to tour Zion Canyon Scenic Drive from the south visitor center to the Temple of Sinawava, a massive rock canyon.

Mt. Carmel Junction to Coral Pink Sand Dunes is another favored road ride. Take Route 89 toward Kanab, and after three uphill miles you'll spot a turnoff sign to the park ten miles away.

Fir and aspen forests enshroud Route 14, a scenic byway from **Cedar City to Cedar Breaks National Monument**. While the paved road is a delight, you'll need stamina and good lung capacity to make the more than 4000-foot climb (25 miles).

When the snow melts, bike lovers hold forth on the trails around Brian Head. Experts enjoy the single-track rides, while those less inclined to tight spaces go for the dirt roads and double-track trails. A relatively easy ten-mile loop in the Brian Head vicinity is the **Scout Camp Loop Trail**. Begin from the Brian Head Hotel, turn south on Route 143 and ride to Bear Flat Road and Steam Engine Meadow. There's a cabin and, you guessed it, an engine on the trail. The trail continues toward Henderson Lake and the namesake scout camp.

Another popular ride is **Pioneer Cabin**, about a six-mile journey on a wide, dirt road that begins from Bear Flat Road. The 1800s-era cabin has aspen trees growing out of its roof!

Dave's Hollow Trail (4 miles) near Bryce Canyon National Park is a pleasant ride through meadows and pine forests that's recommended for all abilities. At the boundary line to the park, about one mile south of Ruby's Inn, is a dirt road that heads west. Follow the road about one-half mile, then turn right about three-fourths mile along the trail. This begins a ride along a mellow, double-track trail that ends at the Forest Service station.

Atop the Aquarius Plateau, highest plateau in the United States, via the true-to-its name Hell's Backbone Road from Escalante, mountain bikers have a party on the spur roads near **Posy Lake** and the **Blue Spruce Campground**.

BIKE RENTALS   For bike rentals and knowledgeable advice, try **Sports Cyclery** (175 West 900 South, St. George; 801-628-1119), **St. George Cyclery** (420 West 145 North, St. George; 801-673-8876), **Zion Canyon Cycling Company** (998 Zion Park Boulevard, Springdale; 801-772-3939), **Bike Route** (70 West Center, Cedar City; 801-586-4242), **Brian Head Cross Country Ski Center** (223 West Hunter Ridge Drive, Brian Head; 801-677-2012) or **Ruby's Inn** (Route 12, Bryce Canyon; 801-834-5341). Fully supported tours may be arranged through **Utah Outback** (12 West Main, Torrey; 801-425-3403).

HIKING

ST. GEORGE AREA TRAILS   Short on time and even shorter on endurance? We have just the place for you. Drive north on Main until it deadends, take a hard right and wind to the top of Red Hill. Park at the base of **Sugar Loaf**, the red sandstone slab with the white DIXIE letters and start walking for a few yards. The view of St. George is nothing short of spectacular.

Snow Canyon offers several excellent hikes. One of the most popular is the short walk to **Johnson's Arch** (.3 mile). Along the way look for the names and dates of early settlers carved into the sandstone. At the end of the trail is the arch cut out of the sandstone wall. Trailhead is at the extreme south edge of the park.

Another popular Snow Canyon hike is to the **Lava Caves** (.3 mile) near the north end of the canyon. If you plan on exploring the rugged caves, believed to have once sheltered Indians, take along a flashlight and good judgment. Watch for the sign along the road north of the campgrounds.

ZION AREA TRAILS   **Zion National Park** is considered one of the best hiking parks in the nation with a variety of well-known trails. A comprehensive list is included in the Zion National Park brochure. Regardless of which trail you choose, expect the unexpected—a swamp, waterfall, petrified forest or bouquets of wildflowers.

Expect company, and lots of it, on **Gateway to the Narrows Trail,** (1 mile) which traces the Virgin River upstream to Zion Canyon Narrows, just one of the tight stretches where 20-foot-wide canyons loom 2000 feet overhead. The concrete path winds among high cliffs and cool pools of water where many visitors stop to soak their tootsies. This easy trail begins at the Temple of Sinawava parking area.

For a more moderate hike, continue past the end of the paved path of Gateway to the Narrows and continue along the **Orderville Canyon Trail** (2.8 miles). Much of the trip involves wading through the Virgin River, at times four feet deep! But, if you don't mind the wet, the narrows is an amazing contrast of Navajo sandstone arches, grottoes and fluted walls looming high over tight chasms. Because of the rapidly changing conditions of the river, the park posts a "narrow canyon danger level" each day. Be aware of that level and also check with rangers for specific tips on forging the river safely.

Angels Landing (2.4 mile) is a strenuous hike that begins at the Grotto picnic area and offers incredible views over the sheer drops of Zion Canyon. Believe it or not, the trail is built into solid rock, including 21 short switchbacks called "Walters Wiggles." The last half-mile follows a steep, narrow ridge with a 1500-foot dropoff. While a support-chain railing is of some help, the trail isn't recommended for the faint of heart or anyone with "high" anxiety.

Another heavily visited trail system is at **Emerald Pools**. The easy, paved trail (.3 mile) to Lower Emerald Pool is shaded by cottonwood, box elder and Gambel oak. Trail's end finds a waterfall with pool below. The more stout-of-heart can venture to the Upper Pool (1.3 miles), a rough and rocky trail. Trailhead is at the Emerald Pools parking area.

Views of the West Temple, Towers of the Virgin and the town of Springdale are the reward at the end of **The Watchman** (1.5 miles), a large, red-brown, 2600-foot crag that overlooks the southern portion of Zion Canyon. Considered moderately difficult, the trailhead is near the entrance to Watchman campground.

Considered one of the most strenuous hikes within Zion, **West Rim Trail** (13.3 miles) takes two days, culminating at Lava Point. Hikers are blessed with scenic vistas including Horse Pasture Plateau, a "peninsula" extending south from Lava Point, surrounded by thousand-foot cliffs. Lightning strikes are frequent on the plateau, and uncontrolled wildfires have left some areas robbed of vegetation. Other views along the way include Wildcat Canyon, the Left and Right Forks of North Creek, Mt. Majestic and the highly eroded Virgin River Narrows area. The trailhead starts at the Grotto picnic area.

CEDAR CITY AREA TRAILS   There are two developed trails within Kolob Canyons. **Taylor Creek Trail** (2.7 miles) follows a small creek in the shadow of Tucupit and Paria Points, two giant redrock cliffs. The creek forks in three directions, but the path straight down the middle goes past two of the three homesteading cabins that still exist in Kolob Canyons and ends at Double Arch Alcove, a large, colorful grotto with a high arch above. The trail starts from the Taylor Creek parking area two miles into Kolob Canyons Road.

The only way to see the world's largest freestanding arch involves a two-day trek along **Kolob Arch Trail** (7 miles), a strenuous descent following Timber and La Verkin creeks. After reaching the magnificent arch, which spans 310 feet from end to end, you might continue on to Beartrap Canyon, a narrow, lush side canyon with small waterfall.

Two highcountry trails are within **Cedar Breaks National Monument**. Both explore the rim but do not descend into the breaks itself. **Alpine Pond Trail** (2 miles) is a loop that passes through a picturesque forest glade and alpine pond fed by melting snow and small springs. Trailhead begins at the Chessmen Meadow parking area.

Wasatch Ramparts Trail (1 mile) starts just outside the visitor center and ends at a 9952-foot overlook of the Cedar Breaks amphitheater. Along the way, pause at Spectra Point, a 10,285-foot viewpoint.

BRYCE AREA TRAILS   Two hours worth of hiking time in Red Canyon can bring big rewards. The **Buckhorn Trail** (1 mile) begins at the campground and ascends high above the canyon past handsome rocks. **Pink Ledges Trail** (.2 miles) is a simple, short jaunt through brilliant-red formations. The trailhead starts near the visitor center. If you don't mind sharing your turf with a horse, try the **Cassidy Trail** (4 miles), named for that famous outlaw, which traverses ponderosa pine and more of those ragged rocks.

Bryce Canyon is hiking central because it's so darn beautiful. Uneasy around hordes of people? Either set out extra early or later in the day—the light shines deliciously on the rocks at both sunrise and sunset—or plan on spending a few days in the back country to wander into castles and cathedrals, animal farms, temples, palaces and bridges. There are more than 60 miles worth of trails on which to wander.

The outstanding **Under-the-Rim Trail** (11 miles) connecting Bryce Point with Rainbow Point could be turned into a multiday trip if side canyons, springs and buttes are explored to their full potential.

Riggs Spring Loop Trail (4 miles) starts at Yovimpa Point and takes best advantage of the Pink Cliffs. More moderate is the **Bristlecone Loop Trail** (.5 mile) that begins atop the plateau and leads to sweeping views of spruce forests, cliffs and bristlecone pines.

One of the most famous, and rightly so, trails within the Bryce boundaries is **Queen's Garden** (.8 mile). Start from Sunrise Point and dive right into this amazing amphitheater. Taking a spur to the **Navajo Loop Trail** (an additional mile) brings you into the Silent City, a hauntingly peaceful yet ominous army of hoodoos. The trail ends at Sunset Point.

In the park's northern section is the **Fairyland Loop Trail** (4 miles). Moderately strenuous, the loop provides views of Boat Mesa and the fantasy features of the fairy area. Near the splitting point for the horse trail is the monolith known as Gulliver's Castle. An easier route is **Rim Trail** (up to 11 miles) along the edge of the Bryce Amphitheater that can be taken in small or large doses.

At **Kodachrome Basin State Park** the trails are short and sweet, offering plenty of satisfaction with little effort. From the **Panorama Trail** (1.5 miles) you get to see the Ballerina Slipper formation. At **Arch Trail** (.2 mile) there is—surprise, surprise—a natural arch. The most arduous of Kodachrome's trails is **Eagle View Overlook** (1 mile), but the valley views make it all worthwhile.

Driving or hiking south of Kodachrome on the dirt road for about 15 miles brings you to **Cottonwood** and **Hackberry Canyons** that merit exploration for their fossils, springs and hidden wonders. Because this is such virgin country, a good topographic map is imperative before setting out.

ESCALANTE AREA TRAILS   There are several access points to the awesome and somewhat mysterious **Escalante Canyons**. A main point of departure is east of town one mile on Route 12. Turn left on the dirt road near the cemetery and left again after the cattle guard. Follow to the fence line and begin at the hiker maze. The trail leads into the upper Escalante Canyon portion of Death Hollow, an outstanding recreation area. For an overnight or three-night trip continue on to where the trails come out 15 miles down the river.

Quite popular is the **Lower Calf Creek Falls Trail** (2.5 miles), about a mile up the highway from the main Escalante Canyon entrance. The trail passes towering cliffs on a gradual incline. You're rewarded with a beautiful waterfall. **The Upper Falls** (5.5 miles) can be reached by a difficult one-mile hike over sandstone and slickrock from the highway.

Plenty of terrain awaits your exploration in **Capitol Reef National Park**, twice the size of nearby Bryce. Trails range from moderate to steep, offering enough unexplored back country that you might not see people for days. Rock cairns mark most trails, while other routes are found with careful study of topographic maps.

Near Route 24 is **Hickman Bridge** (1 mile), a self-guided nature hike to a 133-foot rock rainbow with a gentle enough elevation gain (400 feet) to make it do-able for the whole family. Skirt past the Capitol Dome with its white domes of Navajo sandstone capping the rock. Keep going up the rim, past triple-decker ice cream cone-colored rocks to the overlook (2 miles).

From the **Chimney Rock** (1.8 miles) trailhead, three miles west of the visitor center on a trail with petrified wood, the path winds past the sandstone up switchbacks.

The **Chimney Rock Canyon Trail** (9 miles), which skirts through chocolate-brown canyons, is easier than Chimney Rock Trail but requires a river crossing. Some of the path is on a river bed so don't set out during threatening weather. Arrange for a car at the river's end or return the same way.

South of Route 24, in Capitol Reef, the splendid Waterpocket Fold ridge seems to go on forever. A logical first stop is the flat **Grand Wash** (2.3 miles), which cuts through towering thrones en route through the fold. The trail takes you into narrow canyons and past pockmarked rocks.

A short, steep detour off the Grand Wash to **Cassidy Arch** (1.3 miles) goes from the canyon depths to cliffs. The 19th-century outlaw Butch Cassidy is said to have hidden out in these honeycombs.

From Burr Trail, a rugged road shaves over two miles off the **Upper Muley Twist** (5.5 miles) hike, which offers drama in the form of Saddle Arch and other narrows within the Waterpocket Fold. Access is from Notom-Bullfrog Road and one mile west of the Burr Trail switchbacks.

Lower Muley Twist (12 miles) boasts areas that are steep and narrow enough to "twist a mule pulling a wagon." The colorful route traverses Waterpocket Fold. Start from Burr Trail, off Notom-Bullfrog Road.

Much easier but still spectacular hiking amid sheer walls and similar scenery is **Surprise Canyon** (1 mile), north of The Post turnoff. The Navajo Indians called this the "Land of the Sleeping Rainbows." They were right.

There are only two "trails" in Goblin Valley but plenty of room to wander. **Carmel Canyon** (1.5 miles) is an erosion trail to the Molly's Castle formation. It's on the edge of the Valley of Goblins, a land of funny, little shapes, forms and hideaways in the rock.

Across the park's only road is a trail to the **Curtis Formation** (3 miles). In this parched soil, wild daisies and mule ear seem to miraculously bloom in the spring as does greencantian, an unusual plant that changes shape depending on the season.

Transportation

BY CAR

Route 70 almost slices Utah in two as it runs east-west from the Colorado border. It ends at **Route 15**, Utah's main north-south artery that passes through Cedar City and St. George.

Route 14 branches east off Route 15 at Cedar City toward Cedar Breaks, while **Route 9** heads east from Route 15 to Springdale and the entrance of Zion National Park.

Route 89, a scenic byway, heads south from Route 70 through parts of Dixie National Forest before crossing Kanab. **Route 12** provides a pretty path to Bryce Canyon National Park and Escalante Canyons before bisecting **Route 24**, the only access to Capitol Reef National Park.

BY AIR

SkyWest/Delta Connection serves **St. George Municipal Airport** and **Cedar City Municipal Airport**. Taxi service in St. George includes **Pete's Taxi** (801-673-5467) and **Classy Taxi** (801-628-0005).

BY BUS

Greyhound/Trailways Bus Lines can bring you to Southwestern Utah from around the country. There are stations in St. George (68 West 100 North; 801-673-3457), Cedar City (1355 South Main; 801-586-9465) and Parowan (20 North Main; 801-477-3421).

CAR RENTALS

Rental agencies at St. George Municipal Airport are **Avis Rent A Car** (801-673-3686) and **National Car Rental** (801-673-5098). Other agencies in town include **A-1 Car Rental** (801-673-8811), **Budget Rent A Car** (801-673-6825) and **Dollar Rent A Car** (801-628-6549).

At the Cedar City Municipal Airport, cars can be rented from **Avis Rent A Car** (801-586-3033) and **National Car Rental** (801-586-7059). **Hertz Rent A Car** (801-586-6096) and **Speedy Rental** (801-586-7368) serve Cedar City as well.

GLENN KIM '92

CHAPTER TEN

Southeastern Utah

How best to describe Southeastern Utah? For starters, Teddy Roosevelt, America's quintessential outdoorsman, once traveled here. Then consider the fact that amusement-park thrills and manmade attractions have nothing on this place. Forget the Coney Island roller coaster. Plummet down a 30-degree incline at Moki Dugway or the Moab Slickrock Bike Trail. The rickety bridge to Tom Sawyer Island in Disneyland? You can sway and swing across a genuine suspension bridge over the San Juan River outside Bluff. And Gateway Arch in St. Louis becomes a mere modern toy after you see Mother Nature's natural design at Arches National Park.

This truly is a magic kingdom for the outdoors enthusiast, the naturalist, the archeologist. Leave those luxury resorts, white-sand beaches and gleaming steel museums behind. In this region, the land reigns.

What's really amazing is that Mormon exiles thought they were entering America's wasteland when they fled to Utah in 1847. For this land is anything but barren. Take all the earth's geologic wonders, toss them into a blender and you have Southeastern Utah. An array of mesas abuts dense forests adjacent to broad deserts with red-rock canyons and slender spires thrusting out of semiarid valleys. In this portion of the Colorado Plateau lie the spectacular Arches and Canyonlands national parks, Glen Canyon National Recreation Area (Lake Powell), two national monuments and a host of state parks.

Because Southeastern Utah is so vast and diverse we have divided it into three geographic areas—Lake Powell, San Juan County and Moab. At the heart of the entire region sits Canyonlands National Park. Canyonlands also divides into three sections, which though contiguous are not directly connected by roads. Therefore you will find The Maze section of the park described in the Lake Powell section, the Needles district in the San Juan County listings and the park's Island in the Sky section within the Moab Area listings.

Erosion is the architect of Southeastern Utah. Over the millennia, land masses pushed through the earth's crust, rivers and streams carved deep canyons, wind and water etched mountainsides. On some of the rock walls are pictures and stories left behind by early man that seem to transcend the ages.

The first known people in Southeastern Utah were here long before the Europeans even knew about America. They were called the Anasazi—or ancient ones—and some believe them to be ancestors of today's Pueblo Indians. Evidence of these early builders and farmers is still abundant in the ruins of their homes found among the cliffs, on the mesa tops and in the canyons.

When the tribes disappeared from Southeastern Utah and the Four Corners region around the 13th century, they left dwellings, tools and plenty of personal possessions behind. Theories abound as to what prompted their hasty departure. Some look to about 1276 A.D. when a long drought ruined the harvest and depleted the food supply. There were dangers from marauding bands of fierce nomadic tribes. Others theorize that inexplicable fears caused by religious beliefs may have contributed. Regardless of influences, the Anasazi abandoned the region, and examination of their living spaces and remnants continues to fascinate generations of archaeologists and amateur sleuths.

By the 14th century, the Navajo had become part of the landscape. Today, their reservation sprawls across 16 million acres of Utah, Arizona and New Mexico.

The first known contact by Europeans came in 1765 when Juan Maria de Rivera led a trading expedition north from New Mexico hoping to establish a new supply route with California. That route, which became known as the Old Spanish Trail, opened portions of Southeastern Utah near what is now Moab.

In July 1776, a small band led by Franciscan friars, Fathers Francisco Dominguez and Silvestre Velez de Escalante, ventured from Santa Fe, New Mexico, to Monterey, California. They never made it, but their adventurous journey took them in a great loop through unexplored portions of the region including what is known today as Wahweap Marina at Lake Powell.

When traders finally realized that the crossing of the Colorado River near Moab bypassed more hazardous terrain in Colorado, the 1200-mile Old Spanish Trail opened great portions of Utah to commercial wagon trains. By 1830 the trail began to serve as a major trade route for European expansion into the West.

Nearly a century after the adventurous Spanish priests, a one-armed veteran of the Civil War, John Wesley Powell, led an expedition party on a thrilling and sometimes dangerous 1400-mile row boat trip from Green River in Wyoming to the lower Grand Canyon, charting the Colorado River and the lake that would later bear his name.

To extend its boundaries and promote its principles throughout Utah, the Mormon Church decided to settle the area. Brigham Young sent 42 men down the Old Spanish Trail to Moab. But after an attack by Ute Indians, the settlers departed. Twenty-two years later, however, another group of hearty souls tried again, this time establishing the town of Moab in 1877.

In April 1879, an exploration party scouted the San Juan country and reported that the area could be colonized. A group of 250 pioneers, 83 wag-

ons and a thousand head of cattle left the relative safety of Cedar City in southwest Utah for a 325-mile journey to what is now Bluff. Originally estimated as a trip of six weeks, their arduous journey took six months as they chiseled and chopped their way through sand and rock and at one point lowered wagons down the western wall of Glen Canyon through what is now the legendary Hole-in-the-Rock.

Settlers discovered that Mother Nature rewarded Southeastern Utah with more than scenic beauty. Rich with tremendous natural resources, the land bursts with coal, crude oil, oil shale, natural gas and more. Uranium mining formed the heart of this area until the boom turned bust, but beds of potash and magnesium salts found deep within the soil continue to be mined.

Whether a pioneer Mormon or a modern-day adventurer, people have always found the weather to be a blessing. It gets hot here (summers average in the 90s), but during the other seasons the climate by and large is mild. Winter ranges in the 30s to low 40s, and precipitation is extremely low except in October, when there might be all of an inch of rainfall. Yet within the LaSal and Abajo mountains, skiers, snowmobilers and snowshoers find abundant powder in wintertime.

To this day, Southeastern Utah remains sparsely populated. Towns are small (the largest, Moab, boasts just over 5000 residents) and exude a "pioneer" atmosphere. Tightly clustered buildings set up in traditional Mormon pattern along wide streets, these are sensible towns with a strong backbone. Youngsters still ride their bicycles at sunset or walk hand-in hand to Sunday services. Going out for a drink is more likely to mean a soda than a beer.

Moab now supports a diverse and growing population based on tourism, mining, agriculture and retirement. It is considered one of the most cosmopolitan small communities in Utah and is one of its fastest growing.

Present-day San Juan County has a population of more than 13,000 scattered among farms, hamlets and communities like Monticello, Blanding and Bluff. Most growth can be attributed to natural resource-based industries. The Navajo and Ute reservations comprise a large portion of the southern end of the county, with Native Americans making up about 47 percent of the San Juan population.

In Southeastern Utah, history and geology combine to draw the curious and the hearty. Though man has always explored the region by foot or automobile, the advent of mountain bikes opened up entirely new portals into the back country. John Wesley Powell's historic trip down the Green and Colorado rivers can now be easily run by whitewater enthusiasts. And onetime rugged cattle-drive routes are covered with asphalt for less-intrepid explorers.

Prized nooks and crannies are being "discovered" every day. This glorious land remains ever changing, continually revealing surprises long after any new wonders were thought to remain.

Lake Powell Area

Like life, Lake Powell is grand, awesome and filled with contradictions. Conservationists considered it a disaster when Glen Canyon Dam was built in Page, Arizona, flooding beautiful Glen Canyon and creating a 186-mile-long reservoir that extended deep into the heart of Utah.

Today the environmental "tragedy" is Utah's second most popular tourist destination. Part of the Glen Canyon National Recreation Area that covers one-and-a-quarter *million* acres, the lake boasts 1960 miles of meandering shoreline. Not only is that more shoreline than along the entire west coast of the United States, much of it is in the form of spires, domes, minarets and multi-hued mesas.

The depth of Lake Powell's turquoise waters varies from year to year depending on mountain runoff and releases from Glen Canyon Dam. An interesting cave discovered on one trip may well be under water the next season. The same holds true for favorite sandy beaches, coves and waterfalls. But part of the fun of exploring this multi-armed body of water is finding new hidden treasures and hideaways around the next curve.

The lake can be entered from four marinas accessible by car. **Hite** (Route 95; 801-684-2278) is the most northern facility. **Bullfrog** (Route 276; 801-684-2233) and **Hall's Crossing** (Route 276; 801-684-2261) are neighboring marinas providing convenient car and passenger ferry service. The 20-minute ferry crossing eliminates 130 road miles. **Wahweap Marina** (Route 89; 602-645-2433) near the Glen Canyon Dam offers the most services to boaters, sightseers and overnight visitors.

Dangling Rope Marina (602-645-2969) in mid-lake about seven miles southwest of the entrance to Rainbow Bridge Canyon is a floating refueling stop and supply store accessed only by boat. Enjoy a soft-serve ice cream cone while pumping gas.

Lake Powell's waters usually warm to a comfortable temperature for swimming by May or early June. During the summer months, when the majority of the three million-plus annual visitors come, the surrounding temperatures can exceed a sizzling 100 degrees. Vacationers seek cool relief and a relaxing getaway in this stark desert ocean. Even at peak periods like July 4th and Labor Day weekends, when all the rental boats are checked out and hotel rooms booked, Lake Powell still manages to provide ample shoreline for docking and camping and, as always, clear, blue-green water for aquatic pursuits.

You can become acquainted with Powell from atop its sky-high buttes and adjacent byways, but those truly interested in getting to know the complex personality, curves and quirks must travel by vessel to the quiet box canyons and deep, gleaming pools for an experience akin to spiritual cleansing. Aficionados claim the best season to visit is early fall when rates and temperatures drop to a comfortable level.

Speed boats and houseboats are most popular for exploring, but a smaller water vehicle like a skiff or canoe will give access to outlying areas where you can just pitch a tent or throw down a sleeping bag on the shore.

Groups of friends and family typically rent a fuel-inefficient houseboat, fully equipped with bunks, bathroom and kitchen, as their mobile base and pull along a smaller boat for exploring nooks not easily charted with the lumbering mother ship. Sole concessionaire for Lake Powell is **ARA Leisure Services** (800-528-6154), which rents boats at all marinas except Dangling Rope. Hall's Crossing has a houseboat equipped for the disabled.

Before setting out, the logical place to become acquainted with the second-largest manmade lake in the country is the **Carl B. Hayden Visitor Center** (Route 89, Page, AZ; 602-645-2511). The visitor center has a relief map, changing exhibits and the story of Major John Wesley Powell and his nine companions' charting of the waters by rowboat in 1869 and then again in 1871.

Tours of the adjacent **Glen Canyon Dam,** which was completed in 26 separate vertical blocks by the Army Corps of Engineers in September 1963, are offered at no charge. The dam, a Bureau of Reclamation project, traps the river to provide water storage and hydroelectric power generation for many areas in the West.

Once out on the water, a must-see is, of course, the world's largest stone arch, **Rainbow Bridge National Monument.** Located about 50 water miles from either Wahweap, Bullfrog or Hall's Crossing marinas, "Nonnezoshi"—or rainbow turned to stone, as it's called by the Navajos—spans 275 feet. Declared a national monument in 1910, it wasn't until Glen Canyon Dam was completed 53 years later, and the lake started to fill, that the site became a favorite destination. Well touristed and commercialized on countless posters and cards, the stone arch with its awesome girth and prisms of color never ceases to amaze. Rainbow Bridge is reached only by boat, foot or horseback.

South of the awesome bridge, between Warm Creek and Wahweap bays, is **Antelope Island,** site of the first known expedition of whites to the area. Franciscan priests Francisco Dominguez and Silvestre Velez de Escalante trekked across a low point in the river (before it became a lake) and established camp on the island. Nearby **Padre Bay** was also named for the priests. Within these waters is the rock fortress called **Cookie Jar Butte.**

A landmark visible from the Wahweap section of the lake is the hump-backed, 10,388-foot **Navajo Mountain** and the striking Tower Butte, both located on the Navajo Indian reservation. They are good landmarks to keep in mind when your directional sense gets churned in the water.

A primitive Indian "art gallery" is located approximately ten miles east of the Rainbow Bridge Canyon up the San Juan River arm in **Cha Canyon**. You must motor past what are termed the Bob Hope Rock (check out the profile) and Music Temple Canyon to reach Cha's detailed ruins.

When the heat is on, you'll be spending a lot of time in the refreshing, crystal-clear water. Five miles upstream (while some landmarks and obstacles are marked with buoys, a map is still essential) from Dangling Rope Marina is a water cave in Cascade Canyon that invites exploring. If you're more interested in things that swim than swimming, throw in a line and wait for the bass, crappies, pike and trout to bite.

Highly recommended for fishing is the **Escalante River Arm**, located about 25 miles north and east of Dangling Rope. Bridges and arches and ravines also abound in the Escalante's coves. Keep an eye peeled for prehistoric dwellings and drawings on a ledge above the mouth to **Willow Creek**, nine-and-one-half miles from the confluence with the main channel.

Continuing farther into the Escalante arm, at approximately the 20-mile mark, you'll come across **Coyote Gulch** and its natural bridge and pair of arches.

From the main channel, the steep sandstone ridges of the Straight Cliffs and the 100-mile-long rock uplift called the **Waterpocket Fold** loom to the north. Respect must be given to those who were unintimidated by these fortresses. Just imagine being among the 230 or so Mormons who reached the towering canyons above the river in 1880 en route to establishing a new settlement—and not turning back.

Men blasted in solid rock for more than a month to create the **Hole-in-the-Rock**, permitting passage through the earth's mantle. The steep slope and landmark near the mouth of the Escalante River is still worth scaling, although erosion has partially closed the original notch.

North and east of the Hole-in-the-Rock is a little ol' swimming hole called **Annie's Canyon** about 12 miles from Bullfrog Marina. Boaters may notice more traffic and wake when nearing Halls Creek Bay, Bullfrog Bay and the busy marinas. Those on multiday excursions may want to stock up on ice and other necessary items at this point.

About five miles north of Hall's Crossing is **Moki Canyon**. With its ruins and petroglyphs, the area holds many secrets of the Anasazi Indians. Supposedly the canyon was a miniature city back in prehistoric times. From Moki Canyon upstream about five miles are the odd and eerie Moki steps, thought to be hand and foot holds of this same tribe of ancient climbers.

Turn right and follow the next water pocket to Forgotten Canyon. At the end are the **Defiance House Ruins**, believed to have been occupied during the Anasazis' peak years from 1050 to 1250 AD. Defiance House represents the lake's finest restored ruins and petroglyphs and includes unusual animal/man anthropomorphs.

You'll pass by Tapestry Wall on the left side of the channel before coming to the long stretch of water in handsome **Good Hope Bay,** below the mesa of the same name, that's usually a haven for flatwater—a water-skier's dream. The lake twists and turns past a handful of other canyons in the remaining 15 miles to Hite Marina, the start, or end, depending on how you look at it, of Lake Powell.

For more extensive history and sightseeing tips on Lake Powell, Stan Jones' "Boating and Exploring Map" is essential to your enjoyment and is available at any Lake Powell shop.

CANYONLANDS NATIONAL PARK—THE MAZE   Natural boundaries of rock and water divide Canyonlands National Park into three distinct districts—Island in the Sky, Needles and the Maze—and make travel between the sections almost impossible. Island could be considered the park's overlook, Needles leads visitors into the heart of rock country, while the remote Maze fulfills the promise of solitude and renewal that some seek.

Henry David Thoreau would have liked the uncharted territory of Canyonlands' Maze District because it demands self reliance. Services to this section, considered by some to be a "mini-Grand Canyon," are almost nonexistent save for the emergency water available at the **Hans Flat Ranger Station** (46 miles from the Route 24 turnoff via rough dirt road; 801-259-6513). The ranger will probably want to check your vehicle for road-worthiness before allowing you to proceed. Extra gas, and of course plenty of water, must be on hand before proceeding because you may not see another car for days. The Maze remains some of the wildest land in the West and is accessible only by horse, foot or four-wheel drive vehicle.

Puzzle-like chasms twist and turn through no-man's land where the junipers, piñon pine, sagebrush, yucca, juniper and, in the spring, wildflowers, seem surprising given the desert dryness. From Hans Flat it's 34 miles to the Maze Overlook, a good starting point for hikes or for a bird's-eye view of the rock **Chocolate Drops,** which resemble candy bars left too long in the sun.

Hikers who drop into the steep canyon below the lookout are rewarded with eight-foot-tall pictographs at **Harvest Scene.** As with any remnants of ancient art, it is important not to touch these stunning works because human body oils can cause damage over time.

Traversing from one section to another in the Maze can be difficult and confusing because of the puzzle of canyons. Using Hans Flat as your starting point again, drive 35 miles past Bagpipe Butte Overlook and Orange Cliffs to the Land of Standing Rocks. There you'll have the option for further foot exploration of the **Doll House's** redrock spires and massive fins in Ernie's Country. You may actually see more people here than in other sections of the Maze because some backcountry outfitters and rafting companies access the canyons from the edge of the Colorado River. Still, it's far from a thoroughfare.

Horseshoe Canyon, on the northwestern edge of the Maze about 28 miles from the Route 24 turnoff, contains the prehistoric rock-art collection of the **Great Gallery.** Considered some of this country's best preserved pictographs and painted art, the gallery is full of haunting, life-size drawings of people, animals and the ubiquitous hump-backed flute player named Kokopelli. There is evidence that a pre-historic Indian culture, as well as the later Anasazi and Fremont tribes, dabbled on these walls.

LAKE POWELL AREA HOTELS

At the **Defiance House Lodge** (Bullfrog Marina; 801-684-2233), cool desert room colors mimic the canyon hues outside. Marble basins, tile floors and fluffy towels are standard fare in all 48 rooms. Deluxe units have balconies. Moderate.

Set on a cliff overlooking Lake Powell's westernmost bay is **Wahweap Lodge** (Wahweap Marina; 602-645-2433). Featuring airy rooms with decor similar to its sister property (the Defiance House Lodge), Wahweap gets bonus points for its large swimming pool and manicured grounds. Moderate.

Three-bedroom housekeeping cottages with linens, kitchens and utensils are a viable option for families. Cottages are available at **Bullfrog** (801-684-2233), **Hall's Crossing** (801-684-2261) and the **Hite** (801-684-2278) marinas. Moderate.

Even those who don't enjoy roughing it in a tent and sleeping bag will take to the great outdoors experience on a **houseboat.** Under Lake Powell's silent, starry skies, waves gently rock the boat, providing the perfect tonic for deep sleep. During the day, is there a more relaxing pastime than reclining on the boat's flat-topped roof with book or drink in hand? The mobile floating homes come equipped with all-weather cabins, bunk beds, showers, toilets and kitchens. Three sizes of boats sleep up to 12 people. **Lake Powell Resort & Marinas** rents houseboats at the Wahweap (602-645-2433), Bullfrog (801-684-2233), Hall's Crossing (801-684-2261) and Hite (801-684-2278) marinas. Moderate-to-deluxe-priced depending on the season and the number in the party.

LAKE POWELL AREA RESTAURANTS

Restaurants are few around Lake Powell as most visitors opt to eat on their houseboats or at their campsites. But realizing that people need a break, ARA Leisure Services, which operates as the sole concessionaire for the National Park Service in Lake Powell, has two better-than-average restaurants in its on-shore hotels.

At the Bullfrog end of the lake is the **Anasazi Restaurant** (Defiance House Lodge; 801-684-2233). The restaurant sits perched above the marina and serves Continental cuisine. Steaks, chops and Southwestern specialties please most palates, especially those who've eaten houseboat food for a week. Moderate.

Cornish game hens, slabs of prime rib and plenty of chicken dishes are well prepared and served with salads and generous side orders at the **Rainbow Room** (Wahweap Lodge & Marina; 602-645-2433). Considering the volume of traffic handled, the food is surprisingly good. Save room for one of the homemade desserts. Moderate.

LAKE POWELL AREA NIGHTLIFE

At Lake Powell, enjoy a sunset cruise, with or without dinner, on the **Canyon King Paddlewheeler** (602-645-2433) from Wahweap. This is a favorite time of day to be on the lake because natural-rock amphitheaters appear to change colors before your very eyes as the late afternoon sun makes its curtain call.

LAKE POWELL AREA BEACHES AND PARKS

Glen Canyon National Recreational Area—Glen Canyon Dam confines the waters of the Colorado River forming Lake Powell, the second-largest manmade reservoir in the world. The 1869 square-mile area harbors countless inlets, caves and coves sheltering Anasazi Indian ruins that are ever-changing because of the water level. Marinas are found at five separate locations on the lake: Hite, Bullfrog, Hall's Crossing, Dangling Rope and Wahweap. All kinds of water sports, from skiing to windsurfing, kayaking to inner tubing, have their place at Powell.

Facilities: Hotels, restaurants, picnic areas, restrooms, groceries and visitor centers; information, 602-645-2471.

Camping: There are 400 sites at five campgrounds: Bullfrog, Hall's Crossing, Lee's Ferry, Hite and Wahweap; $7 per night. RV hookups are available through a private concessionaire (602-645-2433) at Wahweap only. There is back-country camping with a permit. Camping is not allowed within one mile of marinas and at Rainbow Bridge National Monument.

Getting there: Both Routes 95 and 89 lead to Lake Powell.

Rainbow Bridge National Monument—Greatest of the world's known natural bridges, this symmetrical, salmon-pink sandstone span rises 290 feet above the floor of Bridge Canyon. Rainbow Bridge sits on 160 acres within Glen Canyon National Recreation Area. Tours of the monument leave regularly in the summer season from Wahweap and Bullfrog marinas; during the rest of the year there is sporadic service out of Wahweap.

Facilities: Restroom; information, 602-645-2471.

Getting there: Accessible by boat, on foot or by your own horse. To go the land route means traversing mostly unmarked trails through Navajo Reservation land. Maps are available from the Bureau of Land Management office in Window Rock, Arizona; 602-871-6449.

Canyonlands National Park–The Maze—The Colorado and Green rivers naturally divide this 337,570-acre, unspoiled park into three distinct and separate districts: Island in the Sky, Needles and the Maze. Uncharted and untamed, wild formations of the Maze are enjoyed only after charting a labyrinth of canyons and jumbled rock. Another option for reaching the Maze is from the Colorado River's edge. The seemingly other-worldly formations and Indian artifacts in this 30-mile-wide jigsaw puzzle are found west of the Colorado and Green rivers.

Facilities: None; information, 801-259-6513 or National Park Office (Moab), 801-259-7164.

Camping: There is primitive camping allowed at Land of Standing Rocks and Maze Overlook with a permit; no water available.

Getting there: Located via Route 24 south 46 miles to the dirt road turnoff to the east.

San Juan County Area

Most people come to San Juan County to visit either Canyonlands National Park Needles District or to drive the Trail of the Ancients. Time permitting, the two combined reveal more about the geology and history of Southeastern Utah than almost any other tour.

Route 211 to the Needles sidles along Indian Creek, named for the area's first settlers. As you approach the steep canyon curves leading to Newspaper Rock, sparse desert landscape turns lush and green—is it any wonder Indian tribes settled here?

Blink and you might miss the turnoff to **Newspaper Rock State Park** (Route 211; 801-678-2238). The monument's sign is small, the right turn quick. This tiny park is usually on the "hit and run" list of most visitors. Though somewhat tarnished by graffiti, the huge sandstone panel is etched with fascinating Indian petroglyphs. This "rock that tells a story" is a compendium of Native American history over a 2000-year span. The petroglyphs span three distinct periods, making this giant mural an archaeological find.

Some of the figures, such as the horseman with a bow and arrow, were not made by the Anasazi but were done by later Indians (probably the Ute and Navajo), indicating that the sacred nature of the shrine was abandoned. A quarter-mile interpretive loop around the monument offers a chance to check out native flora and fauna, and some opt to set up camp here rather than amid the starker Canyonlands.

CANYONLANDS NATIONAL PARK—NEEDLES   In the Needles section of Canyonlands National Park (Route 211; 801-259-6568; admission) you tend to feel a part of the scenery rather than a casual and detached observer. With its myriad of roads and trails, Needles is the most user-friendly of the Canyonlands sections. It also features the finest collection of petroglyphs and prehistoric ruins in the park and is positively packed with natural stone sculptures in the form of arches and monoliths.

The adobe-style **Needles Visitor Center** can provide maps and advice to adventurers. From here a paved road leads six-and-a-half miles into the park. Just past the visitor center a quarter-mile loop trail passes **Roadside Ruin**, an ancient Anasazi granary. Down the road, **Cave Spring Trail** loops three-fifths of a mile past a cave and former cowboy camp.

Needles Outpost Store (Route 211, outside Canyonlands Needles District; 801-259-2032) is a necessary stop before heading into the back country. Ice, food, propane, firewood and guidebooks are sold at non-ripoff prices.

Farther along, **Squaw Flat Rest Area** is a fine place to get your bearings and absorb the magic of the orange, rust and white-striped stone fortresses ("the needles") ahead. Then follow the main road to **Pothole Point Nature Trail**, another short (.6 mile) loop that passes a series of potholes formed in the eroding sandstone. The vistas along the way of distant mesas are spectacular. At the end of the road you'll find **Big Spring Canyon Overlook**, gateway to a view of the Colorado and Green rivers' meeting place.

Anasazi Indians left their mark throughout the Needles with Canyonlands ruins dating from 900 A.D. to 1200 A.D. A four-wheel-drive vehicle or well-equipped mountain bike and good pair of legs are key to exploring the **jeep roads** leading to backcountry arches, canyons and the Anasazis' ancient drawings. A dirt road around the park's circumference is a fine way to view the Needles' unique topographic features. But beware, this route is not for the unsophisticated driver.

For a grand view of the Needles section of Canyonlands, be sure to take in the **Needles Overlook**. Getting there means driving back on Route 211, heading north a few miles on Route 191, then turning west on a deadend road. You'll be rewarded with a mesa-top vista that scans the Abajo and Henry Mountains, Colorado River and extends all the way to the park's Maze district.

Fifteen miles south of the Needles turnoff on Route 191, civilization reappears. Named for Thomas Jefferson's Virginia home, **Monticello** is the San Juan County seat. Complete information on the nearby national parks and monuments, state parks and local attractions can be obtained at the **Multi-Agency Visitor's Center** (117 South Main, in the County Courthouse, Monticello; 801-587-3235).

Early area history is revealed at the **Monticello Museum** (80 North Main; 801-597-2716) in the basement of the County Library. Besides Anasazi artifacts, the museum contains articles from pioneer life—an old stove, wagon keg, sewing machine, vanity case, picture albums and flat irons.

Another 20 miles south on Route 191 is **Blanding**, once a trading center for nearby ranches. The log building a few miles farther along is home to **Huck's Museum & Trading Post** (801-678-2329; admission). Owner Huck Acton has assembled a stellar display of pottery and Indian artifacts dating back to Anasazi times. The private collection of arrowheads, beads, pendants, effigy bowls, cooking pots and tools is sure to impress.

One of the gems of the Utah state park system is **Edge of the Cedars Museum and Indian Ruin** (★) (660 West 400 North, Blanding; 801-678-2238; admission). Site of an Anasazi Indian ruin, Edge of the Cedars allows visitors to explore the small village inhabited from 750 to 1200 A.D., even climbing down a wooden ladder into a large underground room. The modern museum details the many cultures—Anasazi, Navajo, Ute and Anglo—that have played a role in regional development. The exhibits include clothing, artifacts, ceremonial objects and tools as well as video presentations. The museum walls showcase reproductions of ancient Indian pictographs.

TRAIL OF THE ANCIENTS   A scenic, historical and archeological tour of southern San Juan County begins at Edge of Cedars, just south of Blanding, and follows a counterclockwise, 125-mile loop that includes more than a dozen sites of interest such as Natural Bridges National Monument and the cities of Mexican Hat and Bluff. The trail derives its name from Anasazi, "the ancient ones," and much of the tour passes ancient ruins of this now-extinct tribe. Detailed maps are available at the museum.

Just west of Blanding a paved access road from Route 191 leads across a swinging natural bridge to the **Westwater Ruin** cliff dwellings, which include five kivas (circular, underground structures used for gathering of kin groups) and open work areas. The dwelling was occupied from around 1150 A.D. to 1275 A.D. Unfortunately, much of the ruin has been destroyed by vandals searching for ancient relics.

From Route 191, the trail turns west onto Route 95, passing Cottonwood Falls, Butler Wash and Comb Ridge. Only a large depression, almost 80 feet in diameter, marks the great kiva at **Cottonwood Falls**. Looking south from the eastern end of the hole, a prehistoric road may be spotted. **Butler Wash** houses the highly developed stonework remains of a 20-room dwelling area plus several smaller Anasazi structures. The cliff houses can be viewed from an observation area at the end of a mile-long hiking trail. **Comb Ridge** is an eroded monocline, or bending of the earth's crust in a single direction, and extends some 80 miles south into Arizona. Before man's ability to blast solid rock, the ridge was a natural barrier to east/west travel.

The highway continues to cut through the red walls of **Arch Canyon** where centuries of erosion have chiseled and sculpted massive sandstone formations. Seven ancient towers, thought to have been built more than 900 years ago, are clustered high atop the rim of **Mule Canyon**. Three of the seven are visible at the site and considered a rare find because only a few such tower-like ruins are still standing.

At the actual **Mule Canyon Ruin and Rest Stop** are an excavated, 12-room Anasazi pueblo with a pair of kivas and a tower, all extremely well preserved and stabilized. The Bureau of Land Management has even constructed a sheltering ramada over the kiva, affording extra protection and interpretive signs offering clues to its history.

Later explorers of the region included an 1879 scouting party that lost its way while looking for the Hole-in-the-Rock Trail. The scouts climbed to the top of **Salvation Knoll,** from where they were able to regain their bearings and continue their search for a passable route to the east.

What the scouting party didn't spot was **Natural Bridges National Monument** (Route 95; 801-259-5174; admission). Records show it wasn't discovered by white men until 1883. Home to three of the largest known natural bridges in the world, the park maintains a visitor center, hiking trails, campground and paved, nine-mile loop road. Each mammoth stone bridge can be viewed by walking a short distance to an overlook. Archeological sites can be seen from perches along the rim.

The monument area is mostly desert-like with a smattering of piñon-juniper trees, shrubs and grasses among the white sandstone. While ancient Indian tribes lived in the area, the canyons were apparently too small to sustain the farming activities of many families. Nonetheless, Horsecollar Ruin, the cliff dwelling remains of one community, can be viewed.

The three bridges, which resemble arches but are formed solely by flowing water, are known as Owachomo, Sipapu and Kachina. Taken from the Hopi language, **Owachomo** or "rock mounds" is so named for the large, rounded rock mass found nearby and is the oldest of the three bridges with only a narrow strip of nine-foot-thick rock remaining in the center of the bridge. **Sipapu,** a fat-topped spur of rimrock, is the largest bridge in both height (220 feet) and span (268 feet). Its name means "the place of emergence." The "younger" **Kachina Bridge** was found to have prehistoric pictographs resembling kachinas (dancers). White Canyon floodwaters, frosts and thaws are still enlarging Kachina Bridge.

Backtrack from Natural Bridges and turn south on Route 261 to continue the Trail of the Ancients tour. Still primitive, by today's standards, is **Grand Gulch** where Anasazi habitation was omnipresent. Found within the 50-mile-long canyon system (managed as an outdoor museum) are six representative sites from both Basketmaker and Pueblo periods. Extensive remains of Anasazi dwellings, tools and artwork may be seen. Travel is limited to horseback riders and hikers.

Like stepping into a new world, **Muley Point Overlook** abruptly jolts travelers from cedar forests to austere desert scenes as it peers over the meandering San Juan River stretching across arid canyon country far below. In the distance, keen observers can spot the monolith-filled Monument Valley. Be warned: Route 261 leading to Muley Point travels over the Moki Dugway, a graveled, three-mile series of tight (and we mean tight!) switchbacks ascending to the lookout.

Descending from the overlook, the road leads into the **Valley of the Gods**, which, with its unique rock formations jutting hundreds of feet into the air, is considered a mini-Monument Valley.

An interesting offshoot is **Goosenecks State Park** (Route 261; 801-678-2238). From the canyon rim of the park, you can view the San Juan River 1000 feet below forming a series of "gooseneck" switchbacks as it winds its way toward Lake Powell.

Continuing on the Trail of the Ancients, **Mexican Hat** (two miles west of the Route 163 intersection with Route 261) is a tiny community separated from the Navajo Indian Reservation by the San Juan River. Its name comes from a stone formation resembling an upside-down sombrero just outside town. There are a few trading posts, motels, cafés, service stations and an RV park.

The Trail next heads east on Route 163 passing to **Sand Island**, primary boat launch for the San Juan River. Petroglyph panels here showcase five Kokopelli flute players—mythological Indian figures.

At the intersection of Routes 163 and 191 is the tiny town of **Bluff**. While the Mormons first settled Bluff in 1880, some archaeologists believe Paleo Indian hunters may have stalked bison herds through the area 11,000 years ago. Kiva and cliff dwellings confirm the presence of Anasazi tribes. Visitors to the town (the oldest community in San Juan County) may view sandstone Victorian-style homes left by early settlers, some of whom are buried in the historic **Pioneer Cemetery** overlooking the town. The cemetery is easy to get to: just follow the Bluff Historic Loop past Rim Rock Drive to the end of the road.

The **County Jail**, a hand-hewn sandstone structure in the center of town that was originally erected as an elementary school in 1896, now houses the Bluff Library. **St. Christopher's Episcopal Mission** two miles east of Bluff on Route 163 is a unique house of worship built of native sandstone. The Navajo Madonna and Child stand on the site of the original church, which was destroyed by fire.

Approximately three miles east of Bluff, across a swinging footbridge that spans the San Juan River, is the **Fourteen Window Ruin** cliff dwelling (also known as the Apartment House Ruin). Take the dirt road on the south side of the highway to the bottom of the hill. After crossing the rickety bridge and coming to the clearing, the ruins can be spotted straight ahead in the rock. For closer inspection of these honeycombed dwellings, walk the additional mile on the dusty trail.

Those with ample time may want to stay on the Trail of the Ancients into Hovenweep National Monument in Colorado. If not, Route 191 goes north from Bluff through the Ute Indian Reservation back to Blanding.

SAN JUAN COUNTY AREA HOTELS

As tourism generates most of this area's summer economy, hotels are numerous. Yet with few exceptions, most are of the motel variety designed to provide a clean bed and bath but little else.

Top of the line in every way, **Days Inn Monticello** (North Main, Monticello; 801-587-2458) won't disappoint. The two-story complex is decorated in soft blues, gray and mauve. Rooms are large with ample drawer space. Adding to the hotel's popularity are complimentary "heavy duty" continental breakfasts, a huge indoor swimming pool and a whirlpool spa. An outdoor lawn area features lawn chairs and gas grills. Moderate.

Without question the **Grist Mill Inn Bed and Breakfast** (★) (64 South 300 East, Monticello; 801-587-2597) is an exquisite property. Originally an old flour mill, the meticulously restored inn maintains many original features like hand-hewn rough timber beams and loft ceilings. Six rooms, each with private bath, are scattered among three stories for ultimate privacy. Antiques, lace curtains, overhead fans and clawfoot tubs add to the luxury. Guests awake to a full country breakfast. Other amenities include indoor whirlpool, television room, library and on-site country store featuring local handcrafted gifts. Moderate.

Though nothing to write home about, the **Best Western Wayside** (195 East 2nd North, Monticello; 801-587-2261) is nevertheless a good place to hang your hat for a night or two. Some rooms are nondescript motel style; others are ballroom-size with stark, white walls, brass fixtures, writing desks and rose-colored carpets. The on-site swimming pool is a plus as are the tastefully landscaped grounds. Budget to moderate.

Budget-minded travelers will appreciate **Navajo Trail National 9 Inn** (248 North Main, Monticello; 801-587-2251). Immaculate rooms have typical hotel decor but offer large, yellow-and-blue-tile showers. For a few extra dollars, a kitchen can be yours complete with stove, refrigerator and microwave.

The **Old Hotel Bed & Breakfast** (118 East 300 South, Blanding; 801-678-2388) should be called "Grandma's House." Four generations of the same family have called the property home, and the two sisters who run the inn dote on each guest like a favored relative. Even when every other area hotel is full, they manage to find an empty sofa for a stranded traveler.

Seven bright and spacious rooms all have private baths and are filled with country knickknacks—antiques, patchwork quilts, throw pillows and tiny framed prints. A generous breakfast is served on the sun-filled, enclosed porch. Budget.

One of the better properties in the area, the **Best Western Gateway Motel** (88 East Center, Blanding; 801-678-2278) boasts nicely appointed rooms and a congenial staff. Contemporary appointments in blues and earthtones are used in both the large lobby area and 59 spacious units. The swimming pool and children's playground are nice extras. Budget to moderate.

Rooms at the **Prospector Motor Lodge** (591 South Route 191, Blanding; 801-678-3231) range from good to so-so. Many have knotty-pine walls, rose-pattern bedspreads and tile baths. Others are more plastic with laminate furniture. Still, the single-story, red-brick motel is immaculate. Just ask to view a room first. Budget.

Designed by a student of architect Frank Lloyd Wright, the **Cliff Palace Motel** (132 South Main, Blanding; 801-678-2264) has many unusual features, including floor-to-ceiling windows, indirect lighting in bathrooms and dressing areas, tiled seats in showers and built-in luggage racks. Sixteen rooms are appointed with white bedspreads, upholstered chairs and blue shag carpeting. Budget.

Claustrophobics will find the **Kokopelli Inn** (Route 191, Bluff; 801-672-2322) somewhat confining, but the 26 rooms are spotless. Surprisingly, baths are oversized, and there are walk-in closets. Free continental breakfast in the summer. Budget.

There's something very inviting about the **Recapture Lodge** (Route 191, Bluff; 801-672-2281). An oasis of shade trees populates the site, shielding guests from the hot Utah sun. There are 32 homey rooms, nothing fancy, but quiet and comfortable. Lawn chairs, ideal for lounging, line the upper deck. A nice-sized swimming pool provides another way to beat the heat. Adventuresome souls can arrange geologist-guided tours of the nearby canyons, cliff dwellings and Indian sites through the lodge. Budget.

SAN JUAN COUNTY AREA RESTAURANTS

Don't expect to watch your cholesterol in San Juan County. Basic country cooking is standard fare, with a real salad bar about as rare as a rosebush in the desert. Hearty, homemade dishes make **Juniper Tree** (133 East Central, Route 666, Monticello; 801-587-2870) a popular dinner choice. Steaks, prime rib, fish and spaghetti are served with huge chunks of bread and a trip to the soup/salad bar. Locals rave about the pinto-bean soup. The only question is, "What is that fluffy, purple concoction at the salad bar?" Dinner only. Moderate.

An adobe exterior replete with *vigas* houses **La Casita** (Route 666, Monticello; 801-587-2959). The menu of burritos, chimichangas, enchiladas and burgers is priced in the budget-to-moderate range. Family-friendly, La Casita also caters to extra-hungry hombres with the "wild burrito."

A quick pizza fix may be had at **Wagon Wheel Pizza** (164 South Main, Monticello; 801-587-2766). Fresh deli sandwiches, calzones and pizzas are prepared in a flash. Take out or hunker down in a red-leather booth under mock Pepsi-Cola tiffany lamps. Budget.

A safe bet for breakfast, lunch or dinner is the **Chuckwagon Café** (296 North Main, Monticello; 801-587-2531). You can't miss the giant painted mural of an old chuckwagon on the side of the restaurant. The menu features burgers, sandwiches, fried chicken and the like. Budget.

Sit-down restaurants are in short supply in Blanding with the **Elk Ridge** (North Route 191; 801-678-9982) and **Kenny's Restaurant** (140 Continental; 801-678-9986) almost interchangeable. Both offer typical country cooking—chicken-fried steak, burgers, chicken—and hearty breakfasts. Locals usually favor Elk Ridge because it has a small salad bar, and the homemade cherry pie is scrumptious. Budget.

Surprisingly, it's in the tiny town of Bluff where you'll discover some of the best dining. **Cow Canyon Restaurant** (★) (Route 191; 801-672-2208) changes its entrées weekly. They feature Tex-Mex, vegetarian and sometimes even French cuisine. One week the choices might be spinach lasagna, Greek salad or stuffed butternut squash. Desserts range from a frozen yogurt cup to ice cream splashed with Kahlua and baked almonds. Housed in an old log-and-brick trading post, Cow Canyon's ambience more than matches the food. Open Thursday through Sunday, dinner only. Budget to moderate.

The Navajo Taco—fry bread topped with pinto beans, lettuce, tomato, cheese, onion and red or green chili—supposedly originated at **Sunbonnet Café** (Historic Loop, Bluff; 801-672-2201). Log-cabin walls and high tongue-and-groove ceilings provide an authentic Western touch. Sandwiches, hamburgers, steaks and chicken are served, along with the pinkest pink lemonade you'll ever see. Closed Sunday. Budget.

SAN JUAN COUNTY AREA SHOPPING

As gateway to Navajo tribal lands, San Juan County is blanketed with trading posts. Best of the lot is **Cow Canyon Trading Post** (Route 191, Bluff; 801-672-2208), a log-and-brick structure dating from the 1940s. Jewelry, pottery, rugs and ethnographic artifacts of the Navajo and Ute are well displayed and honestly priced.

Other trading posts selling sandstone folk art, pottery, silver jewelry, pipes, papooses and rugs are **Thin Bear Indian Arts** (1944 South Route 191, Blanding; 801-678-2940), **Blue Mountain Trading Post** (South Route 191, Blanding; 801-678-2570) and **Hunt's Silversmith Shop** (146 East Center, Blanding; 801-678-2314), **Burches Trading Post** (Route 163, Mexican Hat; 801-683-2221), **San Juan Inn Trading Post** (Route 163, Mexican Hat; 801-

683-2220), **D&A Trading Post** (Route 191, Bluff; 801-672-2224) and **Twin Rocks Trading Post** (Historic Loop, Bluff; 801-672-2341).

After perusing the wares for sale at **Cedar Mesa Pottery** (333 South Main, Blanding; 801-678-2241) take a behind-the-scenes tour of the pottery factory. Here, you can watch Indian artisans create and decorate their hand-painted pottery.

SAN JUAN COUNTY AREA NIGHTLIFE

In San Juan County, **The Olde Bridge Bar and Grille** (San Juan Inn, Route 163 and the San Juan River, Mexican Hat; 801-683-2220) is open Monday through Saturday for over-the-bar beer sales, while the grill offers dinner nightly.

SAN JUAN COUNTY AREA BEACHES AND PARKS

Newspaper Rock State Park— Hiking and camping within this 50-acre park are encouraged, and the lush, evergreen area provides sharp a contrast to nearby Canyonlands.

Facilities: Restrooms; information, 801-678-2238.

Camping: There are eight sites.

Getting there: From Monticello take Route 211 northwest 15 miles, then Route 191 southwest for 11 miles.

Canyonlands National Park–Needles District—Sculptured rock spires, arches, canyons and potholes dominate the landscape. Grassy meadows like Chesler Park offer striking contrasts to the mostly bare rock. Traces of the Anasazi Indians can be found throughout the area in well-preserved pictographs and petroglyphs. The meeting place of the Colorado and Green rivers, before they join forces and rumble down to Lake Powell, can be seen from Confluence Overlook. If Island in the Sky is the observation deck for Canyonlands, then the Needles could be considered the main stage—you start out right at ground level and become immediately immersed in its unfolding tale.

Facilities: Picnic areas, visitor center and restrooms; information, 801-259-6568, or National Park Office (Moab), 801-259-7164.

Camping: There are 26 primitive sites; $6 per night.

Getting there: Proceed south from Moab on Route 191 for 40 miles, then 35 miles southwest on Route 211.

Natural Bridges National Monument—Three natural bridges, including the world's second and third largest, are within this 7779-acre, canyon-like park first discovered by white pioneers in 1883.

Facilities: Restrooms and exhibit hall; information, 801-259-5174.

Camping: Permitted at 13 primitive sites. No water available anywhere in the park.

Getting there: The park is located on Route 95 about 50 miles west of Blanding.

Goosenecks State Park—An impressive example of "entrenched meander," Goosenecks is a 1000-foot-deep chasm carved by the San Juan River as it winds and turns back on itself for more than six miles while advancing only one-and-one-half miles west toward Lake Powell.

Facilities: Restrooms, picnic area and observation shelter; information, 801-678-2238.

Camping: Primitive camping is allowed within the park. No water is available.

Getting there: The park is located nine miles northwest of Mexican Hat off Route 261.

Moab Area

Movies made Moab famous, but the area has a lot more going for it than this. Used as a home base for many who explore Southeastern Utah, the city has a well-preserved, colorful history. Add to this two wonderful national parks in the region, a neat loop drive, even a winery. What more could you want?

Moab truly is an oasis in the wilderness. Red-rock cliffs really do meet verdant valleys, all in the shadow of the towering LaSal Mountains. First settled in 1855 by missionaries, Moab is laid out in typical Mormon fashion with large, square blocks, wide streets and huge poplar trees. And as in Southwestern Utah, the word "Street" is simply not used in the names of thoroughfares. What you might call Main Street back home is simply known as Main here. The city takes its name from a remote biblical kingdom east of the River Jordan. Present-day Moab is "sporting central" for the lean-and-mean lycra-wearing crowd. Spring is high season in Moab, as thousands of ski bums and heat-seekers flock here for desert warmth.

Moab serves as gateway to both Arches National Park and Canyonlands National Park—Island in the Sky. For area information, stop at the **Moab Visitor Center** (805 North Main/Route 191; 801-259-8825).

Moab's rich history is preserved in the **Dan O'Laurie Museum** (118 East Center; 801-259-7985). Though the collection is small, it is comprehensive, examining the geology and paleontology of Moab's beginnings. Dozens of photographs recount the development of mining, ranching, early transportation and the Old Spanish Trail. There's even the old switchboard that served all of Moab until 1951.

Star Hall, just northeast of the museum, is the start of the **Moab Historic Walking Tour** of 23 homes and commercial structures. Pick up a map at the visitor center.

It was young geologist Charles Steen who first discovered uranium deposits in the region, touching off the rush of miners. The "uranium king" built a **million dollar home** (900 North Route 191) overlooking the Moab Valley and rivers. The house is now Mi Vida Restaurant (801-259-7146).

Director John Ford put the area on the map when he filmed the 1949 classic *Wagonmaster* here. Ford returned to film *Rio Grande* the following year, and Hollywood has favored it ever since. A detailed guide to area movie locations—including *The Greatest Story Ever Told, Cheyenne Autumn, Indiana Jones and the Last Crusade* and *Thelma and Louise*—is available at the visitor center.

Film buffs will revel in the memorabilia of the **Hollywood Stuntmen's Hall of Fame** (100 East 100 North; 801-259-6100; admission). Costumes, weapons, cowboy boots, stunt equipment, posters and more pay homage to the derring-do of stunt people. Action films and oldtime cliffhangers are shown in the museum's movie theater.

ARCHES NATIONAL PARK Traversing the width and breadth of Arches National Park (Route 191, five miles north of Moab; 801-259-8161; admission) on the paved road that author Edward Abbey deplored in his book *Desert Solitaire* (a must-read for any visitor) is easy—maybe too easy. To truly experience the greatest number of natural arches in the country, get out of your car and wander. You won't want to miss the sensation of sandstone beneath shoe, the delicious scent of juniper and sage, even the hauntingly lonely sound of whistling desert wind on the short hiking trails.

The world's largest concentration of natural stone arches, extraordinary products of erosion, makes this 73,378-acre park one of the most spectacular in red-rock country. Sandstone panoramas formed by weathering, movement of the earth's crust and erosion range in size from three to 306 feet. Natural monoliths in this semiarid land resemble everything from city skyscrapers to a gaggle of women and a whale's orb: The interpretation is in the eye of the beholder.

Make your first stop the **Visitor Center** for a bevy of maps and other publications as well as a slide show orientation, geology museum and history exhibit. Rangers can point out many of the best attractions.

From the visitor center the main park road climbs into the heart of the arches region. **Moab Canyon**, a multi-hued example of geological slippage, opens to view about a mile from the center. About six million years ago activity along the Moab fault caused one section of the canyon to shift resulting in rock formations on the bottom of one side that are identical in age with those on the far side of the canyon.

Farther along at the **South Park Avenue Overlook** you'll see giant sandstone rockfaces that rise sheer on either side of a dry creek bed.

Appearing to defy gravity is **Balanced Rock,** a formation that looks like it might fall from its pedestal at any moment. A short but strenuous trail (.3 mile) can be taken to examine all the boulder's vantage points.

One of the easiest areas to visit is **Windows,** about 12 miles from the visitor center via the main park road and Windows turnoff. Four large arches that provide natural picture frames for distant panoramas can be effortlessly viewed. The North and South Windows are a short walk in one direction from the parking lot. Take a jaunt the other way and see the Turret Arch. Splendid Double Arch is just across the road. Preludes to the panoramic windows via the Windows road are Garden of Eden viewpoint, providing sweeping views to the north, and Elephant Butte.

Balanced Rock marks the start of a rough, four-wheel-drive road into the more secluded Willow Flats and **Herdina Park** sections where backpackers can shed the crowds. Herdina Park's claim to fame is that it's the home to five mini-canyons and the unusual **Eye of the Whale Arch.** With a little imagination, you can see the beast's orb.

Those with heavy-duty vehicles may want to venture another ten miles to the vast and scenic Klondike Bluffs, home to the **Tower Arch,** a hole in a wall of solid rock, and minarets that form the **Marching Men.**

The park's northern section, where the main park road ends, has the largest grouping of spires and openings-in-the-rock. No less than seven arches can be viewed in **Devil's Garden,** the park's longest maintained trail. The most distant of these arches is the Double O, about a two-mile trek from the trailhead that feels longer under the hot desert sun. If stamina allows, hike an extra quarter-mile on a more primitive trail to the ominous **Dark Angel** formation.

Halfway to the trail end is **Landscape Arch.** At 306 feet long (and at one spot only six feet thick) it's one of the world's longest natural stone spans. **Navajo Arch**—did it protect Indians at some juncture?—is one-and-one-half miles from the trailhead. Piñon plants, junipers—the most common tree in the park—the Mormon tea plant, the obnoxious prickly pear and evening primrose and Indian paintbrush flowers dot the area. Pick up an interpretive brochure at the visitor center before setting out to enhance your understanding of the desert garden.

From Devil's Garden it's about one mile south on the main road to the fins (yes, they do look like fish fins) of up to 100 feet high in **Fiery Furnace,** which does not live up to its threatening name on hot days. Indeed, the pinnacles provide a degree of relief when temperatures scorch.

Traveling back toward the park entrance, take the first turnoff to the left and drive two miles to the **Delicate Arch (★)** trailhead. Set aside several hours to really enjoy this graceful monument that stands 65 feet high, with a 35-foot opening. Arguably Utah's most beautiful natural wonder, the sensuous bit of slickrock stands boldly against the desert and distant LaSal Mountains. Some early explorers interpreted the arch as being a bowlegged cowboy! The one-and-a-half-mile trail skirts the historic **Wolfe Ranch**, sole remains of a 19th-century cattle operation that somehow survived more than a generation in this harsh land. Those unable or uninterested in hiking to Delicate Arch can drive an additional mile from the trailhead to the **Delicate Arch Viewpoint** and gaze from there.

CANYONLANDS NATIONAL PARK—ISLAND IN THE SKY   On your way to Island in the Sky, be sure and stop at **Dead Horse Point State Park (★)** (Route 313; 801-259-6511; admission). An isolated, 7000-acre island mesa, 6000 feet above sea level and surrounded by steep cliffs, Dead Horse Point State Park showcases 150 million years of canyon erosion, buttes, pinnacles, bluffs and towering spires plus the Colorado River 2000 feet below. Views from the park overlook 5000 square miles of the Colorado Plateau including the LaSal and Abajo mountain ranges.

If ever you doubted Utah scenery could steal your breath away, this promontory will change your mind. Depending on weather and time of day, the Colorado River Gorge below is an artist's palate of ever-changing hues. For a spectacular view of the park, you can't beat the back deck of the Visitor Center. Nearby paths also offer an interpretive guide to regional flora. But don't make the center your only stop. From there drive another mile-and-a-half to the park's majestic overlook. It won't disappoint.

Wilder and less trodden than the Arches is its neighbor, Canyonlands National Park—Island in the Sky district. It's a broad, level mesa serving as observation deck for the park's 527 square miles of canyons, mesas, arches and cliffs. From this vantage point the visitor can enjoy views of the two powerful rivers that constitute the park's boundaries, the Colorado and Green, and three mountain ranges, the LaSals, Abajos and Henrys.

Just past the **Island in the Sky Visitor Center** (Route 313; 801-259-6577; admission) on the left side is the **Shafer Canyon Overlook** and the winding Shafer Trail Road, which swoops down the canyon to connect to the **White Rim Trail**, so named for the layer of white sandstone that forms its line of demarcation. The White Rim parallels the Colorado and later the Green River forming a belt around the Island in the Sky's circumference. Permits are required for campsites along the relatively level trail, which can be comfortably covered by foot, bike or sturdy four-wheel-drive vehicle in two to four days.

Back on top of the mesa that is the Island, enjoy a bird's-eye view of **Lathrop Canyon** and the Colorado River via the Mesa Arch path. Short and sweet, this trail provides a vantage point for distant arches like Washer Woman, menacing Monster Tower and Airport Tower.

Just one-quarter mile west, near the intersection of the park's only two roads, are the Willow Flat campground and the true-to-its-name **Green River Overlook**, a fine contrast to the muddy Colorado. On the road's north side is the short trail to **Aztec Butte** where you'll find Indian ruins.

At the end of this side road, see the bulbous **Whale Rock** jutting out of its parched home near the geologic paradox of **Upheaval Dome**, a 1500-foot-deep crater with a questionable origin. Theories are divided whether this was a natural occurrence or meteor-created. Weird, moon-like craters with peaks spring from its center. Viewing the different stratified layers of the dome provides a glimpse into its millions of years of geologic history.

At the most southerly end of the main road is the **Grand View Point Overlook**. From this vantage point at 6000 feet above sea level, Utah's geologic contrasts become crystal clear. There are totem pole-like spires and the rounded LaSal and Abajo mountains in the distance. The Colorado River cuts so deeply in the canyon below that it's invisible from the overview. Columns and fins and other contorted rocks comprise a gang of soft sandstone structures called **Monument Basin**. By traversing the White Rim trail it's possible to get a closer look at these monuments.

SOUTH FROM MOAB Utah's only commercial winery now has a tasting room three miles south of Moab. **Arches Vineyard** (2182 South Route 191; 801-259-5397) uses 50 acres of premium grapes in and around the Moab area. The winery went into production during the late 1980s, and now everyone can taste the fruit of its labors. Besides sampling the various whites and reds, you can walk through the winery itself. But remember, Utah law prohibits the sale of packaged alcoholic beverages on Sunday, so only tastings and tours are available that day.

Mountains meet red rock along the **LaSal Mountain Loop Drive (★)**. The round-trip ride from Moab is about 60 miles from start to finish and can be driven in either direction. Plan on a minimum of three to four hours to fully enjoy the views and side trips in the evergreen-laden forests that rise 4000 feet above the red rock. Look for the road marker about eight miles south of Moab off Route 191. Turn left and head into the hills.

The land seems to change almost immediately as sandstone gives way to forests and foothills. A popular fishing hole and windsurfing spot, **Ken's Lake**, is off to the left, via a dirt road. Another few miles farther and you're at the Pack Creek Ranch, which operates riding trips in the summer and backcountry skiing excursions during the winter. Continuing on the LaSal Mountain Loop Drive brings you to a turnoff on the right called Geyser Pass. This road accesses a popular area for cross-country skiing.

Back on the loop road another few miles are turnoffs on the right to scenic lakes Oowah and Warner and a U.S. Forest Service campground. At this point the scenery may make it difficult to remain focused on driving.

Three miles farther on the left is the back entrance to Moab via Sand Flats Road. It's a 20-mile bumpy ride back into town. If you choose to continue on the loop road to the summit, you'll be rewarded with sweeping views of the Castle Valley below.

Nearby on the left side is a turnoff to the **Pinhook Battlefield Monument** and burial grounds. Here, eight members of a posse were laid to rest after battling Indians.

Across the loop on the right is the rough road to the site of an 1890s gold camp called **Miner's Basin.** This ghost town is reported to have produced gold ore in excess of $1000 per ton. Note: A four-wheel-drive is often needed to get to the 10,000-foot-elevation spot.

Beginning your descent into the Castle Valley brings you to Gateway Road on the right side—it's the rear entrance to Gateway, Colorado—and the abandoned mining town of **Castleton,** which boomed in the early 1900s with a hotel, two grocery stores, a school and two saloons.

The desert returns past Castleton as you ease into the truly stunning **Castle Valley.** At left is the volcanic remnant **Round Mountain.** There are the **Priest and Nuns** rock formations (yes, they do resemble a padre and his faithful sisters) jutting heavenward to your right, as well as the landmark **Castle Rock** that's been featured in more commercials than Joe DiMaggio.

In another four miles the loop road merges with Route 128 and the scenic river route back to Moab. A worthwhile stop before returning to the city is at the Big Bend picnic area for swimming, camping and picnicking.

Fifteen miles south of Moab is **Hole n' the Rock** (Route 191; 801-686-2250; admission). You can't miss the gargantuan white letters painted onto the cliffside announcing the place. Attractions like this you either love or hate, and those intrigued by a 5000-square-foot home and gift shop inside solid sandstone will love it. Check out the sculpture of Franklin D. Roosevelt on the rock face above the entrance.

Southwest of Moab at the end of Route 279 is the **Anticline overlook,** a 2000-foot-high mesa overlooking archlike rocks, the mighty Colorado, Dead Horse Point and Arches National Park to the north. Here Canyonlands travelers can see where they've been and where they're going.

MOAB AREA HOTELS

Don't be put off by the plastic and neon along the Route 191 strip through Moab. While generic, two-story motels dominate, a few blocks off the main drag are some charming inns that welcome weary travelers with a personal touch.

Proving once again that a book shouldn't be judged by its cover, the **Westwood Guest House** (★) (81 East 100 South; 801-259-7283) is a gem set in a bland, brick, apartment-house facade. A country motif fills the seven three-room condominium apartments. Antique iron bedsteads covered with handmade patchwork quilts are complemented by overstuffed easy chairs and wooden rockers. Each unit has a predominant color scheme—pink, blue, apricot, yellow—that pervades down to the washcloths and potpourri. Fully equipped kitchen. Budget to moderate.

Southwestern decor dominates the **Canyon Country Bed & Breakfast** (590 North 500 West; 801-259-5262), a favorite among mountain bikers. Fresh flowers enliven the five nicely appointed bedrooms, and an inviting living room is filled with a mini-library of books. Budget to moderate.

The pink-adobe exterior with hanging dried chilis makes the **Kokopelli Lodge** (72 South 100 East; 801-259-7615) easy to spot. Though small, the eight rooms are clean, and the service is friendly. Cyclists appreciate a secured area set aside for bikes, and continental breakfast is served on a garden patio each morning. Moderate.

Best of the "strip" motels is the **Best Western Greenwell** (105 South Main; 801-259-6151). Seventy-two rooms are conventionally furnished in pinks, mauves and blues with queen-size beds and sitting areas. Bonuses include the on-site restaurant, a rarity in Moab, and outdoor swimming pool. Budget to moderate.

A Colonial-style brick exterior houses **The Landmark Hotel** (168 North Main; 801-259-6147). Thirty-five units feature tile baths, individual air-conditioning and hand-painted panoramic murals above the beds. Offering a pool and guest laundry, the motel is popular among families, especially large ones who appreciate the rooms with three queen beds and extra-thick walls. Moderate.

Slick Rock Inn (286 South 400 East; 801-259-2266) blends the charm of an old house with modern amenities. Lace curtains, antique mirrors and soft quilts sit aside Southwestern-style tables and rugs. Guests make extensive use of the inn's resource library and curl up on the plush mauve sofa or one of two high-back chairs in front of a cozy fire. All five rooms share baths, with guests provided robes and slippers. Rates include full breakfast. Moderate.

A complete make-your-own breakfast is the best reason to try **Cedar Breaks Condos** (Center and 4th East; 801-259-7830). The half dozen one- and two-bedroom condominiums have full bath, kitchen and living room decorated with plants and collages of Indian petroglyphs. Upstairs units feature private balconies, and a full breakfast (no extra charge) is stocked daily for guests to prepare at their leisure. Moderate.

Certainly off the beaten track, hidden behind a storage center and a trailer park, is the **Lazy Lizard International Hostel** (1213 South Route

191; 801-259-6057). You can't go wrong at the cheapest sleep in Moab. Both the dormitory and private rooms are clean, and bedding is provided. Popular with a European clientele. Budget.

Nestled in the foothills of the LaSal Mountains just 17 miles southeast of Moab, **Pack Creek Ranch** (LaSal Mountain Road; 801-259-5505) is a slice of the Wild West complete with red-roofed log cabins and bunkhouse. Twelve cabins have been refurbished in Southwestern style, including woven rugs and bent-willow furniture. All have refrigerators—and most feature stone fireplaces with a plentiful wood supply. Hollyhocks and day lilies line walkways between the cabins and paths to the main lodge/dining room. Lithe aspen trees surround the outdoor swimming pool. Package rates include meals and horseback riding in summer. Pack Creek is also an ideal winter basecamp for cross-country skiers. Deluxe.

Art and archaeologic finds predominate at **Castle Valley Inn** (424 Amber Lane, Castle Valley; 801-259-6012), 17 miles east of Moab. Rare and valuable discoveries from Southeast Asia furnish the bed and breakfast. Filipino art, seven signed Ansel Adams prints, rugs from the Orient and excavated treasures are combined with handcrafted furniture. The eight units all have private baths, and an outdoor hot tub offers spectacular views of both the red-rock monoliths and mountains. Moderate to deluxe.

MOAB AREA RESTAURANTS

Locals say Moab restaurants have improved greatly of late to meet demands of a more sophisticated, traveling public. As the town is a center for so many outdoor activities, burning calories have created a demand for decent fueling spots.

Pizza reigns supreme at **Eddie McStiff's** (57 South Main; 801-259-2337), Moab's oldest legal brew pub. Pastas, salads, sandwiches, and steaks are offered, but the best bets are the special combination pizzas like the Happy Caper topped with prosciutto, garlic, capers, gorgonzola and mozzarella cheeses. Beverages, including homemade root beer, are served in mini-pitchers, a nice touch for parched desert thirsts. Budget to moderate.

Looks are deceiving at **Main Street Broiler** (★) (606 South Main; 801-259-5908), a tiny, streetside structure that's barely noticeable. But the budget-minded can enjoy gourmet grilled hamburgers in a basket and ooh, so-crisp fries and onion rings.

It's back to the '50s at **Westerner Grill** (331 North Main; 801-259-9918), a slice of Americana that's open 24 hours. Red-leather booths, original chrome counter and red carpet drive the nostalgia home. Fare hot off the grill includes breakfast standards (anytime), hamburgers, liver and onions, pork chops, chicken-fried steaks and homemade chili. Great for middle-of-the-night munchies. Budget.

It's no secret Utahns love their ice cream (they consume more per capita than any other state in the nation), and parlors in the desert seem as prolific as jack rabbits. **Back to the Soda Fountain** (38 North Main; 801-259-7232) won't disappoint any ice cream connoisseur. Thick, frosty shakes, sodas, floats and sundaes are fashioned with homemade ice cream. The menu also features cherry phosphates—remember those?—Key lime fizzes, an assortment of sandwiches and hearty soups. Budget.

Ciao or chow: Italian cuisine is **Catarina's** (51 North Main; 801-259-6070) claim to fame. The menu is a moderately priced affair of typical Italian entrées with spaghetti, calzones, lasagna, shrimp and chicken dishes.

What looks like a log fort from the outside is actually a haven for American/German and European cuisine. **Sundowner Restaurant** (North Route 191; 801-259-5201) boasts a bountiful salad bar, enticing entrées and luscious homemade desserts. Moderate.

Vegetarians flock to **Honest Ozzie's Café & Desert Oasis** (60 North 100 West; 801-259-8442) closely followed by anyone with a sweet tooth. Though tables are a tight squeeze, high-backed booths, linen tablecloths and the soft songs of a guitarist add to the peaceful nature. Menu selections run the gamut from Mexican to Oriental to vegetarian. And homemade desserts like Amaretto cheesecake and honest carrot cake more than make up for the under-salted main courses. There's even an extensive tea list. Healthy breakfasts are also a specialty. Closed for lunch. Budget.

Pack Creek Ranch Restaurant (LaSal Mountain Road, 17 miles southeast of Moab; 801-259-5505) is the closest you'll find to a gourmet establishment. Oil lamps softly illuminate tables, as do the wagon-wheel chandeliers. The menu reflects ranch-house life with mesquite-broiled steaks and seafood, fresh fish, prime rib, barbecue chicken and roast duckling. Dinner includes an extensive salad bar, fresh vegetables, rice or potato and homemade dill rolls. Reservations are a must. Deluxe.

MOAB AREA SHOPPING

Admittedly, Moab is not a mecca for shoppers. Souvenir and T-shirt shops are primarily what you can expect to find. Still, there are a few noteworthy exceptions.

The Shop (33 North Main; 801-259-8623) represents local artists selling pottery, paintings, furniture and bead work from the Ute Reservation. With a potter's wheel in the rear of the store, there's even the opportunity to witness, first hand, some of the work in action.

Moab Mercantile & Gallery of Fine Art (5 North Main; 801-259-2985) also showcases several local artists with an emphasis on prints and photos. Across the hall, **Hogan Trading Co.** (5 North Main; 801-259-8118) carries an impressive variety of Indian art such as kachina dolls, pottery and alabaster sculptures.

What must be one of the most comprehensive collections of books on the Southwest can be found at **Back of Beyond Bookstore** (83 North Main; 801-259-5154). Edward Abbey, Tony Hillerman and others with local ties take up the most shelf space, and there is a plethora of works on the outdoors, natural history and the environment. Popular novels are stocked, too.

The hub for sports of all sorts, **Rim Cyclery** (94 West 100 North; 801-259-5333) sells practical outdoor gear, footgear, regional guides and, of course, tools of the trade. Wise-cracking mechanics proffer knowing advice about destinations if you seem credible. "Cool central" for serious sporting athletes, or at least those who look the part.

MOAB AREA NIGHTLIFE

Utah's strict liquor laws mean an abbreviated bar scene. Moab fares better than most with a few nightspots.

Poplar Place Pub & Eatery (100 North Main; 801-259-6018) is a low-key but inviting establishment in the heart of town. Live entertainment every Friday and Saturday ranges from live folk to soft pop. The crowd is laid-back and the simple menu fare tasty.

Live music and dancing on weekends keep **Rio Colorado Restaurant and Bar** (2 South 100 West; 801-259-6666) hopping.

The **Sportsman's Lounge** (1991 South Route 191; 801-259-9972) has a huge dancefloor and live country music for two-steppin' every weekend.

One of the oldest nightly entertainments in the Moab area is **Canyonlands By Night** (1861 North Route 191; 801-259-5261), a boat trip at sunset up the Colorado River. Complete with light and sound show, the voyage offers a unique perspective on river landmarks. May to October only.

"The Canyons Edge," a multimedia production of the Native American story and Southwestern landscapes, is shown nightly at the Hollywood Stuntmen's Hall of Fame (100 East 100 North; 801-259-7750; admission) through the summer.

MOAB AREA BEACHES AND PARKS

Arches National Park— Popular with plenty of easily accessible geologic wonders, the park is a magnet for the recreational-vehicle crowd and backcountry enthusiast alike.

Facilities: Picnic areas, visitor center and restrooms. Guided walks may be arranged through the ranger station; information, 801-259-8161.

Camping: There are 54 sites at **Devil's Garden** (★); $7 per night. For groups, Juniper Basin site is highly recommended.

Getting there: Located on Route 191, five miles north of Moab.

Dead Horse Point State Park—This 7000-acre mesa has been preserved as a popular park that offers innumerable possibilities for hikers, campers and other outdoor enthusiasts.

Facilities: Picnic areas, visitor center and restrooms; information, 801-259-6511.

Camping: There are 21 sites with hookups; $7 per night.

Getting there: From Moab go north on Route 191 nine miles, then Route 313 for 23 miles.

Canyonlands National Park–Island in the Sky District—This "island" mesa, 6000 feet in elevation, features rugged and beautiful terrain veined with hiking trails. The sparse vegetation and rain on the Island does not keep wildlife like foxes, coyotes and bighorn sheep from calling this land their home.

Facilities: Picnic areas, visitor center and restrooms; information, 801-259-6577 or National Park Office (Moab), 801-259-7164.

Camping: There are 12 primitive sites; no water available.

Getting there: From Moab go north on Route 191 nine miles, then Route 313 for 26 miles.

The Sporting Life

RIVER RUNNING AND BOAT TOURS

The mighty Colorado River weaves its way through the desert rock of Southeastern Utah en route to its final destination in the Gulf of Mexico. Burnt sienna-colored water rushes boldly in some sections, slowing to a near crawl in others. Kayaking, canoeing, whitewater rafting and jetboat tours are abundant throughout the region.

At Lake Powell, you can "see Rainbow Bridge and leave the driving to someone else." Guided full-day and half-day tours of the monument are available from **Wahweap Marina** (602-645-2433) and **Bullfrog Marina** (801-684-2233). Shorter sightseeing tours from Wahweap explore Antelope and Navajo canyons, and from Bullfrog an early-evening cruise takes you past ancient ruins.

To explore canyons such as Westwater (northeast of Moab via Route 70) by kayak contact **Tag-A-Long River Expeditions** (452 North Main, Moab; 801-259-8946) or **Western River Expeditions** (1371 North Main, Moab; 801-259-7019).

Like ducks in a shooting gallery, you can't miss finding a professional river-running company along the Moab highway. All enjoy good reputations and can verse travelers in the water's idiosyncracies. Try **Adrift Ad-**

ventures (378 North Main; 801-259-8594), **Canyonlands by Day** (1861 North Route 191; 801-259-5261), **North American River Expeditions** (543 North Main; 801-259-5865) and **Sheri Griffith River Expeditions** (2231 South Route 191; 801-259-8229).

SWIMMING

Desert summers heat up like a microwave oven. When temperatures soar into the 90s and above, any body of water looks good. Many people opt for a dip in the Colorado or Green rivers and, of course, in Lake Powell.

For swimming, fishing, picnicking and nonmotorized boating in the Monticello area try **Lloyd's Lake**, on the road to Abajo Peak, about three miles west of town. Another good swimming hole is the multipurpose **Recapture Reservoir** about five miles north of Blanding. Turn west off Route 191 and follow the signs. And one of the most popular spots for swimming is at **Big Bend Recreation Area**, 12 miles north of Moab. Don't stray too far from shore, however, as strong currents are likely.

LAKE POWELL HOUSEBOATING AND WATER SPORTS

The best way to see Lake Powell is from the stern of a boat with the breeze passing through your hair and water sprays cooling the temperature. Powell's vertical red-rock cliffs merge with the navy-blue sky and fly by like movie backdrops.

If you don't bring your own water toys, **Lake Powell Resorts & Marinas** offers plenty for rent at the Wahweap (602-645-2433), Bullfrog (801-684-2233), Hall's Crossing (801-684-2261) and Hite (801-684-2278) marinas. Flat-topped houseboats are available (see "Lake Powell Area Hotels" above). They only average two miles per gallon, so many groups also rent a powerboat or jet skis for exploring Lake Powell's 1960 miles of shoreline. Waterskis, tubes, bobsleds, kneeboards, and water weenie-like "wavecutters" are available. A word to the wise—Don't be in a big hurry to check-out boats. Lake employees seem to operate on a "desert clock" and the time-conscious visitor only adds stress to a vacation by trying to hurry the process.

CLIMBING

Experienced climbers can test their mettle on the precipices near Fisher Towers, Arches National Park and in the Potash region near Moab and Indian Creek east of the Canyonlands Needles entrance. Sunbaked walls make summer climbing a drag, but temperatures are generally pleasant during the rest of the year. Deep, sunless canyons are also prime ice-climbing spots in the winter. For gear, a partner or climbing advice, check in with **Rim Tours** (94 West 100 North, Moab; 801-259-5223).

(Text continued on page 442.)

Up the River With (or Without) a Paddle

Running the rivers in Utah allows a pure view of the land from deep within the canyons. It's a different world, thousands of feet away from manmade distractions. Sometimes the only sounds are the whoop of a crane, the river's gurgle or a paddle dipping into the water. Novices shouldn't be deterred by the challenging Class 5 rapids of sections in Cataract Canyon; rafting is big business in Southeastern Utah, and tours are offered in all degrees of difficulty. Because of the rivers' idiosyncracies, it's wise to verse yourself in their courses before taking the plunge.

Along the Colorado River northeast of Moab via Route 70 is **Westwater**, which packs a real punch in a relatively short jaunt. Pre-Cambrian, black-granite walls line the deep canyons and stand in marked contrast to the red-sandstone spires above. Westwater, with 11 telling sections sporting names like Skull Rapid, is a favorite destination for kayakers and other whitewater junkies.

The most heavily used section of the Colorado River is below **Dewey Bridge** off Route 128, a popular put-in place for daytrippers and weekend warriors. When runoff peaks, there are a few mild rapids between here and Moab. But for most of the year expect to kick back and enjoy a scenic float. **Fisher Towers, The Priest and Nuns** rock formations and **Castle Valley**—backdrop of many favorite Westerns—can be lazily viewed from a raft, kayak or canoe, or in low water on an air mattress or inner tube.

Floating along the sinuous Green River and in the rapidless **Labyrinth and Stillwater canyons** is a first choice for families and river

neophytes more interested in drifting past prehistoric rock sites than paddling through a wild ride.

When the Colorado meets the Green River in the heart of Canyonlands National Park, crazy things happen. Below the confluence is the infamous **Cataract Canyon**. No fewer than 26 rapids await river runners in this rambunctious section of whitewater. During the period of highwater (usually May and June), Cataract can serve up some of the country's toughest rapids, aptly named Little Niagara and Satan's Gut. When the river finally spills into Lake Powell at Hite Crossing, 112 miles downriver from Moab, boaters breathe a sigh of relief at having made it through in one piece.

Unique to the **San Juan River**, another tributary of Lake Powell that's well used by rafters, are sand waves. These rollercoaster-like dips and drops are caused by shifting sands on the river bottom of this rapidly running waterway. Below the town of Mexican Hat, the San Juan meanders among deep goosenecks through the scenic Cedar Mesa Anticline and charges through reasonable rapids before spilling into Lake Powell.

Moab's main highway is lined with competitive outfitters offering everything from single-day floats to overnight excursions. Those seeking rushing rapids must be willing to put up with frigid mountain runoff in early spring. By mid-summer, the rivers are warmer and more mellow.

Businesses ready to help you get your feet wet include **Tag-A-Long River Expeditions** (452 North Main, Moab; 801-259-8946), **Adrift Adventures** (378 North Main; 801-259-8594) and in the San Juan River area, **Wild Rivers Expeditions** (101 Main, Bluff; 801-672-2244).

WINTER SPORTS

The only commercial ski area in the region, Blue Mountain in the Abajo range near Monticello, is now defunct. But nordic aficionados still criss-cross the slopes, ski the trees and camp-out in snow caves.

The LaSal Mountains are the second-highest range in Utah, so adequate white stuff is rarely a problem. Snow-filled meadows beckon cross-country skiers. Guided backcountry tours are provided through **Shellenberger's La Sal Mountain Adventure** (2200 Munsey's Drive, Moab; 801-259-8986). The **Four Corners School of Outdoor Education** (East Route, Monticello; 801-587-2859) rents cross-country skis by reservation.

HORSEBACK RIDING AND PACK TOURS

Clippity-clopping on leisurely horseback rides is one of the best ways to explore the LaSal Mountains or the nearby national parks. Trail rides and pack trips can arranged through **Ed Black Trail Rides** (Mexican Hat; 801-727-4285), **San Juan Horseback Tours** (Mexican Hat; 801-683-2283), **Pack Creek Ranch** (LaSal Mountain Road, Moab; 801-259-5505) or **Sunset Trail Rides** (South Route 191, Moab; 801-259-6574).

GOLF

The desert heat seems to keep golf courses from springing up in South-eastern Utah, but the few available ones are well maintained, albeit not championship in caliber. Blanding's golf course has only eight holes, requiring duffers to play one hole twice! San Juan County offers the nine-hole **San Juan County Golf Course** (549 South Main, Monticello; 801-587-2468) and the **Blanding Golf Course** (550 West 100 South; 801-678-2791). In Moab, there's the **Moab Golf Course** (2750 East Bench Road; 801-259-6488).

BICYCLING

The Moab area has become the mountain-biking central for gearheads throughout the West. Miles and miles of dirt, sandstone and paved trails within a 40-mile radius offer options for fat-tire enthusiasts of all abilities.

Outfitters are an absolute necessity for a tour of the remote **Canyonlands-Maze District**. You can zigzag on the slickrock trails in Teapot Canyon en route to the rock fins of the Doll House. The inaccessibility of the Maze ensures that few others will traverse your cycling tracks.

Canyonlands is spectacular from any vantage point, but to really enjoy its splendor from the ground up, take the 100-mile round-trip **White Rim Trail**. The trip typically takes about four days and meanders through rainbow-colored canyons and basins, skirting the Colorado and Green rivers. Since it's almost impossible to carry enough water and supplies in your panniers, a supported trip from an outfitter is recommended. The trail starts 40 miles from Moab via Routes 191, 313 and Shafer Trail Road.

Gold Queen Basin in the Abajo range near Monticello winds through nine miles of fragrant aspen and pine stands to the Blue Mountain skiing area. Mountain greens provide stark contrast to the redrock country in the north. Take the ski area road due west of Monticello and follow the signs.

By far the most popular ride is **Slickrock**, a technically demanding grunt located a couple miles east of downtown Moab on Sand Flats Road. Slickrock has become so well known that in spring cyclists line up wheel-to-wheel at the trailhead. Super steep to the point of being nearly vertical in some sections, Slickrock's 10.3-mile trail can take up to six hours to complete. But canyon, river and rock views, coupled with thrilling descents are dividends to those willing to work. Not for the faint of heart, leg or lung.

Kane Creek Road begins as a flat, paved, two-lane that hugs the Colorado River. It's the gateway to numerous biking trails. Access Kane Creek from Route 191, just south of downtown Moab.

The **Moab Rim Trail**, about 2.5 miles from the intersection, is a short route for experienced cyclists that climbs steadily from the trailhead. Views of the LaSal Mountains and Arches vie for your attention; don't forget to look for ancient petroglyphs on rock walls.

Several miles down Kane Creek Road the pavement turns to dirt as it climbs through the canyon. You can head to toward the **Hurrah Pass Trail** (17 miles) at this point. Another fun ride, **Behind the Rocks** (25 miles), ends on Kane Creek Road. Pick up the trailhead 13 miles south of town via Route 191. The trailhead will be on the right side of the road marked Pritchett Arch. As its name suggests, ride behind the rocks and through Pritchett Canyon. Consult a detailed topographic or bike map before embarking on these journeys, as it is easy to get lost amid the sandstone.

There may be other traffic on the famous **Kokopelli's Trail**, but you're as likely to share space with animals as humans. Native Americans considered the humpbacked Kokopelli to be a magic being, and the trail more than lives up to its namesake. Single-track trails, four-wheel-drive roads, dirt-and-sand paths for traversing mesas, peaks and meadows, you'll find them all along the 128 miles. Detailed maps showing access points are available at bike shops and the Moab Visitor Center.

Follow your nose to **Onion Creek** four-wheel-drive trail. The colorful, easy-to-moderate, 19-mile trail, with views of rock, river and mountains, saves its toughest hill until the end. Take Route 128 north 20 miles from Moab; watch for the turnoff between mileposts 20 and 21, near the road to Fisher Towers.

Hidden Canyon Rim is also called "The Gymnasium." The eight-mile trip can be completed in three hours by almost anyone. About 25 minutes from Moab via Route 191 to Blue Hills Road. Trailhead is approximately three-and-a-half miles from the road.

When the desert turns furnace hot, cyclists pedal for the hills. In the LaSal Mountains near Moab, try **Fisher Mesa Trail**. The 18-mile round-trip passage appeals to less-experienced riders. Drive 15 miles north of Moab on Route 128 to the Castle Valley turnoff. Take the road about 13 miles to where the pavement ends. Look for Castleton/Gateway Road. The trail begins on the left side off this road about four miles from the turnoff.

BIKE RENTALS   For friendly advice, bike rentals or to arrange fully supported tours try **Kaibab** (37 South 100 West, Moab; 801-259-7423). **Western Spirit Cycling** (38 South 100 West, Moab; 801-259-8732) also does the White Rim, Lockhart Basin and Kokopelli's trails. **Slickrock Adventures Inc.** (78 South Main, Moab; 801-259-6996) specializes in excursions to the White Rim. Also try **Rim Cyclery** (94 West 1st North, Moab; 801-259-5223) and **Nichols Bike Stop** (497 North Main, Moab; 801-259-7882). In San Juan County, stop by **Monticello Cyclery** (248 South Main, Monticello; 801-587-2138).

HIKING

Expect the unexpected when hiking in the Utah desert. For around the next bend there could be Indian petroglyphs, a stunning rock bridge or, be prepared—a rattlesnake.

LAKE POWELL AREA TRAILS   If you can tear yourself away from the water, Lake Powell has plenty of petroglyphs, arches and ruins waiting to be explored.

Up the Escalante River arm, about 25 miles from Hall's Crossing marina is **Davis Gulch Trail** (1.5 miles). Climb through the lovely "cathedral in the desert" and the Bement Natural Arch to what some consider one of the lake's prettiest sections.

John Wayne, Zane Grey and Teddy Roosevelt all visited the Rainbow Lodge. It's now the **Rainbow Lodge Ruins**. The trail (7 miles) begins about a mile past Rainbow Natural Bridge National Monument and skirts painted rocks, cliffs and Horse Canyon en route to its destination in the shadow of Navajo Mountain.

Take the left-hand spur from the monument and head toward Elephant Rock and Owl Arch via the **North Rainbow Trail** (6 miles).

From the Glen Canyon Dam, there is a short hike to the shores of the lake and a lovely arch in a recently charted area called **Wiregrass Canyon** (1.5 miles). Drive about eight miles north of the dam on Route 89 to Big Water. Turn east on Route 277 to Route 12 and continue four-and-one-half miles south on Warm Creek Road to the start of Wiregrass Canyon.

SAN JUAN COUNTY AREA TRAILS   Like spires reaching for the sky, the striped rock formations of **Canyonlands Needles district** beckon visitors to explore their secrets. A trail starting at Squaw Flat meanders through Elephant Canyon with optional sidetrips to Devil's Pocket, Cyclone Canyon and Druid Arch. Depending on your chosen route, the trip can be as long or as short as you choose.

Chesler Park (3 miles), one of the park's most popular routes, is a desert meadow amid the rock needles. Accessible from the Elephant Hill trailhead.

Lower Red Lake Canyon Trail (8.5 miles) leads to the gnarly Cataract Canyon section of the Colorado River. Start this steep and demanding multi-day hike at Elephant Hill trailhead.

A spur of the Trail of the Ancients, **Butler Wash** (.5 mile) interpretive trail is exceedingly well marked with cairns and trail symbols. After crossing slickrock, cacti, juniper and piñon, the hiker is rewarded with an Anasazi cliff-dwelling overlook. Take Route 95 east from Blanding. Turn right between mile markers 111 and 112.

Several scenic hikes are found within **Natural Bridges National Monument**. Paths to each bridge are moderate in difficulty, and you may encounter some steep slickrock. But the National Park Service has installed handrails and stairs at the most difficult sections. **Owachomo Bridge Trail** (.2 mile) is the shortest of three hikes providing an up-close and personal view of the bridges.

MOAB AREA TRAILS   **Arches National Park** teems with miles of trails among the monoliths, arches, spires and sandstone walls. **Delicate Arch Trail** (★) (1.5 miles) sports a 480-feet elevation change over sand and sandstone to Delicate Arch. Along the way, you'll cross a swinging bridge and climb over slickrock. The most photographed of all the famous arches, Delicate Arch invites long, luxurious looks and several snaps of the Instamatic.

Another Arches favorite, **Windows** (.5 mile or less) culminates with an opportunity to peer through the rounded North and South Windows, truly one of nature's greater performances. This easy and accessible trail starts just past Balanced Rock at the Windows turnoff.

Canyonlands National Park provides both short walks and long hikes for exploring some of its most outstanding features. **Upheaval Dome Crater View Trail** (.3 mile) is a short hike to the overlook of dramatic Upheaval Dome in the Island in the Sky section of Canyonlands. You can also opt to traverse the entire dome via the **Syncline Loop Trail** (4 miles), an arduous route with a 1200-foot elevation change.

Neck Spring Trail (5 miles) leads through the diverse landscape of the Canyonlands—Island in the Sky district. From the trail, hikers can view seasonal wildflowers and the sandstone cliffs of the Navajo Formation. The trail follows paths that were originally established by animals using the springs, so don't be surprised if a mule deer or chipmunk crosses your path.

A stream will be at your side for the length of the **Negro Bill Canyon Trail** (2 miles), a favorite Moab stomping ground. Negro Bill ends up at Morning Glory Bridge, the sixth-longest rock span in the United States. At canyon's end is a spring and small pool. From Moab, take Route 128 three miles east of the junction with Route 191.

Transportation

BY CAR

From the Colorado border, **Route 70** heads due west forming the northern boundary of the region. **Route 191** travels north-south, passing through Moab, Monticello and Blanding as well as the entrances to Arches and Canyonlands National Parks. Those traveling west from the Colorado border should opt for **Route 128**, a scenic byway that connects with Route 191.

Route 95 branches off Route 191 west toward Natural Bridges, while both Route 95 and **Route 276** lead to Glen Canyon National Recreation Area and Lake Powell.

BY AIR

Few visitors to Southeastern Utah choose to come by commercial air. Those who do use Alpine Air (800-253-5678), which services **Moab's Canyonland Field**. The only taxi service around, aptly named **259-TAXI** (801-259-8294), provides shuttle service from Canyonland Field to Moab.

Visitors to Lake Powell fly into Page, Arizona's **Wahweap Airport**. Page is served daily by SkyWest Airlines. In Utah, airstrips help connect vast desert distances divided by mountains, canyons and rivers. There are public landing fields near the Bullfrog and Hall's Crossing marinas.

BY TRAIN

The nearest **Amtrak** (800-872-7245) station servicing the Moab and San Juan County areas is a whistle stop in Thompson, about 30 miles north of Moab. You will take one of three trains—the "Zephyr," "Desert Wind" or "Pioneer"—depending on your destination.

CAR RENTALS

Rental agencies in Moab are **Certified Ford Rental** (801-259-6107) and **Thrifty Car Rental** (801-259-7317). Both also offer four-wheel-drive vehicles, a must for exploring the backcountry roads and byways. Others strictly renting four-wheel-drive vehicles in Moab include **Farabee Rentals**

(801-259-7494), **North Main Service Center** (801-259-5242), **Slickrock 4x4 Rentals** (801-259-5304) and **Tag-A-Long Expeditions** (801-259-8946).

JEEP TOURS

Much of the rugged, undeveloped wilderness remains inaccessible to regular vehicles. For that reason, many visitors opt for a jeep tour. Four-wheel-drive trips may be arranged through **Adrift Adventures** (378 North Main, Moab; 801-259-8594), **Canyonlands Tours** (543 North Main, Moab; 801-259-5865), **Lin Ottinger Tours** (600 North Main, Moab; 801-259-7312) or **Tag-A-Long Expeditions** (452 North Main, Moab; 801-259-8946). You can also rent your own four-wheel-drive vehicle for exploring.

NATURE WALKS

Customized nature walks throughout the region with special emphasis on plants and wildlife may be arranged through **Off the Beaten Track** (801-686-2304). Full and half-day naturalist hiking trips are offered by the **Canyonlands Field Institute** (1320 South Route 191, Moab; 801-259-7750), which also sponsors seminars, workshops and field trips.

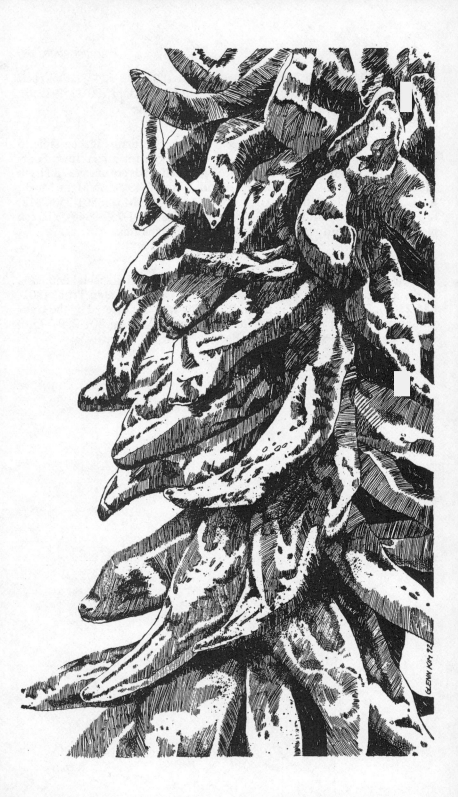

CHAPTER ELEVEN

Southwestern Colorado

From the Anasazi, who built their remarkable cliff dwellings here 700 years ago and then mysteriously disappeared, to the 19th-century miners who made millions in the silver and gold fields, Southwestern Colorado has always been synonymous with adventure. Today, myth and dreams surround this region that is home to Native Americans, cowboys who work cattle in the high country and tourists who flock to its mountain meadows and peaks.

Arguably the most picturesque mountain range in the Americas, the local San Juans compare favorably with the Swiss Alps.

Three hundred yearly days of sunshine and reliable water supplies cascading out of snow-capped mountains were probably two big reasons the Anasazi became the first known settlers of the area—the same reason for today's thousands of yearly visitors. Originally nomadic, the Anasazi eventually settled the fertile mesas, raising beans, corn and squash in the lush river valleys flowing out of the San Juan Mountains.

They first lived in caves or pit houses dug out of the ground, weaving baskets of yucca and hemp that earned their nickname—Basketmakers. They had no written language—historical records consist of paintings and carvings on cave walls that can still be seen today. Combined with other archeological artifacts, including the architecturally unique dwellings made of rock dating back to 550 A.D., visitors now find only mute evidence of these early inhabitants.

The later Cliff Dwellers built the multistory cliff side and mesa top dwellings that are best preserved in Mesa Verde National Park's 52,000 acres, the first national park to be dedicated to preserving manmade artifacts. Other

Anasazi sites are more remote and less well known, such as the Sand Canyon Pueblo—possibly the largest ruin in the Southwest. The Ute Mountain Tribal Park surrounds Mesa Verde on three sides and contains stabilized but unrestored cliff dwellings.

These ancient Indians dispersed around 1200 A.D., gradually drifting away from Mesa Verde and nearby locations, losing any traceable cultural identity. They left behind intact buildings as well as the mystery surrounding their departure. Was it brought on by drought, famine, warfare? To this day, no one knows for certain.

Later tribes—the Ute, Pawnee and Navajo—passed through, claiming the land by the 1600s. Around the same time, Spanish explorers stopped long enough to leave their mark.

The town of Silverton was founded in 1874, Cortez, now a small ranching community and access point to ancient and modern Indian lands, was first settled in 1889. Dolores, favored today by anglers, hikers and river runners, sprang to life when the railroad came to town in 1891, prospering for 60 years until the trains pulled out for good in the mid-20th century.

The railroad company built bridges over raging rivers and blasted through vertical rock cliffs to provide lucrative service to the mines, which were churning out millions of dollars in gold and silver ore. As the boom continued and money flowed out of the mountains, the region grew to include gunfighters, prostitution, gambling and rowdy saloons. Today, many of the towns created by the mining and agriculture boom have found a new life catering to tourists eager to explore this rugged corner of the world.

The physical geography of Southwestern Colorado cuts through two distinct landscapes. The jagged peaks of the San Juan Mountains attain heights above 14,000 feet near Silverton. Then the western edge of the Rockies drops off and the peaks merge with the Colorado plateau—characterized by dramatic mesas, buttes and graceful sandstone configurations carved over eons by wind and water.

Today's visitor to the southwestern corner of Colorado can experience the best of the region's scenic beauty and history. The largest city in this mountain region is Durango, population 12,000. Second is Cortez, with 7000, trailed by the smaller communities of Dolores, Mancos, Hesperus and Silverton. Far from interstate highways, each of these communities showcases the region's rich and varied history.

The towns are separated by vast reaches of trails to hike or ski, rivers to run or fish, forests to camp in or hunt, deserts spotted with ruins and canyons to ride in or explore. An outdoor-lover's mecca, Durango hosts several mountain-biking competitions—there are hundreds of miles of world-class bike trails on and off the roads of the entire region. Equestrians, hikers and backpackers trek the hundreds of pristine wilderness trails preserved from development. River rafters, canoeists and kayakers ply the waters of the Animas and Dolores rivers, claiming some of the most challenging whitewater in the world. Controlled hunting for deer and elk still attracts aficionados from far and wide, and the fishing is good. Add top-class skiing, world-class archeological digs and warm hospitality served up with a historic Western flare and you have an idea of how the heirs of cowboys and Indians are doing things today in this holy place known to the Utes as "the rim of the little world."

Durango-Silverton Area

Steam trains sending up billowing clouds as they wind along river canyons. Brick office blocks, saloons with mirrored back bars, newspapers with handset type and grand hotels where the furniture is museum quality. Remote trails leading up through alpine forests to remote mountain lakes. Resorts accessible only by rail or helicopter. Chuckwagons and Native American galleries. Is there any reason not to visit Durango and Silverton?

Each of these mountain towns has a distinctive spirit that will immediately transport you back in time. The largest community in these parts, **Durango** is a shady Animas River town with historic boulevards, one of the West's most popular tourist railroads and classic Victorian architecture. More placid, Silverton comes to life in the summer when the frontier-style hotels, restaurants and shops cater to the tourist trade. A well-preserved mining town, this community is an ideal base for jeep and fishing trips, hiking, mountain biking and tracking down ghost towns. Unspoiled and well preserved, here's your chance to slip back into the 19th century.

First laid out in 1882 to haul an estimated $300 million in gold and silver out of what is now the San Juan National Forest, the **Durango & Silverton Narrow Gauge Railroad** (479 Main Avenue, Durango; 303-247-2733; admission)—a National Historic Landmark and a National Civil Engineering Landmark—is the biggest attraction in these two towns.

This train out of yesteryear belches black, billowing gusts of smoke and cinders, exactly as it did in 1891. It still carries more than 200,000 passengers each year over the 45 miles of track between Durango and Silverton, one of the most stunning rail trips anywhere. In keeping with the historic responsibility of one of the longest remaining narrow-gauge routes, authentic orange-and-black 1880s Victorian-style coaches and open gondola cars are pulled by coal-fired, steam-powered locomotives originally made for the Denver & Rio Grande Railroad between 1902 and 1925. All equipment is kept in top condition at the station roundhouse in Durango. The roundhouse is open for **Yard Tours** (479 Main Avenue; admission) of the locomotive service area, turntable, machine shop and car shop where impossible-to-find parts are fashioned from scratch and the train cars are restored and serviced.

The train chugs through remote areas of the national forest, crossing the Animas River several times, running parallel to the river for much of the route. These areas are accessible only by the train, on horseback or on foot. There are no roads through these steep-sided narrow gorges, pine forests and undisturbed lands that look much the same as they did in the 1880s.

The trip takes three-and-a-half hours each way, with a two-hour layover in Silverton, covering an elevation gain of nearly 3000 feet from Durango. Although winter service was offered at one time, the train currently operates from early May to mid-October. Starting in September, fall color is an exceptional time on the tracks when the forest colors envelop the swaying train cars. Hop aboard anytime for the lonesome train whistle, clattering metals and clouds of coal smoke that harken back to times when fortunes and accompanying romance rode the rails.

A small collection reveals the manmade and natural history of the region at the **Animas School Museum** (31st Street and West 2nd Avenue, Durango; 303-259-2402; admission). Exhibits featured in the turn-of-the-century schoolhouse include Anasazi artifacts, an Audubon room and the pioneer "Joy Cabin."

The **Center of Southwest Studies** (Fort Lewis College, College Heights, Durango; 303-247-7456) is part of the Fort Lewis College Museum and Archive. Displays include Southwestern and Native American artifacts, as well as books, documents and maps pertaining to the historic background of the entire Four Corners region.

For a soothing dose of history updated in a modern context, **Trimble Hot Springs** (6475 County Road 203, Durango; 303-259-0314; admission) offers refreshing access to an ancient mineral hot springs favored by Chief Ouray and his Ute warriors. Now it's listed as a National Historic Site. The property includes an Olympic-size natural-hot-springs pool, a therapy pool and private hot tubs. This spot is a particular favorite with weary bike riders, hikers and skiers.

Molas Pass, 40 miles north of Durango on Route 550 at 10,910 feet, is the highest point on the road between Durango and Silverton. The views make you feel as if the world is at your feet. Maybe it is.

Silverton, "the mining town that never quit," is a historic testament to the boom years of the mining industry, with virtually every building on Greene Street dating to the turn of the century. The entire town is a registered National Historic Landmark. Among the most informative of these Victorian-era structures is the County Jail, built in 1902 and now home to the **San Juan County Historical Museum** (1567 Greene Street; 303-387-5838; admission). Exhibits detail early-day Silverton life, mining history and the natural history of the San Juan Mountains. Next door to the old jail, the **San Juan County Court House** (1512 Greene Street; 303-387-5671) is capped by an ornate gold-painted dome and clocktower. It was built in 1907 and is still in use today.

The **Silverton Standard and Miner** (1257 Greene Street; 303-387-5477) is the oldest continuous newspaper and business in western Colorado. The frame building it occupies housed a general store when it was constructed in 1875.

Completed in 1901, the **American Legion Hall** (1069 Greene Street) was the original home of the Western Federation of Miners. The brick structure contains a large dance hall on the second floor, now used for local theatrical productions. Legionnaires use the downstairs for a bar and meeting rooms.

The **United Church of Silverton** (1060 Reese Street; 303-387-5325) was constructed in 1880 to house Silverton's Congregational Church at a time when the first call to worship was achieved by pounding on a saw blade. Constructed of stone, it is the oldest Congregational Church structure in the state still offering services, though the denomination has changed.

Today the town's public library, **Carnegie Library** (1111 Reese Street; 303-387-5770) was erected in 1906. The interior furnishings are largely original period antiques, and the lower level has been restored through a mammoth local effort to provide library services. The library replaced a series of free reading rooms that had been scattered throughout the community since the 1880s.

Thirteen miles northeast of Silverton, accessed by following Greene Street East, is **Animas Forks,** a ghost town where gold and silver ore were mined in the 1880s. Abandoned structures include houses, foundations and basic mine structures. A four-wheel-drive vehicle is recommended for the ride that passes through several shallow river beds as it follows the Animas River to its headwaters.

DURANGO-SILVERTON AREA HOTELS

The best-known historic hotel among many in the region is the **Strater Hotel** (699 Main Avenue, Durango; 303-247-4431). Built in 1881, it is a repository of the largest collection of antique Victorian walnut furniture west of the Mississippi and has been certified as a museum. Each one of its 93 rooms is different; comfortable and impeccably cared for, they are furnished with antiques, and all have modern tiled bathrooms. A restaurant and a spa room with a jacuzzi are added amenities. The building is a Durango landmark, located two blocks from the Durango-Silverton Narrow Gauge Train Station. Perhaps best of all, rates are in the moderate range. Reservations may be scarce at times during the summer.

A block closer to the train station, the **General Palmer Hotel** (567 Main Avenue, Durango; 303-247-4747) is another Victorian-era structure, although this one is furnished mainly with reproductions. The 39 rooms are individually decorated with four-poster beds, pewter and brass lamps, etched glass and hand-crocheted bedspreads. Most are on the small side and some "inside rooms" have no windows, though all are well maintained. Moderate to deluxe.

Jarvis Suite Hotel (125 West 10th Avenue, Durango; 303-259-6190) features studios, one- and two-bedroom suites tastefully decorated with contemporary European furnishings. Rooms are small but compensated by cozy living rooms and full kitchens. Rates are moderate to deluxe and represent an especially good deal for families who use the sleeper sofa in the living room.

On the bare-bones end of the spectrum is the **Durango Hostel** (543 East 2nd Avenue; 303-247-9905). Less expensive than some camp sites, with men's and women's dorms, as well as two private rooms decorated in Salvation Army-style decor, there is a kitchen where you can fix your own meals. The budget rates do provide you with a roof over your head.

Located 16 miles north of Durango, **Tamarron Resort** (40252 Route 550 North; 303-259-2000) offers 350 spacious units with kitchens, exposed-timber beams and contemporary Western furnishings. All deliver expansive views of the beautiful high country north of Durango. The resort has a huge indoor-outdoor pool, saunas, whirlpool, children's program, golf, tennis, cross-country ski trails, horseback riding, ski shuttle to nearby Purgatory and two dining rooms. Ultra-deluxe.

At the north end of town, the 20-room **Edelweiss Motel** (689 Animas View Drive, Durango; 303-247-5685) has ordinary wood-paneled rooms with tiny kitchenettes. It is not fancy, though clean and quiet. Use of a hot tub and sauna are included in the budget rates. There is a fruit orchard on the grounds, views of the Animas River and the narrow gauge train tracks are across the street. The restaurant is one of the best in Durango.

Tall Timber (★) (SSR Box 90A, Durango, CO 81302; 303-259-4813) is among the most highly regarded properties in the United States. Accessible by the narrow gauge train or helicopter only, it is situated in the heart of the San Juan National Forest in a pristine and peaceful valley, five miles from the nearest road. For privacy seekers who relish comforts, there are ten luxurious modern units with fireplaces and decks. Guests may use an indoor-outdoor pool, sauna, whirlpool, nine-hole golf course, tennis court, ski and hiking trails and an exercise room. Horseback riding and fishing are also available. Ultra-deluxe rates include meals and transportation to the resort. Four-day minimum stay.

Silverton's **Alma House** (220 East 10th Street; 303-387-5336) was built in 1898 and has been restored in keeping with that era. The small rooms are simply appointed with modern amenities, including queen-size beds, as well as antique dressers, brass lamps and period wallpaper. Some rooms share a bath. Open May 15 to September 25. Budget.

The Grand Imperial Hotel (1219 Greene Street, Silverton; 303-387-5527) offers 40 rooms with private baths and oak pull-chain toilets. Rooms feature antique decor such as brass beds, brocade settees and crystal chandeliers converted from candles to electricity. There are a restaurant and a saloon, complete with bullet holes in the back bar. Open mid-March to October 1. Moderate.

The nicest bed and breakfast in the entire region is **Blue Lake Ranch** (16919 Route 140, Hesperus; 303-385-4537), about 15 miles west of Durango. The 100-acre property includes a main house with four antique and flower-bedecked suites, as well as a three-story log cabin overlooking the water. There are flower and herb gardens and fresh eggs every morning provided by resident chickens. Deer are frequent visitors. Rates are deluxe with breakfast included.

DURANGO-SILVERTON AREA RESTAURANTS

For a touch of the continent in the heart of the Rockies, the **Edelweiss Restaurant** (689 Animas View Drive, Durango; 303-247-5685) offers German, Italian and American cuisine prepared expertly in a casual and friendly atmosphere. The menu includes weinerschnitzel, bratwurst, canneloni Florentine, braised pheasant and prime rib, as well as vegetarian entrées and imported draft beers. Moderate.

Although far from any ocean, the **Red Snapper** (144 East 9th Street, Durango; 303-259-3417) nevertheless manages to offer remarkably fresh seafood at moderate prices. Cajun shrimp, blackened snapper and Colorado trout are among selections that vary daily. All this is served in a stylish contemporary setting highlighted by 200 gallons of aquariums filled with tropical fish. The 40-item salad bar is the best in town, and for dessert, Death by Chocolate should not be missed.

The **Palace Grill** (3 Depot Place, Durango; 303-247-2018) wins recognition year after year as one of Durango's most popular restaurants in local opinion polls. A location adjacent to the narrow gauge train station and its 200,000 yearly visitors does not hurt business. The Victorian decor is attractive and the service verges on stiff formality, a rarity in these casual parts. All in all, an attractive packaging for unimaginative dishes: prime rib, broiled sirloin steak, fried shrimp or duck. Deluxe.

One probably thinks of Mexican food in the Southwest, and the best in town can be found in a small drive-in on a side street. **Griego's** (1400 East 2nd Avenue, Durango; 303-247-3127) offers smothered burritos and tacos, as well as burgers and shakes, at budget prices. Eat in your car or at a picnic table. Griego's North, on Main Avenue, has a dining room, but the food is not as good.

Another local favorite in the budget range is the **Durango Diner** (957 Main Avenue; 303-247-9889). Nothing fancy here, just plain formica counters and tables, fast service and huge servings of standard breakfast and lunch selections such as bacon and eggs, pancakes, homemade hash browns, sandwiches and homemade pies—all spiced with local gossip, making this a good place to find out what is going on around town.

At **Carver's Bakery and Brew Pub** (1022 Main Avenue, Durango; 303-259-2545) you can dine casually at on fresh salads, eggs Benedict, sandwiches and locally brewed beer. Budget.

Chip's Place (4 County Road 124, Hesperus; 303-259-6277) is worth the 12-mile drive from Durango. Again, nothing fancy—plastic chairs, cinderblock walls—but Chip's has been inducted into the Cheeseburger Hall of Fame. The super-chili cheeseburger is spectacular, the corned-beef sandwiches may be the best west of the Hudson River, and steaks are more tender and tasty than you will find locally at any price. The budget-priced menu will make you think you have gone back in time.

The best Italian food in the area is found at another budget-priced restaurant, **Mama's Boy** (32225 Route 550 North, Hermosa; 303-247-9053). Ambience is zilch, with small, crowded tables overlooking gas pumps at a service station, but the pizza is primo. Also check out the antipasto, eggplant parmesan and Eastern-style heroes.

Silverton is justifiably un-renowned for dining. Most restaurants cater to the narrow-gauge train passengers who have an hour or two layover at lunch time. Open year-round, however, is the **French Bakery** (1250 Greene Street, 303-387-5423), located on the ground floor of the Teller House Hotel. Victorian decor cannot mask the standard fare of burgers, soups, salads and a somewhat more imaginative assortment of pastries. No one would mistake this place for a Parisian café. Budget to moderate.

DURANGO-SILVERTON AREA SHOPPING

Durango's Main Avenue and side streets are chock-a-block with gift shops and galleries. The best one in town, featuring fine art, T-shirts and contemporary Western and Native American crafts, is **Toh-Ahtin Gallery** (145 West 9th Street; 303-247-8277). Another location offers prints, posters, artwear, jewelry and original art, **Art on Main** (965 Main Avenue, Durango; 303-247-5450).

For an interesting assortment of antiques, collectibles, railroad memorabilia, used and rare books, try **Southwest Book Trader** (175 East 5th Street, Durango; 303-247-8479).

Unusual gifts collected from travels around the world and local crafts are available at **Jodie's Haircuts and Boutique** (102 East 8th Street, Suite 213, Durango; 303-247-0300).

If your head is simply aching for a custom-fitted cowboy hat, try **O'Farrell Hat Co.** (598 Main Avenue, Durango; 303-259-2517). They make hats by hand, the old fashioned way, and have produced customized models for Ronald Reagan and George Bush.

An influx of **factory outlets** to Durango has brought Ralph Lauren, Benetton, Levis, London Fog and other name-brand discounters to the small downtown area.

Silverton contains a plethora of take-your-pick gift shops clustered mainly along Greene Street between 11th and 14th streets. None stand out. All seem to offer souvenir rocks, T-shirts, jewelry, cowboy hats, leather goods, train whistles, as well as practical area guidebooks, maps and camping gear.

Silverton Mountain Pottery (Blair Street) has original stoneware made from Colorado clay. Every piece is handmade in Silverton with Silverton materials.

DURANGO-SILVERTON AREA NIGHTLIFE

Among seasonal nighttime offerings are the **Bar D Chuckwagon** (8080 County Road 250, Durango; 303-247-5753), with its chuckwagon supper and Western show; the **Diamond Circle Theatre** (699 Main Avenue, Durango; 303-247-4431), featuring live turn-of-the-century melodramas; and the **Durango Pro Rodeo** (La Plata County Fairgrounds, 25th Street and Main

Avenue; 303-247-2308), presenting professional rodeo events on Tuesday and Wednesday evenings.

Aside from these activities, nightlife is pretty much limited to restaurants, bars and a few movie theaters. The **Sundowner Saloon** (3777 North Main Avenue, Durango; 303-385-4410) offers free country-and-western dance lessons.

The **Diamond Belle Saloon** (699 Main Avenue, Durango; 303-247-4431) features an antique gold-leaf filigree back bar, a honky-tonk piano player, waitresses dressed in 1880s saloon-girl finery and bartenders with garters on their sleeves.

Farquahrt's (725 Main Avenue, Durango; 303-247-5440) is an antique-filled rock-and-roll bar with live music nightly.

Silverton's nightlife makes Durango seems like Manhattan by comparison. Try the **Hub Saloon** (1219 Greene Street, 303-387-5527), a Victorian-appointed bar in the Grand Imperial Hotel.

DURANGO-SILVERTON AREA PARKS

San Juan National Forest—The site is huge. The national forest covers two million acres of Southwestern Colorado, offering hundreds of miles of trails and the San Juan Skyway, a scenic byway connecting Durango, Silverton, Telluride and Cortez. Also here are rivers for fishing, swimming and boating, hunting grounds and some of the most spectacular scenery of alpine lakes, cataracts and waterfalls you'll ever see. Unusual geologic formations and historic mines add to the splendor. Deer, elk and eagles live in the pine and aspen forests that are a special treat during fall when bright colors are abundant. With the towering elevations found here (peaking at 14,000 feet), snow is usually on the ground in the high country until July and may fall again as early as September.

Facilities: Picnic areas, restrooms, restaurants and groceries in towns within or adjacent to the forest; information, 303-247-4874. *Swimming, boating and windsurfing:* Good. *Fishing:* At Vallecito Lake or Lemon Reservoir among other sites, for trout, kokanee salmon, bluegill and crappie.

Camping: There are 75 campgrounds throughout the forest; less-developed sites are free while standard ones are $5 to $7; reservations, 800-283-2267.

Getting there: Located north and south of Cortez, and extending east to Pagosa Springs, when you reach Southwestern Colorado you are in the forest. The national forest extends from Telluride to the New Mexico border, from McPhee Reservoir to Pagosa Springs, 47 miles east of Durango. Main access is via Routes 160 and 550.

Weminuche Wilderness—One of the nation's largest wilderness areas, Weminuche consists of 459,000 acres set aside by the federal government to retain its primeval character. The average elevation of the area is 10,000 feet and there are 400 miles of hiking trails. Hiking and horseback riding are allowed through this very rugged slice of the scenic West. No motorized vehicles permitted.

Facilities: None; restaurants and groceries are available in communities outside the wilderness area; information, 303-247-4874. *Fishing:* Permitted.

Camping: Backpack camping is allowed, but permits are required for six or more people.

Getting there: Located 26 miles northeast of Durango, main access is via hiking trails at Vallecito Reservoir, from trails outside of Silverton or Purgatory ski area, or via the Durango-Silverton Narrow Gauge Railroad.

Cortez-Dolores Area

Many of Southwestern Colorado's most fascinating destinations are a short drive from popular Mesa Verde. One of the finest Indian preserves in the Americas, the Ute Mountain Tribal Park offers a Native American-led look at Anasazi country. You can also see another side of this region's special heritage at Lowry Ruins and Hovenweep National Monument, straddling the Colorado-Utah border. Because each is slightly off the beaten track you'll be able to enjoy a leisurely uncrowded visit to this magical region.

The scrubland desert north of the San Juan River is broken by mesas and isolated canyons where pre-Columbian Pueblo Indians lived until around 1300. Established on the Colorado-Utah border in 1923, **Hovenweep National Monument** (40 miles west of Cortez off Route 666; 303-529-4461) contains 784 acres and six groups of ruins. These ruins are most noted for the substantial size of the community they once housed, as well as their square, oval, circular and D-shaped towers, indicating sophisticated masonry skills. Some of the walls stand 20 feet high despite the total deterioration of ancient mortar over the centuries.

Square Tower Ruins, the only site accessible by car, are the best preserved. Hikes of varying lengths through piñon and juniper trees take you to all other sites. Noteworthy ruins include the two pueblos of **Cajon Ruins**, located in Utah, which are the least well preserved, having been heavily vandalized before the monument was established, and **Holly, Hackberry Canyon, Cutthroat Castle** and **Goodman Point Ruins**, located in Colorado.

Sixteen miles north of Hovenweep lies a smaller National Historic Landmark, **Lowry Pueblo Ruins** (unmarked road off Route 666, eight miles west of Pleasant View; 303-247-4082). The site, believed to have housed 100 farmers who raised corn, beans and squash for fifty years until 1140 A.D., contains one of the largest circular communal gathering spots, known as kivas, yet discovered in the Southwest. The site also contains 40 rooms, some of which were three stories tall, and eight smaller kivas. It is here you will find the **painted kiva** with its five layers of ancient plaster paintings, covered by a modern roof to help preserve it.

Considered one of the world's largest collections of ancient Indian artifacts, the **Anasazi Heritage Center** (27501 Route 184, Dolores; 303-882-4811) is adjacent to the 12th-century Dominguez and Escalante Ruins. Materials from the excavations of these ruins are displayed in the very fine museum operated by the Bureau of Land Management. There are hands-on displays involving computers and microscopes, as well as *metate* stones for grinding corn, a loom and a partially reconstructed full-size pit house. Many of the museum items were rescued prior to the flooding of a local valley—retrieved from an area now under water at Dolores's McPhee Dam and Reservoir.

The **Crow Canyon Archaeological Center** (23390 County Road K, Cortez; 303-565-8975; admission) is a school and research center developed to create a greater understanding of the prehistoric Anasazi who populated the Four Corners area. Visitors who have made advance reservations may take day tours of the laboratory research facilities and a working archeological site, or sign up for cultural education programs led by Pueblo scholars. One of the sites where excavations are in progress is the **Sand Canyon Pueblo**, located on an unsigned road near the research center and thought to be the largest ruin yet uncovered in the Southwest. A tiny museum off Main Street in downtown Cortez, the **Cortez Center** (25 North Market Street; 303-565-1151) offers displays on the Basketmaker and Pueblo periods of Anasazi culture, as well as informative videos on various aspects of Anasazi life.

South of Cortez and surrounding nearby Mesa Verde on three sides, the **Ute Mountain Tribal Park** (Towaoc; 303-565-3751; admission) has long been considered sacred ground by the Ute Mountain tribe whose reservation encompasses the park. Following the Mancos River valley, the site contains hundreds of surface ruins, cliff dwellings, petroglyphs and paintings. Maintained as a primitive area and administered by Native Americans, this is one of the most evocative Anasazi sites in all of southwestern Colorado.

Visitors must make reservations for a daily guided tour with a tribe member who drives ahead of you in his vehicle while you follow in yours. The tours cover nearly 100 miles in six hours—stopping numerous times to walk through fields littered with thousands of distinctive pottery shards, to stand beside pit houses and burial mounds, to hike to petroglyphs, rock paintings and sentinel posts, or to scale ladders as high as thirty feet to reach excavated but unrestored Anasazi ruins, left intact much the way they were 800 years ago. Bring water, food and a full tank of gas. A day here is physically exerting and there are no facilities available.

Sleeping Ute Mountain west of the tribal park is a landmark you cannot and should not miss. From its head to the north, to its feet to the south, this mountain with an elevation of more than 9800 feet appears to be an Indian lying on his back with his arms folded across his chest.

CORTEZ-DOLORES AREA HOTELS

Strip motels and chains predominate, but there are a few unusual choices.

An original railroad hotel has been in operation for 95 years in Dolores. The **Rio Grande Southern** (101 5th Street; 303-882-7527) is the oldest building in town. It has six small rooms decorated with reproduction antiques and local artworks. A full breakfast is included in the budget rates. There is also a restaurant.

A real get-away-from-it-all bed and breakfast is located between Cortez and Hovenweep National Monument. **Kelly Place** (14663 County Road G, Cortez; 303-565-3125) is situated on a secluded dirt road, miles from anywhere. Set in the midst of a piñon-juniper forest and sandstone canyons, the five rooms are large and comfortably furnished in contemporary Western style. There are Indian ruins on the 100-acre property which guests can help excavate. Pottery and weaving instruction in the Anasazi style, as well as classes in canning, quilting, tanning, blacksmithing or farming with draft horses are added features. Moderate.

CORTEZ-DOLORES AREA RESTAURANTS

Here we truly begin to stretch in seeking the best restaurants. Chains are well-represented along with a number of small cafés serving undistinguished food. However . . .

In the budget range, **Ponderosa Restaurant & Lounge** (Route 145 and 8th Street, Dolores; 303-882-7910) serves burgers, sandwiches, homebaked pies, cinnamon rolls, cookies, muffins and sourdough Danish in a setting of nouveau K-Mart decor. This spot is convenient to McPhee Reservoir.

Old Germany Restaurant (Route 145 and 8th Street, Dolores; 303-882-7549) looks like a Bavarian cottage. The restaurant serves cod, shrimp,

German-style sausage and Bavarian specialties, imported beers and German wines. Budget to moderate.

Stromsted's (1020 South Broadway, Cortez; 303-565-1257) is on the south end of town, built into a hillside, with interesting woodwork in the dining room and a deck affording views of Mesa Verde and Sleeping Ute Mountain. The steaks, seafood and barbecued ribs are the best in town. Moderate in price.

Genuine Mexican food is served at plant-bedecked **Francisca's** (125 East Main Street, Cortez; 303-565-4093). Budget-to-moderate-priced entrées include *chile rellenos*, chimichangas and stacked enchiladas. Also popular are the Blue Curaçao margaritas.

Western hospitality with no frills might help describe the **M&M Truckstop and Restaurant** (7006 Route 160, Cortez; 303-565-6511). Open 24 hours, this is the locals' choice for breakfast anytime. Eggs with refried beans, pancakes served in multiples of five, french fries made from real potatoes, steaks, sandwiches and everything else on the menu are budget-priced.

CORTEZ-DOLORES AREA SHOPPING

The gift shop at the **Anasazi Heritage Center** (27501 Route 184, Dolores; 303-882-4811) offers a small selection of original Native American crafts.

In Cortez, the gift shop at **Cortez Center** (25 North Market Street; 303-565-1151) has some of the best prices in the region on a small selection of contemporary Native American pottery, weavings and other crafts.

Mesa Verde Pottery and Gallery Southwest (Cortez; 303-565-4492) has a large selection of Native American pottery crafted on the premises, as well as drums, sandpaintings, collectible Pueblo pottery, kachina dolls, weavings, jewelry and sculptures.

CORTEZ-DOLORES AREA NIGHTLIFE

In Cortez, limited to summer months only, there are Indian storytellers weeknights at the **Cortez Center** (25 North Market Street; 303-565-1151), and Native American dances are performed at the **Cortez Visitor Center** (808 East Main, 800-253-1616) next to the City Park.

During the rest of the year try the **M&M Truckstop and Restaurant** (7006 Route 160; 303-565-6511). It is open 24 hours and likely to be the liveliest place in town after dark. Dolores' **Ponderosa Restaurant & Lounge** (Route 145 and 8th Street; 303-882-7910) may offer a semblance of nightlife at times.

CORTEZ-DOLORES AREA PARKS

Hovenweep National Monument—This 784-acre park straddles the Colorado-Utah border. Here you will find six major sites of Indian ruins in nearly mythic Colorado plateau country. Camping, hiking and bike riding are allowed in the slickrock canyon country characterized by sweeping unobstructed vistas of the pastel high desert.

Facilities: Picnic sites, pit toilets; restaurants, food, gas and supplies are available in Cortez, at Hatch Trading Post (16 miles west) or Ismay Trading Post (14 miles southeast); ranger station/information 303-529-4461

Camping: There are 30 tent sites; no water; $5 per night.

Getting there: Located 49 miles west of Cortez, access is via McElmo Canyon Road, three miles south of Cortez or by the Pleasant View Road, 20 miles north of Cortez.

McPhee Reservoir—This 4500-acre manmade lake is located northwest of Dolores and offers a full range of recreational opportunities, most centered around the developed areas at Lone Dome, House Creek, the Great Cut Dike and the McPhee Recreation Area. Open since the late 1980s, the lake is snuggled in between mountains to the west and the desert to the east.

Facilities: Picnic sites, restrooms, showers, hiking, groceries, water; ranger station/information, 303-882-7296. *Boating:* Boat ramps, marina. *Swimming:* Good. *Fishing:* Permitted.

Camping: McPhee Campground has 71 sites (eight with hookups); $6 to $12 per night. House Creek Camp has 43 sites (three with hookups); $8 to $10 per night.

Getting there: It's located northwest of Dolores, main access is via Route 145.

Ute Mountain Tribal Park—This is a primitive area surrounding Mesa Verde on three sides. There are limited facilities, and access is restricted to group tours or those who reserve an Indian guide for backpacking, biking or horseback trips through the 125,000 acres of rugged canyon country and prehistoric Indian ruins. Surrounding the once-lush Mancos River Valley, the arid parklands sprawl through cactus and sage-studded habitats for elk, deer and mountain lions.

Facilities: Picnic tables, restrooms; restaurants and food available in Cortez; information, 303-565-3751, ext. 282.

Camping: Allowed in three designated areas; $5 per night.

Getting there: The park is located 12 miles south of Cortez across from Ute Mountain Pottery in Towaoc, access is via Route 666.

Mesa Verde Area

Mesa Verde National Park (Route 160; 303-529-4465; admission) is the number one tourist attraction in Southwestern Colorado, drawing 700,000 visitors yearly to its deserted canyons, outstanding views and preserved archeological ruins. Ascending the highway to this legendary plateau, you'll enjoy panoramic views of the Four Corners region. Easily reached by a convenient loop drive, each of the cliff dwellings, pit houses and other Anasazi ruins is an authentic Southwestern treasure. Tucked inside sandstone cliffs, many of these dwellings are inaccessible today. Those you can visit, thanks to guided tours, make it clear that these Native Americans were among the leading architects of their day.

Although major cliff dwellings and mesa-top ruins may be seen from overlooks on roadways, visits to other ruins are strenuous, requiring hikes varying in altitude from 6040 feet to 8572 feet, aided by steps and ladders.

Traveling up the steep entrance road for four miles, **Morefield Village** is the site of the of the park's only campground and the starting point for three hiking trails most popular for panoramic views. The shortest trail (about one mile) leads to **Point Lookout** at the tip of the mesa.

Nine miles farther along the road is the **Far View Visitor Center**, the commercial hub of the park and location of most visitor services. The visitor center displays contemporary Native American arts and crafts.

In summer only, **Wetherill Mesa** may be accessed from a turnoff at Far View. It is a rugged 21-mile ride to the **Step House** and **Long House Ruins,** containing 1400-year-old subterranean pit houses from the Basketmaker period and 800-year-old structures from the Classic Pueblo period around 1200 A.D.

The main park ruins and a fascinating archeological museum are clustered around **Chapin Mesa**, 21 miles from the park entrance, a minimum 45-minute drive. The museum contains exhibits and artifacts detailing the history of the Anasazi as well as the development of the national park. From here you can take a short hike to **Spruce Tree House**, one of the major park ruins (which can also be viewed from an overlook). Other significant ruins and isolated cliff dwellings, carved improbably out of sheer rock faces. are accessible via two loops on the **Ruins Road**. The westerly loop, a paved road well marked with signs, leads over its two-mile length past several interesting sites, including **Square Tower House**, pit houses and Pueblo ruins, **Sun Point** overlook at the edge of **Fewkes Canyon** and **Cliff Canyon** and the **Sun Temple Ruins**. The easterly loop is approximately the same length, also paved. It leads through similar pine, scrub brush and sage hillsides along the mesa top to numerous view sites as well as the **Cliff Palace** and **Balcony House Ruins**.

Guided interpretive tours led by park rangers are conducted at all major cliff dwellings during the summer. In winter, guided tours are offered to Spruce Tree House only, weather permitting. Although the park is open year-round, park roads may be closed due to weather conditions in winter months. Winter is the least crowded and most haunting time to visit the park.

MESA VERDE AREA HOTELS

The only motel within the national park is the **Far View Lodge** (P.O. Box 277, Mancos, CO 81328; 303-529-4421). It is actually a fairly modest place in a spectacular setting. Each of 150 rooms is standard motel style, with Indian print bedspreads and a balcony offering 100-mile views across the mesa country. Rates are moderate, and there is a restaurant. Open May to October.

For a truly *hidden* lodging experience travel deep in the San Juan National Forest, travel 20 miles north of Mancos along a gravel road. Prices are budget rate at "Jersey Jim," and you won't be troubled by noisy neighbors. However, you'll have to climb several flights of zigzag stairs en route to your room, a glass-lined facility measuring 15 feet square. But once you arrive the views are extraordinary. Jersey Jim, it seems, is a **fire lookout tower (★)** that has been converted into a wilderness version of an efficiency apartment. Sleeping up to four people (bring your own sleeping bags), it contains a stove, refrigerator and lanterns. For information call the National Forest Service at 303-533-7716.

For dudes and dudettes, **Lake Mancos Ranch** (42688 County Road N, Mancos; 303-533-7900) offers 17 units accommodating 60 guests in private cabins or ranch house rooms. Decor is plain—Western wood-paneled rooms with wooden furniture—but guests do not come here to stay inside. They come to enjoy horseback riding, fishing, jeeping and the great outdoors. There are a pool and supervised children's programs. Rates are deluxe, with meals included. Riding is extra. Minimum stay is one week.

MESA VERDE AREA RESTAURANTS

The best restaurant in this area is seven miles east of the national park entrance. **Millwood Junction** (Route 160 West, Mancos; 303-533-7338) serves budget specials nightly, moderately priced dinners and a memorable Friday night seafood buffet in a comfortable rough-hewn, wood-paneled dining room. Regular menu items include châteaubriand and baby back ribs, as well as stuffed chicken with blueberries and hazelnuts, crab lasagna or sea scallops in a phyllo pastry with a strawberry Normandie sauce. The salad bar is a meal in itself, but save room for homemade ice cream, black-bottom pie or a raspberry torte.

Within the national park you will find three restaurants operated by the concessionaire (303-529-4421). The **Far View Terrace Café** and **Spruce Tree Terrace** are budget-priced cafeterias offering Navajo tacos, burgers, sandwiches and salads. The moderately priced **Metate Room**, at Far View Lodge, serves New York strip steak, a beef and vegetable Mexican sauté, fried shrimp and other Mexican and American dishes.

MESA VERDE AREA SHOPPING

Mesa Verde National Park (303-529-4421) has a gift shop and bookstore located at the park headquarters on Chapin Mesa, as well as a gift shop at the Far View Visitors Center. The bookstore is well stocked with research relating to the entire Southwestern Colorado region.

MESA VERDE AREA NIGHTLIFE

Nightlife in this neck of the woods consists largely of looking at expanses of stars in a clear sky. **Millwood Junction** (Route 160 West, Mancos; 303-533-7338) has occasional live music.

MESA VERDE AREA PARKS

Mesa Verde National Park—In the high-canyon country between Cortez and Mancos, the park offers scenic roads leading to short trails to Native American ruins and stunning mesa-top views of the desert and the mountains. Maintained by the National Park Service, the area contains the most accessible concentration of prehistoric cliff dwellings in the United States.

Facilities: Restrooms, groceries, gas, showers, laundromat; ranger station and visitor centers open in summer only; motel and restaurants in the park; all services operate mid-May to mid-October only, although the park is open year-round; information, 303-529-4465.

Camping: Morefield Campground (303-529-4474) has 477 sites including 15 with hookups; $8 to $15.50 per night.

Getting there: Located 36 miles west of Durango, the entrance to the park is on Route 160, seven miles east of Cortez.

Lake Mancos State Recreation Area—This park is located ten miles from Mesa Verde. The lake is situated at 7800 feet, surrounded by 338 acres of mature ponderosa pine forest laced by hiking and horseback trails.

Facilities: Picnic sites, restrooms, showers; groceries and restaurants five miles away in Mancos; information, 303-533-7065. *Boating:* Permitted. *Swimming:* In the coves.

Camping: There are 33 sites including two primitive tent sites; $9 per night.

Getting there: Located northeast of Mesa Verde, the park is situated north on Route 184 in Mancos to County Road 42, then four miles farther to County Road N.

The Sporting Life

HORSEBACK RIDING, PACK TOURS AND LLAMA TREKS

There are still plenty of horses in this part of the West, and you can ride gentle or spirited steeds for an hour, a day or as long as you can take it, pal. In addition, you can hike with a llama that carries your gear over terrain ranging from high desert to forested alpine trails.

Call **Over the Hill Outfitters** (3624 County Road 203, Durango; 303-247-9289 and 13391 County Road 250; 303-259-2834), **Southfork Stables** (28481 Route 160 East, Durango; 303-259-4871), **Wit's End/Meadowlark Ranch** (254 County Road 500, Bayfield; 303-884-4113 in summer; 303-884-2966 in winter), **LDK Outfitters** (Silverton; 303-387-5861), **Silver Trails** (600 Cement Street, Silverton; 303-387-5869), **The Outfitter** (410 Railroad Avenue, Dolores; 303-882-7740), **The Trappers Den** (37101 Route 160, Mancos Valley; 303-533-7147) or **Echo Basin Ranch** (43747 County Road M, Mancos; 303-533-7000).

Day hikes with llamas or llama leasing are available from Durango's **Buckhorn Llama Co.** (1834 County Road 207; 303-259-5965) or the **Turnbull Llama Co.** (455 High Llama Lane, Durango; 303-259-3773).

RIVER RAFTING AND KAYAKING

Whether the rivers are raging during spring runoff, or relatively calm, waterborne sports are always a good way to explore desert canyons or mountain streams. The upper stretch of the Animas River from Silverton to Rockwood offers the only two-day class V whitewater trip in the West and is suitable for expert kayakers only. The lower reaches may be rafted. The Dolores River is considered tops for whitewater in late May.

Contact **Southwest Adventures** (P.O. Box 3242, Durango, CO 81302; 303-259-0370), **Four Corners Marine** (360 South Camino del Rio, Durango; 303-259-3893), **Durango Rivertrippers** (720 Main Avenue, Durango; 303-259-0289), **Humpback Chub River Tours** (P.O. Box 1109, Dolores, CO 81302 or P.O. Box 759, Moab, UT 84532; 800-882-7940) or **Peregrine Outfitters** (447 Grand Avenue, Mancos; 303-533-7235).

(Text continued on page 470.)

Skiing the Best—The Southwestern Rockies

Many experts think some the best skiing in the world is found in the southwestern Rockies of Colorado. The snow is deep, averaging more than 300 inches a year of feather-soft powder; temperatures average ten degrees higher than more northerly resorts. Telluride and Purgatory offer unparalleled vertical terrain amid crowning mountain beauty. It's only because the areas are harder to reach than better-known ski resorts that they tend to stay less crowded.

Telluride—It's the mountain! Top elevation is an ethereal 11,890 feet, with a vertical drop of 3522 feet, offering distinct ski terrain for all level of skiers. Experts enjoy controlled, out-of-bounds skiing, but must be willing to hike half an hour or more to reach the sites.

The growing popularity and powerful reputation of Telluride has been helped by scheduled airline service into Telluride Regional Airport—the highest commercial airport in the United States at elevation 9086 feet.

Telluride opens in late November. Some special programs offered include, "Ski week," emphasizing a daily two-hour class focusing on physical, mental and social aspects of skiing.

The entire old mining town of Telluride is a National Historic Landmark. Victorian structures predominate. The **New Sheridan Hotel** (231 West Colorado Avenue; 303-728-4351), where William Jennings Bryan delivered his famous "Cross of Gold" speech in 1904, is a gem.

Need a place to hang your ski boots? You can stay in the New Sheridan Hotel—in the opulent historic style of antique Victoriana, at a bed and breakfast in a restored home such as the **Dahl House** (122 South Oak Street; 303-728-4158) or at an increasing number of modern condominiums close to the slopes.

One of the most beautifully located guest ranches in the West is **Skyline Ranch** (P.O. Box 67, Telluride, CO 81435; 303-728-3757), open year-round. They have seasonal ski tours or horseback trips. Ski-in, ski-out lodging, lift-ticket sales, equipment rentals, ski school, restaurant and nursery services are located in the **Mountain Village Base Facility** (P.O. Box 307, Telluride, CO 81435; 303-728-3856) and a new slope-side Doral Telluride Resort is planned. For reservations and information call 800-525-3455.

Purgatory is north of Durango and around 100 road miles from Telluride, though actually just over the hill—the hill being ridges of the San Juan Mountains, roughly 14,000 feet high.

The area covers 630 acres with good snow and mild weather, all adding up to record-breaking ski days year after year. The difference here, for some, is in the vertical terrain. Purgatory has long been considered an intermediate skier's nirvana. Now, however, an area called The Legends has boosted the overall ski field by 25 percent and added nine advanced trails with a vertical drop of 2000 feet. Nevertheless, a good portion of the resort's business comes from a low-key, fun-loving trade, compared with Telluride's trendier skiers.

Half of Purgatory is considered mid-level terrain, and there is a separate Columbine Station area for beginners. It is serviced by its own triple chairlift, providing novices with a private, pristine spot for learning the basics. A justified claim to fame here is that there is rarely a lift line, even during peak season. Purgatory serves 300,000 skiers yearly, the most of any Southwestern Colorado area. Five triple chairs and four doubles help.

Purgatory-Durango opens in late November. Every adult beginner at Purgatory can get a free half-day lesson with the purchase of a lift ticket, and the excellent instructional programs also include group lessons, as well as individualized classes.

Condominiums line the base of Purgatory's slopes. Ten miles south is highly rated **Tamarron Resort** (see "Durango-Silverton Area Hotels" above) with free ski buses. Durango is 25 miles south, offering various lodging-ski-transportation packages through hotels such as the **Strater Hotel** (see "Durango-Silverton Area Hotels" above). The **Durango Lift** (303-259-5438) offers inexpensive bus transportation between Purgatory and Durango.

See you on the slopes!

BOATING AND CANOEING

Gentler than whitewater, lakes and reservoirs are fine for small boats and canoes. For canoes and boats of various sizes at Vallecito Lake contact **Shorty's** (Vallecito Lake, Bayfield; 303-884-2768), **Butch's** (14810 County Road 501, Bayfield; 303-884-9450) or **Mountain Marina** (14810-A County Road 501, Bayfield; 303-884-9450).

At McPhee Reservoir, rentals are available from **Beaver Creek Marina** (P.O. Box 636, Cortez, CO 81321; 303-882-2258).

HUNTING AND FISHING

Anyone with a license can hunt big game, such as deer and elk, and fish for stocked rainbow, cutthroat and brown trout. A number of outfitters make their livings by knowing where these babies may be found. Try **Buck's Livery** (Route 550 North, Durango; 303-259-5675), **Colorado Outback** (2612 North College Drive, Durango; 303-259-1021) or **Ron-D-View Ranch** (Durango; 303-563-9270). **San Juan Outfitting** (186 County Road 228, Durango; 303-259-6259) arranges high-country pack trips to hunt elk, deer or bighorn sheep, using bow and arrow, muzzleloading rifles and regular rifles.

The best fishing is found north of Durango at Haviland Lake, Lemon Lake or Vallecito Lake. For fishing trips call **Duranglers** (801-B Main Avenue, Durango; 303-385-4081) or check with other outfitters.

Fly fishing is good on the Dolores River. McPhee Reservoir is stocked with trout, kokanee salmon, large- and smallmouth bass, perch, bluegill and catfish. **Circle K Ranch** (26916 Route 145, Dolores; 303-562-3808) arranges guided, outfitted trips for hunting and fishing.

SKIING, SNOWMOBILING AND DOGSLEDDING

In an average year it snows more than 300 inches in the high mountains. Traditionally, locals play in the snow rather than moan about it.

Downhill and cross-country skiing or snowmobile rentals are available at **Purgatory-Durango Ski Resort** (Route 550 North, Durango; 303-247-9000) and **Hesperus Ski Area** (9848 Route 160, Hesperus; 303-259-3711).

Cross-country skiing is very good at **Hillcrest Golf Course** (2179 County Road 238, Durango; 303-247-1499), **Bear Ranch** (42570 Route 550 North, Durango; 303-247-0111), the areas of the **San Juan National Forest** (701 Camino del Rio, Durango; 303-247-4874) and **Mesa Verde National Park** (303-529-4421 in summer, 303-533-7731 in winter).

Dog-sled trips are arranged by **Black Feather Mushers** (1630 County Road 214, Durango; 303-247-8281).

GOLF

To tee off, try **Hillcrest Golf Club** (2179 County Road 238, Durango; 303-247-1499), **Tamarron Resort** (40292 Route 550 North, Durango; 303-259-2000) and **Conquistador Golf Course** (2018 North Dolores Road, Cortez; 303-565-9208).

TENNIS

Tennis anyone? In Durango there are courts at the **Durango High School** (2390 Main Avenue; 303-259-1630), **Fort Lewis College** (College Heights; 303-247-7010) and **Mason Elementary** (301 East 12th Avenue; 303-247-3524). In Silverton there are courts in **Memorial Park** at the northeast end of town. Cortez has courts in **City Park** (830 East Montezuma Avenue; 303-565-7877).

BICYCLING

Fast becoming one of the most popular sports in the region, mountain biking has taken off in a big way, due in part to the popularity of two events. The Iron Horse Bicycle Classic, held yearly over Memorial Day weekend, pits riders against the narrow-gauge train in a 50-mile race over two 10,000-foot mountain passes from Durango to Silverton. The best bike riders always beat the train. And the first unified World Mountain Biking Championship was held in Durango in 1990. The championship course at Purgatory is open to riders in the summer. The terrain for biking is challenging and scenic. The variety of roads and trails on public lands is immense.

In the Durango-Silverton area **The Animas Valley Loop** is considered easy by locals who always ride at 6500 feet, but it is mostly flat, rising only 280 feet, and can be ridden in 15- or 30-mile versions. The long route follows County Road 250 north out of Durango and up the east side of the Animas Valley, crossing the main Route 550 at Baker's Bridge and heading back to Durango via County Road 203, on the west side of the valley.

A beautiful intermediate ride is **Old Lime Creek Road**, between Silverton and Cascade Creek, north of Purgatory. It starts 11 miles south of Silverton, off Route 550, and follows the old highway for 12 miles past beaver ponds and a brick retaining span called the "Chinese Wall," which once separated stage coaches from a sheer drop down the steep mountainside.

The **Animas City Mountain Loop** follows an advanced five-and-a-half-mile trail that gains 1250 feet in elevation. It starts off of 4th Avenue, north of 32nd Street, in Durango, and offers stunning views of Falls Creek, the Animas Valley and the West Needle Mountains from the top of a tilted mesa.

In the Cortez-Dolores area the **Horseshoe Ruins Trail** starts 23 miles south of Pleasant View off the road to Hovenweep. It is an easy ten-mile loop through the rolling mesa country that predominates in this area. It takes you to Horseshoe, Holly and Hackberry Ruins within the national monument. The **Cutthroat Castle Trail** starts in the same place, circling north over similar terrain into Hovenweep Canyon and past the Cutthroat Castle ruin. The 17-mile loop is for intermediate riders.

Several easy-to-intermediate rides may be found on roads through **Mesa Verde National Park** (P.O. Box 277, Mancos, CO 81328; 303-529-4421 in summer, 303-533-7731 in winter), particularly in the spring and fall when the air is cooler and there are fewer cars on the roads.

BIKE RENTALS   Rent your bikes at **The Outdoorsman** (949 Main Avenue, Durango; 303-247-4066), **Hassle Free Sports** (2615 Main Avenue, Durango; 303-259-3874) or **Durango Sports Co.** (3101 Main Avenue, Durango; 303-259-4600) and **Southwest Bicycle and Sport** (540 East Main Street, Cortez; 303-565-3717).

HIKING

DURANGO-SILVERTON AREA TRAILS   Numerous hiking trails are found in the San Juan National Forest and Weminuche Wilderness Area. Backpacking trips of several hours to several days are possible. Forest service maps and information are available from the Animas Ranger District, 303-247-4874.

The southwest portion of the 469-mile **Colorado Trail,** connecting Durango and Denver, begins in the La Plata Mountains, west of Durango atop Kennebec Pass. Access is at the end of County Road 124, in Hesperus or via Junction Creek from downtown Durango. This trail offers rugged hiking through alpine wilderness ranging from 7000 to 11,000 feet in altitude.

Perins Peak Trail (5 miles) is a difficult loop trail starting at the end of 22nd Street in Durango. It takes you through pine forests and includes a ten-foot cliff that must be scaled to afford scenic views of Durango and the La Plata Mountains to the west.

Needle Creek Trail (14 miles) is accessed via the narrow-gauge railroad that will drop off passengers in Needleton for rugged hiking in the Weminuche Wilderness. Hikers then flag the train down for the return trip to Durango or Silverton. The trail leads to Chicago Basin, Mount Eolus (14,084 feet), Sunlight Peak (14,059 feet) and Windom Peak (14,087 feet).

Elk Creek Trail (8 miles), also accessed via the train at Elk Park, leads hikers to the Continental Divide above Elk Creek Valley.

Cascade Creek Trail (4 miles) begins 26 miles north of Durango on the east side of Route 550. It leads to the Animas River. Seven miles farther on the **Animas River Trail** you will end up in Needleton and the Weminuche.

CORTEZ-DOLORES AREA TRAILS   The big attraction to hikers in this part of Colorado is the numerous Anasazi Indian sites in the slickrock and canyon country. Hikes along mesa tops afford 100-mile views on clear days.

Navajo Lake Trail (5 miles) begins at Burro Bridge campground off West Fork Road, 12.5 miles east of Dolores and then 24 miles up Forest Road 535. The trail leads to Navajo Lake, at 11,154 feet, which sits at the foot of 14,000-foot El Diente Peak.

Hovenweep Trails are accessed via short marked trails within the national monument leading to the Cajon Ruins in Utah, or in Colorado, to Holly Ruins, Hackberry Canyon Ruins, Cutthroat Castle Ruins and Goodman Point Ruins. The trails wind through arid mesa country, mostly treeless scrublands that see few visitors. Since there are no roads for vehicles, hiking or biking are the only ways to see these ruins.

Ute Mountain Tribal Park contains numerous hiking trails leading to excavated and unexcavated Anasazi ruins along a 25-mile stretch of the Mancos River. You must have an Indian guide with you at all times. The most popular hiking trail covers 13 miles from the park entrance following the river and affording views of wildlife as well as sites of archeological interest.

MESA VERDE AREA TRAILS Hikes in this region of Indian country pass through piñon and juniper forests, canyons, mesas and archaeological sites, including cliff dwellings. Hiking within the national park is limited to five well-marked trails, and hikers must register at the ranger's office. It is very hot in the summer. Bring water.

Petroglyph Point Trail (3 miles) begins on the Spruce Tree House Trail adjacent to the park office and museum. It travels along the mesa top leading to ancient rock art at Petroglyph Point.

Spruce Canyon Trail (2 miles) also begins on the Spruce Tree House Trail and leads into forested Spruce Tree Canyon at the base of the mesa.

Transportation

BY CAR

Southwestern Colorado is a large, sparsely populated area with few major roads along the vast stretches of desert and forest lands and dispersed communities. The main north-south highway connecting Durango and Silverton is **Route 550**. From Durango to Cortez the main road is **Route 160**, which is also the access road to Mesa Verde National Park. It veers south in Cortez and shares a designation with **Route 666** for 20 miles. At that point Route 160 heads west to the Four Corners Monument and Arizona, while Route 666 continues south into New Mexico.

Cortez and Dolores are connected by **Route 145**. Dolores and Mancos are connected by **Route 184**, which meets Route 160 in Mancos.

To reach Hovenweep National Monument the main access is south of Cortez on Route 160 to **McElmo Canyon Road**, only partially paved, or north of Cortez, via Route 666 to the **Colorado turnoff** at Pleasant View, which also passes Lowry Ruins.

BY AIR

The main airport with scheduled service for the entire region is Durango's **La Plata County Airport**. Much smaller, and with far fewer flights daily, is the **Cortez-Montezuma County Airport**. For ski buffs, there's **Telluride Regional Airport**.

Durango is served by America West Airlines, Continental Express, Mesa Airlines and United Express. Cortez is served by Mesa Airlines and United Express. Telluride is serviced by Mesa Airlines and Continental Express.

BY BUS

Greyhound/Trailways Bus Lines and **Texas, New Mexico and Oklahoma Coaches** offer scheduled service through Durango (275 East 8th Avenue; 303-259-2755) and Silverton (Silverton Drive-In, 12th and Greene streets; 303-387-5658).

CAR RENTALS

In Durango, contact **Avis Rent A Car** (303-247-9761), **Budget Rent A Car** (303-259-1841), **Dollar Rent A Car** (303-259-3012), **Hertz Rent A Car** (303-247-5288) or **National Car Rental** (303-259-0068). In Cortez, call **Budget Rent A Car** (303-565-1287) or **Hertz Rent A Car** (303-565-8140).

PUBLIC TRANSPORTATION

The only scheduled public transportation in Southwestern Colorado is the **Durango Lift** (303-259-5438) which operates within the city limits year-round and offers winter service between Durango and Purgatory-Durango Ski Area.

TAXIS

Service in Durango is offered by **Durango Transportation** (303-259-4818). In Cortez, call **Cortez Taxi** (303-565-1073).

HELICOPTER TOURS

For helicopter tours of Mesa Verde National Park, contact **Kenai Helicopters** (P.O. Box 1078, Cortez, CO 81321; 303-565-9340).

JEEP TOURS AND FOUR-WHEEL DRIVE TRIPS

A relatively comfortable way to see the back country is by traveling in a four-wheel-drive vehicle. Guided tours are offered by Durango's **Absolute Adventures** (303-259-2291). Jeep rentals are available in Silverton from **Silverton Lakes Campground** (P.O. Box 126, Silverton, CO 81433; 303-387-5721) or **Triangle Service Station** (864 Greene Street; 303-387-9990).

SCENIC FLIGHTS

A true bird's-eye view of Durango, the Animas Valley and the majestic San Juans from the plexi-glass cockpit of a quiet glider is offered by **Val-Air Soaring** (27290 Route 550 North; 303-247-9037). For airplane charters or scenic flights contact **Gregg Flying Service** (Animas Air Park, Durango; 303-247-4632).

STAGE COACH TOURS

The **Mesa Verde Stage Line** (303-533-7264) offers horse-drawn stagecoach tours from Mancos into Weber Canyon, below Mesa Verde. Three-day advance reservations are required.

Index

Hotel, restaurant and trail names have not been included here unless cited as a sightseeing or historical attraction.

Silva House, 134
Silver City: hotels, 351; restaurants, 351;
shopping, 352; sightseeing, 343, 349-50;
visitor center, 350
Silver City-Grant County Airport, 359
Silver City Museum, 350
Silver Reef: sightseeing, 380-81
Silver Reef Museum, 380
Silverton area. *See* Durango-Silverton area
Silverton Standard and Miner, 453
Sitting Bull Falls, 337
Skiing, 77, 218, 322-23, 354, 468-69, 470
Sky Harbor International Airport, 171
Slaughter Ranch, 197
Sleeping Ute Mountain, 461
Slide Rock State Park, 56, 66-67
Smokey Bear State Historical Park, 333
Smoki Museum, 59
Snakes, 12
Snow Canyon State Park, 366, 370
Snow Lake, 353
Snowmobiling, 470
Socorro area, 314-16; hotels, 315; restaurants, 315-16; sightseeing, 314-15; trails, 325-26
Sonoita: shopping, 214
South Central New Mexico, 338-47; hotels, 342, 344; nightlife, 345-46; parks, 346-47; restaurants, 344-45; shopping, 338-41; trails, 356-57
South Mountain Park, 143
South of Phoenix, 165-66; hotels, 165-66; restaurants, 166; shopping, 166; sightseeing, 165
South Rim (Grand Canyon): hotels, 44, 46; map, 24; nightlife, 48; restaurants, 47; shopping, 48; sightseeing, 42-43; trails, 80-82; visitor center, 42-43
Southeastern New Mexico, 330-38; hotels, 334-35; nightlife, 336-37; parks, 337-38; restaurants, 335-36; shopping, 336, sightseeing, 330-33; trails, 356
Southeastern Utah, 409-47; history, 410-12; Lake Powell area, 413-19; map, 411; Moab area, 428-38; San Juan County area, 419-28; sports, 438-46; transportation, 446-47
Southern Arizona, 175-223; east of Tucson, 196-208; history, 176; maps, 177, 183; south/west of Tucson, 208-17; sports, 217-21; transportation, 222-23; Tucson, 178-95; weather, 175
Southern Navajo Country, 93-99; hotels, 95-96; nightlife, 98; parks, 98-99; restaurants, 96-97; shopping, 97-98; sightseeing, 93-95; trails, 122

Southern New Mexico, 329-59; history, 329; map, 331; South Central New Mexico, 338-47; Southeastern New Mexico, 330-38; Southwestern New Mexico, 347-54; sports, 354-58; transportation, 358-59
Southern Utah University, 378
Southwest: animals, 11-12; calendar of events, 17-23; geology, 4-5; history, 5-10; map, 3; plants, 10-11; seasons, 16-17; visitor information, 23
South/West of Tucson, 208-17; hotels, 211-12; nightlife, 215; parks, 215-17; restaurants, 212-13; shopping, 213-14; sightseeing, 208-10; trails, 221
Southwestern Art and Cultural Adventures, 144
Southwestern Colorado, 449-75; Cortez-Dolores area, 459-63; Durango-Silverton area, 451-59; history, 449-50; map, 451; Mesa Verde area, 464-67; sports, 467-73; transportation, 473-75
Southwestern New Mexico, 347-54; hotels, 350-51; nightlife, 352; parks, 353-54; restaurants, 351-52; shopping, 352; sightseeing, 347-50; trails, 357-58
Southwestern Utah, 361-407; Bryce area, 385-92; Cedar City area, 377-85; Escalante area, 392-97; history, 362, 364; map, 363; St. George area, 365-71; sports, 397-406; transportation, 406-407; Zion area, 371-77
Spanish cultural group, 24
Spanish History Museum, 291-92
Spence Hot Springs, 265
Sportfishing, 397. *See also* Fish and fishing
Springdale: hotels, 375; nightlife, 376; restaurants, 376; sightseeing, 371-73
Squaw Peak Recreation Area, 143
Stables Art Center, 252
Stage coach tours, 475
Stanton: sightseeing, 69
State Capitol (New Mexico), 230
Storrie Lake State Park, 248, 250
Strawberry: sightseeing, 162
Strawberry Schoolhouse, 162
Summerhaven: hotels, 181-82; restaurants, 187
Sumner Lake State Park, 309
Sunset Crater National Monument, 51
Supai: hotels, 46; sightseeing, 43
Superstition Mountain/Lost Dutchman Museum, 153
Superstition Mountains, 152-53

Also Available From Ulysses Press

HIDDEN BOSTON AND CAPE COD
This compact guide ventures to historic Boston and the windswept Massachusetts coastline. 228 pages. $7.95

HIDDEN COAST OF CALIFORNIA
Explores the fabled California coast from Mexico to Oregon, describing over 1000 miles of spectacular beaches. 468 pages. $13.95

HIDDEN FLORIDA
From Miami to the Panhandle, from the Keys to Cape Canaveral, this award-winning guide combs the state. 492 pages. $14.95

HIDDEN FLORIDA KEYS AND EVERGLADES
Covers an area unlike any other in the world—the tropical Florida Keys and mysterious Everglades. 156 pages. $7.95

HIDDEN HAWAII
A classic in its field, this top-selling guide captures the spirit of the islands. Winner of the Lowell Thomas Award. 384 pages. $14.95

HIDDEN MEXICO
Covers the entire 6000-mile Mexican coastline in the most comprehensive fashion ever. 444 pages. $13.95

HIDDEN NEW ENGLAND
A perfect companion for exploring from Massachusetts colonial villages to the fog-shrouded coast of Maine. 564 pages. $14.95

HIDDEN PACIFIC NORTHWEST
Covers Oregon, Washington and British Columbia. Seattle sightseeing, Oregon beaches, Cascades campgrounds and more! 528 pages. $14.95

HIDDEN SAN FRANCISCO AND NORTHERN CALIFORNIA
A major resource for travelers exploring the San Francisco Bay area and beyond. 444 pages. $14.95

HIDDEN SOUTHERN CALIFORNIA

The most complete guidebook to Los Angeles and Southern California in print. 516 pages. $14.95

CALIFORNIA
The Ultimate Guidebook

Definitive. From the Pacific to the desert to the Sierra Nevada, it captures the best of the Golden State. 504 pages. $13.95

DISNEY WORLD AND BEYOND
The Ultimate Family Guidebook

Unique and comprehensive, this guide to Orlando's theme parks and outlying areas is a must for family travelers. 300 pages. $9.95

DISNEY WORLD AND BEYOND
Family Fun Cards

This "guidebook you can shuffle" covers Orlando's theme parks with a deck of 90 cards, each describing a different ride or exhibit. $7.95

DISNEYLAND AND BEYOND
The Ultimate Family Guidebook

The only guidebook to cover all Southern California theme parks. Includes three chapters of daytrip possibilities for families. 240 pages. $9.95

FLORIDA'S GOLD COAST
The Ultimate Guidebook

Captures the tenor and tempo of Florida's most popular stretch of shore-line—Palm Beach, Fort Lauderdale and Miami. 192 pages. $8.95

FOR A FREE CATALOG OR TO ORDER DIRECT   For each book send an additional $2 postage and handling (California residents include 8% sales tax) to Ulysses Press, 3286 Adeline Street, Suite 1, Berkeley, CA 94703. Or call **1-800-377-2542** or 510-601-8301 and charge your order.

About the Authors and Illustrator

Richard Harris, author of the introductory, Northwestern Arizona, Central New Mexico and Southern New Mexico chapters, has lived in Santa Fe, New Mexico since 1982. He has written six guidebooks (including *2 to 22 Days in the American Southwest*), contributed to Fodor's guides and edited more than 60 travel books.

Laura Daily is an award-winning freelance journalist living in Snowmass Village, Colorado. She has published widely in national magazines and newspapers and contributes travel features to Copley News Service. Together with Madeleine Osberger she co-authored the Utah and Northern New Mexico chapters.

Madeleine Osberger, a longtime reporter for the *Aspen Times*, has written for a variety of newspapers and magazines, including the *Chicago Tribune*, *Newsweek*, *Rocky Mountain News* and Associated Press. A columnist for the *Skier News*, she has also contributed to *Snow Country* and *Ski Management*.

Carolyn Scarborough, who penned the Southern Arizona chapter, is an award-winning freelance writer living in Phoenix. A former travel editor of *Southern Living* magazine and member of the Society of American Travel Writers, her writing credits include more than 300 published articles in magazines and newspapers across the country.

Mary Ann Reese, author of the Northeastern Arizona chapter, was associate travel editor at *Sunset* magazine for 17 years, covering Arizona and New Mexico. She also wrote wilderness and urban stories about the West and foreign countries. Earlier, she was London Bureau Chief for the *Stars and Stripes* newspaper.

Ron Butler, author of the Central Arizona chapter, is based in Tucson, Arizona. He has held editorial staff positions at *True* and *Penthouse* magazines. He is the author of *The Best of the Old West* (Texas Monthly Press) and *Fodor's Guide to New Mexico*. His work has appeared in *Travel & Leisure*, *Travel Holiday* and *Ladies Home Journal*.

Steve Cohen lives in Durango, Colorado and writes extensively about the Southwest. Author of the Southwestern Colorado chapter, he has also written for the *Los Angeles Times*, *Denver Post* and *Miami Herald*. He is a member of the Society of American Travel Writers and has written several guidebooks including *Adventure Guide to Jamaica*.

Glenn Kim is a freelance illustrator residing in San Francisco. Born in South Korea, he received a degree in illustration from San Francisco's Academy of Art College. In creating the illustrations for this book, he used the Native Americans and their arts for inspiration. His work also appears in Ulysses Press' *Disneyland and Beyond* and *Disney World and Beyond*.